ROGER STEVENSON
APRIL, 1993

THE CATALOGUE
OF
HEALTHY FOOD

THE
CATALOGUE
OF
HEALTHY
FOOD

BY

JOHN TEPPER MARLIN

WITH

DOMENICK M. BERTELLI

BANTAM BOOKS
NEW YORK · TORONTO · LONDON · SYDNEY · AUCKLAND

THE CATALOGUE OF HEALTHY FOOD
A Bantam Book/August 1990

Photo credits: pages ii and 48 © Walnut Acres; pages xiv and 138 ©
Seth Rothman; page 2 © Dennis Malone; page 10 © Patrick Cragin;
page 26 © Ron Funt; page 58 © Doug Speakman; page 60 © Arrowhead Mills; page 82 © Simon Benepe (courtesy of Greenmarket);
page 96 © R. A. Byers; page 140 © Tree of Life, Inc. (Taft Photog-
raphy); page 154 © Robert Fruré, Hammersnest Production;
page 166 © Richard Sandler

Library of Congress Cataloging-in-Publication Data

Marlin, John Tepper.
 The catalogue of healthy food in America / by John Tepper Marlin with Domenick Bertelli.
  p. cm.
 Includes bibliographical references.
 ISBN 0-553-34858-2
 1. Natural foods. 2. Natural foods—United States—Catalogs.
3. Natural food restaurants—United States—Directories. I. Bertelli,
Domenick. II. Title. III. Title: Healthy Food in America.
TX369.M375 1990
641.3′02′029—dc20   90-30621
            .   CIP

Published simultaneously in the United States and Canada

Bantam Books are published by Bantam Books, a division of Bantam
Doubleday Dell Publishing Group, Inc. Its trademark, consisting of the
words "Bantam Books" and the portrayal of a rooster, is Registered
in U.S. Patent and Trademark Office and in other countries Marca
Registrada, Bantam Books, 666 Fifth Avenue, New York, New York
10103

PRINTED IN THE UNITED STATES OF AMERICA

0 9 8 7 6 5 4 3 2 1

CONTENTS

AUTHOR'S THANKS

For collaboration, guidance, and help, I thank:

• My octogenarian parents—my vegetarian mother, Hilda van Stockum Marlin, for showing me the joys of both a writing career and vegetarian eating, and my father, Ervin R. Marlin, for showing by example a life of moderation in food as all else.

• My organic-gardener wife, Alice Tepper Marlin, who has provided insightful comments on this book at each of many stages.

• The Bircher-Benner Clinic in Zurich, Switzerland, pioneer in preventive medicine and making healthy food tasty, inventor of the much-imitated "Muesli"; especially Dr. Dagmar Liechti von Brasch (Dr. Bircher-Benner's niece), my physician during two long visits to the Clinic, who gave me durable nutritional advice.

• Domenick M. Bertelli (Harvard '91–'92), my dedicated and skilled assistant for this book. A Californian, his prior work at a fast-food restaurant and food-processing plant made him an advocate of additive-free foods and sustainable agriculture. He directed assembly of Chapters 7 and 10 during the summer of 1989, then took a year off from college to finish the work. His father, Dr. Domenick J. Bertelli, steered us clear of some chemistry errors; blame me for any that remain.

• Six other student interns: Matthew Beasley (University of York '89), David Caceres (Harvard '88), Mark Holford (NYU graduate journalism student), Drew Kiriazides (NYU '91), Soo Mee Pak (Yale '88, NYU Medical School '92), and Kate Ryder (Exeter University '90). They persevered in their task of helping to synthesize articles, books, questionnaire responses, and interviews into a book of guidance and reference.

• My agent for the book, Joseph Spieler, who suggested the idea to me, sold it, and maintained his interest in it to the end; copy editor Pat Vance, who capably and thoughtfully took pains to go through a more challenging job than he anticipated; Bantam Books editor Barbara Alpert, who ably guided us on content, format and design; and Martin Moskof, whose careful design work will surely impress the reader.

• My vegetarian daughter, Caroline, and my son J.J., who have helped try out new healthy restaurants and foods and have engaged in lively and ongoing debate over their merits.

• Food growers and vendors who responded to our questionnaires, officials who cooperated with interviews, and the many people who took the time to answer innumerable questions of detail.

• Advisers who read parts of the book and made substantial contributions: Ken Ausubel, Paul Bergman, Dr. Jeffrey Buckner, Annemarie Colbin, Dr. Geraldine V. Cox, Karyn Feiden, Stuart Fishman, Nikki Goldbeck, Ben Goldman, Dr. Thomas H. Haines, Dr. Michael F. Jacobson, Allen E. Kaye, Alice Tepper Marlin, Elaine Marlin, Dr. Randal R. Marlin, Dr. Patricia McArdle, Dr. Michael McCally, Dr. Elisabeth Paice, F.R.C.P., Dr. Warren Sherman, Rena Shulsky, Hilda van Stockum Marlin and Dr. Shelley Weinstock. Responsibility for errors remains with me.

• Libraries and agencies where we did some of our research, especially the Center for Medical Consumers of the Judson Memorial Church, the Harvard Club of New York Library, the New York Public Library, and the Westminster (London) Central Research Library.

• My teachers at Harvard College, where I earned an A.B. degree; Oxford University (Trinity College), where I earned B.A. and M.A. degrees; and the George Washington University, where I earned a Ph.D. degree in economics.

• You, the reader, for making the effort to take from the book the messages and resources that apply to you, and for your determination to use them to make a better life. I salute you.

Bon appétit, and bonne santé!

John Tepper Marlin
New York City
February 17, 1990

PREFACE

Michael F. Jacobson, Ph.D.
Executive Director
Center for Science in the Public Interest

Twenty years ago, a small number of Americans started eating what they thought was the most healthful food possible: Brown rice, whole-wheat bread, homemade soups, organically grown vegetables, and the like. Almost universally they were derided as "health-food nuts" and "food faddists" by journalists, scientists, and almost everyone else, who were smugly eating their Sugar Frosted Flakes, Coke, McDonald's hamburgers, and Wonder bread: "Hey, don't worry about the pesticides!—They're good for you." "Vegetarians are Commies and weaklings!" "Whole-wheat bread is no better than white bread."

Well, somewhere along the line, something happened. The medical evidence piled up so high that dietary revolution occurred while most Americans were waiting in line at Burger King. The Surgeon General of the United States urged Americans to cut down on the briny soups that Campbell's advertised as "Health Insurance." He urged people to cut way back on the saturated fat that is abundant in the beef that the beef industry said "gives us strength." The Surgeon General wasn't alone: The National Cancer Institute, American Heart Association, and even the usually benighted U.S. Department of Agriculture all said that we've been eating wrong. The meat loaf, whole milk, butter, Coke—everything that we had been taught made America great had to go! And the so-called health-food nuts multiplied faster than rabbits.

It turned out that the real food faddists were not the ones out there stuffing themselves with lentils and home-brew yogurt. The real food faddists were (and still are) Betty Crocker and Ronald McDonald. It was their foods and those of their food manufacturing compatriots, literally oozing with fat and cholesterol, soaked through with salt, practically crystalline with sugar, and laced with an alphabet-soup of additives, that were killing people. It was greasy creations like fast-food double-cheeseburgers that promoted heart disease and cancer. It was the sodium in processed foods that promoted high blood pressure and stroke. It was the dyes that caused hyperactivity in some kids. It was the sulfites (remember when some people made fun of brown, health-food apricots, which were not treated with sulfite?) that killed asthmatics by anaphylaxis.

Health-conscious people have dragged the food industry, literally groaning and screaming, into the modern era. Since the big food manufacturers, supermarkets, and restaurant chains wouldn't deign to provide the healthiest foods, people set up their own companies. It all started with the food co-ops and hippie restaurants of the '60s. Then health-food companies, with their potions and pills, began offering some healthful processed foods. Supermarkets saw tiny natural-foods groceries turn into substantial competitors and gingerly began offering whole-grain breads, yogurt, and a few other "alternative" foods. then about ten years ago food manufacturers realized that they could promote foods on the basis of nutrition, not just color, taste, and convenience, and began dishing up more nutritious canned goods and frozen meals.

Each much-publicized health scare creates a new cadre of healthy-food devotees, both among consumers and producers. A National Academy of Sciences report on pesticides several years ago shocked people by giving official credence to the much-bandied-about notion that pesticide contaminants in food were likely causing many cancer deaths. The 1989 Alar controversy gave the biggest boost ever to organic farming. A 1987–1988 campaign against tropical oils (coconut, palm, and palm-kernel oils), which are loaded with saturated fat, persuaded most food manufacturers to switch to more healthful oils.

As more and more people began caring about the

nutritional value and safety of their food, resources became available. First, many new vegetarian cookbooks made their appearance. Then nutrition information began appearing on food package labels. Then came nutrition information on shelf-markers in some supermarkets. But life was still difficult. Where do you eat if you're travelling or new to a city? What do you eat if your town isn't blessed with pre-eminent natural-foods stores, such as Alfalfa's, Bread & Circus, Mrs. Gooch's, or Whole Foods? Where can you take some visiting, health-conscious relatives out to eat without short-circuiting Grandpa Joe's pacemaker?

The answer to all those questions are in John Tepper Marlin's **The Catalogue of Healthy Food**. It's a treasure chest of restaurants, grocery stores, mail-order firms, and retailers that offer the kind of healthy food that everyone in the food industry should be providing.

While it's not a nutrition textbook, the **Catalogue** provides a highly readable guide to where the science of nutrition is at as the decade of the '90s begins. Marlin's inquiry into this murky science may leave some traditional scientists muttering, but rest assured that he always has your health as his top priority. He's not bamboozled by professors who consult for industry or by self-proclaimed consumer groups that are funded largely by the food, chemical, and other industries (American Council on Science and Health comes to mind). And he's not embarrassed to explore for you some of the biodynamic yins and yangs that set most nutritionists' teeth on edge, but in deciding ultimately what food is healthy, he rests on the solid ground, where it exists, of scientific evidence (though I have several small reservations, such as on his views on hydrogenated oils).

The success of most books, including this one, will be measured by the number of copies people buy. But in the long run, this book's success can be measured against a more significant criterion. By shedding light on the nooks and crannies of the production of healthy food, it will speed along public appreciation of how the foods they eat affect their health and will hasten the day that healthy food is available everywhere, from fast-food joints to giant supermarkets. I do not believe it is too far-fetched to relate improved American health from better eating to significant lengthening of our life expectancy and greater productivity and happiness. This book will, I believe, play a part in this process.

FOREWORD

Victor W. Sidel, M.D.
Distinguished University Professor of Social Medicine
Montefiore Medical Center/Albert Einstein College of Medicine

This book is a valuable and timely guide for people seeking to pick their way through the changing and conflicting nutritional propaganda that daily bombards them. It can be of great value if used judiciously to make choices within and among the essential food groups that should be a part of a healthy diet. Indeed, as John Tepper Marlin points out clearly in Chapter 3, the real issue is not eating "healthy foods" but maintaining a "healthy diet." This book can help in attaining this goal.

As we fine-tune our diets, let's not forget how lucky we are. We must fight for policies and programs to help other people—in the United States and in poor countries—who lack the opportunity to eat healthy diets or to live productive, satisfying, and healthy lives. For some one-fifth of the world's population, a constant or recurring problem is the inability to obtain adequate quantities of nourishing food. The consequent hunger, despair, malnutrition, and premature death are tragedies for those who suffer them and for all of us in affluent countries who stand by and permit such suffering. The tragedy is compounded by the fact that the world is capable of producing sufficient food to feed all of its people adequately; social, economic, and political factors have led to the maldistribution of the food that already exists and to artificial barriers to the production of more. Compared to this problem, the eating puzzles faced by affluent people pale in significance.

Nonetheless, many people in the United States and other affluent countries search for—and some badly need—the ability to choose wisely among the extraordinary and oftentimes dysfunctional variety of foods that are available to them. Some, such as the over 30 million people who live in poverty in our nation, are severely limited in their ability to obtain healthy food. Most of us, however, with almost unlimited ability to choose among available foods, may need help in choosing from the cornucopia of items stocked in U.S. supermarkets and food stores.

The barrage of food advertising is devastating. It is worsened by a constant stream of new scientific data, often presented in the popular media or even in the scientific community with no commentary relating the new data to data gathered in previous studies or to indicate the relevance of the new data to choices among foods. All in all, the conflicting data are conducive to a new nutritional problem—Nutritional Data Indigestion! For this problem, Marlin's calmly reasoned book is a fine, just-in-time response.

INTRODUCTION

"Learn how to make food our medicine and not medicine our food."
—Hippocrates

This book is all about making connections—between you and food providers, between food and disease, and between food and the environment. If the 1960s showed up a new social awareness, the 1970s a new self-awareness, and the 1980s new health-awareness, the 1990s could see the integration of our consciousness of society, self, and health; this book may help with such a process.

The book progresses from Part I, *What* people should eat, to Part II, *Who* produces what people should eat, and *How* to buy direct, and Part III, *Where* people can buy what they should eat from an outlet near them—a restaurant, a supermarket, a natural-food store or other source.

Who Can Use This Book

We've written this book for everyone who cares about their health, or the health of someone they love.

Professionals in health care—physicians, dietitians, complementary practitioners, regulatory agency officials, attorneys, journalists—and their clients will find the book of value both for its summaries of what we know and for information available nowhere else.

This book will also be of special interest to people who have a business stake in the food industry—the growers, distributors, processors, retailers and restaurants who have a special responsibility for healthy food.

How to Use This Book

If you are a specialist, interested only in the listings of food producers, retailers, and restaurants, you may wish to turn directly to the *product listings* in Chapter 7 or the *geographical listings* in Chapter 10, which are reference directories for sources of particular foods and regional food vendors. Other substantial *listings of food sellers* are provided at the end of Chapters 6 and 8. In addition, *lists of organizations and agencies* involved in food, mostly nonprofit and regulatory bodies, are provided at the end of Chapters 3, 4, and 5.

If you are interested as a consumer in the broader dietary issues raised in Chapters 1 to 3, you may use this book as:

1. *An introduction to the subject of nutrition*, not to replace textbooks or formal training, but to provide a quick update for consumers of a changing field. For this purpose, Part I will suffice.

2. *A self-improvement vehicle*, to lose weight or otherwise reform one's eating patterns. Part I provides the information on what we need to do. But an *intellectual* appreciation of the material will not suffice. The decision to *become healthier* must be made. Scientists are increasingly in agreement that the major killers of Americans can be controlled by making significant changes in our diets. The trouble is, these changes may require substantial lifestyle adjustments. Reducing fat intake, for example, may mean virtually eliminating red meat and whole milk. The benefits of deciding to live a healthier lifestyle may include a new sense of physical integrity and self-control; but first, the control must be exercised. Starting with a few changes can sometimes have a dramatic effect, generating a new feeling of well-being. The directories and tables in Chapters 3, 7, 9, and 10 provide ample resources for starting to make healthy food choices.

3. *A way to try out healthy cuisines.* A natural-food retail store offers many foods that most Americans have never eaten and wouldn't know how to cook. Healthy-food restaurants, whether they offer a macrobiotic, vegetarian or "natural" cuisine, provide a good way to learn about new, healthy dishes. For someone used to eating hamburgers every evening for dinner, such restaurants bridge the chasm between ignorance of healthy food and knowledge of it, and they help *train one's taste buds.* They are all places that care what the food does to people's health, not just how it tastes. Many manage to make food tasty as well as healthful; these are the ones we have sought to include in Chapter 10.

4. *An entrée into an alternative lifestyle*, either out of curiosity or habit. For this purpose, vegetarian restaurants and wholefood stores provide an excellent *doorway*, literally. Most have bulletin boards and stacks of alternative newspapers in their foyers, showing how to reach other parts of the alternative-living networks (complementary health practitioners and classes, for example). In Chapter 10 we list good places to start with for every U.S. state, and a few Canadian provinces.

How We Collected Information

We relied primarily on four methods of gathering information about food growers and sellers:

1. In the second half of 1989 we mailed over 4,000 *questionnaires* to producers, distributors, restaurants, and retailers, to identify their terms of sale, products, and specialties. We received about a 45 percent response rate from retailers, 35 percent from restaurants, and 20 percent from distributors and growers, who have fewer dealings with the public. Some questionnaires were unusable either because they were inadequately completed or because the information revealed them as inappropriate for this book. To identify outstanding sources of healthy food, we asked respondents to tell us the names of their favorite suppliers. These referrals have been ranked in Chapters 8 and 9, and were used to assign diamonds (♦) in Chapters 7 and 10. The hearts (♥) were assigned based on personal experience.

2. We *interviewed* food producers, distributors, retail stores and restaurants. We also contacted association executives, consultants, and researchers to obtain overall information on the food industry. Based on hundreds of interviews, we assigned diamonds (♦) and hearts (♥) to rate companies and groups in Chapters 3 through 6, in the same way as in Chapters 7 through 10—a diamond means positive third-party endorsements, a heart means my personal endorsement.

3. We *researched* food contaminants, dietary guidelines, growing methods and products through library searches, subscriptions to 25 health newsletters and journals, and interviews and ongoing contacts with dozens of officials of government agencies and nonprofit groups.

4. We *verified* the general background material with a panel of experts, who were sent copies of the chapters in their areas of expertise, and the details of the listings with hundreds of phone calls.

Criteria for Entries

- Only healthy foods are included—no supplements, treatments, or personal-care products, valuable though they may be for the health of some people. We just provide information on the healthiest food and how best to buy it.

- For Chapters 8 and 10, we included only businesses for which we could verify information directly with the people involved, through phone calls or questionnaires.

- In selecting vendors, we preferred those with low-fat, high-fiber (fruit, vegetable, grain) options, based on data in Chapters 2 and 3. We also preferred vendors of food grown without synthetic pesticides or additives, based on data in Chapters 4 and 5.

- We excluded many businesses that do not sell directly to the public.

A Caution and Plea

The wise reader who decides to embark on a change in diet based on the dietary information in Chapters 1 to 3 will consult with a qualified dietary adviser as described in Chapter 3. Similarly, the wise reader will not rely on our directories in Chapters 7 and 10 in place of normal consumer caution—restaurant and store managements change.

If you disagree with a listing and think we have misjudged or omitted a good vendor company, participate in the process by returning the INFO-FORM in the back of this book. Your help will make an updated edition of this book even more useful. We will be glad to send a questionnaire for the next edition to any company you recommend.

If the INFO-FORM has already been removed from this copy, send your nomination or comments to JTM Reports, Inc., 9th Floor, 30 Irving Place, New York, NY 10003. Thank you for caring.

Seeds of Change is a prominant group in the effort to maintain the genetic diversity of various species of plants. They have managed to combine these efforts with research in sustainable agriculture on their farm off the old Santa Fe Trail in New Mexico.

PART 1
WHAT FOOD IS HEALTHY

Milly's in San Rafael California received the most recommendations of any restaurant in our surveys with accolades coming from as far away as Wisconsin and Georgia. The offerings at the restaurant are reasonably priced and exclusively vegetarian.

DIET AND DISEASE

*Health is a positive state of wellness, beyond the mere absence of sickness,
just as peace is more than the absence of war.*

What is Healthy Food?

This book is designed to provide the context and information for the practice of healthy eating. We have evolved into an information society, but we have little to show for it when it comes to our understanding of nutrition and the connections between food, disease, the environment, and ourselves.

The next four chapters seek to make these connections and address the question: "What is Healthy Food? What Should We Eat?" First, what do we mean by "healthy" and "food"?

Healthy. Health is a positive state of wellness,[1] beyond the mere absence of sickness, just as peace is more than the absence of war and encompasses a positive sense of justice among people. The absence of sickness is just a first test of health. This is not just a linguistic distinction. It is at the heart of a problem with Western medicine, which—as we shall discuss in Chapter 3—focuses mostly on disease, not health.

The idea of health as wholeness is rooted in the Anglo-Saxon origin of the word, from the Old English word hael (wassail means "your health"), which is also the source of the modern English words "hail", "hale", "heal", and indeed "whole" itself.

We use the word "healthy" to refer to both people and food. When referring to *people*, the word means "possessing good health; hale or sound (in body)." When referring to *food* or diet, the word means "conducive to health; wholesome, salubrious; salutary." These are the first and second definitions in U.S. and British dictionaries.

Food. Food may be defined as "any solid or liquid which when swallowed can supply any of the following: (a) material from which the body can produce movement, heat, or other forms of energy, (b) material for growth, repair, or reproduction, (c) substances necessary to regulate the production of energy or the processes of growth and repair."

Under this definition, our discussion of food includes alcohol, even though alcohol also has drug-like properties. Tobacco is in no way a food, but because it is so deeply implicated in the killer diseases that affect Americans we will have reason to refer to it many times in this book.

Another definition of food refers to its component *nutrients*. Thus food is defined as "material consisting essentially of protein, carbohydrate, and fat used in the body of an organism to sustain growth and vital processes, repair tissues, and furnish energy." As we shall discuss at more length in the next two chapters, *carbohydrates* provide the body with energy and may also be converted into body fat; *fats* and *alcohol* provide energy in more concentrated form than carbohydrates and may also be converted into body fat; finally, *proteins* provide materials (*amino acids*, of which 20 are "standard" and nine are "essential")[2] for growth and repair, and can also be converted into carbohydrates.

In addition to these major nutrients, food provides *minerals*, which are used for growth and repair, and *vitamins*, which help regulate body processes. Vitamins differ from *hormones*, which also regulate body processes, in that they cannot (except for vitamin D) be manufactured within the body and must be externally supplied; hormones are all made within the body. *Enzymes* are special proteins that accelerate the rate of certain chemical reactions as catalysts (i.e., without themselves being affected).

Not considered nutrients, but important to bear in mind, are water, which is necessary for life (and may contain valuable minerals), and *fiber*, which we discuss at greater length in Chapters 2 and 3.

Specifically excluded from this book are sources of *supplements*, i.e. concentrations of vitamins or minerals taken for medicinal purposes, either as pills, capsules, or special liquid tonics or meals. This is not necessarily to say that overcoming dietary shortcomings in this way is always improper. Physicians have used vitamin and mineral supplements (sometimes in megadoses, as we shall discuss in Chapter 3) to treat nutritional deficits in their patients.

It's just that for most people eating a healthy diet, supplements simply aren't necessary. As several nutrition guides say: "If all the nutrients we need can come from food, why not just get them from food?"[3]

America's Killer Diseases

Leading Causes of Death, 1986. In much of the world, the No. 1 health problem is lack of food; millions of people die each year from starvation. In America, however, the No. 1 enemy of health is excess—the self-destructive way we eat, the alcohol and other beverages we drink, and the quantity of non-nutrients or anti-nutrients we ingest, such as tobacco. Here, thousands die each year from diseases caused in large part by hazardous diets and, to a lesser extent, tainted food.

The two leading killers of Americans in 1986, the latest year for complete published mortality data, were cardiovascular diseases and cancer. They account for two-thirds of the deaths in this country. Cardiovascular diseases (heart disease, strokes, and other vascular diseases) caused 46 percent of deaths; cancer caused another 22 percent. See Table 1–1.

Table 1–1.
Ten Leading Causes of Death, 1986

1	Heart diseases, total	36.4%
2	Cancer, total	22.3%
3	"All other" diseases*	8.8%
4	Strokes	7.1%
5	Accidents, suicide	6.0%
6	Lung diseases	3.6%
7	Pneumonia, influenza	3.3%
8	Diabetes mellitus	1.8%
9	Ill-defined conditions	1.5%
10	Infections, parasites	1.5%

*Residual category.[4]
Source: *Vital Statistics of the U.S.*, 1986, II, *Mortality*, B, Table 8–9.[5]

High-Mortality States. Not all U.S. states have the same mortality rates. The Centers for Disease Control collected information on death rates from "chronic" and "largely preventable" diseases—coronary heart disease and stroke; chronic obstructive pulmonary disease, lung cancer, breast cancer, and colorectal cancer; and cirrhosis and diabetes. Death rates from these diseases in 1986 range from a low of 326.8 deaths per 100,000 in Hawaii to 517.6 deaths per 100,000 population in Michigan. The ten "best" and "worst" are shown in Table 1–2.

The mortality data of some of the "worst" states clearly show the cost in abbreviated human life of industrial activity and coal mining. They are also interesting in the context of organic or sustainable farming, to be discussed in Chapter 5. Several states with the highest mortality rates (New York, Delaware, Indiana) have been the slowest to show interest in reducing use of toxic chemicals in the growing of food.

Table 1–2.
Death Rates, Chronic/Preventable Diseases

Rank	State*	Death Rate, 1986
"Best Ten"		
1	Hawaii	326.8
2	North Dakota	361.1
3	Utah	361.7
4	New Mexico	382.0
5	Texas	387.6
6	Minnesota	388.4
7	Idaho	394.9
8	Arizona	396.2
9	Nebraska	398.3
10	Colorado	400.3
"Worst Ten"		
42	Illinois	487.9
43	Indiana	490.6
44	Rhode Island	491.0
45	South Carolina	493.2
46	Delaware	494.2
47	Kentucky	497.2
48	Ohio	501.2
49	New York	508.5
50	West Virginia	512.5
51	Michigan	517.6

*The District of Columbia is counted as a state.
Source: Centers for Disease Control, *Morbidity and Mortality Weekly Report*, January 19, 1990.[6]

U.S. Trends. Of the two leading killers, heart disease has been declining in recent years, but cancer continues to increase.

Heart disease and related artery diseases increased 167 percent as a cause of death between 1900 and 1970, from 148 to 394 deaths per 100,000 population. But since then, deaths from this cause have been decreasing, to 312 per 100,000 in 1988.[7]

Cancer deaths, however, have been increasing steadily, from 68 per 100,000 in 1900 to 199 in 1988.[8] Of the 985,000 new cases of cancer in 1988 (five-year average survival rate 49 percent), 152,000 were lung cancers (survival rate 13 percent), 152,000 were breast cancers (survival rate 74 percent), and 105,000 were colon cancers (survival rate 54 percent).[9]

International Comparisons. Despite its wealth, the United States does not have the world's highest life expectancy. Switzerland and Japan head the list of 13 countries with higher life expectancies shown in Table 1–3. Of the five diseases most commonly linked to diet, coronary heart disease and cancers of the colon and breast are common in the United States and Europe but have a low incidence in Japan, while cancer of the stomach and cerebrovascular disease are common in Japan but relatively infrequent in the United States.[10]

The low-fat Japanese diet is credited with that country's low rates of coronary heart disease and cancer of the

Table 1–3.
Life Expectancies, Selected Countries

Rank	Country	Life expectancy at birth (years)
1	Switzerland	78.0
2	Japan	77.8
3	Sweden	77.3
4	Canada	77.1
4	Netherlands	77.1
4	Spain	77.1
7	Greece	77.0
8	Italy	76.7
9	Australia	76.1
10	Austria	75.4
10	Belgium	75.4
12	West Germany	75.4
13	France	75.4
14	United States	75.3

Source: *Statistical Abstract of the U.S.*, 1989, 109th ed., Table 1405, pp. 817–818.

Table 1–4.
Life Expectancy at Birth
U.S. vs. Japan, 1955–86

	U.S.	Japan
Males		
1955	66.7	63.6
1965	66.8	67.7
1975	68.8	71.7
1980	70.0	73.4
1986	71.3	75.2
Females		
1955	72.8	67.8
1965	73.7	72.9
1975	76.6	76.9
1980	77.5	78.8
1986	78.3	80.9

Source: Japanese data from *British Medical Journal*, 23–30 December, 1989. U.S. data from National Center for Health Statistics.[13]

breast and colon. While its expenditure on health care has been comparatively small, Japan has a population-wide health-care program and has engaged in several successful public health campaigns, including one to reduce salt intake that is credited with reduced mortality from stroke and stomach cancer.[11] Deaths from strokes fell between 1980 and 1986, a 45 percent decrease for men and 66 percent for women.[12]

The upshot of the preventive measures by the Japanese is that their life expectancy moved ahead of the United States between 1955 and 1986. (See Table 1–4.) In 1955, men had a life expectancy of 66.7 years in the United States and 63.6 years in Japan; in other words, boy babies in the United States could expect to live over three years longer than those in Japan. The figures for girl babies in 1955 were 72.8 and 67.8—U.S. girls could be expected to live five years longer than Japanese girls.

Life expectancy increased in the U.S. between 1955 and 1986, but at a much slower rate than in Japan. So in 1986 a boy baby in the U.S. could look forward to 71.3 years of life, versus 75.2 years for a Japanese baby. From three years shorter, life expectancy of the Japanese male became four years longer, a gain of seven years. The figures for women in 1986 were 78.3 years in the U.S. and 80.9 in Japan—from five years shorter, Japanese women could expect to live two-and-a-half years longer, a gain of over seven years.

British analysts attribute "an important part" of the improvement in Japanese life expectancy to the country's diet. The Japanese diet is still low in fat (even though the Japanese urban diet has doubled its fat content in relation to the rural diet, the current level provides only about half the fat intake of the West) and is high in the ratio of polyunsaturated to saturated fat (over three times the ratio in the West).[14]

Relating Diet and Disease

At least one-fourth of all adult Americans were dieting in 1988.[15] Some say as many as half of Americans are dieting. Others say that they aren't dieting, they are only trying to control their weight. See Chapter 3, Note 18, for references. The verb "to diet," meaning to go on a temporary stringent low-calorie eating program, is falling into disfavor because short-term changes in eating have produced only short-term changes in health (and the changes may be hazardous or counter-productive, or both).[16] However, the noun "diet," meaning the sum total of calories, nutrients, and other substances consumed daily, is very much alive.

Diseases. Diet is increasingly being identified as a cause of the two leading killers of Americans, cardiovascular diseases and cancers:

Cardiovascular diseases, heart and artery (cerebrovascular) illnesses, are linked closely to smoking, ingestion of saturated fat and alcohol, and lack of exercise; heavy caffeine intake adds to the risk.

Cancers have been linked to smoking, alcohol, and ingesting toxic chemicals; cancers of the colon and breast have been linked to the Western-style diet.

These degenerative diseases pose a greater challenge than the earlier killers—cholera, smallpox, tuberculosis and typhoid. The earlier killers had a simpler etiology (cause). The relationship between the disease and the bacillus or other invader was straightforward. They required changes in lifestyle, such as greater attention to public and private sanitation, but not as pervasive a reexamination of lifestyle as we now confront.

Part of the difficulty today is that the degenerative diseases don't have a single cause, i.e. they are *multi-factorial*. They depend on factors that are widely believed to include diet but may also include the individual's living and work environment. Scientific proof of a relationship be-

Table 1–5
Prevalence of Acute and Chronic Conditions
Number per Thousand Pop., 1988
Ranked by Frequency

Condition, *Acute* or Chronic	Millions Affected	No. per 1,000
Influenza (flu)	106	442
Non-flu respiratory illnesses[17]	103	428
Injuries	59	246
Parasites	54	223
Sinusitis, chronic	34	140
Arthritis	31	130
Hypertension[18]	29	122
Orthopedic impairments	27	112
Hay fever, allergic rhinitis	22	93
Hearing impairments	22	93
Heart disease	20	84
Digestive system disorders	15	63
Bronchitis, chronic	12	49
Hemorrhoids	11	46
Asthma	10	41
Dermatitis, including eczema	9	38
Migraine headaches	9	38
Visual impairments	8	35
Varicose veins, lower limbs	8	35
Diabetes	6	26
Kidney and bladder disorders	6	26
Tinnitus	6	26
Sebaceous skin cysts and acne	6	26
Indigestion, frequent	6	26
Cataracts	6	26
Hernia of abdominal cavity	5	20
Constipation, frequent	4	20

Source: National Center for Health Statistics, 1989.[19]

tween a disease and multi-factorial causes is more difficult than between a disease and a single cause.

Besides the two leading killer diseases, a variety of acute and chronic conditions interfere with people's state of wellness. In Table 1–5, the acute conditions are italicized.

To link possible causes to a disease, scientists and doctors rely on several approaches: theories, epidemiology, population studies, and animal and laboratory experiments.

Theories. The time-honored way of approaching disease etiology is to consider what *might* or what *ought* to cause it, by analogy with other diseases. Then if statistical data or experiments support the theory, a case for its validity is developed. A successful treatment is more credible if the physician has a theory for why it should work.

Epidemiology. Epidemiology is the statistical study of the incidence of death and illness in different regions, among exposed and non-exposed populations, and over time. Experts agree that the major killers today, the degenerative diseases such as heart disease and cancer, are caused by multifactorial or "lifestyle" factors, as opposed to a single cause such as a bacterium or virus (though oncologists

haven't given up on viral activation as a cause of cancer). Of the factors, the major ones are diet (including alcohol consumption) and tobacco; the main secondary ones are exercise and occupation.

Population Studies. A controlled test or trial is ordinarily a "double-blind" experiment in which the subjects are divided into two or more groups. Neither they nor those making the measurements know which participants are in which group. However, for dietary and lifestyle factors this test is difficult to conduct, because people generally know what they are and are not eating.

So instead, population studies are also used. *Retrospective* studies ask people with a disease about their past dietary and other habits; the difficulty is that people don't always remember very precisely. *Prospective* studies quiz a large group and monitor them over a period of time. *Intervention* trials involve a group that is selected to make dietary changes while a control group makes none. *Case-control* studies attempt to identify causes by analyzing genetic and retrospective differences (diets and lifestyles) between people with a disease and a matched sample of people with no signs of the disease.

Animal, Laboratory, and Computer Simulation Experiments. Those favoring animal experiments for testing the effects of chemicals argue that: (1) Tests can provide valuable information to save human lives; (2) On short-lived small animals, experiments can show the effects of food or substances over several generations; and (3) Conditions for groups of animals can be controlled in ways that would be unacceptable for human population studies. Animal rights activists argue that these conditions are unacceptable for animals as well, and that the standard procedure of administering toxins until half of the sample group dies (the so-called LD50, for lethal dose 50 percent) is unnecessarily wasteful of animal life. Because of activism against this test, its use was down 96 percent between 1979 and 1985.[20]

Many people distinguish morally between testing on animals for medical purposes as opposed to testing ordinary consumer goods like cosmetics, for which the so-called Draize Test for eye irritation is used. Another significant distinction is whether or not the tests are administered humanely, for example using a pain killer if pain is entailed.

Laboratory and computer simulation experiments entail combining food components and other elements to simulate what happens inside the human body. The Ames Test replaces animal tests with laboratory tests on bacteria; tissue and cell culture cultures are being used instead of both the LD50 and Draize tests; human skin patch tests are being used instead of the LD50 test; and computer simulation models have been developed that satisfy FDA approval requirements.[21]

A question raised about all such tests is the threshold of danger. Experiments on animals may use doses that are much higher than humans would ever be exposed to; some essential nutrients at high enough doses are carcinogens.

Doubt also remains about the extent to which conclusions from animal and laboratory experiments apply to humans. In many cases, no substitute exists yet for animal studies. But at Johns Hopkins and Rockefeller Universities, and at companies like Mobil and Procter & Gamble, effective substitutes for many tests have been developed.[22]

What We Eat

Early Dietary Research. The research of Sir Robert McCarrison in India during the early part of this century showed the importance of diet in the prevention of disease. As Director of Nutrition Research in India he traveled extensively throughout the subcontinent. He observed that peoples of the north, such as the Hunzas and Sikhs, were considerably healthier than those of the south, such as the Madrassis. They lived longer, had lower infant mortality, and had fewer diseases requiring surgery. The key difference between these communities was the food they consumed. The Hunzas ate wholemeal flour, uncooked green vegetables, fresh fruit, sprouted grains, fresh whole milk and occasionally fresh meat. The southern peoples "survived on a diet of largely refined foods such as white rice, little milk and dairy produce plus a few generally overcooked vegetables."

McCarrison fed two groups of rats the diets of the northern Indian people and the typical British person. The rats on the northern Indian diet were healthy and happy. But by the 60th day the stronger rats on the British diet started to kill and eat the weaker rats, who suffered from diseases of the lungs, stomach/intestine, nerves—the same diseases that afflicted people in England and Wales. Sir Robert decided three factors were essential: (1) Food must be grown in healthy soil, (2) It should be eaten whole, and (3) It should be eaten fresh.[23]

Fast Food, Short Life. Most people want to live a long and healthy life. What they eat has a lot to do with whether they achieve that goal. So why do so many Americans eat unhealthy food? To note Sir Robert's recommendations—why do we eat food not grown in healthy soil, heavily processed, and not fresh? Mostly because unhealthy food is all around us—in fast-food outlets, in our kitchens, in the vending machines, and on the coffee carts in our offices—and because Americans have a taste for it.

Still, we do want to be healthy, and reasonable people will make the effort. Choosing to eat healthy food takes some effort at first. We have to break away from unhealthy routines and unhealthy junk food. If we make the effort, it is possible to make healthy eating a habit. One way is to know how to look for food that is both healthy and palatable.

Most Americans live and work in urban areas, and the problems with our eating begin with the tendency of urbanized Americans to do everything in a hurry. At mealtimes, this means fast food. We eat too quickly and settle for easy-to-prepare, "tasty" meals full of saturated fats, sugar, salt, and hazardous chemicals described in Chapter 4.

Even those who think they are ensuring a healthy diet with careful purchases at the supermarket must note reports that produce and processed food are not always what they seem. Federal standards permit levels of harmful chemicals in our food that are cumulatively hazardous, especially where children are concerned. Labels on processed foods may deceive us about the health value of the food. For example, a label claiming "no cholesterol" may be on foods heavy in saturated fats; one saying a food contains "unsaturated" oil may mislead if the oil is hydrogenated, because the process saturates some oil and creates trans-fatty acids that may behave like saturated fat.

So shopping for healthier food isn't always easy. But this book will help you be a savvy consumer. The more there are of you, the more established food growers and sellers will respond to market demand and devote greater attention to disclosing and reducing harmful ingredients in food.

Economic Factors in the Sale of Food. Why have we strayed so far from the path of good nutrition? Much of it relates to the economics of the food industry. To ensure a variety of foods on a year-round basis while keeping down food costs and maintaining farm incomes, the U.S. Department of Agriculture (USDA) has urged efficiency on American farmers. This pursuit of efficiency continues, often to our detriment, as food is passed on to fast-food outlets and supermarkets.

On the farm, in the name of efficiency, fertilizer companies promote petroleum-based chemical fertilizers to replace more time-consuming natural farming methods that use compost and crop rotation to maintain the fertility of the soil. As with human beings, the first small dose of a farm chemical may seem harmless enough. But eventually the land, like the body, becomes addicted to the chemicals—farmers have to add more and more of them to maintain crop production because the natural aeration and fertility of the soil is depleted as the water is gradually poisoned (this subject is discussed in more detail in Chapter 5).

The same goes for the handling of fungi, insects and weeds. Organic farmers can cope with these pests without toxic chemicals. But it takes skill and time. Synthetic pesticides are easier to use. The problem is that the chemicals don't kill just fungi, harmful insects and weeds. They also affect the health of humans, animals, and the soil.

In the meat industry, animals bred for slaughter are injected with antibiotics to cope with their decreased resistance and increased susceptibility to disease as they are crammed, for economic reasons, in compartments where they can hardly move. Cows are injected with hormones to increase their milk supply, bulls to increase their meat yield. Farmers who fight the trend face declining incomes as the increased production from hormone-injected cows keeps milk supply up and prices down. Many overseas buyers refuse to accept hormone-injected American beef.

On down the food line, retailers face very clear economic pressures. The higher the price of the items on their shelves and the lower the spoilage rate, the more money they make. Raw produce is hard to handle in bulk, is low in price relative to processed food, and has a higher spoilage rate. Markups on raw produce are higher than other items, but because of the heavy staff needs and wastage, profits may not be. The economic pressure on the retailers is to provide processed food—cooked, baked, canned, frozen, mixed with yet more chemicals to lengthen their life on store shelves. Some food is even irradiated to lengthen its shelf life, as we note in Chapter 4.

Finally, fast-food outlets have proliferated—places that spray French fries with sugar and cook them in beef fat, and serve high-fat hamburgers loaded with salt. Some fry chicken chunks with so much saturated oil that they are even fattier than the hamburgers. For example, a McDonald's plain hamburger has 13 grams of fat (3 teaspoons of fat, with 4.4 grams of fat per teaspoon), 45 percent of the 263 calories. That's bad enough, but a Dairy Queen Chicken Sandwich or a Burger King Specialty Chicken Sandwich has 40 grams of fat, three times as much fat as the hamburger, accounting for over *half* the calories![24]

These figures aren't isolated examples of American eating habits. *One-fifth* of the U.S. population visits a fast-food restaurant every day, and the calories from a typical meal are 40 to 55 percent fat[25]—twice the recommended amount.

The food industry is, by its own terms, efficient. Some components of the industry express an inability to make decisions in favor of public health because of competition. However, competition can be used in favor of public health if consumers choose to use their power in that direction. Growers and manufacturers are very dependent on high-volume retailers, i.e. the supermarket chains; the retailers therefore do have great potential influence on the food industry. Supermarket executives need some sense that consumer interests in healthy food are not "media-driven responses to unproved hypotheses, or worse, cycles of fashionable eating . . ."[26]

It's time we consumers support those who have bucked economic pressures to maintain our supply of healthy food.

Consumption Data. Since 1977, as we discuss in Chapter 3, the Federal Government has been urging U.S. consumers to eat more grains and vegetables, and less fat. How in fact have consumers been reacting to this advice? The information in Table 1–6 can help answer this question.

Between 1978 and 1988, we Americans did seem to take dietary advice to heart. *We cut consumption of red meat by 71 pounds per person, i.e. by 39 percent.* We increased fish consumption by 10 percent, and poultry by 8 percent. We took in a little less fluid milk and cream, but still consumed 236 pounds a year (about 30 gallons). We consumed 15 percent more fats and oils, not so good, but this 8-pound increase surely doesn't wipe out the fat reduction from cutting out 71 pounds of red meat, especially since a result of the decline in meat consumption is that ranchers and supermarkets are making every effort to lower the fat content in the meat that they sell.

During the same decade, we consumed 16 percent more fresh fruits, a good sign, slightly offset by a decline in processed fruits. Our consumption of vegetables was up by 36 pounds per person, 22 percent, but mostly in the form of canned and (a growing category) frozen products. Bean consumption was up, and sugar down; but the drop in sugar consumption was more than totally offset by the increase in corn sweeteners and (not shown in Table 1–6)

Table 1–6
U.S. Food Consumption Per Capita, Pounds

Selected Foods	1978	1988	Change
Red meats (carcass wt.)	186.1	115.1	−71.0
Fish (edible wt.)	13.6	15.0	+1.4
Poultry (edible wt.)	53.8	57.3	+4.5
Fluid milk and cream	239.0	236.2	−2.8
Fats and oils	55.6	64.1	+8.5
Fresh fruits	83.3	96.9	+13.6
Processed fruits	19.1	15.5	−3.6
Fresh vegetables*	100.5	100.3	−0.2
Canned vegetables*	52.8	82.8	+30.0
Frozen vegetables*	10.9	17.5	+6.6
Dry beans	5.9	7.9	+2.0
Sugar (refined)	93.1	62.4	−30.7
Corn sweeteners	42.6	70.1	+27.5
Wheat flour	112.0	127.5	+5.5

*Excluding potatoes.
Source: USDA, Economic Research Service[27]

low-calorie sweeteners. Wheat flour consumption was up by 5 percent.

The overall *20 percent increase in U.S. consumption of fruits and vegetables over the decade* is a very positive development. The director of the British Heart Foundation believes that "this is a very important factor" in the drop in U.S. (and Australian) deaths from heart disease.[28] In Britain, dietary change overall is slow and mixed, but heart disease and cancer rates are falling among younger people because compared to a generation earlier they are like us smoking less, consuming less fat, and eating more fruits and vegetables.[29]

This suggests that consumers are making health-oriented decisions in their supermarkets, which should encourage manufacturers and retailers to ensure that healthy food will find a place in supermarkets over the long term.

Government Regulation and Advice

Food Regulation. Who is responsible for our health? The government? Yes, in part. The USDA inspects every one of the 6,600 U.S. slaughterhouses and processing plants every day, for disease. But it doesn't necessarily keep diseased food off the market—a substantial percentage of the chickens that pass inspection have salmonella.

The U.S. Food and Drug Administration (FDA) has primary responsibility for food and drug safety. It monitors proposed new human and veterinary drugs to make sure they are safe and efficacious (i.e., they do what the pharmaceutical company claims) and inspects fruit, vegetables, seafood, eggs and milk. However, it has fewer than 700 food inspectors and lab scientists to cover the entire country as well as the flow of foreign imports. It examines less than 1% of domestic seafood and no more than 3% of imported seafood.

The FDA's inspection efforts are supplemented by state agencies. State agencies monitor dairy facilities, with the FDA simply checking that they inspect dairy farms on a regular schedule. Each state has its own approach to food regulation and inspection. Many states, as we shall see in Chapter 5, spell out the meaning of "organic" food, and Maine even defines "natural" food and has detailed regulations for disclosure of post-harvest treatment of food. But a state like Delaware has no regulations for labeling food that has been grown with farm chemicals or has been treated after harvest with chemicals or radiation.

The FDA and USDA require that some food labels disclose the ingredients of processed food in order of weight. Exceptions occur for foods like ice cream provided they are made with standard ingredients (the USDA regulates the *minimum* butterfat for ice cream and ice milk). The Federal label law has many shortcomings—for example, the requirements for disclosure of waxes and colorings are not enforced. We discuss health claims on food labels at the end of Chapter 2.

In a democracy, government can only be as effective as public opinion permits, and the interests behind the status quo are strong. The interests behind change are (in the earliest stages) scattered and weak. By using this catalogue and reporting to us on the INFO-FORM in the back of this book, you can help protect your own health. You can also send a signal to the large growers and food processors that it's time to pay attention to the health concerns of consumers.

Consumers must continue to be concerned about foods that have been produced or preserved with toxic chemicals like aldicarb, which was found in such strength in California watermelons in 1985 that 180 people became sick from them.[30] In this book we provide information on the extent of risk we face and how to minimize it in our food buying.

The Federal Government, after years of neglect of the impact of toxic pesticides[31] on our soil, water, and food, has (in a remarkable story told in Chapter 5) turned its attention to these issues. The USDA has begun a program to show farmers how to reduce the use of pesticides in farming.

In subsequent chapters we list trade associations for growers, names of U.S. Environmental Protection Agency (EPA) and FDA regulatory units and key state counterparts, and nonprofit organizations concerned with public health.

Dietary Advice, Controversy. As the imbalance between what Americans eat and what they should eat becomes clearer year by year, pressure has grown for the U.S. Government to lend its authority to guidelines for public use.

In the 1970s this idea was originally resisted for several reasons. First, the U.S. medical leadership has had a history of not being very interested in nutrition, in part because of its historical battles with practitioners who have advocated more attention to nutrition. For example, it has been slow to recognize the significance of diet in health care, as evidenced by the scarcity of instruction in nutrition in U.S. medical schools.[32] This is, fortunately, changing among younger doctors and medical students, who are demanding more nutrition-related instruction; but it takes time to change the entrenched position of a profession's leaders.

Second, although it is clear that certain groups of Americans should change their diets, some experts resist directing this advice to the entire population. For example, only a few Americans are in imminent danger of death if they do not reduce their salt intake. However, telling everyone to reduce salt intake is like asking everyone to be immunized. Even though only a few people might be exposed to smallpox, everyone gets the vaccine. Better everyone cut down their salt intake, because the risk of having *too little* sodium in the U.S. is almost nil, and the risk of having too much is for some people high. Similarly, even though the need to reduce intake of saturated fats depends on risk factors such as a person's blood cholesterol level, the risk in the U.S. of someone with adequate calorie intake consuming *too little* fat is almost nil.

Finally, some people believe that a government should not issue population-wide advice unless it is absolutely certain of its facts. Such people urge delay on the basis that studies are not convincing enough, or that the theories behind them are weak. Those who favor government action respond that if the preponderance of evidence points in a certain direction, the public should be so informed.

In 1987, the medical establishment took a major step by initiating a dietary campaign to persuade the public to reduce its intake of saturated fat—the National Cholesterol Education Program. The American public gets 42 percent of its calories from fat; we are being urged to reduce this to 30 percent or less. (Other experts recommend cutting fat intake further, to 20 percent or even 10 percent.)[33]

The Vegetarian Option. Since a large portion of the fat we consume comes from animal products (eggs, dairy and meat), the campaign against fat has given vegetarianism a new U.S. respectability. It helps that vegetarians are healthier than the general population—they are more likely to be at a desirable weight, they have lower cholesterol levels; consequently they experience fewer deaths from heart disease and cancer; and they also have less diabetes, fewer hernias, and better digestion.[34] Animal rights advocates have joined the ranks of health-motivated vegetarians.

Vegetarian diets are gaining adherents, and new vegetarians are seeking organic foods and wholefoods. This in turn has helped natural-food stores and even supermarkets sell more fresh organic produce and prominently display a range of healthy products such as whole-grain bread, whole brown rice, and muesli.[35]

We're not saying you shouldn't eat meat at all. Just that a well-informed move toward the vegetarian diet appears to be the right direction for us, as we shall see in Chapters 2 and 3.

Some argue that it's not enough to be a vegetarian— the vegetables must be organically grown and cooked as little as possible, just boiled enough to kill bacteria such as listeria. We get to this subject in Chapters 4 and 5.

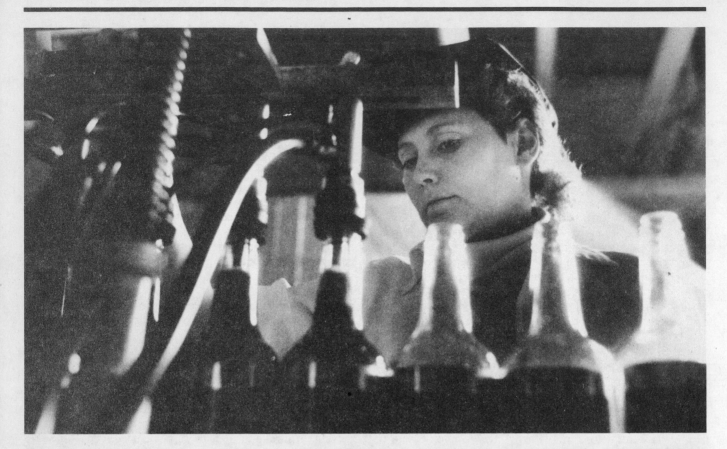

Denise Beach of **Eden Foods** monitors the bottling of Organic Soy sauce in the companies plant in Clinton, Michigan. Eden makes many organic products from soy-milk and flour to dry roasted tamari almonds (bottom). The Company was one of the pioneers in organic certification and was one of the most highly acclaimed companies in our surveys.

HOW TO IDENTIFY
HEALTHY FOOD

"The unexamined meal is not worth eating."
—After Socrates[1]

If what we eat affects our health, how do we know what's best? This chapter looks at how foods may be classified, analyzed and identified, to help us choose what's healthy, in preparation for looking at healthy diets (Chapter 3) and food hazards (Chapter 4).

We briefly review three traditional classifications relating to food, two Eastern (Asian) and one Greek. Then we look at food families from the perspective of Western science, and at the components of food. Finally, we look at the uses and abuses of food labeling.

Three Traditional Food Classifications

Two simplified versions of complex Eastern theories relating food and health have developed substantial followings in the United States. Similar theories were propounded in ancient Greece.

Macrobiotic Yin and Yang. Chinese philosophers divide everything in the world into two categories: yin and yang. Yin originally meant the "shady side of the hill" and yang meant "the sunny side of the hill." Yin stood for coolness and darkness—night, moon, female. Yang stood for heat and light—sun, day, male. From this organizing principle the entire macrobiotic (from the Greek words "great" and "life") diet was introduced to Europe and the United States in the 1950s and 1960s as part of a larger philosophical system by George Ohsawa, born in Japan Sakurazawa Nyoiti.[2] Ohsawa learned his diet and philosophy from Sagen Ishizuka, a Japanese army doctor, who had concluded, based on self-experimentation, that whole brown rice was the best food for bodily and mental balance, which he saw as the essence of health and happiness. The macrobiotic-style diet was originally developed 300 years ago by a scholar, Ekiken Kaibara, whose essential advice was: "eat less, sleep less, and desire less."[3]

A brief macrobiotic explanation of the life of the salmon may help explain the philosophy. Salmon eggs are salty, which makes them hot and therefore yang. Since the ocean is also yang, salmon eggs must be deposited in a yin place. So the salmon seeks something yin, unsalty and cold, i.e. fresh water. It swims upstream and there it lays the eggs. Now the baby salmon that emerge from the eggs are yin, and they are attracted to the ocean. After four years in the ocean they become strong and yang, so that when they are ready to spawn they instinctively are drawn back to their yin birthplace to deposit the yang eggs.[4]

The first U.S. macrobiotic lectures featured Ohsawa speaking on Long Island in 1960; the first macrobiotic store was established in New York City.[5] Two leading promoters of macrobiotics in the United States are Ohsawa's disciples Michio Kushi, who heads the Boston-based Kushi Foundation, and Herman Aihara, who heads the George Ohsawa Macrobiotic Foundation in Oroville, Calif.[6] The organizations offer publications and courses on macrobiotics.

Macrobiotics stresses balance and harmony in living. It prescribes a diet of foods that avoid the two extremes of yin and yang. Ohsawa believed it would be easier for Westerners to understand yin and yang if he reversed the traditional Chinese concept that earth is female and heaven male. For his purposes earth and the contractive force became yang, and heaven and the expansive force were yin. Yin is therefore for macrobiotics that which moves outward and dissipates, while yang is that which pulls together and organizes.[7] Thus leaves are yin, while roots are yang. Leafy foods, like spinach, are on the yin side; foods that are from roots, like carrots, are on the yang side.

Extreme yin foods include milk, coffee, sugar, alcohol and tropical fruits and vegetables. Extreme yang foods include cheeses, meat, poultry and eggs. Avoiding both extremes is the macrobiotic diet, which goes in heavily for whole brown rice and locally grown and sea vegetables.[8]

The diet excludes, besides meat and dairy products,

peppers, potatoes, and tomatoes (all members of the night-shade family); bananas, citrus fruits, spinach; all canned and frozen foods, because they are non-local; and honey, refined sugar, and supplements. A macrobiotic *meal* is unquestionably healthy as a change from the fatty American diet; an exclusively macrobiotic *diet* requires very careful planning to avoid malnutrition.[9]

Yoga Gunas. Indian philosophers developed a number of intricate classifications, *gunas*, for foods based on such factors as weight and oiliness. These classifications were first recorded at length in India's Vedic medicine, developed by the Aryans who migrated to India in 1500 B.C. (therefore also called Aryuvedic medicine). The word Vedic refers to the vedas or "sacred lore" of the Aryans. In Vedic medicine an illness is brought by one of the gods—Varuna brought dropsy, Rudra shot painful arrows, and Yakshma and fire demon Takman brought fever. Remedies included plants like Kushtha, considered an offspring of the gods.[10] The 22 gunas were related to characteristics of the gods. Religion and science were, we might say, unified.

Yoga teachers follow the vegetarian beliefs of the Indian religions.[11] They believe that the meat of dead animals has lost its life force, whereas freshly harvested plants retain their life force. As George Bernard Shaw, a vegetarian, put it: "Think of the fierce energy concentrated in an acorn! You bury it in the ground, and it explodes into a giant oak. Bury a sheep and nothing happens but decay."[12]

The complexity of Vedic medicine is simplified by yoga teachers to three gunas: tamas, rajas and sattva.[13] Like the yin-yang continuum, tamas is at one extreme and rajas at the other. Students are taught that the healthiest way is to seek sattva, the middle.

• *Tamasic* foods have lost their life force and promote lethargy. They reduce alertness and energy. They promote irritability and degeneration through such ailments as obesity, arthritis, and hardening of the arteries. Examples of tamasic foods are rotten or fermented fruits and vegetables; meat (especially if not fresh); or dried red chili peppers.

• *Rajasic* (from the word raja, king, i.e. "royal") foods are stimulative. They are of high quality, but detract from calmness. Fresh meat is rajasic, initially (later, it becomes tamasic and promotes lethargy). Coffee, tea, tobacco, and fresh green chili peppers are rajasic. Rajasic foods may be appropriate for people who need stimulation—warriors and rulers, for example—but not for scholars or priests.

• *Sattvic* foods promote a balanced state of quiet energy, of calm alertness. Sattvic foods include fresh fruit, whole grains, and fresh milk.

The macrobiotic and yoga-vegetarian diets have a great deal in common. Both stress grains, fresh fruits and vegetables. The main difference between the two diets is that yoga is lacto-vegetarian; it permits (fresh) milk. Macrobiotics forbids non-locally grown fruits and vegetables, but in some forms permits fish; yoga simply insists that fruits and vegetables be fresh.

Both diets differ from the strict vegetarian diet, which does not permit milk but normally puts no restrictions on the distance that fruits and vegetables have traveled. Vegans are strict vegetarians with the additional restriction that they do not eat any animal products, such as eggs or honey.

Because of the yoga emphasis on fresh food, yoga centers are often associated with the sale of food. In New York City, for example, one of the most popular natural foods stores is attached to and operated by the Integral Yoga Institute on West 13th Street.

Greek Humors. Greek medicine flowered in the 5th Century B.C. Its most prominent practitioner was Hippocrates, the Father of Western Medicine, who was born on the island of Cos. Many books on medicine have been ascribed to him, but most of them are available only in Greek, Latin, German, or French.[14]

Hippocrates's therapy was primarily focused on dietary adjustment, and he wrote several books on diet. He used drugs to reinforce diet and only in the last resort attempted surgery (which was then riskier and more painful without today's anesthesia and antibiotics).[15] His *On Diet* describes man as being constituted of two elements, fire and water, with the qualities of hot and dry, cold and moist. He then analyzes the four bodily fluids (i.e., humors) according to the same categories and shows how diet can affect these humors. In his *On Sound Diet*, he says that food should be eaten to balance the qualities of the seasons. Thus in winter we should eat foods that keep the body hot and dry, and in summer eat foods that keep the body cool and moist.[16]

Theophrastus used this analysis to describe geniuses as melancholic, basically cold and dry, but with hot elements that must be kept tempered with appropriately bland foods and living style to avoid emotional instability. The three other categories of people depended on the degree of dominance of the other three humors. In sanguine people, the healthy blood fluids predominate; in choleric (bilious) people, yellow bile predominates; in phlegmatic people, phlegm predominates. Each needed a different dietary regimen. They were described in medicine passed on by the Arabs to the West in the Middle Ages, and the four humors were widely in use during that period. Some 20th-Century psychiatrists such as E. Kretschmer believe these ancient classifications of people are scientifically valid.[17]

The thrust of Greek medicine was to seek balance and moderation. Thus hot food would be mixed with cold, dry would be mixed with moist. Just as the Chinese sought to balance yin and yang and Indians balanced the lethargic and stimulative forces, Greeks also searched for the middle way, in food as in everything else.

Western Science

Western Science has a much more detailed perspective on food than the traditional classifications, complex though they were. The analytical approach of science has generated an explosion of information, and our ability to measure and process food is in many ways extremely beneficial. But science has unfortunately lost the unifying principle that underlies traditional thinking about food. As Einstein said, "science without religion is lame."[18] The gospel of moderation, where still preached, is overwhelmed by more insistent news and advertising messages.

Agronomists have one system for describing foods, chemists another, biologists at least two ways of classifying food, and manufacturers yet another.

Agronomy. Agronomists and farmers commonly divide plants into categories based on when and how they are harvested.

Roots or tubers grow in the ground and are mostly harvested in the spring or fall, like beets, radishes, rutabagas and turnips. Some are harvested year-round, like carrots, garlic, ginger, onions, potatoes, and yams.

Shoots, leaves or stems, such as asparagus, greens (chard, kale, mustard or spinach) and lettuces, are generally harvested in the spring or fall. Exceptions are cabbage, celery, green onions and parsley, which are harvested year-round.

Buds, like artichokes, broccoli, and cauliflower, are picked in the spring and fall.

Fruits, like avocado, cucumber, eggplant, green beans, peas, snow peas, summer squash (crookneck, scalloped and zucchini), and sweet corn, are harvested in the summer. Berries and orchard fruits are picked in late summer or fall.[19] Note that the use of the word "fruits" here is the biological or botanical one that we shall define when we discuss food families in the next section.

Chemistry. Chemists are able to identify foods based on whether they form acids or alkalis (base) when consumed. Some people who devise theories about balancing food believe it is important to distinguish between *acid-forming* foods such as grains, meat, and sugars, which are heavy in carbohydrates, and *alkali-forming* or basic foods such as all fruits and vegetables except legumes, which are high in acid-forming protein (dairy products are in the neutral range, although some cheeses can be acidic).

Although its usefulness in nutritional analysis is limited, the acidity-alkalinity measure has been well developed, the pH (for *parts Hydrogen*) scale, developed in 1909 by Danish chemist S. P. L. Sørenson. The pH is the number of parts of hydrogen ions per 10^n, or more formally, "the negative logarithm of the hydrogen ion expressed in moles per liter." The hydrogen ion concentration in pure water is 10^{-7}, so a pH of 7 is defined as neutral—the pH of distilled water, which lacks the input of alkaline carbon dioxide from the atmosphere, is closer to 5.5.[20] Salt water is alkaline. The lower the number, the more acidic the substance. Digestive fluids in the

stomach are intensely acidic, with a pH of 1. Baking soda is intensely alkaline, with a pH of 12.

When we classify foods according to acidity, we are interested in their effects on the body; thus we may taste citric acid in lemons in our mouth, but after being metabolized the acids break down while the minerals leave an alkaline residue; this is true of all fruits and vegetables with the exception of cranberries, plums, and prunes (we don't count legumes and grains, which are separate families and, as we shall see, are acid-forming).[21]

Biology. Biologists classify plants and animals using a hierarchy of life. At the top of the hierarchy are the *kingdoms*, the largest unit of scientific classification. These kingdoms are organized largely on the basis of food—what the organism eats and whether it can manufacture its own food. The two main kingdoms are animals (*Animalia*) and plants (*Plantae*). The other three kingdoms are bacteria, protists and fungi. Bacteria (*Monera*) are single-celled organisms that lack a membrane-enclosed nucleus and mostly feed on other organisms, though some, like the cyanobacteria (blue-green algae), can synthesize their own food. Protists (*Protista*) are predominantly single-celled but contain a membrane-bounded nucleus and may be both plantlike or animal-like in their food habits. *Fungi* have cells with walls, like plants, and tend to be included with plants in discussions of food; however, unlike plants they cannot synthesize their own food and must feed on other organisms, living or dead; yeast is a single-celled fungus but most fungi are multi-celled, such as bread molds, fruit molds, mushrooms, and toadstools.[22]

The plant and animal kingdoms are divided largely on the basis of what they eat. Plants are *autotrophic*, meaning they can synthesize their own food. Animals are *heterotrophic*, meaning they cannot synthesize food and must feed on plants or other animals.

Biologists and organic chemists study the way plants synthesize, i.e. manufacture, food by combining (in a complex process that depends on the presence of chlorophyll) carbon dioxide, water, and sunlight to generate oxygen, glucose (a sugar), and water. The equation is:

$$6CO_2 + 12H_2O + light \rightarrow 6O_2 + C_6H_{12}O_6 + 6H_2O$$

The process starts with the energy from sunlight's exciting chlorophyll molecules in plants. The new energy is transferred in part to new adenosine triphosphate (ATP) molecules, which are a major source of energy found in all living things. It also initiates a chain reaction by which a hydrogen ion and two electrons are added to a nicotinamide adenine dinucleotide (NADP+) to form NADPH. The hydrogen in NADPH is then in steps transferred to carbon dioxide to form a three-carbon compound, phosphoglyceraldehyde (PGAL). PGAL can in turn be combined and rearranged to form the six-carbon sugar glucose.[23] Carbon dioxide has become sugar.

For photosynthesis to work, plants must have chlorophyll, water, carbon dioxide, and sunlight. This means a surface to absorb sunlight and exchange gases, a source of water, and a connection between the two. The first photosynthesizers were the blue-green algae bacteria, but as they evolved the plant functions became specialized into leaves (to catch the sunlight and exchange oxygen for carbon dioxide), roots (to supply water and other nutrients), and stalks (to connect leaves and roots, raise the plant's leaves above other plants, and keep the fruit away from hungry animals).

The interrelationship of plants and animals is fundamental to their natures. Plants stay in one place and create carbohydrates and oxygen out of carbon dioxide, water, and sunlight. Animals move around and eat plants and one another, burn carbohydrates, and convert oxygen into carbon dioxide.

This interrelationship was illustrated in an experiment by the English chemist Joseph Priestley in 1772. He showed that a mouse and a plant in separate closed jars died quickly, whereas when they were put in the same jar they lived.[24] Also, most plants require outside assistance for their propagation through cross-pollination by bees and birds and through seed spreading by birds and other animals (winds and tides also serve this purpose). Some seeds have evolved to be digested and spread by birds.

Food Families

Understanding something about food families will help you (1) Plan a balanced diet and (2) Deal with food intolerances through dietary experimentation, since an intolerance for a food in one family makes it more likely you will be intolerant to other foods in the same family.

Each of the biological kingdoms is subdivided into *phyla*. Modern biology uses a classification system largely created by 18th-Century Swedish naturalist Carolus Linnaeus. The system follows Aristotle by separating animals into those that have backbones and red blood (the phylum *Chordata*) and other phyla of animals that don't. In the plant kingdom, the large phylum *Spermatophyta* is composed of seed-bearing plants, which they reproduce from ovules that develop into seeds when fertilized.

Phyla are divided into *classes*—mammals (*Mammalia*) constitute a class of red-blooded animals that have hair on their bodies and feed milk to their young; angiosperms (*Angiospermae*) constitute a large class of seed-bearing plants that reproduce from ovules that are enclosed and protected in an ovary. As we shall see when we discuss fruits and berries, with a few exceptions they are all plant ovaries. Classes are in turn divided into families, subfamilies, genera, and species. A particular species is identified with two Latin names, the genus first, with the initial letter capitalized, and the species second in lower case.

In the plant kingdom, *Taylor's Encyclopedia of Gardening* describes 191 families, 1,800 genera, and 9,200 species and varieties.[25] Of these, it singles out the 20 most important families for gardeners, which include nine vital food families: grass, palm, cabbage (or mustard), rose, pea (or legumes), rue (or citrus), carrot, mint and daisy families.

In this chapter we review the following food categories: 1. Fruit, 2. Grains and Legumes, 3. Garden Vegetables, 4. Nuts, 5. Fungi (Mushrooms), 6. Dairy Products, 7. Eggs and Other Animal Products, 8. Fish (including Shellfish), 9. Meat.[26]

We can broadly define certain diets based on these nine categories. Fishless *macrobiotic* diets are taken entirely from categories 1–4, and even exclude certain foods within these four categories (e.g., tomatoes and other members of the potato or nightshade family, and any processed grains); however, most macrobiotic diets allow some fish (Category 8). *Strict vegetarians* and *vegans* eat only from categories 1–5; strict vegetarians eat honey, which is an animal product (category 7), while vegans do not. *Lacto-vegetarians* eat only from categories 1–6. *Lacto-ovo-vegetarians* eat only from categories 1–7. *Lacto-ovo-pesce-vegetarians* eat only from categories 1–8. *Lacto-ovo-pesce-pollo-vegetarians* eat from categories 1–8 and also eat chicken; i.e. they don't eat (red) meat, but they eat everything else.

Many individuals develop personal diets based on a history of food *allergies*, which are usually detectable using allergy tests, or (more broadly) food *intolerances*, which do not show up in allergy tests. We identify a few of the foods most frequently associated with intolerances in Chapter 4. The following catalogue of food families will be a valuable reference for this purpose.

1. Fruits and Berries

Botanically, fruits are the ripened ovaries—edible or not—of flower-bearing plants, which are a family of plants within the angiosperm class (plants with ovaries), which is believed to have developed around the time the dinosaurs became extinct. The five basic groups are: (1) fruits made up of the ovaries of several flowers (mulberry, fig, pineapple); (2) those made up of several ovaries of a single flower (strawberry, blackberry, raspberry); (3) fleshy fruits from a single ovary (grape, plum, apple, cranberry, currant, blueberry, tomato, eggplant); (4) dry fruits that do not split (wheat, acorn, maple); and (5) dry fruits that split (pea, mustard).

We will follow common usage in calling tomatoes and eggplants in category 3 vegetables (not berries), and legumes and the cabbage family in category 5 also vegetables (not fruits). Conversely, we will overlook that strawberries, blackberries and raspberries are botanically not true berries because they are made up of more than one ovary.

The major fruit and berry families follow. An occasional vegetable like greengage shows up in one of the fruit families. **Banana** Family (*Musaceae*): banana, plantain, Musa arrowroot. **Citrus or Rue** Family (*Rutaceae*): orange, lemon, tangerine, clementine, grapefruit, lime, citron, ugli (all are species of the same genus). Kumquats are in this family. **Currant** Family (*Saxifragaceae*): blackcurrant, redcurrant, whitecurrant, gooseberry. **Grape** Family (*Vitaceae*): grapes, muscatels, raisins. **Heath** Family (*Ericaceae*): extended family that includes the huckleberry family (*Vacciniaceae*), of which the main genera are the blueberry (*Vaccinum*) and the (inferior) wild huckleberry (*Gaylussacia*); the cranberry is also a member of this family. **Mulberry** Family (*Moraceae*): mulberry, fig, hops. **Palm** Family (*Palmaceae*): extended family which includes coconut (*Cocos*), date (*Phoenix*), African oil palm (*Elaeis*). **Rose** Family (*Rosaceae*). The main subfamilies are: 1. *Rosoideae*: blackberry, raspberry, wineberry, cloudberry, loganberry (all in the same genus); strawberry and rosehip. 2. *Pruo-ideae:* plum, prune, apricot, greengage (recommended medicinally by the sickness-ridden Dr. Blenkinsop in Bernard Shaw's *The Doctor's Dilemma*), cherry, peach, nectarine, sloe (all in the same genus); and almond. 3. *Maloideae:* apple, pear, quince, medlar, loquat. The kiwi fruit is in a category of its own, *Actinidia chinensis;* it grows on a woody vine native to the Yangtze Valley of China, and was brought to New Zealand, where it was first cultivated in 1906.

2. Grains

Grains are all members of the grass family (*gramineae*), which is the most important family in the human diet. Note that buckwheat is not botanically a grain and is listed below under Garden Vegetables. The following are the major grain subfamilies and species.

Corn Subfamily (*Panicoideae*): corn (a food to which a substantial number of people are intolerant), sorghum, sugar cane, pearl millet. **Millet** Subfamily (*Chloridoideae*): finger millet. **Rice** Subfamily (*Bambusoideae*, i.e. from the bamboo subfamily): rice, wild rice. **Wheat** Subfamily (*Pooidae*): wheat, rye, barley, oats. Food intolerance is more likely to be caused by wheat than the other members of its subfamily.

3. Garden Vegetables

Garden vegetables, other than most legumes, are all alkali-forming. **Buckwheat** Family (*Polygonaceae*): buckwheat, rhubarb, sorrel, dock. **Cabbage or Mustard** Family (*Cruciferae*, so called because the stems make a cross). The following are members of the same species: cabbage, cauliflower, brussels sprouts, broccoli, kohlrabi, kale and rutabaga. Other family members are: mustard, turnip, rapeseed, radish, horseradish, cress, peppercress, watercress. **Carrot or Parsley** Family (*Umbelliferae*): carrot, parsnip, celery, celeriac, fennel, parsley, aniseed, caraway, dill, cumin, coriander. **Cucumber or Gourd** Family (*Cucurbitaceae*): cucumber, melon, muskmelon, watermelon, marrow, zucchini, gourd, squash, pumpkin. **Daisy or Composite** Family (*Compositae*): lettuce, chicory, dandelion, endive, artichoke (globe or Jerusalem), salsify, sunflower, safflower, chamomile. **Mint** Family (*Labiatae*): mint, basil, marjoram, oregano, rosemary, sage, thyme, savory (genus *Satureia*). **Onion or Lily** Family (*Liliaxeae*): asparagus, onion, leek, shallot, garlic, chives. **Potato or Nightshade** Family (*Solanaceae*, from the Latin for quiet, an allusion to the narcotic properties of some of the species in the family). This family is noted for leaves that may have poisonous properties. Edible plants include: potatoes (not including yams or sweet potatoes, which are a family on their own, together with the nightshade family making up the phlox order), eggplant, tomato (genus *Lycopersicum*, Greek for wolf-peach, a possible allusion to its once being thought poisonous), aubergine, sweet peppers, paprika, chili peppers, cape gooseberry. **Spinach or Goosefoot** Family (*Chenopodiaceae*): spinach, spinach beet, chard, beetroot, sugar beet.[27]

4. Legumes, Nuts

Pea or Legumes or Pulse Family (*Leguminosae*, a member of the Rose Order): Beans, broadbeans, soybeans, lentils, peas. They are acid-forming or are at least neutral. Legumes are described in *Taylor's Encyclopedia of Gardening* as "perhaps the most important family of plants to the gardener because it includes pea, bean, clover, vetch, peanut, soybean, and many other crop plants." Among plants, it is second in importance to the human diet after the grass family. It includes licorice and some poisons. The word legume describes both the pea family and the pea-pod which is characteristic of the family members (it should not be confused with the French word "legume," which means vegetables of any kind). Peanuts, species *Arachis hypogaea*, also called goobers and groundnuts, are in a separate subfamily of legumes, genus *Arachis* (Greek for a pea-like plant). Other legumes are: anazi, adzuki, chick peas/garbanzo, haricot beans (the species includes kidney beans, baked beans and flageolets, and their green forms as snap beans, string beans and green beans), soybeans, lentils, split peas, broad (fava) beans, butter beans, mung beans, lima beans, chick peas, black-eyed peas, navy beans, pinto beans, carob, runner beans, green beans, snap beans, string beans, mangetout peas. Undercooked beans cause "favism"—a form of anemia—in a few people who are genetically susceptible to this toxin.

Nuts are an alternative source of protein for vegans and strict vegetarians. Besides the Cashew Family (with 18 species) and the Walnut Family (with 10 species), the other nuts are spread out among at least eight families. However, people who have an intolerance to one kind of nut tend to have intolerances to others. **Cashew** Family (*Anacardiaceae*): cashew, pistachio, mango. **Walnut** Family (*Juglandaceae*): walnuts, pecans.

5. Fungi (Mushrooms)

This kingdom includes the huge group of flowerless plants that contain no green coloring and are wholly parasitic or live on the dead remains of other plants. Besides mushrooms, the edible fungi include puffballs, truffles, morels, chanterelles, yeast and mycoprotein.

6. Dairy

Milk is a white liquid provided by the breasts of mammals to feed their young. Human milk is 1.1 percent protein by weight, cow's milk 3.7 percent; that is one reason that human milk is more easily digested (another is that less of the protein in human milk curdles in stomach acids). A substantial majority of people are intolerant of milk because they do not have enough lactase enzymes to digest more than a pint or so a day without severe gas symptoms.

Goat and sheep milk, sometimes used besides that of cows, has a greater concentration of short-chain fatty acids, which gives their milk and cheese a stronger odor and flavor.[28]

Pasteurized milk has typically been heated to a minimum of 144 degrees Fahrenheit for a minimum of 30 minutes, to kill bacteria; it may be heated for a shorter period if the temperature is higher. Milk offered for public sale must be pasteurized under most state laws, and Federal law requires interstate shipments of packaged milk to be pasteurized. *Homogenized* milk has been forced through a small nozzle that breaks up milk's globules into smaller ones that are more uniformly distributed throughout the fluid.

Butter is made by churning cream. *Buttermilk,* strictly speaking, is what is left over after butter is removed from the churned cream and the resulting liquid is slightly soured and thickened by airborne bacteria. Commercial buttermilk may be made like yogurt but at a lower temperature, by adding bacteria to skim milk.[29] *Ghee* or clarified butter is made by heating butter until boiling, then skimming off the white fat.

Cultured, i.e. fermented, milk foods help along the process of digestion of lactose, because the fermenting bacteria eat it. This makes the cultured products acceptable to those whose lactase enzymes are inadequate to digest much milk. This does not, however, help people who are *allergic* to milk products, because the allergy is not to the sugar in milk but to the proteins, which are not affected by the fermentation (we discuss allergies at more length in Chapter 4).

Yogurt is made by adding two bacteria, *Lactobacillus bulgaricus* and *Streptococcus thermophilus,* to milk and keeping it warm for four hours.

Cheese is started the same way as yogurt, except that rennet is added along with the starter bacteria. Rennet encourages the micelles of casein (fat globules) in milk to clump together as curds; the liquid whey is then removed.

7. Eggs and Other Animal Products

Eggs are like milk and seeds in that they were designed by nature to provide food for young animals and plants. While other birds (especially ducks and geese, from the duck family, for example) lay eggs that are eaten by humans, the most commonly eaten eggs come from *Gallus domesticus,* the hen that supplies our supermarkets. Eggs of all birds and fowl contain virtually the same proteins and can therefore be considered one food. Shell color of eggs has to do with genetics, not feed. Leghorn hens lay white eggs, Rhode Island Reds brown, while robins lay blue ones.[30]

Honey in North America is produced by the honey bee, *Apis mellifera,* which collects nectar from flowers and thereby also assists the flowers in cross-pollination (which starts the process of generating seeds). Nectar is mostly sugar. Honey is more concentrated sweetness than sugar, because in ripening in the beehive it is reduced almost entirely to the monosaccharides glucose and fructose, whereas granulated table sugar is a disaccharide—when using honey in recipes calling for sugar, the ratio of 110–125 sugar to 100 honey is suggested. Honey tastes good, but so far no extraordinary healthy qualities have been proven.[31]

8. Fish and Shellfish

Fish, from fossil dating, were the first animals with backbones. They fall into two main categories: bony and cartilaginous. **Bony** fish all share a special type of protein called parvalbumin to which some people are allergic. **Cartilaginous** fish include shark, ray, skate, dogfish.

Fish feed on microscopic plants, the *phytoplankton,* found in open water. This food is richest where the water is coolest. So cool seas support more fish, the cold water cod, haddock, halibut, herring, and sardine.

Plankton is also more abundant near the shore, where the water is fertilized by what the rivers bring with them to the sea. Thus the best fishing areas tend to be near the shores rather than mid-ocean.

Shellfish is a term that covers a wide range of species. **Crustaceans** are a phylum that includes crab, lobster, crayfish, shrimp, prawn. **Mollusks** are a phylum that includes mussels, cockles, winkles, oysters, clams, scallops, squid, cuttlefish, octopus, snails.

9. Meat and Poultry

Meat means red meat, although it is sometimes used to include poultry, in which case a distinction would be made between "red meat" and "poultry meat." Meat is a good source of protein and many vitamins and minerals. The bad news is that it is also a major source of saturated fat, cholesterol, calories, and unwanted chemicals.

The leanness of meat is rated by voluntary classification system developed by the USDA which uses the terms Prime, Choice, and Select. Some companies now market their meats under the Lite or Lean label as well. The fat content, calories, and cholesterol content of meats in these categories are graded as follows: Prime is 6.2 to 14.0 percent fat; Choice is 3.9 to 10.2 percent fat; Select is 2.5 to 7.6 percent fat; and Lean/Lite is 1.7 to 10.6 percent fat.[32] Meat is composed of four main families:

Cattle Family (Bovidae): cows, sheep and goats (the latter two are in the same subfamily). Beef is the largest segment of American agriculture, 20 percent of all farm sales and 45 percent of all livestock, 36 percent by weight of all meat consumed in the U.S. in 1988.

Pig Family (Suidae): pigs. Pork tends to be fattier than beef, but it has maintained its market share because it is inexpensive.

Deer Family (Cervidae): venison. Americans don't eat a lot of deer, for any of three possible reasons: the taste is too strong, or deer are (luckily for them) not commercially viable (hard to domesticate, not enough meat), or because

Table 2–1
Latest RDAs and Recommended Intakes, 1989 vs. Actual Intake, 1985

| Nutrient | RDAs/Recommended Intakes, 1989 | | Actual Intake | |
	Men	Women	1985	Percent Change, 1960–85
Calories	–	–	3,500	12.9
Fat (grams)	–	–	169	18.2
Saturated (grams)	–	–	61	1.6
Monounsaturated (grams)	–	–	68	17.2
Polyunsaturated (grams)	–	–	33	65
Cholesterol (milligrams)	–	–	500	–10.7
Carbohydrates (grams)	–	–	413	9.5
Protein (grams)	63	50	104	8.3
Vitamins				
A (micrograms RE)[35]	1,000	800	1,610	24.8
A, carotenes (micrograms RE)	–	–	660	57.1
A (international units)	3,333	2,667	9,700	36.6
B_1, Thiamin (milligrams)	1.5	1.1	2.2	15.8
B_2, Riboflavin (milligrams)	1.7	1.3	2.4	9.1
B_3, Niacin (milligrams)[36]	19	15	26	23.8
B_6, Pyridoxine (milligrams)	2.0	1.6	2.1	10.5
Folate (micrograms)	200	180	299	3.8
B_{12} (micrograms)	2.0	2.0	10.1	3.1
Biotin (micrograms)*	30–100	30–100	–	–
Pantothenic Acid (milligrams)*	4–7	4–7	–	–
C (milligrams)	60	60	115	15
D (micrograms)[37]	5	5	–	–
E (milligrams)[38]	10	8	16.1	38.8
K (micrograms)	80	65	–	–
Minerals and Trace Elements[39]				
Calcium (milligrams)	800	800	910	–1.1
Chloride (milligrams, min.)*	750	750	–	–
Chromium (micrograms)*	50–200	50–200	–	–
Copper (milligrams)*	1.5–3.0	1.5–3.0	1.7	6.3
Fluoride (milligrams)*	1.5–4.0	1.5–4.0	–	–
Iodine (micrograms)	150	150	–	–
Iron (milligrams)	10	15	17	19.7
Magnesium (milligrams)	350	280	330	3.1
Manganese (milligrams)*	2.0–5.0	2.0–5.0	–	–
Molybdenum (micrograms)*	75–250	75–250	74	–
Phosphorus (milligrams)	800	800	1.540	3.4
Potassium (grams)*	2.0–3.5	2.0–3.5	3.5	–2.3
Selenium (micrograms)	70	55	–	–
Sodium (grams)*[40]	.5–2.4	.5–2.4	–	–
Zinc (milligrams)	15	12	13	7.4

*These are not RDAs, but ranges of recommended intakes.

Source: National Research Council, *Recommended Dietary Allowances*, 10th Edition, p. 284, facing table, and p. 253 (sodium, chloride, and potassium), and *Statistical Abstract of the U.S.: 1989*, Table 197, p. 122.

of the reluctance of Americans to eat Bambi.

Rabbit Family (Lepidorae): hare, rabbit. Rabbit is a very nutritious and economical food that hasn't caught on in the United States so far, for reasons that are thought to relate to the special status of the Easter Bunny. It would help to give the meat in supermarkets a new name.

Poultry also has four main families. **Chicken or Pheasant** Family (Phasianinae): chicken, pheasant, partridge, quail. **Duck** Family (Anatidae): duck and goose. **Pigeon** Family (Columbidae): pigeon, squab. **Snipe** Family (Scolopacidae): snipe, woodcock.

Food Components

Human beings as chemical structures are 65 percent oxygen, 18 percent carbon, 10 percent hydrogen, 3 percent nitrogen and 4 percent minerals.

These elements combine in compounds. For example, most of the oxygen and hydrogen combine to make water, which constitutes nearly two-thirds of our weight; 17 per cent is protein, 14 percent are fats, and a small percentage at any one time are carbohydrates (the rest is minerals). The keys to life are the carbon atoms, which combine with hydrogen to form carbohydrates. They combine with oxygen and hydrogen to form fats and (with the addition of nitrogen) chains of protein molecules.

In the following listing of food nutrients and other components, we identify the need for the component, symptoms of deficiency if appropriate, the Recommended Dietary Allowance if one exists, and the best sources for the component in food. Additional information is also provided where significant.

Recommended Dietary Allowances (RDAs). RDAs are established for different categories of individuals by the Food and Nutrition Board, which operates under the aegis of the National Research Council, the operating agency of the National Academies of Sciences and Engineering and the Institute of Medicine. These RDAs are used by the FDA for establishing U.S. Recommended Daily [sic] Allowances (USRDAs) which are in turn used by manufacturers for purposes of showing the nutritional content of food. The USRDAs cited in this chapter were based on the 1980 RDAs. They are calculated very simply, by taking the highest of the RDAs for each nutrient. This is usually the RDA for men, but for iron the women's RDA was used because it is higher than the men's RDA.

The most recent RDAs, the 10th Edition, were established in October 1989 by the Food and Nutrition Board of the National Research Council, subject to review by the Council's Report Review Committee.[33] A listing of the latest RDAs, and recommended intakes where information is inadequate to establish RDAs, is provided in Table 2–1.[34]

The RDAs shown are for males 25–50 years old, 5'10" tall, 174 pounds, and females 25–50 years old, 5'4" tall, 138 pounds. Where a single figure is cited in the text it means the RDA is the same for both groups. Special consideration must be given to the needs of children, adolescents, and pregnant and lactating women. For these groups, professional nutritional advice should be sought; we will not always attempt to cover every population subgroup in the discussion that follows.

To help you appreciate how small the dietary allowances are, a gram is roughly one-third of a tenth of an ounce (.035 ounces). An ounce, 28.3 grams, is the typical manufacturer's serving size of breakfast cereals—a half cup to a cup, depending on the cereal density (people who eat cereals usually eat more than the serving size for breakfast). Cottage cheese and yogurt serving sizes are typically 4 ounces, 113 grams.

So the only weights in the RDA chart that are substantial enough to measure outside a laboratory are (1) protein, about three ounces per day, (2) calcium, and (3) phosphorus, of which we need about a gram each per day, less than the weight of salt in a typical fast-food hamburger. A cup of skim milk has 30 percent of the USRDA for calcium and 20 percent of the USRDA for phosphorus.

If we compare the RDAs with average intake, we see that the American diet is well supplied with many nutrients, in excess of the minimum RDA for men in every nutrient. However, the daily intake of some groups may be substantially higher and of others substantially lower.

Americans have been eating 13 percent more calories since 1960, but their intake of dietary cholesterol is down by 11 percent. The most rapid increases in vitamin intake are in vitamin A (up 25–57 percent between 1960 and 1985, depending on which measure you look at) and vitamin E (up 39 percent).

Carbohydrates. Most of the weight of food we eat is carbohydrates. They provide energy we need for nerve and muscle operations and for repair of body tissues, and with fiber to aid digestion. A general deficiency of carbohydrates is shown most dramatically by athletes who burn up their energy and lose the ability to move, or by people in cold climates who don't have enough stored energy to stay warm. Although the National Research Council has not established an RDA for carbohydrates, it provides an "energy allowance" of 2,300 to 2,900 calories (more formally, "kilocalories" or Calories, to show that the unit used for human energy is 1,000 times the unit used in physics) per day for men and 1,900 to 2,200 calories per day for women.[41]

Carbohydrates are made by green plants during *photosynthesis* (the food-making process). Chemically, a carbohydrate molecule is composed approximately of an atom of carbon and oxygen for every two atoms of hydrogen. Carbohydrates are either simple or complex.

Simple carbohydrates are *sugars*, which provide energy and nutrients over a short period of time. *Glucose* and *fructose* are sugars that are rapidly absorbed by the body's cells; they have the same chemical composition, $C_6H_{12}O_6$, but are structured differently. *Sucrose* is a *disaccharide*, i.e., composed of two molecules, one of glucose linked to one of fructose with a molecule of water removed; it must be broken down into its components by adding back the water molecule during digestion. Similarly, *lactose*, milk sugar, is another disaccharide that must be broken down during digestion to its component molecules of glucose and *galactose*, before it reaches the colon or the sugar will ferment and create painful carbon dioxide gas. To break down lactose, an enzyme called lactase is needed. This is created naturally by the body and is at its maximum soon after birth; thereafter it declines to a stable minimum between the second and fourth year of life.

Complex carbohydrates include starch and glycogen. As we shall see, these are considered much healthier to eat than the simple carbohydrates (sugars). The complex carbohydrates are all composed of long chains or strings of glucose molecules.

Starch, because it must be broken down by the digestive system, provides energy and nutrients that are released over a longer period of time than sugars, providing more stability and reliability to the body's functioning. Its chains of glucose molecules must be broken down by the digestive system. Good sources are whole-grain bread, cereal, pasta, and rice, and corn, legumes and potatoes.

Glycogen is similar to starch in that it is also made up of strings of glucose molecules and some of the strings are readily digestible. It therefore provides a useful storage of energy in the liver, muscles, or tissues.

Fiber (*cellulose*) is technically a complex carbohydrate, because its molecules are, like starch, composed of chains of glucose molecules. But it is usually (for example, in government reports) given its own classification because it is an "unavailable" carbohydrate, largely indigestible (except by horses and cattle, which have stronger bacteria in their stomachs). While not considered essential to human life, fiber plays an important part in preventing certain diseases, notably colon cancer, by adding bulk to food and thereby aiding in the digestive process. Good sources besides whole grains are vegetables from the cabbage or mustard family.[42]

Some "fad diets" push a low-carbohydrate or non-carbohydrate daily menu, which would exclude bread. Promoters of such diets fail to mention that any weight loss is temporary and the medical consequences could be serious and permanent. When its carbohydrate store is depleted after 12 to 16 hours, the body can only use fats (and proteins) for energy; this improper breakdown of fats leads to the formation of ketones, in a condition called ketosis. Ketosis causes headaches and upsets the body's acid-base balance; more seriously, in a pregnant woman it can cause brain damage in the fetus. A low carbohydrate store also causes a glucose deficiency in the kidney, which excretes water and needed minerals. The quick weight loss that a fad dieter experiences is just dehydration.

Alcohol. Although not healthy, alcohol is a significant source of energy, providing 7 calories per gram (midway between fat at 9 calories/gram and carbohydrates and protein at 4 calories/gram) when metabolized; it can also be converted into fat.

Fats. Some fatty acids found in dietary fat are essential; they are also concentrated calories (they combine with carbohydrates to create heat and energy), and they carry fat-soluble vitamins. They are necessary, but in the American diet the problem is not a deficiency but an excess. Much current dietary research and controversy are focused on fats.

Fats are of three types: saturated, monounsaturated, and polyunsaturated. *Saturated* fats are the most hazardous to health, and are found heavily concentrated in animal products and tropical oils (e.g., coconut and palm oil). *Monounsaturated* fats such as olive oil and rapeseed (canola) oil are considered the healthiest. *Polyunsaturated* fats are in vegetable oils such as safflower oil. They are less harmful than saturated fats but are considered less beneficial than the monounsaturated fats. *Trans-fatty acids* are formed by partial *hydrogenation* of unsaturated fats in vegetable oils. Hydrogenation converts some polyunsaturated fats into saturated fats and others into trans-fatty acids. Unfortunately, hydrogenation may destroy the beneficial features of polyunsaturated fats and makes them act more like saturated fats. A writer for the American Heart Association concludes that hydrogenation is "equivalent to

saturation" in its effect on blood cholesterol; others say it's not as bad as saturation.[43]

A high concentration of saturated fats in the diet causes a buildup of blood cholesterol (cholesterol in the human blood, also called serum cholesterol), which has been associated with higher incidence of heart disease. This cholesterol is of several types, of which the most important to know about are: (1) low-density lipoprotein (LDL), so-called "bad" cholesterol, which distributes cholesterol to body tissues, and (2) high-density lipoprotein (HDL), so-called "good" cholesterol, which collects cholesterol and carries it away from body tissues. Some people

are predisposed genetically to having too much LDL cholesterol in their blood; this is thought to make them more vulnerable to heart disease.

Blood cholesterol should be clearly differentiated from dietary cholesterol, i.e. cholesterol found in animal products, which is not considered as hazardous for the general population as it once was (as opposed to saturated fat, which scientists now point to as the culprit in the high rate of heart disease in America). People at high risk should monitor their intake, which for the average American comes about 40% from egg yolks, 40% from dairy products, and 20% from meat.

The scientific basis for identifying saturated fat as the villain in the dietary piece comes from a wide range of scientific studies.

For example, epidemiologists have monitored what happens when people migrate from one country to another. They find that the U.S.-born children and grandchildren of Japanese immigrants tend toward having the same diseases as other Americans.[44] They have tried to find in the U.S. lifestyle an explanation for the change in the disease patterns of the Japanese families, and their suspicions center now on the high-saturated-fat U.S. diet.

Problems may be found with any one study, for reasons that we discussed in Chapter 1. But it would be fair to say that there is "a 98 percent consensus" on the broad recommendations of U.S. dietary guidelines—i.e., to cut down on saturated fats and increase intake of complex carbohydrates.[45]

Protein. Derived from the Greek word for "first," dietary protein is essential for growth and repair of any animal's body tissues, and for building blood and antibodies to fight infection. Protein in food contains a range of 20 *amino acids*, of which 20 are "standard" types that make up antibodies, enzymes, hemoglobin, and hormones. Of the amino acids, nine are considered "essential" in that the body cannot synthesize them and they must be found in the food we eat; they are histidine, isoleucine, leucine, lysine, methionine, phenylalanine, threonine, tryptophan, and valine.[46]

Considerably smaller portions of protein are now considered necessary than was thought a few years ago. The National Research Council uses an RDA of 0.8 grams per kilogram of body weight, i.e. 63 grams of protein a day for men, 50 grams a day for women (see Table 2–1 above). The British Department of Health and Social Security recommended only 40 grams a day per person—just a pint of milk and 2 ounces of cheese.

One source of protein is meat, poultry, eggs, and dairy products. Some have contended that only such animal products have a complete range of the essential amino acids. However, this is no longer thought to be so much the case. Vegetarians were told in the first edition (1971) of Frances Moore Lappé's *Diet for a Small Planet* that when eaten together, grains and legumes *complement* one another and provide a full range of protein, all anyone needs. Lappé provided recipes for combining grains (as in rice and beans, wheat and peanuts) with legumes to provide a full range of amino acids, all the protein anyone needs. In the revised (1982) edition of her book Lappé places much less emphasis on the protein issue, concluding: "With a healthy, varied diet, concern about protein complementarity is not necessary for most of us."[47] An RDA of 63 grams of protein is barely two ounces.

Vitamins. First identified in this century, vitamins are essential nutrients for avoiding certain diseases. The first vitamin to be identified was vitamin B_1. Kanehiro Takaki, surgeon-general of the Japanese navy, noted in 1882 that beriberi cases were greatly reduced by adding meat and vegetables to sailors' rice diet. Christiaan Eijkman, a Dutch medical officer in the East Indies, showed in 1900 that people who ate white, polished rice in prison camps suffered from beriberi while those who ate brown, whole rice did not. Frederick G. Hopkins of Cambridge University showed in 1906 that for rats to grow properly they needed certain "accessory food factors." Casimir Funk, a Polish biochemist working in London, in 1912 claimed to have isolated the anti-beriberi factor from rice hulls and named it the "vitamine." Originally scientists thought that there were just two vitamins, the fat-soluble vitamin A and the water-soluble vitamin B. Two Americans, biochemist Elmer V. McCollum and physician Joseph Goldberger, subsequently showed that the fat-soluble and water-soluble vitamins were both mixtures of separate elements.

The fat-soluble vitamins—A, D, E, K—dissolve, and are carried, in fats. The other, water-soluble, vitamins dissolve, and are carried, in water. The "B-complex" vitamins, originally thought to be one vitamin, now include over 15 elements. They are grouped as the B Majors (B_1, B_2, B_3) and B Minors (a long list that includes folic acid, B_6, and B_{12}),[48] because a diet with an adequate amount of the B Majors seems also to supply an adequate amount of the B Minors.

Initially, scientists named vitamins with letters of the alphabet. As further research identified the chemical composition of the vitamins, descriptive names were also used. For the most recent discoveries, the letters have been dispensed with completely. The following list includes the most important vitamins.

Vitamin A was the first fat-soluble vitamin to be discovered. It is extremely important for healthy eyes, healthy skin, and resistance to disease, including certain cancers. A deficiency contributes to night blindness. The USRDA is 5,000 international units (IUs), or 1,500 micrograms RE (retinol equivalent)—one IU equals 0.3 micrograms of RE units of vitamin A. The RDA for vitamin A is 1,000 micrograms (1 milligram) of RE for men and 800 micrograms (0.8 milligram) of RE for women. This is equivalent to 6 milligrams of beta-carotene. The reason for the difference in RDA units is that vitamin A comes primarily in two forms: (1) the preferable form, as *carotenoids*, of which the best-known is beta-carotene (found in dark green leafy vegetables and other green vegetables, carrots, and other orange, red and yellow vegetables and fruits), which the body converts into vitamin A and (2) the more concentrated form, from meat and dairy products in which the vitamin A comes as *retinol*, already available for the body's use without having to be converted. The carotenoids are recommended over retinol because they have antioxidants that may inhibit cancer, and by not being preformed they are less likely to produce toxic levels of vitamin A. Excessive intake of preformed vitamin A (doses of 25,000 international units or more) has been linked to birth defects and bone abnormalities. Best sources of vitamin A are apricots, broccoli, cantaloupe, carrot (a large one has 6.6 milligrams of beta carotene), dandelions (1 cup cooked has 8.4 milligrams), kale, spinach, sweet potato (a medium-sized one has 5.9 milligrams); try to eat the equivalent of a carrot a day.[49]

Vitamin B_1, Thiamin (also sometimes spelled thiamine), is important for muscles and the nervous system, and conversion of carbohydrates into energy. A deficiency results in beriberi, a disease of the nervous system that still occurs globally, but rarely in the United States. Its USRDA is 1.5 milligrams. The RDA is 1.5 milligrams for men and 1.1 milligrams for women. Best sources for thiamin are wholemeal baked products, eggs, legumes (peanuts, soy flour, peas), organ meats, pork, and certain supplemented breakfast cereals (check the package to see how much of this vitamin is included).

Vitamin B_2, Riboflavin (originally called vitamin G), is needed for growth, healthy eyes and skin, appetite, cells' use of oxygen (respiration), digestion, and healthy nerves. A deficiency is shown by inflamed lips and a sore tongue, and scaliness of skin around the nose and ears. Its USRDA is 1.7 milligrams. The RDA is 1.7 milligrams for men and 1.3 for women. Best sources of riboflavin are asparagus, broccoli, cottage cheese, yogurt, and supplemented (check label) breads and cereals.

Vitamin B_3, Niacin, also called nicotinic acid, is needed for growth, for healthy skin and nerves, and to help the body's cells use oxygen and other nutrients. Deficiency is shown by pellagra, a disorder of the skin, intestines, and nervous system. Niacin's USRDA is 20 milligrams. The RDA is 19 milligrams for men and 15 for women. Best sources are fish (especially water-packed tuna, mackerel, salmon), poultry breast, lean meat (especially veal), whole-grain or supplemented (check label) breads and breakfast cereals. Milk and eggs have little niacin but contain *tryptophane*, a pellagra-preventive amino acid that substitutes for niacin to supply some of the body's needs.

Vitamin B₆, Pyridoxine, is needed for growth and nerves. Its USRDA is 2 milligrams. The RDA is 2 milligrams for men and 1.6 for women. Best sources are legumes (especially kidney beans, but also lentils, lima beans, peas, soybeans), poultry, sunflower seeds, brown rice, vegetables (broccoli, brussels sprouts, carrots, cauliflower, corn, potato, spinach), fish (salmon, tuna).

Vitamin B₁₂, Cyanocobalamin, promotes longevity, is required to metabolize protein, fat and carbohydrates, and contributes to a healthy nervous system and appetite. Deficiency symptoms include nervous disorders, anemia, and weakness in walking and speaking. Its USRDA is 6 micrograms. The RDA was reduced to 2 micrograms for men and women. Best sources are fish (especially halibut and salmon, also haddock), meat (hamburger), milk, poultry, soy products (including miso, tempeh), seaweed. Vegans (i.e., strict vegetarians eating no meat, eggs, or dairy products), in particular vegan nursing mothers, have a special need for vitamin B₁₂; the National Research Council says that this deficiency can be *"but rarely is"* produced by a vegan diet.[50] An injection of a tiny amount of B₁₂ lasts for a year or more and helps cure pernicious anemia.

Folate and Folacin are generic terms for compounds that are nutritionally and chemically similar to folic acid (also called pteroylglutamic acid, or PGA).[51] Folate is important for the development of red blood cells. Its USRDA is 400 micrograms (0.4 milligram). The 1989 RDA is reduced to

200 micrograms for men and 180 micrograms for women. During pregnancy the RDA is increased to 400 micrograms per day. Folate is widely available in food. Best sources are liver, yeast, leafy vegetables (beets, broccoli, cabbage, spinach), legumes (chickpeas, pinto beans, soybeans), orange juice.[52]

Biotin (was once called vitamin H before it was found to be part of the B-complex group) assists in metabolizing protein, carbohydrates, and fats. Since this and the following vitamin have never been observed lacking in humans, no RDA is established, only a range of recommended intake of 30–100 micrograms/day for men

and women. Best sources are liver, egg yolk, soy flour, cereals, and yeast.[53]

Pantothenic Acid is an oily substance that helps synthesize adrenal hormones and other essentials for functioning of the metabolism. No RDA is established, only a range of recommended intake of 4 to 7 milligrams a day for men and women. Best sources are liver, whole grain cereals, and legumes.[54]

Vitamin C, Ascorbic Acid is needed to maintain body cells, blood vessels, and tissues; to maintain the body's resistance to disease and ability to heal its own wounds; to build strong bones and teeth; and to aid in iron absorption and the metabolism of folacin and proteins, the formation of collagen (which keeps cells together), and the manufacture of chemicals used in the brain. An extreme deficiency of vitamin C causes scurvy, which is evidenced by sore and spongy gums, a loosening of teeth, bleeding under the skin, and fatigue. The British knew that citrus fruits staved off scurvy, which is why their sailors had a good supply of limes on board and were called "limeys." Vitamin C is also promoted as a possible aid to preventing cancer, for example by reducing nitrosamines. Adults require about 10 milligrams of vitamin C per day to avoid overt symptoms of scurvy. After about 200 milligrams per day, the National Research Council concludes that vitamin C is excreted with the urine. The 1989 RDA continues to be 60 milligrams per day, but was increased to 100 milligrams per day for smokers.[55] Best sources are fresh fruit (cantaloupe, grapefruit, oranges, pineapple, limes) and vegetables such as broccoli, brussels sprouts, cabbage, cauliflower, spinach, sweet potatoes, tomatoes.

Vitamin D is composed of about ten fat-soluble vitamins, chemically related to steroids; two are important nutritionally. They control, and are essential for, absorption of calcium and phosphorus and release of calcium stored in the bones; they are necessary for healthy bones and teeth. A deficiency leads to rickets, a condition of soft and deformed bones. An excess of vitamin D also leads to serious bone changes. The RDA is 5 micrograms for men and women. Vitamin D₂ is created with ultraviolet irradiation of a crystalline steroid alcohol *ergosterol*, which is found in yeast, molds, and ergot (a dark sclerotium, a mass of hardened interwoven threads, of grass seed fungi). Vitamin D₃ is found in fish-liver oils, eggs, margarine, and as an additive to milk; it is also formed by the skin when exposed to sunlight or ultraviolet rays.

Vitamin E, Tocopherol, is a group of fat-soluble vitamins that prevent destruction of fatty acids and vitamin A and are essential for maintaining red blood cell membranes. A deficiency contributes to infertility, degenerative muscle changes or vascular abnormalities. The RDA is 10 milligrams for men, 8 for women. The best sources of vitamin E are vegetable oils, wheat germ, nuts, whole-grain breads and cereals.

Vitamin K is needed for blood clotting. Intestinal bacteria ordinarily manufacture vitamin K. The RDA is 80 micrograms for men, 65 for women. Best sources are green leafy vegetables such as cabbage, cauliflower, kale, and spinach.

Minerals and Trace Elements. Although minerals and other very small ("trace") elements constitute only 4 percent of our weight, they are vitally important for controlling bodily functions. Some of them, like calcium, potassium, phosphorus, and sodium, are required in substantial amounts. Others are needed only in tiny amounts. Trace minerals have a variety of functions, including contributing to the processes described for other nutrients. Many experts believe that adequate intake of other nutrients in food will usually provide enough of such minerals.[56] However, some specialists in food sensitivities maintain that a certain percentage of people need idiosyncratic extra quantities of some minerals.[57]

Calcium is required for strong teeth, bones, and the proper functioning of the blood (clotting) and transmission of nerve impulses. The RDA is 800 milligrams for both men and women. Best sources are dairy products (milk, cheese), green vegetables (cabbage, broccoli, watercress), eggs, almonds, brazil nuts, wholemeal bread, potatoes, soy flour, dried apricots and oatmeal.

Chloride is essential for maintaining fluid and electrolyte balance, and is an essential part of the gastric juices. Losses tend to accompany sodium depletion, e.g. through sweating. No RDA, but a minimum level of 750 milligrams per day is suggested. The main dietary source is sodium chloride, salt, which provides about 6 grams a day of chloride in the American diet along with 4 grams of sodium.

Chromium is needed for maintaining normal glucose metabolism. Deficiency results in diabetes-like symptoms. A recommended intake range of 50–200 micrograms for men and women was tentatively established in 1989. A high availability of chromium is found in brewer's yeast, calf's liver, American cheese, and wheat germ.

Cobalt is essential for the functioning of vitamin B_{12}. However, no evidence has been adduced that inadequate cobalt has ever been consumed, so no RDA or any other guideline has been established.

Copper is necessary for all vertebrate animals. Deficiency results in anemia, skeletal defects, nervous disorders, and other ailments. No RDA is established, for lack of data. Instead, a recommended intake range of 1.5 to 3 milligrams a day has been established. Liver is the best source of copper, followed by seafoods, nuts, and seeds.

Fluoride is good for the teeth (increases their resistance to decay) and bones. Researchers claim that heavy doses of fluoride have been helpful for women suffering from osteoporosis. Mottling of the teeth occurs in children ingesting concentrations of 2 to 8 milligrams per kilogram. No RDA is established for fluoride, but a recommended safe and adequate range is 1.5 to 4 milligrams per day. Best sources are fluoridated water, tea, and the soft bones of fish like sardines and salmon.

Iodine is necessary to form thyroid hormones, which regulate the rate at which the body uses energy. A deficiency causes goiter, which has also been caused by an excess of iodine, above 2 grams per day. The RDA is 150 micrograms for both men and women. Best sources are iodized table salt (introduced in the 1920's), which provides 75 micrograms or half the RDA per gram, and seafood. Bread made with iodates to oxidize the dough provide 500 micrograms per 100 grams of bread.

Iron is needed for healthy blood (it makes hemoglobin in red blood cells) and vitality. The RDA is 10 milligrams for men and 15 for women (reduced from 18 in the 1980 edition of the RDAs). The ingestion by children of iron supplements meant for adults can be lethal (all it takes is 3 grams to kill a 2–year-old child), and most of the 2,000 annual U.S. cases of iron poisoning are of this nature. Iron is found in meat; eggs; legumes such as baked beans, soy beans and soy flour and lentils; grains such as wholemeal flour and bread, wheat germ, and oatmeal; and in yeast, nuts, dried fruit (prunes and raisins), potatoes and leafy green vegetables and watercress.

Magnesium is necessary for many physiological processes, including bodily use of calcium and potassium. When magnesium deficiency was induced in patients, the symptoms were nausea, muscle weakness, and irritability. Large amounts of magnesium are not toxic except for people with kidney disease. Many of the cases of magnesium deficiency and excess are iatrogenic—failures of the physician or hospital to monitor magnesium intake adequately. The RDA is 350 milligrams for men, 280 milligrams for women. Magnesium is available in all unprocessed foods, especially nuts, legumes, and unmilled grains. Over four-fifths of magnesium is destroyed by removing the germ and husk of cereal grains. Green vegetables are also rich in magnesium.

Manganese is essential for all animals. Deficiency signs in animals and institutionalized humans include poor reproductive performance, slow growth, birth defects, bone malformation, and poor glucose tolerance. No RDA has been set, but a range of recommended intake is from 2 to 5 milligrams per day for men and women. The RDA is easy to obtain; whole grains and cereal products are rich in it.

Molybdenum is a part of several enzymes that are important for digestion. A deficiency in goats results in poor weight gain, reduced consumption and shortened life expectancy. A recommended range of intake of 75 to 250 micrograms is suggested by the National Research Council. Best sources of molybdenum are milk, beans, breads and cereals.

Phosphorus is used with calcium in forming bones and teeth, and aids in regulation of the acid-base relationship; it is important for healthy nerves. The RDA is 800 milligrams for men and women. Best sources are dairy products, meat, fish, and egg yolk.

Potassium is used, along with sodium, in regulating body fluid volume; it is also important for transmission of nerve impulses. It plays a role in controlling hypertension, and the fact that low intakes of potassium occur among blacks may contribute to their higher rates of hypertension. No

RDA has been established for potassium, because it is widely available in a healthy diet, and a diet that includes ample unprocessed fruits and vegetables will include 8 to 11 grams a day of potassium. The 1989 RDA report suggests that 1.6 to 2 grams are required. Best sources are unprocessed fruits (bananas, oranges, raisins) and vegetables, and milk (provides about 1.3 grams per liter; a liter is slightly larger than a quart).[58]

Selenium plays a role in hydroperoxide breakdown; it has a close metabolic tie to the antioxidant vitamin E. A deficiency shows up in increased incidence of Keshan disease, a failure of heart muscles or valves; one researcher speculates on the possible involvement of a cardiotoxic virus that is encouraged by a selenium deficiency. Animals with selenium deficiency have responded well to vitamin E supplements. The RDA for selenium is 70 micrograms/day for men and 55 micrograms/day for women. Best sources of selenium are seafoods, kidney, liver, other meats, and grains depending on the soil where the grains were grown.

Sodium regulates body fluid volume. Not much is needed for this purpose, no more than 2 grams per day, about 5 grams (one teaspoon) of table salt, which is about 40 percent sodium. No RDA has been established; however, the

National Research Council suggests that a safe minimum intake would be 0.5 gram per day, and a safe maximum would be 2.4 grams.[59] Sodium occurs naturally in milk and other foods except vegetables. Processed food is commonly heavily laced with sodium; one fast-food hamburger and fries will have over 2 grams of sodium. So the difficulty for Americans is to keep sodium intake down.

Zinc is a component of enzymes that are involved in most of the key processes of metabolism; it is an essential element for all life on earth. Zinc deficiency produces loss of appetite, slow growth, changes in the skin and testicles, and changes in the immune system; a deficiency during pregnancy can lead to birth defects. Zinc is acutely toxic, causing intestinal irritation and vomiting, at the 2 grams level; immune response impairment occurs with smaller doses over a period of time. The RDA for men is 15 milligrams per day, and for women 12 milligrams per day. Regular zinc supplementation above the 15–milligram level should not be undertaken without qualified medical supervision. The major sources of zinc in the American diet are meat, eggs, seafoods, and cereal.

Manufacturers' Labeling

If agronomists and farmers look at food in terms of seasons, and biologists in terms of inputs to chemical reac-

tions or as families of living things, then marketing and advertising people see food as potentially lucrative accounts. The attitude of manufacturers is like that of the diner waitress in the *New Yorker* (July 31, 1989) cartoon who assured her customers: "You want organic, we'll make it organic." If the public wants oat bran, fiber, low-sodium, no-cholesterol . . . the manufacturers will give it to them that way, or at least they will accentuate the positive and, laws permitting, will eliminate the negative.

Label Hype. These days, the laws permit a great deal on labels. The spate of health claims in the 1987–1990 period, which we shall discuss further in Chapter 3, has revealed a number of misleading nutritional labels, some of which cross the line into fraudulence. We aren't just talking about Beech-Nut Nutrition Corp.'s mislabeled apple juice, which contained little or no apple juice,[60] but about labels that mislead by providing misidentification, by omitting key information, or by providing information in a way that is not easily understandable by the consumer. Here are a few of the abuses:

Cholesterol-Free more often than not borders on fraud by playing on the ignorance of many consumers, who have heard that high cholesterol is bad and think that a cholesterol-free food is *ipso facto* healthy. It ain't so. No plant has cholesterol; it is manufactured by animals; but saturated vegetable fats like palm oils are just as unhealthy for most people as high-cholesterol animal fats, and are worse for most people than high-cholesterol seafood. Those who have a high blood cholesterol are urged to keep their dietary cholesterol below 300 milligrams, but for the general population dietary cholesterol is not as important to watch as fats, especially saturated fats. Phil Sokolof, an Omaha building materials manufacturer who had survived a serious heart attack, was so upset about the misleading nature of "No Cholesterol" claims on foods heavily laden with saturated fats from tropical oils that he spent $2 million on newspaper ads attacking them. As a result, 12 large food companies have committed themselves to removing these oils from their food.[61]

Diet foods must meet one of the two criteria for low-calorie or reduced-calorie foods, listed below.

Fat-Free claims, as in "95 Percent Fat-Free," are based on weight. Such a product with 100 grams and 100 calories per serving is 45 percent fat, because the 5 grams of fat each carries 9 calories. This is well above the federally recommended 30 percent fat in our diets (and many people believe it should be even less).

Ingredients must be listed in order of weight, but to disguise the sugar content several different sweeteners are used. Thus a breakfast cereal might list wheat, corn syrup, brown sugar, and honey, in that order, when the combined sweeteners would be the No. 1 ingredient if combined!

Lite or Light is legally meaningless. It could refer to color, alcohol content, texture, sodium content, or fat, as well as calories. Other words should be looked for, such as low-calorie, which does mean something. In the case of low-fat ice cream, look for the words "ice milk," which is a legally meaningful term (specified by the USDA). If it means low-calorie, check the calories. Sara Lee's Light Classics French Cheesecake has more calories than the original version; it was referring to texture.[62]

Low-Calorie foods must have fewer than 40 grams per serving and must have fewer than 0.4 calories per gram. Reduced-calorie means the food must have one-third fewer calories per serving than the regular product. Unfortunately, the low-calorie version may simply have been diluted with water, or may have had the serving size reduced.

Low-Fat claims are meaningless, except that manufacturers who use them must list saturated and unsaturated fatty acids, and dietary cholesterol.

Low-Sodium foods, such as soups, may only be reduced by one-third, and may still be high in relation to the maximum amounts recommended per day. *No Salt Added* doesn't necessarily mean the product has no salt. Any claims about sodium or salt require that the label list the amount of sodium. Check the ingredients. A low-sodium product may not have more than 140 milligrams per serving; very low sodium, no more than 35; and sodium-free or salt-free, less than five. When U.S. manufacturers of a snack food eliminate the salt and offer it as a new product described as "salt-free," they should be careful about exporting to Canada. The sensible Canadian authorities require that a product described as "salt-free" must have very low traces of sodium; otherwise, the label must read "no salt added." In any case, eliminating salt is rarely enough to make an unhealthy product healthy.

Natural is a legally meaningless term except in Maine, where it is defined by state law, and when applied to red meat and poultry, when its meaning is defined by the USDA. Many natural ingredients, as we shall see in the next two chapters, are unhealthy.

No Sugar and *No Sugar Added* claims should be looked at with suspicion. Check the ingredients. A barbecue sauce that claims "no sugar" lists corn syrup as its second ingredient.[63]

Oat Bran products may not have much oat bran in them; and in any case, the importance of oat bran in particular (as opposed to the general need for more complex carbohydrates and fiber, which is widely agreed on) is a matter of dispute.[64]

Serving Size is often underestimated to disguise the true calorie intake. For example, most people eat two ounces of breakfast cereal, but the typical serving size is one ounce.[65]

Unspecific Oil Listings in ingredients. Some products will have a listing such as "soybean and/or palm oils"—it makes a difference which one! Soybean oils are unsaturated fats, palm oils are saturated. Consumers have a right to know which it is.

The label that may take the cake is in a place of honor in the Goldbecks' Museum of Food Labels. It is "Rodenbery's Butter-Maple Syrup"—no butter, no maple syrup.[66]

A New Approach. Many cartoons have poked fun at the incomprehensibility of current nutrition labels. One shows a scruffy juvenile sitting on the curb eating a chocolate bar and reading the string of chemical names for emulsifiers, stabilizers, and so forth. Another has the long list of ingredients running off the edge of the package, finishing with "Continued on Next Package."

Clearly, many food labels require a high degree of technical knowledge to decipher. The Center for Science in the Public Interest has proposed a radical new approach to food labeling, to maximize the nutritional information to the public. It proposes adding, next to the amount of a particular nutrient, whether a product is high, medium, or low in this nutrient. It also proposes requiring a clear pie chart on every label showing the proportions of nutrients in percentages.[67]

Seals of Approval. Given public confusion over what products are healthy, a new idea has arisen, for certifying organizations to lend their seals of approval to individual products.

In Chapter 5, we shall see that these seals are being widely used by certified organic farmers to distinguish their products from others that are labeled "organic" without any evidence of what that means.

Another seal of approval is being offered by the American Heart Association, to vouch for the heart-healthiness of products. But the value of this seal may be limited if the Association does not identify the criteria by which it awards the seal. Also, FDA Acting Commissioner James S. Benson wrote to the American Heart Association at the end of January 1990 warning them that their program was "risking regulatory action" and that it was a "very real possibility that the FDA would find one or more foods under your program to be misbranded."[68] The FDA may have brought the situation on itself, as *The New York Times* has editorialized, by delaying "urgently needed rules to clarify what claims may be made."[69]

A seal that has been in operation for some time in Colorado is the HealthMark, which is used to designate products, restaurants, and grocery shelves. It has been awarded to 170 restaurants in the Denver area, 15 products, and two supermarket chains. It also offers one-day and three-day educational programs.

Label Laws. Food grading and product labeling are monitored by three organizations: the USDA for dairy, poultry, and meat products; the FDA for standards of identity of processed foods; and the Federal Trade Commission for misleading trade practices.

As of early 1990, detailed nutritional labels are required only for foods that make health claims or are nutritionally fortified. Packaged foods must only list ingredients that make up more than 5 percent of the weight in descending order by weight. If the food is synthetically made, it must say "imitation." Foods that carry nutritional claims must list serving size, calories, carbohydrates, fat, and sodium in milligrams per serving size; and protein and at least five essential vitamins and two minerals as percentages of the USRDAs.

Some practices are stopped cold. For example, in April 1989 an administrative Federal Trade Commission judge enjoined Kraft from claiming that its Kraft's Singles cheese slices contain as much calcium as five ounces of milk (the actual amount of calcium was equivalent to about three ounces of milk).[70] Campbell's soup was stopped from claiming a canned soup was high in calcium when it was shown that the calcium came from the milk that was to be added to the contents of the can.

But we need better information about our food, along the lines suggested by the Center for Science in the Public Interest. The Surgeon General suggests that all food la-

bels (not just those that make health claims) carry the following information: "calories, protein, carbohydrate, fats, cholesterol, sodium, and vitamins and minerals. To the extent permitted by analytical methods, manufacturers should disclose information where appropriate on the content of saturated and unsaturated fatty acids and total fiber in foods that normally contain them. Descriptive terms such as 'low calorie' and 'sodium reduced' in compliance with Food and Drug Administration's regulations for food labeling may also be helpful, and the expanded use of these terms should be encouraged."[71]

As of the opening of Congress in 1990, two bills were before the Congress to reform food labeling. One, S. 1425, was introduced by Senators Howard E. Metzenbaum (D-OH) and John E. Chafee (R-RI), and would expand food labeling requirements along the lines suggested by the Surgeon General. The bill was before the Committee on Labor and Human Resources. In the House, a similar bill, H.R. 3652, was introduced by Rep. Henry A. Waxman (D-CA) and was reported out of the Committee on Energy and Commerce. To express your support or other opinion on these bills, write to or call their sponsors at the addresses listed under "U.S. Congress" at the end of Chapter 3.

Selecting Healthy Food

We have looked at food through the eyes of ancient thinkers and modern scientists, of farmers and chemists, producers and consumers. How in practice, does one use food identification to eat in a healthy way?

The first step is to become more aware of what is in foods by regularly consulting the labels that food processors are increasingly required to put on products. As the 1988 Surgeon General's Report says: "Food labeling offers opportunities to inform people about the nutrient content of foods so as to facilitate dietary choices. Food manufacturers should be encouraged to make full use of nutrition labels."[72]

No one food is by itself healthy. The key to selecting healthy food is to make it part of a healthy diet. The fact is, ancient admonitions to look for the middle way, moderation, in our handling of food is exactly what the RDAs come down to—we must obtain our nutrition in a certain middle range, not too much and not too little.

Mainstream medicine and science now generally agree that Americans eat too much fatty food and sugar, and not enough vegetables. Some dietary advisers recommend making whole grains the major dietary staple, along with legumes and (usually) fish. These recommendations are examined in Chapter 3.

The major areas of dispute are the need to make population-wide pronouncements (as opposed to advice to certain groups of people at special risk of contracting some diet-related diseases) about the desirability and hazards of meat and poultry, eggs and dairy products, salt, and fiber. Most people agree that skim milk products are healthy, as are moderate amounts of lean meat and skinless poultry. To be sure that what we eat corresponds to these positive attributes, we need better food labeling. The two bills before Congress would address this need.

But a growing school of thought stresses the importance of attitude in maintaining health. A macrobiotic guru has said that a calm, cheerful person is following the essence of the macrobiotic regimen regardless of his or her diet. In other words, it may be healthier to eat franks and beer with thanks and cheer, than bread and sprouts with dread and doubts.[73] Fortunately, these aren't our only two options!

Unicorn Village in North Miami Beach, Florida is a restaurant, market, and boutique rolled into one complex. The restaurant has been recognized as outstanding for over a decade and features live jazz to complement a fantastic view. The deli has over 75 items for takeout and the boutique offers a wide range of books and gifts.

3

THE HEALTHY DIET

"Concerns about nutrition and health have expanded . . . to encompass the effects of typical American dietary patterns on the incidence of chronic diseases . . ."
—Secretary Otis R. Bowen, M.D., 1988.

Uncle Sam's Dietary Research

Most Americans eat an unhealthy diet. One estimate reckons that two-thirds of Americans die from diseases caused by poor diet.[1]

In particular, *Americans eat too much saturated fat,* which several Federal studies have linked to heart disease and cancer. Diet is the most important contributing factor to heart disease and is linked to one-third of all cancer deaths.[2] These figures don't include tobacco smoking, which accounts for another third of cancer deaths and kills even more people through heart disease and emphysema.[3]

Early Dietary Debates. In 1977, the U.S. Senate Select (McGovern) Committee on Nutrition and Human Needs urged Americans to avoid being overweight and recommended that we reduce fat intake to 27–33 percent of calories.[4]

But in 1978, the American Heart Association recommended a higher maximum fat intake range, 30–35 percent of calories[5] and in 1980 the National Academy of Sciences' Food and Nutrition Board, in its semi-decennial update of the RDAs described in Chapter 2, recommended reduction of fat intake to no more than *35 percent* of calories.

In the same year, the Board sought to minimize the importance of fat and cholesterol. It issued *Toward Healthful Diets,* a set of guidelines that pooh-poohed concerns about fat and cholesterol. Investigations following the report, labeled a "fiasco," uncovered that it was written in part by a consultant to the egg industry.[6]

The Institutes' Initiatives. The official U.S. health research bodies, the National Institutes, date back to the Hygienic Laboratory at the U.S. Marine Hospital on Staten Island, N.Y. In 1948, instead of joining the British

Government in the creation of a comprehensive health service, the U.S. Government opted to expand the country's health research with the creation of nine health research institutes, under the umbrella name of the National Institutes of Health.

In keeping with the disinclination of U.S. medicine to place much importance on preventive medicine or diet, the Institutes in the 1960s and 1970s mostly channeled Federal money to medical researchers, accounting for about one-third of such funding.

The National Cancer Institute therefore took an important step in 1982 by funding a report by the National Academy of Sciences on how diet affects the incidence of cancer.[7] The Academy's Committee on Diet, Nutrition, and Cancer recommended reducing fat intake to 30 percent of calories, back down to the McGovern Committee's recommended level. Two years later, the Academy and the Institute published these dietary guidelines as *Cancer Prevention;* they recommended a varied diet, avoiding obesity through increased physical activity, and reduced fat intake.[8]

In 1984, the federally supported Coronary Primary Prevention Trial found that lowering people's blood cholesterol reduced the incidence of fatal heart attacks.[9] This conclusion led to the 1985 creation of the National Cholesterol Education Program under the aegis of the National Heart, Lung and Blood Institute. The program recommends that Americans cut their fat intake by nearly one-third, from 42 to 30 percent of calories.

The Surgeon General's Report, 1988. While the Institutes' initiatives were important, they lacked the impact of a national health policy. Demurrers could argue that they were minority views. This situation changed in 1988, with the appearance of *The Surgeon General's Report on Nutrition and Health.* It was presented both by the Surgeon

General, Everett Koop, M.D., Sc.D. and the outgoing Secretary of Health and Human Services, Otis R. Bowen, M.D. The report pulled no punches, and marked a unique turning point in public policy toward nutrition and disease.

The Foreword by Secretary Bowen said: "This [Report] marks a key event in the history of public health in the United States. . . . It responds to the increasing interest of scientists, health professionals, and the American people in the role of diet in health promotion. Within recent years, concerns about nutrition and health have expanded beyond the need to prevent deficiencies to encompass the effects of typical American dietary patterns on the incidence of chronic diseases that are leading causes of death and disability in this country. . . . This Report reviews the scientific evidence that relates dietary excesses and imbalances to chronic diseases. On the basis of the evidence, it recommends dietary changes that can improve the health prospects of many Americans. Of highest priority among these changes is to reduce intake of foods high in fats and increase intake of foods high in complex carbohydrates and fiber."[10]

The Surgeon General went on to do something that earlier guidelines avoided—to urge the medical profession to incorporate more nutrition education in physician training. The report said: "Improved nutrition training of physicians and other health professionals is needed. Training should emphasize basic principles of nutrition, the role of diet in health promotion and disease prevention, nutrition assessment methodologies and their interpretation, therapeutic aspects of dietary intervention, behavioral aspects of dietary counseling, and the role of dietitians and nutritionists in dietary counseling of patients."[11]

The Surgeon General's specific recommendations for diet do not greatly differ from the 1985 consensus dietary report prepared jointly in 1985 by the U.S. Department of Agriculture and the U.S. Department of Health and Human Services (DHHS), *Dietary Guidelines for Americans*,[12] discussed in the next section. Both reports recommend weight control, reduced fat intake, increased starch and fiber intake, and minimal use of alcohol (no more than two drinks a day) and sodium. The Surgeon General places less emphasis on eating a variety of foods (omitted, perhaps because of his concern about "overconsumption"[13]) and reducing intake of sugar (demoted from a general recommendation to one restricted to those who are vulnerable to cavities, especially children). But he adds three new dietary recommendations or "issues" for certain population groups: adequate calcium (especially for adolescent girls and adult women), fluoride (especially for those in communities that do not have fluoridated water), and iron (especially for children, adolescents, and women of childbearing age).[14]

Uncle Sam's Dietary Recommendations

The first half of this chapter is organized according to the categories in the 1985 USDA-DHHS consensus guidelines, for which many explanatory pamphlets are widely available. We review them and discuss their rationale.

1. Eat a Variety of Foods

No single food provides all the vitamins and minerals a person needs. Most nutritionists recommend that we eat a "balanced" diet. The "Basic Four" Food Group Plan, devised by the USDA with heavy emphasis on protein and the strong support of the U.S. dairy, egg, and meat industries,[15] suggests that we select our food so as to have 2–4 servings per day from each of the following four food groups: (1) Vegetables and fruits (4/day), (2) Grains (4/day), (3) Dairy (2/day), and (4) Meat, poultry, fish, legumes, eggs, nuts (2/day).[16]

Recent recommendations from other studies would add that grains are better whole, with bran intact; and that the brands and varieties of dairy, meat, and poultry products we select should all be low in fat. Fish should be on the menu at least twice a week.[17]

Vegetarians have been told to eat legumes (as we saw in Chapter 2, the peas and beans family) with whole grains to obtain the full range of amino acids for adequate protein intake. More recently, the concern about obtaining enough protein has been questioned, but even so the advice to mix legumes with grains still has validity as a way to plan variety and balance into meals. Strict vegetarians (who don't consume dairy products) need to make special efforts to obtain enough calcium, iron and vitamin B_{12}.

The main thrust of this dietary guideline is to avoid fad diets that concentrate on one food at the expense of others, and to obtain needed vitamins and minerals from a variety of foods rather than eating a narrow diet that requires food supplements or artificial foods (half of all Americans regularly consume low-calorie foods and beverages).[18] On the other hand, many health practitioners believe that certain groups of Americans may need supplements, especially if they live in cities, are elderly, consume less than 1,500 calories a day,[19] or are on the verge of an illness. Such supplements may be consumed as enriched foods like cereals, many of which provide substantial percentages (25 percent or more) of the USRDAs, which should suffice for many people. Tablets provide higher concentrations of supplements, but can be hazardous. Respect the upper limits recommended in the RDAs provided in Chapter 2. We discuss supplements again later in this chapter when we review the types of dietary advisers.

2. Maintain Desirable Weight

Overweight people are more at risk for deadly heart diseases, high blood pressure, and diabetes. Obesity also contributes to the risks associated with some cancers.[20]

Obtaining adequate nutrients would be no problem if we didn't have to limit our overall intake of food. But we do, or we will get fat. Sugar, other highly processed foods, alcohol, and fat all add calories without their share of needed nutrients.

Fat in our food is bad not only because too much predisposes us to heart disease and cancer and adds weight. Such fat-, salt-, and calorie-laden staples as "fatfurters" and "shamburgers" (to use Ralph Nader's terms for high-fat ground meats) contribute to the American problem of obesity.

The latest (1983) Metropolitan Height and Weight Tables are shown as Tables 3–1 and 3–2.

Table 3–1
Metropolitan Weight Tables

Height	Small	Medium	Large
Men			
5'2"	128–134	131–141	138–150
5'4"	132–138	135–145	142–156
5'6"	136–142	139–151	146–164
5'8"	140–148	145–157	152–172
5'10"	144–154	151–163	158–180
6'0"	149–160	157–170	164–188
6'2"	155–168	164–178	172–197
6'4"	162–176	171–187	181–207
Women			
4'10"	102–111	109–121	118–131
5'0"	104–115	113–126	122–137
5'2"	108–121	118–132	128–143
5'4"	114–127	124–138	134–151
5'6"	120–133	130–144	140–159
5'8"	126–139	136–150	146–167
5'10"	132–145	142–156	152–173
6'0"	138–151	148–162	158–179

Source: Metropolitan Life Insurance Company. Weights in pounds at ages 25–59 based on lowest mortality from 1979 Build Study. Frame size is based on elbow measurements.

The median (typical) weight for men is in fact above the top of the medium frame range for every height. For 5'2" it is 142 pounds, 5'4" 148 pounds, 5'6" 158 pounds, 5'8" 167 pounds, 5'10" 173 pounds, 6'0" 183 pounds, 6'2" 194 pounds, 6'4" 227 pounds.[21]

The median weight for American women is slightly above the top range for a medium frame for every height except 5'6", where it is three pounds below the upper level.[22]

The Metropolitan Weight Tables were first produced in 1942; they were redone in 1959 and again in 1983. The 1983 figures were several pounds (over ten in some categories) higher than in 1959. The American Heart Associa-

tion said in 1983 that the earlier figures should have been continued because they are a better reflection of optimal weight.

The Government Tables. Some argue that the Metropolitan Tables are misleading, for three reasons:[23]

1. They assume people should keep the same weight throughout life. "But there's just overwhelming evidence now that as you go through life it's in your best interest to lay down some fat," says Dr. Reubin Andres, clinical director of the Gerontology Research Center of the National Institute on Aging. His research indicates the weights in the Metropolitan Tables are "just right" for those in their early 40s, but should be lower for younger people and should be higher for older people. Dr. William R. Hazzard, director of the Johns Hopkins Center of Aging, agrees. Most experts won't go that far, but many agree that obesity is a more serious heart disease hazard for people under the age of 45 than for those who are older. On the other hand, some argue that mortality data are skewed against thin people because the figures may include smokers and people dying of wasting diseases, who are thin but not healthy.

2. They assume men of the same height should weigh more than women. Dr. Andres doesn't see the need to provide different weights.

3. They require users of the tables to figure out their body frame size by measuring the width of their elbow. Dr. Andres calls the body-frame distinctions "speculative."

The Gerontology Research Center has developed alternative tables shown in Table 3–2. These tables are favored over the Metropolitan Tables by *Consumer Reports*.[24]

Table 3–2
GRC Weight Tables by Age Range
Recommended Weights for Both Sexes

Height	20–29	30–39	50–59	60–69
4'10"	84–111	92–119	107–135	115–142
5'0"	90–119	98–127	114–143	123–152
5'2"	96–127	105–136	122–153	131–163
5'4"	102–135	112–145	130–163	140–173
5'6"	109–144	119–154	138–174	148–184
5'8"	116–153	126–163	147–184	158–196
5'10"	122–162	134–173	156–195	167–207
6'0"	129–171	141–183	165–207	177–219
6'2"	137–181	149–194	174–219	187–232
6'4"	144–191	157–205	184–231	197–244

Source: Gerontology Research Center, National Institute on Aging. Weight ranges, in pounds, are for people without shoes or other clothing. People in their 40s should use the Metropolitan Tables.

A distinction not made on any weight tables is whether body fat is on the hips, buttocks, and lower body (the "pear" shape) or the abdomen (the "apple" shape). Columbia University obesity specialist Dr. Theodore B. Van Itallie sums it up: "If your obesity is in your haunches, you're at lower risk than if it's in your paunch." Two old explanations were that abdominal fat cells are larger than average and are more closely linked to the liver. The latest explanation, in the January 1990 issue of the *New England Journal of Medicine*, doesn't contradict the older theories. It provides evidence that pear-shaped people have higher levels of high-density lipoprotein, HDL ("good") cholesterol, which is heart-protective. Body shape tends to explain a lot of the difference among people's HDL levels, provides biological support for the attractiveness of small waists, and accounts for much of the previously observed difference between male and female HDL levels.[25]

Getting the Message from the Weight Tables. Whatever weight table you use, you can determine whether you are underweight, the right weight, overweight, obese, or very obese.

You are *underweight* if you are below the lower level of the range. A risk of being underweight, especially for women, is osteoporosis, a dangerous bone sponginess; the risk is reduced by getting enough exercise and calcium (either through milk or other calcium-rich food, or through supplements).

You are *overweight* if you are above the upper level, or 10 percent above the midpoint, of the range for your height. This is generally not considered a serious health problem.

You are *obese* if you are more than 20 percent above the midpoint of the range for your height. This is a serious health problem. One-fourth of American women and one-eighth of American men are said to be obese.[26] According to the National Institutes of Health, obese people are more at risk for adult diabetes, hypertension, elevated blood cholesterol, and cardiovascular disease.[27]

You are *very obese* if you are 40 percent or more above the midpoint for your range. The American Cancer Society finds that such people are more at risk for breast, colon, rectal, and uterine cancer.[28]

What should you do if your weight is too high? I would like to be able to say that cutting down on fat and calories intake in favor of complex carbohydrates will do the trick. It will help, long term, since dietary fat makes a big contribution to obesity. But it won't usually produce rapid changes in weight. For that, special diets are needed. Don't try it without the supervision of qualified advisers, because rapid weight loss diets can be hazardous, especially high-protein diets.

But the key to controlling obesity may have less to do with diet than exercise. A Stanford University study placed 32 middle-aged, sedentary male volunteers on a progressive running-based exercise regimen; no other changes in lifestyle were asked of them. Result: The men who ran the most miles lost the most weight. Yet the more body fat they lost, the more they ate. So reducing calories in our diet seems less important than burning them up![29] This conclusion is reinforced by the Health and Nutrition Examination Surveys showing that the thinnest people generally consume the most calories.[30] A 1989 study finds that a higher mortality rate is linked to being among the least fit 20 percent of a population group. To rise above this high-risk group, all it takes is a half-hour's brisk walk per day.[31]

Roy Walford, M.D., professor of pathology at UCLA medical school, is a longevity expert who advocates reduced weight for almost everyone. He notes that mice fed a restricted-calorie diet lived longer than controls that were fully fed.[32] From this, Walford concludes: "Information is already available to enable one to live to be more than 120 years old if he begins early enough and adheres religiously to a lifelong regimen of dietary restriction."[33]

However, no real evidence exists that this regimen will work. The apparent long life of underfed rats is explained by Professor Edward Masoro, chairman of the physiology department at the San Antonio Health Science Center of the University of Texas. He says the typical lab diet *shortens* rats' lives because it is too generous and high in protein for animals allowed to eat whenever they want. Cutting rations allows rats to live closer to a normal life span. But people eat so many different kinds of diets—most with economically controlled rations—that if a magic life-extending diet existed "it would have been stumbled on already."[34]

So Walford's ascetic regimen may not make people live longer. It may just *feel* longer.

But we should keep an open mind. As gerontologist Andres says: "Some things that sound absolutely dippy eventually turn out to be right. And yet, most things that sound dippy *are* dippy—or worse."[35]

3. Avoid Too Much Fat, Saturated Fat, and Cholesterol

Americans generally should consume less fat and dietary cholesterol. These hazards are especially dangerous for those at high risk, as measured by blood cholesterol levels.

Blood cholesterol elevation is a significant factor contributing to the risk of coronary heart disease, the No. 1 cause of death among U.S. adults. It is also strongly linked to high blood pressure, which is another risk factor for heart disease. Heart attacks are the ultimate sign of heart disease and mean that muscles in the heart have been destroyed by lack of oxygen and the tissues have died. The medical term for heart attack, "myocardial infarction," is derived from three Latin words meaning muscle, heart, and tissue death (infarction is from the same root, farcire, as the word "farce"; the arteries are stuffed with fatty plaque and the blood can't get through, so the tissues die).[36]

A heart attack is fatal in only one out of three cases; many people survive a heart attack, reform their lifestyle, and go on to live a long life. If a heart attack destroys 10 percent of the muscle tissue around the heart, the heart is still strong enough to function well, especially if the patient is willing to make the necessary dietary (reduce fat consumption) and other lifestyle (increase exercise, reduce stress) changes.

The National Heart, Lung and Blood Institute urges

Americans to reduce their blood cholesterol level to below 200 milligrams per deciliter, and to consult with their doctor for further attention if the level exceeds the high-risk level of 240, which is true of *one-fourth* of U.S. adults.

Epidemiological data suggest, in rough terms, that a nonsmoker with no hypertension and a blood cholesterol of 200 milligrams per deciliter might not reach the critical stage of cardiovascular disease (i.e., 60 percent coverage of artery surfaces by atherosclerosis) until age 70. If blood cholesterol is 250, the age drops to 60. If blood cholesterol is 300, the age drops to 50.[37] This is not to say exactly that life expectancy drops 10 years for an increase of 50 in the blood cholesterol level; it does suggest that people with high blood cholesterol are likely to see their quality of life deteriorate much faster than those who are below the high-risk range. Subtract another 10 years from the above figures for smokers, and yet another 10 years for those with hypertension—a smoker with hypertension and a blood cholesterol level of 300 would reach the critical stage of cardiovascular disease at age 30![38]

Studies show that treatment of high blood cholesterol by diet (and, in extreme cases, drugs) reduced the incidence of heart attacks among treated patients and that treated patients lived longer than an untreated control group.[39]

The total blood cholesterol level is not the sole risk factor to be measured in a blood test. Another important one is the level of HDL ("good") cholesterol, which does not attach itself to tissues. If this level is significantly above 35 milligrams per deciliter it offsets the previously mentioned hazard of having a total cholesterol level above 240.[40]

Some physicians and patients have absorbed the principle that the lower the ratio of LDL to HDL the better, and have proceeded to use a rule of thumb such as that the LDL:HDL ratio should be less than 2 (for example, an LDL of 140 would be acceptable if HDL is 75 or higher). Such ratios may be comforting but are not considered meaningful based on current knowledge.[41]

Fat, especially saturated fat, is the major culprit in contributing to high blood cholesterol. The National Heart, Lung and Blood Institute recommends fat intake be kept below 30 percent of calories, i.e. 10 grams of fat (90 calories) for every 300 calories. But many nutritionists say it is not enough to reduce our intake of fat to 30 percent, and urge us to take the figure down further. Dr. Walford urges us to keep it below 20 percent of calories; the Pritikin program attempts to reduce it to 5 or 10 percent.[42]

A diet low in fat, saturated fat, and cholesterol will tend to be lower in calories, since fat has 9 calories per gram vs. 4 calories per gram for protein and carbohydrates (alcohol has 7 calories per gram). This guideline therefore supports the previous recommendation to keep our weight down. Avoiding fat also appears to lower the risk of cancers of the breast, uterus, prostate, colon and rectum.

To illustrate the link between fat and calories, consider milk and cream. (See Table 3-3.) A line has been drawn through the middle of the table to show that any dairy product above 2 percent fat exceeds the recommended fat-to-calorie intake of 30 percent.

Table 3–3
Calories from Fat in Milk and Cream

Type of Milk/Cream (Calories per Cup)	Percent Fat	Percent Calories from Fat
Skim (88)	0.2	2
Low-fat, 1% (100)	0.1	18
Low-fat, 2% (145)*	2.0	30
Whole (159)	3.5	48
Half-and-half (324)	11.7	79
Light cream (506)	20.6	88
Heavy cream (838)	37.6	96

*Non-fat milk solids added.

Source: USDA, *Nutritive Value of American Foods*, 1988.[43]

According to USDA data, a cup of unfortified skim milk has only a trace of fat, so that it derives only *2 percent* of its calories from fat.[44] Low-fat, "2%" milk commonly has calories added by non-fat milk solids; even so, it gets *over 30 percent* of its calories from fat—more than the maximum ratio of fat to total calories we are advised to consume! A cup of whole milk is 3.5–4 percent fat by weight (must be a minimum of 3.25 percent according to USDA standards) and gets *48 percent* of the cup's 159 calories from fat. In other words, whole milk gets 50 percent more of its calories from fat than is advised. Half-and-half's calories are *79 percent* fat, light cream's 88 percent, and heavy cream's 96 percent. Even higher are mayonnaise, which gets *99 percent* of its calories from fat; and butter and vegetable oils, which get *100 percent*.[45]

Saturated fat is the worst. It is found in animal foods (meat, poultry, and dairy products), *and* in coconut and palm oils, *and* to some extent in hydrogenated oils—which also contain trans-fatty acids that act on the body much like saturated fat. National guidelines recommend keeping our intake of saturated fatty acids to under one-third of total fats (i.e., below 10 percent of total calories).

Of the 8.5 grams of fat in a cup of whole milk, more than half of it (4.7 grams) is saturated.[46] Only one-fifth of the fat in margarine is saturated.[47]

To avoid saturated fat, limit consumption of animal products, the so-called tropical oils (palm oil, palm kernel oil, coconut oil), and hydrogenated oils. Avoid *any* deep-fried foods, which are usually cooked in saturated fats. Consume skim milk, low-fat cottage cheese, and no-fat yogurt; dairy products without the fat still provide the calcium. Eat fish, but avoid fish packed in oils high in saturated fats. Avoid pastries and popcorn popped in (or topped off with) oil. Choose low-calorie salad dressings, but watch out for artificial ingredients (see Chapter 4). Avoid adding fats to food during cooking—broil, bake or boil, don't fry!

Fatty meats are high in saturated fatty acids and should be avoided. That means eschewing frankfurters, fatty hamburgers, and lunch meats (bologna, pepperoni, salami), which can have a very high fat and additive content, and fried poultry or poultry skins.[48] However, including *lean* meat in a balanced diet is not viewed by most mainstream nutritionists as hazardous; meat is high in protein, vitamins and minerals, especially iron and zinc. As consumers become more aware of the need to avoid saturated fats, meat producers and supermarkets are attempting to reduce the percentage of fat in the meat they sell. Check any general claims against the label, and remember that the easiest way to reduce fat content in lunch meats is to add more water; the number to look for is not grams of fat per serving but *calories from fat as a percentage of total calories*, remembering to count nine calories for each gram of fat.

Cholesterol in food (*dietary* cholesterol) is found in meat, eggs and dairy products. It is a hazard, since it is believed to contribute to blood cholesterol in humans. The National Heart, Lung and Blood Institute recommends keeping dietary cholesterol below 300 milligrams per day.

Dietary cholesterol is not considered as serious a contributor to high blood cholesterol as saturated fat,[49] so that foods high in dietary cholesterol but low in fat—shellfish, for example—are not as hazardous as fatty frankfurters or lunch meats. But individuals with blood cholesterol in the high-risk area should consult with physicians about limiting their intake of dietary cholesterol.

Certain findings about the link between blood cholesterol and a higher risk of heart attacks are widely accepted:[50] (a) In middle-aged men, high blood cholesterol increases the risk of a heart attack.[51] (b) Reducing one's cholesterol level by 20 percent has been shown to slow or reverse the formation of plaques on the arteries, which is considered a major cause of heart attacks. (c) Changing one's diet alone can reduce blood cholesterol by about 10 percent or more.[52]

Some researchers and journalists[53] have raised questions about research on cholesterol. For example, they point out that the population studies chosen for blood cholesterol research have been mostly groups of middle-aged men. Do the findings apply to the elderly (heart surgeon Michael DeBakey didn't think so, but a new article in the *Journal of the American Medical Association* says they do),[54] to children, and to women (who have a much lower risk of getting a heart attack before menopause)?[55] An open question is whether reduced blood cholesterol has any re-lated hazards, such as perhaps at some low level increasing the likelihood of cancer or other disease.

High blood pressure is another risk factor for heart disease, and diet has been found to be related to high blood pressure—notably excessive salt intake and inadequate potassium and calcium;[56] excessive intake of alcohol; and excessive calorie intake and obesity. The same balanced low-fat diet that reduces the risk of heart disease would reduce the risk of high blood pressure.

Many doctors in the past have preferred to prescribe drugs to lower blood pressure rather than bother with the more time-consuming and often thankless task of educating their patients about the need for dietary and life-style changes. But even the *Essential Guide to Prescription Drugs* recommends dietary changes as the "primary treatment for all individuals with elevated blood lipid levels."[57] Diuretics, commonly prescribed for patients with high blood pressure (50 million prescriptions in 1988), raise blood cholesterol for a substantial number of patients by 5 to 10 percent and reduce potassium in about one-third of patients. Beta blockers, also prescribed for high blood pressure (30 million prescriptions in 1988) can reduce HDL ("good") cholesterol.[58]

From a practical point of view the advice for avoiding cardiovascular disease is three-fold: (1) Don't smoke; (2) Eat a low-fat, natural[59] diet (avoiding alcohol and salt[60]); and (3) Exercise regularly.

4. Eat Foods with Adequate Starch and Fiber

Most Americans eat too little starch—the main food conveyed by the label "complex carbohydrates"—in relation to the other food in their diets. Nutritionists therefore recommend that we eat more fruit and vegetables, whole grain breads and cereals, and legumes (peas and beans).[61]

Starch, as we saw in Chapter 2, is a complex carbohydrate composed of long chains of glucose (one of the three basic sugars) molecules folded back on themselves. The body converts starch into *maltose*, which is then converted into glucose. In its raw state, starch is hard to digest; cooking makes the chains unfold somewhat and makes the food easier to digest. Good examples of starchy foods are potatoes and beans. Many other vegetables, grains, and fruits are high in starch.

Fiber is a name for the indigestible parts of food, especially *cellulose*. As we saw in Chapter 2 cellulose is, like starch, composed of chains of glucose molecules, but is structured differently so that it is insoluble and is poorly digested and absorbed, even with cooking (cattle can digest cellulose because their stomach has super-bacteria to break it down). Fiber has a water-retaining capacity that creates a sponge-like matrix, a bulking effect, and a binding capacity in the gastrointestinal tract; it also effects chemical exchanges. Although research is still under way to clarify causal links, some studies conclude that the increase of bulk from fiber has significant beneficial effects.

The most incontrovertible evidence is that fiber reduces colon (and rectal and intestinal) cancer. This is presumed to be either because fiber shortens the time carcinogens (including harmful bile acid and salt residues) are in contact with the intestines and colon, or because fiber dilutes and binds to bile acids.

Fiber is also thought, by substituting for foods high in fat and cholesterol, to reduce blood cholesterol and the risk of heart disease. It helps prevent diverticulosis, an outward bulging of small pockets in the large intestine. Finally, by slowing down food intake and adding bulk, it is believed to curb appetite and assist in long-term weight loss.[62]

Though fiber in our diets has many benefits, it has not been considered an essential dietary nutrient. The traditional view is that an essential nutrient is a substance that must be present to *sustain life*, and strictly speaking fiber doesn't qualify. A more recent view is that substances necessary for *optimal health* are essential. This definition accepts fiber as an essential nutrient.

Nutritionists recommend that people consume 20–35 grams of fiber a day, two to three times the 11 grams/day that Americans eat. Exceeding 35 grams/day is *not* recommended, because it could cause dehydration and demineralization (fiber carries out with it calcium, iron, and zinc), and could interfere with the creation of vitamin A.[63] People can get all the fiber they need by eating a variety of fruits, vegetables (especially legumes) and *whole* grains. Most cooked vegetables have 2 to 3 grams of fiber per half cup. Most fruits have 3 to 4 grams per serving. Legumes have 4 to 9 grams of fiber per half cup. Cereals generally have under 3 grams of fiber per serving, although some new bran cereals have up to 13 grams of fiber per serving.[64]

Easy ways to increase one's intake of fiber are to substitute (1) whole wheat bread and whole-grain cereals for white bread and processed cereals, (2) unpeeled (unwaxed) apples for apple juice, and (3) potatoes in their skins for mashed potatoes.

5. Avoid Too Much Sugar

Americans obtain nearly one-fourth of their calories from sugars, the simple carbohydrates that include fructose, glucose, lactose, and sucrose. They are urged to cut this to no more than 10 percent, substituting complex carbohydrates like grains for sugar.[65]

For many Americans, sugar-sweetened soft drinks are their biggest single source of refined sugar. A regular soda in a can contains 11 teaspoons of sugar, sucrose (glucose and fructose bonded together), and not a trace of redeeming nutritive value.[66] In 1986, Americans drank 30 gallons per person of soft drinks, nearly one-third of the 96 gallons of non-alcoholic beverages (excluding vegetable

juices) they consumed. The second-place drink was coffee, 27 gallons, which adds just sugar and a drug, caffeine, to the diet. In third place was milk, 26 gallons, most of it whole milk. The other significant beverages were tea (13 gallons) and fruit juices, mostly citrus (6 gallons).[67]

Better than soft drinks are fruit juices, because along with their fructose they have vitamin C and a few other nutrients; but the sugar is still there and orange juice actually has a calorie *more* per fluid ounce (15 vs. 14) than a cherry soda.

Sugar provides nothing but calories and is not a good food source to be playing such a major role in the American diet because it is often consumed in foods devoid of vitamins and minerals. As a simple carbohydrate, it is metabolized very rapidly which invites dramatic shifts in energy levels. Evidence suggests that sugar may play a role in a wide range of problems from tooth decay and hyperactivity to obesity, diabetes, and heart disease.

That it causes tooth decay is perhaps the best substantiated of these claims, but many observers point out that any carbohydrate that remains on tooth-surfaces for long periods of time promotes cavities. Childen are especially at risk of tooth decay if they do not have fluoridated water. Studies examining the relationship between sugar consumption and hyperactivity are contradictory, some even concluding that sugar intake reduces hyperactivity. A possible explanation of this is that large sugar doses trigger large releases of insulin, which in turn lead to "downs."

Claims about sugar intake causing obesity are hard to sort out because high levels of sugar intake correlate too closely with high levels of fat intake in most people and population studies. Most claims about sugar causing diabetes rely on evidence that it promotes obesity (which in turn quite clearly increases the incidence of diabetes in those with a genetic predisposition to the disease). The argument that sugar causes heart disease takes many complex forms. One says that 10 to 20 percent of the population develop raised blood-lipid levels upon ingestion of any carbohydrate. Other theories state that since sugar can be converted to fat, large amounts of sugar lead to more fat circulating in the bloodstream of anyone who eats too much of the stuff. Less plausible theories state that sugar contributes to heart disease because sucrose leads to salt-retention. Studies show, though, that a high-sugar diet does not lead to sustained increases in the blood-pressure of healthy people.

Some see a way out in diet sodas, which contain artificial sweeteners—aspartame (Nutrasweet) and saccharin (cyclamate was banned in the U.S. by the Nixon Administration)—and no calories. The soda manufacturers are delighted to offer us diet sodas because the artificial sweeteners are cheaper than sugar. However, some experts are still extremely worried about their carcinogenic potential, and the American Dietetic Association recommends not having more than three diet sodas per day. In any case, by maintaining but not satisfying the taste for sweetness, low-calorie sweeteners have been found to be poor and even counterproductive approaches to losing weight. Diet sodas (and other diet products) in practice tend to be consumed in addition to, not instead of, other beverages and food. The best way to quell a sugar craving is with a small carbohydrate snack.

So best of all is to go easy on the sweet beverages, whether sweetened with sugar or fake sugar, and go for plain herbal teas, seltzer water, skim milk, vegetable juices, or just water—all of which are low in sugar.

6. Avoid Too Much Salt

Salt is 40 percent sodium, and a high sodium intake may contribute to high blood pressure, especially in someone with a family history of the condition. High blood pressure can lead to heart attacks, strokes, and kidney diseases.[68]

One controversy over sodium in the diet is whether or not people need to care how much sodium they consume above a certain level, because after a certain amount of intake the impact on blood pressure seems to taper off.

Another controversy relates to the population vs. patient-specific debate we discussed in Chapter 1—does someone who is not at risk for high blood pressure need to worry about sodium? Sodium "may be a problem if you are among the one-in-five Americans who is hypertension-prone, and among the one-in-three of the hypertension-prone who is salt-sensitive."[69]

A problem with this approach is that young people not at risk may get a taste for salt and then have difficulty eliminating salt when they are older and develop hypertension.

To regulate body fluid volume, people need 500 milligrams, half a gram, of salt per day—above that, the less the better, preferably no more than 2 grams of sodium per day, recommends the Center for Science in the Public Interest.

To lower salt intake, watch the sodium content of processed foods, especially soups and meat. Fast-food outlets are big offenders. Choose low-sodium alternatives whenever available. Instead of using salt, season with lemon juice, herbs, spices, or other natural and nutritious flavorings.

7. If You Drink Alcoholic Beverages, Do So in Moderation

Americans in 1986 drank more beer than any other single beverage—41 gallons a year per person, 86 percent of all alcoholic beverages. Wine was in a distant second place, accounting for 4 gallons per person, 9 percent of alcoholic beverage consumption. Consumption of distilled spirits has been declining, and in 1986 was 2 gallons per year per person.[70]

Heavy drinking is associated with many health problems, including increased likelihood of accidents. Heavy drinking is associated with cancers of the mouth, throat, esophagus and liver. The risk of cancer is especially high for heavy drinkers who smoke.

Alcohol intake is unwise for those who are trying to lose weight, because alcoholic drinks are high in calories while providing virtually no vitamin and mineral nutrients.

The Surgeon General recommends limiting alcoholic beverages to at most two drinks a day. The American Heart Association recommends no more than 1.7 ounces per day.[71] Pregnant women are advised not to drink at all—one of every 500 U.S. babies is severely damaged by fetal alcohol syndrome.[72]

Orthodox Medical Opinion on Diet

In the early decades of this century, physicians were less organized than they are today, but it is clear that many paid great attention to diet, disease prevention, and naturopathic remedies.

The Consolidation of U.S. Medical Orthodoxy. For over two decades (mostly the 1930s and 1940s) the editor of the *Journal of the American Medical Association*, Morris Fishbein, M.D., fought systematically to replace pluralism in the American medical profession with an orthodoxy built around three types of treatment: drugs (especially the new wonder drugs), radiation, and surgery. Dr. Fishbein battled unorthodox practitioners, with a list of enemy "quacks" that grew to 300,000.[73]

In his quackbuster role, Dr. Fishbein's bête noire was Harry M. Hoxsey, who ran cancer clinics with treatment centered on his herbal tonic. Fishbein co-authored a 1948 article, targeted at Hoxsey, which began: "All the other wicked medical fakes, firing hope and darkening it to despair, pale beside the savagery of the cancer charlatans. They look like men, they speak like men, but in them, pervading them, resides a quality so malevolent that it sets them apart from others of the human race."[74]

Hoxsey sued Fishbein for libel and a year later won. Fishbein was subsequently forced out of his AMA post, but the FDA and its state government allies carried on a war against Hoxsey's flourishing clinics. Texas finally forced Hoxsey out of his main clinic in 1957 and closed it in 1960. In 1963 Hoxsey persuaded his long-time assistant Mildred Nelson to continue his treatments in a Tijuana-based clinic.[75]

An effective documentary movie, *Hoxsey: Quacks Who Cure Cancer?*, tells more than Hoxsey's story. It provides a unique insight into the history of American medical politics. Hoxsey's treatment, for example, was banned without having been tested and in the face of a determination by two Federal courts that his herbal tonic had therapeutic value. Medical historian Pat Ward found expert support for therapeutic merits of herbs in the tonic, and concludes that Dr. Fishbein's purple prose was characteristic of "the low level of discourse and the emotional—rather than analytical—tone that has characterized the American medical profession's response to unorthodox remedies."[76]

Criticism of Medical Inattention to Diet. The newly orthodox leadership of the American Medical Association and related scientific and governmental bodies (like the EPA, FDA, and Surgeon General) did not, until the prodding of the McGovern Committee in 1977, focus on the potential use of diet in preventing or curing diseases. Drugs were considered the therapy of choice because they were better controlled, more measurable, and worked faster than herbal ("quack") remedies or long-term dietary and lifestyle changes.

Critics have said that orthodox American medicine has been trapped by its unhealthy relationships with food and chemical trade associations, large food-processing companies, and above all, the pharmaceutical companies.

Drug manufacturers sponsor medical conferences, provide free travel for doctors, and in 1988 advertised in the *Journal of the American Medical Association* to the tune of $38 million, which was one-fourth of the AMA's operating budget.

Those who have argued that too many government experts and medical leaders are beholden to industry associations or individual companies have gained the ear of Congress. Senators Harry M. Reid (D-NV) and Joseph I. Lieberman (D-CT) have called for an investigation into possible conflicts of interest among the EPA panelists who reviewed the registration of the farm chemical Alar.[77] The panel was composed almost entirely of people consulting for the chemical industry.

Failure of Most Medical Schools to Teach Nutrition. Many establishment institutions agree that orthodox medical schools have neglected nutrition. For example, the National Academy of Sciences, which concluded that "many U.S. medical schools do not teach nutrition . . . More than half the schools provide less than 20 hours. . . . and only 20 percent report that nutrition is taught entirely as a separate course. The distribution of nutrition subjects that are taught is uneven. . . . Of 6,000 questions from National Board examinations administered between 1980 and 1984, 3 percent to 4 percent were, at least in part, related to nutrition; however, the distribution of questions among the basic sciences and clinical specialties was uneven. Several topics, such as obesity and undernutrition, were strongly emphasized. Such topics as osteoporosis and the relationship between nutrition and cancer were overlooked. . . . In the committee's judgment, faculty responsibility for nutrition teaching is not clearly defined . . . The majority of medical students believe that instruction in nutrition is inadequate and that when nutrition is incorporated into other courses, as opposed to being a discrete course, its impact is lost."[78]

Medical student leaders are very clear in expressing their feeling that medical students are being short-changed. In 1985, the President of the American Medical Student Association testified: "Medical education has traditionally focused on the principles of acute episodic health-care delivery, overlooking the concepts and application of nutrition and preventive medicine. Nutrition is not well taught, if taught at all, in most medical schools . . . Because of this deficiency, *most physicians-in-training in the United States enter their professional life not equipped with the skills or attitudes to apply nutritional concepts in their practice of medicine.*"[79]

Why Don't They Teach Nutrition? Why, a lay person might well ask, would anyone oppose teaching nutrition? From interviews with doctors and published materials I offer some possible answers.

1. Hospital Economics. Hospitals need medical students to staff the front line and students need the experience that internships give them. Medical school becomes training for the intern experience, when the young graduates are on call for 72 hours at a stretch. Medical schools and hospitals fear that the interns will botch up and embarrass them or worse; this fear is transferred to the students, who learn to focus on "acute episodic" emergency room skills.

2. Medical School Psychology. Exams, curriculum, and clinical training in medical school convey to students that medicine has two ends, hard and soft. The hard, "yang" or macho (à la M*A*S*H) end is surgery, prescribing strong drugs, setting broken bones; this is important, manly stuff. The soft "yin" end is prevention and nutrition, less important, left to the "pink-collar" professionals like the dietitians. The task of hard medicine is to find the invading bacteria or bacilli and to map a campaign to kill the invaders with drugs, radiation, or surgery. The military model explains incidents of student and postgraduate resident abuse. Four out of five fourth-year students in a near-100 percent student survey at one medical school reported they had been abused.[80]

3. Fee-for-Service Health Insurance and Medical Career Economic Planning. Like students of any other professional discipline, medical students keep an eye on their future career prospects. In this light, nutrition does not offer much attraction in an environment of health care service reimbursement, which favors hard over soft medicine. Government and private health insurance policies and practices tend to query mere "cognitive services" to patients when reimbursement is requested. The best a physician can expect an insurer to pay is $75 for nutritional counseling and then only if the diagnosis is hyperlipidemia (high blood cholesterol), diabetes, or renal disease; insurers even query consultations about food allergies.[81] Why would medical students choose a preventive-care career, when health insurers will unquestioningly fork over tens of thousands of dollars for cancer or heart disease treatment?

Recent Changes in Orthodox Medicine. Orthodox attitudes toward nutrition began changing in the late 1970s. In 1974 Dr. Charles E. Butterworth reported a high frequency of iatrogenic (doctor-caused) malnutrition in hospital patients. He found, among other things, that attending physicians were depriving patients of nutrition while they gave them tests and did not provide any supplements.[82]

Negative side effects of pharmaceuticals are spilling over from the pages of the *Physicians Desk Reference* into the public consciousness. Patients are increasingly aware of the prevalence of these side effects and of iatrogenic illnesses caused by misprescribed, overprescribed, inadequately explained, or poorly monitored pharmacological medication. Criminal investigation of frequent flyer mileage rewards to physicians for prescribing Inderal LA offered by Wyeth-Ayerst (American Home Products) do not give medical consumers any reason for confidence in the objectivity of drug prescribing. Wyeth-Ayerst has settled a Massachusetts investigation for $195,000 but still faces a

Federal inquiry.[83] Searle is now also under attack for offering inducements to physicians for prescribing CALAN SR.[84]

While substantial lip service has been paid to the need to improve nutrition education in U.S. medical schools, a 1986 survey of medical students found that 85 percent of them were unhappy with the quantity and 60 percent with the quality of this education.[85]

Changes are on their way, driven by economics. Health care has simply become too expensive. Corporations are looking for ways to cut premiums while maintaining care for employees, and are attracted to group practice and health maintenance organizations like Kaiser Permanente, a good idea suggested by Bernard Shaw eight decades ago. Government and private health insurers are desperately looking for ways to reduce reimbursements, at the same time as the plight of those who have no health insurance is becoming a national scandal. Minneapolis and Saint Paul have led the way in encouraging health maintenance organizations in their region to compete in providing health services at a moderate cost.

Meanwhile, the cost-benefit calculus of economists emphasizes that conventional medicine is "not curing much more cancer than a generation ago," in the words of a 1984 report,[86] while the bulk of the credit for decline (e.g., by the previously cited director of the British Heart Association) in cardiovascular disease goes not to drugs or surgery but to dietary changes.

Those who are designing health care payment systems for the future talk about the need to reform the "Relative Value Scale" (RVS) for paying health practitioners. Up to now the RVS has been primarily fee-based, driven by demand for services and ability of the patient to pay; this is good for famous surgeons but bad for routine but important medicine. Researchers are now looking at a more equitable resource-based RVS, driven by the cost in time and other resources to provide a service. In the Congress, the Senate Finance Committee and House Ways and Means Committee have appointed a Physician Payment Review Commission, which is looking at these issues in connection with Medicare Part B (physician) payments. Their work will be used in reforms of Medicare and in discussions of the possibility of National Health Insurance.[87] One desirable outcome of the changes would be that a physician will have the time and inclination to tell patients who are eating self-destructively how they should modify their diets.

As governments, insurers, patients, and practitioners for different reasons have become dissatisfied with the adequacy of orthodox medicine and cast their therapeutic nets more widely, some of the lines between orthodox and preventive medicine have become blurred and others have been crossed.

One reason is that even with the best will in the world it would take time to produce a generation of physicians properly trained in nutrition. But with the slow pace of change at the medical schools and in the medical specialties, the public must confront the fact that it will take many years to produce nutrition-trained M.D.s in large numbers. Even then these people won't make much difference in overall medical practice for decades because the new-model M.D.s will constitute a small fraction of the M.D.s in private practice.

Expect change. What is orthodox today may be shown false tomorrow. Not long ago a cigarette company was allowed to advertise that "More Doctors Smoke Camels than Any Other Cigarette," and attach information making Camel-smoking part of a good health-care regimen.[88]

What is strange today may become orthodox tomorrow. The originator of radiation therapy for cancer was denounced for 30 years before the technique was accepted by the American College of Surgery.[89] In Dr. Morris Fishbein's day, chemotherapy was quackery. Five methods of cancer therapy that were on the original 1971 list of "unproven methods" (which was read by some as a pronouncement that practitioners of these methods were quacks or quasi-quacks) were subsequently removed and became respectable. These methods include hyperthermia, heat therapy, which is now being promoted as "the fifth modality in cancer therapy," along with surgery, radiation, chemotherapy and immunotherapy.[90] (However, laetrile has still not been shown effective and could be harmful.) Even though some zealous defenders of orthodoxy consider non-traditional dietary therapists collectively worthless at best and dangerous at worst, it is unwise to suppress them totally.

Complementary Dietary Therapists

During the period when orthodox medicine dismissed diet as a central contributor to health, a number of *complementary* (also called alternative, holistic, integrated or preventive) health practitioners emerged, promoting a different view of the role of food in contributing to health. The term complementary medicine makes clear that its practitioners do not prescribe drugs or perform surgery. Complementary dietary practitioners seek to cure patient disorders, where appropriate, by identifying and filling nutritional needs, or eliminating illness-causing foods. Some advise their clients to take supplements; most simply recommend a change in eating habits. They are the medical or paramedical equivalents of the organic or sustainable agriculture practitioners discussed in Chapter 5.

A growing number of Americans are being drawn to one element or another of the complementary health care system, which ranges from vegetarian diets (which many orthodox medical experts applaud) to transcendental beliefs that go beyond the scope of this book on food, although as we saw in Chapter 2 they have historically been part of medical practice. The full extent of public use of non-traditional treatments was revealed by the Louis Harris poll in 1986. More than one-fourth of the public (27 percent) reported having used one or more non-traditional treatments in 15 treatment areas (the percentage would be higher if more areas were included)! Of those who have sought treatment in one of the 15 treatment areas, *60 percent* of the public used non-traditional treatments (of this figure, 26 percent used only non-traditional treatments, and 34 percent used both acceptable and non-traditional treatments); only 40 percent relied exclusively on acceptable treatments.[91]

While some orthodox doctors advise their patients about nutrition as a disease-preventive regimen, they more commonly consider diet as a topic to be used as a therapy for certain diseases, once diagnosed. The details of a therapeutic diet are then left to a dietitian, to whom the patient is referred. Sometimes the dietitian's role is filled by a complementary health practitioner.

Some U.S. complementary practitioners have taken extensive training. For example the four-year, accredited naturopathic medical schools in Seattle and Portland cover the essentials of conventional medical practice in their first two years, then focus in depth on preventive medicine and natural remedies for disease. But many states require no training to practice complementary therapies that don't require drugs. Some orthodox doctors see no harm in complementary practices and even encourage their patients to seek a "third opinion;" others worry that such alternatives might substitute improperly for what they consider real medicine.

Complementary Practice in Europe. Complementary medicine has a long history in Europe. Bernard Shaw comments on a thriving heterogeneous medical industry in his famous preface to his 1906 play, *The Doctor's Dilemma,* and concludes that medical theories are "a matter of fashions."[92] Today, complementary practitioners are used by one in four people in Belgium, one in ten in Denmark, one in four in Finland, and one in eight in Britain.

Complementary medicine in Europe tends to be used by women more than men, and by higher income groups more than the rest of the population. One reason for complementary medicine being an upper-income option is that on the Continent complementary practitioners must be physicians, with full medical training; in some countries (e.g., Belgium, Finland, France, and The Netherlands), practicing medicine of any kind without such full training is a criminal offense. In Britain and Denmark, complementary medicine is mostly a private option, costing more than using free or nominal-cost public health services.[93]

The British attitude is that the complementary practitioners can't do much harm, and might do a lot of good both to the patient and (by taking some of the load) to the overburdened and underfinanced public medical sys-

tem. The fact that Royal Family patronizes complementary practitioners, and protects medical herbalism by Royal Charter, greatly helps their status. A survey of general practitioners in a community in England found that 76 percent had referred patients to medically trained complementary practitioners during the previous year and 72 percent had referred patients to non-medically trained practitioners.[94]

As the Single European Act of 1992 looms, and European governments scramble to harmonize their disparate practices and standards, some guidelines may emerge that will be helpful to the United States. The Council of Ministers of the European Community has directed that all drugs and remedies be reviewed by the end of 1990; that ways be explored for integrating complementary medicine in existing systems of health care delivery; and that complementary practitioners be required to complete three years of tertiary education.[95] "Sooner or later the nettle of scientific validation of complementary medicine will have to be grasped. So far little has been done: complementary practitioners have generally been unwilling to submit their work for assessment, and governments have lacked the political will to fund research."[96]

Two U.S. Extremes. A popular advocate for unorthodox nutritional views, Gary Null, hosts radio talk shows and compiles books that espouse a very-low-fat diet, strenuous exercise, and ample supplements.[97] He scorns middle-of-the-road "prudent diets" of the Federal guidelines, saying: "If people are consuming foods or engaging in lifestyles that cause disease, suggesting that moderation be exercised is like suggesting that they try to get moderately better."

All very well, but Null's attacks on conventional doctors can be outlandish. Example: "Traditional physicians often fail to see any connection between diabetes, heart disease, and high blood pressure."[98] To the contrary, it is elementary knowledge that obesity is one of the threads that connect all three. Informed listeners and readers may be put off by his uneven and selective documentation[99] and above all by his mail-order selling of a full line of his own supplements.

The medical establishment has its feisty defenders. Prominent among them is Dr. Victor Herbert, whose J.D. (law degree, acquired in mid-career) is now woven in next to his M.D. on his lab coat. He is an entertaining defender of the medical and food industry status quo. His articles seeking to expose health fads and quacks provide documentation of his perspective, even though they are clearly advocacy-oriented. He rightly attacks indiscriminate use and advocacy of nutritional supplements,[100] but in his exasperation he tars his opponents with an excessively broad brush, while whitewashing those whom he counts as his allies. Sample Herbert quote: "Health food gurus sell us poison and call it food while denouncing the safe food supply in the United States and other Western countries as poison."[101]

In his lectures, Dr. Herbert highlights an amusing and telling stunt, getting his pets certified as nutritionists. He shows slides with his poodle and cat next to "Professional Nutritionist" certificates for Sassafras Herbert and Charlie Herbert, which he obtained from the American Association of Nutritional Consultants sometime before 1983.[102] However, valid credentials do not dazzle Dr. Herbert, who scorns two-time Nobel Prizewinner Dr. Linus Pauling for advocating megadoses of vitamin C, as well as conventionally trained but unorthodox cancer therapists or sponsors of fad diets or treatments.[103]

To his credit, Dr. Herbert is willing to take on a glamorous diet doctor like Stuart Berger, whose fame implies his ability to pay lawyers to fight back.[104] But the quackbusters' enlistment of health insurers, state medical licensing boards, and state governments to threaten workaday complementary physicians for tests or treatments that are conventionally "not medically indicated"[105] is disconcertingly reminiscent of Dr. Fishbein's era.

Dr. Herbert engaged in courageous dietary self-experimentation in 1961 with his partner Louis W. Sullivan (now Secretary of Health and Human Services) to identify the threshold and effects of folic acid deficiency and thereby establish its minimum RDA.[106] But his quackbuster activism reduces an American's options for conducting similar experiments under medical supervision to address illnesses that conventional medicine fails to cure.[107] *Most clients of complementary practitioners are educated and use orthodox physicians as well.*[108]

In major tests, such as the 1976 Proxmire Amendment (to the Food, Drug, and Cosmetic Act), which voided attempted FDA rulemaking for vitamin labels, Federal politicians have lined up on the side of freedom of choice in health care,[109] because the public wants it. When asked which disease they feared most, 77 percent of those surveyed in a 1985 AP/Media General poll said cancer; *half* of those surveyed favored allowing complementary cancer clinics to operate in the United States (many clinics have been exiled to places like Tijuana, Mexico) and said they would seek unapproved treatments if they were diagnosed as having cancer or other serious diseases.[110]

Many traditional doctors acknowledge that complementary nutritional approaches could be helpful and are noninvasive and therefore don't pose the same threat that, say, unlicensed surgeons would. But a few worry that dietary cures or preventive health regimens could nonetheless be hazardous without the supervision of a trained doctor (example: a high-protein weight-loss diet). A few seek professional sanctuary in the line from Pope, "A little knowledge is a dangerous thing,"[111] implying that complementary practitioners are all less well trained than conventional ones, which is just not fair, as we shall see.

Vegetarian/Vegan Diets. Since elevated blood cholesterol is associated with eating saturated fats, and animal fats are the main culprits, one solution is to give up eating meat and dairy products, as strict vegetarians and vegans do. Meat is still a luxury today for most people on earth. The Japanese, who could afford to eat as much meat as Americans, choose not to (though they are eating much more meat now than they used to) and live longer than Americans and Europeans.

Vegetarians choose not to eat meat for religious-moral reasons (respect for animals, for example, or concern about what they see as the wasteful use of global resources in producing meat) or because they believe it is unhealthy.[112]

Dr. Max Bircher-Benner, the previously mentioned Swiss doctor, was a pioneer in vegetarianism. Soon after he began his career in 1891, he found by trial and error that a diet of raw fruit and vegetables cured a gastric disorder. Years later, after further experiments, Dr. Bircher-Benner concluded that food processing was removing little-understood but vital nutrients.[113] He said that by eating poorly, people were relegating themselves to a state of semi-disease, "the twilight zone of ill health."[114]

American vegetarian guru Dr. John McDougall pursued a career path similar to that of Dr. Bircher-Benner. Having completed his conventional medical training without learning about nutrition,[115] McDougall discovered the benefits of vegetarianism through clinical practice. McDougall joined other doctors in concluding that the main culprits contributing to heart disease were what he called "feast foods"—mostly animal protein. These "feast foods" are increasingly implicated not just in heart disease but also cancer, in part because pesticide residues in American food are much more concentrated in meat (and to a lesser extent dairy products) than in plant foods.[116]

Dr. Dean Ornish, at the 1989 meetings of the American Heart Association, presented evidence that a vegetarian diet, along with yoga meditation and exercise, reversed atherosclerosis without the help of drugs.[117]

Vegans eat plants only, no animals or animal products, some even avoiding honey, leather or down. Vegans are at risk of having vitamin B_{12} and calcium deficiencies, because relatively few plants contain these nutrients, and questions have been raised about the absorbability of the nutrients from plants. However, vegans can obtain vitamin B_{12} from kelp, oats, seaweed, soybean (preferably as soy meal or tempeh), whole wheat bread.[118] The best plant sources for calcium are almonds and other nuts, beans, broccoli and other greens, seaweed, sesame seeds, tahini, sunflower seeds, and almonds.[119] The vitamin B_{12} deficiency is a special concern for vegan mothers nursing infants, who may develop anemia or nervous disorders. For those who don't mind invasive solutions, an injection of B_{12} takes care of this problem and lasts a year or more.

Raw food is a focus of some vegetarian diets. Heat destroys a portion of many enzymes and some nutrients, notably vitamin C, folic acid, and vitamin A; other nutrients like iodine leach into the water in which food is boiled and are lost when the water is thrown out. Raw food enthusiasts want to capture these lost nutrients.

But digesting uncooked starchy foods may be difficult, and raw food requires more care to avoid ingesting dangerous bacteria that are killed by cooking.[120]

Even the strongest advocates of raw food do not insist everything be raw, only that vegetables not be overcooked and that some raw food be eaten daily, especially at the start of a meal.[121]

Organic food is also stressed by many complementary dietary advisers, both vegetarians and carnivores. As we shall see in Chapter 5, "organic" means grown without the addition of synthetic (especially petroleum-based) compounds. People seek out organic food both for their own health and for the health of farmers and the environment. The availability of organic food is one of our major criteria for including businesses in the directories in Chapters 7 and 10, so we cover the subject with care in Chapter 5.

Macrobiotic diets, which we reviewed already in Chapter 2, are a specially restricted form of pesce-vegetarianism. The diet is supposed to approximate the traditional Japanese diet, but this could be valid only if fish is on the menu; some versions of the diet are vegan and exclude fish. The U.S. macrobiotic diet goes beyond vegetarianism in excluding foods such as the nightshade family (potatoes, tomatoes, eggplant, peppers), non-locally grown food, and dairy products. It has a useful way of classifying foods and provides specific guidance on the cooking and seasoning of foods. For some, macrobiotics is a spiritual outlook, so that someone may be said to be macrobiotic regardless of what he or she eats.

Some elements of the macrobiotic diet are clearly beneficial by the standards of the 1988 Surgeon General's Report. It is high in fiber, lower in fat, moderate in protein, and makes people more conscious of what they are eating.

Adherents of the diet make many claims for it, including its value in arresting such cancers as Hodgkin's disease.[122] However, only a minority of orthodox physicians give this much credence. The *University of California, Berkeley Wellness Letter* is ruthless: "Not only is there no evidence that any kind of macrobiotic diet can cure cancer, but it can actually contribute to malnutrition and weight loss."[123] Also, a few cancer patients who have stabilized on the Gerson regimen (three meals a day plus raw juices hourly) have reportedly deteriorated rapidly when switched to a macrobiotic one.[124]

However, cancer patients undergoing chemotherapy are sometimes advised by orthodox oncologists (cancer specialists) to adopt a macrobiotic diet to avert dangerous interactions between synthetic chemicals in processed food and the toxic synthetic chemicals prescribed in chemotherapy to poison the cancer cells; this concept is given wide credence, as is the idea that nutritionally planned vegetarian diets can prevent (not cure) cancer.

The nutritional hazards of the dairy-free diet relate to possible deficiencies of calcium, iron, and vitamin B_{12}. But adequate calcium can be obtained by taking care to eat leafy green vegetables, tofu, and the soft bones of fish; iron deficiency can be offset by finding a good source of vitamin C; and vitamin B_{12} deficiency is rare.[125] Parents should know that very young children (under 8) fed a macrobiotic diet grow up shorter and lighter than children whose diets include dairy products—not that children necessarily suffer health-wise from being smaller than their peers.[126]

Whatever the merits of a *strict* macrobiotic diet, some macrobiotic meals in a diet unquestionably help Americans adjust their eating in the right direction. If our diet is skewed toward being too high in saturated fat and too low in fiber, a good way to change is tasty macrobiotic food, to offset the idea that low-fat food must be bland and unappetizing. In Chapter 10 we include some first-rate macrobiotic restaurants.

Selecting Your Own Dietary Adviser

Don't be bashful if you decide all this diet stuff is too complicated to figure out without help. People like Bo Derek, Clint Eastwood, and George McGovern all have nutritionists they consult with. No reason you shouldn't too, if you are prepared to pay the fee.[127]

But where does one find such an adviser? Starting from the premise that you want what you eat to contribute to your health, let's review the types of qualified people from whom you might seek dietary advice. The guiding question is: "Does the practitioner use diet as a central aspect of his or her therapy?" We therefore exclude, for example, practitioners of acupuncture, osteopathy (which seeks to treat ailments by identifying and untangling or relaxing pinched nerves), and homeopathic medicine, whose practitioners believe that ailments can be treated by very small amounts (in pills, drops or ointments) of substances that could produce symptoms of the illness in healthy people.[128] While some broad-scope practitioners of these therapies include nutrition, this is not their central focus.

Clinical Ecologists. Clinical ecologists, who are mostly M.D.s, examine the relationship between the environment, including a person's diet, and any symptoms the person may be experiencing. If clinical ecologists suspect that an individual might have a food intolerance, they recommend elimination of the offending food(s) from the patient's diet. Orthodox medicine as represented by the American Academy of Allergy and Immunology pronounced clinical ecologists' theories "speculative and unproven,"[129] but their ideas are gaining a following, as indicated by a balanced report prepared by the American College of Physicians in mid-1989.[130]

Chiropractors (D.C.s). Like osteopathic physicians, many of whom have training equivalent to M.Ds, doctors of chiropractic focus their treatment on the alignment of bones. But chiropractors are probably the most frequently consulted dietary advisers in the U.S., considering the fact that 21 percent of the public has consulted them and a large percentage of them give nutritional advice.[131] Most chiropractors have taken nutrition courses—more than the average M.D. but less than most clinical ecologists, dietitians, naturopathic physicians, nutritionists, or orthomolecular practitioners. Chiropractors have no clinical training in nutrition and no therapeutic nutrition on their board exams. Some states specifically permit chiropractors to give nutritional advice; others forbid them to do so. A significant amount of supplement sales are made through chiropractors.

Conventional Physicians (M.D.s). As we have already noted, M.D.s have historically been given little education or training in nutrition. Of 34 medical schools surveyed in the National Academy of Sciences' 1985 study of medical schools, fewer than half covered the following topics (in relation to nutrition) in their curricula: adolescence, allergy, cancer, central nervous system, cultural variations, dental caries, drug-nutrient interactions, immune response, prudent diet, vegetarianism.[132] In the tests of the National Board of Medical Examiners, no questions were found on any of the following: food fads, food intolerance and allergies, nutrition in cancer patients, nutrition in the aged, osteoporosis, parenteral and enteral [intravenous] nutrition, popular diets, role of nutrition in the immune response, vitamin A metabolism.[133] This is not to say that some M.D.s have not obtained a high level of nutritional training. One group of such M.D.s has been clustered in the American College of Nutrition, led by Mildred S. Seelig, M.D., who in January 1990 told me she was still saddened by the slow rate of change of the medical profession in recognizing the importance of nutrition in health. The American College's 1,000 members are mostly M.D.s, Ph.D.s, and Sc.D.s (Doctors of Science); information on it is provided at the end of this chapter, under "Nutrition."

Dietitians (R.D.s). A registered dietitian is someone who has had at least (1) an undergraduate degree with about 70 hours of nutrition or food science, and (2) further training and successful completion of a board examination as required by state law or the American Dietetic Association (see Directory at the end of this chapter), or both.[134] Nearly three-fourths of R.D.s have master's-level degrees. Nearly half the states require or offer licenses or certificates for dietitians. Some have mandated licensing of dietitians, making it illegal to practice nutritional advice without a license. Eight states license or certify dietitians who voluntarily apply for such state licensing or certification, or protect the use of the professional title; other individuals are permitted to practice.[135] Since dietitians commonly work on referral from, or in an institutional environment along with, orthodox physicians, they are rarely challenged as a complementary adjunct to conventional medicine. The other therapies, even though most of their practitioners have spent longer in training, are not always so easily accepted, in part because they seek to build an independent medical practice.

Wholefood Cooking Schools. An increasingly popular way that people are learning about diet is through health-oriented cooking schools, which focus on using natural foods or wholefoods. The oldest such school in the United States is the Natural Gourmet Cookery School in New York City, founded in 1977. It trains teachers of cooking, and its 60 graduates have established schools throughout the country.

Wholefood Store Staff. A study by Louis Harris for the FDA says that 5 percent of the American population consults "health products salespeople"—i.e., the staff in health-food or wholefood retail stores—for advice about diet, supplements, and other health matters. Those who encounter problems with non-traditional treatments in 15 surveyed treatment areas are *nearly as likely to tell a wholefood store staffer* (16 percent) *as a physician* (19 percent)![136] One reason is that some wholefood store staff members are highly knowledgeable about their products and how they contribute to health, and their advice is free to anyone who walks in the door. However, sales staff are unlikely to be qualified, nor should they want, to assume responsibility for a buyer's health. Casual health advice to an essentially healthy customer could be helpful and at worst will encourage the customer to buy unnecessary and costly specialty foods or supplements. But if this advice substitutes for consultation with a qualified health practitioner, it could be hazardous.

Naturopathic Physicians (N.D.s). Naturopathic medicine is practiced by doctors of naturopathy, who describe it as "a medical discipline that works to support the natural healing mechanisms of the body when treating disease."[137] They contrast their approach with conventional, "allopathic" medicine, practitioners of which prefer to use surgery, synthetic drugs, and radiation,[138] and whose view of the task of medicine is to kill alien invaders in the body. Naturopathic physicians study basic medical sciences and diagnostics, but their treatments are prevention-oriented and non-invasive, and may include dietary modification, supplementation or fasting. Other treatments may include herbal medicine, homeopathy, physical medicine, exercise therapy, counseling, oriental medicine, or minor surgery. About 1,000 medically trained naturopathic physicians are practicing in the United States, and eight states license them as primary care doctors. The Council on Naturopathic Medical Education, recognized by the U.S. Department of Education, recognizes two graduate-level naturopathic medical schools—the National College of Naturopathic Medicine, established in Portland, Oregon, in 1957, and the Bastyr College of Medicine in Seattle, Washington, founded in 1978. Consumers should be aware of the distinction between qualified N.D.s who have been through four-year graduate training, and some naturopaths who have had only brief correspondence-course training.

Nutritionists. A nutritionist is, like a dietitian, focused exclusively on diet and its relationship to health. The difference between them is that the qualified nutritionist is expected to be (1) better trained, at least to the level of an M.S. (Master of Science) degree,[139] and (2) more clinically independent than the dietitian. About 15 percent of the population has consulted a nutritionist of some sort. However, consumers should be aware that not all "Nutritionists" have advanced degrees. A significant portion have obtained their credentials through a correspondence course, sometimes accompanied by one or more tests. Three major correspondence courses are offered by (1) the National Institute of Nutritional Education, (2) Dr. Jeffrey

Bland, and (3) the American Association of Nutritional Consultants (the group that gave certificates to Dr. Herbert's poodle and cat). They require their students to take tests for some certificates (Dr. Bland's is a series of multiple-choice chapter-by-chapter tests self-administered by the student and mailed in to be evaluated), but they do not offer the advanced-degree training that is expected of a professional nutritionist offering clinical advice. In fairness to those who offer and take the correspondence courses, students are mostly either natural food industry personnel who do not intend to practice as clinical nutritionists, or are already medically trained, as M.D.s or chiropractors, for example, and are simply seeking to extend their education conveniently.

Orthomolecular Practitioners. Orthomolecular medicine was so named in 1968 by Dr. Linus Pauling, two-time winner of the Nobel Prize, who has advocated large doses of vitamin C to prevent colds and other illnesses. Physicians and psychiatrists pursuing this approach to therapy are trained conventionally and then specialize in this area. The concept is to "put nutrition first," working to create the right balance of chemicals in the body or brain, if necessary by prescribing large doses of vitamins or minerals. Many orthomolecular practitioners specialize in psychiatric disorders.[140]

Should We Be Free to Choose? Some people believe that what they eat is their own business, and that they should be free to consult whomever they please regarding diet and nutrition.

Others worry that people who are untrained, or unprincipled, or both, will displace trained physicians and nutritionists and will prey on unsuspecting or poorly informed individuals. They fear fraudulent misrepresentation of credentials by such individuals and, worse, that clients might be put into potentially dangerous "quack" diets. They wish to protect consumers from this possibility of fraud and seek to prevent the practice of dietary advice without a license.

The argument for permitting some latitude for alleged quacks to operate in does not depend on there being no concomitant risks. Consumers are entitled to be told the truth about a practitioner's qualifications and methods; even with the truth, consumers may make "wrong" choices. However, restricting choices means that the people doing the restricting may also make wrong choices, and these errors may be far more serious for society. The benefits to consumers at large from having medical practitioners' views continually open to challenge is substantial. This system has costs, too. The focus of government attention should be on disclosure, not on putting people out of business if they don't practice the same medicine as everyone else.[141]

Non-Governmental Fraud-Chasers

The unofficial fraud-chasers are primarily the medical societies and independent litigators. The medical societies can discipline or expel their members, but must (like independent lobbyists or litigators) go after non-members through lobbying for the enactment or enforcement of state medical licensing laws. Complementary practitioners have successfully defended themselves against such activities by appealing to Federal courts under antitrust laws.

Medical Associations. The AMA was in 1987 found by a U.S. District Court to have engaged in restraint of trade by prohibiting, under the AMA Principles of Medical Ethics, the association of physicians with "unscientific practitioners,"[142] in this case chiropractors, against whom they mounted a strong campaign. The AMA has been judicially advised that it doesn't have a U.S. health-care monopoly.

But state medical associations have been more successful in squelching complementary practices. In Arizona, for example, an insurance equity bill, requiring health insurance companies to reimburse insured persons for the services of certain complementary practitioners, was passed by both houses of the legislature but was vetoed by the governor. In Oregon, regulations that would have applied to naturopathic physicians passed the senate but were blocked by the head of a committee from getting to the house floor. The Oregon Medical Association in 1989 revoked the license of Lynn Anderson, M.D., for using homeopathy and nutrition to treat cancer.

"Quackbusters." The National Council Against Health Fraud, Inc. (self-described as "Quackbusters") was organized in 1977 as a California group. It became national in 1984 to replace an annual congress that brought together the American Medical Association and the FDA (the annual meeting had been publicized in an unfavorable light by the National Health Federation and was terminated; a new, independent group was needed to fill the vacuum). Dr. Herbert, previously mentioned,[143] in his spare time serves as a Quackbuster expert witness against medical practitioners who are targeted for litigation or regulatory attention. In 1989 contributions were solicited for the Herbert Anti-Quackery Litigation Fund, based in Kansas City.[144]

Watchdogs over the Food Industry. While a number of observers of the food industry occasionally call attention to misleading labeling by large food companies, the Center for Science in the Public Interest is the most active and persistent monitor of deceptive claims of this type. Its 180,000 members, who receive the *Nutrition Action Healthletter*, are an important interest group for future action on labeling.

Government Fraud-Chasers

Governments are involved in dietary matters at the Federal, state and local level. At the Federal level, the main administrative issue is food labeling; however, the research and public statements on diet of the National Institutes of Health have a broader significance than labeling. The state level is the focus of licensing battles for complementary therapies. At the local level the issues of labeling and licensing arise in connection with consumer protection.

Federal Regulation of Health Claims on Food. For 81 years prior to 1987, the FDA effectively prohibited any health claims on foods. It took the position, codified in the Code of Federal Regulations, that such claims would put foods into the drug (medicine) category, as the Food and Drug law requires; any drug requires several years of FDA testing to ensure its safety and efficacy.

The FDA prohibition against health claims was successfully challenged in 1984, when Kellogg Company put health claims on its All Bran cereal. The FDA, under pressure from deregulatory champions in the food industry, at the Office of Management and Budget, and in senior posts at the Department of Health and Human Services (its parent agency), did not act to end Kellogg's action. Even an urgent letter from Dr. Sanford Miller, then Director of the FDA's Center for Food Safety and Applied Nutrition, to the FDA's Commissioner saying "The time for the FDA to act is now" had no effect. Instead, the FDA did nothing and starting in February 1986, the word was out in the food industry that it was open season on health claims. In 1987 the FDA issued a proposed rule that would permit health claims on food, with some limitations.[145] This legitimized the health claims initiatives and removed any remaining obstacles to companies that wished to follow Kellogg's example.

The food and advertising industries quickly responded to the new promotional opportunities. By 1989, *40 percent of new products and one-third of the $3.6 billion in food advertising, carried health claims*. Example: "This food is low-sodium, and therefore reduces hypertension and the likelihood of your having a stroke." The tag line "CHOLESTEROL-FREE" on high-fat palm, palm kernel, or coconut oil products would by itself not put the product under the FDA's purview (a claim would have to be included that the absence of cholesterol would cure or prevent heart disease or some other illness), even though the statement can be highly misleading. Abuses clearly occurred during the free-ranging 1988–89 period, for example some deceptive promotional practices by fiber and supplement manufacturers.[146] On the other hand, some argue that health claims on food have had a positive effect in drawing people's attention to nutrition.

The FDA reopened its sanctions against food vendors making health claims in 1989, seeking an injunction to prevent a small food company, U.S. Health Club, Inc., from marketing Exachol, a lecithin product. In the first round a New York Federal District Judge agreed with the company that the FDA was inconsistent in its enforcement by ignoring much larger companies making no less misleading claims.

The FDA proposed new regulations for controlling the health claims on food and food supplements to the House Government Operations subcommittee on human resources, chaired by Rep. Ted Weiss (D-NY). As revised two months later, the new regulations permit health claims on a product label only if they are not deemed misleading and if they describe one of the following four connections between food and disease: (1) Fiber may reduce the risk of colon cancer and heart disease; (2) Low fat may reduce the risk of cancer and heart disease; (3) Low salt may reduce the risk of high blood pressure; and (4) High calcium may help prevent the bone disease osteoporosis.[147]

Rep. Weiss and others in Congress are understandably deeply concerned about the legislative function being preempted by an executive agency. "Congress, not FDA, is empowered to change the law that prohibits health claims on food labels," he said. However, a bill (H.R. 3562) introduced by Rep. Henry A. Waxman (D-CA), Chair of the Subcommittee on Health and the Environment of the House Committee on Energy and Commerce, would make the Constitutional issue moot by providing more detailed direction to the FDA on food labeling, including health claims; this bill was out of Committee and before the House as this book went to press. A related bill is before the Senate Committee on Labor and Human Resources, chaired by Senator Edward M. Kennedy (D-MA), having been introduced by Senators Howard Metzenbaum (D-OH) and John E. Chafee (R-RI).

Federal Monitoring: Proposed Council. The Nutrition and Health Act of 1989 (S.1739) calls for the creation of a Federal Council on Nutrition and Health to monitor the relationship between nutrition and health by tracking nutrition research, promoting nutrition education, and maintaining a clearinghouse of information in this area. The bill, backed by the National Nutrition Coalition, was introduced by Senator Tom Harkin (D-IA); co-sponsors include Senators Rudy Boschwitz (R-MN) and Strom Thurmond (R-SC).[148]

Orthodox vs. Complementary: My View

Having spent a great deal of time reading and listening to both sides of the orthodox vs. complementary medicine debate, I have developed a lay point of view that might be of interest to the reader.

Finding and consuming healthy food is *not* dependent on where one seeks medical care. However, some practitioners are more interested in diet than others, and this may affect one's choice of physician and dietary adviser.

Complementary practitioners address two different markets. One is definitely upscale, the naturopathic physician with a professional clientele or a cancer clinic with saunas, recreational facilities and fine cuisine. The other is relatively poor, the storefront "botanica" or part-time healer with natural remedies.

The case for government protection of the upscale clientele is weak if the clientele can be shown to know exactly what it is doing in patronizing the complementary practitioner. Data suggest that clients of complementary practitioners often have a conventional doctor and go to the complementary practitioners with their eyes open.[149] If conventional medicine offers cancer patients, for example, unacceptable treatment options (slash, burn, poison), why wouldn't people want to consult with complementary practitioners? The fact that, according to University of Chicago Professor Norman Farnsworth, six of the nine herbs in Hoxsey's tonic have immune-enhancing or anti-tumor properties suggests the possibility that complementary cancer treatments may not always be baseless hucksterism.[150]

I do worry about less educated people who may put off until too late treatment for a serious illness beyond the skills of a complementary practitioner. But the quality of conventional medicine offered to the poor in the U.S. is so often hurried and inadequate that a trained complementary practitioner's care may be no worse and could be better. For the substantial number of poor people who haunt health clinics seeking a sympathetic ear, a complementary practitioner could be a godsend, provided conventional care is available and counseled when needed—and for the harried conventional doctor too.

Some defenders of orthodox medicine equate complementary practice with quackery. But in the case of cancer, at least the complementary practitioners use techniques that are non-invasive and thereby obey Hippocrates's first principle: "Do no harm." Much surgery is unnecessary or marginal, and is undertaken primarily because the patient has the insurance or bank account to pay for it. A *Scientific American* article says that the number and kind of surgical procedures performed in an area correlates better with the number of surgeons and their specialties than with the variety of diseases.[151]

Orthodox practitioners for years had just two answers to cancer: surgery and radiation; any other approach was quackery. Later, oncologists added chemotherapy, a treatment that they had rejected. Even so, all three are all unattractive options; some patients would rather keep looking for other choices. They should have that right.

Why can't oncologists work *with* complementary practitioners—offering conventional therapy and suggest to the patient that complementary practitioners might also be able to help? In China, where cancer is the leading cause of death, Western methods of treatment are used along with traditional remedies to offset the toxicity of chemotherapy and the stress of surgery; success rates are reportedly higher than when either treatment is used independently.[152]

Without doubt, quacks flourish in America. Hope springs eternal in the human breast, and in any age some unscrupulous people are ready to step in to feed that hope. But in their zeal to attack the unconventional, I believe quackbusters overstate the adequacy of conventional treatments and unfairly smear the work of qualified complementary practitioners. Those M.D.s who keep an open mind about new fields such as clinical ecology (which places renewed emphasis on nutrition for prevention and cure of disease) are to be applauded. Finally, I hope that medical students will be encouraged in every possible way to study nutrition and to give diet greater attention in their clinical work.

Dietary Advisers

The following organizations provide information to the public on dietary or nutritional issues, with the goal of preventing or curing diseases such as cancer and heart disease. To limit the length of the list, educational and referral organizations have been sought rather than medical practitioners. A few significant industry groups have also been included.

Organizations that are not italicized offer conventional nutritional advice on eating a balanced diet, avoiding fat, and so forth, without seeking to use nutrition as a primary therapy for coping with life-threatening disease. Organizations that are italicized offer referrals to complementary medical practitioners, or information on complementary practices.[153] Our main criterion for including an organization is its accessibility and potential usefulness to the consumer, rather than its point of view.

A diamond (♦) indicates that an organization has been strongly recommended to me by other people for its work relating diet and disease. A heart (♥) means I have had personal experience of the commitment of the group to making this connection and helping people with referrals.

American Medical Association (AMA), 535 North Dearborn, Chicago, IL 60610. (312) 645-5000. The AMA is not as entrenched in its scorn of nutritional therapy as it was earlier in the century. The pleasant public information people at the AMA say that nutrition is becoming more important to its members, as evidenced by the 27 resolutions on "Foods and Nutrition" passed or reaffirmed at the 1979–89 annual or interim meetings,[154] the changed focus of the *Journal of the American Medical Association*, and increased interest in the preventive and nutritional medicine specialties for M.D.s. (see the College of Preventive Medicine below under "P" and the American Board of Nutrition under "N"); these are two of 79 medical specialties. But AMA members with an interest in these specialties tell me that while the modest trend toward more interest in nutrition is welcomed, the profession and its medical schools haven't come very far yet.

Botanicals: See Herbal.

Cancer Control Society, 2043 North Berendo, Los Angeles, CA 90027. (213) 663-7801. Lorraine Rosenthal.

Sends a substantial packet of information on complementary cancer treatment clinics, practitioners and patients. A December 1989 packet included flyers on the following three Tijuana-based clinics, which use botanical or nutritional therapies: Gerson Therapy Center, Vista Medical Center; St. Jude International Clinic; Hospital Santa Monica (run by the controversial Dr. Kurt Donsbach).♥

Cancer Institute, National (NCI), U.S. Department of Health and Human Services, National Institutes of Health, Office of Cancer Communications, Bethesda, MD 20892. Call (800) 4–CANCER to order publications or ask questions; your call will be routed to a regional agency under contract to the NCI; in the New York City area the agency is the Memorial Sloan-Kettering Cancer Center. Cancer rates have risen steadily since 1900, despite the NCI's having spent, between 1938 and 1986, $15.5 billion in Federal appropriations for cancer research. According to an article by the former editor-in-chief of the NCI journal, age-adjusted mortality rates over the period provided "no evidence" that the efforts "have had much overall effect."[155] The NCI publishes a consumer guide, *Everything Doesn't Cause Cancer: But How Can We Tell Which Things Cause Cancer and Which Ones Don't?*♦

Cancer Research, American Institute for, 1759 R Street, N.W., Washington, DC 20009. (800) 843–8114. The AICR is the only national cancer organization with a primary focus on the relationship between diet and cancer. Offers a variety of public health education programs related to diet and cancer, for consumers and health professionals. Publications include *Dietary Fiber to Lower Cancer Risk* (1988).♦

Cancer Therapies, Foundation for Alternative (FACT), P.O. Box HH, Old Chelsea Station, New York, NY 10011. (212) 741–2790. Ruth Sackman, President. Chapters in Boston, Detroit, Philadelphia. This small 20-year-old clearinghouse for cancer patients helps steer patients to a complementary therapy on a one-to-one basis (they also have a directory, but believe "directories are confusing"). No fee; the organization is non-profit, supported by contributions. Membership is $10 and covers a publication that appears roughly bimonthly.♥♦

Cancer Victors and Friends, International Association of, Inc., 7740 West Manchester Ave., #110, Playa del Rey, CA 90291. (213) 822–5032. Marie Steinmeyer, President. Sixteen chapters. This 28-year-old independent non-profit institution sends out on request a list of cancer clinics and treatment centers. Annual membership is $20.

Cancer: American Society of Clinical Oncology. Its subcommittee on unorthodox therapies prepared "Ineffective Cancer Therapy: A Guide for the Layperson," *Journal of Clinical Oncology*, 1983:1, pp. 15–163.

Cancer Society, American, 1599 Clifton Road, NE, Atlanta, GA 30329. (404) 320–3333, FAX (404) 325–2217. G. G. Marion, Vice President, Creative Services. Has 57 divisions, located in every state and Puerto Rico. Has published *Unproven Methods of Cancer Management* (1971, 1982).

Environmental Medicine, American Academy of, P.O. Box 16106, Denver, CO 80216. Asked us not to include their phone number. This is the new name of the Society of Clinical Ecologists. All full members of the Academy are physicians, about half M.D.s, half D.O.s (Doctors of Osteopathy). Will refer individuals to clinical ecologists in their area; write requesting a list. Trains physicians in environmental medicine.

Health Fraud, National Council Against, Inc., P.O. Box 1276, Loma Linda, CA 92354. (714) 824–4690. William T. Jarvis, Ph.D., President. Originally a southern California organization, the group became national in 1984 and has 2,500 members rallying under the "Quackbuster" logo. It seeks out and exposes quacks, educating the public about "untruths and deceptions," serving as a clearinghouse of information on "health misinformation, fraud and quackery," and by "encouraging legal action against law violators."[156] Who is a quack? Dr. Jarvis is outraged by food faddists, i.e. people with "exaggerated beliefs in the effects of food upon health and disease . . . based on magical thinking about food." Dr. Jarvis borders on calling all "nutrition educators" quacks because he says they stress "the importance of individual nutrients and the dramatic results of neglecting these in the diet. The psychology of this approach favors food faddism," because "the very act of examining a subject, e.g. a nutritional substance, in great detail tends to exaggerate its importance."[157]

Health Freedom Lobbyists: *National Health Federation* **(NHF),** 212 West Foothill Boulevard, P.O. Box 688, Monrovia, CA 91016. (818) 357–2181: Veronica Nerio, Executive Director. (703) 754–0228: Clinton Miller, Legislative Advocate, Box 528, Gainesville, VA 22065. About 80 chapters throughout the United States. Favors deregulation of medical practice and in 1976 achieved an extraordinary victory. The FDA had asked Congress for authority to limit vitamin pill potency, as part of an anti-quack program pursued with the American Medical Association. The NHF proposed counter-legislation restricting the FDA's ability to regulate food supplements not shown to be dangerous or mislabeled. To the surprise of many experts, the NHF proposal passed as the Proxmire Amendment to the Federal Food, Drug, and Cosmetic Act. The NHF refers callers to complementary health practitioners—M.D.s, D.C.s (chiropractors), dentists, homeopaths. Membership of $20/year covers its monthly news journal. Targeted in a report by the American Council on Science and Health (see under Industry Groups).[158] In 1989 John Parks Trowbridge[159] became NHF's Chairman.

Health Statistics, National Center for, Room 157, 3700 East-West Highway, Hyattsville, MD 20782. (301) 436–8500. Keepers of such important reference materials as the cause-of-death data summarized in Chapter 1.

Heart Association, American, National Center, 7320

Greenville Ave., Dallas, TX 75231. (214) 373-6300. Conducts research and disseminates information on reducing disability and death from cardiovascular diseases and stroke. Has initiated a program for certifying food products that are heart-healthy (see Chapter 2).♦

Heart, Lung and Blood Institute, National, National Institutes of Health, 9000 Rockville Pike, Building 31, Room 4A21, Bethesda, MD 20892. (301) 496-4000. Claude Lenfant, Director. Expressed strong praise for study by the Preventive Medicine Research Institute showing that diet and other lifestyle changes could reverse atherosclerosis without drugs.[160] Offers a free brochure, "Eating for Life"; write to the above address for your copy.

Herbal Medicine: *Botanical Council, American,* P.O. Box 201660, Austin, TX 78720. (512) 331-8868. Mark Blumenthal, editor. Publishes *Herbalgram*, which prints news about medicinal uses of herbs, one of the two main branches of naturopathic medicine.♥♦

Herbal Medicine: *Botanical Medicine Institute,* P.O. Box 33080, Portland, OR 97233. Educates conventional and complementary health practitioners and the public in clinical uses of herbal medicine. Publishes a bimonthly newsletter.

Herbal Medicine: *NAPRALERT.* (312) 996-7253. This international database of botanical medicine is directed by Norman Farnsworth, Ph.D., Professor of Pharmacognosy, University of Illinois at Chicago, in collaboration with the World Health Organization.[161]♦

Herbal Medicine: U.S. Department of Agriculture, *Germ Plasm Services Laboratory,* Building 001, Room 133, BARC-West, Beltsville, MD 20705. James Duke: (301) 344-2612. This lab is expert on medicinal properties of herbs and other food; is especially interested in plants that are associated with cancer cures.♦

Industry Group: American Council on Science and Health (ACSH), 1995 Broadway, 18th Floor, New York, NY 10023. (212) 362-7044. Elizabeth M. Whelan, Executive Director. ACSH describes itself as "founded in 1978 to provide scientifically balanced evaluations of issues involving food, chemicals, the environment, lifestyle, and health."[162] However, both the Center for Science in the Public Interest and Consumers Union have drawn attention to ACSH's funding sources. CSPI says that ACSH "despite its august-sounding name, is heavily financed by food, chemical, and oil corporations and trade associations."[163] Consumers Union calls ACSH "an advocacy group largely supported by the chemical, food, and agricultural industries (but self-described as a consumer group)."[164] ACSH is losing its battle to protect industry from the implications of rational public policy.[165]

Industry Group: *Council for Responsible Nutrition,* 2100 M Street, N.W., #602, Washington, DC 20037. (202) 872-1488. Association of manufacturers, wholesalers, and distributors of nutritional supplements.

Industry Group: International Life Sciences Institute, 1126 16th Street, N.W., Washington, DC 20036. (202) 659-0074. Research and educational group supported by food manufacturers.

Industry Group: *National Nutrition Coalition,* 1050 Thomas Jefferson Street, NW, 6th Floor, Washington, DC 20007. (202) 298-7208. Nancy Macan. Recently established group of 16 natural foods organizations led by the National Nutritional Foods Association, lobbying for a Federal Nutrition Council.

Industry Group: *National Nutritional Foods Association (NNFA),* 150 Paulerino, Suite 285-D, Costa Mesa, CA 92626. (714) 966-6632. FAX (714) 641-7005. Burton Kallman, Ph.D. Original sponsor of the National Nutrition Coalition. Trade association of companies and individuals in the natural foods business.♥♦

Medical Colleges, Association of American, 1 Dupont Circle, N.W., #200, Washington, DC 20036. (202) 828-0400. Medical schools are including more nutrition in their courses of study.

National Academy of Sciences/National Research Council, 2001 Wisconsin Ave., N.W., Washington, DC. (202) 334-2000. Sponsors and disseminates research on health, diet and other issues. The National Academy is an honorary association that works through the National Research Council, which obtains contracts and grants from government agencies and foundations and is also the operating arm of the National Academies of Sciences and Engineering. The Academy and Council also operate the National Academy Press.♦♦

Natural Gourmet Cookery School, 48 West 21st Street, #202, New York, NY 10010. (212) 645-5170. Annemarie Colbin, founder and director, and author of several successful vegetarian cookbooks. Trains would-be vegetarian cooks and also teachers of natural cooking. Provides a home delivery service. Two of the reference points of her teaching are the ancient Chinese yin-yang continuum and five-element phases (three of the elements are the same as the Greek elements that go back to Hippocrates—fire, water, and earth; the Chinese phases include metal and wood instead of the Greek "air").[166]♥♦

Naturopathic Physicians, American Association of (AANP), P.O. Box 20386, Seattle, WA 98102. (206) 323-7610. This national organization of licensable naturopathic doctors of naturopathy (N.D.s) is a federation of two dozen state naturopathic organizations. It offers referral services for naturopathic physicians in each state, and includes several specialty societies.♥♦

Nutrition, American Board of, 9650 Rockville Pike, Bethesda, MD 20814. (301) 530–7110. Certifies M.D.s and Ph.D.s as clinical nutritionists (C.N.s); exams are held biennially. The annual postgraduate course enrolls about 100 people, including some R.D.s who take the course for credit rather than certification. The Association for Clinical Nutrition, at the same address, publishes *The Journal of Clinical Nutrition,* available for $40, of which $5 is for membership in the Association. Send a stamped self-addressed envelope and they will send you a list of C.N. physicians near you who accept private patients.♦♦

Nutrition, American College of, 722 Robert E. Lee Drive, Wilmington, NC 28412. (919) 452–1222. Mildred S. Seelig, M.D., Executive Director. Founded in 1965 to rectify the failure of most orthodox medical practitioners to pay adequate attention to nutrition. Its 1,000 members are mostly M.D.s, Ph.D.s, and D.Sc.s (Doctors of Science), with a few R.D.s (Registered Dietitians) and nurses.♥♦

Nutrition and Healthcare, Coalition for Alternatives in (CANAH), P.O. Box B-12, Richlandtown, PA 18955. (215) 346–8461. CANAH's main goal is enactment of a Healthcare Rights Amendment that would guarantee to all individuals the right to "choose and to practice the type of healthcare they shall elect for themselves or their children . . ."[167] Annual $20 membership covers a quarterly newsletter.

Nutrition and Preventive Medicine, National Academy of, 303 N. 52nd Street, #225, Lincoln, NE 68504. (402) 467–2716. Carroll Thompson, M.D., Director. Open 10 a.m. to 2 p.m. most days, Nebraska time.

Nutrition Institute, Community, 2001 S Street, N.W., Washington, DC 20009. (202) 462–4700. Rodney Leonard, Executive Director. Publishes well-regarded newsletter, $70 for the first year. In response to a tripling of salmonella poisoning from chicken, recommends not eating chicken.♥♦

Nutrition: American Dietetic Association, 216 West Jackson Boulevard, #800, Chicago, IL 60606. (800) 621–6469 or (312) 899–0040. Division of Government Affairs, 1667 K Street, N.W., Washington, DC 20006. The ADA's Commission on Dietetic Registration establishes and enforces standards for certifying registered dietitians (R.D.s) and "dietetic technician, registered" (D.T.R.s), and accredits undergraduate and internship programs in dietetics. Sponsors National Nutrition Month. Battles prejudice against a "pink collar profession" through its own PAC, lobbying to get Congress to recognize dietitians the way physical therapists and social workers are, as independent health practitioners. Publications include the *Journal of the American Dietetic Association* and Mary

Abbott Hess, R.D., and Anne Elise Hunt, *Pocket Supermarket Guide* (1989). About 2,000 R.D.s specialize in individual counseling, and are organized in the Consulting Nutritionist Practice Group. You can make contact with this group and obtain a list of practitioners near you by contacting the American Dietetic Association.♦

Nutrition: Center for Science in the Public Interest (CSPI), 1501 16th Street, N.W., Washington, DC 20036. (202) 332–9110. Michael Jacobson, Ph.D. Offers mainstream nutritional advice, especially in its newsletter, *Nutrition Action Healthletter,* and at the same time is a strong consumer advocate, coming down hard on fat, salt and pesticides in food; drawing attention to mislabeling by food processing companies; and advocating tougher federal nutritional and hazard labeling laws.♥♦♦

Nutrition: *Ceres Press,* P.O. Box 87, Woodstock, NY 12498. (914) 679–8561. David and Nikki Goldbeck. Publishes *Goldbeck's True Food* Newsletter, $14/year. Well developed concept of healthy food as natural food in a sustainable world♥♦

Nutritional Education Association, Inc., 3647 Glen Haven, Houston, TX 77025; mailing address P.O. Box 20301, Houston, TX 77225. (713) 665–2946. Ruth Yale Long, Ph.D., Nutritionist. Educates the public about the importance of good nutrition for health, through publications and personal consultation.

Orthomolecular Medicine: *Huxley Institute for Biosocial Research,* 900 North Federal Highway, #330, Boca Raton, FL 33432. (305) 393–6167. (800) 847–3802, 8 a.m.–2 p.m. PST. Provides a list of orthomolecular physicians. Home of the American Schizophrenic Association.

Preventive Medicine, American College of, 1015 15th Street, N.W., #403, Washington, DC 20005. (202) 789–0003. Founded in 1954, this medical specialty society certifies M.D.s in four areas of preventive medicine; nutrition is a small component. Its 2,000 members are all M.D.s.

Preventive Medicine: *American College of Advancement in Medicine,* 23121 Verdugo Drive, #204, Laguna Hills, CA 92653. (800) LEADOUT. This organization of 400 preventive medicine practitioners, all of whom have M.D. or D.O. (Doctor of Osteopathy) degrees, is prepared to provide individuals with a referral to a member in their area.♦

Preventive Medicine: *CANHELP,* 3111 Paradise Bay Road, Port Ludlow, WA 98365. (206) 437–2291. Patrick McGrady, Jr., Founder. Provides clients with information on complementary therapies. The client sends all written test results (no x-rays) with a cover letter describing any special complications. CANHELP sends back a list of referrals and a bill for $400. If the cost seems too high, a less expensive option is the World Research Foundation, listed below, which provides a similar service.

Preventive Medicine: *European Council of Integrated Medicine,* P.O. Box 177, 3830 AD Leusden, The Netherlands. 31–33–96939. G. J. (Bert) van Lamoen, Managing Director. The Council also has a Belgian address: Rue des Echevins 71, 1050 Brussels. FAX 32–2–68–380. Is planning for the realignment of national health policies as Europe integrates in 1992.

Preventive Medicine: *Foundation for Alternative Medicine,* P.O. Box 59, Liberty Lake, WA 99019. (509) 255–9246. Marge Jacobs, Secretary/Treasurer. Attempts to evaluate complementary therapies.

Preventive Medicine: *Project CURE,* 140 North Foster Street, #200, Dothan, AL 36303. Investigative Office: 1101 Connecticut Ave., NW, #403, Washington, DC 20036. (800) 552–CURE. Tammy Jordan, Human Relations Specialist. Founded in 1979 by Robert DeBragga and other cancer patients, Project CURE has become a major lobby for an alternative view of health care. It prepares systematic abstracts of complementary health therapies and provides an objective evaluation. Makes available John M. Fink's directory, *Third Opinion,* and other useful literature.♦

Preventive Medicine: *World Research Foundation,* 153 Ventura Blvd., #405, Sherman Oaks, CA 9103. (818) 907–5483. Steve and Laverne Ross, Founders. Nonprofit group with a library and computer database of all medical therapies. Will search its database for clients at a charge of $43 including shipping. Branch offices in West Germany and China.♥♦♦

U.S. Congress, House of Representatives, Committee on Government Operations, Subcommittee on Human Resources, Washington, DC 20015. Rep. Ted Weiss (D-NY), Chair. (202) 225–2548. Has held hearings to question FDA's permitting health claims on food in contravention of the law, which says that a health claim makes a food into a drug, and that drugs must be tested for safety and efficacy.

U.S. Congress, House of Representatives, Committee on Energy and Commerce, Subcommittee on Health & the Environment, Washington, DC 20015. Rep. Henry A. Waxman (D-NY), Chair. (202) 225–2927. Waxman introduced H.R. 3562, which would change the food labeling law and would legislate how the FDA should handle health claims on food; as of early 1990 the bill was out of Committee and before the House.

U.S. Congress, Senate, Committee on Labor and Human Resources, Washington, DC 20510. Senator Edward M. Kennedy (D-MA), Chairman. A bill that would reform FDA labeling regulations was introduced by Senators Howard Metzenbaum (D-OH) and John E. Chafee (R-RI). Senator Tom Harkin (D-IA) has introduced a bill for a National Nutrition Council. Senators Harry M. Reid (D-NV), (202) 224–3542, and Joseph I. Lieberman (D-CT) are investigating the EPA's permitting Alar use.

U.S. Food and Drug Administration (FDA), U.S. Department of Health and Human Services (HHS),Louis Sullivan, M.D., HHS Secretary, Parklawn Building, 5600 Fishers Lane, Rockville, MD 20910. FDA Acting Commissioner James F. Vincent, Room 14–71, (301) 443–2410. Alexander Grant, Associate Commissioner for Consumer Affairs, Room 1685, (301) 443–5006; Consumer Inquiries, (301) 443–3170. Regulations Department, (202) 485–0187. Congressional Liaison, (301) 443–3793. During 1983–89, the FDA was praised by the food and drug industries for deregulatory actions, but was criticized by Congressional leaders for failure to enforce the law concerning health claims on food.[168] The FDA inspects fruit, vegetables, seafood, eggs and milk, in conjunction with state agencies, and sets standards of identity for food. Has published *Cancer Quackery: Past and Present* (Rockville, Md.: FDA Consumer Publications, July/August, 1977).

Vegan Society, American, 501 Old Harding Highway, Malaga, NJ 08328. (609) 694–2887. Founded in 1960, is based on the principle of "ahimsa," Sanscrit for "not killing." Teaches people to live without animal products.

Vegetarian (Macrobiotic): *Kushi Institute for One Peaceful World,* P.O. Box 1100, Brookline Village, MA 02147. (617) 738–0045. Michio and Aveline Kushi. Another 20 macrobiotic centers, located in all regions of the country, are included in John M. Fink, *Third Opinion,*[169] available from Project CURE.

Vegetarian Society, North American, P.O. Box 72, Dolgeville, NY 13329. (518) 568–7970. Affiliated with vegetarian groups throughout the United States. Members contribute $12/year, get a quarterly publication.

The owners of **Walnut Acres** in Penns Creek, Pennsylvania have been growing organically since the 40's and now ship their fresh, baked, dried, and canned goods all over the world by mail.

4

FOOD HAZARDS
AND HOW TO AVOID THEM

Singly, each question might have been answered satisfactorily.
Cumulatively, the questions helped change American attitudes toward food safety.

Health hazards in food were dramatized for the American public in March 1989. An effective publicity campaign led by Meryl Streep (on behalf of Mothers and Others for a Livable Planet) about the adverse effect on children of foods containing pesticides, notably apples and apple products sprayed with the chemical Alar, came in the wake of the government's recall of Chilean grapes after two grapes were found poisoned with cyanide. Many questions were already being raised about the safety of beef, chicken, eggs, fish, milk and pork. Singly, each question might have been answered satisfactorily. Cumulatively, the questions helped change public attitudes toward food safety.

We will look at hazards from foods in their natural state, then at hazards added during the growing stage, and finally at hazards added during the processing and distribution stage. We then describe the agencies and groups working on these problems, and conclude with a listing of such groups.

Hazards from Nature

In Chapter 2 we referred to certain plants, for example in the Nightshade family, as being poisonous, and we noted that it was important to cook plants such as legumes to reduce natural toxins. Some plants manufacture their own toxins to fend off natural enemies such as insects and birds. In Chapter 3 we noted that excessive consumption of animal fat is the main culprit in certain degenerative diseases. In fact toxins are present naturally in all plant and animal foods.

Hippocrates admitted this when he wrote admiringly of the adaptation of the human race to the available food in nature. "I am of the opinion," he said, "that man used the same sort of food [as animals], and that the present articles of diet had been discovered and invented only after a long lapse of time.

"For when they suffered much and severely from this strong and brutish diet, swallowing things which were raw, unmixed, and possessing great strength, they became exposed to strong pains and disease, and to early deaths."[1]

Professor Bruce N. Ames, chairman of the biochemistry department of the University of California at Berkeley, has studied natural hazards, and has become the world's most famous neo-Hobbesian—Hobbes having summed up the life of man in the state of nature as "solitary, poor, nasty, brutish, and short."[2] Ames has it in for Mother Nature.

Having devised a way to test for carcinogens by mutating bacteria in the laboratory instead of by killing animals (the Ames Test that we introduced at the end of Chapter 2), Ames first discovered many new carcinogens among synthetic chemicals and was for a few years a hero of both environmentalists and animal lovers. Then he found many of these carcinogens occur naturally in food, and decided that synthetic chemicals weren't so bad. "Natural cancer agents in our diet," he concluded, "are 10,000 times more plentiful than the synthetic ones."[3] He adds, soberly: "It is important not to divert society's attention from the few really serious hazards, such as tobacco or saturated fat [or, he adds elsewhere, alcohol], by the pursuit of hundreds of minor or nonexistent hazards."[4] But his message is to minimize the hazards of synthetic pesticides in food.

His many critics have accused Ames of "trivializing cancer risks," of neglecting to note that the synthetic chemicals cause diseases other than cancer, and of failing to note the danger of unpredictable interactions among carcinogens. Consumers Union said dismissively that Ames's view "is founded not in science but in political philosophy." Only about 20 natural constituents of food have been found to cause any cancer in animals.[5]

Among the problems with Ames's research cited by Consumers Union are: comparing too few examples (he compared only 14 synthetic chemicals and 15 natural substances) to develop a full picture of relative risks; minimizing pesticide risks by using banned pesticides (DDT and EDB) as his only examples; and using inappropriate assumptions about the ingestion of certain foods that exaggerate a person's likely exposure to natural carcinogens.[6]

Consumers Union also sides with the view that people have had generations of experience to cope with the existence of natural poisons, but the hazards are still not fully understood for new synthetic poisons that are thrust upon society willy-nilly by businesses for profit. It says: "Nature may not be benign, but it's blameless." When chemical producers aren't benign, they aren't blameless. On this basis, synthetic chemicals are morally intolerable where natural chemicals are not.[7]

New York University Professor Arthur Upton, former director of the National Cancer Institute, worries that Ames's hypotheses might be used to justify a laissez-faire policy toward toxic synthetic chemicals: "I am concerned that we are doing things to the environment that may be very deleterious to us in the long run, and hard to reverse."[8]

Aflatoxin is a prominent example of a chemical produced by Mother Nature. It is a potent carcinogen produced by the *Aspergillus flavis* mold, which can sometimes infect peanuts, corn, and other grains during the growing stage but more commonly attacks after harvest, during storage. It became a major concern in 1989 after dangerous concentrations were found in corn samples from the 1988 growing season. The FDA responded with a "don't panic" statement, admitting that the contamination was worse than usual, but that the standard for human consumption (20 parts per billion) had not been compromised. Instead, the more contaminated samples (up to 300 parts per billion) were said to be earmarked for livestock feed. Because aflatoxin breaks down into non-toxic elements in cooking, finished corn products generally test within safe levels, but corn oil, peanuts, and peanut oil can still be a risk.

Botulinum (*Clostridium botulinum*) is a spore-forming bacterium which can produce a deadly toxin and an illness, botulism, that can be fatal. The spores are more resistant to heat than other micro-organisms, and can re-infect food if not totally destroyed. This is why special care is taken in canning food to heat it to high enough temperatures to ensure that all organisms are killed. Even so, canned soups in the United States (and hazelnut yogurt in Britain) have in recent years caused outbreaks of botulism.[9]

Histamines, Lectins, and Peptides. As we shall see later in this chapter, these three potential irritants are especially associated with allergic reactions or food sensitivities. *Histamines* are found in aging cheese, fish, and sausage. *Lectins* are legume toxins that occur naturally in kidney beans and other legumes. They must be inactivated by boiling the legumes for ten minutes, and discarding the water. *Peptides* and other allergens are found in a variety of foods.

Other hazards described below under "diseases caused by improper handling" actually are hazards found in nature that we know how to remove but have failed to. Example: trichinosis in pork.

Hazards Added During Growth

Chemicals, The Price of Farm "Efficiency." American farming after World War II racked up steady improvements in efficiency, assisted by government subsidies of farm research and farmer education. Fewer and fewer farmers were needed to produce the nation's food, and the farm population dropped from 22 million in 1880 to 10 million in 1970—from 44 percent of the total population to a mere 5 percent. Yields per farmer and per acre soared and American agriculture became the marvel and envy of the world.

These improvements were based on (1) more sophisticated farm machines, (2) new hybrid seeds, and (3) newly introduced and initially more effective farm chemicals (fertilizers and pesticides).

But the innovations carried with them a mortgage on the future. The high cost of the farm machines, and farmers' need to borrow money to pay for them, contributed to farm consolidation and, in the 1980's, insolvencies among overextended farmers. Since hybrid seeds don't reproduce themselves predictably, farmers became addicted to a $10-billion-a-year habit of buying new seeds each season.[10] Farm chemicals are credited with helping the world's farmers grow enough food to feed everyone on earth, if the produce were only distributed equitably.[11] But the problems accompanying the innovations that made this possible were inadequately appreciated.

The Growth of Pesticide Use and Potency. To spur yields, American farmers were encouraged by the U.S. Department of Agriculture (USDA) to use more farm chemicals.[12] Arsenic was an early farm chemical, but not until 1947 did the U.S. have a national law specifically regulating pesticides (the British and French had acted to protect the consumer 56 years earlier), just as DDT was coming into widespread use. DDT replaced less effective earlier pesticides and made possible the consolidation of smaller truck farms into the larger monocultural farms that are the core of modern American agribusiness. Then, in 1962, Rachel Carson's *Silent Spring* brought home to the American public the full range of DDT's hazards—its persistence in the food chain and its cumulative deadly effects. A decade later, in 1972, Federal law forbade Americans from using DDT, effective at the beginning of 1973.[13] DDT is still found in the soil and in root crops, but some of the species that were endangered by DDT have started to come back.

Still, use of other pesticides grew apace and peaked in 1982 with 880 million pounds of chemical powder and spray deposited on U.S. farms, about four pounds of chemicals per American. The USDA had done its work—farm productivity had doubled, but at the expense of a ten-fold increase in the use of pesticides between 1942 and 1982.[14]

The weight of pesticides in use has been declining since 1982, to 430 million pounds in 1988 (Table 5-1 in

Chapter 5 shows this trend). But the cumulative amount of residual chemicals in the soil and groundwater has been growing, and the potency and toxicity of the chemicals has been increasing, more than offsetting the decline in weight.[15] More than half the chemicals are deposited on corn, wheat and soybean crops in the Midwestern Grain Belt.

The U.S. Environmental Protection Agency (EPA) has found 46 kinds of pesticide residues in the ground water of 26 states.[16] Another source says 77 chemicals have been detected in well water in 39 states.[17]

Pesticides in Use.[18] Chemical pesticides are mostly petrochemical derivatives used to battle fungi, insects and weeds. A number, like DDT, have been banned—i.e., their EPA registrations were involuntarily cancelled. Others have been cancelled through agreements with manufacturers that may permit further testing. Cancellations in the 1970s included several chemical cousins to DDT, organochlorines: aldrin, BHC, chlordane and dieldrin (all withdrawn by agreement); endrin, heptachlor and toxaphene.[19] Other cancelled or discontinued chemicals include cyhexatin, a miticide, and DBCP (dibromochloropropane), a soil fumigant. Residues of chemicals that have been cancelled in the U.S. persist in the soil of U.S. farms, and continue to be found in food, especially root crops like potatoes and carrots. The chemicals may also be used abroad and may be found in imported food.

Five supermarket chains in 1989 said they would refuse to stock foods that had been treated with alachlor, captan, or EBDCs; would ask food suppliers to disclose all pesticides used to grow food and vegetables; and would encourage growers to phase out the use of 64 pesticides identified by the EPA as potential carcinogens.[20] The five chains have 1,200 outlets and sales of $8 billion (annual U.S. supermarket sales are $300 billion): Bread & Circus Wholefood Supermarkets, Newton, Mass.; Raley's, Sacramento, Calif.; ABCO Markets, Phoenix, Ariz.; Amerinian Brothers Produce, San Jose, Calif.; and Provigo Inc., Montreal, Quebec (owns Petrini Supermarkets in the U.S. Middle West).

The following pesticides, identified by their generic names, are selected from a much longer list as being both (1) especially hazardous and (2) at least until recently still in common use. Some commodities are exemplified as those on which the pesticides are used, based on amounts of residues detected in samples.[21] Possible hazards from use are identified in parentheses—a carcinogen has been shown to cause cancer in animals, a mutagen to mutate genes in animals. The EPA classifies a carcinogen as A, meaning it causes tumors in humans; B-1 and B-2, meaning it definitely causes tumors in animals (B-1 is stronger than B-2); or C, meaning some evidence exists that it causes tumors in animals.

Acephate, insecticide used on celery, legumes, peppers (carcinogen, mutagen). Systemic, cannot be washed off (not that other chemicals without this identification are easy to wash off, especially since growers or distributors started coating some produce with wax).

Alachlor, herbicide that is the most widely used in the U.S., used on corn, peanuts, and soybeans (carcinogen). Has been detected in drinking water in 18 states.[22] Not detectable by FDA's routine lab tests.[23] One of three pesticides that five supermarket chains in 1989 said they would not permit on products they sell.

Aldicarb, insecticide used mainly on potatoes, also on citrus fruit and soybeans (highly toxic). Systemic, cannot be washed off.

Captan, fungicide used to protect many seeds and such fruits as apples, cherries, grapes, peaches and strawberries (carcinogen, mutagen). One of three pesticides that five supermarket chains in 1989 said they would not permit on products they sell. All but 24 uses were restricted in February 1989; permitted uses include all seed uses, plus plant bed treatment, pre-harvest and post-harvest treatments for the fruits mentioned above and some others.

Chlorothalonil, fungicide used on cantaloupes, cauliflower, celery, legumes, tomatoes, watermelon (carcinogen, chronic disease effects, mutagen).

EBDCs (ethylene bisdithiocarbamates), fungicide used on about one-third of U.S. fruits and vegetables. However, the FDA cannot detect EBDC residues with routine lab tests. The FDA has a special test to monitor residues, but it takes a month to process, too long to prevent consumers eating the food with the illegal residue levels.[24] One of three pesticides that five supermarket chains in 1989 said would keep products off their shelves.

Lindane, insecticide used on leafy vegetables (carcinogen, chronic disease effects); same formula as is used in Kwell, for head lice. Use has been restricted by the EPA.

Methyl Parathion, insecticide used on cantaloupes and strawberries (carcinogen, chronic disease effects, mutagen).

Parathion, insecticide used on broccoli, carrots, cherries, oranges, peaches (carcinogen, mutagen).

Permethrin, insecticide used on 60 crops, including corn, soybeans, and tomatoes (carcinogen).

Phosmet, insecticide used on apples, pears and sweet potatoes (carcinogen, mutagen).

Trifluralin, herbicide used on carrots (carcinogen, chronic disease effects). Cannot be washed off.

Chemical Fertilizer and Growth Regulators. In addition to pesticides, the methods that brought about the "green revolution" (meaning greater productivity from use of farm chemicals) have involved the use of other farm chemicals.

One is overuse and misuse of nitrogen-based chemical fertilizers in conjunction with over-farming. This has contaminated groundwater supplies with carcinogenic nitrites and has had other consequences described in Chapter 5.

Another is the use of growth regulators like *Alar*, which has become a symbol of the hazards of farm chemicals added during growth. It is Uniroyal's name for the spray known generically as daminozide, used on red apples to control their growth. It permeates the apple and can't be washed off. When cooked, it breaks down into the more dangerous carcinogen UDMH, which *Consumer Reports* (May 1989) reported finding at a level of as high as 0.5 parts per million in affected applesauce, apple juice and other (cooked) apple products. The hazard is cancer from the accumulation of the chemical in the body. This is especially serious for young children who eat a lot of apple products and for whom the accumulation is more serious because they weigh less than adults for whom maximum tolerances were set by the EPA.

Factory Farming. Breeders of cattle, swine and poultry in their search for efficiency have added new doses of antibiotics, salmonellae, and hormones to the American diet.

Antibiotics in preventive doses are added to the animals' diets because as they are crowded together more tightly for maximum output the incidence of disease, and the size of "dead piles" where diseased animals were dumped, increased to unacceptable levels. Preventive doses of antibiotics have kept the animals out of the dead piles, at the price of treating them as if they were always sick. It works, for now. But the practice has been linked to the declining effectiveness of antibiotics in people, already a growing problem because of indiscriminate use of broad-spectrum antibiotics. The more an antibiotic is in use, the more encouragement is given to the breeding and evolution of new strains of bugs that are resistant to these antibiotics. In 1960, under *15 percent* of human staphylococci infections, which cause food poisoning, pneumonia, and skin and bone infections, were resistant to penicillin. By 1988 the figure had risen to *over 90 percent*.[25]

Salmonellae (about which we say more in the next section) are breeding in new strains resistant to antibiotics. Growth of these bacteria in chickens is encouraged by the close proximity of the birds to one another, by the feeding of parts of dead chickens to live ones, and by the unsanitary conditions of the mechanized slaughterhouse assembly line.

Hormones are injected into cattle, swine and chickens, to encourage them to grow or produce eggs or milk faster. The bovine growth hormone (BGH), bovine somatotropin, has been found to increase the milk output of cows by 25 percent.

Use of hormones in animals is forbidden in Britain and Continental Europe, but the FDA pronounced BGH safe. A professor at the University of Illinois Medical Center believes the FDA acted prematurely, noting that more than 20 animal studies suggest the hormone could be absorbed from milk into the human bloodstream where it would create hormonal effects and cause allergies.[26]

The makers of Ben & Jerry's Homemade ice cream say the company will not purchase milk from cows that have been given BGH. A company spokesman, Alan Parker, said: "The issue goes to the heart of what kind of farm community we want in this country and what kind of food it will raise."

Five supermarket chains—Kroger (1,200 stores in 30 states), Safeway (1,100 stores in the West and Washington, D.C.), Stop & Shop (116 stores in New England), Supermarkets General (based in New Jersey), and Vons Companies, Inc. (based in El Monte, Calif.)—also announced they will not sell milk or milk products from cows that have been treated with BGH. They say they do not want to sell a product containing an experimental drug.[27]

Several organizations are concerned not only about the obvious hazards to humans cited above but also with the inhumane way that factory farming treats the animals, which are effectively caged for their entire lives. These groups include the Farm Animal Reform Movement, Food-Animal Projects, and the Humane Farming Association; their addresses and other information are included in the listing at the end of this chapter.

Hazards Added During Processing

Take, for example, an onion headed for processing into a package of your favorite soup. After exposure to pesticides and potentially dangerous chemicals in the water supply and soil, it is picked, thrown into a truck, and taken to a dehydration plant. There it may be washed with a fungicide to prevent mold and tossed into a bin, which might be a little rusty. Our onion might get kicked around a little before it makes it to the dicing stage. Then it rides along a conveyor belt, where it can come into contact with grease and other undesirable materials. Once dehydrated, an anti-caking agent such as calcium stearate—a metallic soap of fatty acids—may be applied prior to shipment to a warehouse. There the onions might be sprayed with another anti-fungal agent or may absorb pesticides used to keep the warehouse free of rats and bugs. From there the onions will be shipped off to a factory to be added to the other ingredients to make the processed soup.

Chemicals are added to other vegetables and fruits to regulate their harvesting period or reduce damage during transportation. They are also added to lengthen shelf life, or improve taste. Some pose potential hazards, despite food industry statements that preservatives are mostly harmless and essential to efficient food distribution.

Also, some supermarkets and smaller stores routinely fumigate with or spray pesticides around the produce area (yes, even areas marked "organic food," as we note in the next chapter) to eliminate flying or crawling insects.

Additives. Among the chemicals added to food during processing are the following.[28]

Antioxidants (in the excellent European number system for additives, the E300s) are added to prevent fatty foods from becoming rancid, and to protect the loss of fat-soluble vitamins from oxidation. Used in cheese spreads, chewing gum, and vegetable oils. Examples: butylated hydroxytoluene (BHT), butylated hydroxyanisole (BHA), dodecyl gallate (dodecyl 3,4,5), octyl gallate, propyl gallate (propyl 3,4,5 trihydroxy-benzene), trihydroxy-benzene. A reviewer of this book who works for the Chemical Manufacturers Association tells me that BHA and BHT are anti-carcinogens.

Artificial Colors (the E100s) are added for cosmetic purposes, often to compensate for the loss of color during processing. Used in such foods as beer, canned vegetables, and soft drinks. Examples: aluminum, brilliant blue FCF, caramel, indigo carmine (indigotine), patent blue, pigment rubine (lithol rubine RK), tartrazine. In late January 1990, the FDA banned Red Dye No. 3 because it was found to cause cancer in animals.

Emulsifiers and Stabilizers (the E400s), to permit oil and water to mix, make mixtures smoother, and slow the rate at which baked goods go stale. Used in baked goods, ice cream, salad dressings. Examples: calcium disodium EDTA (calcium disodium ethylene diamine-NNN'N'tetra-acetate [sic]), esters (acetic, citric, lactic, or sucrose) of mono- or diglycerides of fatty acids.

Flavor Enhancers, used like salt to accent the taste of processed food. Used in canned vegetables, frozen foods. Examples: calcium dihydrogen di-L-glutamate (calcium glutamate), inosine 5-disodium phosphate (sodium 5-inosinate), monosodium glutamate (sodium hydrogen L-glutamate, MSG), potassium hydrogen L-glutamate. Those who have studied MSG claim that people's adverse reaction to it, the so-called "Chinese Restaurant Syndrome," cannot be reproduced in careful trials, and is therefore considered idiosyncratic, like a food allergy or intolerance.[29]

Preservatives (E200s), to defend products against microbes that would spoil or poison the foods, and thereby to increase the products' shelf life. Used in such foods as banana skins, beer, cider, citrus fruit skins, dehydrated vegetables, dried fruit, fruit juices and syrups, sausages, and wine. Examples: benzoic acid, calcium benzoate, calcium sulphite, calcium hydrogen sulphite (calcium bisulphite), ethyl 4-hydroxy-benzoate (ethyl para-hydroxylbenzoate) and its sodium salt, potassium benzoate, potassium metabisulphite (potassium pyrosulphite), propyl 4-hydroxy-benzoate (propyl para-hydroxybenzoate) and its sodium salt, sodium nitrate (chile saltpeter), sodium nitrite, sodium sulphite, sodium benzoate, sodium hydrogen sulphite (sodium bisulphite), sodium metabisulphite (disodium pyrosulphite), sulphur dioxide. The FDA has a difficult-to-comprehend standard of identity requiring that processed meat labeled bologna include sodium nitrites (which can be converted by the body into seriously carcinogenic nitrosamines)![30]

Sweeteners (E420s), used to sweeten food, either in concentrated form (chemicals with many times the sweetness of sugar) or bulk form (chemicals with about the same sweetness as sugar). Used in diet soft drinks, low-calorie yogurt, dietary desserts. Examples: aspartame (Nutra-Sweet), cyclamate (banned in U.S., being reconsidered), saccharin, in the concentrated forms; sorbitol and xylitol in bulk form. Some experts warn against consuming more than three diet sodas per day.

Irradiation. Food may be irradiated to prolong shelf life. Ionizing radiation is unquestionably useful to distributors and retailers because it kills any bacteria or insects that might be in food, while at the same time slowing the ripening/aging process. In the absence of safety questions, the food industry would irradiate many foods in supermarkets that are neither canned nor frozen.

Consumer and legislative resistance to food irradiation is based on environmental, nutritional, and safety concerns. A half dozen accidents at nuclear irradiation facilities have contaminated products as well as workers and local communities.[31] Irradiation has been found to kill some of the food value, the vitamins that play an important part in digestion and nutrition.[32] It encourages the growth of aflatoxin and creates carcinogens such as formaldehyde and hydrogen peroxide in some foods. It also creates other chemicals that have not been fully examined and tested.

As of late 1989 three states had banned food irradiation—Maine, New Jersey and New York. Gov. Mario A. Cuomo of New York noted that state agencies with oversight believed irradiation was harmless, and that his support of the ban was based on intense consumer pressure. The New York ban delays the manufacture, sale and distribution of radiation-exposed food for two years. Outgoing Gov. Thomas Kean of New Jersey also imposed a two-year moratorium.[33]

Britain still has a ban on irradiation as of early 1990. The government has considered lifting the ban, but 12 supermarket chains announced that they would not stock irradiated products, and associations of fruit and vegetable wholesalers said they would join with the Coalition against Food Irradiation to lobby for continuing the ban. The Coalition cites the following safety issues: effects of irradiation on food additives, pesticide residues and packaging; vitamin loss; destruction of benevolent bacteria in food; and the possibility that irradiation causes cancer. Food writer Egon Ronay, who founded the Coalition, says the burden of proof is on the irradiators to show that the process is safe.[34]

During the British debate, Professor Donald Louria, M.D., chairman of the department of preventive medicine and community health at New Jersey Medical School claimed that the FDA had ignored key findings in three of five studies that showed abnormalities in rats and dogs that were fed irradiated food. He concluded that the FDA's basis for approving irradiation had "major flaws."[35]

The British Nutrition Foundation, which is supported by the food industry, opposes allowing food irradiation until a way is found to apply suitable labeling, controls, and inspections to such foods. The Foundation's fear is that consumers may be misled into believing that food is wholesome merely because bacterial tests are unable to prove otherwise.[36]

Packaging. Food is packaged in ways that may be unhealthy. *Aluminum* in cans or cooking trays has been said to leach into food, and high levels of aluminum absorption have been linked to Alzheimer's disease. *Dioxin,* a proven carcinogen, has been found in milk cartons. *Lead* may leach into canned food through the soldered seams or be spattered into food during canning. Most cans in American stores are now welded, with a smaller black seam instead of the previous wider, silver seam; some cans, such as those used for Health Valley products, are even coated with an enamel to protect against leaching of metals from the cans to the food inside. However, cans imported from abroad may still use soldering. Hazard: impairment of neurological development (a major issue for children).

Diseases Transmitted Through Improper Handling

While bacteria and parasites occur in nature, they are ordinarily killed by cooking. The following diseases are among the most serious ones transmitted through careless handling of food during distribution and processing.

Campylobacter is one of the two bacteria that the USDA says infects one-third of all raw poultry sold in the United States. The vast majority of the 2 to 4 million campylobacter cases a year in humans are caused by food, and about half of them are attributable to chicken. Hazard: gastrointestinal illness; long-term effect is rheumatoid arthritis; can be fatal; C. jejuni is implicated in Guillian-Barre syndrome.

Hepatitis A is a fecally transmitted disease resulting from unclean processing or handling of food. Hazard: jaundice, fever; may require weeks for liver to recover. More than 25,000 incidents were reported in 1987.

Listeria (*Listeria monocytogenes*) bacteria have been found in cheese. Hazard: encephalitis, commonly fatal.

Salmonella (*Salmonella typhimurium*) is a bacterium transmitted in raw poultry, meat, milk and eggs. Hazard: Fever, stomach cramps. In 1987, 51,000 incidents and 500 deaths were reported in the U.S. The head of the USDA Inspection Service told *60 Minutes* in 1987 that one-third of *all* poultry offered for sale in the United States is contaminated either with salmonella or campylobacter. The television program staff did their own check and found that over half the chickens they purchased had salmonellosis. By late 1989 the situation had not improved, to the point where Rodney Leonard of the Community Nutrition Institute was advising his newsletter readers not to eat chicken. In Britain, cases of food poisoning rose from 17,000 in the first six months of 1988 to 24,000 in the same period in 1989; more than one-third of them were salmonella infections. Some cases were related to pork, especially stuffed pork that is cooked ahead of purchase and then chilled.[37]

Shigellosis is a fecally transmitted, highly contagious disease resulting from unclean processing. Hazards: Diarrhea, stomach cramps.

Trichinosis is a parasitic disease carried by pork if inadequately cooked. Hazard: muscular pain, fever, edema (swelling caused by accumulation of water), and dyspnea (shortness of breath).

Typhoid (*Salmonella typhosa*) was found in canned corn beef from Argentina a decade ago. Hazards: fever, diarrhea, prostration, headache, intestinal inflammation.

Food Allergies and Intolerance

A food allergy is defined as any adverse reaction to food in which the immune system can be shown to be involved. A food allergy can reveal its symptoms in many ways, such as: fatigue; rapid weight change; puffiness of face, hands, abdomen or ankles; palpitations, especially after eating; heavy sweating unrelated to exercise.[38]

The traditionally defined allergy operates through mast cells, which are gathering points in our tissues, especially around the bronchial tubes, the nose and the gut. The Immunoglobulin E antibody, or protein molecule, attaches itself to the mast cell. When an antigen, the target molecule to which the antibody binds, binds more than one Immunogobulin E molecule on the mast cell surface, the mast cell degranulates. Degranulation means the mast cell releases histamines, which increase secretions that cause discomfort—i.e., the allergic reaction.

Food allergies are detected clinically through the use of a scratch test (either on the surface of the skin or more recently through an injection) or radioallergosorbent test (RAST).

However, these tests do not detect food intolerances not related to Immunogobulin E. While such intolerances cannot be shown to be related to the immune system, the symptoms (headaches, pains, coughing) are improved when certain foods are removed from the patient's diet. Clinical ecologists (whom we described in Chapter 3) believe that these food intolerances account for 95 percent of food *sensitivities*, an umbrella term to describe both traditionally measurable allergies and food intolerances.[39]

Immunological reactions to food are idiosyncratic; one person's meat may be another's "poison." However, this book has a two-fold population-wide message: (1) Quite unpleasant illnesses may be caused by individual food sensitivities, and (2) These sensitivities may, because of the accumulation of poisons in food, be increasing.[40]

Causes of Food Sensitivity. Some foods are more likely than others to have natural poisons that cause problems for individuals with food sensitivities.

Enzymes of some tropical fruit may have a bad effect. Pineapple and papaya contain powerful protein-breaking enzymes that can attack the membranes of any body cell, including the mast cells. This may cause the mast cells to degranulate, releasing histamines and causing discomfort. It is not advisable to eat raw papaya or pineapple on an empty stomach because of the damage that may be done to the stomach lining by these enzymes. (Canned pineapple is safe because the heat used in canning inactivates the enzyme.)

Histamines (from the Greek "histos," meaning "mast") are molecules of a chemical, $C_5H_9N_3$, your body generates and uses to communicate to other parts of the body the presence of an invading entity. High concentrations of histamines cause allergic reactions. The causes are found most commonly in well-ripened cheese, sausages kept for a long time, and inadequately refrigerated fish (mackerel and tuna). The liver normally detoxifies histamines within 12 hours. But anyone with a weak liver should avoid histamine-rich foods. The liver is weakened by the drug isoniazide (used to treat tuberculosis), by viral hepatitis, and cirrhosis.

Lectins are produced in particularly high concentrations by certain legumes. They are also found in snails, and in wheat, where they may be responsible for producing celiac (abdominal) disease. Lectins bind to carbohydrate molecules on the surface of all cells and make red blood cells clump together; they are inactivated by boiling for a few minutes. The powerful lectin in kidney beans can cause serious diarrhea and abdominal pain if the beans are inadequately soaked and cooked; fortunately, ten minutes in boiling water is sufficient, and canned beans are generally boiled even longer. Discard at least once the water that legumes are boiled or soaked in (raw soy beans contain chemicals that inhibit the ability of trypsin enzymes to digest proteins; broad beans contain vicine, which can cause favism, a type of anemia).[41]

Peptides are small protein-like molecules that are in several foods and, like lectins, bind to mast cells and make them degranulate. Peptides are found in egg whites, strawberries, crustacean shellfish, tomatoes, fish, pork and chocolate.

Other foods that appear to trigger mast cells are buckwheat, sunflower seeds, mango and mustard. Half of all patients who suffer from this mast cell triggering, which is known as false food allergy because no allergy is measured, have been said to suffer from a magnesium deficiency.[42]

If you are chronically sick or have headaches, something in your diet may be causing it. A systematic dietary testing regimen, supervised by a doctor (clinical ecologists specialize in this), can determine whether a particular food is causing distress. The two most common approaches are: (1) Eliminate all foods except pears and lamb (which are rarely involved in food intolerances), adding foods one by one and monitoring their impact; (2) Eliminate the most likely offenders one by one, starting with refined sugars, then fruit (on the sugars of which yeast may be feeding) and white flour.[43]

Pressures on the Regulators

The presence of poisons in our food is defended by growers and manufacturers on the grounds either that the toxicity is low or that the dose is low. True enough, if the dose is large enough almost anything will kill you. On that basis, the Meat Board stresses that dioxin is found in very small doses in meat. However, Diane Courtney, head of the Toxic Effects Branch of EPA's National Environmental Research Center, told the Subcommittee on the Environment of the Senate Commerce Committee that dioxin is "by far the most toxic chemical known to mankind."[44]

The record shows that regulatory authorities respond to trade association pressures. Daminozide (Alar) and its breakdown product UDMH were first recognized as strong carcinogens in 1973. EPA staff attempted to cancel Alar's registration in 1985, based on two findings: (1) Daminozide causes cancer in animals and (2) Its effects are concentrated and aggravated when daminozide breaks down into UDMH, as it does when apples are heated for apple sauce or for pasteurized apple juice.

EPA management in 1985 referred the proposal to its Scientific Advisory Panel, seven of whose eight members were employed as consultants to the chemical industry while they were on the panel. At least one member was hired by Uniroyal to consult on Alar after the panel's judgment was rendered; another member was hired by Uniroyal to consult on another chemical. The panel decided that the studies cited by the staff were flawed and that new studies should be conducted, to be presented in 1990.[45]

How to Avoid These Poisons

The only way to avoid the poisons is to know what you are buying, and to take certain precautions. Salmonella bacteria and seafood parasites can be killed by thorough cooking. Mold toxins like aflatoxin can be reduced by cooking. Other chemical toxins including many pesticide residues are *not* eliminated or reduced by cooking; we must avoid the foods that carry them.

Smart Shopping. Other risks in food are minimized by: (1) Learning more about how our food is produced, and (2) Buying products that are least likely to have the poisons in them. If one is convinced, as the Federal Government is not, that existing radiation levels in milk are hazards, the way to avoid the hazard is to join the vegans and macrobiotics and not drink milk at all or not to drink milk that comes from dairies located near nuclear facilities. The challenge is to find out where the milk in your city comes from.

Similarly, shopping for organic food is one way to avoid added farm chemicals, but the effectiveness of this approach depends on knowing where to buy the food. In Chapter 10 we list restaurants and retail stores that offer organic produce. Some supermarket chains (such as Safeway) have long been concerned about chemicals in food and have acted to keep certain products (e.g. Alar-treated apples) out of their stores. One may ask: "Do stores with such policies actually test what they sell? Or do they simply rely on representations of vendors?" Independent groups have tested apples in stores that claimed their apples were Alar-free, and many were found to be impregnated with Alar.

Food Handling at Home. To avoid botulism and other illnesses from careless food handling at home, keep all working surfaces clean and wash hands frequently; do not mix raw and cooked foods, or use the same utensils on them; keep raw foods at the bottom of the refrigerator, separate from prepared foods; use FIFO (first in, first out) inventory control in your refrigerator; foods cooked for later use should be covered outside the refrigerator while cooling; re-heated foods should be brought to a high temperature and recooked thoroughly; frozen food, especially meat and poulty, should be allowed adequate time to thaw so that it will be cooked thoroughly.[46] Be careful when using a microwave oven not to rely on it to kill parasites and bacteria; the microwave heats up water molecules but doesn't necessarily kill micro-organisms. Meat, poultry, and other food that has been open for a few days should be cooked throughly over a regular stove.[47]

Support Your Friends. One way to avoid poisons in foods is to support farmers and retailers who are seeking to bring you healthier food, and consumer organizations working to encourage government agencies to do a better job of protecting America's food.

Consumer Groups and Key Government Agencies

The following consumer groups, and a few government agencies, are among those carrying the battle against toxic chemicals in food to the media and to legislators. (Another list of organizations at the end of Chapter 3 is oriented primarily to nutrition and preventive medical practice, and the list at the end of Chapter 5 is oriented primarily to organic agriculture.)

A ♥ means that from personal contact I can vouch for the commitment of the organization to consumer safety or health, and its effectiveness; a ♦ means that I have had significant third-party testimony to this commitment and its effectiveness.

Americans for Safe Food, Roger Blobaum, Executive Director, 1501 16th Street, N.W., Washington, DC 20036. (202) 332-9110. Project of Center for Science in the Public Interest. Coalition of more than 40 consumer and environmental groups lobbying against tainted food.♥♦

Cancer Information Service, a program of the National Cancer Institute, one of the National Institutes of Health. (800-4-CANCER). The number connects you directly to a regional center under contract to the National Cancer Institute that can answer questions about cancer and carcinogens.

Center for Science in the Public Interest (CSPI), Michael F. Jacobson, Ph.D., Executive Director, 1501 16th Street, N.W., Washington, DC 20036. (202) 332-9110. This Ralph Nader-inspired group seeks to improve public understanding of nutrition and poisons in food. Prepared *Eater's Digest: The Consumer's Factbook of Food Additives* and publishes *Nutrition Action Health Letter,* a first-rate monthly that highlights the fight against additives and poor diets.♥♦♦

Clean Water Action Project, 317 Pennsylvania Ave., SE, Washington, DC 20003. (202) 547-1196. Exercises considerable political influence. "The only major environmental group working to organize rural Americans," says the *Utne Reader.*[48]♦

Community Nutrition Institute, 2001 S Street, N.W., #530, Washington, DC 20009. (202) 462-4700. Rodney Leonard, Executive Director. Non-profit publisher of fine newsletter costing $70 for new subscribers.♥♦

Environmental Defense Fund, 257 Park Avenue South, New York, NY 10010. (212) 505-2100. Concerned with national environmental legislation; litigates over issues such as pollution.♦[49]

Farm Animal Reform Movement (FARM), P.O. Box 70123, Washington, DC 20088. (301) 530-1737. A smaller version of People for the Ethical Treatment of Animals. Lobbies against factory farming, hormones, preventive feeding of antibiotics to animals. Newsletter is sent free to contributors; has 15,000 members.

Food & Water, Inc., 225 Lafayette Street, #612, New York, NY 10012. (800) E FE or (212) 941-9340. Walter Burnstein, Executive Director, or Michael Colby, Associate Director. New organization, quickly drew attention to its opposition to food irradiation.[50]

Food Animal Concerns Trust (FACT), Chicago, IL. (312) 525-4952. Focuses on treatment of animals for food, with a view to helping the consumer make choices that are healthy for those who eat animals, the animals themselves, and the farmers.

Greenpeace, 1436 U Street, NW, Washington, DC 20009. (202) 462-1177. Broad-based environmental group lobbying against pesticides on farms (as well as wildlife and disarmament). Has a flair for media, as may be measured by its 1.8 million U.S. member and offices in 18 countries. Membership costs $20/year; members receive a newsletter.♦♦

Humane Farming Association, 1550 California Street, #6, San Francisco, CA 94109. (415) 485-1495. Largest organization devoted exclusively to animal rights. Dedicated to protecting animals, consumers, and family farmers (is not exclusively vegan in orientation). Has 55,000 members, who for a contribution of $15 or more get a newsletter.♦

Humane Society of the U.S., 2100 L Street, N.W., Washington, DC 20037. (202) 452-1100. Dr. Michael Fox, author of *Agricide,* Vice President for Farm Animals, Bioethics. Million-member ($10/year, quarterly magazine) organization, addresses treatment of farm animals and dangers to consumers from maltreatment.

National Business Center for Food Safety, 1050 Commonwealth Ave., Suite 301, Boston, MA 02215. (800) 338-2223 or (617) 232-8080.

National Coalition Against Misuse of Pesticides (NCAMP), 530 Seventh Street, SE, Washington, DC 20003. (202) 543-5450. Thomas L. Oates, information coordinator. National coalition of grassroots groups working to control use of pesticides. It serves as a clearinghouse for information on the use and misuse of pesticides, and alternatives to them. Publishes newsletter five times a year and a monthly technical report. Individual membership is $20/year.♦

National Coalition to Stop Food Irradiation, P.O. Box 59-0488, San Francisco, CA 94159. (415) 626-2734. Nora Cousens, legislative director. Founded in 1984 to protest food irradiation. Has over 90 chapters and supporting organizations. Individual members pay $25/year and receive a newsletter.

National Toxics Campaign, 37 Temple Place, 4th Floor, Boston, MA 02111. (617) 482-1477. John O'Conner, Executive Director. Consumer Pesticide Project, 10 Gold Mine Drive, San Francisco, CA 94131. (415) 826-6314. Works through local citizen pressure to get pesticides out of the food chain.

Natural Resources Defense Council (NRDC), 40 West 20th Street, New York, NY 10011. (212) 727-2700. John Adams, Executive Director. Also 90 New Montgomery Street, San Francisco, CA 94105. (415) 777-0220; FAX (415) 495-5996. Actively involved in lobbying against uncontrolled use of pesticides. Sells two books on pesticides: *Intolerable Risk: Pesticides in Our Children's Food* ($6 for Executive Summary) and *Pesticide Alert: A Guide to Pesticides in Fruits and Vegetables* ($8.50). Membership $10/year. Meryl Streep leads NRDC's grassroots group *Mothers and Others for a Livable Planet,* at the New York address. A copy of *For Our Kids' Sake: How to Protect Your Children from Pesticides in Food* costs $7.95 payable to Mothers and Others. On the Alar issue, in the words of the *Utne Reader,* NRDC and Mothers and Others "hit a home run."[51] ♥ ♦♦

Northwest Coalition for Alternatives to Pesticides, (454 Willamette, #210, 97401) P.O. Box 1393, Eugene, OR 97440. (503) 344-5044. Norma Grier, Executive Director. Five-state coalition of groups seeking controls on pesticides. Publishes quarterly journal sent to members. Individual members pay $25/year; individual subscribers pay $15/year.♦

People for the Ethical Treatment of Animals (PETA), P.O. Box 42516, Washington, DC 20015. (301) 770-7444. Mediawise nonviolent animal rights group, opposed to exploitation of (including eating; they are vegan in outlook), or testing on, animals for any reason. Publishes an effective fact booklet, "The Realities of Animal-Based Agriculture." It has 270,000 members, and is growing fast; membership is $15/year.♦

Pesticides Action Network—North America Regional Center Pesticide Education Action Project, (220 Golden Gate Ave., 9th Floor, 94102) P.O. Box 610, San Francisco, CA 94101. (415) 771-7327 or (415) 541-9140. Monica Moore, Executive Director. International coalition of organizations opposed to misuse of pesticides.

Pesticide Hotline, National Pesticide Telecommunication Network, (800) 858-7378. Call this EPA-funded number any time, 24 hours a day, seven days a week, for information on the content, use and antidote for any pesticide. The hotline is operated by qualified personnel at Texas Tech University, Thompson Hall, Room S-129,

Lubbock, TX 79409. They handled 34,000 calls in 1989. They have all the brand names on hand and can answer your questions on hazards and how to use chemicals right away, or refer you to another source.♥

US Department of Agriculture (USDA), Administration Building, 12th Street and Jefferson Drive, S.W., Washington, DC 20250. Arthur Whitmore, Press Office: (202) 447-4026. Ben Blankenship, Public Information: (202) 786-1504. Herman Delvo, Pesticides: (202) 786-1456. Stephen Crutchfield, Water Quality: (202) 786-1444. The USDA regulates meat and poultry, inspecting for disease as well as proper labeling. It also helps make markets for U.S. agricultural products. Problem: The USDA both regulates farm product contaminants and promotes agricultural products, so "There is a conflict of interest at the Department," says Jean Mayer, President of Tufts University and a prominent nutritionist.[52]

US Environmental Protection Agency (EPA), Waterside West Building, 401 M Street, S.W., Washington, D.C. 20460. William K. Reilly, Administrator, Room 1200. (202) 382-4700. External Affairs Office, (703) 557-7102; FAX (703) 557-8244. Fungicides: (703) 557-1900. Insecticides: (703) 557-2400, 557-2386, 557-7400. Herbicides: (703) 557-1850. Monitors and regulates air, water, and soil quality; and pesticides.

US Food and Drug Administration (FDA), Department of Health and Human Services (Louis Sullivan, Secretary), Parklawn Building, 5600 Fishers Lane, Rockville, MD 20857. (202) 443-2410: Commissioner (Vacant), Room 14-71. (301) 443-5006: Alexander Grant, Associate Commissioner for Consumer Affairs. The Consumer Affairs Office of the FDA in 15 years has grown from one person to 33. The FDA inspects fruit, vegetables, seafood, eggs and milk, in conjunction with state agencies. It is responsible for but does not inspect the quality of commercially sold bottled water. It also sets the standards of identity for food labels.

Valley Action Network, P.O. Box 5592, Fresno, CA 93755. One of four chapters of the California Action Network, based in San Joaquin. Brings to the attention of the public the pollution of water and land by chemicals. Membership $15/year for individuals.

Water Hotline, (800) 426-4791. This EPA-funded service will answer questions about drinking water safety.

Harlan Lundberg stands knee-deep in a field of rice straw that remains on the field after harvest each fall. Most rice farmers burn their straw, in the belief that it contributes to plant disease. Behind Harlan is a "roller," made out of recycled earth-mover tires. **Lundberg Family Farms** uses it to flatten the straw into a tight mat, lying close to the hard, clay soil. This begins the process of transforming a pesky liability for most farmers, into a valuable asset for the Lundbergs.

PART 2
WHO PRODUCES HEALTHY FOOD

Combines harvesting grain destined for **Arrowhead Mills.** The Hereford, Texas based company was the most widely acclaimed wholefood producer in our surveys.

ORGANIC FARMING AND ITS IMPORTANCE

The way food is grown also affects the health of the producer and the environment.

This chapter focuses on healthy and unhealthy ways of growing food, and shows how we can tell if the food was grown in a healthy way.

What Makes Organic/Natural Food Healthy?

Up to now, we have looked at healthy food strictly from the *consumer*'s viewpoint. But the way food is grown also affects the health of the *producer* and the *environment*. A food can hardly be deemed healthy if it injures its producers; it must be healthy to work with. And how can we deem a food healthy if its production poisons the soil, the water we drink, or the air we breathe? Its production must help preserve the environment.

Some advocates for purer food would make a case for organic food and organic farming based on the consumer's perspective alone—the food is safer to eat. Others who argue for a reduction in the use of chemicals do so out of concern for producers, or the environment, or both.

We review here the arguments for growing food without toxic chemicals and then provide information so the consumer can make choices based on how the food was produced.

Organic Foods. In the context of food and farming, organic means *grown without synthetic chemicals;* but as we shall see in this chapter, only a few states have laws that define and restrict the use of the word.[1] Organic farming means growing without using synthetic compounds to fertilize the soil, kill insects or weeds, or control the growth, ripening, transportability or perishability of farm products. Acceptable fertilizers for organic farming include composts and manures, mined and untreated mineral rock powders, and nitrogen-fixing crops such as legumes. Acceptable pesticides include products (mostly natural and derived from plants) that have minimal adverse impact on soil, health,

and the environment. Weeds are usually controlled by cultivation techniques.

The basic principles of organic farming were codified in 1981 by the West German-based International Federation of Organic Agriculture Movements: (1) To work as much as possible within a closed system (minimal waste), and to draw upon local resources. (2) To maintain the long-term fertility of soils. (3) To avoid all forms of pollution that may result from agricultural techniques. (4) To produce foodstuffs of high nutritional quality and sufficient quantity. (5) To reduce to a minimum the use of fossil energy in agriculture. (6) To provide farm animals living conditions appropriate to their physiological needs and to humanitarian principles. (7) To make it possible for agricultural producers to earn a living and develop their potentialities as human beings.

"Natural" Foods. "Natural" foods are prepared without artificial ingredients. Natural foods should not contain additives such as chemical colorants or preservatives, artificial flavors or flavor enhancers, highly refined grains, sweetening agents, processed fillers, or any other product that depends on advanced factory technology rather than culinary skills. Strictly interpreted, "natural" food should not have been subjected during the growing period to synthetic fertilizers or pesticides. However, most people do not go this far, and will accept a conventionally grown carrot as natural if nothing synthetic is added to it between harvest and consumer. Organic food may be thought of as natural food at its best.

Because the term "natural" is regulated only in Maine and for meat products, manufacturers feel free to use the term loosely to create an image of wholesomeness, thereby cashing in on the demand for chemical-free food. The term can be controversial. As explained by Nikki and David Goldbeck, who have written extensively about natural foods: "Indeed, 'natural' cheeses contain artificial coloring and preservatives; 'natural' ice creams are not only loaded with sugar but may include such untraditional ingredients as vegetable gum and mono- and diglycerides; 'natural' breads are often made of refined white flour and are fortified with synthetic nutrients; some 'natural' cereals are more highly sweetened than processed varieties; foods that are 'naturally flavored' may also contain artificial flavoring, preservatives, thickeners, and colorants. Even margarine, a totally fabricated product, has been described as 'natural' by some manufacturers."[2]

To eliminate such confusion, the Goldbecks prefer the term "wholefoods," which are "foods that are free of chemical additives and left in the whole, unprocessed state or processed as little as possible to render them suitable for eating." The Goldbecks describe their "wholefoods philosophy" as a reaction against the scientists' "oversimplistic cause-and-effect" approach to health problems and the food industry's "revolving fads of nutrients, additives, and the like." Their philosophy appeals to common-sense logic and evidence. They believe that by relying on wholefoods as much as possible, people will have the best chance of receiving all the "known, as well as the yet unknown nutrients." At the same time they avoid new synthetic chemicals with which the human digestive system has had little evolutionary experience.[3]

Michael Jacobson, executive director of the Center for Science in the Public Interest, does not like to stretch the meaning of the word "healthy" (he even prefers "healthful" as applied to food). He wants to apply the same kinds scientific tests to determine which foods are healthy foods as are used by the FDA to decide whether a drug is *safe* (non-toxic) and *effective at doing what the drug company claims it will do*.

Jacobson agrees with the Goldbecks on the importance of considering the health of producers and the environment, but argues that this is a separate issue from consumer safety and health. "Don't confuse the needs of the environment with the consumer's need for healthful food," he says.

Organic vs. Sustainable Farming

The term "sustainable" or "low-input" as applied to farming means "reduced use of purchased inputs, especially synthetically produced chemicals." Washington doesn't want to say "organic," in part because this term has greatly distressed the chemical industry lobby and in part because organic farming is a big leap for farmers hooked on regular use of synthetic pesticides. Indeed, with the proliferation of terms referring to different degrees of organic farming, a new term has been invented (by I. Garth Youngberg, whom we will introduce in the next section), "alternative agriculture,"[4] covering all the various moves away from conventional farming practices.

Growing Local Interest in "Sustainable" Farming.
According to a definition used by Stephen Viederman, president of a foundation that supports work on the issue, "sustainable" or "alternative" agriculture programs are simply broader terms for efforts to reduce the use of pesticides without necessarily achieving the purity required of fully organic farming.

By another definition used by USDA officials, "low-input" and "sustainable" agriculture programs seek to reduce *all* purchased inputs (e.g., by replacing purchased fertilizer by composted manure and uneaten plants), not just pesticides, for reasons that go beyond the hazards of putting toxic chemicals on food. Among other benefits, low-input agriculture is cheaper for the farmer, less hazardous to farm workers, healthier for the soil, and less likely to pollute regional groundwater.

Either way, sustainable agriculture is the grower's view of the objective of pesticide-free food. Not only are the people who eat food free of synthetic chemicals better off, but the earth is also better off. Synthetic fertilizers and pesticides cumulatively and rapidly *destroy the land's ability to produce* healthy food. That's why sustainable agriculture is considered by its adherents as the socially and inter-generationally responsible approach to agriculture. Defenders of farm chemicals note that natural farming practices can also be destructive and deplete the soil. True enough. Sustainable agriculture is not just the absence of synthetic chemicals; it is also the positive practice of soil maintenance.

In the late 1970s, motivated in part by the scarcity of oil earlier in the decade, the USDA was interested in the potential for reduced agricultural reliance on petrochemicals. With some interest in the subject on the part of President Carter, a strong supporting study was published by the USDA in 1980, the *Report and Recommendation on Organic Farming*.

In 1982, however, with the oil crisis deemed over, President Reagan's Agriculture Secretary, John Block, terminated the job title of the report's author, Garth Youngberg, and declared organic farming a "dead end."[5] Youngberg went on to found the influential Institute of Alternative Agriculture.

The reasons for a new interest in sustainable agriculture have to do only partly with increased consumer awareness of the hazards of chemicals and the growing interest in organic food. They also have to do with the farmers' own economics and environmental issues.

Motives for Shifting to Organic Farming. In the 1960s and 1970s a number of farms were started by individuals and groups who were concerned about the poisoning of the earth and the need to get back to a simpler life.

Some farming philosophies, such as Bio-Dynamic farming, are strongly motivated by a spiritual desire to respect the rhythms of the universe and of nature.

Commercial farmers, however, are motivated mainly by one thing in shifting to organic farming: *consumer demand*. California grape-grower Jack Pandol explains his initiation of organic farming on 110 of his acres: "If this is what people want, we're willing to give it to them." Growers and packers saw the serious damage to the sales and income of the apple industry in 1989 because of the Alar scare, and they don't want the same thing to happen to them.

Consumer demand doesn't necessarily originate in fear. Many restaurant chefs in the San Francisco area and elsewhere are demanding organically grown vegetables because they and their customers prefer the taste to that of chemically grown produce.

The growing demand for organic food is creating a demand for organic farmers, which has in turn spawned a sales force of private pest control advisers, who instruct farmers and supermarkets how to keep pesticides out of the food they sell. One such adviser is ProAg, which caters to the very large growers and has 50,000 acres of California farms under contract.

Another pest control adviser is the Oakland-based NutriClean, which has a program guaranteeing "no detectable residues." To the dismay of organic farmers in California, NutriClean also certifies growers who use nonorganic pesticides that don't leave residues. In response, NutriClean President Stanley Rhodes charges that organic growers use dangerous botanical pesticides and try to hide their use. We may be seeing an early skirmish in major wars of words among proponents of different organic labels in the 1990s. The battles will be waged with the education of consumers in mind; consumer decisions will decide who wins. They may also feed the demand for stronger certification and regulatory programs to ensure the purity of food.

Grassroots Origins/Foundation Support. During the mid-1980s, interest in sustainable agriculture was a grassroots matter, driven above all by (1) the financial problems of farmers and their interest in reducing the cost of their inputs, and (2) pollution of groundwater by chemical fertilizers and pesticides. The organic food movement played varying levels of importance.

Foundation support of sustainable agriculture projects ran at about $5 million a year in 1988–89. The largest donors were the Jessie Smith Noyes Foundation in New York City and the Northwest Area Foundation in St. Paul, Minn., followed by the Wallace Genetic Foundation and the Joyce Foundation in Chicago. The Rockefeller Brothers Fund has made grants to study the policy issues in this area.

So during the mid-1980s, the sustainable agriculture and organic food movement was kept flowing by an interplay among true believers, government actions and foundations. By 1989, organic agriculture was described as "on the verge of changing from a movement to an industry." Growers, distributors, retailers, governments, agricultural scientists and economists were increasingly "responding to consumer concerns about food safety by exploring organic agriculture."[6]

A Harris poll conducted at the end of 1988 found that of a random sample of adults, 84% would choose organic produce if given a choice and 49% would be willing to pay more for it.[7]

Flor Heden, vice president of Texas's Whole Foods Markets, the state's first certified-organic retailer-wholesaler, summed it up well in mid-1989. She crowed: "We are mainstream!"

Motives for Switching to Sustainable Agriculture. Sustainable agriculture got a scientific boost in September 1989 when the National Academy of Sciences produced a report that proposed to shift most of American agriculture to natural cultivation, and recommended that the USDA increase by a factor of ten (to $40 million) its spending for research on sustainable farming methods. The USDA welcomed the report, saying the "time was right" to consider such changes.[8] The USDA had already started in this direction in 1987 with its Low-Input/Sustainable Agriculture (LISA) program, a tiny Congress-initiated reversal of its historic emphasis on synthetic fertilizers and pesticides. The amount of funding of LISA, however, in comparison with the USDA's enormous budget dedicated to encouraging use of synthetic pesticides, prompted one participant in a late-1989 Washington conference to say: "LISA isn't even a drop in the bucket—it's a vapor."

LISA is not purist about its mission, in part as a gesture to the chemical industry lobby and in part because for some types of farming and in some areas of the country eliminating synthetic fertilizers and pesticides will take time and a lot of training. The thrust of LISA's message to farmers is to reduce inputs to the farm and waste from it—which means reducing chemical (and other) purchases and maximizing internal recycling practices such as composting. Same church as the organic movement, different pew (in the back, near the door).

One motive for sustainable agriculture is concern about the environment—above all, seepage of chemicals into groundwater and depletion of topsoil at a rate of three billion tons a year in 1982.[9] Although usage of toxic chemicals has declined since 1982, their toxicity levels have risen.

In Chapter 4 we saw how pesticides have made their way into our food and water. Farmers are being forced to review their practices with an eye to maintaining the productivity of their earth and the purity of their water. For farmers not inherently concerned about such environmental damage, government regulations—at the county, state and federal levels—are capturing their attention. In Iowa, groundwater pollution was clearly the primary motivating force in the passage of several recent laws relating to use of pesticides on farms.

The ending of traditional crop rotation and complementary-crop planting, coupled with the heavy use of irrigation, has also depleted farmland resources and contributed to soil erosion. An estimated 75 percent of U.S. topsoil, which took billions of years to form, has been lost since the arrival of Columbus—most of it during the half-century since the Depression. As a result, almost one-third of U.S. cropland is showing a steady and serious decline in productivity.[10]

Another motive for farmers is their personal safety and that of their workers. Each year, pesticides poison some 45,000 individuals, sending 3,000 to the hospital and killing 200.[11] These are acute effects that hint at the enormous long-term cumulative impact of pesticides on farmers and other Americans.

Farmers are also paying attention to organic farming methods because of a loss of confidence in the availability, cost, and effectiveness of chemicals. Costs are high in part because it may cost as much as $50 million to bring a new chemical to market, and then the product must undergo time-consuming and unpredictable government scrutiny. Bruce Beretta, a McFarland, Calif., almond grower who is moving toward organic practices, says simply: "We did it for economics."

Availability is a problem because companies making chemicals for small crops may be unable to afford the cost of developing or re-registering a product. For example, the Uniroyal Chemical Company in October 1989 confirmed that it was ending production of Alar in the United States (it may still be produced in Elmira, Ontario). The company said it had asked the EPA to cancel its registration of the chemical because environmentalists and apple growers had successfully lobbied to have Alar withdrawn from the U.S. market, and the overseas market was too small to sustain its production.[12] Since World War II, pesticide use has increased ten-fold, yet loss of crops to insects has doubled.

One reason for the apparent loss in effectiveness of pesticides is that broad-spectrum toxic chemicals are killing off natural predators that used to keep pests in check.[13]

Another reason is that the target populations of these chemicals has become resistant to them. Driscoll Strawberries, in Watsonville, Calif., had to seek organic insect control methods because the two-spotted spider mite had become resistant to one of the insecticides in use against it, and at the same time an alternative chemical was pulled off the market. Similarly David Brown, a California orange grower for Sunkist, says he has been using more chemicals every year with no apparent diminution in the pest population; he is moving toward organic methods on his own, while the cooperative he works with has created a group to look at alternatives to chemical pesticides.

Recent Trends. As Table 5-1 shows, the quantity of farm inputs fell sharply between 1980 and 1986, in part because the farm economy was depressed and farmers just weren't prepared to pay as much for inputs.

Use of farm chemicals peaked in 1981 with an index of 129 (i.e., the amount of chemicals used was 29 percent higher in 1981 than in it was in 1977, the base year for the index).

The sharpest increase in farm inputs between 1960 and 1981 was in use of farm chemicals, from 32 to 129. The sharpest decreases in farm inputs between 1981 and 1986 were in use of farm chemicals, from 129 to 109, and use of machinery and power. The financial difficulties of farmers clearly played a part in reduced purchase of inputs. But something else was afoot—what we would have to describe as a reexamination of some of the assumptions on which the buildup in inputs were based.

Our Crazy Laws

Indeed, the assumptions underlying farm purchases of inputs were heavily influenced by the Federal Government.

Table 5-1
Quantity of Farm Inputs, 1977=100

	1960	1980	1986
Total, all inputs	99	103	87
Farm labor	177	96	80
Farm real estate	103	103	93
Machinery and power	83	101	76
Farm chemicals	32	123	109
Feed, seed, breed	77	114	102
Taxes and interest	95	100	91
Miscellaneous	77	96	110

Source: *Statistical Abstract of the U.S.: 1989*, 109th ed., Table 1106, p. 640.

As consumers, we should know that some of the most anti-consumer legislation concocted in Washington, D.C. has been farm programs. Efforts to shelter farmers from price changes have been the object of derision in elementary economics courses. As we shall see, many farm programs don't help farmers and some haven't helped anyone at all.

How USDA Pressures Promote Petrochemicals. Since World War II, USDA and Extension Service experts have been encouraging farmers—through subsidized educational and incentive programs, including requirements for Federal financing—to exchange their agricultural diversity for larger farms producing only two or three crops a year, with the help of petroleum-derived fertilizers and pesticides.

Most U.S. cropland—70 percent—is enrolled in a USDA commodity program (i.e., a program by which the USDA subsidizes production or non-production). A farmer deciding to rotate into a soil-building crop, in place of the corn previously grown, could lose commodity program benefits for five years. The USDA's "base acreage" system rewards farmers for maximum yields per acre—instead of maximum revenue from produce sales in the marketplace, which would be much more favorable to organic farming. This system discourages not only crop rotation and diversification, traditional ways of helping the soil rejuvenate itself, but mixed crop-livestock operations and reduced application of fertilizer and pesticides.[14]

So, of the 25 states with the most farms, only one, Ohio, showed an increase from 1988 to 1989. The size of the average farm grew in one year from 453 to 456 acres, reflecting both the farm crisis that gripped most of the country and the continued trend toward concentration. Between 1982 and 1989 the number of U.S. farms dropped from 2.4 million to fewer than 2.2 million.

New USDA programs—notably ATTRA and, as we shall discuss, LISA, both listed in the directory at the end of this chapter—work toward reducing the amount of pesticides and other inputs on farms. But these programs are miniscule compared to the impact of the major USDA programs.

Recent Developments in U.S. Farm Laws. Federal and state officials have been slow to show concern about the impact of growing methods on the quality of American food. The overall thrust of the USDA's activities has been toward greater use of toxic farm chemicals. The EPA's effectiveness may be summed up by its handling of Alar in 1986, when it knew of the chemical's hazards and still referred the issue to a committee of experts tied to the chemical industry.

Similarly, cosmetic standards for fruit are set by Federal and state governments and producer trade associations. These standards place heavy pressure on farmers to use high levels of pesticides, says the California Public Interest Research Group.[15] The government-mandated prettiness of the fruit forces farmers to use about twice the volume of pesticides that would otherwise be needed, keeps supply down, and pushes up consumer prices.

This thrust of Federal and state policies was slowed dramatically in the latter half of the 1980s. Garth Youngberg, the previously mentioned participant in the process, cites three crucial developments: (1) Prices for commodities dropped, putting a squeeze on farmers, who began to question the need for their heavy investments in fertilizers and petrochemical pesticides; (2) Federal officials wondered why the country was spending $30 billion a year on agricultural subsidies to promote intensive farming and superannuate 160 million of the nation's 380 million farming acres; (3) Environmental concerns were returning to the forefront of the national consciousness.

So Congress in 1985 overrode chemical-industry opposition to Federal support of organic or low-input farming issues. The first small initiative—the Low-Input/Sustainable Agriculture (LISA) program—was authorized in 1985 and was funded to start in 1987. The Agriculture Department had in 1982 rejected Carter-era sustainable agriculture initiatives, but Congress was impressed by grass-roots activity in this direction.[16] Elements of the turnaround included a surge of public concern among Americans about their health, a strong Surgeon General, some activist farmers, and a sequence of frightening news stories showing the dangers of chemicals in food and water.

Federal legislation is the most appropriate way to handle the food industry because most of the food we eat travels through several states on its way to the consumer. State laws are better than nothing, but sooner or later it will become clear that it is too much to expect consumers to keep track of the vagaries of the food labeling laws in 50 states. Demand is growing for national labeling and certification standards.

In Congress, as this book goes to press, the 1990 Farm Bill promises to expands the low-input sustainable agriculture program.

Even more important a signal for the future is that Senator Patrick J. Leahy (D-VT), Chairman of the Senate Agriculture, Nutrition and Forestry Committee, in late 1989 introduced S. 1896, a bill that would encourage organic farming. The bill is discussed in the next section.

How Organic?

Because of the widespread use of pesticides and the fact that traces linger in the soil for years, no food can be assumed to be pesticide-free even if no pesticides were used to produce it. Chemical lab tests are sensitive and usually pick up some levels of pesticides, so the goal of pesticide-free food is elusive. But the goal of production without toxic pesticides is a reasonable one.

Transitional steps must be taken toward sustainable farming methods. Think, therefore, of certified organic farming—meaning no addition of synthetic chemicals during the growing periods—as an *objective*, with certain milestones along the way.

Reduction in use of synthetic chemicals is the first step (usually accompanied by increased recycling of farm by-products). This is, however, a direction rather than an achievement measurable by the consumer. Consumers will want to know: "Is this product produced without synthetic pesticides, or not?" During the transitional period, it is hard to know, because pesticide residues remain from prior years, making monitoring difficult. But the consumer is supporting organic farming and healthy food in the larger sense by purchasing from farmers who are making a best effort to reduce their use of chemicals.

Transitional Organic. This label can be misleading, because it can range from a farm where no synthetic fertilizers or pesticides are used but the grower is complying with the three-year waiting period (during which time the soil is expected to lose a sufficient amount of its chemical residues) to a farm that has made only marginal reductions in the use of chemicals.

Farmers want a Transitional Organic label because it means they can sell right away—not at the same price that organic produce commands, but at a higher price than conventional produce. Otherwise they have to wait three or four years before they can get a return on their investment in organic farming.

Consumers may choose not to buy transitional organic products on the reasonable supposition that policing a farm that is just starting to go organic is difficult. Faced with a pest that threatens to destroy a crop, the farmer may be tempted to rescue it with an emergency spraying, and then not report it; any residues found in the food could be attributed to leftover pesticides from prior years. A farmer established in the organic business would be less likely to need emergency spraying and would be more likely to be found out if he did resort to it.

On the other hand, consumers should consider carefully the importance of buying transitional organic food because of the value of this gesture in supporting transitional farmers and recognizing their efforts. The risk from transitional organic food is in any case presumably less than from food without any regular pesticide monitoring, i.e. most of our food.

Certified Organic. Being certified organic is the best way for a farmer to convince a consumer that synthetic chemicals have not been used during the growing of the produce being sold. The oldest of the certification programs active in the United States is the Demeter label, which certifies that the farmer has been following the Bio-Dynamic farming methods promoted in 1924 by Rudolf

Steiner. The major groups are included in the listing at the end of this chapter.

Certification groups are often interested in more than providing organic food to the public or tapping a promising market. Often deeper philosophical bases underlie their promotion of organic practices. The membership of the Natural Organic Farmers Association, for example, showed a broad spectrum of primary concerns at their 1989 summer conference in Williamstown, Mass. Such issues as "basic organic gardening," "composting for farms," and "Integrated Pest Management" were reviewed at seminars that also included in-depth discussions with the agricultural commissioners or their surrogates in seven northeastern states. However, much of the discussion focused on the preservation of the family farm. Indeed, most conference participants argued that sustainable agriculture is impossible under any other system.

A National Organic Logo? As mentioned above, Sen. Patrick J. Leahy (D-Vt.) in November 1989 introduced a bill that would "promote the production of organically produced foods by establishing a national standard for organically produced products."

Titled the *Organic Foods Act of 1989*, S. 1896, the bill requires the Secretary of Agriculture to develop a list of non-toxic pesticides that would be acceptable for organic farmers to use, with the advice of a National Organics Board composed of organic farmers and specialists.

The bill calls for a national organic label. The requirement would be three years non-use of toxic pesticides for plant commodities, or use of organic feed for livestock for a minimum of the final 60 percent of the animals' slaughter weight.

While a national organic logo would have great significance for the interstate organic market, it would not necessarily supersede the state certification programs. The national standard, if enacted, would most likely be less stringent than the standards of some states. The state standards would then take on the character of an extra level of consumer assurance.

State Laws Favoring Organic or Sustainable Agriculture. States support sustainable agriculture in many ways. The most important things they do are to:

1. Tax Farm Chemicals. Iowa's 1987 Groundwater Protection Act taxes synthetic fertilizers and pesticides and uses the revenue for programs to reduce the use of such chemicals. The Act raised pesticide registration fees, imposed a 0.1 percent pesticide sales tax and a $.75/ton tax on anhydrous ammonia. Defenders of farm chemicals argue that natural fertilizers also contaminate the groundwater.

2. Earmark Oil Overcharge Funds. Since 1982, Exxon and other oil companies have been paying money to the states through the U.S. Department of Energy to settle Federal prosecution for violating Federal oil price laws. Several states, including Iowa, Minnesota and Wisconsin, have earmarked the money for programs to reduce farm use of chemicals.

3. Adopt or Certify Organic Standards. In 1980, only California and two other states had laws regulating organic agriculture. However, as of October 1989, 17 states had adopted regulations defining what "organic," "certified organic," or "transitional organic" should mean on a label: California, Colorado, Iowa, Maine, Massachusetts, Minnesota, Montana, Nebraska, New Hampshire, North Dakota, Ohio, Oregon, South Dakota, Texas, Vermont, Washington, and Wisconsin (details on each state's laws are provided at the end of this chapter).

In addition to setting standards, five states (Minnesota, New Hampshire, Texas, Washington and Vermont) employ staff to monitor compliance, and other states (such as Iowa, Kansas, Oklahoma and Wisconsin) are weighing doing so.

Organic food standards have been extended in some states to include what is sometimes called organically raised meat or poultry, meaning cattle or fowl that are raised (1) primarily on natural vegetation and not on processed feed (which is sometimes found to include not only chemicals but also ground-up animal parts), (2) without the use of antibiotics except to treat illness, (3) without the use of growth-inducing hormones.

Not all certifications for poison-free farming necessarily relate to toxic chemicals. For example, it would be desirable to require handling of peanuts to minimize the potential for aflatoxins. To deal with such possibilities, Wyoming is considering a law that would give the state's agriculture department powers to set standards for any commodity and certify that these standards are being met by a particular farmer.

4. Certify Independent Soil Testers. Private soil testers tend to accompany their reports with recommendations for commercial fertilizers with which they have ties; they do not describe sustainable alternatives. Iowa and Minnesota offer to certify independent labs that are not tied to sale of chemicals.

5. Finance Alternative Farms. Several states have established low-interest loan funds for small alternative farms. Minnesota in 1988 created a $1 million revolving fund for loans of up to $15,000 for this purpose, at an interest rate of 6 percent. Texas funds are deposited in low-interest-bearing accounts with banks that under a "linked deposit" system promise to relend the funds to alternative farmers at a low interest rate.

6. Provide Alternative Farming Education. Programs of education in alternative farming methods take two main forms. A few land-grant universities are offering courses and degrees in the area. The University of California at Santa Cruz offers a good four-year course and a Ph.D. program in agroecology and sustainable agriculture. The University of Maine at Orono also has a good four-year program. It and the University of Vermont offer undergraduate degrees in sustainable agriculture. Other good programs are offered by Ohio State and Iowa State (through its Leopold Institute). The other form is direct education of farmers. Many state agriculture departments provide information to farmers on low-input farming techniques. Programs of this kind are in place in California, Iowa, Minnesota, Texas and Wisconsin, and are under consideration in Ohio.

7. Promote Composting. Massachusetts is launching a program to promote use of compost in farms and gardens. The program first identifies compost appropriate for farm use that would otherwise go to landfills. It then redirects this compost to farms.

8. Offer Marketing Assistance. Some states help farmers market organic produce. Wyoming marketed a branded Lean Beef in San Francisco to determine the degree of consumer demand for beef from cattle that were hormone-free, grass-fed and spared antibiotics unless sick. (The useful result of the trial was that over 30 percent of consumers surveyed were willing to pay 25 percent more for such beef, and the overall demand for beef in the participating stores rose 50 percent.)

New York and Vermont have supported the establishment of marketing cooperatives. Texas is working with supermarkets to persuade them to sell Texas-certified organic food. Texas and Colorado have encouraged farmers to form associations of organic food growers. Since sale of food locally reduces the need for chemicals and other processing to extend food life, many states support farmers' markets. California, Massachusetts, and Texas have extensive programs to support local sale of farm produce. Other states like Connecticut produce lists of farmers' markets.[17]

Prospects for Organic Farming

Transitional Problems. Experts think the transition from heavy use of synthetic chemicals will take many years and will require a substantial change in public attitudes toward food and farming. For example, the USDA programs that discourage diversification are still in place.

Even in California, the nation's leader in growing organic food, the trend is taking time. The number of organic farms is growing rapidly, as we discuss below, but many of these farms are necessarily small (ten acres or so; five a minimum) because organic farming is labor-intensive.

Apart from attitude and legislative obstacles, the process will take years for two practical reasons.

First, weaning a farm from pesticides takes time because chlorinated hydrocarbons like DDT have been shown to remain in the soil for many years, and the same pattern is feared for other pesticides. In addition to the 1,500 fully organic farms in California, many others are in transition to organic status. California has a short transitional period (one year; most certification programs require three years), but even so the transition is difficult. A compromise approach is to follow the Integrated Pest Management philosophy, i.e., using pesticides only as a last resort. This appeals to large growers and food processors, perhaps for the same reason that it is problematic for consumers. It can be a slow, gradual process that is hard to monitor because it is based on intentions and best efforts, not results.

Second, certain regions of the United States like California are relatively resistant to pests because they have a dry climate. A moist climate like Florida is a different matter. Some crops might not be cultivable there, and in the southeast generally, using organic methods. Stricter regulation of pesticides in this part of the country might mean some fruits and vegetables would not be growable there any more. This would pose national economic adjustment problems because Florida alone produces half the nation's winter vegetables. However, some organic farms producing fruits and vegetables do thrive in Florida and elsewhere in the southeast, and their savings in pesticides present a strong motivation to go organic. "Even now, the cost of pesticides is killing farmers there," says Charles Benbrook, staff director for the National Academy of Sciences report on use of chemicals in agriculture.

Long-Term Viability of Organic Farming. Some argue that organic farming is not a viable route to the future, that the productivity of American farms is inextricably linked to the use of chemicals. In our survey of large food producers and supermarkets, we got the impression that their executives think the organic farm movement is a hangover from the 1960s.

Others, however, believe that continued pesticide use at current levels is dangerous to consumers and will affect the long-term viability of American farms. The National Academy of Sciences is in this camp. Charles Benbrook, cited above as director of the staff that helped prepare the Academy's report on pesticides, concludes: "You don't need any of the worst chemicals."

Virtually all surveyed farmers who use organic methods say they improve the fertility of the soil and reduce the risk to farmers themselves. Even farmers not committed to organic methods agree.[18]

Studies of sustainable agriculture methods conclude that they are workable, but that they require skills that conventional farmers may not have. "There is nothing magical about sustainable agriculture . . . that guarantees its success, even in good times. And in bad times, many regenerative farms fail along with their conventional chemical-intensive cousins. It takes excellent management skills to succeed in any style of farming, but it seems that sustainable agriculture is more of a challenge. . . . Some [sustainable] farmers report somewhat lower yields than their neighbors, but the yield sacrifice is frequently more than offset by cost reductions."[19]

Promising New Trends. Three promising trends offer hope that the movement toward larger farms and increased use of chemicals will be reversed. One is that the figures maintained by the USDA do not take into account gardeners, people who grow food almost entirely for their own use, usually on an acre or less. An intermediate category of "market gardeners" consists of people who grow primarily for their own use or as a hobby but end up with substantial extra crops that they sell in the marketplace; these farm-gardens are in the 1-to-5 acre range depending on crops and region (commercial growers tend to have at least five acres). Judging from the increased public interest in organic food and the popularity of organic farming fairs and farmers markets, we may see a resurgence of gardening by individuals who want to get back in touch with where their food comes from.

Second, in the state with the largest amount of fruit-and-vegetable farming, California, we see a counter-trend to farm consolidation and increased chemical use. In this state, which produces over half (about 53 percent) of all the vegetables grown in the United States, and over two-fifths (42 percent) of its fruits and nuts, the number of organic farms *doubled* from 1988 to 1989, to 1,500.[20]

This is still only a small fraction, 1.8 percent, of the 84,000 farms in California, and probably an even smaller fraction of the farms' output, since organic farms tend to be smaller than the average U.S. farm. However, it is a trend that is likely to continue.

Finally, increased local interest in organic farming and certification in other states suggests that the California experience is not isolated.

How to Identify Organic Produce

In March 1989, the Alar (apple) and Chilean grape scares contributed to making more Americans conscious of food safety. The immediate reaction of many was to avoid suspect food and seek organic food. Organic food vendors (mostly small stores) were overrun, because the supply is small—even in California, the vanguard state of the natural foods industry, only 1 percent of the produce is organically grown.

Increasing the supply of organic food without diluting its quality, or adding an unacceptable premium to its price, has become a pressing concern. The problem is giving the consumer some confidence in the product. Government agencies inspect many agricultural products, but generally do not measure their pesticide content, so they have not been able to attest to the organic purity of produce. Indeed, the cost of pesticide testing and the near-impossibility of detecting some pesticides make it impossible to be sure of their absence.

A retail store can serve as a source of consumer confidence, and should want to know what pesticides, if any, were used on the produce it sells. But most stores lack the resources for proper inquiry. Organic/natural food retailers have a special responsibility to know who their suppliers are. The retail stores we list in Chapter 10 include some outstanding ones, worth a special trip.

It comes down to knowing where food comes from and relying on the practices of the grower-producer. Most of the hundreds of restaurants and stores that responded to our surveys say they rely on the assurances of the growers and distributors. This is fair enough in a rural area if the farmer is nearby and known to the store or restaurant, but such assurances are not enough for food labeled "organic" that is purchased in an urban area or at a distance from the grower.

How Can Consumers Identify Organic Food? The increasing demand for organic food requires a system for identifying it; thus the United States desperately needs national standards for organic food, along the lines of Senator Leahy's bill, described above. At present, food is defined in different ways by those states regulating food la-

beling or organic certification, and by private certifying agencies. To support Senator Leahy's bill or further initiatives, contact him at the address listed at the end of this chapter alphabetically under U.S. Congress.

In 1973 Oregon became the first state to pass laws that define "organic" and impose penalties for mislabeling. California followed in 1979 and its law has served as a national model, although it is sometimes criticized as insufficiently rigorous.

Other states define "certified organic" and impose penalties for mislabeling food. For example, Texas does not define "organic" (though it does define "certified organic"); "organic" therefore means whatever the producer wants it to mean. Unless the label says "*certified* organic" and provides the name and logo of the certifying agency, the consumer is out of luck. We'll return to this later in the chapter.

Organic Labeling Fraud. Sad to report, some products are labeled as organically grown when they are not. Farms that practice sustainable agriculture account for only a half-million to a million acres,[21] about 1 percent of all farming acreage in the U.S. Until the supply of organic produce catches up with the demand, opportunities for fraud will continue to tempt some farmers and distributors.

Stories of fraudulent labeling abound. It's like the legendary "pâté d'alouette" that was described as 50% lark, 50% pork—meaning: one lark for every pig. A processed food might be labeled "organic" even if only some of the ingredients in it are organically grown. Some specific examples:

- Chilean grapes were recalled by importer Jack Pandol of Delano, Calif., after the cyanide scare in March 1989. Pandol says a Texas supermarket chain had labeled many of its grapes "organic" even though Chile grows no organic grapes. Under the 1989 Texas law the supermarket chain did nothing illegal.

- Bonner Packing Co. of Fresno, Calif., sells raisins certified as organically grown by two independent certification agencies, Farm Verified Organic and the Organic Crop Improvement Association. Christopher Steggall, a field representative for Bonner, recently purchased by Dole (itself owned by Castle & Cooke, which, alas, by one rating system has the dubious distinction of being America's least socially responsible food company[22]), says he receives calls "all the time" from growers claiming to have organically grown raisins. However, when he asks for soil samples, the growers back off.[23]

- One California farmer was discovered buying up second-rate farm products cheap and reselling them as organic at a premium.

- An East Coast grower told us about another farmer whose peach crop was damaged by a hail storm. To try to cut his losses he raised the prices and tried to sell the scarred fruit as organic.

- A Southern California carrot packer, Pacific Foods

(not to be confused with the Pacific Gardens label of a highly responsible organization, Associated Cooperatives, also in California), labeled carrots as organic when they were not. The organic food industry (not the state) identified the fraud and, with the help of the media, pressured the state to stop it.[24]

Look for Organic Farmers' Self-Identification. Legitimate organic growers have an interest in making it clear to consumers that they are maintaining standards, and many of them have cooperated in forming farmer-owned certification groups. At least one group (Farm Verified Organic) was created by food processors and has maintained a high level of credibility. Some states, as we shall see, have laws for identifying and certifying organic farmers.

In the United States, new certification groups turn for guidance to the custodian of standards, the Organic Foods Production Association of North America. Other highly influential certification organizations are *California Certified Organic Farmers, Demeter, Farm Verified Organic, Natural Organic Farmers Association*, and the *Organic Crop Improvement Association*—all listed in the directory at the end of this chapter.

The most influential state standard for "organic" is probably California's Health and Safety Code Section 26569.11 (see the directory, under California), both because California exports so much produce and because the law was imitated in other states. Be warned that state monitoring of compliance with Section 26569.11 is weak (see Dr. Sheneman's comments under the California entry under Consumer Assistance Agencies in Chapter 6); most malefactors are brought to justice by competitors. Outside of California, use of the standard on shipments to other states borders on fraudulence.

Documented Organic. Documentation means a written record that includes a grower's field locations, their histories, growing practices and so forth. The field locations are important because of airborne drift or waterborne runoff of pesticides from a neigboring farm. The documentation should show what kind of farming is done on all borders. The information should show how long the farmer has farmed each field without pesticides. The issue is whether the fields have been free of pesticide use for longer than the transition period, which is usually one to three years before planting. The residues of DDT, which was banned effective at the beginning of 1973, have been found to linger indefinitely. The idea behind a transition period to organic growing is to minimize the residual pesticides from prior years' sprayings. The growing procedures should show what forms of pest control were used.

Being documented is a pro-consumer, inexpensive step for growers who are eager to sell their products as organic but are unable or do not wish to be certified (which would be the best assurance for the consumer).

A situation that could be abused is one in which the grower is maintaining only a portion of production as organic. The grower must document which parts of the farm are organic and how they are protected from pesticides in use on the rest of the farm.

To help retailers get documentation on growers, a valuable service collects the information, attests that it is on file, and summarizes it for users such as retail stores. This is Merchandising Organic Foods, listed alphabetically at the end of this chapter. Stuart Fishman, who founded the company, has developed a useful documentation form that he uses to survey growers.

Documented and Verified Organic. Once growers document their farming practices, the next step is to have them evaluated and verified. Consultants, private agencies or government agencies may provide this service.

Verified No Detectable Pesticide Residues. Several supermarket chains, including Sacramento-based Raley's and northeastern Stop & Shop, have brought in NutriClean to check their produce for detectable levels of pesticide residues. The farms that supply such produce may or may not be organic.

The president of NutriClean, Stanley Rhodes, says testing for pesticides makes it possible for supermarkets to offer consumers produce that is free of detectable residues of 14 pesticides suspected of causing cancer. Growers may be able to pass NutriClean's standards without incurring the expense or trouble of organic farming methods.[25]

Some organic farmers are suspicious of what seems to be a short-cut to consumer protection. Others see it as a possibly helpful adjunct to the system.

Checking on Post-Harvest Handling

Organic food may be pristine when it leaves the farm, but not when it goes into your shopping cart. It is worth paying some attention to what happens when food goes from farm to store.

Standards for Post-Harvest Food Handling. American consumers also need a set of standards for food handling and processing—what happens to food *after* it is harvested. Even "organically grown" food may have synthetic chemicals added to delay spoilage or improve its appearance.

Labeling laws should require the final product to disclose any unhealthy additives. Federal law requires that shipping containers identify post-harvest chemicals and waxes that seal them in the produce, but stores discard the containers and (contrary to law) usually don't pass on the information to shoppers.

Starting in 1990, Maine requires every store that sells treated produce to display a sign saying: "Produce in this store may have been treated after harvest with one or more post-harvest chemicals." Within two days of a request, any shopper must be told what chemicals were used. Untreated produce must also be identified. This path-breaking disclosure requirement was the work of the Maine Organic Farmers and Gardeners Association.

Distribution Standards. Distribution standards relate to maintaining the freshness of the product. Some supermarkets that advertise produce as organic have been reported to fumigate the produce area with chemicals overnight, on a regular schedule, to prevent the intrusion of flying or crawling insects. They are even said to spray the produce area directly with insecticide. The Texas Department of Agriculture is one of the first agencies to certify retailers as well as farmers and distributors. Unless retailers are monitored, organic food could be sprayed at the last link in the chain.

Biological Pest Control (Publications and Sources)

The references in this section are restricted to organizations and books that focus fairly narrowly on biological (i.e., without synthetic chemicals) pest control.

Bio-Integral Resource Center, P.O. Box 7414, Berkeley, CA 94707. Publishes quarterly newsletter with information on pests and how to control them with minimal use of toxic chemicals.

Biological Urban Gardening Services (BUGS), P.O. Box 76, Citrus Heights, CA 95610. (916) 726-5377. Steven Zien. Educates urban gardeners in the use of natural pesticides and techniques for maintaining healthy plants. $10/year membership includes quarterly newsletter.

Birnes, Nancy, *Cheaper & Better* (Harper & Row, 10 East 53rd Street, New York, NY 10022). One chapter includes directions for homemade, plant-derived, safe pest control mixtures.

Bountiful Gardens Ecology Action, 5798 Ridgewood Road, Willits, CA 95490. Sells natural pesticides.

Johnny's Selected Seeds, Foss Hill Road, Albion, ME 04910. Sells biological and botanical insecticides.

National Coalition Against the Misuse of Pesticides (NCAMP), 530 7th Street, S.E., Washington, DC 20003. (202)-543-5450. A $20 membership includes the organization's quarterly newsletter.

Natural Gardening Research Center, P.O. Box 149, Sunman, IN 47041. Natural pest control products.

Nichols Garden Nursery, 1198 Pacific, Albany, OR 97321. Sells pyrethrum powder, a non-toxic pest control product.

Organic Gardening Magazine (Rodale Press, 33 East Minor Street, Emmaus, PA 18098). This venerable monthly was promoting organic methods when they were much less fashionable. It's good value at $13.97/year.

Rodale's Garden Insect, Disease, and Weed Identification Guide (Rodale Press, 1989). Identifies over 200 garden pests and ways to control them organically. 325 pp., $16.95.

Yepson, R., Jr., *Rodale's Encyclopedia of Natural Insect & Disease Control* (Rodale Press, 1989). Latest organic controls for defending plants from their natural enemies. 496 pp., $24.95.

Farm Certification and Education (Directory of Agencies and Groups)

This section, through the end of this chapter, covers agencies and groups devoted to the certification and education of organic farmers, and to labeling of farm products for consumers. The organizations are broadly dedicated to the advancement of organic farming through certification, education, regulation and research. Certain groups of organic food growers have conferred the right to use their logo (symbol) on products that have been certified as conforming to their guidelines. These groups are *italicized* in the list below. Their logos, used on produce farmed according to their standards, are shown.

We have also included governmental and educational groups because from state to state the role that governmental agencies and private associations play overlaps considerably. State laws often give teeth to privately generated organic farming standards by referring to them in legislation prescribing labeling practices and prohibiting certain farming methods. The Federal Government, through the EPA, FDA and USDA, also has had something to say about such practices, and with Congressional interest should play a larger role in the coming years.[26]

Meanwhile, the expertise in organic farming is spread out around the country. A good start in identifying such expertise is to get the list of organizations that have received USDA sustainable farming research money, the LISA grant recipients. This list is available free from Neill Schaller at LISA (see under "L" in the alphabetical directory at the end of this chapter.)

We have appended a ♥ or a ♦ to some entries based on our personal experience with or third-party testimony to the agency or business. These are less scientifically applied than in Chapter 10, where they are based on written questionnaires; we offer them to be helpful to the reader and in the spirit of humility, not as our or anyone else's last word.

♥ means **impressive personal contact,** whether through a visit or on the phone, that convinced us that the people we spoke with had an unusual level of commitment to the consumer of organic food—or to farming methods that are of direct importance to the consumer.

♦ means **enthusiastic third-party testimony,** usually from several sources, to such commitment. When we heard such enthusiasm from five or more sources we attached a second ♦.

Agrisystems International, 125 West Seventh Street, Wind Gap, PA 18091. (215) 863-6700. Tom Harding. Consultant to farmers on transition to organic methods. Played a significant role in creation of the Organic Crop Improvement Association.

Alabama has no certification or labeling law and we are unaware of any certification organizations active in the state.

Alaska Department of Natural Resources, Division of Agriculture, 3700 Airport Way, Fairbanks, AK 99709. (907) 745-7200. Mark Weaver, Director. Alaska has no certification program, but organic growers in the state can be documented by various agencies. The Division of Agriculture publishes a *Food & Farm Products Directory* which in 1988 starred the entries for organic growers.

Alternative Energy Resources Organization, 44 N. Last Chance Gulch, No. 9, Helena, MT 59601. (406) 443-7272. Al Kurki, Executive Director. Regional clearinghouse on organic farming. Quarterly magazine available for $15/year.♦

Americans for Safe Food, 1501 16th Street, N.W., Washington, DC 20036. (202) 332-9110. Roger Blobaum. Coalition of over 80 groups working to increase the availability of safer food. Tracks state organic food certification and labeling laws. Membership is free and includes quarterly newsletter. Has published Dan Howell, *Organic Agriculture: What the States are Doing,* available for $3. ASF is a project of the Center for Science in the Public Interest (CSPI), at the same address. (See also the entry for ASF in Chapter 4 and for CSPI in Chapter 3.)♥♦

Appropriate Technology Transfer for Rural Areas (ATTRA), P.O. Box 3657, Fayetteville, AR 72702. (501) 575-7570. Toll-free (800) 346-9140. Information service designed for farmers and advisers on organic farming, operated by the National Center for Appropriate Technology under a grant from the U.S. Department of Agriculture, which received an appropriation of under $1 million in FY 1989 for this purpose. Can provide farmers the latest information on the fast-changing certification and labeling laws in different states.♥

Arizona has no certification or labeling law. Organic growers in the state tend to seek documentation from private agencies and often look to California for standards.

Arkansas farmers are mostly certified by the Ozark Organic Growers Association, listed next. The state puts out a list for consumers of growers that sell directly to the public and farmers' markets. The organic growers listed in the publication are few and far between, but consumers have a shot at finding organic produce at the farmers' markets listed at the end of the directory. Write to University Extension, Lincoln University, 900 Moreau Drive, Jefferson City, MO 65101 for a copy.

Arkansas: *Ozark Organic Growers Association,* HCR 72, Box 34, Parthenon, AR 72666. (501) 446-5783. Nonprofit marketing cooperative serving about 130 small-farmer members in Arkansas, Missouri and Oklahoma. Certifies farms and helps market their products. This aggressively strict certification group has been prepared to deny certification to a farmer for having a can of the herbicide Roundup on his farm (it was, he said, for killing weeds in the parking lot; OOGA said no way).♦

Bio-Dynamic Farming and Gardening Association, Inc., P.O. Box 550, Kimberton, PA 19442. (215) 327-2420 or (215) 935-7797. Roderick Shouldice, Administrative Director. Provides technical help for those engaged in biodynamic farming, which is a highly structured and spiritually oriented organic farming movement promoted by Rudolf Steiner and his followers. The Asso-

ciation's membership dues are $20/year, which includes its quarterly magazine. The Association has 1,000 members, 250 of whom are farmers. Bio-Dynamic farmers and their products are certified under the Demeter (see below) label.♥

California Action Network, P.O. Box 464, Davis, CA 95617. (916) 756-8518. Lobbying organization, works for and can take a lot of credit for better California laws relating to farming standards. Organized forums for California organic food sellers to discuss AB 2012, and used the grass roots information to improve the bill. Publishes its *Organic Wholesalers Directory and Yearbook,* selling for $22.♥♦♦

California Certified Organic Farmers (CCOF), P.O. Box 8136, Santa Cruz, CA 95061. (408) 423-2263. Bob Scowcroft, Executive Director. Strong certification and educational organization working closely with its 14 active chapters. Its seven paid staff members and 200 serious volunteers monitor 525 organic farmers. CCOF visits each certified farm an average of twice a year—ranging from a minimum of once a year to a maximum of seven times in a year. "A Sunday morning surprise visit gets respect," says Scowcroft. CCOF is recovering from the October 1989 earthquake, which destroyed its offices (miraculously, all certification records survived). It is seeking to become a chapter of the Organic Crop Improvement Association (see below) and to develop an online electronic bulletin board to permit consumers to check immediately on the history and status of all CCOF-certified grower crops. CCOF's one-year transitional period will go to three years by 1992. Publishes a thorough *Certification Handbook* which includes a "List of Permitted and Prohibited Materials." Individual membership is $15/year, which covers a quarterly newsletter.♥♦♦

California: Committee for Sustainable Agriculture, P.O. Box 1300, Colfax, CA 95713. (916) 346-2777. Otis Wollan, Executive Director. Sponsors annual Ecological Farming Conference. Advocates stronger organic farming laws. Publishes weekly market report for produce grown or sold in California, *OMNIS* (sample copy available for $1 plus stamped self-adddressed envelope). Membership of $15/year covers well-put-together quarterly newspaper with legislative updates and other information.♥

California Department of Health Services, 714 P St., Room 400, Sacramento, CA 95814. 916 445-2263. Frank Nava, Chief, Food and Drug Field Operations Section. Administers one of the earliest state regulations of organic food labeling. Its Health and Safety Code Section 26569.11–17, enacted in 1979, regulates the use of the word "organic" on food labels. It provides detailed definitions of what qualifies (covering milk and meat as well as fruits and vegetables), requiring, for example, that an organic farm must be pesticide-free for one year before it can plant foods to be labeled "organic." (California Certified Organic Farmers and California Action Now in 1989 promoted a bill, AB 2012, that would, among other things, increase this period to three years. California is being pressured by Minnesota and Ohio laws prohibiting the labeling of any produce as organic if it comes from a state where the transition period is less than three years.) The Code requires reference to Section 26569.11 on health food product labels that assert a product is organic. California doesn't itself certify a grower or a product as organic, simply requiring that organic producers maintain records producible on demand to the Department of Health Services. The Code has no systematic enforcement provisions, but exposes a duplicitous producer to civil as well as criminal action. Organic farming in the state constituted about 1 percent of all produce farming in 1988. Large growers are looking hard at moving to organic farming methods. Projections are that 10% of California's crops will be organically grown by the end of the century. Thanks to its organized organic farmers, California has one of the country's best organic food labeling laws. Even so, a variety of new labels not covered under the California law are appearing: "No spray," "pesticide-free" (firms like Nutriclean are responding to a consumer demand for on-site inspection). The bottom line is: *In California, if a food is labeled "organic," it means something, but even here it's safer to shop in a conscientious retail store.*

California Institute for Rural Studies, P.O. Box 530, Davis, CA. (916) 756-6556. Researches agricultural issues and educates farmers. Sponsors the Alternatives in Pest Control Education Fund. Membership of $15/year covers use of library, 20% discount on publications, and early notification of research results.

Canadian Organic Growers, P.O. Box 6408, Station J, Ottawa, ON, Canada K2A 3Y6. (519) 699-4481. Provides technical assistance and publishes a quarterly newsletter and *The Canadian Organic Directory* (compiled by Tomás Nimmo of Organic Farm Services, listed below), available postpaid for US$10 to U.S. addresses, C$10 to Canadian addresses. Dues are C$12/year. It has four chapters and about 1,500 members. *Canadian Organic Producers Marketing Cooperative, Ltd.,* Box 2000, Girvin, Sask. S0G 1X0. (306) 567-2810. Alfred Moore, President. *Organic Crop Improvement Association (Canada) Inc.,* 35 Alexandra Blvd., Toronto, ON M4R 1L8. Many other organizations of organic/sustainable farmers are active in the Canadian Provinces. **Alberta:** Sustainable Agriculture Association. **British Columbia:** 7 organizations. **Manitoba:** Sustainable Agriculture Movement of Manitoba. **New Brunswick:** OCIA New Brunswick and Sustainable Agriculture for the Valley Ecosystem. **Nova Scotia:** OCIA Nova Scotia. Organic Growers Co-op. Sustainable Agriculture Club. **Ontario:** OCIA Ontario, P.O. Box 8000, Lindsay, ON K9V 5E6. (705) 324-9144, ext. 243. Larry Lenhart. 7 other groups. **Prince Edward Island.** 4 groups. **Quebec:** 14 groups, including the publisher (price: C$.75) of a list of organic/sustainable farming groups in Canada; write to: Ecological Agriculture Projects, P.O. Box 191, Macdonald College, 21, 111 Lakeshore Drive, Sainte Anne de Bellevue, QC H9X 1C0. (514) 398-7771. Stuart Hill, Director. **Saskatchewan:** 3 groups.

Carolina Farm Stewardship Association, see North Carolina.

Center for Rural Affairs: see Nebraska.

Colorado Department of Agriculture, Division of Plant Industry, Denver, CO. Colorado became the fourth state to pass a certification law (House Bill No. 1211, adding new Article 11.5 to Section 1, Title 35, CRS, 1984, passed June 1989). This law includes a labeling law (it defines both "certified organic" and "organic"). The Division of Plant Industry has been monitoring pesticide use for some time. It is a state with a rapidly growing organic movement. Certification standards for growers are being developed by the Colorado Organic Producers Association, listed next.

Colorado Organic Producers Association, 23242 Highway 371, La Jara, CO 81140. (719) 274-5230. Serves as a promoter of organic-sustainable agriculture and a network for distributors and retailers of organic and healthy food. Anyone can become a non-voting member of COPA and receive their marketing directory (including about 60 farmers, retailers, and distributors) for $25.

Connecticut Department of Consumer Protection, Food Division, 165 Capitol Avenue, Hartford, CT 06106. (203) 566-3388. The Department of Consumer Protection is the primary oversight agency to monitor food labeling. Certification efforts are in the hands of Natural Organic Farmers Association (see below). The state's Agriculture Department helped fund the Natural Organic Farmers Association chapter's useful guide to growers and retailers of healthy food in Connecticut, but otherwise has no involvement (as of late 1989) in organic farm certification.

Delaware Department of Agriculture, Division of Production and Promotion, 2320 South duPont Highway, Dover, DE 19901. (302) 736-4811. Chemical-industry-dependent Delaware does not have an organic certification program. Charts for 1982-83 show that the southern most third of the state had a very high level of pesticide usage. The Department of Agriculture knew of only one organic producer in the state, market gardener Sharon Carson (she knew of only one other, Scott & Kathy Miller, transitional organic berry and fruit farmers).

Delaware: Sharon Carson, R.D. 2, Box 277, Delmar, DE 19940. (302) 846-2571. Sharon and Kent Carson have attempted to form an Eastern Shore "organic growing group" made up of farmers, market gardeners, gardeners and consumers on the "Eastern Shore" peninsula of Delaware and parts of Maryland and Virginia. They produced an *Eastern Shore Organic Directory* (available for $5) in February 1990. ♥

Demeter Association. (West of the Mississippi:) 4214 National Avenue, Burbank, CA 91505. (818) 843-5521. (East of the Mississippi:) P.O. Box 6606, Ithaca, NY 12851. Certifies organic food and farms that meet the standards of biodynamic farming, minimizing waste to the outside world. Farmers enter into a contract with the association and pay an application fee of $150; once certified they pay a small royalty on the products they sell. The Demeter Education Foundation, at the same address, sells its newsletter for $5/year. See also Bio-Dynamic Farming and Gardening Association, Inc., above.♥♦

Eden Acres, Inc., 12100 Lima Center Road, Clinton, MI 49236. (517) 456-4288. Jean Winter. Sells *The Organic Network*, a computer-generated listing of organic growers and clinical ecologists, for $15. The value of the listing is limited because it is old (1984-dated edition sold to me in late 1989) and, in contrast to the excellent annual directory sold by the California Action Network (listed above), provides virtually no information about the listed farms or individuals other than their names and addresses.

Eden Foods Inc., 701 Tecumseh Road, Clinton, MI 49236. (517) 456-7457. Ron Roller, Director. Martha Johnson, Marketing Director. Offers a testing and certification program for growers in North America. Has certified its own products but as of 1990 will also have its products certified by the Organic Crop Improvement Association, so that the products will be marked "double certified." Not connected to Eden Acres, above.

Farm Verified Organic (FVO), P.O. Box 45, Redding, CT 06875. (203) 544-9896. FAX (203) 544-8409. Michael B. Marcolla, executive committee chairman. Also FVO Program, Mercantile Development Inc., 274 Riverside Avenue, P.O. Box 2747, Westport, CT 06880. (203) 226-7803. International nonprofit organization, founded 1984, to certify organic produce. Trademark licensed to food companies in 15 countries. Documents and verifies production procedures to ensure compliance with regulations and laws. Certifies organically grown produce. Provides technical assistance to over 200 members with over 250,000 acres under cultivation. This processor-initiated organization is the largest certification group that is neither state-run nor owned and controlled primarily by farmers. It is therefore somewhat suspect among farmers. It has, however, so far largely overcome these suspicions by its scrupulous attention to detail and documentation.♥♦

Florida Organic Growers, P.O. Box 365, High Springs, FL 32643. (904) 454-3487. Has about 200 members, and has developed guidelines, "Certification Standards for Florida Certified Organic Growers," and a "FOG" logo. The standards cover organically bred livestock.

Florida Department of Agriculture & Consumer Services, Mayo Building, Tallahassee, FL 32399. (904) 488-9682. Arthur F. Perry III, Division of Marketing. The State of Florida does not yet have any certification or labeling standards, but is actively considering them.

Georgia Department of Agriculture, Agriculture Building, Capitol Square, Atlanta, GA 30334. Brenda B. James, Public Relations. Georgia has no labeling or certification law. The state publishes a list of farmers markets,

of which by far the most important (FY 1988 sales $204 million) is the one for Atlanta, in nearby Forest Park, GA.

Georgia Organic Growers Association, P.O. Box 567661, Atlanta, GA 30356. (404) 621-4661: message center. (404) 786-8051: Honey Rubin, Public Affairs Coordinator and a co-founder (in 1981). (404) 253-0347: Larry Conklin, Certification Director and a co-founder. Between 1985 and 1989, the Association grew from 50 to 350 members. Began certification in 1990 with the assistance of OFPANA, using California Certified Organic Farmers paperwork as a guide. Prepares standards for commercial growers and arranges for verification. Transition period is three years; growers are registered during this period but may not use the Association's logo (as of late 1989 it did not plan to have a Transitional Organic logo). In addition, is working with the University of Georgia Extension Service to establish a paper trail for growers seeking to reduce their use of chemical sprays following gradual Integrated Pest Management methods. Bi-monthly newsletter, sent to members (dues are $15/year).♥♦

Illinois Department of Agriculture, Division of Marketing, State Fairgrounds, P.O. Box 19281, Springfield, IL 62794. (217) 782-6675. FAX (217) 524-5960. Publishes a buyer's guide that includes "health food" listings but does not identify organic growers, certified or otherwise. The state has no labeling or certification law and there are no major certification groups active in the state.

Indiana Sustainable Agriculture Association, 807 South Green, Crawfordsville, IN 47933. (317) 362-4946. Dave Swaim. Provides technical assistance.

Institute for Alternative Agriculture, 9200 Edmonston Road, #117, Greenbelt, MD 20770. (301) 441-8777. I. Garth Youngberg, founder. This interesting foundation-supported organization was started in 1983 by a refugee from the USDA, which had closed its ears to the need for reduced use of chemicals on farms. It is now a source of hard scientific data about sustainable agriculture and serves as a lobby (2,000 members) for it in Washington. Its founder is a folk hero for the sustainable agriculture revolution. His organization is the most important advocate in the U.S. for sustainable agriculture. It joined forces with Americans for Safe Food in holding an influential conference in March 1989 on reducing chemicals on farms and in food. Membership is $15/year, which covers the quarterly journal. It also publishes a monthly newsletter and the proceedings of its annual conference on alternative farming methods.♦♦

International Federation of Organic Agriculture Movements (IFOAM), RD 1, Box 323, Kutztown, PA 19530. Bernward Geier, Executive Secretary. This is the U.S. base of the worldwide membership organization with strong European ties. Distributes newsletter and other publications, and holds conferences.

Iowa, Department of Agriculture and Land Stewardship. Iowa, worried about its groundwater, in 1987 imposed a tax on farmers who use chemical fertilizers and pesticides, with the money going to fund research on sustainable agriculture. A law (Senate File 2262) defining organic farming standards was passed in 1988 to take effect July, 1989. The transition period for farms to become organic starts at one year and by mid-1991 becomes three years. Vendors of organic agricultural food (except beef or pork) must keep records of such sales for three years, and must have a sworn statement of compliance with organic food standards or face a fine of up to $500. The Iowa Department of Agriculture is empowered, but not required, to monitor compliance with the law.♦

Iowans for Organic Food Standards, 22 East Court Street, Iowa City, IA 52240. (319) 351-7888. Hilary Strayer. Membership group created in 1987 to support Iowa's organic farming law passed the following year.

Iowa, Practical Farmers of, Route 2, Box 132, Boone, IA 50036. (514) 432-1560. Richard Thompson. Provides technical assistance.

Iowa State Natural Food Associates, RR Box 153, Epworth, IA 52045. (319) 744-3157. Ron & Val Lucas. Organization of growers and consumers dedicated to promoting sustainable agriculture.

Kansas State Board of Agriculture, Marketing Division, 109 SW 9th Street, Topeka, KS 66612. (913) 296-3737. Has developed a "From the Land of Kansas" logo and distributes a directory of food producers that use it. However, it doesn't identify which products are organically grown. Kansas is considering an organic labeling law.

Kansas Organic Producers, P.O. Box 153, Beattie, KS. (913) 353-2414. Judy Nickelson. Founded in 1975, provides education and certification.

Kentucky Department of Agriculture, Capital Plaza Tower, Frankfort, KY 40601. (502) 564-4696. Ward "Butch" Burnette, Commissioner. The state does not have laws to certify or label organic food, and does not maintain any list of producers or sellers of organic foods.

Low-Income/Sustainable Agriculture (LISA) Program, CSRS/SPPS, USDA, Room 342, Aerospace Building, 14th & Independence Avenue, SW, Washington, DC 20250-2200. Neill Schaller, Program Director: (202) 447-3640. Jane M. Ross, Public Affairs: (202) 447-2929; FAX (202) 475-3179. Patrick Madden, Manager, Field Operations: (818) 242-7082. After the USDA rejected an initiative toward organic farming in the early 1980's, Congress adopted the concept and the Food Security Act of 1985 (Title 14, Subtitle C, Section 1463, relating to Agricultural Productivity Research) authorized the LISA program in the teeth of Reagan Administration opposition. LISA stands for reduced chemical inputs into farming and reduced waste through greater recycling. The program was funded with an appropriation of $3.9 million for FY1988 and $4.45 million for FY 1989 under the Agricultural Productivity Act. LISA's four regional host institutions received 371 proposals for research and education

projects in 1988 and 431 in 1989; out of those the institutions selected 49 in 1988 and as of August 1989 was supporting 78 ongoing projects. For FY 1990 $15 million has been requested.[27]♥♦

Maine Department of Agriculture, Bureau of Agricultural Marketing, Food and Rural Resources, Station 28, Augusta, ME 04333. (207) 289-3491. Provides lists of farmers' markets throughout the state and certified organic growers. Maine passed a law (Section 1.7 of MRSA c.103) specifying the meaning of organic and natural. Transition period is 2-3 years. Growers, processors and retailers must retain records for two years. The Department of Agriculture is not required to monitor or enforce compliance. Farmers are mostly certified by an independent group, Maine Organic Farmers and Gardeners Association, listed next. This group is responsible for the tough new Maine Post-Harvest Treatment Labeling Law. Starting January 1990, the law requires retailers to post a prominent sign if produce has been chemically treated after harvest. Retailers must also label untreated produce and answer consumer requests for information about treatment, within 48 hours of a request. Since September 1989, retailers must label produce from countries that permit use of U.S.-banned pesticides.

Maine Organic Farmers and Gardeners Association, P.O. Box 2176, Augusta, ME 04338. (207) 622-3118. Nancy Ross, Executive Director. This well-organized group has 2,200 broadly based members ("anyone who eats") and a staff of eight people. It certifies 70 farmers, as of late 1989, and will provide a list of them on request. It sets up apprenticeship programs and provides technical assistance. It runs the hugely successful annual Common Ground Country Fair, which *The New York Times* has called "the nation's pre-eminent exhibition not only of the purer production techniques, but also of a self-reliant rural life style." Maine Organic Farmers and Gardeners Association has sponsored some pioneering Maine labeling laws (country of origin, post-harvest treatment) and will provide information on them. Individual membership dues of $20/year cover an attractive 32-page bimonthly newspaper. It also sells a cookbook, *Bountiful Harvest*, for $12 postpaid.♥♦♦

Maryland: Alternative Farming Systems Information Center, 10301 Baltimore Blvd., #304, Beltsville, MD 20705. (301) 344-3704. Provides technical assistance on sustainable agriculture.

Massachusetts Department of Food and Agriculture, 100 Cambridge Street, Boston, MA 02202. August Schumacher, the Department's Commissioner, has invested $1.3 million of his budgets during 1986-88 to help many farmers cut down substantially on their pesticide use. The Department also publishes a good list of farmers' markets. (See also entry for Massachusetts chapter of Natural Organic Farmers Association.)

Merchandising Organic Foods, 5628 SW Miles Court, Portland, OR 97219. (503) 245-5640. Stuart Fishman, founder and operator. This interesting information service documents claims of growers to organic status. The service is used by retail stores and restaurants that are looking for suppliers of hard-to-get organic food, a situation that is likely to continue for several years as demand for organic food outstrips supply. To be documented, growers fill out a documentation form from Merchandising Organic Foods. They can then identify themselves as "documented organic." For $50, Merchandising Organic Foods will produce for a grower an evaluation in the form of a Summary Report comparing the grower's farming practices with a specific set of organic standards. This evaluation may then be used by the grower, Merchandising Organic Foods, and point-of-sale vendors as promotable information on the grower's products. Documentation is no substitute for certification because it isn't verified; however, it has a value independent of certification because it provides independent comparative information on growers' practices. Merchandising Organic Foods prepares an occasional newsletter for its clients.♥ ♥

Michigan Department of Agriculture, P.O. Box 30017, Lansing, MI 48909. (517) 373-1058. Gary P. Bauer, Center for Agricultural Innovation and Development. As of early 1990, did not certify organic farms or define the term organic, but a spokesman for Organic Growers of Michigan said that the state was much more receptive to organic farming issues than it has been in the past. The state's ranking by the Centers for Disease Control as having the highest mortality rate in the United States for "chronic but preventable" diseases (see Chapter 1) may help along the process of reform.

Michigan, Organic Growers of, 6359 Euclid, Marlette, MI 8453. (517) 635-2864. Joe Scrimger, Treasurer. Developed certification standards back in 1974. Certifies growers and assists in marketing. Scrimger's bean and grain farm is certified by Organic Crop Improvement Association and Farm Verified Organic as well. Requires pesticide-free soil for three years prior to full certification, but offers a Certified Transitional logo. Working on state laws and official recognition of organic certification. Annual membership $22/year. A list of organic growers in SW Michigan is available from Sheila LeBeau at (616) 468-6102. To subscribe to a quarterly publication on organic farming in Michigan, contact Pat Whetham, 11230 West Mt. Morris Rd., Flushing, MI 48433; (313) 659-8414.

Minnesota Department of Agriculture, 90 West Plato, St. Paul, Minneapolis, MN 55107. (612) 296-1486. Minnesota passed a law (RD864) effective 1988 that requires growers and vendors to keep records for three years on produce labeled organic, with a three-year transition period. The Department of Agriculture has the right to demand records and inspect any facility where organic food is grown, processed or sold. It also has an important feature—funding for the promotion of organic farming. This law was superseded in 1988 by a new law that allowed the legislature to designate a certification organization as having the right to certify growers on behalf of the state. In

other words, the state was in the certification business by delegating the power contractually to a private agency.

Minnesota: Land Stewardship Project, 14758 Ostlund Trail, N., Marine, MN 55047. (612) 433-2770. Ron Kroese, Executive Director. Patrick Moor, Managing Director. Assists farmers in Minnesota wishing to reduce use of chemicals. Promotes "farmland ethics" through educational programs for children and adults. Annual $20 contribution covers a quarterly newsletter.♥ ♦

Minnesota: Organic Growers and Buyers Association (OGBA), P.O. Box 9747, Minneapolis, MN 55440. (612) 674-8527. Yvonne Buckley. Certifies growers in Minnesota and some other states, offers marketing assistance, and lobbies for laws favorable to organic farming. In 1989, received a $100,000 grant from the Minnesota legislature to promote organic farming.

Mississippi Organic Growers Association, Route 1, Box 442, Lumberton, MS 39455. (601) 796-4406. Tom Dana, contact person. Initiated a certification program and then abandoned it because members are small-scale organic farmers selling mostly to local buyers who know the growers and don't require certification.

Missouri Department of Agriculture, P.O. Box 630, Jefferson City, MO 65102. (314) 751-2613. FAX (314) 751-2868. Jim Anderson, Division of Market Development. Publishes consumer guides that include organic growers. Missouri is served, along with Arkansas and Oklahoma, by the Ozark Organic Growers Association, listed above under Arkansas: Ozark.

Montana, Organic Certification Association of, P.O. Box 871, Helena, MT 59624. (406) 848-7381. Steve Elliott. Formed in 1988, this Organic Crop Improvement Association chapter certifies farmers. Membership dues are $10.

Montana passed a law (HB 646) effective in 1986 defining the meaning of organic. A two-year transition period to organic farming is required. Enforcement is effected through third-party action, for which attorneys' fees may be recovered. Labels must refer to the Montana law if using the word "organic" (Section 4, MCA). As in Maine, pesticide residues must not exceed 10 percent of the permissible levels specified by the FDA.

National Institute for Science, Law and Public Policy. Has prepared *Healthy Harvest III, A Directory of Sustainable Agriculture Organizations, 1987–88,* which lists organic growing associations, food distributors, journals of organic farming, seed sales, training programs and so forth in the United States and abroad. May be purchased for $10.95 (plus $1 postage) from Potomac Valley Press, 1424 16th Street, N.W., #105, Washington, DC 20036.

National Research Council, National Academy of Sciences, 2101 Constitution Avenue, N.W., Washington, DC 20418. (202) 334-3062. Charles M. Benbrook, Executive Director. The Board on Agriculture produced an important report in 1989 showing the feasibility of sustainable agriculture.♦♦

Natural Food Associates, P.O. Box 210, Atlanta, TX 75551. (214) 796-3612. John M. Ellis, President. Publishes *Natural Food and Farming.*

Natural Organic Farmers Association (NOFA), RFD #2, Sheldon Road, Barre, MA 01005. (508) 355-2853. Julie Rawson or Jack Kittredge (Editor, *Natural Farmer*). The individual state chapters of NOFA are extremely independent, with their own newsletters and events. In attempting to contact any of the following chapters (covering New England minus Maine and Rhode Island, plus New Jersey and New York) note that most NOFA farms tend to be on the small side, selling most of their commercial produce through brokers. Many NOFA members are gardeners who grow only for their own consumption. You may get an answering machine the first time you call a NOFA number and hear a cock crowing in the background when you get through; even then, you may not reach the person you want right away, because NOFA members mostly don't sit around in offices all day. To attend the annual NOFA conference (at Hampshire College, Amherst, Massachusetts on Aug. 3-5, 1990), contact Julie Rawson. NOFA follows a strict certification process, with a three-year transitional period and no "Transitional Organic" certification or logo. To join NOFA and get a copy of its newsletter, *The Natural Farmer,* as well as a discount on its annual conference, individuals should send $25 to one of the following NOFA chapters: *NOFA-Connecticut,* Box 386, Northford, CT 06472. Or: 51 Mott Hill Road, East Hampton, CT 06424. (203) 267-4289: Mary and Charles Brown, Membership. Or: Old Solar Farm, 153 Bowers Hill Road, Oxford, CT 06483. (203) 888-9280: Bill Duesing, President. Connecticut started its certification program in 1989 with 18 certified farms. The NOFA chapter has produced an excellent guide to organic growers and retailers in the state. *NOFA-Massachusetts,* RFD #2, Barre, MA 01005. (508) 355-2853: Julie Rawson, Treasurer & Membership. Or: 153 N. Main Street, Natick, MA 01760. (508) 655-2204: Martin Gursky and Lynda Simkins, Co-Presidents. This strong chapter certified 25 farms in 1989, and publishes the "Food for Life" guide to organic growers in the state. *NOFA-New Hampshire,* Route 1, Box 516, Andover, NH 03216. (603) 648-2521. Geri Veroneau, Membership, or Rich Estes, President and Treasurer. Certifies farmers in New Hampshire under contract to the State Agriculture Department. *NOFA-New Jersey,* R.D. #2, Box 263A, Pennington, NJ 08534. (609) 737-9183. Al Johnson, Treasurer. Certification starts in 1990; 13 farms were pre-certified as of late 1989. *NOFA-New York,* P.O. Box 454, Ithaca, NY 14851. (607) 648-5557. Pat Kane, Administrative Secretary (one of the few paid NOFA officers). The largest NOFA chapter, NOFA-NY is growing rapidly with 950 members in late 1989 and 66 certified farms. It offers several very useful publications. The state of New York is the least cooperative of any state government with NOFA.[28] *NOFA-Vermont/Vermont Organic Farmers,* Quail John Road, East Thetford, VT 05043. (802) 785-

2698. Wendy Cole, Membership. As of late 1989, the certification of 23 farms was renewed from a previous year and nearly 30 more farms had applied for certification (see Vermont below).[29]♥ ♥

Nebraska: Center for Rural Affairs, P.O. Box 405, Walthill, NE 68067. (402) 846-5428. Marty Strange. Founded in 1973, provides technical assistance on sustainable agriculture to farmers and teachers in Nebraska and neighboring states.♦

Nebraska Department of Agriculture, P.O. Box 94947, Lincoln, NE 68509. (402) 471-2341. Todd R. Ibach. Following a 1986 law (LB1016) modeled on the Minnesota law, the Department of Agriculture sets standards for organic farming and labeling. The law specifies a three-year transition period. Only the Organic Crop Improvement Association as of mid-1989 was authorized to certify farms on behalf of the state. In previous years Demeter and Farm Verified Organic have been active in the state.

Nebraska, Organic Crop Improvement Association Chapter, RR1, P.O. Box 163, Marquette, NE 68854. (402) 854-3195. Michael R. Herman, President. This fast-growing OCIA chapter expected to have certified 35 farmers by the end of 1989 and 70 by the end of 1990. Will not make available a list of growers (they say it is OCIA policy, but other chapters make their grower lists available); instead, they will circulate buyers' names to members. Membership is $50 a year.♦

Nebraska Sustainable Agriculture Society, P.O. Box 736, Hartington, NE 68739. (402) 254-2289. Sam Welsch. Dedicated to reducing chemical use in agriculture. Newsletter available free. Membership starts at $10/year.

Nevada Department of Agriculture, P.O. Box 1110, Reno, NV 89510. (702) 789-0180. Sandra M. Walsh. Most fruits and vegetables sold in Nevada come from California. As of late 1989 the state did not have any organic food laws and did not maintain any kind of listing of organic food producers or sellers.

New Alchemy Institute, 237 Hatchville Road, East Falmouth, MA 02536. (508) 564-6301. John Quinney, Executive Director. Kurt Teichert, Site Manager. Researches environmentally sound agricultural practices. (Founder John Todd heads up Ocean Arks International.) Membership, $35/year, covers quarterly magazine (available to non-members for $8/year) and reduced prices for Natural Organic Farmers Association-certified produce and other items.♥

New England Small Farm Institute, P.O. Box 939, Belchertown, MA 01007. The Institute was established in 1978 to foster the growth of financially viable organic farms. In conjunction with Natural Organic Farmers Association, it offers apprenticeships on its 180-acre farm, which also serves as home to the national office of OFPANA.

New Hampshire Department of Agriculture, Caller Box 2042, Concord, NH 03301. (603) 271-3788 or 271-3685. Vicki Smith. Statute RSA 426: 6-10 (effective 1986) broadly defines organic food and permits the Department of Agriculture to issue further regulations; inspect growers, manufacturers and retailers; issue certificates; and issue orders to enforce compliance. Pesticide residues for organic food may not exceed 1 percent of FDA permissible levels. New Hampshire in 1989 became the third state (after Texas and Washington) to certify organic growers. The Department of Agriculture has delegated first-line responsibility for certification of growers and monitoring of compliance with the law to the New Hampshire Natural Organic Farmers Association, contracting with the Association to conduct the certification and monitoring (see entry under Natural Organic Farmers Association).

New Jersey, Cornucopia Network of, Inc., 12 Terrace Avenue, Nutley, NJ 07110. (201) 667-0079. Donald B. Clark. Fosters farmers markets and educates New Jersey residents about farm, food and environmental issues. Annual $15 membership covers quarterly newsletter. (See also entry for New Jersey chapter of Natural Organic Farmers Association.)

New Mexico: Organic Growers Association, 1312 Lobo Place, N.E., Albuquerque, NM 87106. (505) 268-5504. Sarah McDonald, Secretary. Technical assistance on sustainable agriculture.

New York State Department of Agriculture and Markets, 1 Winners Circle, Capital Plaza, Albany, NY 12235. (518) 457-4188. Richard T. McGuire, Commissioner. Provides lists of supermarket chains and farmers' markets in New York State. If an organic labeling or certification law is passed, this agency would administer it—at least under the terms of an organic farming bill, AB 7429, introduced by Assemblywoman Gloria Davis, Chairman of the Task Force on Food, Farm, and Nutrition Policy. The staff director of the oversight committee in the state Assembly is Joseph Barnett, (518) 455-5573 or (518) 455-5203. (See also entry for New York chapter of Natural Organic Farmers Association.)

North Carolina Department of Agriculture, Division of Marketing, P.O. Box 27647, Raleigh, NC 27611. (919) 733-7887. Jeff Morton, Horticulture Section Manager. The state does not have organic food labeling or certification law. Provides a list of retailers that sell organically grown produce. The two certification groups active in the state are the Organic Crop Improvement Association, which does not offer a transitional program (meaning that would-be organic farmers must face three years of not being able to use the organic label), and CFSA, which does offer such a program.

North Carolina: Carolina Farm Stewardship Association (CFSA), P.O. Box 551, Pittsboro, NC 27312. (919) 663-2429. Kate Havel. Membership association of organic producers and consumers. Certifies organic farmers in both North and South Carolina under standards that were developed in conjunction with OFPANA. About 25 farms were certified as of the end of 1989; new entrants into the program are certified as transitional organic. Prepares a directory and publishes a newsletter. Has been awarded a LISA grant. Publishes standards for organic gardening, accepts registration from farmers, examines the registrations and arranges for inspection of applicant farms. If a farm passes inspection, it receives an Organic Production Certificate; no specific crops or animals are certified. Membership is $12/year, covers quarterly newsletter. Publishes book of farming songs.

North Dakota (mostly): Northern Plains Sustainable Agriculture Society, RR1, Windsor, ND 58493. (701) 763-6287. Fred Kirschenmann, President. Provides technical assistance and information only. Newsletter subscription $5/year. Annual dues, $10.

North Dakota Department of Agriculture, 600 East Boulevard, State Capitol, Bismarck, ND 58505-0020. (701) 224-4757. John Sandbakken. Prepares a buyer's guide that includes a section on organically grown produce. The state's organic labeling law (SB 2511) became effective in 1987, using the California model of defining the term "organic." Requires a transition period of three years. Vendors of organic food are made responsible for maintaining records to prove the source of the food. Certification programs must comply with state organic standards but otherwise operate independently. Farm Verified Organic's national technical office is based in Medina, N.D. The other certification agency active in the state is the Organic Crop Improvement Association.

North Ozark Organic Growers Association, Route 1, Box 145A, Urbana, MO 65767.

Northwest Area Foundation, West 975, First National Bank Building, Saint Paul, MN 55101. (612) 224-7490. Terry Tinson Saario, President. This foundation has made a substantial and early commitment to sustainable agriculture.♥♦

Noyes (Jesse Smith) Foundation, 16 East 34th Street, New York, NY 10016. (212) 684-6577. Stephen Viederman, President. Largest private supporter of sustainable agriculture in the U.S., according to *Foundation News*. Viederman is a true believer.♥♦

Ocean Arks International, 1 Locust Street, Falmouth, MA 02540. (617) 540-6801. John Todd, President. Researches and tests techniques for sustainable fishing.♦

OFPANA. See Organic Foods Production Association of North America below.

Ohio Department of Agriculture, 65 S. Front Street, Columbus, OH 43215. Steven D. Maurer, Director: (614) 466-2732. Division of Marketing and Communications, Reynoldsburg Laboratory Divisions, 8995 East Main Street, Reynoldsburg, OH 43068; Julie Kirk, Secretary: (614) 866-6361. The Director of Agriculture has established a Standard of Identity for Organic Foods effective in 1989 under Administrative Code 901:3–8. To use the state-authorized logo, growers must have a record of three years' freedom from use of synthetic chemicals and must be certified by an agency approved by the state, such as OEFFA-OCIA. The Division of Marketing and Communications makes available a better listing of organic growers than any other source we have come across—a detailed computerized list that shows for every farm its acreage, market area and how every crop on each farm is sold.♥

Ohio Ecological Food and Farm Association (OEFFA), 65 Plymouth Street, Plymouth, OH 44865. (419) 687–7665. Holly Fackler. Broad-based, loosely knit association of chapters of growers and consumers. Offers certification program approved by the Ohio Director of Agriculture, marketing assistance, and bulk purchasing programs. OEFFA has within it an Organic Crop Improvement Association chapter for farmers who need internationally recognized certification. Membership, $20/year, includes newsletter.

Ohio: Firelands Organic Producers Association, Route 2, 1716 Remelle Road, Monroeville, OH 44847. (419) 663–2361. Jim Hemminger.

Oklahoma is considering an organic food labeling law.

Oklahoma: Kerr Center for Sustainable Agriculture, Box 588, Poteau, OK 74953. (918) 647–9123. Free monthly newsletter (3,000 distribution). Technical assistance on sustainable agriculture.

Oregon Department of Agriculture. In accordance with its organic food regulation (Administrative Rule Chapter 603–23–100–110) effective 1985, growers must keep records for two years of all substances applied to the soil or plants. Organic food must not have pesticide levels exceeding 10 percent of FDA permissible levels. The Department of Agriculture is charged with enforcement. A 1989 law, replacing one dating back to 1973, defines "organic" by describing farming procedures and materials that are acceptable. It permits organic food to have up to 10 percent of the allowable tolerance levels (under Federal law) for pesticide residues; organic farmers argued that to set the standard lower would ignore the fact that pesticide residues remain in the soil from an earlier era. The Department was given the authority to levy fines on violators of up to $15,000.

Oregon Tilth: P.O. Box 218, Yualatin, OR 97062. (503) 692–4877. Lynn Coody, President; Yvonne Frost, Certification Director. The Oregon Tilth has produced an important "Transitional Document" to address the difficult problems to be faced by conventional farmers seeking to go organic.♦

Organic Crop Improvement Association (OCIA), 3185 Township Road 179, Bellefontaine, OH 43311. (513) 592–4983: Betty J. Kananen, Administrative Director (volunteer). International farmer-owned group for certification of organic farming methods and produce, plus manufacturers, processors and brokers. OCIA is proud of its code-based audit trail, which is designed to permit identification of every OCIA-certified package from point of sale to the consumer back to date and place of harvest. OCIA is concerned that a break in the audit trail at its weakest links would destroy public confidence in a certification program and therefore that the full trail should be promptly available to any person inquiring about it. Prepares and distributes its Certification Standards, which for some years have required three years of transition before a farm can be certified organic. OCIA does not have a "Transitional Organic" label—a reason OCIA has been slower to get much of a foothold in states where organic farms are scarce and farmers need to get under way quickly. Membership dues start at $75/year for member farmers at large. The decentralized operations include 27 chapters in North America, Mexico, Peru and other foreign countries. Several chapters in Canada are listed above under the Canadian . . . entry. Several important OCIA chapters are listed under their state headings, for example Montana, Nebraska, Ohio and Pennsylvania. Other sample U.S. chapters are: OCIA-North Carolina, P.O. Box 32133, Raleigh, NC 27622, which certifies growers in Virginia as well as North Carolina. OCIA-Wisconsin, P.O. Box 52, Viroqua, WI 54665 (Dave Engel). Overall, OCIA is given credit for setting very high organic farming standards; for example, it led the way toward the three-year transitional period. On the other hand, its enormous reach is not matched by equivalent staff resources; the work is done almost entirely by volunteers. In the face of the impending organic farming workload, it is fair to guess that OCIA will either have to hire staff or its strained resources will become unequal to the task of enforcing its high standards. Questions are already being raised about the validity, for example, of OCIA-Mexico's certification of sesame seeds.♥♦

Organic Farm Services, Box 230, Heidelberg, Ontario N0B 1Y0, Canada. (519) 699–4481. Tomás L. Nimmo. Consulting services on the promotion of organic farming throughout eastern North America.♥

Organic Farmers Associations Council, c/o Organic Foods Production Association of North America (see below). The first assembly of the Council in December 1989 attracted representatives from over 30 organic farm organizations. The Council sponsors an excellent magazine, *Organic Farmer,* which is available quarterly for $10/year from *Rural Vermont* at (802) 223–7222.♥

Organic Food Network, c/o American Fruitarian Society, 6600 Burleson Road, P.O. Box 17128, Austin, TX 78760. (512) 385–2841.

Organic Foods Production Association of North America (OFPANA), P.O. Box 31, Belchertown, MA 01007. (413) 323–6821. Judith Gillan. A producer trade association convened with the encouragement of IFOAM, it includes processors and distributors as well as grower groups, promoting standards and certification of organic farming methods and produce. Its excellent *Guidelines for* the *Organic Foods Industry* includes a good discussion of documentation and verification, and is sold for $10 plus $2.50 postage. Voting members, who are in the organic food business, pay $100/year for membership, non-voting members $25/year.

Ozark Organic Growers Association (OOGA): See Arkansas: Ozark . . .

Pennsylvania Department of Agriculture, 2301 North Cameron Street, Harrisburg, PA 17110. (717) 787-4737. Boyd E. Wolff, Secretary. Publishes *A Consumer's Guide to Direct Marketing,* showing farmers' markets and roadside stands through the state, identifying organic farmers. Does not have an organic certification or labeling law.

Pennsylvania Chapter, Organic Crop Improvement Association, RD2, Volant, PA 16156. (412) 530-7220. Ronald Gargasz is the contact for the chapter as well as being elected President of OCIA for 1989-90.

Rhode Island Organic Certification Committee, Earth Care Farm, 89 Country Drive, Charlestown, RI 02813. (401) 364-9330. Mike Merner. The Committee has developed certification standards with guidance from OFPANA, and designed its first application form, for which the deadline was May 1989.

Rhode Island Department of Environmental Management, Division of Agriculture, Roger Williams Building, 22 Hayes Street, Providence, RI 02908. (401) 277-2781. Dennis Martin. The Division of Agriculture produces some interesting information sheets, including detailed charts of the Rhode Island growing seasons and a list of roadside stands, but it so far does not have a state organic certification or labeling program in place. "We intend to work with interested parties during the coming year," says the Division, "to promulgate rules and regulations for a Rhode Island Organic Certification Program" (see previous entry).

Rodale Institute, Box 323, RD1, Kutztown, PA 19530. (215) 683-6383. Richard Wheeler, Managing Director. Nonprofit organization reorganized, after a large gift of stock from Anna Rodale (widow of J. I. Rodale, founder of Rodale Press) at the beginning of 1990 with three divisions: (1) Rodale Research Center, which does biological experimentation; (2) Information Exchange, which picks up the work of the Regenerative Agriculture Association, and (3) Global Opportunities, a futuristic think tank.♥♦

Rodale Press, 33 E. Minor Street, Emmaus, PA 18098. (215) 967-5171. Robert Rodale (son of J. I. Rodale, the late founder), President. Publishes *Organic Gardening* magazine, books and other publications. Send a self-addressed stamped envelope to *Organic Gardening*'s Reader Service and they will send free information to get someone started on the search for certified organic food.♦

South Carolina: See North Carolina, Carolina Farm Stewardship Association.

South Dakota Department of Agriculture, Anderson Building, 445 East Capitol, Pierre, SD 57501. (605) 773-3375. Gloria Hansen. The organic food law (Senate Bill 214), enacted in 1988, defines organic food and specifies prohibited fertilizers. Synthetic compounds are prohibited during growing, manufacturing and processing. The transition period is three years. Vendors must maintain records to prove that food labeled organic is in compliance with standards. The Department of Agriculture is required to create a system for ensuring compliance, which may include required records and inspections.

Tennessee Department of Agriculture, Division of Marketing, Ellington Agricultural Center, P.O. Box 40627, Nashville, TN 37204. (615) 360-0160. FAX: (615) 360-0194. Kevin Hosey. Prepares directories of growers that feature organic farmers. Does not certify organic growers and does not have an organic labeling law. Besides the newly formed Tennessee Sustainable Agriculture Marketing Association, two other groups exist in the state that are oriented more toward gardeners than commercial farmers—the Alternative Growers Association and the Organic Growers Association of Tennessee.

Tennessee Sustainable Agriculture Marketing Association. Route 8, Box 31, Crossville, TN 38555. (615) 484-0937. Louise Gorenflow. This new organization of the 20 to 30 commercial organic growers in the state has as its goal the development of certification standards and a certification program to be operated independently of the state. It is modeled on the Carolina Farm Stewardship Association (CFSA) described above, with input from OFPANA. It has chosen not to become a chapter of the Organic Crop Improvement Association because OCIA doesn't provide a "Transitional Organic" logo, and the organic farmers in Tennessee are worried about their incomes during the three years of compliance with OCIA standards without the payoff in higher consumer demand from certification.

Texas Department of Agriculture (TDA) Organic Certification Program, P.O. Box 12847, Austin, TX 78711. (512) 463-9883: Keith Jones, Consumer Services. 463-7467: Robert Maggiani, Direct Marketing. FAX (512) 475-1618. The Texas program is extremely interesting, both for its virtues and its shortcomings. On the positive side: (1) The Texas certification program has been led by Jim Hightower, the State's energetic, reform-minded, and visionary Commissioner of Agriculture, who has courageously taken on the Cattleman's Association and Farm Bureau; the new rule creating organic markets for Texas products is a tribute to his skill and determination, and to the research and planning of the Department of Agriculture. (2) When the voluntary certification program was instituted in 1988, Texas was the first state in the nation to institute its own organic farming certification law (Washington was second). (3) Texas adopted the three-year transitional period from pesticides (two years from fertilizers); by adopting the three-year period, it has made this the standard, and California is likely to follow soon. (4) Texas was the first U.S. certification agency to adopt a Transitional Organic logo, an idea that is being widely discussed and has already been imitated by New Hampshire. (5) The Department thought 150 farmers would inquire about certification; in fact, more than 1,100 farmers asked for information and application forms. (6) The program has been moving ahead rapidly, and as of late 1989, 100 growers had been certified. (7) Texas has the only state program that certifies manufacturers, distributors, and retailers as well as growers. (8) The Texas program establishes *good standards* for certified organic food and hired Keith Jones to manage the program and conduct most inspections; five TDA inspectors help him enforce compliance—any food processor, manufacturer or retailer must keep records proving the organic nature of food so labeled, "verified by a traceable audit trail,"[30] and is open to unannounced inspections from the TDA; all records are open to the public unless they contain information that can be shown to be in the nature of trade secrets or otherwise legitimately confidential; any violator of the law, misidentifying food as *certified* organic can be prosecuted under the Texas Deceptive Trade Practices Act. (9) Texas is one of nine states that have decided to regulate health claims on food (suing, for example, Quaker Oats for claiming that oat bran reduces cholesterol). On the negative side: (1) Texas intentionally chose, for the time being, not to have any standards for food that is labeled simply "organic" so long as it does not make any other claims, including that it is certified; a TDA spokesman says that to have taken on the organic labeling issue in 1988 would have entailed a "huge fight" and would probably have resulted in legislation that would in the end have been weaker than the path TDA is pursuing. (2) Private certification officials wonder if the TDA, or any government agency, will be up to the challenge of responding promptly to inquiries about the audit trail; TDA replies that organic food regulation is properly a governmental job and will increasingly be seen as such. (3) Some observers think that TDA should contract with a nonprofit certification organization to do the certification, as is the case with New Hampshire and Washington; but the Texas Organic Growers Association didn't get under way until 1987.[31] The bottom line is: *Buy "Certified Texas (TDA) Organic" with confidence. Ignore for now any uncertified "organic" label on a product (1) sold in Texas or (2) produced in Texas and sold in another state without an organic labeling law.*♥♦

Texas: Natural Food Associates, P.O. Box 210, Highway 59 South, Atlanta, TX 75551. (214) 796-3612. Bill Francis, Executive Director.

Texas Organic Growers Association, Route 1, Box 50-B, Thrall, TX 75678. (512) 856-2868. Ralph Ware, General Manager. Established in 1987; has been working with the TDA on the state's new organic certification program. Producer-owned marketing cooperative.

Tilth Producers' Cooperative, see Oregon Tilth and Washington Tilth. Tilth is just another word for farming, from the word "till" (as in "till the soil").

U.S. Congress, Senate, Committee on Agriculture, Nutrition, and Forestry, Washington, DC 20510. (202) 224-2035. Senator Patrick J. Leahy (D-VT), Chairman. The 1990 Farm Bill expands the sustainable agriculture initiatives that were first included in 1985. Leahy's proposed *Organic Foods Act,* S. 1896, would establish a national standard for organic foods.

U.S. Department of Agriculture (USDA), Administration Building, 12th Street and Jefferson Drive, S.W., Washington, DC 20250. Arthur Whitmore, Press Office: (202) 447-4026. Ben Blankenship, Public Information:(202) 786-1504. Douglas Bowers, Agricultural History: (202) 786-1787. Herman Delvo, Pesticides: (202) 786-1456. Stephen Crutchfield, Water Quality: (202) 786-1444. Dave Smallwood, Food and Nutrition Policy and Food Away from Home: (202) 786-1864. Judy Putnam, Food Consumption: (202) 786-1879. John Ginzel, Meat Demand: (202) 786-1285. Ron Sitzman, Aquaculture (fish farming): (202) 447-3244. Lee Christensen, Broilers and Eggs: (202) 786-1714. Jim Miller, Dairy Products: (202) 786-1770. Ben Huang, Fruits and Nuts: (202) 786-1884. Primary responsibility for pesticides was moved from the USDA to EPA in 1972. The USDA has two tiny activities that help the healthy food cause: the Low-Income/Sustainable Agriculture (LISA)♥♦ Program and the Appropriate Technology Transfer for Rural Areas (ATTRA)♥ program (see separate entries for these two programs).

U.S. Environmental Protection Agency (EPA), Waterside West Building, 401 M Street, S.W., Washington, D.C. 20460. Lee M. Thomas, Administrator, Room 1200. (202) 382-4700. Monitors and regulates air, water and soil quality. Since 1972, has been responsible for pesticide monitoring.

U.S. Food and Drug Administration (FDA), Department of Health and Human Services (Dr. Louis Sullivan, Secretary), Parklawn Building, 5600 Fishers Lane, Rockville, MD 20910. Commissioner, Room 14-71. (202) 443-2410. Inspects fruit, vegetables, seafood, eggs and milk, in conjunction with state agencies. See entry in Chapter 3 for full description of the FDA's position on food labeling.

Vermont Department of Agriculture, 116 State Street, Montpelier, VT 05602. (802) 828-2427. (802) 828-2416: Amanda Legare. (802) 828-2500: Steven F. Justis, Marketing Specialist, Agricultural Development Division. Distributes an attractive general directory to agricultural products in the state, and also a list of organic growers. The Department has for years inspected dairy and meat products to comply with Federal standards. More recently the state has passed an organic labeling law and the Department monitors compliance with it. Natural Organic Farmers Association-certified organic farmers carry the Vermont Organic seal, with the Vermont Department of Agriculture address. The job of certification has essentially been delegated to Natural Organic Farmers Association.

Vermont Organic Farmers—Vermont Natural Organic Farmers Association, 15 Barre Street, Montpelier, VT 05602. (802) 223-7222. Enid Wonnacott, Administrator. Vermont Organic Farmers (VOF) is the certification program for Vermont Natural Organic Farmers Association (see Natural Organic Farmers Association above). It publishes guidelines, *Standards and Applicant Information,* modeled on those promulgated by OFP ANA. About 50 farms applied for certified organic status in 1989, and half (renewals from 1988) were certified as of the fall of 1989. Certified members of VOF pay $100/year.♥

Virginia Department of Agriculture and Consumer Services, Division of Marketing, P.O. Box 1163, Richmond, VA 23209. Steven W. Thomas, Administrator—Fruit, Vegetable & Peanut Marketing. Publishes a list of farmers' markets. A task force within the Department is investigating the possibility of Virginia establishing an organic farming certification program.

Virginia Association of Biological Farmers, Box 252, Flint Hill, VA 22627. (703) 676-3263. Diana Bird. Technical assistance on sustainable agriculture.♦

Washington State Department of Agriculture, 406 General Administration Building, Olympia, WA 98504. (206) 234-5042. Vern Hedlund, Director, Inspections, Dairy and Food Division; MilesMcEvoy, organic food certifier. Washington and Texas were the first states to establish their own organic farming certification programs, in 1988. Washington's organic labeling law (Substitute House Bill No. 297, April 1985, adding a new chapter to Title 15 RCW) gave the state's Department of Agriculture a staff to certify organic growers (on a voluntary and fee-paying basis), require records, and otherwise enforce compliance with the law. By 1991 the transition period will be three years for pesticides and two for fertilizers. Producers must provide a sworn statement to the buyer that the food was grown organically, and must maintain records to prove it. Backup records must be retained for two years. Vendors must identify the producer at the point of sale and in advertising. Violators are liable for the cost of an investigation plus $1,000. The Department works with the Washington Tilth on maintaining standards for organic farming in the state.♦

Washington Tilth (Tilth Producers Cooperative, TPC): 1219 East Sauk Road, Concrete, WA 98237. (206) 853-8449. Diane Jerkins, Deborah Pelham. TPC lobbies the state legislature for organic food laws, then works with the state's Department of Agriculture to implement it. Members pay $25/year and receive a bimonthly newsletter. The 34-page handbook, *Standards and Guidelines for Oregon and Washington Tilth Certified Organically Grown,* costs $7.♥♦

West Virginia Department of Agriculture, Marketing & Development Division, State Capitol, Charlestown, WV 25305. Robert L. Williams, Division Director. Refers inquiries about organic farming to the Mountain State Organic Growers and Buyers Association.

West Virginia: Mountain State Organic Growers and Buyers Association, Route 10, Morgantown, WV 26505. Keith Dix, President. Newly formed in 1989.

Wisconsin Department of Agriculture, Trade & Consumer Protection, 801 West Badger Road, P.O. Box 8911, Madison, WI 52708. (608) 267-3311. Will Hughes. The Department was authorized by a law (1987 Wisconsin Act 278) effective in 1988 to establish standards for organic food. The Department publishes a first-rate guide to the state's farms and their products, *Take Home . . . Something Special from Wisconsin,* which is described as a "direct marketing guide" and sounds as though it would include mail-order information; in fact it is restricted to helping people looking for roadside stands, pick-your-own farms, and farmers markets. It includes a useful chart of crops and their harvest dates, and also a guide to festivals in the state. Wisconsin has a chapter of the Organic Crop Improvement Association.

Wisconsin Natural Food Associates, Inc., 6616 County Trunk Highway I, Waunakee, WI 53597. (608) 846-3287. Esther Horsted, Paul White. Recognizes organic growers under its Grower Approval Program. Annual $7 membership dues cover a quarterly bulletin and newsletter.

Wisconsin Organic Growers Association, Route 1, Box 160, Spring Valley, WI 54767. (715) 772-3104. List of members available.

Wisconsin Rural Development Center, Inc., P.O. Box 504, Black Earth, WI 53515. (608) 767-2539. Denny Caness, Executive Director. Margaret Krome, Project Director. Seeks to reform statewide agricultural policies in the direction of sustainable systems.♦

Wyoming Department of Agriculture, Division of Marketing and Promotion, 2219 Carey Avenue, Cheyenne, WY 82002. (307) 777-6577. FAX: (307) 777-6869. Charleen Garofalo. (307) 777-6577. Colteen Cailteux. Publishes the *Wyoming Agricultural Trade Directory,* listing farms and their crops (only a few are organic producers), and *Wyoming Agriculture: A Directory,* listing state, regional and federal officials and organizations, and other references. The state had no labeling or certification laws as of mid-1989.

Frank Mikulski's stand at the **Union Square Greenmarket** in New York City usually does a brisk business. Mikulski's stand sells vegetables from his farm in Goshen, New York.

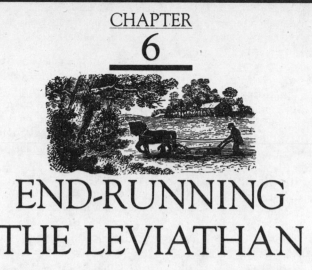

END-RUNNING
THE LEVIATHAN

*Co-ops are a compatible form of organization for people opting out of the
mass food distribution system.*

This chapter discusses ways to avoid the mass food distribution monster, by ordering food directly from smaller producers, processors, or distributors. Two practical ways to gain independent access to food are to use food co-ops or order by mail. These options are especially important for people living in areas poorly served by wholefood stores.

The Leviathan. The Biblical prophets wrote of terrifying aquatic monsters called Leviathans, and in 1651 Hobbes, mentioned in Chapter 4, called the government a Leviathan that makes peace among people at the price of controlling them.

Today, corporate farmers, large food-processing companies, distributors and supermarket chains, in conjunction with chemical companies, have created a Food-Providing Leviathan for the American people. It is enormous and on its own terms impressively efficient. But it can be hazardous.

Like a huge oil tanker, the Leviathan can be painstakingly turned toward a new course, adapting to new concerns about chemicals in agriculture, and food additives, and making healthier food widely available.

For the time being, though, the Leviathan is drifting. An informal survey we took shows why.

Survey. We sent a questionnaire to 150 food-processing companies, including the major wholefood processors and the largest conventional food manufacturers. We asked them about sustainable agriculture, labeling laws, the products they make, and general trends in the food industry. Most of the companies we highlight in this book responded to such questions and indicated great interest in the issues. But conventional food manufacturers responded tentatively, indifferently, and incompletely, if at all.

Respondents, in fact, fell almost entirely into two

schools. The first, composed of representatives of the wholefood industry, mostly expressed concern that labeling laws were too lax, said they supported sustainable agriculture, were forthcoming about any additives in their products, and did not think that, on the whole, processed food products today were more healthful than those made 10 years ago.

The other group, composed of conventional food manufacturers, mostly indicated that present labeling laws were adequate, claimed sustainable agriculture was not viable, left all the questions about food additives blank, and asserted that, on the whole, the processed food products of today are healthier than those of the early 1980's.

Access to Food

Until the Leviathan turns, finding healthy food will take care and effort. Buying from a wholefood store or the wholefood section of the supermarket is the simplest way to buy healthy food. Such stores are surveyed in Chapter 8 and are listed in detail in the geographical directory in Chapter 10.

You can also grow your own food and buy direct from farmers, either by visiting them or going to a farmers' market. We will briefly look at these options, and then focus on a solution that can work for almost anyone—buying from or through a co-op.

Grow Your Own Food. Although this book emphasizes how and where to purchase healthy food, one healthy and money-saving way to proceed is to buy seeds or seedlings and grow some of your own food. Lettuce, tomatoes (from seedlings) and zucchini are fairly easy to grow; other good starter vegetables are peas, beans, radishes, and summer squash.

Gardeners can achieve four to six times the yield of professional farmers because of the closer care they can provide the plants. The average vegetable garden has 600 square feet. Over half of all U.S. households have gardens of some kind, and they produce 18 percent of the country's food.[1]

For those who lack a piece of property to garden on, or who want to join others, a vegetable garden can become a community project. Some successful community gardens have even flourished in urban vacant lots. My family and I participated in one of these for several summers in Chelsea, a neighborhood in Manhattan, and our gardening group won a prize for the effort. For assistance in forming a community garden contact the American Community Gardening Association at the University of California Cooperative Extension Service, (213) 744-4341.

Direct Buying from Producers. Healthy food is available directly from food producers, cooperative warehouses, and the relatively small commercial distributors that sell directly to consumers.

The two basic ways of having food shipped direct are by mail (U.S. Postal Service or United Parcel) or by truck (either the producer's or one belonging to a distributor). The truck delivers either to the individual's home, or to a specified drop-off, which in some cases is a wholefood store willing to accept such deliveries. Orders can be placed by phone or mail. In either case, one would normally obtain from the seller a price list with details on minimum orders, prices for different quantities, methods of shipping, acceptable methods of payment, and so forth.

Increasingly the facsimile (fax) machine is providing the speed of a phone call with the convenience and accuracy (although not yet all the legal protections, as we shall see later in this chapter) of mail.

Farmers' Markets. Many cities now have farmers' markets, which like their historical antecedents are a way for producers and consumers to meet and do business face to face. They are usually regulated by state agriculture departments, which also have lists of such markets for consumer use. For the name and address of your state agriculture department, check the alphabetical directory at the end of Chapter 5.

Support the farmers who are making the effort to have their produce certified as organic.

How to Buy Food Through Co-ops

The distinctive feature of cooperatives is that they are owned by their members. The International Cooperative Alliance at a 1966 meeting summarized cooperative principles under six headings: open membership, economic democracy, limited return on invested capital, patronage rebates, education and cooperation among cooperatives.

What's Special About Co-ops. Testifying to a House Committee in June, 1989, the head of the National Rural Cooperative Development Task force described the uniqueness of the co-op form of ownership as follows: "The cooperative model is an ideal mechanism to overcome the principal competitive disadvantages of rural areas . . . lower population densities and the resultant higher service costs and smaller markets. Cooperatives can aggregate capital, people, business and member-user inputs, outputs, and services into large enough units to be economically competitive."[2]

Public perceptions of co-ops vary greatly among countries. In the Soviet Union, co-ops are the predominant form of free market activities. In European countries like Denmark and West Germany, co-ops are mainstream institutions. In the United States, co-ops are sometimes considered socialistic!

The majority of co-ops in the United States are in the food business, where being a co-op means doing business in a special way. I did not start writing this book with any brief for co-op ownership. However, I have been impressed with the extent to which the wholefood industry has been held together by co-ops. Co-ops are a compatible form of organization for people opting out of the mass food distribution system.

For one thing, food co-ops tend to be small. They are mostly organizations of small farmers or household customers. Some co-ops get to be fairly large, but they are still tiny compared to the food conglomerates. Buying co-ops are most often limited by the difficulties in organizing buyers. The ones that insist on being volunteer-run have a self-limiting small size, which tends to keep the organizations close to the needs of the members. The cooperative warehouses are in turn owned by the buying co-ops, which maintains the link to the consumer.

My endorsement of co-ops is not based on any feeling that anonymous stock ownership of companies is necessarily bad, or that co-ops are all perfect. Rather, the record of co-ops in caring about the food they sell seems better than that of the large stockholder-owned companies that make up the bulk of the American Food Leviathan. Cooperatives not only provide a way to save money and buy superior quality food; they also provide members with information about food, nutrition and organization, while supporting small farmers and ecologically sound farming practices.

Co-op personnel also tend to be nice people who haven't been reduced to automatons at a checkout counter; they care intensely about their work, as you will find if you phone them.

How to Organize a Buying Club or Food Co-op. Most distributors don't sell to individuals or families because their minimum order quantities for economical shipping are higher than most individuals or families can use. By joining other buyers in a "buying club" or food co-op, individuals can get the benefits of bulk buying. One guess is that about 4,000 buying clubs now operate in the United

States, of which 80 percent carry organic produce, at prices between 5 and 30 percent below what supermarkets charge for comparable products.[3]

Japanese households make far more use of buying clubs. They are estimated to belong to a million such clubs, with an average of ten members each. One large buying club has over 300,000 members and a staff of 700 people to handle orders.[4] It combines the functions of buying clubs and the U.S. co-op warehouses discussed later in this chapter.

In a buying co-op, someone orders food each month, and the co-op members pick up their orders. The co-op manager usually starts out being a volunteer, with other members also volunteering to help. Sometimes the co-op grows so large that the manager is paid (the job may rotate among members). Sometimes the pickup depot becomes so active that it converts to being a co-op store.

The best number for a co-op is 10–15 people. The problem with having a co-op that is too small is that the bulk minimums (typically 25–pound or 50–pound bags) will be too much for the group to absorb, limiting choice and leading to a large quantity of "extras" (leftover goods).

A buying co-op is best organized through an existing group such as a tenants association, a church or a school group. A major concern will be to find an appropriate place to have the food delivered, preferably with an area where volunteers can break down bulk shipments into smaller sizes for each family. The best locations are church halls, schools, community centers or other civic buildings, or homes of members who have ample garages. Remember, if you are having food delivered by truck, the location must be accessible to large trucks.

Prior to the organizational meeting a co-op warehouse catalogue might be distributed. At the meeting, a name is selected and tasks are typically assigned to volunteers for three committees: ordering, distribution, and bookkeeping, as well as a steering committee to meet at least every three months. A central coordinator or manager is also selected for a period of at least six months, and is often paid a nominal fee for assuming this important role. The main organizational matters to decide are how often to buy (most order once a month, some every two months), membership requirements such as an initial fee ($5–$25 is typical), and minimum hours for volunteering or an extra charge for non-working members. It would be a good idea to have someone from another co-op attend the meeting and describe how their co-op works.[5]

How Buying Co-ops Order Food. The most difficult problem in a buying co-op is handling the orders. Two constraints operate: one is that nothing can be ordered below the minimum amount for a bulk order; the second constraint is that amounts above the minimum must usually, but not always, add up to another minimum.

For example, organically grown brown rice produced by Community Mill & Bean is listed in the September-October 1989 pricelist of the Hudson Valley Federation of Cooperatives as available in 10- or 25–pound bags, with a price of 81 cents/pound for the smaller bag and 78 cents/pound for the larger one. The questions for the buying co-op are: First, do they have enough orders to get to a single 10–pound bag? Second, can they make it up to the next tier, 25 pounds, where the price drops somewhat?

Rice keeps for a long time. But the order size becomes more complicated for goods that have a shorter life span, for example bread.

Buying co-ops tackle this problem in one of three ways (or in some combination of them):

1. Auction (two hours, under 30 people). This approach takes about two hours and works best when the co-op has fewer than 30 members. All the members of a buying co-op come together for an order meeting. All of the members have previously gone over and checked off on the catalogue of the co-op warehouse or other distributor the things they want.

A facilitator who has an eye on the clock (otherwise meetings will take even longer than two hours) reads off each section in the catalogue and finds out if anyone wants something from that section. Then, in order, the meeting proceeds through the section to consider items for which someone has an order. Members indicate they want to order by raising a hand with a number of fingers extended. In the case of the organic brown rice, one finger would mean one pound of rice. Someone counts fingers, and announces that they have, let us say, 22 pounds ordered. The coordinator could then say: "Will we go to 25 pounds, or should we only order two 10–pound bags?" At that point, some members may raise their order to get to 25 pounds.

Generally, if the total order is less than half the minimum required, the order is dropped. If the order is over one-half the minimum it will be brought up again at the next auction meeting. Some buying co-ops rotate sections within a catalogue to increase interest, ordering from the first half only (or third if they meet at least every four weeks) at one meeting, and the remaining half at the next meeting, with a special list of commonly ordered or perishable items coming up at every meeting.[6]

2. Silent Auction (one hour, 20–40 people). Under the Silent Auction or Sign-Up method, instead of responding to a calling out of the items to be ordered, members write down their orders on 40 or more large (roughly 1' by 2') poster cards. These cards are prepared ahead of time and are taped on tables or walls around a room. Each card has an item identified with the order number at the top, with one card for each item commonly ordered plus a few extras for new items. Each card is covered with clear contact paper, and the current price of the item is written in before the meeting in grease pencil so that the card can be re-used.

When members arrive, they write in their orders in grease pencil. As they do this, they can communicate with one another to encourage signing up for a particular item that needs buyers.

At the end of the 45 minutes or so that it will take for members to write in all their orders, everyone takes a card or two and adds up the total amount of the order for that item. (At this point a regular auction may be held for items that exceeded 50% of the minimum order but were less than 100%.)

When orders have been agreed upon, members adjust their individual order sheets to match the final order quantity, and they turn them in; these sheets are then used as a check later when the orders are delivered and broken down.[7]

3. Min-Max (no meeting needed, any number). For groups that don't want long meetings, the min-max approach is by far the easiest. Each member writes down the smallest order they would like to place, and the largest. The order is then phoned in or mailed (or faxed!) to the compiler, who simply adjusts each order to the amount that will make up an even bulk order.

The compiling job usually takes two people two to four hours. In large (over 50 members) buying co-ops, the orders are consolidated for groups of about ten each, and the consolidated orders are then combined again for a final order to the distributor.

Larger Co-ops

The above methods may look time-consuming, but consider that in two or three hours you can take care of most of your shopping for the month, and you may save time in the long run. Meanwhile you have had a chance to share information with your neighbors about a common interest, food.

Even easier is to join an existing retail co-op, such as those listed in Chapter 10. These co-ops have a large enough base to stock their shelves like regular markets. Members, who usually have to buy a share and volunteer a few hours a month, are often subsidized by the purchases of non-members who patronize the market but choose not to join.

Many different formulas are used for figuring prices. Example: member prices are five to ten percent over cost, non-member prices are 25 percent over cost. This makes

food cheaper for members. Further discounts are usually available for bulk orders or case orders for those who want to use the co-op like a buying club. You may not save as much money as you might through a smaller buying club, but retail co-ops can provide a good middle-ground between convenience and choice.

Help for Setting Up Your Buying Co-op

The following organizations, in addition to at least two of the co-op warehouses (Blooming Prairie and Ozark Cooperative Warehouse) listed later in this chapter, provide assistance in setting up a food co-op. The books that are listed are available for purchase in the catalogues of many of the co-op warehouses, which also sell computer programs.

At the end of the following entries a diamond (♦) means we have heard great things about the organization; a heart (♥) means we have personal experience of the group's commitment to the consumer.

California Association of Cooperatives, 1563 Solano Ave., #243, Berkeley, CA 94707. (415) 524–8826. Matt Kuman. Started in 1988, it has 70 members ($40/year), publishes a newsletter approximately four times a year. Provides technical assistance (supported in part by a grant from the Mutual Service Insurance Corporation) to people seeking to establish or manage co-ops.♥♦

California Department of Consumer Affairs, 1020 N Street, Sacramento, CA 95814. (916) 445–1254. Steve Baker: (916) 324–7191. Published *How to Form a Pre-Order Club*, available free on request.

Cooperative Grocer Magazine, Box 597, Athens, OH 45701. (614) 448–7333. Dave Gutnecht, Editor. Circulates to 2,000 co-op retail stores. $18/year for six issues.♥

Labor Relations and Research Center of the University of Massachusetts at Amherst, 111 Draper Hall, Amherst, MA 01003. (413) 545–4875. Publishes *Workplace Democracy*.

National Cooperative Business Association, 1401 New York Avenue, N.W., #1100, Washington, DC 20005. (202) 638–6222. Paul Hazen. Publishes the *NCBA Cooperative Business Journal*. Sells *How to Organize a Cooperative* for $5.75, postage included. Maintains a computerized listing of food-buying co-ops; call and find the one nearest you. Ask for free catalog of publications.

U.S. Department of Agriculture (USDA), Administration Building, 12th Street and Jefferson Drive, S.W., Washington, DC 20250. Public Information: (202) 786–1504. Publishes *How to Start a Cooperative* (1986), designed for farm co-ops.

Food Sources for Buying Co-ops

Buying co-ops can purchase food directly from producers or manufacturers, from medium-sized distributors, or from co-op warehouses.

1. Direct Purchase.

The most direct approach for a buying co-op is to purchase from producers. Ordering direct from producers is attractive because of the connection it makes between consumers and producers. This connection is valuable for both sides. It helps consumers appreciate the work that goes into the food they eat. It can also be useful in planning for the use of seasonal food, in ensuring a supply of high-quality food, and in identifying and avoiding hazards associated with specific foods.

The economic benefits of forming a buying club or food co-op depend on the price reductions offered by the producer or food processor. Two examples follow:

Associated Cooperatives, 322 Harbour Way, #25, Richmond, CA 94801. (415) 232-1111. Owned by co-op retail stores in California. Manufactures Pacific Gardens brand products, including cookies made with 100% organic ingredients. These cookies retail for $1.89 in stores, but sell for $14.90 for one case of 12 (versus $22.08 at retail). Ordering 10 cases knocks the price down 10 percent or more.♦

Jasmine & Bread, RR #2, Box 256, South Royalton, VT 05068. (802) 763-7115. In the spring of 1990 it sold its mustard for $5/jar (6½-ounce size) including shipping costs when ordered two-at-a-time through the mail. This is about the same price as in wholefood stores. However, when you order a dozen jars of mustard, they cost only $34 ($2.83 each, versus the $5 price for the smaller shipment), plus a UPS shipping charge of $2–$3 to New York City. The *shipped* cost is therefore only about $3/jar, a 40% saving for multiplying the order by six.

For a listing of products and producers see Chapter 7.

2. Medium-Sized Distributors.

A buying co-op can handle a few direct connections with producers. However, especially in the beginning, the easiest approach is to pick out a distributor and order from its catalogue.

Large distributors to health-food stores won't sell to non-commercial purchasers at all. Some smaller ones will sell to buying clubs of six or more households. Three examples follow.

In this and the next section, a diamond (♦) at the end of a listing is assigned based on our survey in Chapter 8 or from independent testimonial from experts within the co-op community. Two or more diamonds represent multiple third-party testimony as described in Chapter 8; these double-diamond companies will be cited again in Chapter 8, as will many others. A heart (♥), again, means we have had personal experience of the company's commitment to the consumer.

Mountain Ark Trading Company, 120 South East Avenue, Fayetteville, AR 72701. (800) 643-8909 or (501) 442-7191. They sell to anyone ("Nation-Wide Mail Order," $1 for catalogue) and accept credit cards. For bulk orders ($100 minimum purchase), they offer (1) special prices (e.g., $21.99 for a 25–pound bag of organic brown price) on bulk items such as grains, beans, noodles, nuts and seeds, dried foods, and oils; and (2) a per-box handling fee of only $2 in addition to freight charges. They note that UPS freight charges go down when an order exceeds 200 pounds.[8]♥

Mountain Peoples Warehouse, 110 Springhill Bvld., Grass Valley, CA 95945. (916) 273-9531. This company has some degree of employee ownership, but is not a co-op. Do not confuse with Mountain Warehouse in Durham, N.C., which is a co-op listed in the next section.♦♦

Neshaminy Valley Natural Foods (accent on the "a" in Neshaminy), 5 Louise Drive, Ivy Land, PA 18974. (215) 443-5545. Jim Lyons gets his produce from Albert's Organics. He guarantees that all the produce he sells is from the Certified Organic category (as opposed to transitional and uncertified organic categories, which are also available from the distributor), with one exception—the lotus root he gets from California or China is generally not organically grown.♥♦♦♦

For a full listing of distributors around the country, see the end of Chapter 8.

3. Co-op Warehouse Distributors.

Because of the reluctance of commercial distributors to sell to buying co-ops, an important network of co-op warehouses has grown up. It is the spinal cord of the wholefood industry. The key organizations in this network are listed below.

Blooming Prairie, 2340 Heinz Road, Iowa City, IA 52240. (319) 337-6448. Sharon Lake, Purchasing Manager; Sue Futrell, Marketing Manager. Wrote and published *The Blooming Prairie Buying Club Manual* and the *Manual on Bookkeeping for Buying Clubs*, which emphasizes the financial side of running a buying club. *This is the most highly recommended of all the co-ops*, and is a major distributor in the Midwest.♦♦♦

Blooming Prairie Natural Foods, 510 Kasota Av. SE, Minneapolis, MN 55414. (612) 378-9774. Sue Futrell. Was set up under the auspices of Blooming Prairie in Iowa City. Sells rice, beans, flour.♦♦♦

Clear Eye, RD.1, Box 31, Savannah, NY 13146. (315) 365-2816.

Common Health Warehouse Cooperative, 1505 N. 8th St., Superior, WI 54880. (715) 392-9862. They deliver to northern Minnesota, northern Wisconsin, the upper peninsula of Michigan, North Dakota, Montana, and parts of South Dakota, and Wyoming.♦

Coopérative La Balance, 1249 De Condé St., Montréal, PQ H3K2E4. (514) 931-2936.♦

Federation of Ohio Cooperatives, 320 Outerbelt St., Columbus, OH 43213. (614) 861-2446.♦♦

Horizon Distributors/CRS Workers' Co-op, 3450 Vanness, Vancouver, BC V5R5A9. (604) 439-7977.♦

Hudson Valley Federation, serves southeastern New York, western Connecticut and parts of New Jersey, PO Box 367, Clintondale, NY 12515. (914) 883-6848.

Michigan Federation of Food Cooperatives, 727 W. Ellsworth, Ann Arbor, MI 48104. (313) 761-4642. They own People's Warehouse and the Daily Grind Flour Mill that provides the organic grains and flours they distribute.♦

Mountain Warehouse, 1400 East Geer Street, Durham, NC 27704. (919) 682-9234.♦♦

North Coast Cooperative, 3134 Jacobs Av., Eureka, CA 95501. (707) 445-3185.♦

North Farm Cooperative, 204 Regas Road, Madison, WI 53714. (608) 241-2667.♦

Northeast Cooperatives, Box 1120, Quinn Rd., Brattleboro, VT 72701. (802) 257-5856.♦♦

Nutrasource, 4005 6th Avenue South, Seattle, WA 98108. (206) 467-7190. This company is not itself a co-op, but is owned by co-ops. It was originally privately owned but was purchased by the Puget Consumers Co-op (a retail store) and others, including an Employee Stock Ownership Plan.♦♦

Ontario Federation of Food Coops, 22 Mowat Avenue, Toronto, ON M6K3E8. (416) 533-7879.♦

Orange Blossom Cooperative Warehouse, Burt Polansky (buyer), 1601 NW 55th Place, Gainesville, FL 32606, Mail to: PO Box 4159, Gainesville, FL 32613. (904) 372-7061.

Ozark Cooperative Warehouse, Box 30, Fayetteville, AR 72701. (501) 521-4920. Publishes the *Buying Club Manual: How to Organize a Pre-Order Co-op (or Buying Club)* with *Ozark Cooperative Warehouse,* which includes a sample order form, a sample co-op newsletter, and job descriptions for all the people involved in running a buying co-op. Also sells computer programs for running a buying co-op.♦

Roots and Fruits Cooperative Produce, 510 Kasota Ave. SE, Minneapolis, MN 55414. (612) 379-3030. This co-op leases space in the same building as Blooming Prairie Natural Foods but is a produce wholesaler.♦♦

Tucson Cooperative Warehouse, 359 S. Toole, Tucson, AZ 85701. (602) 884-9951.♦

The Nuts and Bolts of Ordering

What Can Be Shipped. Just about anything you buy in a store can be shipped by mail. But be sure you have a system for accepting delivery at your end, preferably someone at home or a doorman, or at least a safe back door and a notice to the trucker that it's OK to leave the shipment at the door.

Frozen food will typically be shipped via UPS overnight or Second Day Air in an insulated container with dry ice in it—a lot of wasteful packaging and energy use, and a higher price to pay for the packaging. (Frozen food is shipped to stores in refrigerated trucks.) Farm produce is generally shipped only by truck with minimal packaging—just a sturdy bag; the low ratio of value to weight of the items means that UPS shipping and related packaging is not cost-effective either for the buyer or the seller.

People working in distribution warn that just because something is in a wholesale catalogue, it isn't necessarily ready to be shipped out. Some 2 to 5 per cent of wholesale catalogue items are out of stock at a given time. Retail stores can call around to different distributors when they run out of something that is in demand; distributors may sell out more easily.

Delivery Time and Shipping Charges. The terms of delivery—delivery time, shipping charges, payment, damage coverage—vary greatly depending in large part on whether you are dealing with a distributor who will ship to you direct by truck, or a small producer who must rely on an outside shipper, usually UPS.

For a *distributor,* the truck routes are set in advance. You are told when a truck will be in your area, and you must get your order in—by phone or mail—two days or so ahead of the delivery. For example, in the case of Neshaminy Valley Natural Foods, a medium-sized distributor based in Pennsylvania, the truck is in Manhattan one day a week between 7 a.m. and 7 p.m., and one must get the order in by 4 p.m. two days before (the order may be changed up until noon the day before). Clear Eye Natural Foods, which distributes primarily in upstate New York, schedules a truck run to a given location once a month. It prints its truck route schedule four months in advance in its newspaper-style price list; orders must be in several days before the run.

Distributors will send orders out by UPS when buyers are outside of their truck delivery area, but they don't like it because UPS packaging is so labor-intensive. The good news for buyers is that distributors usually *do not charge* when they deliver by truck, at least if the order is large enough. Clear Eye Natural Foods delivers free for orders that are over half a ton, but charges $5 for orders between

750 and 1,000 pounds and $10 for orders below 750 pounds (and above the minimum truck-delivery order size of 500 lbs. or $500). Free truck delivery is an important feature when comparing costs between alternative suppliers.

A *small producer* doesn't have company trucks to deliver direct to you. Their goods are commonly picked up for resale by a distributor or by a buyer (a local restaurant or retailer) with its own truck. To sell direct to small buyers, the small producer must use UPS. The advantage of UPS over the U.S. Postal Service is that UPS picks up from the producer daily and ensures the goods will be taken from the point of pickup to point of delivery. Typical time for a UPS delivery is 2 days locally and 3 days across the country. If mustard is sold at $3.75/jar through the mail, vs. $4.98 at a city health-food store, and two jars are mailed for a UPS charge of $1.75, the shipping cost for a two-jar order makes it cost just a little less than the health-food store. The advantage of ordering directly is more obvious if the nearest wholefood store is not conveniently located, or does not carry the mustard. If the goods are highly perishable or are coming from the other side of the country, or both, you can pay extra for UPS second-day or next-day delivery, but this will cost an extra $10 or so. UPS charges are almost always added on by the grower or distributor to the buyer's bill. Buying locally grown food saves money and does the environment a favor by reducing energy used in transportation.

Payment. Many *distributors*, who are watching every dollar, want a check in advance or C.O.D., and don't accept credit cards because they can't afford the percentage the bank takes on the charges.

Small producers are more likely to accept Visa, Master-Card and American Express because they deal a lot with first-time orders. Credit cards ensure that they will get paid. They are also eager to do business directly with consumers because they make more money on these sales. Many of them like the direct contact with customers rather than the impersonal relationship they have with a big distributor. For a new customer, a seller will almost always want a credit card number, money in advance, or a good reference that can be checked out.

Damage and Returns. UPS insurance covers damage in transit. If goods come by truck, the distributor usually guarantees them and will replace an item if damaged.

Most sellers will accept return of products shipped in error, or spoiled, or defective. Some will pick them up or pay the return postage. For returns that are the buyer's error, some charge may be imposed. Clear Eye Natural Foods charges a "$2 restock fee" per item or unit.

Consumer Mail Order Rights

Under Federal Trade Commission (FTC) rules, mail and phone orders have certain rights.

Mail Orders. Mail orders are defined as orders that are sent in by mail (whether paid for by credit card or check) *or* orders that may have been placed by phone but are paid for by check. In either case, if they keep copies of their mailings, both sides of the transaction should have a paper trail covering the transaction.

The consumer's rights under these conditions are covered by the FTC's Mail Order Rule, adopted in 1975. It requires that (1) orders be shipped within 30 days of receipt, or within a time period specified in an advertisement, or that (2) the merchant promptly refund on demand the consumer's payment if the consumer chooses to cancel the order because of the delay.

Another advantage of mail orders is that they are covered by U.S. Postal Service regulations prohibiting interstate mail fraud. You may have recourse to the U.S. Postal Service inspectors and attorneys as well as FTC regulations.

Phone-and-Charge Orders. One way to place your order is to phone it in and charge it to a credit card. If you do this, you are not covered by the FTC's mail-order protections. *This applies to fax orders as well.*[9]

However, you have some protection. Under the Federal Fair Credit Billing Act, phone-and-charge orders entitle the consumer to dispute credit card charges for merchandise that failed to arrive. However, they have only 60 days from the charge to inform the credit card company of non-delivery of the merchandise. Therefore avoid advertisements where orders are promised after 60 days from payment.

The FTC has been considering since 1984 a change in its rules to extend mail order protections to phone-and-charge orders.

General Consumer Guidelines. The important advice for consumers, besides checking out a company ahead of time (for example, through the Better Business Bureau), is to keep a record of your order and payment and follow up promptly when the 30–day period has expired or when defective merchandise arrives.[10]

Finding Suppliers

Survey Results. We asked all of our respondents to name their favorite producers/brands. Many did not respond to this portion of the questionnaire and many big names like Tree of Life got far more recommendations under the distributor category (see Chapter 8). We received over 1,000 questionnaires. The number of recommendations is low in relation to the questionnaires returned, because each re-

Table 6–1
Most Recommended Wholefood Producers

Votes	Company
82	Arrowhead Mills, Hereford, TX
81	Health Valley, Montebello, CA
69	Eden Foods, Clinton, MI
38	Lundberg Family Farms, Richvale, CA
32	Little Bear Organics, Pacific Palisades, CA
29	Knudsen & Sons, Chico, CA
25	Fantastic Foods, Inc., Novato, CA
24	Hain Food Co (PET), Los Angeles, CA
22	Barbara's Bakery, Novato/Petaluma, CA
21	Westbrae, Downey/Ennerville, CA
19	After the Fall, Brattleboro, VT
16	Spectrum Naturals/Oils, Petaluma, CA
15	Alta Dena Dairies, City of Industry, CA
14	Cascadian Farms, Concrete, WA
13	Shiloh Farms, AR
12	Tree of Life, St. Augustine, FL
10	Walnut Acres, Penns Creek, PA
9	Little Bear, Minneapolis/Winona, MN
8	Erewhon (non-U.S. Mills) NE/Los Angeles, CA
8	Twin Lab, Ronkonkoma, NY
8	Ventre Packing/Enrico's, Syracuse, NY
7	Garden of Eatin, Los Angeles, CA
7	Organic Farms Inc., Beltsville, MD
7	White Wave, Boulder/Denver, CO
6	Colonel Sanchez, Venice, CA
6	San J, San Francisco, CA
6	Shelton's, Pomona, CA
5	Corr Sodas, Robert J., Chicago, IL
5	Frontier Co-op Herbs, Norway, IA
5	Nature's Path/Manna, Richmond, BC, Canada
5	New Morning, Leominster, MA
5	Pacific Rice, Woodland, CA
5	U.S. Mills/Erewhon, Newtown Upper Falls, MA
4	Celestial Seasonings, Boulder, CO
4	Imagine Foods/Rice Dream, Palo Alto, CA
4	Jaffe, Imperial, CA
4	Lakewood, Miami, FL
4	Nasoya Foods, Leominster, MA
4	Purity Foods, Okemos, MI
4	Rainbow Light, Santa Cruz, CA
4	Worthington Foods, Worthington, OH
3	Albert's Organic, Los Angeles, CA
3	Amy's Kitchen, Petaluma, CA
3	De Boles, Garden City, NY
3	Earth's Best, Middlebury, VT
3	Guistos, So. San Francisco, CA
3	Heinke's Juice Co. (Weider), Paradise, CA
3	Island Springs, Vashon, WA
3	Maine Coast Vegetables, Franklin, ME
3	Mercantile Foods, Redding, CT
3	Nature's Best, Torrance, CA
3	Neshaminy Valley, Ivyland, PA
3	Pizsoy, Cherry Hill, NJ
3	Solaray, Ogden, UT
3	Spring Creek Natural Foods, Spencer, WV
3	Timber Crest Farms, Sonoma, CA
3	Vegetarian Health, Chicago, IL

Source: National mail survey by the author, summer and fall 1989. The "votes" were all write-ins; no ballot was provided.

spondent was asked to provide just a short list of nominees, and many chose not to answer this question. The ranking below of 57 growers and manufacturers is a rough guide to the country's most widely respected healthy-food suppliers. However, the industry is changing rapidly and includes many rising stars. (See Table 6–1.)

The top-rated companies are Arrowhead Mills, which produces grains and grain products, and Health Valley, which offers a full range of packaged goods.

Two of the companies on this list—Barbara's Bakery and Celestial Seasonings—rate highly in *Shopping for a Better World*, the guide to socially responsible companies prepared by the New York-based Council on Economic Priorities.[11] Another highly rated wholefood producer was Dolefam (makes Monk Oil olive oil).

Directory of Producers and Manufacturers. The product directory in Chapter 7 provides good leads for you as an alternative or backup to your local health-food store, for example in order to have the food delivered directly, or to have the wider choice (and usually lower prices) that direct purchase provides.

We do our best to give you up-to-date information, but can't be sure that when you use the directory every piece of information will still be accurate. Our directory cannot substitute for your own investigation when you are ready to buy. If you find that a piece of information is outdated, we would appreciate your letting us know by using the INFO-FORM on the last page of this book.

Consumer Assistance Agencies

The following resources may help in checking on on current laws or a possible supplier, or following up on nondelivery or other problem. It would take up too much space to describe all the consumer affairs advocates in each city and state, but a few are provided from four large cities and the two largest states as examples.

California Department of Health Services, Food and Drug Branch, 714 P Street, Sacramento, CA 95814. (916) 445–2263. Dr. Jack Sheneman, Food and Drug Scientist. State equivalent of the FDA. Enforces all state laws relating to the manufacture and packaging of food products, including organic food labeling. Dr. Sheneman is frank about the fact that policing organic food is a low priority, compared to "monitoring the functioning of artificial heart valves," and that fraudulent labeling is up to local district attorneys to act on. He says that California's organic food law is used by growers and distributors outside of California to identify goods they are shipping to other states. Since the goods never enter the State of California, Dr. Sheneman doesn't even have an opportunity to police the validity of the labeling. He considers such use misrepresentation bordering on fraud. The Los Angeles office is at 1449 West Temple, Los Angeles, CA 90026. (213) 620–2965. Other offices are located throughout the state.

Chicago, Department of Consumer Services of the City of, 121 N. LaSalle, Chicago, IL. (312) 744–4092.

Council of Better Business Bureaus, 4200 Wilson Boulevard, #800, Arlington, VA 22209. (703) 276–0100. James H. McIlhenny, President. Umbrella organization for nearly 200 affiliated Better Business Bureaus throughout the U.S. and Canada.

Direct Marketing Association, 1101 17th Street, N.W., Washington, DC. (202) 347–1222. Chester G. Dalzell, media relations manager.

Los Angeles, Consumer Affairs Office of the County of, 500 West Temple, Los Angeles, CA. (213) 974–1452.

New York, Better Business Bureau of Metropolitan, 257 Park Avenue South, New York, NY. (212) 533–6200. Barbara Berger Optowsky, President.

New York City, Consumer Affairs Department of, 80 Lafayette Street, New York, NY 10005. (212) 577–0111. Mark Green, J.D., Commissioner. Newly elected Mayor David Dinkins has installed a vigorous activist for consumer rights, who has considerable enforcement power through his ability to rescind store licenses.♥

New York State, Consumer Protection Board of, 250 Broadway, New York, NY 10007. (212) 587–4908. Consumer advisers will take complaint information and attempt to mediate a solution. Gross offenses are referred to Attorney General Robert Abrams for legal action.

New York State Department of Agriculture and Markets, 1 Winners Circle, Albany, NY 12235. (518) 457–5368. Maurice Guerrette, Director, Food Inspection Services. Inspects and regulates supermarkets, bakeries, delis, farmers' markets, and manufacturing plants, with a few exceptions—the USDA enforces Federal meat standards, and New York City's Department of Health inspects restaurants. New York City office: Two World Trade Center, 27th Floor, New York, NY 10047. (212) 488–4823.

U.S. Federal Trade Commission, Pennsylvania Ave. at 6th Street, N.W., Washington, DC 20580. (202) 326–2180. Office of Public Affairs. Joel Brewer, attorney, Bureau of Consumer Protection.

U.S. Postal Service, 475 L'Enfant Plaza, S.W., Washington, DC 20260. (202) 268–2284: Office of the Consumer Advocate. Peter Wheeler, attorney.

Washington, Better Business Bureau of Metropolitan, 1012 14th Street, N.W., Washington, DC. (202) 393–8000.

General Mail Order

Chapter 7 lists many companies that specialize in one item (e.g., amaranth flour) or a single category of items (e.g., soy products). The following directories list businesses that will sell many retail items to you. They are meant to serve people who do not live near wholefood stores, or are looking for products not sold in stores. The first list, "Mail Order Houses," is of establishments that mainly sell by mail. The second list, "Retailers/Producers That Take Mail Orders," identifies companies that will sell by mail on request.

Many retail stores will fulfil mail orders on a limited basis. If you can find such a store within a 200–mile radius, you could end up saving a lot on postage.

The first, shorter, list is arranged alphabetically by company name; the second, longer, one is arranged by state.

1. Mail Order Houses (Companies with Large Mail Business)

Allergy Resources Inc., 195 Huntington Beach Dr., Colorado Springs, CO 80921. (719) 488–3630. **Type of Business:** Mail order distributor. **Sells to:** Retailers and the public. **Sells:** "All your allergy needs delivered to your door." Condiments, baking goods, baking substitutes, flours, milk substitutes and powders, wheat-free and gluten-free products, grains and meals, sprouting seeds, dried rice and beans, oils, pasta, cereals, and accessories. **Certification:** Asserted 60% organic. **Prices:** Some discounts available on large orders. **Shipping:** UPS. **Minimum Order:** Varies. **Catalogue Available?** Yes.

Deer Valley Farm, RD#1, Guilford, NY 13780. (607) 764–8556. **Type of Business:** Grower, manufacturer, and distributor since 1947. **Sells to:** Retailers and mail order to the public. **Sells:** Dried beans, dried fruit, whole grains, flours and meals, sweeteners, fresh vegetables, baked goods, processed grain products, and meat. **Organic?** Asserted Organic (50%). Member of NY-NOFA. (See Chapter 6 for more).

Diamond K Enterprises, Jack Kranz, R.R. 1, Box 30, St. Charles, MN 55972. (507) 932–4308. **Type of Business:** Manufacturer, retailer, wholesaler, broker and mail-order distributor. **Sells to:** Retailers and the public. **Sells:** Dried and fresh beans, flours and meals, grains, nuts, processed grain products, seeds, oils and dried fruits. **Organic?** Asserted organic. **Credit:** V M. **Prices:** Discount for large orders. **Hours:** M-Sat, 8–5. **Shipping:** All USA areas served usually allow 1–2 weeks for delivery. **Minimum Order:** None. **Catalogue Available?** Yes.

Gravelly Ridge Farms, Star Route 16, Elk Creek, CA 95939. (916) 963–3216. **Type of Business:** Mail order distributor. **Sells to:** Retail stores and the public. **Sells:** A wide variety of organic fresh fruit, dried fruit, vegetables, and grains. **Certification:** CCOF certified. **Hours:** M-F and Sunday, 9–6. **Shipping:** They ship perishables on the same day they are harvested. Availability depends on season. **Minimum Order:** None.**Catalogue Available?** Yes.

Green Earth, 2545 Prairie St., Evanston, IL 60201. (800) 322–3662, (312) 864–8949. **Type of Business:** Retail store and mail-order distributor. **Sells to:** The public. **Sells:** They specialize in organic food and have a wide selection of organic produce, organic grains, and meat from organically grown animals. **Organic?** Most of their goods are certified organic, agency varies. **Credit:** V M. **Hours:** 10–7 daily. **Shipping:** They ship Monday through Thursday by UPS or Federal Express (if necessary). They ship their perishable orders in reusable styrofoam containers within cardboard boxes with call tags. **Minimum Order:** None. **Catalogue Available?** Yes. **Comments:** They actively support sustainable agriculture and ecologically sound practices.♦

Healthfoods Express, Lin Martin, President, 181 Sylmar, Clovis, CA 93612. (209) 252–8321. **Type of Business:** Mail order distributor. **Sells to:** Public. **Sells:** Vegetable meat analogs, granola, wheat, cheese substitute, soybean milk, coffee and tea substitutes. **Certification:** None. **Credit:** Visa and Mastercard. **Prices:** 10% discount on case orders, $3 discount on first order of $30 or more and 5% bonus discount on all non-sale items to be used on subsequent orders (done through a system of awarding bonus points. **Shipping:** UPS. **Minimum Order:** Suggested $30, but any order accepted. **Catalogue Available?** Yes.

Jaffe Bros. Inc., E. Jaffe, PO Box 636, Valley Center, CA 92082. (619) 749–1133. **Type of Business:** Mail order distributor. **Sells to:** Retail stores and the public. **Sells:** Beans (chick peas, kidney beans, lima, navy, pinto, black-eyed peas, black turtle beans), grains (barley, buckwheat, corn, popcorn, millet, oats, rice, wheat), dried fruit, nuts and nut butters (almond, sesame, tahini, peanut, cashew, macadamia). **Certification:** Asserted organic. **Credit:** V, M, and C.O.D. **Prices:** Discounts on 20lb, 25lb, and 50lb cases. **Hours:** M-F and Sundays 8–5. **Shipping:** Normally within 2 days. **Minimum Order:** None. **Catalogue Available?** Yes.

Macrobiotic Wholesale Company, 799 Old Leicester Hwy, Asheville, NC 28806. (704) 252–1221. **Type of Business:** Mail order distributor. **Sells to:** The public. **Sells:** Macrobiotic products. **Other:** They also deliver goods by common carrier. No minimum order. Some organic products.

Moksha Natural Foods, 724 Palm Ave, Watsonville, CA 95076. (408) 724–2009. Toll-free (800) 274–8778. **Type of Business:** Mail order distributor. **Sells to:** The public. **Sells:** A wide variety of goods from tomatoes to cornmeal to truffles. **Organic?** Asserted 10–15%. **Credit:** V M. **Prices:** 10% off case orders. **Shipping:** Orders are sent out within a week of receipt by UPS. **Minimum Order:** $15. **Catalogue Available?** Yes. **Comments:** They are new to the business, but seem to have made a good start. Their catalogue is very attractive and straightforward.

Mountain Ark Trading Co., Robb Boyd, Frank Head, 120 South East Avenue, Fayetteville, AR 72701. (501) 442–7191, (800) 643–8909. **Type of Business:** Distributor. **Sells to:** Stores and the public—mail order retail all over the world. **Sells:** Organic coffee, condiments (including Umeboshi products, and organic lime vinegar), dried beans (including turtle, pinto, and anazi), dried fruit, whole grains (including teff, and quinoa), flour and meal grains, processed grains (including Japanese pastas and seitan), sourdough bread, herbs, nuts, nut butters (peanut, tahini, sesame, almonds), oils (sesame, corn, olive), soy products (tempeh, natto, soymilk and starters), sweeteners (rice syrup, barley malt, amesake), soups, teas (bancha, barley, lotus root, dandelion, burdock), beer (beer home processing kits), sea vegetables and fish (in season). **Volume:** Approaching $1 million a year. **Organic?** Asserted organic, 70%. Some products are labeled as certified organic, depending on which farm produces them. They look for official state certification or grower documentation. **Pricing:** Two prices for all products: retail and bulk. **Credit:** V M AE. **Prices:** Generally lower than retail. A bulk price list comes with the catalog. **Hours:** M-F 8–5, Sat 8–12. **Shipping:** Ships UPS or (especially for those who only have a Post Office box or otherwise can't accept UPS) parcel post. **Minimum Order:** None for retail, $100 for bulk orders. **Catalogue Available?** Yes.♥

New American Food Co., David Johnson, PO Box 3206, Durham, NC 27705. (919) 682–9210. **Type of Business:** Mail order distributor. **Sells to:** Public. **Sells:** Baked goods, beans, beverages, candy, cereals, whole wheat flour, apple juice, applesauce, nuts (peanuts, cashews and almonds), oils, pasta, rice, soy products and salsa. **Organic?** Asserted 60% organic, rely on the certification of suppliers. **Credit:** V M AE. **Prices:** No discount for bulk. **Hours:** 24 hours. **Minimum Order:** None. **Catalogue Available?** Yes.

Timber Crest Farms, 4791 Dry Creek, Healdsburg, CA 95448. (707) 433–8251. FAX (707) 433–8255. **Type of Business:** Mail-order distributor. **Sells to:** The public and distributors. **Sells:** A wide range of organic dried fruits and vegetables, nuts, and gift packs. Organic: apples, apricots, diced mixed fruit, mixed fruit, peaches, pears, prunes (3 sizes), monukka raisins, Thompson Raisins. Non-organic: cherries, dates, white figs, mission figs, mango, papaya, pineapple chips, pineapple rings, star fruit, almonds, brazil nuts, cashews, filberts, pistachios, wheat nuts, Tomato bits, pasta sauce, tomato halves, dried tomato chutney, dried tomato tapenade, apple butter, pear butter, and plum butter. **Organic?** They assert that most of their products are organically grown CCOF. No sulfiting agents used on any products. **Credit:** M V AE. **Prices:** Most "Sonoma" items are 8–12 oz and cost around $4. Gift packs run from $10–$30. "Timber Crest" bags are typically 5 lbs and cost $13–$46. **Shipping:** Extra postage charges for Alaska, Hawaii, and Canada ($.50 per small "Sonoma bags" and $4 for bigger, 5lb. "Timber Crest" bags). **Minimum Order:** None. **Catalogue Available?** Yes, 13 pages with photographs of the products.

Walnut Acres, Walnut Acres Road, Penns Creek, PA 17862. (717) 837–0601. **Type of Business:** Grower, manufacturer, mail order distributor, and retailer. **Sells to:** Distributors, retailers and mail order to public. **Sells:** Baked goods (cookies, breads, muffins, pancakes), dried beans, whole grains, flours, pasta, rice, cheese, oils, nuts and nut butters, dried fruit, soy products, spices, fruit juices, canned soups and canned vegetables. Fresh fruit, meat, vegetables, tempeh, tofu and yogurt available at store only. **Organic?** 100% organic for fresh produce (OCIA), and 80% for processed goods. **Credit:** V M. **Prices:** 25% off retail for wholesale orders. **Hours:** M-Sat 8–5. **Shipping:** Orders shipped worldwide within 3 working days of receipt. **Minimum Order:** $300 for wholesale; none for retail. **Catalogue Available?** Yes. **Comments:** Walnut Acres, one of the oldest organic farms in the country (dating back to 1946), is one of the most frequently recommended mail-order distributors we have come across and they make or sell a lot of terrific products.♦♦♦

2. Retailers/Producers That Take Mail Orders

For more details on these companies, including ratings, see Chapter 10 or, if so identified, Chapter 8. The idea is to use this list to find retailers near you, and then to check on what they sell in detail in Chapter 10 (or 8).

Alabama

Huntsville, **Pearly Gates Natural Foods,** Myrna Copeland, 2308 Memorial Parkway S.W., Huntsville, AL 35801. (205) 534–6233.

Arkansas

Huntsville, **Eagle Agricultural Products,** Inc., Gary and Kathy Turner, 407 Church Ave., Huntsville, AR 72740. (501) 738–2203.

California

Arcata, **Mad River Farm Country Kitchen,** Susan Anderson, PO Box 155, Arcata, CA 95521. (707) 822–7150.

Costa Mesa, **Mother's Market & Kitchen,** 225 E. 17th St., Costa Mesa, CA 92627. (714) 631–4741.

Elk Creek, **Gravelly Ridge Farms,** Star Route 16, Elk Creek, CA 95939. (916) 963–3216.

Fullerton, **Health Foods,** 115 E. Commonwealth, Fullerton, CA 92632.

Huntington Beach, **Mother's Market & Kitchen,** 19770 Beach Blvd., Huntington Beach, CA 92648. (714) 963–6667.

Huntington Beach, **Licata's Nutrition Centers,** 5242 Bolsa Ave., Suite 3, Huntington Beach, CA 92647. (714) 893–0017. Retail Store located in Anaheim.

Lakeport, **Nature's Food Center,** 601 N. Forbes, Lakeport, CA 95453. (707) 263–5359.

Los Angeles, **Melissa's Brand** (World Variety Produce Inc.), Manny Duran or Trudy Hernandez, PO Box 21407, Los Angeles, CA 90021. (213) 588–0151

Mendocino, **Old Mill Farm School of Country Living,** Mail to: PO Box 463, Mendocino, CA 95460. (707) 937–0244.

Nevada City, **Alpine Aire Foods,** Box 926, Nevada City, CA 95959. (800) 322–6325.

Pescadero, **Jacobs Farm,** Sandy, Larry, Box 508, Pescadero, CA 94060. (415) 879–0508. Fax: (415) 879–0930.

Philo, **Dach Ranch,** Mendocino Growers, John Dach, 9201 Hwy 128, Mail to: PO Box 44, Philo, CA 95466. (707) 895–3173; evenings 707–895–3382.

Sebastopol, **Appleseed Ranch,** Paul Kolling, 1834 High School Road, Sebastopol, CA 95472. (707) 823–4408.

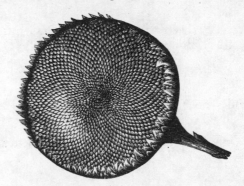

Yuba City, **Sunflower Natural Foods,** 726 Sutter St., Yuba City, CA 95991. (916) 671–9511.

Colorado

Gardner, **Malachite School and Small Farm,** Alan Mace, ASR Box 21 Pass Creek Road, Gardner, CO 81040. (719) 746–2412.

Connecticut

Greenwich, **Greenwich Healthmart,** Chuck Ringel, 30 Greenwich Avenue, Greenwich, CT 06830. (203) 869–9658.

Florida

Gainesville, **Orange Blossom Cooperative Warehouse,** PO Box 4159, Gainesville, FL 32613. (904) 372–7061.

Miami, **Sprout Delights Inc.,** Steven Bern, 13090–2702, N.W. 7th Ave., Miami, FL 33168. (305) 687–5880, (800) 334–2253.

Illinois

Chicago, **New City Market,** 1810 N Halsted St., Chicago, IL 60614. (312) 280–7600.

Downers Grove, **The Fruitful Yield,** Gary Kleinman, 2111 63rd St., Downers Grove, IL 60515. (312) 969–7614.

Evanston, **The Green Earth,** 2545 Prairie St., Evanston, IL 60201. (800) 322–3662, (312) 864–8949.

New Lenox, **Salt of the Earth Natural Foods,** Sue Dite and Barbara Hoyt, Owners, 1340 N. Cedar Road, New Lenox, IL 60451. (815) 485–6525.

Skokie, **The Fruitful Yield,** 4950 Oakton, Skokie, IL 60077. (708) 788–9103.

Indiana

Indianapolis, **Good Earth Natural Food Store,** 6350 N. Guilford Ave., Indianapolis, IN 46220. (317) 253–3609.

Iowa

Laurel, **Paul's Grains, Wayne,** 2475–B 340 St., Laurel, IA 50141. (515) 476–3373.

Maine

Belfast, **Fiddler's Green Farm,** Nancy Galland and Richard Stander, Owners, RR 1, Box 656, Belfast, ME 04915. (207) 338–3568.

Bridgewater, **Wood Prairie Farm,** Jim and Megan Gerritsen, RFD 1, Box 164, Bridgewater, ME 04735. (207) 429–9765.

Maryland

Beltsville, **Organic Foods Express,** Scott Nash, 11003 Emack Road, Beltsville, MD 20705. (301) 937–8608.

Frederick, **It's Only Natural,** 43 E. Patrick St., Frederick, MD 21701. (301) 662–7277.

Massachusetts

Cambridge, **Equal Exchange,** PO Box 2652, Cambridge, MA 02238. (617) 482–4995.

Michigan

Grand Rapids, **Harvest Health Inc.,** Henry Diedering, 1944 Eastern Ave. SE, Grand Rapids, MI 40507. (616) 245–6268.

Midland, **Wysong Corporation,** David Singsank, 1880 N. Eastman Road, Midland, MI 48640. (517) 631–0009.

West Cassopolis, **Roseland Farms,** John and Merill Clark, 27427 M-60 West Cassopolis, MI 49031. (616) 445–8769, (616) 445–8987.

Minnesota

East Bethel, **Nomadic Organics Inc.,** Bill Krahn, Edward Brown, 22921 N.E. Johnson St., East Bethel, MN 55005.

Garrison, **Life-Renewal Inc., Div. Garrco, Inc.,** Ronald M. Holmquist, Highway 18, Box 92, Garrison, MN 56450. (612) 692–4498.

Missouri

Willow Springs, **Plumbottom Farm,** Rt. 3, Box 129, Willow Springs, MO 65793.

Montana

Helena, **Real Food Store,** Laughing Water, Owner/Manager, 1090 Helena Avenue, Helena, MT 59601.

Nevada

Las Vegas, **Ira's Organic Foods Market,** Ira Lovitch, 5643 W. Charleston Blvd #3, Las Vegas, NV 89102. (702) 258–4250.

Las Vegas, **J & J Health Foods,** 3870 E. Flamingo, Las Vegas, NV 89121. (702) 456–7807.

New Jersey

Hightstown, **Nutrition Center,** Becky Russell, Rte. 130, Warren Plaza West, Hightstown, NJ 08520. (609) 448–4885.

Pennsville, **Simply Delicious,** 243–A N. Hook Rd., Box 124, Pennsville, NJ 08070. (609) 678–4488.

New York

Hicksville, **Good Life Natural Foods,** 339 S. Broadway, Hicksville, NY 11801. (516) 935–5073.

New York, **Integral Yoga Natural Foods,** 229 West 13th Street (near 8th Avenue), New York, NY 10011. (212) 243–2642.

North Carolina

Waynesville, **Zoolie's Natural Food Market, Inc.,** Jean & Phil Davis, 208 Haywood Square, PO Box 869, Waynesville, NC 28786. (704) 452–3663.

Ohio

Akron, **Millstream Natural Health Supplies,** Jonathan D. Miller, 1310–A E. Tallmadge Ave, Akron, OH 44310. (216) 630–2700.

Clarksville, **Todd's Fork Creek Company,** 885 N. George Rd., Clarksville, OH 45113. (513) 289–2040.

Pennsylvania

Altoona, **Millenial Health & Books,** 1718 12th Ave., Altoona, PA 16601. (814) 949–9108.

Manheim, **Weavers Natural Food, Inc.,** 15 Market Square, Manheim, PA 17545. (717) 665–6871.

Milesburg, **Rising Sun Organic Produce,** Hope P. Woodring, Box 627 I-80 & PA-150, Milesburg, PA 16853. (814) 355-9850.

New Holland, **Garden Spot Distributors,** 438 White Oak Road, Box 729 A, New Holland, PA 17557. (717) 354-4936. (See Chapter 8 for more.)

Philadelphia, **Health Foods International,** 3585 Aramingo Ave., Philadelphia, PA 19134. (215) 289-5750.

Tamaqua, **Dutch Country Gardens,** Joseph Yasenchek, Box 1122 Rd. #1, Tamaqua, PA 18252. (717) 668-0441.

Valencia, **Frankferd Farms,** T. Lyle or Betty Ferderber, 318 Love Rd., Rd.#1, Valencia, PA 16059. (412) 898-2242.

Rhode Island

Newport, **Harvest Natural Foods,** 1 Casino Terrace, Newport, RI 02840. (401) 846-8137.

Tennessee

Chattanooga, **The Vitality Center,** 1150 Hixson Pike, Chattanooga, TN 37405. (615) 266-5016.

Memphis, **Honeysuckle Health Foods,** 4741 Poplar, Memphis, TN 38117. (901) 682-6255.

Texas

Hereford, **Arrowhead Mills Inc.,** Boyd Foster, PO Box 2059, 110 South Lawton, Hereford, TX 79045. (806) 364-0730, (806) 364-8242.

Vermont

Bethel, **Rathdowney Ltd.,** Brendan Downey-Butler, 3 River St., Bethel, VT 05032. (802) 234-9928.

Burlington, **Origanum Natural Foods,** Catherine Camp, 227 Main St., Burlington, VT 05401. (802) 863-6103.

Chester, **Gourmet Produce Co.,** Richard D. Rommer, RR 3, Box 348, Chester, VT 05143. (802) 875-3820.

Virgin Islands

Christiansted, **Good Health,** Antoine or Pat Murray, United Shopping Plaza, Christiansted, St. Croix, Virgin Islands, VI 00820. (809) 778-5565.

Virginia

Blacksburg, **Eats Natural Foods,** 1200 N. Main St., Blacksburg, VA. (703) 463-2279.

Edinburg, **Magic Garden Produce,** Robert Peer, Rt. 3, Box 304, Edinburg, VA 22824. (703) 459-3376.

Virginia Beach, **Heritage Store,** Box 444, Virginia Beach, VA 23458. (804) 428-0100.

Washington

Chelan, **Bear Foods Wholesale-Golden Florins General Store,** Charlie Bear, PO Box 2118, 125 E Woodin Ave, Chelan, WA 98816. (509) 682-5535.

Ellensburg, **Better Life Natural Foods,** 111 West 6th St., Ellensburg WA 98926. (509) 925-2505.

Seattle, **Ener-G Foods Inc.,** PO Box 84487, Seattle, WA 98124. (206) 767-6660, (800) 331-5222, in WA (800) 325-9788, FAX: (206) 767-4088.

Wisconsin

Brookfield, **Omega-Life Inc.,** P. O. Box 208, 15355 Woodbridge Rd., Brookfield, WI 53005. (414) 786-2070.

Wyoming

Caspar, **Wyoming Natural Foods,** 242 S. Wolcott, Caspar, WY 82601. (307) 234-4196.

Organic Farms Inc. is one of the largest distributors of organics in the United States, supplying much of the East Coast with everything from pasta and tamari to fruit juices and carrots.

7

PRODUCT GUIDE

*Caution: Many products claim to be a "good source" of something like oat bran
when the something amounts to nothing more (health-wise and-quantity wise)
than pixie dust. Check the fine print on the label.*

The focus in the following Product/Producer Directory is on food only, not vitamins, or mineral supplements, or health-care products. (We cover garlic, but not concentrated garlic. We cover herbs, but not herb capsules.)

General Rules for Finding Good Products

You are more likely to get whole, pesticide-free foods in natural-food/wholefood stores, but it is not a certainty. Even in these stores you should read the labels to make sure.

For a complete treatment of labeling laws and standards see Chapter 2. The following are some hints for sorting out the claims you might find on a product label:

1. Be wary of "all natural" claims. The term is legally meaningless (except in Maine and in meat products) and does not imply that products are free of pesticides (organic). There are also natural additives that are not good for you (e.g. coconut oil). Sometimes it does denote food that is better for you, but not always.

2. If it says "cholesterol-free!" there is a fair chance that all the other brands are cholesterol-free too. Any plant-based product should be cholesterol-free, so don't be impressed by peanut butters or bananas that bear that label.

3. Caution: Many products claim to be a "good source" of something like oat bran when the something amounts to nothing more (health-wise and quantity-wise) than pixie dust. Check the fine print on the label.

4. If it says "lite," check the calories to see just how much "liter" it really is than regular brands.

5. If it says "no salt added," that does not necessarily mean there is no salt in the product. Some cracker companies take this label to mean there is no salt on the outside—meaning there could be sodium in the doughy part.

6. "Fruit Juice Sweetened" is not necessarily an improvement over conventional processed sugar.

7. Sugar-free and sugarless refer only to table sugar (sucrose). Other forms of sugar (like fructose) and artificial sweeteners can be used in these products.

8. Make sure any beneficial claims the product makes are really beneficial. For example, one product we came across claimed it was a good source of simple carbohydrates. Well, so is processed sugar. (Eating complex carbohydrates leads to a more even energy supply between meals).

9. "Premium" and "Gourmet" are often euphemisms for "fatty."

10. A product that claims to be 95% fat-free can still have lots of fat because the claim refers to weight. Whole milk is 96% fat-free but still gets 48% of its calories from fat.

11. Organic foods with lots of saturated fat (e.g. chips or cookies) may be better for you than the same sort of foods with non-organic ingredients. However, it would not be right to say they are good for you. Don't let labels like "eat [these oat-bran potato chips] to your heart's content," soothe you. In the long run your heart will not be content.

12. Be wary of any medical claims listed on food products; these products have not been government-tested for medicinal properties. The FDA has announced that it plans to return soon to stricter standards.

If you are trying to find something we don't list:

• Try the Mainly Mail Order companies in Chapter 6; many of them sell products beyond those we had space to list here.

• Ask someone at one of the establishments in Chapter

10 or call one of the companies listed in this chapter and in Chapter 8; From our experiences, most of the people in these businesses are quite friendly and probably can help you find what you want.

How the List is Organized

We combined some similar foods (e.g. grains) and listed some products under broad general categories such as "beverages" and "convenience mixes."

References are sometimes made to the volume of foreign imports of the listed product. The purpose is to alert buyers to the possibility that growing standards depend on the regulations of a foreign agency. Mexico, for example, has few regulations regarding the use of chemicals on the winter tomatoes that are imported into the United States in large quantity.

Commonly used pesticides are listed for many fruits and vegetables to show the variety of chemicals that are in use. Wax on produce seals in pesticides; otherwise many pesticides can be washed off or reduced by cooking.

We name brand names, producers, and in some cases suppliers and distributors. We try to give a brief description of the product or company and the address and phone number. If the product is available by mail order directly from the company, we usually say so. Many items are available only through stores or in wholesale quantities. If you want to buy some of these products by mail, the stores and cooperative warehouses listed in Chapter 6 can probably accommodate you.

Hearts ♥ denote the companies and brands that are our favorites. Diamonds ♦ indicate how often a company was recommended by businesses we surveyed, magazines that we surveyed, magazines that write on wholefoods, or by our consultants.

PRODUCT/PRODUCER DIRECTORY

Alcohol. See also Beer, Wine. Alcohol is a target of both the Dietary Guidelines for Americans issued by the USDA's Human Nutrition Service and the Surgeon General's Report (see Chapter 3). Alcohol itself has almost no nutritional value but has plenty of calories—7 per gram, nearly as much as fat. Most mixed drinks add even more calories in the form of sugary soft drinks. One or two drinks are not believed to be harmful to healthy non-pregnant adults. However, heavy drinking may cause serious nutritional deficiencies as well as liver disease, hypertension and certain types of cancer (especially if the drinker also smokes). Drinking by pregnant women can cause birth defects in their babies. Furthermore, half of all traffic accidents on U.S. highways are alcohol-related. Cutting back on or cutting out alcoholic beverages is a nutritionally sound way to reduce calorie intake. A jigger of hard liquor has more calories (105) than 12 ounces of light beer.

Almonds. See also Nuts. Thanks in part to an aggressive marketing strategy, almond consumption has boomed over the last 10 years. The average American now consumes more than half a pound of almonds a year. Almonds are a source of fiber and contain small amounts of eight of the nine essential amino acids. Almonds also contain a lot of fat (over 90 percent of the calories) and staggering amounts of sodium in their salted form. The almond industry is quick to point out that most of the fat is polyunsaturated and that a quarter of it is in the form of linoleic acid, a chemical group that is said to help prevent cancer. If you eat almonds go for the unsalted varieties.

Blue Diamond— They don't grow 100% organic, but some of their farmers grow chemical-free and they seem to take integrated pest management seriously.

Amaranth. A "super-grain" that, when blended properly with wheat flour, is reputed to have 20 amino acids (including the nine essential acids) in proper proportions. It is under cultivation in only three states, and is about 20 times more expensive (per bushel) than wheat. It has a particularly high concentration of the amino acid lysine and is high in phosphorous and calcium. Amaranth has a reputation as a super-energizer. See also Grains.

Arrowhead Mills— Organic Amaranth. See listing under Grains.

Cheyenne Gap Amaranth— Amaranth grain and flour (mail order), Arris Sigle, H.C. 1, Box 2, Luray, KS 67649-9743. (913) 698-2457 early until 8 a.m. Central Time, (913) 698-2292 all day. (See listing in Chapter 10.)

Cross Seed Co— Sells Golden Amaranth and Amaranth Pancake & Biscuit Flower Mix (asserted 100% organic), as well as organic beans, grains, and seeds by mail. HC 69 Box 2, Bunker Hill, KS 67626. (913) 483-6163.

Grainaissance Inc.— Amaranth. As they sell through distributors, try a gourmet or healthy food store. 1580 62nd St., Emeryville, CA 94608. (415) 547-7256.

Health Valley— Amaranth Cereals and pilafs with organically grown grain. Also cookies, crackers, muffins, pilaf, whole wheat pasta, and soy milk. Many of their products are also low-salt. Sold through stores.♥♦♦♦♦

Helmuth Country Bakery— A wide variety of Amaranth and wheat baked goods. Available by mail. They assert 10% of their products are organic, some of the ingredients grown on their own organic farm. 6706 W Mills Road, Hutchinson, KS 67501. (316) 567-2301.

New Morning— Crispy Brown Rice w/ Amaranth Cereal. Sold through stores. 24 Jytak Park, Leominster, MA. 01453-5932.♦

Nu-World Amaranth, Inc.— Amaranth in many forms from puffed to flour, Larry Walters, PO Box 2202, Naperville, IL 60567. (312) 369-6819, FAX: (312) 416-8316. (See listing in Chapter 10)

Anazi. See Legumes.

Amazake. A nectar-like beverage obtained by adding koji (cooked grains that have been inoculated with a type of mold) to cooked rice and incubating. It is easy to digest, a leavening agent in baked goods, and a base for non-dairy ice cream.

Grainaissance Inc.— Amazake and Mochi. As they sell through distributors, try a gourmet or healthy food store. 1580 62nd St., Emeryville, CA 94608. (415) 547-7256.

Kendal Food Co.— Organic amazake and almond amazake. Also Mochi.

Apples and Apple Products. In March 1989, the Natural Resources Defense Council (NRDC) reported that many red apples had a dangerously high level of Alar and UDMH, especially for children. Alar is a brand name for daminozide, a ripening and growth regulator. UDMH is its "metabolite," a byproduct after processing. Both Alar and UDMH (a chemical cousin to rocket fuel) are probable carcinogens.

The NRDC predicted that 6,000 U.S. pre-school children might get cancer from such chemicals, since they consume much more processed fruit per pound of their weight than does the rest of the population. *Consumer Reports* agreed with the concern, arguing that since UDMH is thought to be a much more serious carcinogen than Alar, processed apple products—apple juice and apple sauce (so often given to children)—are much more dangerous than plain apples.

Derl I. Derr, a spokesman for apple growers, declared that growers (who suffered a 20 percent drop in apple sales, and a $100 million loss of income) would voluntarily eliminate use of Alar: "by September (1989) . . . levels of Alar will be reduced to virtually zero."[1] But foreign apple growers could use the pesticide and export their apples and apple products to the United States. As is the case with many pesticides, the company that makes Alar (Uniroyal) is free to sell it overseas.

More pesticides can be used on apples than on any other fruit or vegetable and nearly one-third of apples tested by the USDA showed residues. Pesticides most commonly detected are diphenylamine (DPA), captan, endosulfan, phosmet, and Guthion (azinphos-methyl).[2]

Though purchasing organic apples would appear to be a good way to avoid chemical worries, it may not always be a viable one. Says Tomás Nimmo a Canadian organic farming expert: "Organic apple growing is generally a disaster." He suggests that "ecological" growing methods are a realistic, economic survival compromise. (Ecological implies minimal use of non-systemic pesticides on the perimeter of orchards if crop damage becomes critical. Ecologically grown apples are also tested for residues before they are sold.)

Erewhon— Additive-free applesauce available in stores or by mail. 236 Washington St., Brookline, MA 02146. (617) 738-4516.♦

Golden Acres Orchard— Organic apples in season, apple cider vinegar, apple juice; Asserted organic. Front Royal, VA 22630. (703) 636-9611.

Samascott Orchards— Does not use Alar or Captan. Sells apple cherry cider as well as apples and straight cider. Kinderhook, NY 12106.

Sleepy Hollow Farm— Sells certified organic apples and cooking herbs by mail. 44001 Dunlap Road, Miramonte, CA 93641. (209) 336-2444.

Sonoma Gold— Organic applesauce. Appleseed Orchards, Sebastopol, CA 95472.

Tree-Licious Orchards— Does not use Alar or any systemic chemicals. Port Murray, NJ 07865. (201) 689-2906.

Walnut Acres— Additive-free applesauce. Penns Creek, PA 17862. (800) 433-3998, (717) 837-0601.♦♦

Wild Rose Ranch— Grows and sells organic apples (80% of their crop, certified by CCOF) and apple juice via distributor. PO Box 1619, Sebastopol, CA 95473. (707) 823-1480.

Apricots. Because apricots must be eaten soon after picking (3 to 4 days) to avoid spoilage, 9 out of 10 commercially grown apricots are sold in some processed form, usually dried.[3] Apricots are a good source of vitamin A (as their color would suggest), and potassium.

Artichokes. Artichokes are not particularly rich in vitamins (especially after all the boiling required to cook them) but are good sources of fiber. If you dip your artichoke blades, avoid mayonnaise or fatty sauces and try low-fat yogurt with some lemon, garlic, and a touch of salt.

Asparagus. Asparagus grows like a weed in parts of eastern Europe and Central Asia and is grazing fodder for livestock (humans, too, can eat it raw.) It is rich in vitamins A and C and the minerals potassium and zinc (though less so after boiling). Buy asparagus that has tightly closed tips and green color extending two-thirds of the way down the stalk.

Avocado. Avocados are rich in folic acid (14 percent of USRDA), vitamin C (13 percent USRDA), vitamin A (12 percent USRDA), B_6 (11 percent USRDA), potassium (60 percent more than in bananas), and fiber, but contain high levels of fat. California avocados get 86 percent of their calories from fat, and larger Florida avocados get about 76 percent of their calories from that same source. 67 percent of this fat is mono-unsaturated (the type of fat in olive oil) which has been shown to reduce blood cholesterol levels.[4] Still, half an avocado carries one-fifth of the fat the average adult should consume for a whole day.[5]

Adzuki. See Legumes.

Sanctuary Farms— Sells organic Adzuki beans, black soybeans, buckwheat, corn, popcorn, wheat, and beef by mail. Shipping is UPS, no credit on first purchases. RD #1, Butler Rd, Box 184-A, New London OH 44851. (419) 929-8177.

Baby Foods. The widespread public awareness of food hazards (the Chilean fruit-poisoning and the toxic Alar scare) has prompted an increase in the demand for baby foods made from organic ingredients. Organic baby foods still only account for .1 percent of the $1 billion-a-year baby-food business, though.

Earth's Best Baby Food— Buys from growers certified by the Organic Crop Improvement Association (OCIA). They also send representatives to inspect farms and require documented records. Available in 750 supermarkets (mainly in Colorado and New York) and in 1500 natural food stores and diaper service stores in eight cities. The company also publishes a newsletter. PO Box 887, Middlebury, VT 05753. (802) 388-7974, FAX: (802) 388-9274.♦

Heinz, H. J., Co.— Heinz has written to growers that it will not buy food for its baby food brands if it has been treated with any of 13 chemicals now under Special Review by the EPA. PO Box 57, Pittsburgh, PA 15230.

Simply Pure Foods, Inc.— 100% organic baby food—grown under certification standards of Maine Organic Farmers. RFD 3, Box 99, ME 04401. (207) 941-1924.

Summa Organic Baby Cereal— Sells exclusively through health food stores. OCIA certified. Imported by: Purity Foods Inc., 421 Okemos Road, Suite 21, Okemos, MI 48864. (517) 340-7941.

Bananas. They are a great source of potassium, riboflavin, vitamin A, and vitamin C (twice that of apples). The average banana has 105 calories and a lot of fiber.

Most bananas are imported from Latin America because banana plants (they are actually herbs) like warm, constant temperatures. Because of heavy pesticide use on imported bananas, however, you may be better off limiting your intake of store-bought bananas. Use of pesticides in some countries was so severe that field-workers began to suffer markedly higher morbidity and mortality rates. Pesticides residues commonly detected on bananas include diazinon, thiabendazole, carbaryl, DCPA, methamidophos, dimethoate, demeton, and parathion.

Hawaiian Exotic Fruit Co.— Organic bananas (in several varieties), white pineapple, papayas, sweet potatoes, taro, lemons, sweet-corn, and whole ginger-roots. (See Chapter 10 for more.) Box 1729, Pahoa, HI 96778. (808) 965-7154.

Richardson's Seaside Banana Garden— 50 varieties of organically grown bananas available by mail order. 6823 Santa Barbara Ave, Ventura, CA 93001. (Catalogs cost $2.00.)

Beans. See Legumes.

Beef. Beef is the largest segment of American agriculture, with 1987 sales of $34 billion—20 percent of all farm sales and 45 percent of all livestock. Beef constituted 36 percent by weight of all meat consumed in the United States in 1988. It is high in protein and contains many vitamins and minerals. But beef also tends to have a lot of saturated fat. The National Cattlemen's Association provides nutritional information for "trimmed" beef showing that beef has a higher proportion of saturated fatty acids than chicken, pork or fish—8.7 grams (at 9 calories per gram, about 80 calories) in a 3–ounce serving.

The leanness of meat is rated by a voluntary classification system developed by the USDA which uses the terms Prime, Choice, and Select. Some companies now market their meats under the "lite" or lean label as well. The fat content, calories, and cholesterol content of meats in these categories are as follows.[6]

Grade	Percent Fat	Calories	Cholesterol
Prime	6.2–14.0	154–210	60 mg*
Choice	3.9–10.2	132–176	60 mg
Select	2.5– 7.6	120–152	60 mg
Lean or Lite	1.7–10.6	93–184	31–55 mg

*milligrams

Conventional wisdom has increasingly shifted against red meat both for health reasons (it is high in saturated fat and cholesterol) and for ecological reasons (raising beef for food requires seven to ten times the grain needed to sustain a person eating grain directly). Even the advertising campaign for beef has hit some hard times. Meat Board spokesman James ("Real Food for Real People") Garner had to undergo quintuple coronary artery bypass surgery a few years ago.

U.S. consumer groups are concerned that hormones are sometimes put in parts of the animal that will be eaten. Over 60 percent of cattle slaughtered in the United States have been treated with hormones; in January 1989 European countries decided to stop buying hormone-treated U.S. meat. One company says that demand for hormone-free beef has been up 20 percent in 1989 over a 1988, but supply is limited.

According to the Center for Science in the Public Interest, the following stores carry hormone-free beef: A&P, Bread & Circus, City Markets, Clemens Markets, Dominick's Finer Foods, Farmer Jack, First National Supermarkets, Grand Union, Kash 'N Karry, King Kullen Grocery Co, King Sooper, Kings Super Markets, Kroger Co., Puget Consumer's Co-op, Purity Supreme, Schnuck Markets,

Treasure Island, Whole Foods Market.

Concerns about the use of antibiotics in cattle are not invalid, but the use of these drugs, except to treat illness, has decreased drastically over the last few years.[7]

Sometimes suppliers of beef produced without hormones represent their beef as "organic." At present, no federal definition of "organic" exists (although a law was proposed in 1989; see Chapter 5). A handful of states do have laws defining "organic" meat; these laws usually feature strict requirements with regard to use of animal drugs. Private organic certification standards are generally more strict, often requiring that the animal's feed be 100 percent organic as well as requiring humane production practices."[8] Organic beef is worth seeking out, as the majority of pesticide residues ingested by humans come via meat.

Concerns have also been raised about how humanely the animals are treated. Many people become vegetarians primarily because they are repulsed at the methods used to "harvest" cows. Apparently most methods involve sledgehammers or machetes. Growers of organic beef generally do so on a smaller scale and are usually more humane. (See Chapter 4 for more.)

To reach a toll-free meat and poultry consumer information hotline at the Department of Agriculture, call (800) 535–4555 10 a.m.-4p.m. EST. In 1988, the U.S. imported $2.6 billion of beef, veal, and pork, mostly from Australia, New Zealand, Canada and Denmark.[9]

B 3 R Country Meats, Inc.— Meat (all wholesale cuts); All Natural Beef; lamb; fresh carcasses, fresh boxed and frozen portion cuts. Minimum order $1000. M.L. Bradley, Cal Herrmann, PO Box 374, Childress, TX 79201. (817) 937–8870.

Brae Beef— Mail order worldwide of beef and poultry. Greenwich, CT 06831. (203) 869–0106.

Brodman's Organic Beef Farm— Grows organic beef (sold privately and to restaurants). 6409 E. TWP Rd. 8, Republic, OH 44867. (419) 585–5852.

Coleman Natural Beef— In 1988 sold $20 million worth of beef that it grew without hormones or antibiotics. Carried by 400 supermarkets: The Grand Union in NYC, Purity Supreme in New England, A&P in NY and NJ, Bread & Circus in Boston, and Farmer Jack's in Detroit. (about 10% is "organic" and 90% is "natural") Also by mail order. 5140 Race Court, #4, Denver, CO 80217. (303) 297–9393.

Dakota Lean Meats Inc.— Trimmed hormone-free beef available through stores in California and by mail. 136 West Tripp Avenue, Winner, SD 57580. (800) 727–5326.

Food Animal Concern Trust (FACT)— Produces "cruelty-free" eggs and veal. Sold through mid-western markets. PO Box 14599, Chicago, IL 60614. (312) 525–4952.

Green Earth Natural Foods— Mail order in the U.S. and Canada of organic beef, pork, poultry and lamb. Evanston, IL 60201. (801) 322–3662.

Kohler Purelean Beef— Hormone-free, antibiotic-free beef available through stores in Illinois and Wisconsin and by mail. 1115 West Riverside Drive, Kohler, WI 53044. (414) 458–9811.

Larsen Beef— Carried by over 420 supermarkets: Kroger-stores in Atlanta, King Kullen on Long Island, Kash 'N Karry in Florida, and Dominicks in the Chicago area. Dallas, TX 75248. (214) 233–6999.

Laura's Lean Beef— Carried by 140 stores in Kentucky and Southern Indiana including: Kroger, some Foodtown, Randalls, IGA, and Megamarket stores. Winchester, KY 40391. (606) 842–5082.

Lean & Free— They claim that many of their steak cuts have less fat than chicken white meat with no skin. Mail order nationwide. Supplies 6 supermarkets in Arizona, two in Florida. Ackley, IA 50601. (800) 383–BEEF.

Maverick Ranch Lite Beef— Buys cattle and resells only those that test free of hormones and antibiotics. Carried by 200 supermarkets: King Sooper in Denver, Schnucks in St. Louis, Kings Supermarkets in NJ, and Clemens in Philadelphia. No direct sales to the public. 402 North Pine Meadow, Dr., Denver, CO 80216. (303) 294–0146.

Natural Beef Farms Food Distribution Co.— Mail order nationwide of beef, poultry, lamb, veal, and pork products. Chantilly, VA 22021. (703) 631–0881.

Organic Cattle Co., Inc.— Provides beef to several stores in the NYC area. White Plains, NY 10605. (914) 684–6529.

Peace Valley Premium Beef— Hormone-free, antibiotic-free beef. Sold through stores in New York and Ohio and by mail. 125 Hosea Avenue, Cincinnati, OH 45220. (513) 861–2455.

Quality Steaks— Carried in 150 supermarkets: Star Markets in Massachusetts, First National Supermarkets in Nebraska, and ABCO in the Phoenix area. Denver, CO 80216. (303) 355–5575.

Roseland Farms— Organically raised beef, lamb, and grains available through many Midwest stores and by mail. Roseland Farms, 27427 M-60 West, Cassopolis, MI 49031. (616) 445–8769, -8987.

Spray Brothers Farm— Raises organic beef and grains. Terms of sale unspecified. 5960 Spray Lane, Mt. Vernon, OH 43050. (614) 397–4207.

Stapelman's Meats— Hormone-free, antibiotic-free beef available through stores in Florida, North Carolina, and Nebraska. Also by mail. Osman Lockers, Second and State Streets, Box 358, Osman, NE 68765. (402) 748–3971.

Whippoorwill Farms— Sells organic beef, veal, pork and lamb. PO Box 717, Lakeville, CT 06039. (203) 435–9657.

Beer. See also Alcohol. Ounce for ounce, regular beer contains only half the calories of dry wine (12 vs. 23). Sweeter wine has *more* calories (40 per ounce), light beer *fewer* calories (8 per ounce), so that the ratio of calories between sweet wine and light beer is five to one! However, the standard drinking unit for beer drinkers—the beer mug or can—is much larger (12 ounces) than that for wine drinkers (5 ounces).

Alcohol is basically a toxin and can be addicting. It should also be noted that Bruce Ames's study found beer to be 10 times as carcinogenic as Alar, about which such a fuss was made in 1989.

In 1986 (the last year for which figures are available) beer constituted over 85% of all alcoholic beverages drinken and was the most popular beverage in the United States, bar none.[10]

Beverages, Non-Alcoholic. See also Coffee, Fruit and Vegetable Juices, Tea. Some farm goods are processed into liquids not elsewhere mentioned.

Vegetable juice is generally high in vitamins A (beta-carotene form) and C. The sodium content is sometimes astounding, however. Regular V8 has over 17 milligrams of salt per calorie (CSPI recommends no more than 1 milligram per calorie).

If you drink diet-soft drinks, the American Dietetic Association recommends that you not drink more than three cans a day, which is equal to 18 packets of artificial sweetener.[11] See also Sugar and Sugar Substitutes.

Aloe Vera Trading Co.— Organic aloe vera juices (flavored and plain). (Sold through stores, minimum order 5 cases.) 9105 Sovereign Row, Dallas, TX 75247. (214) 630-8086.

Bambu— Coffee substitute. Asserted organic, sold through stores.

California Natural Products— Dacopa Instant Beverage, a caffeine-free drink consisting wholly of roasted juices from Dahlia tubers. PO Box 1219, Lathrop, CA 95330. (209) 858-2525.

Dr. Tima Natural Products— Sodas (no sugar added), cola, soybean milk. 8570 Wilshire Blvd., Beverly Hills, CA 90211. (213) 652-9884.

Ginseng Extra— Sodas. Ginseng Up Corp., New York, NY 10016. Distributed by: Health Trends, Costa Mesa, CA 92626. (714) 957-2599, FAX: (714) 957-2634.

Golden Temple Tea Co.— Medicinal Teas. 3629 10th Ave., Los Angeles, CA 90018. (213) 732-2218.

Hansen Foods Inc.— "All natural" (but not organic) sodas. 14380–G Nelson Ave, City of Industry, CA 91744. (818) 336-7099.

Hi K Kola— Makes sodas high in potassium and low in sodium. Distributed by: Alacer Corp, Buena Park, CA 90622.

Long Life Herbal Teas— Some teas made from organically-grown herbs available by mail. 70–A Greenwich Ave. #220, New York, NY 10011. (212) 580-9252.

Tianfu China Cola— Makes colas with no artificial flavors or sweeteners, preservatives, or caffeine. 110 W. 17th St., New York, NY 10011. (212) 675-5335, FAX: (212) 242-4369.

Vermont Natural Beverage— Pforzheimer sells egg cream and sodas flavored with maple syrup, sold under the "Vermont Natural" label (asserted 90% organic). His cream soda flavors include sparkling maple, raspberry-maple and vanilla-maple. Newport Center, VT 95857. (802) 244-7886.

Blueberries. One of the most commonly eaten berries, blueberries are perhaps the hardiest of the berry group. They contain vitamins C and A and are conducive to drying.

De-Lite Foods Co.— Makes explosion dried blueberries that are apparently ideal for such ventures as trans-Antarctic expeditions (the most recent of which bought 44 pounds). Alma, GA.

Bread and Other Baked Goods. See also Convenience Mixes. For centuries Europeans had been eating bread that appeared dark brown in color. The standard of baking bread was to use the entire wheat kernel (germ, endosperm, bran). It was then discovered that if the wheat germ and bran were discarded, the remaining endosperm would yield, when made into bread, a pristine fluffy light loaf that was more appealing than the hard, dark crunchy kind. What these doughy revolutionists did not realize was that this process stripped many of the nutrients (81 percent of the niacin, 80 percent of the riboflavin, and more than 75 percent of the manganese, iron, and zinc).[12] What we know today as enriched bread is the return of these nutrients to white bread due to the Enrichment Act of 1942. But enriched bread still lacks magnesium, zinc, B_6, and, most importantly, fiber that whole wheat bread has. (Wheat bran has 12 grams of dietary fiber per ounce, as well as 40 percent of the USRDA for both niacin and magnesium, and 15 percent of the USRDA for iron).[13] As described in Chapter 3, fad diets that exclude carbohydrates like bread could be dangerous.

Many efforts are being made to develop food products that are nutritionally fortified with omega-3 oils (see Chapter 4 or Fish). One promising approach has received patent 4,857,326. Paul A. Stitt, a chemist in Manitowoc, Wisc., has created a process (treatment with zinc and vitamin B_6) for stabilizing flaxseed after it has been ground into meal, so that the omega-3 oils can be baked into bread. He and his wife have formed a company, Natural Ovens, which bakes flax-filled breads, cookies and muffins sold in 800 supermarkets in the Midwest.[14]

Buddhist communities like Tassajara or the Zen Center in San Francisco, or Greystone in New York City, are famous for producing high-quality bread from organically grown grains.

Unfortunately, fresh bread made with yeast and without preservatives doesn't keep well and therefore doesn't ship well or cheaply; overnight service is expensive. The local bakery is still a neighborhood treasure. Bread that is offered for sale through the mail is typically made without yeast. Yeastless sourdough bread keeps for about 10 days after receipt without refrigeration, and for a month if you put it in the refrigerator when it arrives.

The Baker— Whole-grain breads made with organic stoneground flour. 60 Bridge St., Milford, NJ 08848.

Baldwin Hill Corporation— Whole wheat bread made with organic flour. Baldwin Hill Road, Phillipston, MA01331.♦

Berkshire Mountain Bakery— Bakes and sells high quality traditional sourdough bread made from organically grown ingredients by mail. Asserted 100% organic. PO Box 785, Housatonic, MA 01236. (800) 274-3412. (413) 374-3412.

Bread Alone— Seven varieties of great whole-grain handmade breads baked in wood-fired brick ovens. Certified 95% organic. They ship UPS on the same day the bread is baked. Also available through some stores and farmers markets (we get ours at Union Square in NYC). They have a brother bakery, Le Moulin de la Vierge, in Paris, France. Rt. 28, Boiceville, NY 12412. (914) 657-3328.♥♥♦

French Meadow Bakery— Organic, yeast-free breads. Asserted 100% organic. Sold through stores.

Gourmet Award— Bread crumbs and stuffing with organic ingredients. Sold through stores.

Helmuth Country Bakery,— A wide variety of Amaranth and wheat baked goods. Available by mail. They assert 10% of their products are organic, some of the ingredients grown on their own organic farm. 6706 W. Mills Road, Hutchinson, KS 67501. (316) 567-2301.

Innisfree Farm— Whole grain breads. Brattleboro, VT 05301. (802) 254-4600.

Just Baked— Organic, yeast-free breads and snacks. Made by Pacific Bakery, PO Box 950, Oceanside, CA 92054. (619) 757-6020.

Lifestream Natural Foods Ltd.— Breads made with organically grown sprouted grains including wheat and rye, Krispbread and whole-rye Krispbread. Sold through stores. Richmond, B.C., CANADA V6V 1J7. (Distributed by Health Valley.)

Manna Breads/Nature's Path— Makes 14 varieties of bread using organic grains, 9 of which use sprouted grains. (Grain certified by OCIA.) Also Organic Manna Flakes, Raisin Bran, and Brown Rice Crisps. Sold through stores, minimum order 100 cases. Nature's Path Foods, Inc., 7435 Progress Way, Delta, BC V6X2P9, Canada. (604) 278-2923.♦♦

Mill City Sourdough Bakery— Bakes sourdough bread with rye, whole-wheat, and 5 other kinds of grain. Certified 100% organic by the Organic Growers and Buyers Association, member of the OGBA and OCIA. Shipping by U.P.S., usual delivery time is 3 days. Available through stores and by mail, 6 loaf minimum, V M and AE accepted. 1566 Randolph Ave., St. Paul, MN 55105. (612) 698-4705.

Mother Nature's Goodies, Inc.— Frozen pies in cases of six: Apple, apricot, blueberry, boysenberry, cherry, pumpkin. They are kept frozen in the mail with insulated containers and dry ice. Yucaipa, CA 92399. (714) 795-6018.

Nature's Storehouse— Whole-wheat breads with no dairy or hydrogenated oils available by mail. Minimum order negotiable. Highway 108, PO Box 69, Lynn, NC 28750. (704) 859-6356.

Oasis Breads— Sprouted breads. 440 Venture Street, Escondido, CA 92025. (619) 747-7390.

Ozark Cooperative Warehouse— Makes breads, dinner rolls, and buns. Sold through their cooperative warehouse. PO Box 30. Fayetteville, AR 72702. (501) 521-COOP.

Pritikin Breads— Breads that conform to the standards of the Pritikin Diet. Health Valley Distributing Co., Irwindale, CA 91706. (818) 334-3241.

Season's Enterprises Ltd.— Makes organic oat bran tortillas. PO Box 965 Racquet Club Dr., Addison, IL 60101. (312) 628-0211.

Shepherdsfield Award Winning Bakery— Whole-wheat bread, rye bread, potato rolls, muffins, cinnamon/raisin bread, flour, and gourmet waffles available by mail. All products made from organically grown grains and baked with no added colorings, preservatives, synthetic fiber, or sythetic coloring. Rt. 4, Box 399, Fulton, MO 65251. (314) 642-1439.

Shiloh Farms— Breads available by mail. (Not strictly organic but close.) White Oak Rd., Martindale, PA 17549. (717) 354-4936.♦♦♦

Sprout Delights Bakery— Sells yeast free breads, rolls, muffins, snacks, and cakes made from sprouted organic grains by mail. Also vegetarian Sprout Burgers and Millet-Barley Burgers. (Asserted 90+% organic, minimum order $20 for public.) 13090 NW 7th Ave, North Miami, FL 33168-2702. (305) 687-5880 or (800) 334-BAKE. FAX: (305) 687-3233.

Summercorn Foods— Wholegrain breads made from organic grain and fresh-milled flour: Whole Wheat Sourdough, 100% Rye Sourdough, Cinnamon Currant Bread, and Italian Bread. Also cookies, breads, soy products, granolas, and nut/fruit mixes available direct at the main bakery, through markets in the Midwest and Southwest, and by mail to areas with no distributors. 401 Watson, Fayetteville, AR 72701. (501) 521-9338.

Walnut Acres— Several varieties of bread made from organically grown grains. Penns Creek, PA 17862. (800) 433-3998, (717) 837-0601. (See listing in Chapter 6 for more.)♦♦

Broccoli. Broccoli is considered the health food par excellence, according to the *University of California, Berkeley Wellness Letter*. It is an excellent source of potassium, calcium and phosphorous. Broccoli is a good source of bioflavonids that together with vitamin C strengthen the body capillaries against breakage or leakage of fluid into surrounding tissues. One cup of cooked broccoli has the same protein content as one cup of cooked corn or rice with only 1/3 the calories. Preparing broccoli (and other vegetables) in water depletes the vitamin benefit of the vegetable. Heat plays a factor in destroying vitamin C, but more importantly, the water soluble vitamins (vitamin C and all the vitamin B complex) are literally washed down the drain. Warning: Farmers are allowed to use dozens of different pesticides on it, including parathion, a possible human carcinogen. Only some of the chemical residues can be washed off or cooked out.

Buckwheat. See Grains (even though it is not a true grain).

Butter, Margarine, and Other Spreads. See also Oils. Butter is heavy in saturated fat, and for decades manufacturers have attempted to sell margarine as a lower fat substitute. (New soy and other spreads are also coming onto the market.)

Margarine also gets almost all of its calories from fat, the difference being that the fat in margarine is unsaturated (margarine, being derived from vegetable oil, also has no cholesterol). Many believe that margarine is therefore healthier than butter. But critics of margarine argue that the process by which margarine is made to harden at the same time destroys the beneficial value of the polyunsaturated oil. The process is partial hydrogenation. It creates so-called "trans-fatty acids" that are new to the human diet. *Goldbeck's True Food* newsletter reports on a few studies with findings that margarine and partially hydrogenated oils elevate blood cholesterol levels in some people by as much as 20 milligrams per deciliter; reduce HDL ("good") cholesterol in pigs; inhibit insulin binding in monkeys; and adversely affect immuno-responses and reproductive performance in some individuals. On the basis of such as yet limited evidence some critics of margarine charge that the new trans-fatty acids act like saturated fats by elevating cholesterol levels, even though they are usually grouped with unsaturated fats on labels and in dietary calculations. The newsletter concludes that many labels make flawed claims about the saturation of the fats: ". . . The whole basis of dietary advice concerning fat is built upon a faulty foundation."[15] Science will surely resolve the dispute with new evidence; the practical point is that *margarine might not be better for you than butter.*

In addition, many people feel that margarine lacks the taste and texture of butter. Some new products try to answer this complaint with hybrid combinations of butter and margarine. Your options are to (1) buy low-calorie margarine (in which water has been blended to reduce the overall fat content), but don't try to cook with it, or (2) use butter and eliminate saturated fats from other areas of your diet, or (3) eliminate both margarine and butter.

For cooking purposes, because of the effects of heat on oils, ghee (the clear component of melted butter) is reputed to be not only much tastier but possibly no worse health-wise than other oils. However, ghee it is difficult to find in stores and takes a minute or two to extract yourself.

If you do buy margarine, the *University of California, Berkeley Wellness Letter* recommends you look for (1) brands that contain at least twice as much polyunsaturated as saturated fat, (2) safflower, sunflower, corn, and soybean oil bases in that order, (3) tubs instead of sticks, as margarine in a tub can be softer and, hence, is often less saturated, and (4) as low a sodium content as possible.

Cabbage. An increasingly popular vegetable because of studies showing the cancer preventing effects of two chemicals naturally found in cabbage: indoles and dithiolthines. Other cruciferous vegetables (the name derives from the "cross-shape" of its flowers) are broccoli, cauliflower and bean sprouts. Cabbage is high in roughage or fiber, which has also been shown to prevent cancer. Cabbage is also a great source of calcium, vitamin A (carotene) and C, and riboflavin. Note: though cabbage alone is excellent, a cole slaw dish contains five times the calories and is high in fat due to the mayonnaise dressing used. Also, sauerkraut has a high salt content. Pesticide residues detected on cabbage include methamidophis, dimethoate, fenvalerate, peremethrin, BHC, and 31 others.[16]

Canned Goods. Check also under particular item (e.g. beans). Beware of and avoid lead-soldered canning with a crimped seam and a silvery, irregular line (generally 1/2 to 3/4 of an inch wide) along the joint. Lead from soldered can seams can get into food during the manufacturing process, through leaching or careless spattering. Although today fewer than 4 percent of foods canned in America are in lead-soldered cans, goods canned in foreign countries still pose a risk. Choose welded cans with a seam that is thin, dark-striped, and smooth. Another potential problem resulting from improperly canned goods is botulism, although only 17 deaths from this were reported in 1987, well down from previous years.

Other metals such as tin and iron can leach into food, but pose no real harm and may be beneficial. For flavor's sake, transfer juices in opened cans into plastic or glass containers.[17]

Cherry Hill Co-operative Cannery— Not all its products are now actually canned. Some come in jars. Products not elsewhere listed include honey, maple syrup, pickles, preserves, salsa. Barre, VT 05641. (802) 479-2558.

Co-op— A line of canned fruits and vegetables with no sugar, salt, additives, or preservatives and as little processing as possible. Sold through stores and co-ops.

Millstone Foods (Loma Linda)— A line of canned vegetarian goods: Burger-like, Nut Meat, Tender Cuts (whole wheat gluten steaks), vege-beans, Vegeburger, Wheat Fries, and many other meat-substitute foods. Sold through stores. Loma Linda Foods Inc., 11503 Pierce Street, Riverside, CA 92515. California only: (800) 442–4917, (800) 932–5525.

Walnut Acres— Canned organic vegetables: Tomatoes, beets, corn, pumpkin, and several varieties of beans. Penns Creek, PA 17862. (800) 433–3998, (717) 837–0601.♦♦

Cantaloupes. See Melons.

Carrots. Carrots are rich in vitamin A, a fat-soluble vitamin that performs an array of functions in our body from maintenance of vision and epithelial tissue (the skin and outer layers of digestive, reproductive and respiratory tracts), growth of bones, to the synthesis of hormones. Carrots actually do not contain pure vitamin A, but have the precursor material, or provitamin, called carotene, which the body changes into active vitamin A or retinol. Carotene has a bright orange pigment that gives color to cantaloupes, mangos, papayas and apricots to name a few. Combined with chlorophyll, carotene gives the deep green color to spinach and broccoli. (It is the carotene pigment which brings the trees in autumn to full grandeur.) Overdoses of carotene-rich vegetables at times give the skin a yellowish tint because carotene is stored right below the skin surface. Taken in excessive quantities, vitamin A can be toxic. Pesticides detected include DDT (banned in U.S. since 1973, but residues still found in root crops), trifluralin, parathion, diazinon, and dieldrin.

Escondido Juice Co.— Frozen carrot juice from organically grown carrots. Sierra Distributing, Oceanside, CA 02054. (800) 621–5640 ext. 584237, (619) 434–9710.

Ferraro's Fine Juices— Organic carrot juice available through retail stores. 1610 S. Magnolia Ave. Monrovia, CA 91016. (818) 357–3339.

Pyramid Juice Company— Makes carrot, celery, and beet juice. (Carrot juice asserted 100% organic, 55% of their juices are organic overall.) PO Box 1303, Ashland, OR 97520. (503) 482–2292.

Walnut Acres— Carrots and other root crops available by mail. Penns Creek, PA 17862. (800) 433–3998, (717) 837–0601.♦♦

Cauliflower. Along with cabbage and broccoli, cauliflower is a cruciferous vegetable. It is a good source of vitamin C, but as evidenced in its white color, low in vitamin A. Pesticides detected include methamidophos, dimethoate, chlorothalonil, diazinon and endosulfan.[18]

Celery. Excellent source of potassium but low in vitamin A and C. Most supermarket celery is blanched to reduce its bitter flavor. But as a result of this process, much vitamin A is lost. Organic celery or the unblanched kind is the best bet for vitamin A. Pesticides residues detected include dicloran, chlorothalonil, endosulfan, acephate, methamidophos. Trimming the leaves and tops off celery stalks may reduce chemical residues.

Cereals. See also Grains, Rice. Because cereal is usually eaten to start one's day, it is probably a good idea to go for cereals with lots of complex carbohydrates and, perhaps, some fiber (which can come from fresh fruit sliced on top of cereal, too). Sugar-filled cereals are usually nutritional disasters.

If you notice small, square black chunks in your cereal, they are (probably) not insect larvae, but "pigmented" apple chunks. Presumably groggy consumers are supposed to mistake them for raisins or dates.

Allergy Resource— Cereals made from organically grown grains and some rare grains, baking substitutes, condiments, wheat-free and gluten-free products, organic flours, rarely-found flours, dried beans, pastas, and cereals by mail. 195 Huntington Beach Dr., Colorado Springs, CO 80921. (719) 488–3630.

American Prairie— Eight varieties of hot and cold cereals with organic ingredients (FVO certifies the cereal; its seal is on the label). Sold through stores. Mercantile Food Company, PO Box 1140, Georgetown, CT 06829.♦

Arrowhead Mills— Hot and cold cereals made with organic ingredients including: Cracked Wheat Cereal, Barley Flakes, Triticale Flakes, and Wheat Bran. Also seeds, whole grains, nuts, beans, and mixes. Overall 75% of products are asserted organic. Sold mainly through stores, but mail order is available for people who do not live near a retail outlet. 110 S. Lawton, Hereford, TX 79045. (806) 364–0730.♥♦♦♦♦

Barbara's Bakery— Cereals (hot and cold) some with organic ingredients (check the label to be sure) and no artificial colorings, additives, or preservatives. Also cookies, and granola bars. Sold only through stores. 3900 Cypress Drive, Petaluma, CA 94952. (707) 765–2273.♦♦♦

Black Ranch— Organic whole grains (oats, red and white wheat, amaranth and rye), rose hips, red clover sprouts, wholegrain flour (wheat, rye, and amaranth), 6 grain cereal. Dave and Dawn Black, 5800 Eastside Rd., Etna, CA 96027. (916) 467–3387. (See Chapter 10, CA, Etna for more.)

Diamond K Enterprises— Sells cereals made from organically grown grain: brown rice and 7-Grain. Also grains, rice, flours, cereals, pancake mixes, birdseed, sunflower seeds, and some dried fruits. Allow 1 to 2 weeks for shipping. (Asserted 95% organic, see listing in Chapter 10 for more.) RR 1 Box 30–A, St. Charles, MN 55972. (507) 932–4308, or 932–5433.

Elam's— High-fiber cereals and mixes. National Baker's services, Inc.

Erewhon— Makes five varieties of organic whole-grain cereals from, variously, wheat and rice.♦♦

Familia— Muesli with unprocessed grains and lots of dried fruit. Imported from Switzerland, sold through stores. Biofamilia AG, CH-6072 Sachseln, SW.♥

Health Valley— A line of cereals with some organic ingredients: Amaranth Crunch with Raisins, Amaranth with Bananas, Amaranth Flakes, Blue Corn Flakes, Fiber 7 Flakes, Healthy Crunch (2 kinds), Real (3 kinds), Sprouts 7, Swiss Breakfast, and Wheat Germ & Fiber. Also cookies, crackers, snack bars, muffins, pilaf, whole-wheat pasta, and soy milk. Many of their products are also low-salt. Sold through stores.♥♦♦♦

Kashi— Cereals. (Not organic, but nutritionally sound and free of preservatives, cholesterol, additives, sugar, and salt.) Sold through stores.

Kolln Oat Cereals— Wheat-free, salt-free, and sugar-free. Edward & Sons Trading Co., Distributor, Union, NJ 07083. (201) 964-8176.

Little Bear Trading Co.— Cereals made from organically grown grains. Also flour, rice, beans, noodles, and vegieburger mixes. Available through healthy food stores and an increasing number of conventional markets. They assert 95% of their products are organic. 226 E. Second St., Winona, MN 55987. (507) 452-6332.♦♦♦

Lundberg Family Farms— Organic brown rice cereals (hot and cold). Also other rice products including flour, and rice cakes. 5370 Church St., Mail to: PO Box 369, Richvale, CA 95974. (916) 882-4551. (Please see Chapter 10 for more.)♥♦♦♦

Manna/Nature's Path— Makes organic Manna Flakes, Raisin Bran, and Brown Rice Crisps, and non-organic Fiber-O's and Hearty-O's. Also makes 14 varieties of bread using organic grains (OCIA). Minimum order 100 cases. Nature's Path Foods, Inc., 7435 Progress Way, Delta, BC, Canada. (604) 278-2923.♦♦

Muesli— A mix of grains and fruit first put together by the Bircher-Benner clinic in Zurich. Imported by U.S. Mills, Inc., Willington, MA 01887. (508) 657-8120.

Pacific Rice— Makes a variety of "100% natural" (but not organic) low-sodium and sodium-free rice cereals including Quick 'n Creamy (brown rice hot cereal), and Vita Fiber Rice Brand. Available through stores. 460 Harter Ave, Woodland, CA 95695. (916) 662-5056. For more info call (800) NOW-RICE.♦♦

Paul's Grains— Sells organic rice, cereals, and beef by mail. 2475-B 340 St., Laurel, IA 50141. (515) 476-3373.

Perky's— Relatively unprocessed, low-sodium cereals. Made by New Morning.♦♦

Walnut Acres— Whole grain cereals, some organic. Penns Creek, PA 17862. (800) 433-3998, (717) 837-0601.♦♦

Cheese. Cheese is made from milk, so the type of milk used determines the fat (saturated) and cholesterol content. Cheese made from buttermilk, such as cream cheese, and from whole milk, such as cheddar, are generally high in fat, while cheeses made from skim milk are lower in fat. The lower the fat, generally, the more rubbery the cheese (e.g. Swiss cheese and mozzarella). Some vegetarians are creating a demand for cheeses made from non-animal rennet. Animal rennet is taken from the stomachs of slaughtered animals. Non-animal rennet comes from plants. Most of the $400 million of cheese imported by the United States in 1988 came from New Zealand and Italy.

Newsweek in May 1989 ran a story suggesting that beef, cheese, and cheese products are good for you in large quantities because they contain CLA (a form of linoleic acid), a substance that, according to researchers at the University of Wisconsin reduces the incidence of cancer in rats. Cheez-Whiz is particularly high in the substance. However, eating cheese products for the beneficial effects of CLA is like drinking sea water to relieve thirst—the net effect is negative, to say the least. To achieve a discernible level of protection, the rats were given a dosage of CLA equivalent to that found in eight cheeseburgers.[19] If you prorate that amount to the increased body weight of a human you could easily be talking 50 cheeseburgers. Cheese, like ice cream, is probably OK in your diet, but only so long as you eat it in moderation and it does not push the fat content of your diet over 15–30 percent.

Eiler's Cheese Market— Cheese made from chemical-free cows and goats. De Pere, WI 54115.

First World Cheese Inc.— Makes Apineace Cheeses and Dr. Cheddar Cheese Alternatives with low cholesterol and low to no sodium. Sold mainly through stores, minimum order 45 cases. 111 Dunneroad, Mapewood, NJ 07040. (201) 378-8600.

Galaxy Cheese Company— Makes Formagg cheese substitute.

Hawthorne Valley Farm— Cheese made from chemical-free cows and goats. Ghent, NY 12075.

Lifeline Food Co.— Makes low-fat, low-salt cheeses with skim milk. Available by mail. 426 Orange St., Sand City, CA 93955. (408) 899-5040.

Lifeway Foods— Makes low-fat cottage cheese, low-fat kefir, and cheesecake. (Minimum order $200, no organic claims) 7625 Austin, Skokie, IL 60077. (312) 967-6558.

Morningland Dairy— Organic raw milk cheeses by mail: Monterey Jack, Hot Pepper Jack, Mild Pepper Jack, Chives Colby, Garlic Colby, Dill Cheddar, Hot & Spicy Cheddar and others. Rt. 1, Mountain View, MO 65548. (417) 469-3817.

Philadelphia Cream Cheese— Does not contain animal rennet.

Schurman's Wisconsin Cheese Country Inc.— Organic cheddar cheese. (Wholesale orders only.) PO Box 776, Beetown, WI 53802. (608) 794-2422.

Smith's Country Cheese— Sells Gouda Cheese by mail. (Also through a farm store.) Winchendon, MA 01475. (617) 939–5738.

Cherries. This high sugar content fruit, as evidenced by its sweet flavor, contains the minerals phosphorus, potassium and calcium. Pesticide residues detected include parathion, melathion, captan, dicloran and diazinon. More than 50 percent of cherry samples tested in 1987 contained pesticide residues. If you eat a lot of cherries, you might want to grow your own or seek out organic cherries.

Chicken. See Poultry.

Chilies. Chilies, or chili peppers, members of the capsicum family, come in a variety of colors and mouth-heating capacities. Three-alarm chilies include Serrano, pica piment (originally grown only in Holland) and Jalapenos. Two-alarm chilies include Fresnos and Poblanos. One-alarm chilies, the mildest, include Anaheims. The Jalapenos are reported to contain an anti-coagulant, reducing the likelihood of blood clots and strokes. Chilies add taste without fat or sodium. They contain potassium and vitamins A and C.

Citrus Fruits. They contain a significant amount of vitamin C. The claims of exponents of the "Grapefruit Diet," that grapefruit has fat-burning capabilities, is a fallacy. Nonetheless, it is a healthy food. Pesticide residues detected include thiabendazole, ethion, methidathion, chlorobenzilate, parathion, and carbaryl.

S.M. Jacobson Citrus— Grows and sells Texas Ruby-Red grapefruit and oranges by mail (100% organic). They say their fruit is at its best after December 1. A 13–pound box costs between $13 and $20 depending on postal zone. 1505 Doherty, Mission, TX 78572. (512) 585–1712.♥

Blue Heron Farm— Organically grown oranges. PO Box 68, Runsey, CA 95679. (916) 796–3799.

Ecology Sound Farms— Sells oranges, certified organic. 42126 Road 168, Orosi, CA 93647. (209) 528–3816.

Starr Organic Produce, Inc.— Organic grapefruit and oranges. PO Box 561502, Miami, FL 33256. (305) 262–1242. Sells oranges and grapefruit.

Valley Center Packing Co.— Sells organic oranges, grapefruit, lemons, and limes year-round, and tangelos, tangerines, asian pears, and apples seasonally in commercial quantities. Ask your local supermarket to give them a call. 28425 South Cole Grade Road, Valley Center, CA 92082. (619) 749–5469.

Coffee. Volumes of research have been published on the adverse effects of caffeine and about the same amount dispelling its negative effects. Problems stem from findings that are arrived at by correlations, not by causal scientific evidence. An example is heart disease. A study at John Hopkins showed that heavy coffee drinkers (over five cups a day, all males) "were two to three times more likely than non-drinkers of coffee to develop coronary heart dis-

ease."[20] The study failed, however, to recognize other risk factors of coronary heart disease that are common among excessive coffee drinkers: high-fat diets, psychological stress, and sedentary lives. Other controversial claims of adverse health effects from caffeine are that it causes cancer and birth defects. Large dosages of caffeine are unquestionably bad for you—French novelist Honoré de Balzac died of a caffeine overdose delivered via coffee (although it took a regular habit of 50 cups a day to do it).[21] Coffee has also been linked to female infertility.[22]

Decaffeinated coffee has become increasingly popular in a nation where coffee as a beverage is becoming less popular. Purveyors of fancy coffee and coffee beans claim that decaffeinated coffees now account for 20–30 percent of their market. A study of restaurants suggests that decaf can constitute up to 40 percent of coffee sales and is particularly popular after dinner.[23] The rationale for the increased popularity of decaf appears to be that manufacturers are now using better beans. When choosing decaf coffee, it is probably safer to choose those that have been through the (Swiss or natural) water process. This method entails soaking the beans to leach out the caffeine and then draining off the water for treatment with ethyl acetate, a substance found in ripening fruit. The water is then re-added to the beans to help avoid dilution of flavor. Methylene chloride, the most common decaffeination agent until recently, was banned in July 1989 for use in hair-spray.

Coffee, like other monocultures, is heavily sprayed with pesticides. In 1988 the U.S. imported $2.5 billion in coffee from Brazil, Colombia and Mexico. Bleaching coffee filters white causes considerable water pollution; non-bleached coffee filters are increasingly available.

Cafe Altura— Organically grown decaffeinated coffee made by Terra Nova, 206 N. Signal St. Suite M, PO Box 1647, Ojai, CA 93023. (805) 646–5535, FAX: (805) 646–3368.

Fiddler's Green Farm— Sells coffee, not certified organic. Belfast, ME 04915. (207) 338–3568.

California Natural Products— Dacopa Instant Beverage—the caffeine-free drink consisting wholly of roasted juices from Dahlia tubers you may have been waiting for. PO Box 1219, Lathrop, CA 95330. (209) 858–2525.

Equal Exchange— Organic Peruvian Coffee by mail. Also gourmet blends and teas. PO Box 2652, Cambridge, MA 02238. (617) 482–4945.

Suzanne's Specialties— Sells organic coffees by mail. 116 9th Street, Steamboat Springs, CO 80487. (303) 879–5731.

Condiments. See also Spices, Sauces.

Ketchup is mostly processed tomatoes, sugar, and salt. Lots of salt. The average ketchup has 156 milligrams of sodium per tablespoon.[24] Barbecue sauces, steak sauces, chili sauces, and cocktail sauces usually have the same problem. Those worried about salt might try tomato paste as a substitute.

Mayonnaise, whether regular, "lite," or cholesterol free, is loaded with fat, which accounts for 80–95 percent of its calories. The "lite" designation just means there is more thickening agent in the mixture so that there are fewer calories (and hence fewer fat-calories) per spoonful. The "cholesterol free" label on some brands is mostly a gimmick, as regular mayonnaise itself has very little (about 5 milligrams per tablespoon).[25] Regular mayonnaise has 4 times as much fat as sour cream. Healthier alternatives are yogurt flavored with mustard and lemon, or minced avocado (guacamole). Homemade mayonnaise is a big hazard because of the risk of salmonella poisoning inherent in any food made with raw eggs. Mustard has a lot of sodium: 188 milligrams per tablespoon for yellow mustard, and an amazing 465 milligrams/tablespoon for the average Dijon variety.[26] The best way to avoid the sodium is to buy dry mustard mixes and make your own low-salt concoctions.

Less common condiments like horse-radish, chutneys (tomato, apple, or mixed fruit) and salsa tend to have less sodium and can add new and interestng flavors to well-worn recipes. To be sure, though, always check the label and go for products where salt is near the bottom.

Arrowhead Mills— Organic sesame tahini. Also cereals, seeds, flours, whole grains, nuts, oils, and mixes. Overall 75 percent of products are asserted organic. Sold mainly through stores, but mail order is available for people who do not live near a retail outlet. 110 S. Lawton, Hereford, TX 79045. (806) 364-0730.♥♦♦♦♦

Chalif— "All-natural condiments" including low-salt and no-salt mustards. Also stir-fry sauce. Sold through stores. PO Box 27220 (1230 E. Mermaid Lane) Wyndmoor, PA 19118. (215) 233-2023.

Cuisine Perel— Condiments and gourmet sauces (asserted 50% organic). Minimum order $300. PO Box 1064, Tiburon, CA 94920. (415) 435-1282.

Deep Roots— Makes salt-free seasonings. Also drypackaged bean mixes, bulk herbs, and sprouts. Deep Roots Trading Co., Roger Spivack, 427 W. 3rd St., Williamsport, PA 17701. (717) 323-2210.

Jasmine & Bread— Tomato apple ketchup, chili sauce, mustard, plum sweet and sour, and other preserves. Their condiments started as "low-sugar, low-sodium" products, but now they say they are almost all "no-sugar, no-salt" products. Products contain maple syrup and honey from Vermont farmers instead of sugar. All fruits and vegetables are pesticide-free. South Royalton, VT 05068. (802) 763-7115.

Kozlowski Farms-Sonoma County Classics— No-sugar-added fruit butters, chutneys, and conserves; mustards, fudge sauces, marmalades, jams, jellies, barbecue sauce, vinegars, syrups. 5566 Gravenstein Hwy., Forestville, CA 95436. (707) 887-1587, FAX: (707) 887-9650. (See Chapter 10 for more).

Loriva Supreme Foods— Organic sesame tahini. Also sesame oil, seeds, flower, and peanut butter. Sold through stores.

Nasoya Foods— Tofu salad dressings, and tofu-based mayonaise made from organically grown soybeans (but not herbs). It is still full of fat, but has less saturated fat than real mayonnaise. Minimum order 100 cases, no minimum for FOB. 23 Jytek Drive, Leominster, MA 01453. (508) 537-0713.♦

Naturally Northwest— This brand of light mayonnaise does not contain eggs and uses organically grown soy products (it still gets about 80% of its calories from fat). Their mustard (which comes in Cajun, Dijon, and Herb varieties) is also "all natural." Pacific Foods, 19480 SW 97th Avenue, Tualatin, OR 97062. (503) 692-9666.

Out To Lunch— Makes Hummus (a garbanzo bean and Tahini spread). Asserted 20% organic. PO Box 2366, Austin, TX 78768. (512) 892-4475.

Premier Japan— Japanese condiments free of artificial additives (no MSG), preservatives, and colors. Also a full line pasta products and sea vegetables. Sold through stores. Distributed by Edward & Sons Trading Co., Box 3150, Union, NJ 07083. (201) 964-8176.

Confections and Cookies. The sugar content often means you are getting "empty calories." This is not to mention the variety of hydrogenated and partially hydrogenated vegetable oils, and artificial colorings, etc. that most commercial cookies contain in disconcerting quantities. Many sweets are also high in fat—commonly over 50 percent for chocolate (the same rule applies as for ice cream: the higher the fat content, the more "premium" the brand). Some sweets are better than others, however, and, as long as you eat them as only an occasional treat, they can be an acceptable addition to your diet.

Barbara's Bakery— Cookies, granola bars, and cereals, with no artificial colorings, additives, or preservatives. Sold only through stores. 3900 Cypress Drive, Petaluma, CA 94952. (707) 765-2273.♦♦♦

Basic Commodities Inc.— Makes some sugar-free candies. PO Box 3267, Toledo, OH 43607. (419) 537-1711. FAX:(419) 531-6887.

Br. Ron Corporation— Makes sprouted brownies (carob and chocolate) and cookies (chocolate chip, oatmeal raisin, and peanut butter among others) with some organic ingredients.

Falcon Trading Co.— Makes organic trail and snack mixes and a line of malt sweet carob and chocolate candies with organically grown fruits and nuts. 1955 17th Ave., Santa Cruz, CA 95062. (408) 462-1280.

Health Valley— A line of cookies with some organic ingredients. Also cereals, crackers, snack bars, muffins, pilaf, whole-wheat pasta, and soy milk. Many of their products are also low-salt. Sold through stores.♥♦♦♦♦

Maramor Kitchens— Makes sugar-free, tropical oil-free carob candies. 1855 E. 17th Ave., Columbus, OH 43219. (800) 843-7722.

Mrs. Densen's Cookie Co.— Makes cookies using whole-wheat (and usually organic) flower and other organic ingredients. (Most of their business is baking for private labels.) 9651 Hwy. 101 N., Redwood Valley, CA 95470. (707) 485-0306.

Nanak's Gourmet Cookies— Chocolate Chip, Chocolate Mint Fudge, French Vanilla Chip, Hazelnut Fudge, and Quinoa Oatmeal Raisin cookies made with organic whole-wheat flour and free of preservatives, etc. Sold through stores. 3629 10th Ave, Los Angeles, CA 90018. (213) 732-1433.

National Ovens of Manitowoc Inc.— Makes sunny millet bread, oat bran delight bread, crunchy granola, energy drink, and fortified flax, available by mail. Asserted 50% organic, affiliated with OFPANA. V M accepted. PO Box 2137, Manitowoc, WI 54221. (414) 758-2500.

Natural Wonders Candy— Plain and peanut nuggets with "a natural vegetable wax coating" (as opposed to beetle-puree) and no artificial colorings. They still have a lot of fat. Sold through stores. California Candies, 3691 Lenawee Avenue, Los Angeles, CA 90016. (213) 204-1400.

Pacific Gardens— Dairy-free, honey-sweetened cookies made with organic whole wheat. Sold through stores.

Pride of the Farm— Cookies with no hydrogenated oils, processed sugars, or preservatives in 10 varieties (1 gluten-free). Sold through stores. J&J Snack Foods Corp.

Queen Bee Garderns— Makes and sells confections made from "natural" ingredients with no artificial colorings, flavorings, or additives. (We cannot vouch for the fat content, though they claim the taffy is low in fat.) 1863 Lane 11½, Lovell, WY 82431. (307) 548-2543.

Richmond Baking— Makes Hi Fiber Cookies ("all natural" but not organic), whole-wheat graham crackers, and granola bars. They do a lot of contract manufacturing. PO Box 698, Richmond, IN 47374. (317) 962-8535.

R.W. Frookie— A line of "all natural" fruit-juice-sweetened cookies with low levels of saturated fat and salt. Soldthrough stores. 375 Sylvan Ave., Englewood Cliffs, NJ 07632.

Summercorn Foods— Cookies made from organic flours, organic raisins, filtered water, and soy-based egg and butter substitutes. Also breads, soy products, granolas, and nut/fruit mixes available direct at the main bakery, through markets in the Midwest and Southwest, and by mail to areas with no distributors. 401 Watson, Fayetteville, AR 72701. (501) 521-9338.

Sunlight Foods Inc./Sunspire— Makes unsweetened, kosher candy (carob and barley) bars (minimum order $500). 2114

Adams Ave., San Leandro, CA 94577. (415) 569-9731, (415) 568-4948.

Tree of Life— Makes cookies from organic ingredients and expeller-pressed oils, sweetened with fruit juice. Also dozens of other items. (Minimum order $150.) They are the largest distributor in the country and sell their goods primarily through stores. (See Chapter 8 for more).♦♦♦

Convenience Mixes. See also Sauces, Soups. A lot of the products that might fit under this category have been placed elsewhere (see cereals). There are some companies that make a variety of healthy mixes for such situations as camping.

Allergy Resource— Baking substitutes, condiments, wheat-free and gluten-free products, organic flours, rarely-found flours, dried beans, pastas, and cereals by mail. 195 Huntington Beach Dr., Colorado Springs, CO 80921. (719) 488-3630.

AlpineAire Foods— Sells a variety of easy to make "Quick Meals" for camping (see Chapter 10, California, Nevada City for more).

Cross Seed Co— Sells Amaranth Pancake & Biscuit Flower Mix (asserted 100% organic), as well as organic beans, grains, and seeds by mail. HC 69 Box 2, Bunker Hill, KS 67626. (913) 483-6163.

David's Goodbatter— Pancake and baking mixes made from organic ingredients: whole wheat buttermilk, wheat free buttermilk, buckwheat buttermilk, rice & oats mix, and Premium Almond and Premium Pecan mixes. Mail orders taken for regions where no retailer or supplier carries their products. No minimum order. PO Box 102, Bausman, PA 17504. (717) 872-0652, FAX: (717) 872-8152.♥

Dear Valley Farm— Cake mixes made from organically grown grains. RD 1, Guilford, NY 13780. (607) 764-8556.

Deep Roots— Makes dry packaged bean mixes (some varieties are organic, some are not—check the label). Also bulk herbs and salt-free seasonings. Deep Roots Trading Co., Roger Spivack, 427 W. 3rd St., Williamsport, PA 17701. (717) 323-2210.

Fantastic Foods Inc.— Packaged convenience mixes including rice, "Nature Burgers," Fantastic Falafel, vegetarian chili, quick pilafs, potatoes au gratin, and pasta salads (not organic, but free of additives). Sold through stores. 106 Galli Dr., Novato, CA 94949. (415) 883-5129.♦♦♦

GEM Cultures— Cultures for tempeh, miso, amazake, shoyu, tamari, sourdough, kefir, soy products. (See Chapter 10) Betty L. Stechmeyer, 30301 Sherwood Rd., Ft. Bragg, CA 95437. (707) 964-2922.

Heartymix Company— Sells a wide variety of baking and food mixes from cake and doughnut mixes to soup mixes to wheatless bread mixes by mail. Also candies and confections. No organic claims, but they say they ". . . manufacture and sell naturally fortified baking and food mixes which are made from, as far as [they] can manage, natural ingredients of high food value." 1231 Madison Hill Road, Rahway, NJ 07065. (201) 382–3010.

Jemolo Enterprises— Makes E-Z Gourmet Brand pre-mixes for muffins, cookies, and breads, powdered drinks, Vita-Mac Pasta, and Meadow Maid milk and ice cream. (Overall they assert that about 50% of their products are organic.) Available through stores under their own brand names or under private labels. PO Box 378 Manteca, CA 95336. (209) 823–5896.

More Than Foods Inc.— Makes grain pilaf mixes and vegetable mixes/side dishes/dinner helpers (brand names are: More than Rice, and More than Potatoes). Asserted 50% organic, available through stores (minimum order 100 cases except in remote areas where it is 1 case.) 1765 Westwind Way, McLean, VA 22102. (703) 734–1998.

Secret Garden— Makes "whole food, all natural soup and entree mixes," including Hearty Chili Mix, Turtle Rice Soup Mix, Wild Rice Hotdish/Stuffing Mix, Mandarin Wild Rice Mix. Most ingredients come from their biodynamic farm. Goods available direct by mail, Visa and Mastercard accepted. Rt. 1, Box 404, Park Rapids, MN 56470. (218) 732–4866.

Shiloh Farms— Pancake and other baking mixes. White Oak Rd., Martindale, PA 17549. (717) 354–4936.♦♦♦

Corn and Corn Products. See also Tortilla Chips and Popcorn. A mold that has infected peanut crops for years has now attacked corn and other grains—aflatoxin, second only to TCDD in its carcinogenic properties based on animal tests. Cooking the corn cuts the aflatoxin. Pesticide residues are detected in less than one percent of the corn analyzed by the USDA. Most common residues are from sulfallate, carabryl, chloropyrifos, dieldrin (banned in 1974) and lindane.

Col. Sanchez Traditional Foods— Makes blue corn chips, tortillas, and biscuits, red chile tortillas, truffles, and blue and yellow corn mesa. Available through stores and by mail order. PO Box 5015, Santa Monica, CA, 90405. (213) 396–2228, FAX: (213) 396 3522.♦♦

Garden of Eatin' Inc.— Blue corn chips, tortillas and chapetis. Check your local retailer. 5300 Santa Monica Blvd., Los Angeles, CA 90029. (213) 462–5406.♦♦

Pleasant Grove Farms— Ed or Wynette Sills, PO Box 636, Pleasant Grove, CA 95668. (916) 655–3391.

Couscous. It may look like rice, but it is really the endosperms of durum wheat. It is the after-product of refining wheat and is not particularly nutritious.

Casbah/Sahara Natural Foods— They sell Organic Couscous and several processed grain products, primarily to distributors. 2820 Eighth St., Berkeley, CA 94710. (415) 548–1868.

Crackers. See Snacks.

Cucumbers. This high-water-content vegetable is a poor source of vitamins. Pesticide residues detected include methanidophos, endosulfan, dieldrin, chlorpyrifos and dimethoate.

Cherry Hill Co-operative Cannery— Organic Pickles and other canned and jarred goods (25% organic overall). MR 1, Barre, VT 05641. (802) 479–2558.

Cultured Vegetables. Cultured vegetables are generally raw vegetables that contain lactobacilli (also available in certain brands of milk). Little literature is available on these products, but if you send a self-addressed, stamped envelope (with two stamps) to Rejuvenative Foods, Box 8464, Santa Cruz, CA 95061, they will send you a "newsletter and lots of free information." (408) 462–6715.

Dates. Dates are generally 60–75 percent sugar and are a good source of nicotinic acid, iron, and potassium.[27]

Ahler's Organic Date Garden— (5–pound minimum order) PO Box 726, Mecca, CA 92254. (619) 396–2337.

Great Date in the Morning— Organic dates, melons, and vegetables (depending on season). Jim Dunn, PO Box 31, 85–710 Grapefruit Blvd., Coachella, CA 92236. (619) 298–6171. (See Chapter 10 for more.)

Lee Anderson's Covalda Date Company— Dates (fresh, processed, and dried), citrus fruits, and pecans. PO Box 908, 51–392 Highway 86, Coachella, CA 92236. (619) 398–3551.

Western Date Ranches— Organically grown Medjool dates. Minimum order 10 cases. Peggy Hartsock, Marketing Manager, PO Box 879, Bard, CA 92222. (619) 572–0192.

Desserts. Sweet desserts tend to be bad for you not so much because they are sweet (though this is a problem), but because they contain lots of saturated fats. Companies that make pre-packaged desserts are not always forthcoming about making the fat content of their products clear. Sara Lee sold "Light Classics" cheesecakes that were not any "lighter" than their regular cheesecakes for over a year before they withdrew advertising suggesting that these products really did contain less fat.[28] The healthiest dessert is probably fresh fruit.

Dips. We give here the same warning we give for all sauces and dressings: beware of fat and salt. Dips are often particularly effective at adding unnoticed fatty calories and salt to your diet.

Emerald Valley Kitchen— Makes a black bean pâté made from organically grown beans.

Dried Fruit. Not all the products called dried fruits are healthy and those that look the prettiest may not be the best. If an apricot still has an orange tint after drying or if a raisin is "golden" that means it has been treated with some kind of sulfur compound. Sulfur destroys the B vitamins and causes allergic reaction in many people (especially asthmatics). Others argue, however, that sulfur protects the vitamin C in fruits. Dried fruit is one category where organic handling markedly detracts from the aesthetics of the food.

Some domestic dried fruit and all imported fruit is fumigated. Sometimes preservatives are added, as well. If the product is domestic, the drier it is, the more likely it has not been drenched by unnecessary chemicals.

Tropical fruit is not all that conducive to drying, so dried tropical fruit is often dipped in saturated sugar solutions to give the final products a pleasant flavor. Keep this in mind when buying things like dried pineapple. Also be sure not to confuse dried bananas with banana chips, as the latter are deep-fat fried.

Dried food is dense food, so it is important to consider just how much you eat at one sitting. Eating 10 dried apricots as a snack is conceivable, but it is doubtful many would eat 10 fresh apricots at once. Eating too much dried fruit and drinking a lot of fluid can result in mammoth—even potentially dangerous—stomach aches. A little dried fruit, though, is a good and nutritious snack, and a good substitute for candy.

Capay Canyon Ranch— Sells organically grown fruit and dried fruit by mail. PO Box 508, Esparto, CA 95627. (916) 662-2372.

Country Grown— Organically grown dried fruits: figs, apricots, and raisins. Also grains, beans, and seeds. Certified by OCIA. Sold mainly through stores, mail order available. Box 2485, Dearborn, MI 48123. (313) 561-0421.

Joe Soghomian, Inc.— Thompson Seedless raisins, jumbo raisins, Zante currants. 8624 Chestnut, Fresno, CA 93725. (209) 834-2772. (209) 834-3150.

Just Tomatoes— Sells unsulfured dried tomatoes, persimmons, and apples. (Not organic, minimum order 1 case.) PO Box 807, Westley, CA 95387. (209) 894-5371.

Moksha Natural Foods— Sells organic dried tomatoes, apricots, and pears (among many other things) by mail.724 Palm Ave, Watsonville, CA 95076. (408) 724-2009.

Natural Foods Inc.— Sells organic raisins and oat bran. Natural Foods Inc., 3040-G Hill Ave, Toledo, OH 43607-2931. (419) 537-1713.

Sowden Bros.— Organic prunes and prune juice. Also other dried fruits. Available by mail. 8888 Township Rd., Live Oak, CA 95953. (916) 695-3750 FAX: (916) 695-1395.

Timber Crest Farms— Dried, sulfur-free, organic fruit (apples, apricots, peaches, pears, prunes), and dried tomatoes. 4791 Dry Creek Rd., Healdsburg, CA 95448. (707) 433-8251.

Van Dyke Ranch— Sells dried fruit—bing cherries,apricots by mail and through a stand. (Please see Chapter 10 for more.) 7665 Crews Rd., Gilroy, CA 95020. (408) 842-5423.

Eggs. Eggs can come from run-around (free range) hens or from hens literally cooped up 24 hours a day in tiers of cages so small that they can't even stretch their wings (battery or factory eggs) depending on the producer. Organic and humane groups work to promote eggs from free-range chickens, which makes certification worth seeking out.

Consumer Reports— argues in its October 1989 issue that eggs are maligned as a food: "[they] are a nutritional bargain . . . a good source of high-quality protein, riboflavin, phosphorous, and vitamins A, D, and B_{12}."

People are eating fewer eggs, in large part, because of concerns about cholesterol. However, some recent studies suggest that the dietary cholesterol has limited effect on blood cholesterol. In any case, most doctors still recommend that, if you eat eggs, you limit your intake to four or fewer a week. So-called "low cholesterol" eggs are probably not worth the extra cost because the cholesterol in an average egg is lower than it used to be and only a few percentage points higher than that in a "low-cholesterol" brand. Another reason eggs are maligned stems from the risk of salmonella poisoning, especially from undercooked eggs (such as those used in products like home-made mayonnaise, egg nog, and chocolate mousse). It causes 500 deaths a year. To avoid catching salmonellosis from eggs, make sure to cook the eggs long enough that no part of either the white or the yellow parts is runny; that means the eggs should be hard-boiled—keep them in the water for seven minutes.

Eggzact— The brand name of a cholesterol-free egg replacement that consists of powdered egg whites available by mail. 6 ounces, the equivalent of 60 eggs, costs $7, postage and handling included. (It is better suited to baking mixes than omelets). Heart Smart Food, PO Box 491, Needham Heights, MA 02194.

Eggplant. A nightshade related to tomatoes and peppers, eggplants are mostly water (94 percent) and therefore a low-calorie food (38 cal/cup). They are fairly versatile and can be cooked in a wide variety of ways. Avoid soft eggplants and large ones, and be aware that eggplant may be waxed for aesthetic enhancement.

Figs. Figs have the highest amount of fiber of any fruit, says the California Fig Advisory Board. Dried figs are 80 percent higher in potassium than bananas, a remarkably good source of calcium (more calcium by weight than in whole milk), almost fat-free and sodium-free. The California Fig Advisory Board inspects all California figs. If the moisture level is allowed to drop to 25 percent, no preservatives are needed. At the 30 percent level, the FDA-approved preservative potassium sorbate is added. California Figs also may contain sulfur dioxide to preserve their golden color. For a useful flyer on the nutritional value of figs, recipes and other information, write to the California Fig Advisory Board, PO Box 709, Fresno, CA 93712. (209) 445-5626; FAX: (209) 224-3449.

Kalashian Packing Co.— Fresno, CA 93721. (209) 237–3665; FAX: (209) 237–4714.

Producers Packing Corp.— Fresno, CA 93792. (209) 275–2191; FAX: (209) 275–0647.

San Joaquin Figs, Inc.— Fresno, CA 93722. (209) 224–4963.

Valley Fig Growers— Fresno, CA 93718. (209) 237–3893; FAX: (209) 237–3898.

Fish. See also Shellfish. Fish has less fat than meat. That is one factor adduced to explain why fish-eaters like the Japanese and Eskimos have much lower rates of heart disease. Another explanation is that fish contains oils that have been shown to be beneficial to the heart and lungs. These oils contain omega-3 fatty acids, which have some anti-inflammatory properties.[29] The fish highest in omega-3 oil generally live in the deep ocean and include herring, sardines, eels, halibut, sablefish, salmon, tuna, mackerel, lake trout, bluefish, and spiny dogfish.[30]

The main problems with fish derive from what they eat or what parasites they carry. Bottom-dwelling inshore fish and even ocean fish may eat debris. Where fish eat affects how polluted they are, so be wary when your neighbor offers you swordfish from the Hudson River or Boston Harbor. Fish from the Great Lakes and elsewhere contain PCBs as well as such pesticides as DDT, chlordane, aldrin, dieldrin and toxaphene (in fact the FDA more frequently finds pesticide residues in fish than in fruit).

Even fish that do not scavenge can be contaminated, for water is one of the main dumping grounds for all kinds of waste. Pregnant mothers should especially avoid lakefish (which contain PCBs) shark, swordfish, large tuna, halibut, and marlin, which can accumulate mercury in their systems.[31] Mercury attacks nerve cells making it bad for the mother and posing serious risk to the fetus.

On average, fish pose a risk of bacterial and viral infection ten times higher than the risk from beef and seven times higher than the risk from chicken.

Other possible hazards arise from the methods employed in modern aquaculture. Fish farmers are following the example of meat producers and injecting young salmon with drugs and hormones to promote growth. The intentional addition of pesticides to fish-tanks to eradicate parasites is also quite common.[32]

It is best to avoid fatty lake trout. Buy, instead, lean ocean fish like flounder, halibut, monkfish, and snapper; and cook it thoroughly to kill microbes (toxics will remain anyway). Be especially careful when cooking fish in a microwave, as many models heat food unevenly. Diseases picked up from fish can be quite nasty and hard to diagnose. When buying tropical fish, like snapper or grouper, buy small fish to avoid ciguatoxin poisoning. If you buy fish in cans like tuna or salmon, go for those products packed in water instead of oil.

A particularly good cookbook on fish is *Eat Fish, Live Better* by Anne Fletcher (Harper & Row) which analyzes in depth a lot of the research on fish and its relationship to better health.

Aquaculture Marketing Service— Canned, and fresh/frozen rainbow trout (hormone-free, pesticide-free, drug-free) raised in mountain spring water available by mail. Minimum order 1 mini-case (12 cans), money back guarantee "to every customer for any reason." UPS delivery takes about 1 week, Fresh/frozen shipped only from Monday to Wednesday. 356 W. Redview Dr., Monroe, UT 84754. (801) 527–4528.

Mountain Ark Trading Company— Sells fish from the North Carolina National Forest area, shipped UPS Second Day Air and packed in dry ice. Fayetteville, AR 72701. (800) 643–8909.♦

The Crawdad Farm— Boyce or Sharon Ward, PO Box 395, Mauriceville, TX 77626. (409) 745–2388. (See listing in Chapter 10.)

Natural Beef Farms Food Distribution Co.— Sells some seafood, too. 4399–A Henninger Court, Chantilly, VA 22021. (703) 631–0881.

Northwest Natural— Frozen salmon and halibut patties. Certified kosher (which means, among other things, no dolphin chunks). Minimum order 25 cases. Peter Lesser, 6644 Sexton Dr., Olympia, WA 98502. (206) 866–9661.

Flour. See also Grains, Convenience mixes.

Allergy Resource— Organic flours (amaranth, soy, barley, buckwheat, corn, millet, oat, rice, quinoa, rye, navy bean) rarely-found flours (Jerusalem artichoke, teff, potato, adzuki, tapioca, pinto bean, lentil, dehydrated poi, and sorgum), baking substitutes, condiments, wheat-free and gluten-free products, dried beans, pastas, and cereals by mail. 195 Huntington Beach Dr., Colorado Springs, CO 80921. (719) 488–3630.

Arrowhead Mills— Organic and chemical-free flours including: Amaranth, Garbanzo, Rice, Triticale, and Whole Wheat White. Also organic Cornmeal (blue, yellow, and high lysine), seeds, whole grains, nuts, beans, cereals, and mixes. Overall 75 percent of products are asserted organic. Sold mainly through stores, but mail order is available for people who do not live near a retail outlet. 110 S. Lawton, Hereford, TX 79045. (806) 364–0730.♥♦♦♦♦

Black Ranch— Organic whole grains (oats, red and white wheat, amaranth and rye), rose hips, red clover sprouts, wholegrain flour (wheat, rye, and amaranth), 6–grain cereal. Dave and Dawn Black, 5800 Eastside Rd., Etna, CA 96027. (916) 467–3387. (See Chapter 10, CA, Etna for more.)

Champlain Valley Milling— Flours: spring bread, pastry, corn & cornmeal, spelt, durum, organic white bread flour, organic white pastry flour, Champ P & W Mix. Also grains. They assert that 75 percent of the goods they sell are organic. Sold mainly through stores, though orders can be picked up at their plant. 110 Pleasant St., Westport, NY 12993. (518) 962–4711.

Cheyenne Gap Amaranth— Amaranth grain and flour (mail order), Arris Sigle, H.C. 1, Box 2, Luray, KS 67649-9743. (913) 698-2457 early until 8 a.m. Central Time, (913) 698-2292 all day. (See listing in Chapter 10.)

Diamond K Enterprises— Sells organically grown and processed flours: amaranth, barley, brown rice, buckwheat, corn, millet, oat, and multi-grain and "pastry" flour by mail. Also cereals, grains, pancake mixes, birdseed, sunflower seeds, and some dried fruits. (Asserted 95% organic, see listing in Chapter 10 for more.) RR 1 Box 30-A, St. Charles, MN 55972. (507) 932-4308, or 932-5433.

Eagle Agricultural Products— Organic flours: corn, rye, rice, soy, unbleached white, pastry. Also white cornmeal. Huntsville, AR. Primarily available through Ozark Cooperative Warehouse (see Chapter 6). PO Box 30, Fayetteville, AR 72702. (501) 521-COOP.

Great Grains Milling Co.— Sells stone-ground flour made from organically grown hard red spring wheat (asserted 100% organic, certification pending). Available direct and by mail. They flush the ground flour with nitrogen, which they say keeps the flour fresh longer. PO Box 427, Scobey, MT 59263. (406) 783-5588.

Helmuth Country Bakery— Sells amaranth flour, puffed amaranth (cereal), egg noodles and snack crackers. Available by mail. They assert 10% of their products are organic, some of the ingredients grown on their own organic farm. Hutchinson, Kansas 67501. (316) 567-2301.

Little Bear Trading Co.— Organic flours. Also cereals, rice, beans, noodles, and vegie-burger mixes. Available through healthy food stores and an increasing number of conventional markets. They assert 95% of their products are organic. 226 E. Second St., Winona, MN 55987. (507) 452-6332.♦♦♦

Loriva Supreme Foods— Organic sesame flour. Also sesame seeds, oil, tahini, and peanut butter. OCIA Certified. Sold through stores. Formerly International Protein Industries. 40-10 Oser Ave, Hauppauge, NY 11788. (516) 231-7940.

Lormak— Organic whole-wheat flour available by mail. Also cracked wheat and buttermilk pancake mix. Rt. 2, Box 58, Concordia, KS 66901. (913) 243-7517.

Natural Way Mills, Inc.— Organic flours including Gold N white flour, Durum flour, W.W. pastry flour, hard white spring wheat and flour, oat bran. Their products are sold mainly through stores, but they will do mail order. Rt. 2 Box 37, Middle River, MN 56737. (218) 222-3677.

Neshaminy Valley— Organic flours in several varieties. Also fruit, nuts, and grains. 5 Louise Drive, Ivyland, PA 18974. (215) 443-5545, FAX: (215) 443-7087.♦

Nu-World Amaranth, Inc.— Amaranth in many forms from puffed to flour. Larry Walters, PO Box 2202, Naperville, IL 60567. (312) 369-6819, FAX: (312) 416-8316. (See listing in Chapter 10.)

Shepherdsfield Award Winning Bakery— Organic stoneground wheat flour available by mail. Also breads, and other baked goods. Rt. 4, Box 399, Fulton, MO 65251. (314) 642-1439.

Todd's Fork Creek Company— Makes and sells organic flours (soy, soft wheat) and corn meal (yellow, red, blue, and white). Some mail orders accepted. Call or write for a price list. 885 N. George Rd., Clarksville, OH 45113. (513) 289-2040.

Frozen Dinners. See also Convenience Mixes, Pizza. One of the most pervasive icons of the 80's, some companies are now marketing frozen dinners that are healthful and tasty. Then again, some frozen dinners still taste like greasy cardboard. Those of the former variety are listed below. They often do not exactly meet our wholefoods/organic criteria, but they are better for you than conventional frozen dinners.

Cascadian Farm— Frozen organic fruits and vegetables. Also organic pickled products and jams. Sold through stores. Concrete, WA.♦♦♦

Healthy Choice Dinners— Makes a line of 10 low-fat, low-cholesterol, low-sodium frozen dinners suitable for preparation in a microwave. Available even in conventional supermarkets.

Jaclyn's— Frozen dinners: grilled tofu in peanut sauce or black bean sauce, with organic rice, tofu, green beans, carrots, and corn. Asserted 40% organic, sold through stores. Also breaded veggies, frozen soups, organic bread crumbs, and pasta sauce. Jaclyn's Food Products, Inc., PO Box 1314, Cherry Hill, NJ 08034. (609) 983-2560.

Stouffer's Right Course— Makes 11 low-fat, low-sodium, low-cholesterol dinners. Available in supermarkets.

Tree Tavern Products— See Jaclyn's.

Frozen Desserts. As a substitute for ice cream, frozen fruit contains no cholesterol or fat and has considerably fewer calories than ice cream.

Rice Dream and *Gone Bananas*— are two tasty, non-dairy frozen treats to look for in your market. Imagine Foods Inc. is also planning a line of organic products in the near future. 299 California Ave. #305, Palo Alto, CA 94306. (415) 327-1444.♦

Rose International— Tofu ice cream mixes as well as soybean milk, tofu, and other soy products. (They assert that 60% of their products are organic.) PO Box 5020, CA 95402. (707) 576-7050.

Ice cream is not a health food. (Really.) For most adults, the cholesterol puts ice cream on a list of things to be eaten sparingly if at all. Frozen yogurt and ice milk are better alternatives. However, some ice cream brands are better than others from a health perspective. We list a few and explain why.

Ben & Jerry's— uses only natural ingredients, except for the candy and cookies it adds to certain flavors. But like other "superpremium" ice cream (Haagen-Dazs and Steve's being the other two leading brands), the ice cream is very high in butterfat. They are currently test marketing a new "lite" ice cream (actually ice milk) that has between half and two-thirds the butterfat.

Damian's Ice Cream— All natural and kosher ice creams. PO Box 115, Boston, MA 02132. (617) 323–6130.

French American Ice Cream Company— Makes Mulberry Street low-fat frozen yogurt and Café Glacé sold through stores. All products sweetened with fruit juice. 1330 North Broadway, Suite 210, Walnut Creek, CA 94596. (415) 934–5858.

Nouvelle Ice Cream Corp.— Non-fat ice creams and sorbets. 1111 E. Francisco Blvd. # 4, San Rafael, CA 94901. (415) 459–6890.

Skinny Dip— A no-fat, virtually sodium-free dessert. Made by Rujac International, Inc. 2628 N. Cullen Ave, Evansville, IN 47715. (812) 479–1014.

Fruit and Vegetable Juices. See also Carrots. Juice is not as filling as fruit and is therefore more likely to be consumed in excess; however, it is much healthier and less likely to be consumed in excess than soda pop. Juice from organically grown fruit is hard to find and is sold mostly locally. In 1988 the U.S. imported $600 million in orange juice, mostly from Brazil and Mexico.

Orange, grapefruit, orange-grapefruit, and tomato juices are all regulated by USDA standards, guaranteeing clear labeling practices. This is not true for other juices and juice blends. In general look for the labels: 100 percent pure juice, 100 percent fruit juice, 100 percent fruit juice blends, or 100 percent fruit juice from concentrate. The labels 100 percent real juice, 100 percent natural, fruit drink, fruit cocktail, and juice beverage are legally meaningless and can be deceptive. Another way to ensure you are getting juice is to look at the order of ingredients (which by FDA regulations must be printed on the container). If high-fructose sweeteners, corn sweeteners, or artificial sweeteners show up on the labels, you know it is not pure juice. Water near the top of an ingredients list is also suspicious, though for some things pure juice would be hard to take. Cranberry juice cocktail, for instance, may be only 20–30 percent pure juice because 100 percent would be unpalatable for most people.[33]

Most tomato and vegetable juices have astounding quantities of salt. Try no-salt and low-salt varieties and you may find that the vegetables taste good by themselves.

After The Fall— Fruit juices, some made from organically grown fruit. After the Fall Products Inc., PO Box 777, Putney Rd., Brattleboro, VT 05301. (802) 257–4616.♦♦♦

Biotta Vegetable Cocktail— A cocktail made from organic carrot, tomato, celery, and beetroot juices with cultured whey. Tasty, too. Made by Biotta AG, CH Tgerwilen,

Switzerland. Distributed in the U.S. by Richter Bros. Inc., Carlstadt, NJ 07072.

Ferraro's Fine Juices— Some organic juices sold through retailers. 1610 S. Magnolia Ave., Monrovia, CA 91016.

Heinke's Inc.— Fruit juices. Paradise, California 95969. (916) 877–4847, FAX: (916) 877–3358.♦

Knudsen and Sons— Juices (apple, gravenstein, pear, concord grape), wine, non-alcoholic beer, Recharge "thirst quencher," preserves, jams, jellies, soft drinks, spritzers. Only some are organic. (200 case minimum) Speedway Ave., PO Box 369, Chico, CA 95927. (916) 891–1517.♦♦♦

Lakewood— Fruit juices, including cranberry, coconut, and peaches 'n' cream. Sold through stores. Miami, FL.

Naked Juice/U-Like Juice— Some organic fruit juices, mostly distributed through stores. 2132 West Hyde Park Blvd., Los Angeles, CA 90047.

Odwalla— Fresh, unpasteurized, and some organic fruit and vegetable juices delivered by truck to Bay Area stores and restaurants. (Minimum order is $50.) Rob Feldman, Caty Mangan, Greg Steltenphol, Drawer O, Davenport, CA 95017. (408) 425–4557.

Organic Farms— Makes organic pear and apple juices. Beltsville, MD.♦♦

Plaidberry— Juices, cakes, pies, and award-winning jams made from organically grown (95%) plaidberries. Expect 4–6 weeks on mail orders, also available in some stores; no minimum order. PO Box 2546, Vista, CA 92083. (619) 727–1122.

Santa Cruz Natural— Organic juices including strawberry-guava, apple-blackberry, orangeade, pear, and lemon-strawberry. Freedom, CA 95019. (408) 728–0515, FAX: (408) 728–0779.

Sierra Distributing— They make some organic frozen juices (including carrot juice) and wheatgrass juice. David L. Lane, 603 1st St. #515, Oceanside, CA 92054. (619) 721–0123.

Garlic and Onions. The flavor properties of garlic are well known and these pungent little bulbs are the center of yearly festivals in Gilroy ("Garlic Capital of the World") and Berkeley, California. Though its efficacy in repelling fanged nocturnal visitors is questionable, the evidence suggests that garlic affects the blood lipid level and helps fight heart disease. It is also credited in some studies as a cancer-fighting agent.[34] Its traditional role as a folk remedy in many cultures (it has been used to combat everything from headaches and baldness to pneumonia and the plague) has been validated by some recent studies, and, while still only esteemed on the fringe of mainstream medicine, it is gaining acceptance.[35] Folk wisdom also suggests that it has invigorating properties that make it effective as an aphrodisiac, or something to eat before going into battle.[36] Garlic is amazingly adept at getting into your blood-stream and it is claimed that if you rub cloves on your feet, garlic will be discernible on your breath within 20 minutes. Garlic is best when served fresh and uncooked. Try it on salads as a substitute for salt and fatty dressings.

If you are buying minced garlic in oil, look for brands with acids to inhibit bacteria growth. Otherwise the product may pose a risk of botulism.

Neither garlic nor onion is particularly rich in any vitamins. Most onions you will find in a store are 90 percent water. Onions can be dehydrated fairly easily, making them well-suited for use in dried food mixes. (Visiting a processing plant where tons of onions have been diced to pieces for dehydration is truly enough to make you cry—like you've never cried before.) It is often hard to distinguish reconstituted onions from fresh ones (try it next time you see a fast-food hamburger).

Pesticide residues detected on onions include DCPA, DDT (residues left from pre-1973 era), ethion, diazinon and malathion.

Arjoy Acres— Garlic and elephant garlic. HCR Box 1410, Payson, AZ 85541. (602) 474–1224.

Arizona Natural Products— Onions and garlic; 8281 E. Evans Rd. #104, Scottsdale, AZ 85260. (602) 991–4414. (See listing in Chapter 10.)

Ecology Sound Farms— Grows organic garlic. Orosi, CA 93647. (209) 528–3816.

Haypoint Farm— Organically grown garlic by mail. Box 292, Sugar Island, Sault Ste. Marie, MI 49783. (906) 632–1280.

Pleasant Grove Farms— Organically grown elephant garlic available through mail order. (Please see Chapter 10 for more.) PO Box 636, Pleasant Grove, CA 95668. (916) 655–3391.

Plumbottom Farm— Garlic braids decorated with flowers by mail (100% organic). Rt. 3, Box 129, Willow Springs, MO 65793. (417) 962–3204.

Walnut Acres— Onions and other root crops available by mail. Penns Creek, PA 17862. (800) 433–3998, (717) 837–0601.♦♦

Grains. See also Amaranth, Bread, Cereal, Flour, Oats, and Rice. Fiber is an important, element in the diet (see Chapter 3). Best sources are grain, fruits (especially figs), and vegetables. Insoluble fiber, like that found in wheat bran is among the more effective ways to reduce your chances of colon cancer. In whole grains the fiber is concentrated in the bran, germ, and endosperm (the parts stripped away to make white bread). Wheat, for example, has 12 grams of fiber and significant quantities of minerals in just one ounce.

We need 45 to 60 grams of protein a day: Grains are a high-protein food, but must be complemented with a legume or a milk product to provide all nine of the essential amino acids. (See Chapter 2 for more on amino acids.)

Arrowhead Mills— Organic Amaranth and Quinoa. Also seeds, flours, nuts, beans, cereals, and mixes. Overall 75% of products are asserted organic. Sold mainly through stores, but mail order is available for people who do not live near a retail outlet. 110 S. Lawton, Hereford, TX 79045. (806) 364–0730.♥♦♦♦♦

Black Ranch— Whole grains (oats, red and white wheat, amaranth and rye), rose hips, red clover sprouts, whole-grain flour (wheat, rye, and amaranth), 6 grain cereal available by mail. Grains certified by CCOF 5800 Eastside Rd., Etna, CA 96027. (916) 467–3387.

Community Mill and Bean— Whole grains, flours and meals, processed grain products (baking mixes), dried soybeans. Sells wholesale quantities. R.D. #1, Route 89, Savannah, NY 13146. (315) 365–2664.

Country Grown— Organic grains (hard red spring wheat, hard red winter wheat, soft white winter wheat, rye, durum, barley, millet, buckwheat, and rice). Also seeds, beans, and dried fruit. Certified by OCIA. Sold mainly through stores, mail order available. Box 2485, Dearborn, MI 48123. (313) 561–0421.

Cross Seed Co— Sells amaranth, whole barley, whole rye, whole oats, hulled oats, hard red winter wheat, soft white winter wheat, triticale, whole buckwheat, whole millet, and popcorn (all asserted 100% organic). Also Amaranth Pancake & Biscuit Flower Mix, as well as organic beans, grains, and seeds by mail. HC 69 Box 2, Bunker Hill, KS 67626. (913) 483–6163.

Diamond K Enterprises— Sells organically grown grains and beans: amaranth (seed), barley (hulled and unhulled), buckwheat (groats and grits), corn (hi lysine and regular), oats (hulled and unhulled), Millet (hulled and unhulled), flax (seed), lentils, mung beans, pinto beans, navy beans, turtle beans, and kidney beans by mail. Also rice, flours, cereals, pancake mixes, birdseed, sunflower seeds, and some dried fruits. Allow 1 to 2 weeks for shipping. (Asserted 95% organic, see listing in Chapter 6 for more.) RR 1 Box 30–A, St. Charles, MN 55972. (507) 932–4308, or 932–5433.

Do-R-Dye Organic Mill— Grains: oats, wheat, rye, corn, sweet corn, and blue corn. Also oatmeal, and flour (rye and whole wheat). Certified organic by OCIA. They sell mainly wholesale quantities, but mail order is available. Box 50, Rosalie, NE 68055. (402) 863–2248.

Family Farms— Organically grown grains sold mainly to bakeries and distributors. Wyo Avenue/Road 9, Orland, CA 95963. (916) 865–3865.

Living Farms— Sells organically grown grains and beans: buckwheat, corn, flax, millet, oats, popcorn, rye, soybeans, triticale, and wheats. Mostly wholesale quantities, but mail orders accepted. Asserted 100% organic. Box 50, Tracy, MN 56175. (800) 353–5320.

M & M Distributing— Whole organic grains: amaranth and blue corn. Sold mainly through stores, but they will do mail orders. Mark and Marcy Jones, R.R.2, PO Box 61-A, Oshkosh, NE 69154. (308) 772-3664.

Montana Flour & Grains— Organically grown grains and flours: hard red wheat (winter and spring), hard and soft white wheat, barley, rye, kamut, and multi-grain mixes. (Some varieties are not organic—inquire for more information. Primarily wholesale quantities but no minimum if there is no distributor in your area.) Ferry Route, Box 808, Big Sandy, MT 59520. (406) 378-3105.

Mosher Products— Grows and sell organic wheat by mail. Also wheat grinders. PO Box 5367, Cheyenne, WY 82003. (307) 632-1492.

National Grain Products Co., Inc.— Processes and distributes some organic grains: buckwheat, rye, whole wheat. Also some organic cereals: granola, oatmeal, wheat. (Asserted 40% organic, most sales wholesale, but no minimum order—smallest bag is 25 pounds.) PO Box 1469 Minnetonka, MN 55345. (812) 476-2215. FAX:(812) 476-8701.

Natural Way Mills, Inc.— Sells organically grown whole grains and flours by mail. Also sells organic dried beans. Rt. 2 Box 37, Middle River, MN 56737. (218) 222-3677.

Neshaminy Valley— Organic grains and flours in several varieties. Also fruits and nuts. 5 Louise Drive, Ivyland, PA 18974. (215) 443-5545, FAX: (215) 443-7087.♦

Quinoa— Grain and flour from organically grown (asserted 90%) quinoa. Also "Supergrain" pastas and spaghetti. Sold mostly in supermarkets (case orders only). PO Box 1039, Torrance, CA 90505. (213) 530-8666. FAX: (213) 530-8764.

Sanctuary Farms— Sells organic buckwheat, corn, popcorn, wheat, Adzuki beans, black soybeans, and beef by mail. Shipping is UPS, no credit on first purchases. RD #1, Butler Rd, Box 184-A, New London, OH 44851. (419) 929-8177.

Granola and Other Bars. Granola is often a symbol of health-consciousness, but many brands are not terribly good for you. Some granola, for instance, has more saturated fat and sugar than ice cream. A typical granola bar gets more than a third of its calories from fat. A chocolate-coated granola bar is likely to deliver half of its calories from fat.[37]

Health Rich— Snack bars with OCIA-certified organic ingredients: Peanut Butter, Oat Bran, Spicy Raisin, Strawberry-Banana, Toasted Sesame. Sold through stores. 1611 Bradley, Lansing, MI 48910. (517) 482-4480.

Health Valley— Snack bars with some organic ingredients. Also cereals, cookies, crackers, muffins, pilaf, whole-wheat pasta, and soy milk. Many of their products are also low-salt. Sold through stores.♥♦♦♦♦

Inter Mountain Trading Co.— Sells Bear Valley brand "High Energy Concentrated Food Bars" that are well balanced and free of additives (though we can't vouch for fat content) PO Box 6157, Albany, CA 94706. (415) 526-3623.

Sprout Delights Bakery— Sells Totally Nuts, Go Bananas, and Just Fruit "high energy healthy snacks." Also yeast-free breads, rolls, muffins, snacks, and cakes (all made from sprouted organic grains), vegetarian Sprout Burgers and Millet-Barley Burgers by mail. (Asserted 90+% organic, minimum order $20 for public.) 13090 NW 7th Ave, North Miami, FL 33168-2702. (305) 687-5880 or (800) 334-BAKE. FAX: (305) 687-3233.

Summercorn Foods— Granolas and nut and dried fruit mixes with some organic ingredients. Also Bread, soy products, and cookies available direct at the main bakery, through markets in the Midwest and Southwest, and by mail to areas with no distributors. 401 Watson, Fayetteville, AR 72701. (501) 521-9338.

Grapefruit. See Citrus Fruits.

Grapes. The grape industry is the world's largest fruit industry. Grapes are the third most cultivated crop in the U.S. and, in 1988, the U.S. imported $300 million in grapes from abroad (mostly from Chile).

In 1989 a Buenos Aires phone tip led to a large-scale search for cyanide-laced grapes. *Time* Magazine devoted the cover of its March 27 issue to the "two tainted grapes" discovered and the "Great Food Scare" that ensued. *Newsweek* also featured the story on its cover that week. This incident was most significant in the way it pointed out the inadequate resources available to test imported produce. This is important because, while only a few Chilean grapes were cyanide-tainted, many are laced with high concentrations of undesirable pesticides and fungicides. Sometimes these chemicals and/or the spraying frequency and intensity reflected would be illegal for farmers in this country. Pesticides detected on grapes include captan, carbaryl, dimethoate, dicloran, and iprodione.

Stephen Pavich & Sons— Organic grapes (wholesale quantities only) Tom Pavich, Partner, Rt 2 Box 291, Delano, CA 93215. (805) 725-1046.

Ham. See Pork.

Herbs. Herbs are increasingly available fresh in supermarkets. They can also be ordered from organic farmers, or grown in a box by your window.

Mallat Family Farm— Herbs and mesclan lettuce by mail. Asserted 100% organic. 29930 Desert Charm Rd., Desert Hot Springs, CA 92240. (619) 342-0065.

Elderflower Farm— Organic culinary herb blends, herb vinegars. and related books by mail. Elderflower Farm, 501 Callahan Rd, Roseburg, OR 97470. (503) 672-9803. See listing in Chapter 10 for more.

Herbs Etc.— All botanicals are picked in the wild or organically grown. Extraction process does not use heat. Santa Fe, NM 87501. (800) 634-3727.

The Herbpharm— Mail-order business, cooking classes, and restaurant. Open Monday to Friday 9am to 5pm; Saturday and Sunday 9a.m. to 6p.m. Fall City, WA 98024. (206) 784-2222.

Mallat Family— Fresh organic herbs and Meclon lettuce available through the mail. They primarily sell to retailers in Southern California. Frank and Regina Mallat, Owners, 29930 Desert Charm Rd., Desert Hot Springs, CA 92240. (619) 342-0065.

McZand Herbal Inc.— Bulk herbs (25-30% organic) sold through distributors across the U.S. PO Box 5312, Venice, CA 90291. (213) 392-0404.

San Francisco Herb & Natural Food— A variety of wildcrafted (picked in their natural habitat) herbs and spices. 4543 Horton St., Emeryville, CA 94608. (415) 547-6345. (800) 523-5142, in California (800) 227-2830.

Sun Isles Spices— Where possible, spices are grown wild. Naturally processed. Free of artificial colors, MSG, cornstarch, dextrin, dextrose, disodium guanylate, disodium inosinate, hydrogenated oils, propylene glycol, salt, sugar, tricalcium phosphate, FDC, and silicone dioxide. Irradiation is not used. Pasadena, CA 91107. (213) 681-5275. FAX: (818) 449-6713.

Honey. Some people assume that honey is a better sweetener than other sugars because it is natural. In reality a comparison of honey to other sweeteners (e.g. table sugar, corn syrup, maple sugar, and molasses), reveals that the nutritional content is about the same. Honey, like table sugar, is a simple sugar (either a monosaccharide or a disaccharide; see Chapter 2). It enters the blood stream at roughly the same rate as table sugar. Simple sugars are called "empty calories" because they are not nutrient dense. Compared to a complex carbohydrate, like a slice of whole grain bread, an equal caloric portion of a simple sugar will not offer the same amount of nutrients. A simple sugar has no fiber and few vitamins or minerals.

Simple sugars have no serious effects on the average person, but some physiological stress is caused by the rapid rate at which these sugars are absorbed. Ingestion of large quantities of glucose (the form that all sugars ultimately take in your body) triggers a release of insulin, which causes a drop in energy within about 30 minutes. As an exception to the low mineral content of sugars, molasses has a lot of iron, because iron is a contaminant from the machines that process the molasses. Honey can cause botulism in infants under one year old, but is safe for older children.[38]

Bullseye Honey Farms— Roger Starks, PO Box 272, Wakonda, SD 57073. (605) 361-0493.

Comvita— Makes a wide range of bee products including honey, fruit honeys, pollen and honey spread, and beenut butter. Made in "nuclear free" New Zealand and distributed by Pacific Resources, PO Box 668, Summerland, CA 93067. (805) 969-1925.

Cherry Hill Co-operative Cannery— Honey. Barre, VT 05641. (802) 479-2558.

Dawes Hill Honey & Royal Jelly— Honey in 7 varieties (alfalfa, clover, wildflower, blueberry, tupelo, orange blossom, buckwheat), honey fruit spreads, pollen, and propolis. Sold through stores. 1143 Elmira Rd., Newfield, NY 14867. (607) 273-7173.

Golden Angels Apiary— Honey (thistle, clove, orange blossom, wild flower, tulip poplar, comb honey), bee propolis (tincture, raw pieces), beeswax (cubes). No chemicals in any stage of the production and operation. Dennis R. Whetzel, PO Box 2-Road 752, Singers Glen, VA 22850. (703) 833-5104.

Honey World— Inc., PO Box 458, Parker, SD 57053. (605) 297-4181.

Island of the Moon Apiaries Inc.— Honey, bee pollen, royal jelly, and propolis Rt 1, Box 320, Esparto, CA 95627. (916) 787-3993.

Jack's Honey Bee Products— Unprocessed honeys in many varieties including, avocado (colored), raw clover, eucalyptus, and sage. Sold through stores. 2602 E. Foothill Blvd., Pasadena, CA 91107.

McCord Apiaries— Sells honey and bee pollen. 1805 Glide Dr., Glide, OR 97443. (503) 496-3277.

Volcano Island Honey Co.— Gourmet honey, including "rare Hawaiian White Honey." (They assert that it is collected without the use of harmful chemicals. Minimum order: $45 for mail order customer. Also available at Bloomingdale's, Dean & DeLuca, and Balducci's in New York City). PO Box 1709, Honokaa, HI 96727. (808) 775-0806.

Hot Dogs. Take the best cuts from an animal, and what do you have left? The stuff most companies put in hot dogs. Few brands contain the rarely-eaten parts described in lore (i.e. snout, heart, spleen, etc.) and if they do it must be listed on the package. Most, however, contain extremely fatty meat; 70% of the calories that come from an average hot dog are attributable to fat.[39] Chicken and turkey franks are not necessarily an improvement over beef and pork hot dogs because the former are likely to contain skin, which is extremely fatty. Hot dogs also generally have sweeteners, salt, fillers (like soy flour or dried milk) and preservatives (like BHT and BHA). They are also likely to contain nitrates, which can become dangerous when cooked. Hot-dog substitutes are an improvement, but even Tofu Pups get more than half their calories from fat.

Bounty of the Sea— Makes Tuna Franks that are 91% fat free, nitrite free, and relatively low in sodium. Also Tuna lunch meat. Sold through stores. Sugar Land, TX 77478. (713) 240–2479.

Heartland Meats/Dakota Honey Hot Dogs— Makes all natural beef hot dogs (asserted 100% organic). Sells in wholesale quantities. PO Box 818, Rapid City, SD 57709. (605) 341–6063.

Not-Dogs— Soy hotdogs that are reputed to be the best tasting.♦

Lightlife Foods, Inc.— Cholesterol-free "Tofu Pups", which have the taste if not quite the texture of regular hot dogs, and "Fakin' Bacon." Greenfield, MA 01302. (413) 772–0991.

Loma Linda— Sizzle Franks, Linketts, Big Franks, and Little Links meat-substitute hot dogs. Also many other meat substitutes. Sold mainly through stores. Loma Linda Foods Inc., Riverside, CA 92515. (714) 687–7800. California only: (800) 442–4917.

Tulasi— Tofu hot dogs. Surrey International, Arlington, NJ.

White Wave— Makes meatless "Healthy Franks". Also soy-milk, tempeh, tofu, soy cheese, meat substitutes, and other soy products (asserted 75% organic). 1550 N 57th Ct., Boulder, CO 80301. (303) 443–8447.♦♦

Ice Cream. See Frozen Desserts.

Jam, Jelly, and Fruit Spreads. The difference between jam and jelly, for those who find it obscure, is that jam has pieces of real fruit in it while jelly is essentially fruit juice, sugar, and gelatin. Nutritionists say jam on bread is better than butter for most Americans, who can tolerate the sugar better than the fat. The problem is, most Americans put the jam on top of the butter.

Cascadian Farm— Organic fruit spreads: raspberry, strawberry, blueberry, and blackberry. Sold through stores. Concrete, WA.♦♦♦

R. W. Knudsen— Fruit Spreads with no artificial colors, preservatives, or added sugar (no organic claims). Sold through stores.♦♦♦

Mad River Farm Country Kitchen— Jams (blackberry, red raspberry, strawberry, boysenberry, blueberry, monmorency cherry, red raspberry rhubarb), marmalades (sunshine and lemon), and cranberry conserves. The strawberry jam and marmalades are made from organically grown fruit. Susan Anderson, PO Box 155, Arcata, CA 95521. (707) 822–7150.

Plaidberry— Juices, cakes, pies, and award-winning jams made from organically grown (95%) plaidberries. Expect

4–6 weeks lay time on mail orders; no minimum order. PO Box 2546, Vista, CA 92083. (619) 727–1122.

Poultney Preserves— Preserves. RR#1, Box 359, Poultney, VT 05764. (802) 287–9163.

Walnut Acres— Sells organic nuts, preserves, and fresh and canned vegetables (see listing in Chapter 10 for more). Penns Creek, PA 17862. (717) 837–0601, (800) 433–3998.♦♦

Juices. See Fruit and Vegetable Juices and Beverages.

Kefir. See also Yogurt. Kefir is a yogurt-like dairy product fermented with kefir wheat. Kefir producers say that for centuries kefir was the most popular dairy product in Europe. Dr. Johannes Kuhl, a European researcher, recommended a wholesome, natural diet reinforced with liberal amounts of lactic acid-fermented products, including sourdough dark bread, sauerkraut and kefir as a protection against cancer. Kefir breaks up the milk curd into very small particles, making it easy to digest—ideal for infants, pregnant women, nursing mothers, convalescents, the elderly, and people who suffer from constipation or have some other digestive difficulty. It has been effective for some people with dairy product intolerance, and helps restore intestinal flora (see acidopholus). Kefir is said to provide 30 percent more protein with one-third fewer calories than yogurt. It has one-third less lactose than typical dairy products.

Lifeway Foods— Nine flavors of kefir, eight of them lowfat, in 32–ounce plastic bottles, three varieties of cheese, and cheesecake. Sold through stores. 7625 Austin, Skokie, IL 60077. (312) 967–1010, FAX: (312) 967–6558.

Kiwifruit. Kiwifruit has twice the vitamin C content of oranges and is a delicious snack alternative.

Ecology Sound Farms— Kiwifruits, persimmons, plums, dried fruit. All certified organic. 42126 Road 168, Orosi, CA 93647. (209) 528–3816.

Green Knoll Farm— Organic kiwifruit available by mail. (Certified by CCOF). PO Box 434, Gridley, CA 95948.

Weiss's Kiwifruit— Sells organic kiwifruit by mail. 594 Paseo Companeros, Chico, CA 95926.

Lamb. See Meat.

Legumes. Legumes are a high-protein food and a healthy substitute for meat and fish protein. However, they are not a *complete* protein—they do not have all of the nine essential amino acids and therefore are best eaten with a protein complement such as grain or rice.

Including all nine amino acids at each meal is very important, because amino acid stores deplete in a few hours. Eating a dish of lentils at noon followed by some whole grain rice at 5 does not work. Your protein must be complete for your body to function properly. Protein deficiencies are rarely a problem for non-vegetarians and conventional wisdom is coming to the view that even most vegetarians get more than enough protein even without careful planning.

Lentils, beans, peas, and certain nuts also contain quantities of so-called "anti-nutrients," which inhibit the digestion of certain minerals or starches. Some preliminary research suggests that this has a beneficial effect in maintaining constant insulin levels and reducing colon cancer.[40]

Navy and kidney beans, chickpeas and soybean offer a higher percentage of protein per gram than lentil beans or peas. Legumes are an excellent source of thiamin (B_1) and niacin (B_3). Pesticide residues commonly detected on green beans include dimethoate, methamidophos, endosulfan, acephate and chlorothalnil.

Some beans, especially lima beans and kidney beans, need to be boiled for a good period of time in an uncovered pot or they can be poisonous. And while even well-boiled lima beans may continue to have that pre-digested wood-pulp taste, the beans are apparently safe.

Arrowhead Mills— Organic Anasazi, Garbanzo, Mung, Pinto, and Soy beans. Chemical-free Black Turtle and Kidney Beans, Lentils, and Split Peas. Also cereals, seeds, flours, whole grains, nuts, oils, and mixes. Overall 75% of products are asserted organic. Sold mainly through stores, but mail order is available for people who do not live near a retail outlet. 110 S. Lawton, Hereford, TX 79045. (806) 364-0730.♥♦♦♦♦

Country Grown— Organically grown beans: pinto, red kidney, black turtle, mung, garbanzo, adzuki, white navy, black-eyed peas, small red chile, split yellow peas, lentils. Also grains, seeds, and dried fruit. Certified by OCIA. Sold mainly through stores, mail order available. Box 2485, Dearborn, MI 48123. (313) 561-0421.

Eagle Agricultural Products— Dried beans (kidney, lima, navy, pinto and soy). Also flours, cornmeal, pastas, cookies, baking mixes, rice and fruit juices. They assert that 95% of their products are organic overall. 407 Church Ave., Huntsville, AR 72740. (501) 738-2203.

Eden— Various organically grown precooked beans in cans and jars including pinto, great northern, and adzuki. Also crackers, oils, processed fruits, soy-milk and other soy products. 30% organic overall. Eden set up organic standards 20 years ago and has now combined those standards with third-party verification through OCIA. Eden Foods, Inc., 701 Tucumseh Road, Clinton, MI 49236. (517) 456-7424, (313) 973-9400.♦♦♦♦

Health Valley— Good vegetarian chili with lentils. Also cereals, cookies, crackers, canned goods and many other products.♥♦♦♦♦

Little Bear Organic Foods— Organically grown refried beans and other Mexican foods. Available through stores. 15200 Sunset Blvd., Suite 202, Pacific Palisades, CA 90272. (213) 454-5452.♥♦♦♦

Little Bear Trading Co.— Produces a full line of canned organically grown beans. Also flour, cereals, rice, noodles, and vegie-burger mixes. Available through healthy food stores and an increasing number of conventional markets. (Yes, there are now two "Little Bears," the company management having divorced.) 226 E. Second St., Winona, MN 55987. (507) 452-6332.♥♦♦♦

Natural Way Mills, Inc.— Sells organically grown whole grains and flours by mail. Also sells organic dried beans. Rt. 2 Box 37, Middle River, MN 56737. (218) 222-3677.

Purity Foods Inc.— Bulk beans. Also dried fruits, nuts, and macrobiotic products. Goods are certified as part of the ERNTEDANK program. Sold through stores. 4211 Okemos Rd. Suite 21, Okemos, MI 48864. (517) 349-7941, -7942, -7943, (517) 349-2262.

Walnut Acres— Canned organic beans: pinto, garbanzo, kidney, green, great northern, and peas. Penns Creek, PA 17862. (800) 433-3998, (717) 837-0601.♦♦

Lemon and Lime. See Citrus fruit.

Lettuce. Lettuce is one of the earliest known vegetables, going back over 2500 years. Iceberg lettuce is the most commonly sold in the United States, but among organic farmers leaf lettuce sells better because it is known by sophisticated buyers to have a higher vitamin and mineral content.

Lettuce is a good source of vitamins A and C, iron, calcium, chlorophyll and many trace minerals. The nutritional value can deteriorate quickly, so it should be eaten as soon as possible after harvesting. Lettuce should be stored in a near airtight container or plastic bag to retain its freshness. It should be rinsed clean on purchase (iceberg drained well) and then refrigerated until eaten.

Commercial lettuce farming starts with chemical fertilization using a broad-spectrum nitrogen fertilizer like ammonium sulfate or calcium nitrate. Pre-emergence herbicides like Kerb and Baylan are commonly used before planting. Government regulations permit 60 different pesticides to be used on lettuce; 43 of them have been detected as being in use. The most common insecticides used on lettuce are phosdrin, a contact insecticide used for aphids and worms and applied every week or two; endosulfan, a chlorinated hydrocarbon (DDT family) usedfor flies; Pounce, sprayed for a variety of pests; and Lannate, sprayed for aphids as often as every week. Fungicides are used on lettuce to prevent diseases such as rot and damping off. Captan is often used as a protective fungicide before symptoms occur; this chemical is believed by many experts to have no level of safe use.

The following organic farming practice is used by John Givens Farm, Goleta, CA. To build up the soil before planting, Givens uses a combination of dairy manure, fish emulsion, foliar kelp spray and compost, along with crop rotation. He says pests are not a problem. Weeds are controlled by hand, tractor cultivation and weed management.

Star Route Farms— Organic lettuce and other vegetables available in the Bay Area of California. Warren Weber, Bolinas CA. (415) 868-0929.♥

Tanimura and Antle— Has replaced insecticides with a vacuum system that removes insects.

Mangoes. Sometimes called the king of fruits in Asia, mangoes are rich in vitamins A and C. Organic mangoes are now imported from Haiti to many conventional supermarkets including, A&P, Albertson's, Food Emporium, Kroger, Shopwell, Shoprite, Sloan's, Kings, and Waldbaum.[41]

Maple Syrup. Maple syrup is a natural, high-calorie sweetener that is typically 60–70% sucrose. Problems with maple syrup stem from paraformaldehyde pellets some harvesters use to increase drainage and lead contamination. Vermont and Canadian growers usually refrain from using paraformaldehyde.[42]

Annie's Enterprises— Maple syrup and maple syrup based products (including mustard and barbecue sauces) made with syrup bled on their own 250 acre "farm." Ann Christopher, RR 1, Box 63, East Calais, VT 05648. (802) 234-5157.

Cherry Hill Co-operative Cannery— Maple syrup. MR 1, Barre, VT 05641. (802) 479-2558.

Coombs Maple— Dana Coombs, Maple Lane, HCR 13, Box 50, Jacksonville, VT 05342. (802) 368-2345.

Shady Maple Farms— 100% pure organic maple syrup. Gary Coppola, RR1, St. Evariste, PQ G0M1G0. (418) 459-6649.

Uncle Joel's Pure Maple Syrup— Organic maple syrup; Rt. 1, Box 270, Hammond, WI 54015. (715) 796-5395.

Vermont Country Maple— Makes maple sugar (largest manufacturer in the world). Asserted 100% organic, available by mail. Box 53, Jericho Center, VT 05465. (802) 864-7519.

Meat. See also Beef, Poultry. Meat is a good source of protein and many vitamins and minerals—but is also a source of fat and unwanted chemicals. Pork and lamb tend to be fattier than beef, and all red meat has more fat than poultry.

We are not ardently against the ingestion of meat, butthere are sound ecological reasons why meat consumption is wasteful. John Robbins'in *Diet for A New America* claims the following: As much as 85 percent of topsoil depletion is directly associated with livestock raising. If the water subsidies afforded the meat industry were removed, a pound of hamburger would cost $35. By far the greatest amounts of pesticides and chemicals (55 percent) are carried into the human food chain through meat and dairy products.[43] Robbins also claims that by switching to a completely vegetarian diet, the average meat-eater could save one acre of trees per year, and dramatically reduce his chances of having a heart attack.[44] His portrayal of the cruelty and unsound practices used in the raising of most beef and chicken is a powerful diatribe against the modern meat, dairy, broiler, and egg industries.

Meat Substitutes (Burgers, etc.). See also Hot Dogs. Vegetarians who like a good burger have dozens of options these days.

Bud Inc.— "Soyfoods for a healthy world," including vegie burgers.

Fantastic Foods Inc.— Packaged convenience mixes including "Nature burgers," (not organic, but free of additives). Sold through stores. 106 Galli Dr., Novato, CA 94949. (415) 883-5129.♦♦♦

Heartline— "Meatless meats." The product comes in dried form and needs to be reconstituted with water. Sold through stores. Lumen Foods, 409 Scott St., Lake Charles, LA 70601. (318) 436-6748.

Island Spring Inc.— Tofu noodles, tofu burgers, tofu dressings, tofu frozen dessert and kimchi, PO Box 747, Vashon, WA 98070. (206) 622-6448, (206) 463-9848.♦

Lightlife Foods, Inc.— Cholesterol-free "Tofu Pups", which have the taste if not quite the texture of regular hot dogs, and "Fakin' Bacon;" Greenfield, MA 01302. (413) 772-0991.

Lifestream Natural Foods— Vegi-Patties. Sold through stores. Richmond, BC V6V 1J7.

Little Bear Trading Co.— Vegie-burger mixes with some organic ingredients. Also many other products available through stores. They assert 95% of their products are organic. 226 E. Second St., Winona, MN 55987. (507) 452-6332.♥♦♦♦

Love Natural Foods— Loveburgers, soy nuggets, and vegetarian T-shirts and prints by mail (no organic claims). 3 Masada Dr., Cohutta, GA 30710. (404) 694-8179.

Millstone Foods (Loma Linda)— A line of canned vegetarian goods: Burger-like, Nut Meat, Tender Cuts (whole wheat gluten steaks), vege-beans, Vegeburger, Wheat Fries, and many other meat-substitute foods. Sold through stores. Loma Linda Foods Inc., 11503 Pierce Street, Riverside, CA 92515. (714) 687-7800. California only: (800) 442-4917 / (800) 932-5525.

Mud Pie Vegie Burger— Frozen vegetable patties made with some organic ingredients (asserted 50% organic). Available primarily through stores or at their restaurantat the same location. 2549 Lyndale Ave., South Minneapolis, MN 98532. (612) 870-4888.

Paul's Organic— Harvest burgers. Made by New Horizons, New York NY.

Sprout Delights Bakery— Vegetarian Sprout Burgers and Millet-Barley Burgers by mail. (Asserted 90+% organic, Minimum order $20 for public.) 13090 NW 7th Ave, North Miami, FL 33168-2702. (305) 687-5880 or (800) 334-BAKE, FAX: (305) 687-3233.

Turtle Island Soy Dairy— Makes Tempeh Burgers, BBQ Tempeh Burgers, Sloppy Joe Tempeh, Meatless Country

Stew, and other Tempeh Products (asserted 20% organic). (See also Meat Substitutes.) Minimum Order $50. PO Box 218, Husum, WA 98623. (509) 493-2004.

Wholesome & Hearty Foods, Inc.— Makes Frozen, Non-soy "Gardenburger", "Gardensausage", and "Gardentaco." An organic burger is "coming soon." Portland, OR 97214. (503) 796-0109.

Melons. See also Watermelon. The three classes of melons are winter melon, muskmelon and cantaloupe. The net-skinned cantaloupe that most Americans are familiar with is actually a muskmelon, while a true cantaloupe rind is scaly or warty (both have orange flesh). Honeydew melon is classified as a winter melon. Cantaloupes and honeydew melons are good sources of vitamin C. Cantaloupes are also rich in vitamin A. All melons are good sources of potassium. In 1988 the U.S. imported $100 million of melons from Mexico. Pesticides detected on cantaloupes include chlorothalonil, dimethoate, endosulfan, methamidophos, and methyl parathion. Pesticides found on watermelons include captan, carbaryl, chlorothalonil, dimethoate, and methamidophos.

Milk. Milk is an excellent source of calcium and protein, particularly for vegetarians. However it can also be a source of unnoticed and unwanted fat. About half the calories in whole milk come from fat and even for two-percent milk, almost a third come from fat. Skim milk is the best choice, containing almost no fat. If the taste of skim milk does not at first appeal to you, going from two percent to one percent, and finally to skim over the course of a few months can make the transition less noticeable. Indeed, for the converted, drinking whole milk after switching to skim feels like drinking cream. In 1987 Americans consumed more skim and low fat milk than whole milk for the first time in history—a positive trend.

Milk with acidophilus contains a species of bacteria that adds nutritional value (B vitamins and certain enzymes) and makes dairy products easier to digest. It also has some medicinal properties and is sometimes recommended for people taking antibiotics because it helps replace the "good" bacteria in your intestines that the antibiotics kill off.

Some companies and nutritionists claim that pasteurization destroys some of nutritious properties of milk, especially the B vitamins and vitamin C. This is disputed by most scientists and public health officials. One thing that is certain is that raw milk can be higher in hazardous bacteria (including salmonella, and tubercle bacillus) which between 1971 and 1984 made several hundred Californians and untold numbers of other people across the country seriously ill. According to Consumers Union, at least 30 Californians died during that span as a result of drinking raw milk.[45] Steuve's Natural, Inc. (a subsidiary of Alta-Dena Certified Dairy) in California was recently issued a court order to stop advertising its raw milk as healthier than pasteurized milk and was fined $123,000 for false advertising and prosecuting expenses. The company is appealing.

In December 1989, the *Wall Street Journal* tested 50 samples of low-fat and skim milk from 10 cities across the country. Using the "Charm II" test, they found that 38% of the samples were contaminated with antibiotics or sulfa drugs.[46] The findings prompted the FDA to do their own tests which initially found contamination more widespread than the *Journal's* survey. Then, in a sudden turnaround, FDA said that they ran further tests and could not confirm the initial findings. The mind-boggling upshot is that the further tests were *less* sensitive than the originals.[47] Because the later tests could not detect the drugs to the same concentrations, but only in concentrations four to six times higher, it is not surprising that, suddenly, no contamination was found in most of the samples. However, even these results are being called into question because some of the samples originally tested as tainted enough that they should have shown up on even the later series. Michael Jacobsen of the Center for Science in the Public Interest said bluntly, "FDA is trying to pull the wool over people's eyes."[48]

Other potential problem areas for milk are (1) High cholesterol (doesn't apply to skim milk), (2) Use of hormones in cows, (3) Pesticides that get into milk from the grains and feed the cows eat (meat and milk are actually significant contributors to the quantity of pesticides ingested by humans—accounting for a much higher percentage than residues from fruits or vegetables), and (4) Dioxin contamination from paperboard containers. A few recent incidents of contaminated animal feed have occurred (see Chapter 3). Also serious concerns have been raised about the way most dairy cows are treated.[49]

Buttermilk lovers should make sure they are getting buttermilk. A lot of "buttermilk" today is made by inoculating reclaimed stale milk with microbes that mimic the buttermilk flavor. Buttermilk in stores may also contain several other unwanted ingredients including artificial colorings and vegetable gums.[50]

Jackson-Mitchell Pharm. Inc.— Goat milk; evaporated, powdered, and fresh (asserted organic, 25 case minimum). PO Box 5425, Santa Barbara, CA 93150. (805) 565-1538.

Miso. When soybeans, salt and a cereal grain are completely fermented, the pasty product is called miso. Miso is a complete protein, containing all nine essential amino acids. It is also low in fat and calories. A few variations of miso are processed in the same way as miso but with one or two differences: Barley miso uses barley as its cereal grain, chickpea miso uses chickpeas instead of soybeans, soy miso contains no grain at all --this pungent miso, which is just soy and salt, adds strong flavor to soups and stew.

GEM Cultures— Cultures for tempeh, miso, amazake, shoyu, tamari, sourdough, kefir, soy products. (See Chapter 10) Betty L. Stechmeyer, 30301 Sherwood Rd., Ft. Bragg, CA 95437. (707) 964-2922.

Great Eastern Sun— Miso Master Misos: Traditional Red, Mellow White, Country Barley, Mellow Barley, and organic soybean miso with some organic ingredients. Sold through stores.

Mitoku— Johsen organic brown rice miso, Mansan organic soybean miso and other soy products. Sold through stores.

South River Miso— Sells organic unpastuerized miso and organic brown rice Koji. South River Farm, Conway, MA 01341. (413) 369–4057.

Mochi. A food made from pounding steamed rice. It is a little sticky, but is pleasantly sweet and fairly easy to prepare.

Grainaissance Inc.— Mochi and Amazake. As they sell through distributors, your local purveyor of healthy or gourmet foods is your best bet. 1580 62nd St., Emeryville, CA 94608. (415) 547–7256.

Mushrooms. Wild mushrooms are on the decline, an indicator of the effects of acid rain. While renowned for better flavor, wild mushrooms are also justly known for poisoning mushroom hunters who pick the wrong ones. Unless you are well-trained in mycology, you probably don't want to risk it. Cultivated mushrooms are rarely organically grown and are often drenched in chemicals. For that reason you should wash mushrooms before cooking or eating them. Mushrooms of various species have been credited with a wide range of medicinal benefits from prevention of heart disease to reduction of cancer risk.

American Forest Foods Corporation— One of the oldest and largest certified-organic growers of shiitake mushrooms in the U.S. (OCIA). Available by mail and through stores under the brand name "Imperial." Minimum order one 12–pack of 1.75 ounce dried shiitake. Rt. 5, Box 84E, Henderson, NC 27536. (919) 438–2674.

Hardscrabble Enterprises, Inc.— Sells oak (shiitake) mushrooms; not certified organic. Paul and Nan Goland, Route 6, Box 42, Cherry Grove, WV 26804. (304) 567–2727.

Mitoku— Sun-dried shiitake mushrooms, and many other products imported from Japan. Available through stores.

Ohsawa— Organic shiitake mushrooms. Also sauces, rice, teas, noodles, and snacks. Chico, CA 95928. (916) 342–6050.

Nectarines. Because nectarines are often picked before fully ripe (so they will travel better) you probably won't get the full flavor from those bought in the store. Even store-bought nectarines are pretty good, though. Sliced nectarines and a little milk make a terrific dessert. They are high in vitamin A and are comparable to bananas in potassium content.

Non-Dairy Creamers. Most are made with coconut oil which is loaded with saturated fat (more than the buttermilk used in ice cream). Powdered skim milk is a better choice.[51]

Nuts and Nut Butters. See also Peanut Butter. Nuts are high in protein, but also in fat. Most of this fat is either stearic or unsaturated, but even unsaturated fat should be eaten only in moderation. An ounce of pistachios (25 nuts) contains 16 grams of fat and gets 84 percent of its calories from fat.[52]

You might help preserve the Brazilian rainforests—buy Brazil nuts, which grow on the *castanha do para* tree, found in the tropical rainforest. One reason the rainforests are being destroyed is that not enough of a commercial market exists for rainforest products.

Blue Heron Farm— Sells organic almonds, walnuts. PO Box 68, Runsey, CA 95679. (916) 796–3799.

DIPASA— Nuts and nut butters (tahini sesame butter). Also bulk dried fruits, breadcrumbs, seeds, quinoa, amaranth, oils, granola cereal, black pepper and oregano. Texas International Commodities 3545 E.14th St., Suite A/B, Brownsville, TX 78521. (512) 546–6666, (512) 546–8235.

Genesee Natural Foods— Sells nut butters (almond, hazelnut, cashew); certification varies. Rt. 449. Genesee, PA 16923-9414. (814) 228–3200 or 228–3205.

Jardine Organic Ranch— Sells organic pistachios, almonds, and walnuts through a stand on the ranch. They also sell in larger quantities to some companies. 910 Nacemiento Lake Dr., Paso Robles, CA 93446. (805) 238–2365, (805) 239–4334. (See Chapter 10 for more.)

Kettle Foods-- Sells peanuts, almonds, cashews, sunflower, hazelnut, and sesame nut by mail. Also Kettle Chips (they assert that 20% of their products are organic, CCOF, Tilth). PO Box 664, Salem, OR 97308. (503) 364–0399.

Kresa Ranch— Sells organic walnut-meat under their own label through supermarkets (primarily on the west coast).

Living Tree Center— Sells organic almonds and almond butter to distributors. PO Box 797, Bolinas, CA 94924. (415) 868–2224.

Neshaminy Valley— Some organic nuts. Also grains, flours and fruits. 5 Louise Drive, Ivyland, PA 18974. (215) 443–5545, FAX: (215) 443–7087.♦

Rancho Shangrila— Sells 100% organic English Walnuts (25–pound minimum). 9340 Ojai-Santa Paula Rd., Ojai, CA 93023. (805) 646–1392.

Rejuvenative Foods— Sells several organic nut-based products: almond butter, halvah, tahini, sesame butter, "Luscious" and "Sweet Luscious" (raw almonds, raisins, sesame seeds, and sunflower seeds). They also sell "Vegidelite", raw sauerkraut, and other cultured vegetables, and the Complete Guide to Raw Cultured Vegetables. (See also Cultured Vegetables.)

Snak King Corp.— Makes trail mixes and nut butters using organically grown nuts (sold through retailers). 9525 Brasher St, Pico Rivera, CA 90660. (213) 692–7711.

Walnut Acres— Sells organic nuts, preserves, and fresh and canned vegetables (see listing in Chapter 6 for more). Penns Creek, PA 17862. (800) 433-3998.♦♦

Oats, Oat Bran. Some research suggests that a daily intake of 39 grams of oat bran will produce a modest reduction in cholesterol. However, a survey of 80 products containing oat bran shows that hardly any of the packages say how much oat bran is in the product.[53]

Don't get caught up in oat-mania. It may be beneficial, but it is no wonder-food. Reducing your intake of saturated fat is a more important step in fighting high cholesterol levels. A recent study done in Boston found that patients who consumed low-fiber refined wheat were able to lower their cholesterol levels just as much as those eating oat-bran (7.5 percent over 6 weeks).[54] The common denominator among both groups? All the subjects ate far less saturated fat than they normally did. Furthermore, even if soluble fiber is beneficial, many other foods have comparable amounts including prunes and kidney beans.

Oat bran, because of its positive reputation, often shows up in miniscule quantities in products where oat bran does not belong, like brownies and beer. The most-mindboggling infusion of oatbran is, perhaps, in potato-chips. The package of Robert's American Gourmet Potato Chips with Oat Bran claims the product is "the chip that's good for you," and encourages you to "enjoy these treats to your heart's content."[55] With all the saturated fat in potato chips, that line is laden with irony.

The exaggerated claims made by some oat-bran pushers have caught the attention of the FDA, which will probably toughen up recently relaxed standards as to what kind of claims food companies can make.

Health Valley— A highly regarded manufacturer (see Chapter 8) that seems to have the largest number of oat bran products on the market.♥♦♦♦♦

Oils. Oils and fats are at the center of the debate over cholesterol. Some scientists argue that dietary cholesterol plays the most important role in increasing serum cholesterol (though their position has eroded considerably); others consider hereditary factors and saturated fat intake more important. In either case, most specialists believe that anyone with a high serum (blood) cholesterol level (over 200 milligrams/liter) should reduce his or her dietary intake of cholesterol, especially such cholesterol-rich foods as eggs, shellfish, milk products and fatty meat. A diet low in cholesterol and high in fiber is recommended. Cholesterol is divided into two kinds: "good" HDL's and "bad" LDL's (see Chapter 3 for more). Whereas butter and other solid fats contain saturated fats that increase LDL's, oils contain mono-and polyunsaturated fats that reduce LDL's and increase HDL's. Oils containing a higher percentage of mono-unsaturated fats (some safflower oils and olive oils) are more effective than oils with a higher percentage polyunsaturated fats (sunflower, corn, soy) in increasing HDL levels. (Exercise also helps increase HDL levels.) Exceptions to this rule are coconut oil and palm oil, which, though both liquid fats, are mostly saturated and hazardous.

Corn oils and peanut oils have a different problem: They may contain aflatoxins (a carcinogen produced by mold).

Consuming a fatty acid known as omega-3, found in fish oils and flaxseed oil, has been found to alleviate some symptoms of heart disease, according to the Heart, Lung and Blood Institute of the National Institutes of Health. Animal studies also suggest that omega-3 oils may help prevent cancer.[56] However, a recent study done by doctors at Beth Israel Hospital in Boston found that fish oil capsules do not help patients who have undergone surgery to open up blocked arteries. Their study, in fact suggested that fish oil was worse than olive oil (the chosen placebo)—which is not to say that olive oil is great for clogged arteries. Of those who had taken the fish oil, 34 percent had a relapse of the occlusion, while only 23 percent of those taking olive oil had their arteries re-clog.[57] Some studies suggest that fish oil is most helpful when consumed with the fish, not in the form of an extract. The evidence is not strong enough for us to fully adopt that claim, but it does seem sensible.

Regular commercial processing usually entails use of petrochemical solvents that must be boiled away at high temperatures. This tends to destroy many key nutrients (especially vitamin E) and leaves undesirable residues. Expeller-pressed oils are those derived by squeezing the seed, grain, or fruit at pressures up to 15 tons per square inch. The higher the pressure, the more heat is generated. At high pressures, the temperature can go over 300°F, which "denatures" the proteins or makes them useless by breaking key bonds. Lower temperatures (in the 120°F – 160°F range) do not damage the oil significantly, but do reduce the yield, making good oils a little more expensive. The term "cold pressed" theoretically means that an oil is expeller-pressed at low temperatures. However the term has no legal definition and is, according to East West's *Shopper's Guide to Natural Foods* "absolutely meaningless when used as an indication of quality."[58] Apparently, even producers of chemically extracted, bleached, deodorized oils can claim their products "cold-pressed" at the whim of their marketing consultants. According to East West, reputable suppliers refrain from putting "cold-pressed" claims on their labels. Good oils are cloudy and maintain a good, strong aroma, color, and flavor, though they may have a shorter shelf-life.

Controversy over tropical oils like coconut and palm oils highlight the sort of dichotomy in the healthful food industries we have often encountered in our research. Some pure natural foods enthusiasts claim that these oils are natural, have been used for centuries, and therefore are better than partially hydrogenated oils with less saturated fats. More compelling however are arguments by consumer advocates like the Center for Science in the Public Interest that these oils are as bad for you as lard. (For more, see the May 1989 issue of CSPI's *Nutrition Action Healthletter*, in which the deceptive advertising campaign of the palm oil industry is dissected.) Giant Supermarkets recently switched from palm and coconut oils in the goods made in their bakery section.

And in case you have ever wondered just what canola oil is, the name comes from CANadian Oil, Low Acid. Essentially, it is rapeseed oil that is very low in erucic acid and saturated fat.

Allergy Resources Inc.— makes flaxseed oil and multi-vitamin omega 3 co-factors, as well as sesame and olive oils. Minimum order one case. Also a range of flours, milk substitute powders, wheat-free, gluten-free baking mixes, cereals, pastas and accessories. 195 Huntington Beach Dr., Colorado Springs, CO 80921. (719) 488-3630.

Arrowhead Mills— Organic Sesame oil. Also cereals, seeds, flours, whole grains, nuts, oils, and mixes. Overall 75% of products are asserted organic. Sold mainly through stores, but mail order is available for people who do not live near a retail outlet. 110 S. Lawton, Hereford, TX 79045. (806) 364-0730.♥♦♦♦♦

Columbus Foods Co.— Makes organic Nature's Secret Canola oil and other vegetable oils. 800 N. Albany, Chicago, IL 60622. (312) 265-6500.

Greek Gourmet— Imports and sells extra virgin olive oil and olives by mail (asserted 100% organic minimum order one case). 195 Whiting St., Hingham, MA 02043. (617) 749-1866.

Hain Pure Food Co.— Oils: corn, olive, safflower, sesame oil, sunflower oil, avocado oil, apricot oil, and others. Also over 200 other products. No organic claims; they sell "natural" foods, but little organic. Available only through stores. Pet Incorporated, 400 South Fourth Street, St. Louis, MO 63102. (314) 622-6716.♦♦♦

Jaffe Brothers— Makes and mails cold-pressed olive oil and sesame oil. PO Box 636, Valley Center, CA 92082. (619) 749-1133.♦

Loriva Supreme Foods— Cold-pressed sesame oil (organic), walnut oil, peanut oil, sunflower oil, and safflower oil. Also organic sesame products. Sold through stores. Formerly International Protein Industries. 40-10 Oser Ave., Hauppauge, NY 11788. (516) 231-7940.

Matol Botanical International— Sells some fish (omega-3) oils and a variety of other oils by mail. 1205-b Amethyst St., Redondo Beach, CA 90277. (213) 379-2089.

Natural Oil Imports— Imports a variety of unrefined expeller pressed oils for health foods.

New Dimensions Distributing— Unrefined vegetable oils, 16548 E Laser Dr Ste. A7, Fountain Hills, AZ 85268. (602) 837-8322.

Omega Nutrition— Organic oils: sesame, hazelnut, sunflower, and flax seed. Sold through stores. 1720 La Bounty Road, Ferndale, WA 98248. (604) 322-8862.

Spectrum Naturals— Organic, cold-pressed flax oil with omega-3. 133 Copeland St., Petaluma, CA 94952.♦♦♦

Spruce Foods, Inc.— Makes organic oils, vinegars, mustards, and snacks. Available in stores. 959 Grant Place, Boulder, CO 80302. (303) 440-0336.

Tree of Life— Makes cold-pressed organic olive oils (among dozens of other things). (Minimum order $150, products sold mainly through stores.) See Chapter 8 for more.♦♦♦

Okra. Perhaps better known as gumbo, okra is high in carotene and contains some B-complex vitamins. Most sources recommend that you not cook it in aluminum or cast iron pans.[59]

Onions. See Garlic and Onions.

Oranges. See Citrus Fruits.

Pancakes and Waffles. See also Bread and Other Baked Goods, and Convenience Mixes. Because they usually contain eggs, make sure they are well cooked to avoid the risk of Salmonella.

Arrowhead Mills— Blue Corn Pancake and Waffle Mix. Also seeds, whole grains, nuts, beans, cereals, and other mixes. Overall 75% of products are asserted organic. Sold mainly through stores, but mail order is available for people who do not live near a retail outlet. 110 S. Lawton, Hereford, TX 79045. (806) 364-0730.♥♦♦♦♦♦

David's Goodbatter— Pancake and baking mixes made from organic ingredients. No minimum order. PO Box 102, Bausman, PA 17504. (717) 872-0652, FAX: (717) 872-8152.♥

Diamond K Enterprises— Sells pancake mixes from organically grown grains: barley, buckwheat, corn, whole wheat. Also grains, flours, cereals, birdseed, sunflower seeds, and some dried fruits. Allow 1 to 2 weeks for shipping. (Asserted 95% organic, see listing in Chapter 10 for more.) RR 1 Box 30-A, St. Charles, MN 55972. (507) 932-4308, or 932-5433.

Granny's Buttermilk Pancake and Waffle Mix— Also Blueberry Pancake and Muffin Mix. Made primarily from organic ingredients. Made by Eagle Agricultural Products, sold through stores.

Heritage Flour Mills— Pancake, muffin, and waffle mixes, cereals, rice, pasta, beans, oils, and whole grain flours sold through their own outlet and other regional stores (asserted 15-20% organic). 2925 Chestnut, Everett, WA 98201. (206) 258-1582.

Lormak— Buttermilk pancake mix with organic whole-wheat flour available by mail. Also cracked wheat and flour. Rt. 2, Box 58, Concordia, KS 66901. (913) 243-7517.

Natural Nectar— Waffles. 8454 Steller Drive, Culver City, CA 90232. (213) 838-8497.

Shepherdsfield Award Winning Bakery— Whole-wheat gourmet waffles (presently only available for local deliveries). Also breads, and other baked goods. All products made from organically grown grains and baked with no added colorings, preservatives, synthetic fiber, or synthetic coloring. Rt. 4, Box 399, Fulton, MO 65251. (314) 642-1439.

Vans International Foods— Makes frozen specialty baked goods including oat bran waffles and 7 Grain waffles with low salt, high fiber and no preservatives. (No organic claims.) Sold through stores. 1751 W. Torrance Blvd,Unit K, Torrance, CA 90501. (213) 320-8611.

Pasta. A nutritious and satisfying food that is easy to prepare, pasta comes in many forms from whole-grain to "enriched" to oriental noodles. It provides lots of complex carbohydrates as well as B vitamins, iron, and some protein. (Traditional pasta does not contain enough protein to approach your USRDA, but some recent products mix the wheat flour with soybean and amaranth flours to make it more adequate.) All forms of pastas are take-offs on the basic theme of flour and water (macaroni) or flour, eggs, and water (noodles). The number of variations on this theme, however, is amazing.

Whole-grain pasta, usually made from durum wheat, has more fiber and nutrients, but generally has a shorter shelf-life. Buckwheat pasta is one of dozens of Asian varieties that are becoming increasingly available in the U.S.

Ramen is a particularly easy to fix variety that is available in many natural food stores. When making the ramen, though, you may only want to add part of the flavor packet as the salt in some varieties is overpowering.

Pastas available today can contain:

1. Amaranth—a grain cultivated by the Aztecs that is nutritionally superior to (but more expensive than) most grains cultivated commercially.

2. Buckwheat (blended in Japan with other grains to make soba or udon)—more closely related to rhubarb than wheat (see Chapter 2). It is high in calcium and lysine and is rich in vitamin E and the B vitamins.

3. Corn—be careful in cooking corn pasta as it tends to disintegrate easily.

4. Kamut—like amaranth a "rediscovered" grain, it has more protein and, reportedly, a particularly good flavor.

5. Potatoes (of all things)—like corn pasta, potato pasta tends to dissolve if cooked too long.

6. Quinoa—another grain reputed to have strong nutritional qualities.

Other mixtures abound, and new ones emerge all the time. Lupini pasta even makes a pasta mixing whole grain wheat and lupin beans, a "high-fiber, high-protein, carotene-containing bean with no flatulence."

While pasta itself is a good nutritional bargain, spaghetti sauces and marinaras are not always so good for you. Many of them contain large quantities of fat and sodium. To avoid fat it is generally better to go for the sauces without meat or flavored with meat. For more, see Spaghetti Sauce.

For more information on pasta, contact the National Pasta Association. Send a check for one dollar to Pasta Sourcebook, 40 W. 57th Street, Suite 1400, New York, NY 10019.

Amy's— Organic Macaroni with a cheddar cheese sauce. Also vegetable pies with organically grown vegetables, organic flour, and "low-fat cheddar cheese sauce."Available through stores. Amy's Kitchen, PO Box 449, Petaluma, CA 94953. (707) 762-6194.♦

DeBoles— Pasta products, including some with organically grown wheat. Check the label. All products are kosher. Sold through stores. 2120 Jericho Turnpike, Garden City Park, NY 11040. (516) 742-1818.

Gabriele— Whole wheat pasta and flavored pastas, some organic. Minimum order $2500. Lou Fusano, Vice President, 17651 E Railroad St., Industry, CA 91748. (818) 964-2324, FAX: (818) 912-1058.

Health Valley— Oat bran pasta dinners with organically grown whole wheat, organic brown rice flour, organic corn flour, and organic soy flour. Box includes low-sodium, low-salt sauce. Also other pastas, cereals, cookies, crackers, snack bars, muffins, and pilafs. Sold through stores.♥♦♦♦♦

Herb's— Premium pastas, some with organically grown amber durum wheat. Available in stores. Made by Schmidt Noodle Co. (a subsidiary of Eden Foods) 701 Tecumseh, Clinton, MI 49236. (313) 973-9400.

La Maison de Soba™— Udon made from organically grown grain. 378 Isabey, St. Laurent, QC H4T IWI. (514) 738-3000.

Lupini Pasta— Sells pasta made from wheat and lupin beans (making the pasta a source of complete protein). (They primarily wholesale, but there is no minimum order. No organic claims.) 10925 Valley View Road, Suite 200, Eden Prairie, MN 55344. (612) 941-4524.

Mitoku USA, Inc.— Whole wheat and brown rice udon imported from Japan. Also soy sauces, misos, sea vegetables, noodles, seasonings, condiments, oils, teas, cereals, beans, herbal and folk remedies, sweeteners, and snacks. Also food processing and cookware equipments. About 25% of products are organic (OFPANA standards), and all conform to macrobiotic quality standards. Sold through stores. PO Box 1343, Clifton Park, NY 12065. (518) 383-6580.

New Morning Farm— Pastas made from all organic unbleached white and whole wheat flours available by mail. Also various vegetables. Rt. 1, Box 25, Amesville, OH 45711. (614) 448-4021.

Noodle Nook— Makes kosher (but not organic) whole-wheat pastas in 10 varieties. 11150 Arrow Rte., Suite A, Rancho Cucamonga, CA 91730. (714) 941-3005.

Ohsawa— Kombu, wakame, and sea palm harvested off the Mendocino Coast in Northern California. Also sauces, rice, teas, noodles, and snacks. Chico, CA 95928. (916) 342-6050.

Pure Sales Inc.— They import organic whole wheat pasta. Minimum order $1,000. PO Box 8708-702, Newport Beach, CA 92658-1708. (714) 540-5455.

Putney Pasta Company— Frozen pasta products with no artificial additives: Tortellini, raviolini, agnolotti, noodles, sauces. PO Box 599, Hickory Ridge Road, Putney, VT 05346. (802) 387-4848.

Quinoa— Supergrain pastas and spaghetti, most ("90%") made with organically grown quinoa. Also grain and flour. Sold mostly in supermarkets (case orders only). PO Box 1039, Torrance, CA 90505. (213) 530-8666; FAX: (213) 530-8764.

Royal Angelus Macaroni Company— They make kosher pasta from organically grown grain. Wholesale quantities only. 5010 Eucalyptus Ave., Chino, CA 91710. (714) 627-7312.

Tree of Life— Among many other things, makes whole wheat pastas from organic durum wheat. (Minimum order $150 -products sold mainly through stores). See Chapter 8 for more.♦♦♦

Westbrae— Organic Genmai Soba. Sold through stores.♦♦♦

Peaches. As their color would suggest, peaches are high in vitamin A and vitamin C. Pesticides found in peaches include dicloran, captan, parathion, carbaryl and endosulfan.

Pears. Pears ripen best once they have been picked and can be a good source of fiber. Pesticides residues detected include azinphos-methyl, cyhexatin, phosmet, endosulfan and ethion.

Ecology Sound Farms— Sells Asian pears, certified organic. 42126 Road 168, Orosi, CA 93647. (209) 528-3816.

Western Shore— Pear wafers with no sulphur available by mail. 11155 Highway 160, PO Box 75, Hood, CA 95639. (916) 775-1637.

Peanuts and Peanut Butter. Peanuts are listed separately from other nuts because they are really a bean (legume), roasted to taste like a nut. Peanuts share with nuts a high fat level. Aflatoxin mold is often a problem with peanuts, but the problem probably gets less attention than it deserves because of lax FDA standards on what is acceptable. Aflatoxin in peanut butter has been staying below 1 part per billion, but even that level is high.

Peanut butter contains 5 grams of protein per tablespoon and fair amounts of niacin, potassium, and magnesium. However, most peanut butters derive over 80 percent of their calories from fat. Most of this fat is not saturated, but peanut butter lovers should still consume it in moderation. Many commercial brands have hydrogenated oils, the health effects of which are questioned by

some dieticians. The "no-cholesterol" tag on some brands is health-hype. Unless a rat falls into the processor, peanut butter, like all plant-based foods, is naturally cholesterol-free. (And just in case the marketing people get carried away, peanut butter is not a good source of oatbran.)

Genesee Natural Foods— Sells peanut butter; certification varies. Rt. 449. Genesee, PA 16923-9414. (814) 228-3200 or 228-3205.

Island Products— Sells a variety of organically grown, salt-free nuts and dried fruit. (Sales are mainly to LA retailers.) 393 N Cypress, Orange, CA 92666. (714) 997-5615. (See Chapter 10 for more.)

Walnut Acres— Sells peanut butter. Asserted organic. Penns Creek, PA 17862. (800) 433-3998.♦♦

Peas. See Legumes.

Pectin. A carbohydrate that serves as a base for jam.

Pomona's Universal— Low-methoxyl pectin that will set regardless of the sugar concentration of the jam. Sold through suppliers.

Workstead Industries— Citris pectin. PO Box 1083, Greenfield, MA 01302. (413) 722-6816.

Peppers. See also Chillies. Peppers are nightshades, putting them in the same family as tomatoes and potatoes. They are good sources of vitamin A and potassium. For chili peppers, the general rule is the yellower the pepper, the more numerous the alarms.

Pies. See Bread and Other Baked Goods.

Pineapple. This popular tropical fruit has a unique sweet flavor that people seem to either love or hate. It is high in fiber, and contains vitamins A, C, and some of the Bs.

Hawaiian Exotic Fruit Co.— Organic white pineapples, bananas (in several varieties), papayas, sweet potatoes, taro, lemons, sweet-corn, and whole ginger-roots. (See Chapter 10 for more.) Box 1729, Pahoa, HI 96778. (808) 965-7154.

Pizza. Pizza is bound to contain a fair amount of saturated fat because cheese contains lots of saturated fat. A slice of pizza with mushrooms and green peppers is still probably better for you than a hamburger.

Graindance Pizza— Made from stone-ground whole-wheat flour (asserted organic), with mozzarella and provolone cheese and tomato sauce; *Soydance Pizza*, lactose-free, with tofu (asserted organic) substituted for cheese; pizza shells and paddycakes. The regular and tofu pizzas have the same calories, 190 per slice, one-fourth of a 9-inch pizza. Check your local wholefoods store. Tomanetti, Inc. (Amberwave Foods), 201 Ann Street, Oakmont, PA 15139. (412) 828-3040, (412) 828-3176.

Pizsoy— A tasty frozen pizza made with buckwheat flour and a soy based mozzarella substitute (the grain + soybean ingredients make it a source of complete protein). Available in stores. PO Box 1314, Cherry Hill, NJ 08003. (609) 354-8036.

Pomegranates. Much esteemed by those who like the tart taste, pomegranates (or rather, their edible seeds) are rich in potassium and citric acid. The outside is leathery and red with what looks like a crown at one end. The inside consists of hundreds of juicy bright red seeds wrapped in white visceral mesh. They are not available everywhere, but for ardent fans, the trees are relatively low-maintenance and can be grown in the right climate.

Popcorn. It is a bit hard to digest and is not especially nutritious, but it is better than some other snacks you might pick up at the movie concession stand. The average American reportedly eats 52 quarts of the stuff a year.[60] Coating popcorn with flavorings (such as cheese or caramel—or even butter and salt) may enhance the eating experience, but it makes the product more unhealthy. Cheese and butter add lots of fat.

The best popcorn from a nutritional standpoint is air-popped popcorn with light salting or garlic powder. Be careful of "air-popped" popcorn you buy prepackaged, though. Bachman Air Popped popcorn is soaked in oil after the air-popping, making it quite fatty. *Orville Redenbacher's Light* is the best you can do for microwavable popcorn.[61]

Country Grown— Organic popcorn. Also seeds, beans, and dried fruit. Not all of their popcorn is organic—check the label. Sold mainly through stores, mail order available. Box 2485, Dearborn, MI 48123. (313) 561-0421.

Health Best— Air-popped organic popcorn. Sold through stores. Health Best, 645 No. Citracado Pkwy, Escondido, CA 92025.

Little Bear Organic Foods— Traditional and lite organically grown popcorn. Also refried beans and corn chips. Available through stores. 15200 Sunset Blvd., Suite 202, Pacific Palisades, CA 90272. (213) 454-5452.♥♦♦♦

Pork. See also Meat. The pork you find in markets today is substantially leaner than pork consumed in previous decades; but may still contain lots of saturated fat. When you buy pork products, go for lean, fresh ham, avoiding cured, smoked, or processed meats as they are likely to contain more fat or unwanted preservatives, or both.

Potatoes. Potatoes offer an adequate amount of protein, along with vitamin C and B, calcium, potassium and iron. The problem with potatoes is that most people peel away the nutrients, so if you include the potato skin in Grandma's potato salad recipe, you will be eating healthier. The skin contains fiber and the minerals manganese, chromium, selenium, and molybdenum. You should avoid consuming the sprouts or any green-colored flesh or skin on a potato, for they contain poisonous alkaloids.[62] Pesticide residues detected include DDT (banned in 1972), chlorpropham, dieldrin, aldicarb, and chlordane.

35 billion pounds of potatoes are grown in the U.S. each year, 65% of which end up as potato chips, french fries, frozen potato products, and dehydrated instant mixes.[63]

Barbara's Bakery— Makes and sells instant mashed potatoes with no sulfiting agents. Sold through stores.♦♦♦

Brown Company— Idaho potatoes, seed potatoes. PO Box 69, Tetonia, ID 83452. (208) 456-2500 or 456-2629.

Cascadian Farm— The largest organic farm in the northwest. The owner, Gene Kahn, grows 300 varieties of potatoes (though only eight in commercial quantities) and has recently launched Cascadian Farm Organic Potato Chips. The fat and salt in most potato chips makes them an unhealthy snack food, but Cascadian does its best to reduce these hazards by "quick-cooking" the chips and salting them lightly. PO Box 568, Concrete, WA 98237. (206) 853-8175.♦♦♦

Poultry. Poultry include all domesticated fowl raised for human uses. Chicken is the most commonly eaten (average consumption in 1987 was 63 pounds),[64] but the category also includes turkey, duck, and goose. Poultry is generally better to eat than beef, veal, or pork, because it has less saturated fat, though duck and goose begin to rival beef in fat levels. When eating poultry, avoid eating the skin to avoid eating lots of unwanted saturated fat.

In 1988, 24 percent of the boneless weight of meat consumed in the United States was chicken. However, far too much chicken (over 20 percent)[65] is consumed in the deep-fat-fried form, which eliminates almost all the health advantages. Kentucky Fried Chicken and a few other chains are test-marketing roast chicken, which is much better for you.

The designation "free-range chicken" implies that the chicken was allowed to roam around in a yard pecking and scratching when it wanted to. Most of the 90 million chickens sold in the United States each week actually spend their whole lives cooped in tiny cages.[66] The USDA recently decided that the term "range" applied to chicken is legally meaningless, so you probably won't find it on packages. To be sure you are getting free-range, ask the meat department manager where you buy meat. Buying free-range also supports smaller farmers in an industry of giants—the largest eight producers (out of more than 100) control more than half the business.

Cooping up so many birds in tight quarters has ramifications beyond the ethical realm. One-third (or more—some estimates claim it is more than half) of all American-raised poultry is infected with salmonella bacteria. This is not a great cause for concern for those who are careful handling the raw fowl. For those who are not, salmonella can lead to intense sickness and even death. Many people recommend washing the birds before putting them in the oven. If you leave a salmonella-infected chicken sitting on your counter, be sure to remember that that patch of counter will likely have salmonella bacteria on it when you move the chicken somewhere else. Ideally you should clean the chicken in one place, clean up afterwards, and wash your hands before getting the chicken out of the oven. Thorough cooking is essential; if the bird is not cooked well enough to kill the bacteria, diarrhea, nausea and fever can result.

In March of 1989 400,000 chickens had to be destroyed in Arkansas because they were contaminated by a cancer-causing pesticide called heptachlor. Heptachlor, which was banned from use on foods in 1977, is still used to treat grain seeds before they are planted. In this instance, heptachlor, which includes a red dye as a warning, might have caused the grain to be mistaken for rust-colored sorghum seeds. The contaminated seeds were then fed to the chickens. Though this was an isolated incident, according to Lester M. Crawford of the USDA, "the public is at risk beacause treated seeds are not being monitored properly." In the mid-1970's, scientists determined the insecticide was especially dangerous for nursing mothers, infants and children. In animal studies, heptachlor caused malignant tumors.[67]

In 1988 the U.S. imported $100 million of poultry and by-products from China, Canada and France.

Turkey contains a neuro-transmitter called serotonin that is elemental in inducing sleep in humans. Some people claim this is the reason people feel like napping after Thanksgiving dinner. But the effects of gluttony are probably more significant.

Health Is Wealth Inc.— Soybean-fed hormone-free chicken and turkey, chicken franks. Sykes Lane, Williamstown, NJ 08094. (609) 728-1998.

Natural Beef Farms Food Distribution Co.— Sells chicken, and turkey. 4399-A Henninger Court, Chantilly, VA 22021. (703) 631-0881.

Preserves. See Jam and Jelly.

Rabbit. Rabbit meat is leaner, more protein dense, and has lower cholesterol content than chicken or fish, but is not widely consumed because many people find the idea of eating such cute little creatures unappealing. (If it were more widely known how cows are "harvested" there might be a similar aversion.) Rabbit also tends to be more expensive than other meats. Also, because it is somewhat dry, it requires more skillful cooking to prevent toughness.

Chez Panisse restaurant— Berkeley, Calif., serves biodynamically (see Chapter 4, Demeter Association) bred rabbits.[68]

Joe Soghomian, Inc.— Thompson Seedless raisins, jumbo raisins, Zante currants. 8624 Chestnut, Fresno, CA 93725. (209) 834-2772, (209) 834-3150.

Radishes. Radishes are members of the cabbage family and some varieties can be eaten for their greens, as well as their roots. Trying radishes other than the conventional red radish can add interesting new tastes to salad—but be careful about using some of the white radishes; they can be as hot as jalapeño peppers. They contain vitamin C and potassium.

Rice. See also Grains. Rice is the main staple for almost half of the world's population and the average inhabitant of the Far East eats more than 100 pounds of rice a year. (The average American eats less than 10 pounds per year).[69] Rice comes in many varieties that offer distinct tastes and textures. In general, brown rice is richer in nutrients than white rice.

Some people predict that rice bran will be the new sensation when the oat-bran craze grows stale.

The Crawdad Farm— Long-grain rice. Boyce or Sharon Ward, PO Box 395, Mauriceville, TX 77626. (409) 745-2388.

Erntedank— Wild rice grown without herbicides and pesticides. Sold through stores. Purity Foods, Inc., 4211 Okemos Road, #21, Okemos, MI 48864. (517) 349-7941.♦

Grey Owl Wild Rice— Rice grown without fertilizers or chemicals. Distributed by Siap Marketing Co., Inc., Box 3003, McIntosh Mall, Prince Albert, Saskatchewan S6V 6G1.

Leech Lake— Organically grown rice. Route 3, Box 100, Cass Lake, MN 56633. (218) 335-8200.

Lone Pine Enterprises— Organic rice (minimum order 5,000 pounds.) PO Box 416, Carlisle, AR 72024. (501) 552-3217.

Lundberg Family Farms— Organic brown rice products (macrobiotic) -including RizCous, flour, cereal, and rice cakes. 5370 Church St., Mail to: PO Box 369, Richvale, CA 95974. (916) 882-4551. (Please see Chapter 10 for more.)♥♦♦♦

MacDougall's California Wild Rice— Rice grown without pesticides and herbicides. Sold through stores. PO Box 5326, Marysville, CA 95901.

Pacific Rice Products— Makes various "100% natural" rice cereals (both hot and cold), Mini-Crispies flavor-coated rice cake snacks, crispy cakes, and Squinkles. 460 Harter Ave, Woodland, CA 95965. (916) 662-6074.♦♦

Polit Farms— A grower of organic rice and corn products sold through stores. PO Box 61, Maxwell, CA 95955. (916) 438-2759, FAX: (916) 438-2759.

Hinode— Rices grown without pesticides and herbicides. Look for the No-Spray label. Rice Growers Association of California.

Secret Garden— Rice soup mixes. Most ingredients come from their own biodynamic farm (which also has a training-apprenticeship program). Goods available direct by mail, Visa and Mastercard accepted. Rt. 1, Box 404, Park Rapids, MN 56470. (218) 732-4866.

Southern Brown Rice— Rice (long, medium, and short grain; brown and wild varieties; Basmati rice and Southern wild blend), brown rice cream, brown rice flour, and rice bran. Also beans. Available by mail. Asserted

95% organic overall, certified by OCIA. PO Box 185, Weiner, AR 72479. (501) 684–2354.

Taste Adventure— Pinto bean flakes and soups (black bean, split pea and curry lentil). No gums, fillers, preservatives, animal products or added fats and oils (No organic claims.) Made by Will-Pak Foods. 769 Battery St., San Pedro, CA 90731. (213) 519–9113.

Walnut Acres— Soups made with organic ingredients. Penns Creek, PA 17862. (800) 433–3998.♦♦

Salad Dressing. The biggest problem with salads is the same one that can afflict pasta dishes: the topping or dressing is often full of fat and sodium. Some are almost as bad as mayonnaise and derive 80–90 percent of their calories from fat. Even "lite" dressings are often loaded with fat. In general, go for vinaigrettes and dressings that do not list oil as the first ingredient. Sodium is trickier to figure, as most labels do not make the sodium content clear. If you can tell, go for a dressing with less than 300 milligrams of sodium. The November 1989 issue of *Nutrition Action* (published by the Center for Science in the Public Interest) has a breakdown of 60 salad dressings available in stores. Their informal recommendations are *Pritikin* Italian, and *Gourmet Garnishes Italian "Ciao."*[70]

Another solution, of course, is to eat your salads without dressing.

Caesar Cardini Foods— "Cardini Natural" dressings with no preservatives, no added sugar, no salt, no MSG, and some organic ingredients (though we cannot vouch for fat content). Check your local healthy food purveyor or supermarket. 1604 West 130th St., Gardena, CA 90249. (213) 516–1470.

Cherry Hill Co-operative Cannery— Sells marinara sauce, mustard and mustard sauce, pickles, preserves, salsa. Barre, VT 05641. (802) 479–2558.

Cook's Classics Ltd.— Additive and preservative-free, low sodium "natural" salad dressings (not organic). 2672 Bayshore Parkway, Suite 900, Mountain View, CA 94043. (415) 968–8665.

White Wave— Organic Tofu Ranch and Tofu Blue dressings. Also other soy-based products (not all of which are organic). Sold through stores. 1990 N. 57th Ct., Boulder, CO 80301.♦♦

Salsa. Salsa is a great addition to many dishes and the perfect compliment for tortilla chips; it should be virtualy fat-free and requires little sodium for good taste. We came across dozens of salsa products claiming to be "all natural." That is sort of like advertising bananas as cholesterol-free. Salsa really doesn't need flavor enhancers or preservatives. The risk with these products comes from possible pesticide residues. These risks are hard to evaluate. However, if you want a higher degree of confidence, try those listed below.

Enrico's— Salsa with some organic ingredients. Also spaghetti sauce, enchilada sauce, and barbecue sauce. Sold through stores. Ventre Packing Co. Inc., 373 Spencer St., Syracuse, NY 13204. (315) 422–9277.♦♦

Tree of Life— Makes thick salsas with organically grown tomatoes and other ingredients. St. Augustine, FL 32085.♦♦♦

Sauces. See also Condiments, Salad Dressing, Spaghetti Sauce, and Salsa. The sauces people put on food often add more fat, sodium, and calories in general than they may realize. A dab of mayonnaise here, some salad dressing there, a lyonnaise sauce on the potatoes, maybe a little barbecue sauce on the hamburger—pretty soon it can add up to hundreds of fatty, sodium filled calories. In general, exercise moderation in eating creamy sauces (including cheese sauces) and sauces that list oil high on the ingredient list.

Chef Albert Leone— "All natural" sauces with no sugar, artificial preservatives, flavorings, and cholesterol and little sodium (fat content is unclear). Seven varieties available through stores. 449 South Beverly Drive, Suite 211, Beverly Hills, CA 90212. (213) 277–1272.

Chalif— Stir-fry sauce. Also "all natural condiments" including low-salt and no-salt mustards. Sold through stores. PO Box 27220 (1230 E. Mermaid Lane) Wyndmoor, PA 19118. (215) 233–2023.

Enrico's— Barbecue sauces with no preservatives or artificial flavors or fillers. Also spaghetti sauce, enchilada sauce, and salsa. Sold through stores. Ventre Packing Co. Inc., 373 Spencer St., Syracuse, NY 13204. (315) 422–9277.♦♦

Mia Tia— Three kinds of inexpensive Mexican ("early California-style") seasoning mixes in powdered form; Enchilada, Taco & Burrito, and Chili Mix.

San-J— Tamari soy sauce, tamari light (25% less sodium), and other sauces. Also crackers. Sold through stores. 2880 Sprouse Dr., Richmond, VA 23231. (800) 446–5500, (804) 226–8383.♦♦

Enrico's— Low-fat, low-salt enchilada sauce, barbecue sauce, spaghetti sauce and salsa. Sold through stores. Ventre Packing Co. Inc., 373 Spencer St., Syracuse, NY 13204. (315) 422–9277.♦♦

Premier Japan— A full line of soy and rice-based sauces. Also condiments and sea vegetables. Sold through stores. Distributed by Edward & Sons Trading Co., Box 3150, Union, NJ 07083. (201) 964–8176.

Sierra Vista Corp.— All natural (but not organic) barbecue sauces. Sold through stores. PO Box Orinda, CA 94563. (415) 548–0675.

Walnut Acres— Barbecue and other sauces. (See Chapter 6 for more.) (800) 433–3998.♦♦

Whole Food Marketing Co.— Distributes "gorilla" sauce, which is low in fat, salt, and calories. Sold through stores. (213) 541–0339.

Wizard's Cauldron— Sauces and condiments with some organic ingredients (asserted 50% organic overall). Box 969, Hillsborough, NC 27278. (919) 732-5294.

Sea Vegetables. Sea vegetables are nutritionally loaded, supplying complete protein, calcium, B_{12} (which three are important for vegetarians), and many minerals. They include alaria, kelp, kanten, kombu, nori, and carrageenan. Except for some nori, most sea vegetables are not cultivated and are harvested from wild plants, making organic standards hard to apply. Sea vegetables absorb pollutants that may be in the water so be aware of their origin before you eat them. Most of the sea-vegetable harvest is dehydrated before it is sold.

The "kelp" brown sea vegetables, such as wakame and kombu, contain algin, which is thought to fix and remove radioactive particles and heavy metals from the human body.

Kombu is said to make good vegetarian soup stock.

Philip K Park Co.— Granular sea kelp (asserted 90% organic.) Minimum order one case. 318 Lake Hazeltine, Dr., Chaska, MN 55318. (612) 448-5151.

Maine Sea Vegetable Company— Alaria, dulse, kelp, and nori. Also "Sea Chips" and "Sea Seasonings." Sold mainly through stores. Franklin, ME 04634. (207) 565-2907.♦

Mendocino Sea Vegetable Company— Wildcrafted sea vegetables from North America harvested in unpolluted coastal locations. Available by mail, orders under $20 (post paid) are subject to a $4 handling charge. PO Box 372, Navarro, CA 95463. (707) 895-3741.

Mitoku USA, Inc.— Hidaka Sun-Dried kombu, San-Riku Sun-Dried Wakame, Boshu Wild Hijiki, and Sendai Select Nori imported from Japan. Also many other products (see listing for pasta). All products conform to macrobiotic quality standards. Sold through stores. PO Box 1343, Clifton Park, NY 12065. (518) 383-6580.

Ohsawa— Kombu, wakame, and sea palm harvested off the Mendocino Coast in Northern California. Also sauces, rice, teas, noodles, and snacks. Chico, CA 95928. (916) 342-6050.

Premier Japan— Chopped kombu, hijiki, instant wakame, and toasted nori. Also full lines of condiments and sauces. Sold through stores. Distributed by Edward & Sons Trading Co., Box 3150, Union, NJ 07083. (201) 964-8176.

Seeds (Edible). See also Nuts. Most edible seeds are listed in the places where people more logically think of them—i.e. nuts. Sunflower seeds, like nuts, have a lot of fat and are often coated with salt.

Country Grown— Organically grown seeds: radish, alfalfa, and red clover. Also grains, beans, and dried fruit. Not all of their popcorn is organic—check the label. Certified by OCIA. Sold mainly through stores, mail order available. Box 2485, Dearborn, MI 48123. (313) 561-0421.

Diamond K Enterprises— Sells organically grown sunflower seeds and oils. Also grains, flours, cereals, pancake mixes, birdseed, sunflower seeds, and some dried fruits. Allow 1 to 2 weeks for shipping. (Asserted 95% organic, see listing in Chapter 10 for more.) RR 1 Box 30-A, St. Charles, MN 55972. (507) 932-4308, or 932-5433.

Loriva Supreme Foods— Organic sesame seeds. Also sesame oil, tahini, flower, and peanut butter. OCIA Certified. Sold through stores. Formerly International Protein Industries. 40-10 Oser Ave, Hauppauge, NY 11788. (516) 231-7940.

Seeds (Plantable). One of the best ways to ensure that your fruit and vegetables are organic is to grow them yourself. While this may be difficult in a city, suburban backyards usually have soil fertile enough to attempt crops (even in the cities there are sometimes community gardens). You will not only get healthier food, but will derive the satisfaction of having grown your own meals.

Domenick Bertelli grew up in a home with a 70 x 40 backyard in suburban northern California that had four grape vines (resting on a simple grape arbor), three apricot trees, a strawberry patch, six or seven boysenberry bushes, two or three raspberry bushes, a plum tree, a peach tree, a lemon tree, an orange tree, five loquat trees, an avocado tree, an apple tree, a pomegranate tree, a cherry tree, and a vegetable patch that usually has tomato plants in two varieties, green peppers, squash, zucchini, and occasionally cucumbers and carrots. And the lawn was plenty big enough for a game of catch. Some of these plants were bought partially grown, but a lot of them grew from seeds. Vegetables just require watering every couple of days (though you should also be prepared to squish or otherwise remove a snail or horn-worm now and again).Trees usually require pruning once a year, which can also furnish raw material for wreaths and holiday fires.

One of the effects of the Leviathan described in Chapter 6 has been to vastly reduce the number of varieties of crops grown. According to an article in *Solstice* magazine, 100 years ago one could find 320 varieties of corn in regular cultivation. Now six varieties make up 71 percent of the harvest.[71] Six varieties also dominate the apple market, although the Clonal Germ Plasm Repository for Apples and Grapes in Geneva, New York has 2,000 varieties in their orchards.

Hybridization, a process of controlled genetic selection, has resulted in crops that are better suited to the machines and methods of agribusiness. However, these efforts to create products from bug-resistant lettuce to square tomatoes, often have the unwanted side-effect of breeding out desirable nutritional and flavor traits. Furthermore, the seed produced by hybrid crops is sterile or useless (the recessive or undesirable traits suppressed in the hybrid generation come out again through genetic variation). Hybridization is important in maintaining and improving agricultural production. But it will take great care and coordination to preserve genetic diversity of given species, elements that may be lacking in an industry where companies come and go very quickly.

Several companies (see below) and organizations are trying to preserve bio-diversity through seed swapping and avoidance of hybrids. They also offer some interesting varieties of various plants that may not be ideally suited to cultivation on a huge scale, but which can add character to your backyard garden and new tastes to home-grown meals.

Abundant Life Seed Foundation— A catalog costs $1. Memberships are also available for $5 to $20. PO Box 772 Port Townsend, WA 98368.

Cross Seed Co.— Sells sprouting seeds (asserted 100% organic) for alfalfa, yellow clover, red clover, turnip, Chinese cabbage, black mustard, fenugreek, radish, and sunflower seeds. Also Amaranth Pancake & Biscuit Flower Mix, organic beans, and grains. HC 69 Box 2, Bunker Hill, KS 67626. (913) 483-6163.

Diamond K Enterprises— Sells organic amaranth and flax seeds by mail (specify sprouting if that is your intent). Also grains, rice, flours, cereals, pancake mixes, birdseed, sunflower seeds, and some dried fruits. Allow 1 to 2 weeks for shipping. (Asserted 95% organic, see listing in Chapter 10 for more.) RR 1 Box 30-A, St. Charles, MN 55972. (507) 932-4308, or 932-5433.

Grain Exchange— A catalog costs $1, an annual membership costs $10. Send a self-addressed stamped envelope to The Land Institute, 2440 East Water Well Road, Salina, KS 67401.

Hartman & Daughters— Will send you a price list if you mail them a self-addressed, stamped envelope. PO Box 20174 Indianapolis, IN 46220.

Peace Seeds— A seed list costs $1 and a catalog and research journal cost $6. 2383 Southeast Thompson St., Corvallis, OR 97333.

Redwood City Seed Co— A seed catalog costs $1. PO Box 361, Redwood City, CA 94064.

Seeds Blum— The owner has built a network of rare-vegetable suppliers. Send $3 for a catalog. Idaho City Stage, Boise, ID 83706.

Seeds of Change— The maintainers of one of the largest organic seed banks in the country, the group also runs the Gila Eco-Agricultural Center, which is breaking new ground (so to speak) in sustainable agriculture. They offer consultancy services in agro-forestry, ecological farm design, organic native seeds, marketing and promotion, environmental restoration, and drought-tolerant crops. 621 Old Santa Fe Trail #10, Santa Fe, NM 87501. (505) 983-8956.♥

Seeds Savers Exchange— They were one of the first groups in the country to organize networks of gardeners to help preserve the genetic variety of many plants. They have an impeccable reputation for dedication and for being good at what they do. An annual membership costs $15 and includes a Winter Year Book. RR 3 Box 239, Decorah, IA 52101.♥

Shumway Seeds— Send $1 for a catalog. PO Box 1, Graniteville, SC 29829.

Southern Exposure Seed Exchange— A catalog costs $3 and a price list $1. PO Box 158, North Garden, VA 22959.

Specialty Seeds, Herbs, and Spices— Sells some organic seeds. Minimum order 100 pounds. 12623 SW Green Drive, PO Box 410. Culver, OR 97734. (503) 546-2801.

Wheatland Seed Inc.— Seeds, whole grains, flours, and meals. (Asserted 30% organic; minimum order 10 tons.) 1780 No. Hwy 69, Brigham, UT 84302. (801) 734-2371.

Seitan. Also known as Kofu. Seitan is a meat substitute made by extracting the gluten from wheat. It is high in protein and has about half the calories of beef. Unlike beef, it has no saturated fat. Its popularity as a meat substitute comes from its texture and, when seasoned, flavor which are somewhat meatlike.

Upcountry Inc.— Makes seitan from organically grown soybeans (Asserted 90% organic). (Minimum order 10 pounds at $2.35/pound.) 25 Church St., Lenox, MA 02140. (413) 637-0452, (413) 637-2073.

Shellfish. Much of the shellfish sold in the United States ($2.7 billion worth in 1988) came from Mexico, Ecuador and Canada. Raw shellfish poses a hepatitis danger. Unlike fish, the crustaceans (shrimp, for example) are high in cholesterol.

Lobsters are the least fatty shellfish and are a good source of B vitamins, protein, calcium and iron. They are high in cholesterol, but contain only half as much as eggs.[72] Lobsters may not be for the squeamish as they should be kept alive until cooked.

Clams, mussels, and oysters tend to be high in protein and minerals, but can also absorb any pollutants in the water. Also beware of "red tides" and other bacterial proliferation that can make shellfish unsafe from time to time.

Snacks. See also Confections, Granola, Potatoes, Tortilla Chips. Some studies suggest that eating between-meal snacks can contribute to better health and alertness because insulin and blood-sugar levels remain more constant. But most people (and we probably speak for your dentist in this) are not ready to abandon the idea of three or four well-balanced meals a day.

The biggest problem with snacking is what people choose to munch on. Television ads will tell you that a candy bar will perk you up, or that potato chips are just the thing. Both items usually get more than half their calories from fat and add other unwanted baggage. Candy bars are loaded with sugar and are generally lacking in nutrition, which means you are eating "empty calories." You won't be as hungry later and may not eat enough things like milk, bread (whole-wheat, of course), and vegetables to give you the nutrients you need (see Chapters 2 and 4 for a more in-depth discussion of dietary needs and philosophies). Furthermore, the rapid increase in blood sugar generated by a candy bar causes your body to pump large quantities of insulin into your blood stream, which actually causes a bit of a let-down about half an hour after you finish. Potato chips are also noticeably lacking in nutrients and loaded with salt.

What to do then? "Fruit and vegetables" is a clichéd answer, but nevertheless a good one. Dried fruit is particularly portable and, while sugary, often contains necessary vitamins and minerals. Muffins and rolls are also good snacks because they often add not only fiber but complex carbohydrates, which will give you energy for a longer period of time.

American Natural Snacks— Makes several varieties of natural snacks. (Asserted 10% organic, sold through stores.) PO Box 1067, St. Augustine, FL 32085. (904) 825-2056.

Bakery de France— "Croissant Chips" with organic flours, no preservatives and no sugar added (the plain and sourdough are better for you than the other flavors). Asserted 80% organic, sold through stores. 1508 Crocker Ave., Hayward, CA 94544. (415) 487-5993.

FiberRich— Bran-crackers that are low-salt and 35% fiber. Sold through stores.

Glenn Foods Corp— Makes Glenny♥s "100% natural" (but not organic) snacks: brown rice treats, moist and chewy bars, sunrise nutrition bars, nookie items, fruit drops. Products have no added wheat, dairy, sugar, salt, or oil. The fat content is good to reasonable for most of their snacks. Sold through stores. 999 Central Ave., Suite 300, Woodmere, NY 11598. (516) 374-0135.

Maine Sea Vegetable Company— Makes "Sea Chips" (corn/seaweed) with little sodium and relatively low fat content for chips (about 36% of calories). Also alaria, dulse, kelp, and nori. Sold mainly through stores. Franklin, ME 04634. (207) 565-2907.♦

Miss Nancy's— Makes Bagel Chips, Pita Chips, and Bagels made with whole wheat flour, oat bran, and no additives, or sugar (not organic). Available through stores. Joshua Enterprises, 197D Greenfield Road, Lancaster, PA 17601. (717) 295-1770.

Omega Nutrition— Sesame snaps sweetened with brown rice. Also oils and fruit leathers. Sold through stores. 1720 La Bounty Road, Ferndale, WA 98248. (604) 322-8862.

Ryvita— Makes high-fiber "crisp-breads" that are relatively low-calorie. Sold through stores.

San-J— Baked crackers made from brown rice with no oil. Also sauces and spices. Sold through stores. 2880 Sprouse Dr., Richmond, VA 23231. (800) 446-5500, (804) 226-8383.♦♦

Snack Cracks— Crackers made from organically grown brown rice. Made by Ohsawa America, PO Box 3608 Chico, CA 95927. (916) 342-6050.

Wasa— Crisp-breads that are high in fiber but low in salt and calories. Sold through stores.

Soy Products. See also Miso, Sauces, Tofu. The biggest advantage of soy milk is that it offers a substitute for milk (and hence a good protein source) for those who have a lactase deficiency, also known as lactose intolerance. (This condition is common among Mediterraneans, Africans and Asians, but rare in Northern Europeans.) Soybean milk is low in sodium, low in fat, high in protein, and generally has fewer calories than dairy milk. Consumption of soy beverages has leaped by 425 percent since 1983 and sales for 1989 were estimated to be $45 million.

Contrary to some claims about soy milk for babies (most notoriously an ad by Eden Foods written in 1983) soy milk is not a substitute for mother's milk or powdered formulas! It does not have adequate amounts of vitamins A, B_{12}, C, or D to meet the standards for baby formula. Even for adults, soymilk, unless specifically marked enriched, is deficient in A, B_{12}, C, D, E, thiamin, pantothenic acid, calcium, and iodine when compared to milk.

Bake to Nature Organic Milling Co.— Soy oat beverage. San Dimas, CA.

Community Mill and Bean— Dried soybeans, whole grains, flours and meals, processed grain products (baking mixes). Sells wholesale quantities. R.D. #1, Route 89, Savannah, NY 13146. (315) 365-2664.

Edensoy— Organic soy milk and other soy products. Eden Foods, Inc., 701 Tecumseh Road, Clinton, MI 49236. (517) 456-7424, (313) 973-9400.♦♦♦♦

Island Spring Inc.— Soy products, soy milk. PO Box 747, Vashon, WA 98070. (206) 622-6448, (206) 463-9848.♦

Kanoa: A Free Spirit— Soy products, soy yogurt. PO Box 77, Pleasant Prairie, WI 53158.

Love Natural Foods— Loveburgers, soy nuggets, and vegetarian T-shirts and prints by mail (no organic claims). 3 Masada Dr., Cohutta, GA 30710. (404) 694-8179.

Mitoku USA, Inc.— Soy products including miso, shoyu, and tamari imported from Japan. Also udon, sea vegetables, noodles, seasonings, condiments, mirin, oils, teas, cereals, beans, herbal and folk remedies, sweeteners, and snacks. About 25% of products are organic (OFPANA standards), and all conform to macrobiotic quality standards. Sold through stores. PO Box 1343, Clifton Park, NY 12065. (518) 383-6580.

Naturally Northwest Pacific Foods— Soy beverages. 19480 S.W. 97th Ave, Tualatin, OR 97062. (503) 692-9666, FAX: (503) 692-9610.

NûTofù— Cheese substitute made from organic soymilk (tofu is asserted 100% organic, asserted 50% overall). Sold through stores. 90 West St., Suite 612, New York, NY 10006. (212) 964-8740.

Ohsawa— Soy products, including Nama Shoyu organic soy sauce. 1330 Fitzgerald Ave., San Francisco, CA 94124. (415) 822–1800.♦

Pacific Soybean & Grain— Distributes a variety of soy products, about 25% of which are organic. 495 De Haro St., San Francisco, CA 94107. (415) 863–0867.

Quong Hop & Co.— Claims to be the oldest tofu company in America (three generations) and the first to commerically use organically grown soybeans (about 80% now, CCOF) and vacuum packing. They make ready-to-eat soy products including: soy milk, tofu in many varieties, tempeh. Sold through markets. 161–G Beacon St., South San Francisco, CA 94080. (415) 873–4444.

Sovex Natural Foods— "Better than Milk?" Soy drink. Box 310, Collegedale, TN 37315.

Surata Soyfoods Inc.— Makes organic soy products including soy and multi-grain tempeh, tofu (firm and soft), soysage, Szechuan baked tofu, and hickory smoked tofu (98% organic, OCIA). No minimum order, though they are mainly a manufacturer and wholesaler. 302 Blair Blvd., Eugene, OR 97402.

Turtle Island Soy Dairy— Makes tempeh products including bulk "Tempehroni," soy tempeh, 5–grain tempeh, and tempeh burgers (asserted 20%) organic. (See also Meat Substitutes.) Minimum Order $50. PO Box 218, Husum, WA 98623. (509) 493–2004.

Vitasoy— Organic soy milk in four flavors and two sizes, other soy products. Also teas, fruit drinks. Jerome Maynard (National Sales Manager), Hilton Tsui (VP Marketing), 99 Park Lane, Brisbane, CA 94005. (415) 467–8888, FAX: (415) 467–8910.

Westbrae— Soy products (some organic), including Malteds soy shakes with half the fat of regular shakes (regular Westbrae soy milks tend to be quite fatty—drawing 40% of their calories from fat).[73] Available through stores. Emeryville, CA 94662. (415) 658–7521.♦♦♦

White Wave— Makes soy milk, tempeh, tofu, soy cheese, meat substitutes, and other soy products (75% organic). 1550 N 57th Ct., Boulder, CO 80301. (303) 443–8447.♦♦

Soups. Like many quick foods, canned and powdered soups rely on oodles of salt for flavoring. The average Campbell's red-and-white soup has 1,047 milligrams of salt (about twice the amount the National Academy of Sciences says we need for a whole day).[74] For an easy to find healthier alternative, Campbell's does have a line of soups for which they add less salt (and charge you more money). The Center for Science in the Public Interest recommends that you buy soups with 300 milligrams of sodium or less and fewer than 5 grams of fat.

Cream soups usually have more fat than water-based counterparts. If a soup calls for milk, use skim milk to help keep down the fat content.

Erntedank— Organic soup mixes. Made by Purity Foods, Inc., 2871 W. Jolly Road, Okemos, MI 48864. (517) 351–9231.♦

Hain— Makes several low-fat, low-salt soups.♦♦♦

Heartymix Company— "All natural" soup mixes. 1231 Madison Hill Road, Rahway, NJ 07065. (201) 382–3010.

Pritikin— Makes a whole line of soups that are within the guidelines of the Pritikin diet, which emphasizes cutting back on fat (to 10% of total calories if possible) and salt.

Secret Garden— Makes "whole food, all natural soup and entree mixes," including 12–Bean Soup Mix, Hearty Chili Mix, Turtle Rice Soup Mix, Cream of Wild Rice Soup Mix, Wild Rice Hotdish/Stuffing Mix, Mandarin Wild Rice Mix. Most ingredients come from their biodynamic farm. Goods available direct by mail, Visa and Mastercard accepted. Rt. 1, Box 404, Park Rapids, MN 56470. (218) 732–4866.

Vogue Cuisine Inc.— Makes "natural," vegetable-based, low-sodium soups. 437 Golden Isles Dr., Hallandale, FL 33009. (305) 458–2915.

Spaghetti. See Pasta.

Spaghetti Sauce. The sauce you choose for your spaghetti or other pasta dish has a lot to do with how good the dish is for you. Pasta itself has virtually no fat and very little sodium. However, the sauce can contain high levels of both these undesirables. According to a study done by *Environmental Nutrition*,[75] you can avoid a lot of the fat by choosing sauces without meat or flavored with meat (a sauce with meat must have at least a 6 percent meat content while one *flavored* with meat must have at least a 3 percent content). Especially good brands with regard to fat are *Chef Boyardee, Pritikin, Weight Watchers, Enrico's,* and *Tree of Life.* Avoiding sodium is trickier. Prego Spaghetti Sauce, No Salt Added is among the best with respect to sodium (containing only 25 milligrams), but it gets 54 percent of its calories from fat. One of the best with respect to fat is Master Choice Pomodoro, but it has an astounding 1,022 milligrams of sodium. The best compromise looks to be *Enrico's,* which has only 1 gram of fat per serving (13 percent of total calories) and 391 milligrams sodium (174 for the No Salt/Sugar Added variety). On the basis of their informal taste test, the Center for Science in the Public Interest affirms Enrico's as a good choice and also endorses Tree of Life.

Enrico's— Low fat, low sodium spaghetti sauces. Also salsa, enchilada sauce, and barbecue sauce. Sold through stores. Ventre Packing Co. Inc., 373 Spencer St., Syracuse, NY 13204. (315) 422–9277.♥♦♦

Jaclyn's— Non-dairy Alfredo Sauce and No Tomato Pasta sauces with no cholesterol, sweeteners, or hydrogenated fats (We can't vouch for the saturated fat content). Sold through stores. Also breaded vegetables, frozen soups, organic bread crumbs, and pasta sauce. Jaclyn's Food Products, Inc., PO Box 1314, Cherry Hill, NJ 08034. (609) 983-2560.

Pacific Gardens— Makes a pasta sauce with organic tempeh and vegetables. Sold through stores.

Tree of Life— Makes pasta sauce with organically grown tomatoes. Also salsa. Sold through stores. St. Augustine, FL 32085.♦♦♦

Spices. See also Herbs. Salt seems to be the overwhelming spice of choice in the U.S. This, of course, does not have to be so. Try using garlic, lemon, herbs, and experiment with spices like curry. Cutting back on salt can make food a lot more interesting. For those who need to cut back on salt, watch out for products called salt-substitutes. Some still contain some salt (sodium chloride). Potassium salts (the main substitute) can be dangerous to those with kidney disease and can interfere with the electric pulses that regulate heartbeat (though it is rare).[76]

AMS Food Trading Inc.— Imports some organically grown spices. Ali Sadeghi, Manager, 220 Montgomery St. Suite 931, San Francisco, CA 94104. (415) 788-6940.

Earth Products— Makes and distributes River Road™, Seasonings, and Kettle Scents®. Minimum order $50. Natural Products, 15368 Mowersville Rd., Shippensburg, PA 17257.

The Herb Patch— Makes salt-free seasonings, mulling spices, and teas. (Mostly wholesale, but some retail. Asserted 30% organic. Middletown Springs, VT 05757. (802) 235-2466.

J. Crow Inc.— Herbs and spices by mail including mulled cider and wine mixes. Also Tibetan manufactured aroma therapeutic incenses. Asserted 80% organic. V M AE accepted. Minimum order $15, most business over $250. PO Box 172; Old Tenney Rd., New Ipswich, NH 03071. (603) 878-1965.

Mitoku— Umeboshi, umeboshi vinegar, and kuzu (more of a thickening agent than a spice), and many other products imported from Japan. All products meet macrobiotic quality standards. Sold through stores. PO Box 1343, Clifton Park, NY 12065. (518) 383-6580.

Ohsawa— Organic Gomashio (sesame seeds to salt, 15:1) and miso condiments. Also sauces, rice, teas, noodles, and snacks. Chico, CA 95928. (916) 342-6050.

Oregon Spice Co. Inc.— Makes several salt-less seasonings, some with organic ingredients. Also sells a wide range of herbs. Minimum order $50.00. Oregon Spice Company, 3525 SE 17th Ave, Portland, OR 97202. (503) 238-0664, FAX: (503) 238-3872.

Parsley Patch— No-salt seasoning blends available in stores or direct by mail (no organic claims). (Parsley Patch is a subsidary of McCormick & Co., Inc.) 211 Schilling Circle, PO Box 208, Hunt Valley, MD 21031. (301) 527-6007.

Starwest Botanicals Inc.— Sells some organically grown herbs and spices. Van Joerger, President, 11253 Tradecenter Dr., Rancho Cordova, CA 95742. (916) 638-8100.

Spinach. Like other dark, leafy vegetables, spinach is a good vitamin source. It is high in vitamin A, iron, and (for a vegetable) protein. Pesticides found on spinach include endosulfan, DDT (pre-1973 residues), methomyl, methamidophos and dimethoate.

Sprouts. Sprouts are a much maligned icon, but are loaded nutritionally. Buying seeds and producing your own sprouts is one of the cheapest ways to get good vitamin-rich food.

Gourmet Produce Company— Grows and sells organic sprouts (wheat grass, sunflower, and radish, certified 100% by VOF). They ship nationwide in refrigerated boxes year-round. RR3, Box 348, Chester, VT 05143. (802) 875-3820.

Squash. Squash comes in summer and winter varieties, both of which are good sources of vitamins A and C and potassium. The designations summer and winter are related to the rate at which the squash grows, the summer varieties maturing much faster. Summer varieties include Crookneck Squash, Spaghetti Squash, and Zucchini. Winter varieties include Acorn Squash, Butternut Squash, and Pumpkins.

Strawberries. Strawberries are sources of vitamin A, vitamin C, and potassium. Strawberries were found to have more pesticide residues than any other fruit researched by the National Resources Defense Council for their 1987 book *Pesticide Alert*.[77] Authors Mott and Snyder found that 86 percent of imported strawberries had residues and that over 60 percent of strawberries overall had residues of more than one pesticide. Thorough washing can remove captan (the most common residue). Other residues are reduced somewhat by cooking and heat processing.[78] Other pesticides found on strawberries include vinclozolin, endosulfan, methamidophos and methyl parathion.

Purepak, Inc.— Sells organic strawberries (mainly to retailers in Southern California). PO Box 588, Oxnard, CA 93032. (805) 485-1127.

Sugar and Sugar Substitutes. See also Honey, Maple Syrup, Snacks. Consumption of processed sugars is often an unhealthy practice because (1) the sugar is often eaten in snacks and drinks that are almost devoid of vitamins and minerals, (2) the sudden infusion of lots of sugar can send your insulin level into sudden frenzies, and (3) eating sugary foods promotes tooth decay. Traditional warnings about sweets making you fat are probably true not so much for the sugar, but for the fat that accompanies it in products like chocolate and ice cream.

Sugar substitutes are becoming increasingly popular—in 1987 the average American consumed 5.5 pounds of saccharin and 13.5 pounds of aspartame.[79] The problem with sugar substitutes is that they do not really help achieve the goal for which they are presumably eaten by most people: weight reduction. Study after study shows that, on average, people who use artificial sweeteners fail to significantly reduce their overall caloric intake. Instead, people rationalize that they can eat ice cream or french fries because they are balancing it with a diet soft drink. Better steps toward weight reduction are to get exercise and to plan one's diet more carefully.

Sweet Potatoes. They are rich in vitamins A and C.[80] Pesticides detected include dicloran, phosmet, DDT (pre-1973 residues), dieldrin and BHC.

Tea. See beverages, herbs. Sales of herbal teas are growing 25 percent a year, as people are becoming aware of the high caffeine and tannic acid content of regular tea. Herbal teas can have toxic components, though, so be sure you really know what you are drinking.

Celestial Seasonings— Herbal teas found in supermarkets. They also have a good record with respect to social responsibility.♦

Mitoku— Herbal teas, some organic. All products meet macrobiotic quality standards. Sold through stores. PO Box 1343, Clifton Park, NY 12065. (518) 383-6580.

Satori— Herbal teas renowned for their taste. Some varieties are certified organic. Many herbs in the non-organic teas come from China, which the company says makes them ostensibly organic. 332 Ingalls St., Santa Cruz, CA 95060. (408) 429-1707. Order line: (800) 444-SATORI.

Tofu. See also Soy Products, Meat Substitutes. Tofu is the curd derived from soy milk. It is an excellent source of protein and calcium. The high calcium content depends on the type of mineral added during the curding period (calcium sulfate or nagari). According to the Surgeon General, adolescent and adult females should increase their intake of calcium. Since it has little taste itself, tofu absorbs the taste of cooking materials it is prepared with. It can therefore be made into a variety of foods that taste like meat, such as hot dogs, hamburgers and lunch meats, with none of the cholesterol of the real meat. It has a fat content of about 15 percent.

Food Plant— Makes tofu, southwestern specialties (e.g. tofu tamales and burritos), salsa, and jelly/jam. Asserted organic, minimum order is $150. They claim to be "the last of the 'hardcore hippie' organizations in a struggle for a better world, redirecting societal cash flow, and protecting the environment." 2889 Tradeswest, Santa Fe, NM 87501. (505) 476-8979.

Homestyle Foods— Organic soy products: tempeh, tofu, and ready-to-eat soy foods. (Minimum order $75). 2317 Bluebell Dr., Santa Rosa CA 95403. (707) 525-8822.

Island Spring Inc.— Soy products: soy milk, tempeh, tofu noodles, tofu burgers, tofu dressings, tofu frozen dessert and kimchi. Sold mainly through stores (mail order through Col. Sanchez—see Tortilla chips). Asserted 98% organic. PO Box 747, Vashon, WA 98070. (206) 622-6448, (206) 463-9848.♦

Lightlife Foods, Inc.— Cholesterol-free "Tofu Pups", which have the taste if not quite the texture of regular hot dogs, and "Fakin' Bacon." Greenfield, MA 01302. (413) 772-0991.

Rose International— Soybean milk, tofu, and other soy products, as well as cholesterol-free cheeses and tofu ice cream mixes. (They assert that 60% of their products are organic.) PO Box 5020, CA 95402. (707) 576-7050.

Summercorn Foods— Tofu made from organic soybeans, tempeh, and soymilk. Also Whole Wheat Sourdough, 100% Rye Sourdough, Cinnamon Currant Bread, Italian Bread, granola, nut & fruit mixes, and cookies available direct at the main bakery or through markets in the Midwest and Southwest. 401 Watson, Fayetteville, AR 72701. (501) 521-9338.

Tofoods Company Inc./Litetrends— Prepared tofu entrees, meat alternatives, and mayonnaise. (Products are developed in conjunction with the Food Science Department of the University of Maryland under a state grant.) PO Box 3763, Silver Spring, MD 20901. (301) 384-1108.

The Tofu Shop— A wide variety of tofu products from organic soybeans. 768 18th St., Arcata, CA 95521. (707) 822-7409.

Tomsun Foods— Tofu/Fruit yogurt. 247 Wells St., Greenfield, MA 01301. (508) 772-7927.

Yves Fine Foods, Inc.— Tofu in several varieties. Vancouver, B.C., Canada V6A 2A8.

Tomatoes. High in vitamins A, B complex, C, potassium, and phosphate. Store-bought tomatoes are usually picked when pink so that they ship better, hence have less flavor. Winter tomatoes are pressure ripened and usually have amazingly little taste. The best tomatoes are deep red and a little bit soft.

In 1988 the U.S. imported $200 million of tomatoes and byproducts (tomato paste) from Mexico and Italy. Pesticides detected in this country include methamidophos, chlorpyrifos, chlorothalonil, permethrin and dimethoate.

A tomato-based salsa dip goes well with tortilla chips. The hot varieties include jalapeno or other hot peppers, for which metabolic benefits are claimed (see above under Peppers). Salsa is said to have been an Aztec dish.

Just Tomatoes Company— Makes unsulfured dried tomatoes (not organic). Minimum order: 1 case. PO Box 807, Westley, CA 95387. (209) 894-5371.

Tortilla Chips. Tortilla chips are usually fried in oil, which means they are bound to have a high fat content. Blue corn chips are claimed to have over 20 percent more protein than yellow corn chips, with less oil and a high lysine and mineral content; combined with legumes, blue corn is said to make easily digested protein with a full complement of the needed amino acids. Many people will also tell you that they taste better.

Col. Sanchez Traditional Foods— Makes blue corn chips, tortillas, and biscuits, red chile tortillas, truffles, and blue and yellow corn mesa. Available through stores and by mail order. PO Box 5015, Santa Monica, CA 90405. (213) 396–2228, FAX: (213) 396 3522. (Please see Chapter 10 for more.)♦♦

Little Bear Organic Foods— Bearitos blue chips are stone ground and organically grown according to California law, with no added preservatives. The chips are thinner than other chips, which means, it is claimed, that they absorb 10 percent less oil (they get about 42% of their calories from fat). The chips are cooked in sunflower, safflower or unhydrogenated corn oil. The package labeling is not very detailed. Sold mainly through stores. 15200 Sunset Blvd., Suite 202, Pacific Palisades, CA 90265. (213) 454–4542.♥♦♦♦

Mexi Snax— Organic tortilla chips. Also (believe it or not) oat-bran tortilla chips. Doug Shannon, 2035 W. Winton Ave., Hayward, CA 94545.

Turkey. See Poultry.

Vinegar. Wines are made when growing yeast oxidizes some of the sugar in fruit juices to make alcohol. Vinegar is made when that alcohol is in turn oxidized to make acetic acid. Fruit and balsamic vinegars have less bite than wine vinegars. If you use these alternative vinegars in salad dressings, you can cut back on the oil and, hence, the fat.

Golden Acres Orchard— Organic apples in season, apple cider vinegar, apple juice; self-certified organic. Front Royal, VA 22630. (703) 636–9611.

Kozlowski Farms-Sonoma County Classics— Jams, jellies, no-sugar-added fruit butters, no-sugar-added chutneys, no-sugar-added conserves, fudge sauces, marmalades, barbecue sauce, vinegars, mustards, syrups. 5566 Gravenstein Hwy., Forestville, CA 95436. (707) 887–1587, FAX: (707) 887–9650. (See Chapter 10 for more.)

Mitoku— Umeboshi vinegar, brown rice vinegar, and many other products imported from Japan. All products meet macrobiotic quality standards. Sold through stores. PO Box 1343, Clifton Park, NY 12065. (518) 383–6580.

Premier Japan— Brown rice vinegar. Also condiments, sauces, and sea vegetables. Sold through stores. Distributed by Edward & Sons Trading Co., Box 3150, Union, NJ 07083. (201) 964–8176.

Spruce Foods, Inc.— Makes organic oils, vinegars, mustards, and snacks. Available in stores. 959 Grant Place, Boulder, CO 80302. (303) 440–0336.

Water. Bottled water may be the only solution to water quality in some areas. In 1988, Americans spent $2 billion on bottled water. In California the average person consumes 15 gallons of bottled water a year (the figure is 6.1 gallons per capita in the rest of the country). Califor-nia Beverage Hotline called bottled water "one of the great consumer markets" of the next decade.[81]

One of the biggest problems with the trend toward bottled water is that it is not fortified with fluoride. Children and adults who drink bottled water instead of tap-water have been shown to have a higher incidence of tooth decay.

By and large, city water is safer than rural water, because it is regularly tested. Major toxins found in water are: chlorinated solvents, trihalo-methanes, lead, PCBs, and pathogenic bacteria and viruses. Before switching to bottled water, have your water tested. Most local governments provide a rudimentary water testing service for a nominal fee. Outside laboratories do a better job and charge more.

In 1987 the EPA neglected 100,000 violations in water systems serving 30 million people for lack of funds.[82] The EPA also found that parts of 38 states were afflicted by pesticide-contaminated water.[83]

If you are worried about lead poisoning from lead welds in your pipes, run your water for a few minutes in the morning to flush out the water that has been in contact with lead (if possible, save this water for other household uses). Lead pipes and pipes with lead welds should be replaced as soon as possible to prevent the serious effects of lead poisoning. The EPA estimates that 42 million Americans drink water with unsafe lead content.

Advertising for bottled water can often be confusing and misleading, so be especially cautious in choosing the bottled waters you buy. Some brands are just as contaminated as tap water. Claims about special waters (i.e. "catalyst altered" or "light") are dubious and should be investigated. You might try the following.

Artesia Waters Inc.— Sparkling Natural Mineral Water, Flavored Mineral Water. Available through stores. 4671 San Antonio, TX 78218. (512) 654–3027.

Aspen Sparkling Mountain Spring Water— Sparkling mineral water.

EnviroSafe— Water purifiers. 6033 Luther Lane, Dallas, TX 75225. (214) 696–8812.

Golden Wilderness— "Natural Artesian Water from the California High Sierras." Clasped Hands, Inc., (818) 368–2253.

Multi-pure— "Point of use" water purification systems. 21339 Nordhoff Street, Chatsworth, CA 91311. (818) 341–7377.

Poland Spring— Home delivery of bottled water to the northeast. Maine. (800) 622–8009.

USA Water Purification Filter— a bone charcoal purifier. Rockland USA, 12215 East Skelly Dr., Tulsa, OK 74128. (800) 331–3654.

Syfo Water Company Inc.— Sells bottled water (1 and 5 gallon sizes) and seltzers and flavored sparking waters.

Walnut Acres— Sells a variety of water filters. Penns Creek, PA 17862. (800) 433–3998.♦♦

The Watertest Corporation— Sends and analyzes mail-order test kits for $40 to $98. Manchester, NH 03101. (800) 426-8378.

Waters (America) Co. Ltd.— Portable pitcher-type water cleaner, called Aqua Minerale, using a mineral sand made from crushed coral reef. Reduces impurities and adds calcium, magnesium and other minerals. A little over a foot high, it weighs under 4 pounds empty. It has three filters, which have a capacity of 150, 300 and 600 gallons respectively (i.e., 2, 4 and 8 month replacement cycles). Costs about $100. 406 Twisted Stalk Dr., Gaithersburg, MD 20878. (301) 258-9571, FAX: (301) 990-7078.

Watermelons. Watermelons are technically not members of the melon family. They have nowhere near the amount of vitamin A the orange melons contain and a much higher percentage of their weight comes from—you guessed it—water.

Wine. See also Alcohol. The malevolent effects of alcohol are much documented: cirrhosis and cancer of the liver, hypertension, fetal alcohol syndrome, and alcoholic psychosis. Nutritionally speaking, alcohol has little to offer and causes the excretion of many needed minerals, especially zinc. Alcohol is also high in calories. On the flip side, drinking alcohol in moderation was found by some researchers to lower the blood pressure modestly. There are two beneficial effects attributed to grape juice that are carried over to wine: an antiviral agent (found in the skin of grapes, hence it would be found only in red wines) and a high potassium content, which reduces high blood pressure.

If you are going to buy wine, you may as well buy organic wine. It is not only more likely to be free from chemical residues, but it can be just as good and often is comparably priced to regular wine. Organic wines are cropping up all over France and California—Veronique Raskin of The Organic Wine Company estimates that there are now 250 varieties.

Chartrand Imports— Sells 25 organic wines, many imported from France, some brought from California (Fitzpatrick winery). He mainly sells to retailers but will do mail orders to areas where there is no outlet (provided it's legal). PO Box 1319, Rockland, ME 04841. (207) 594-7300.

Four Chimneys Farm Winery— Produces wine from organically grown grapes, and fruit wines with no synthetic additives. Available by mail, in stores, in restaurants, and at farmers markets. 5% discounts on orders of 3 or more cases. Cases shipped the day after paid orders are received. RD #1, Hall Rd., Himrod, NY 14842. (607) 243-7502.

Frey Vineyards— Sells California wines made from organic grapes. 14000 Tomki Rd., Redwood Valley, CA 95470. (707) 485-5177.

The Organic Wine Company— imports organic (certified by Nature et Progres) wines from France (minimum order: 3 cases). Check for Domaine de las Bousquette, Cotes-du-Rhone, Chateau du Moulin Peyronin, L.C. Jouglas, Chateau Ballue Mondon, or Blanquette de Limoux where you buy wine. 54 Genoa Place, San Francisco, CA 94133. Phone and FAX: (415) 433-0167.

Wine (Non-Alcoholic). Non-alcoholic wines retain the solid value of wine without its anti-nutritional drawbacks.

Ariél— Non-alcoholic wines "that win prizes against wines with alcohol." Ariél won the gold medal at the 1986 Los Angeles County Fair and has been commended by Howard Goldberg of the *New York Times*, L. Walker of *Wines & Vines*, and J. Gordon of the *Wine Spectator*. The *Vegetarian Times* also heralded Ariél wine as one of the best new products at the 1989 Natural Foods Expo. Look for Ariél Blanc, Ariél White Zinfandel, and Ariél Cabernet Sauvignon. (No organic claims.)

Jungfrau, Petillion, Giovane, and Carl Jung— Organic, non-alcoholic wines available through stores.

Yogurt. Yogurt is reputed to be nutritionally superior to milk because it contains enzymes that make it more readily digestible. Many lactose-intolerant people can eat Yogurt. Yogurt, like milk, can contain pesticide residues if the cows from which it came ate fodder that had been sprayed.

Alta•Dena Certified Dairy— Makes several types of yogurt that are free of artificial colors, preservatives and refined sugars. They also make frozen yogurt mixes. (Alta•Dena was recently purchased by Bongrain SA of France, which also owns Columbo yogurt.) City of Industry, CA.♦♦♦

Brown Cow Farm— Low-fat and non-fat yogurts sweetened with honey or fruit juice. Sold through stores. 190 Seely Hill Rd. Newfield, NY 14867.

Mountain High Yoghurt— Makes "100% natural" yogurt without preservatives or additives. The yogurt is sweetened with honey and is 99% fat free. Available in many grocery stores in the west. 1325 West Oxford, Englewood, CO 80110. (303) 761-2210.

Springfield Creamery Inc.— Makes low-fat and non-fat dairy products. Also honey yogurt, cream cheese, sour cream, and kefir. 29440 Airport Rd., Eugene, OR 97402. (503) 689-2911.

Stars— Frozen yogurts sweetened with fruit juices. No organic claims; sold through stores. PO Box 40429, San Francisco, CA 94110. (415) 695-0604.

Zucchini. See Squash.

Seeds of Change maintains a large organic seed bank all through their farm near Santa Fe, New Mexico. The group runs the Gila Eco-Agriculture Center and offers consulting in ecological farm design, agro foresty, and enviromental restoration.

PART 3
WHERE YOU CAN BUY HEALTHY FOOD

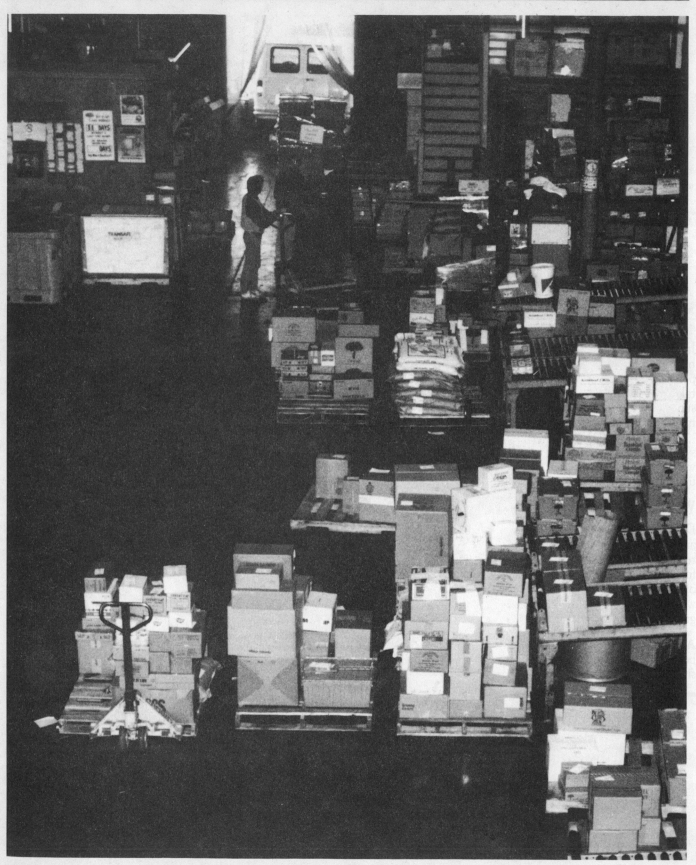

Tree of Life is the foremost distributor of healthy food in the United States. They shipped $50 million worth of goods through the St. Augustine warehouses (pictured here) in 1988 and may have doubled that in 1989.

CHAPTER 8

THE DISTRIBUTION
OF HEALTHY FOOD

*In 1987 farmers retained a meager 20 cents of every dollar consumers spent on
fruits and vegetables and a pitiful 7 cents of each dollar spent on grains.*

In Chapter 6, we suggested you try growing your own
healthy food, or buy it direct from a farmer or distributor,
perhaps through a buying co-op or farmers' market. This
takes time, and you may not have it. So we must consider
supermarkets, grocery stores, wholefood stores, or restaurants.

In this chapter we look more closely at the distribution
system for healthy food. Consumers have a right to know
who is handling their food between the time it is picked
up at the farm and the time they buy it in the store.

What Distributors Do

Distributors buy food in bulk from farmers, repackage it,
and sell it to retail stores or other volume buyers such as
restaurants or institutions. Distributors may also engage in
food processing such as canning, freezing, or baking. Tree
of Life, for example, is a distributor and also manufactures
what it claims to be the only salsa made with organically
grown tomatoes.

A Growing Role. Distributors and food processors have
been taking an increasingly large share of the food dollar
since 1970 (see Table 8–1).

Table 8–1
Farmer's Share of the Food Dollar, 1987 vs. 1970

Food (spending, billions)	1987	Farmer Share	1970
Meat products ($110)	31¢		42¢
Poultry/eggs ($30)	34¢		44¢
Dairy products ($54)	34¢		41¢
Fruits/vegetables ($86)	20¢		23¢
Grains ($51)	7¢		15¢

Source: *Statistical Abstract of the U.S.: 1989*, Table 1104, p. 639.

The three areas where farmers receive at least 30 cents of
the consumer's food dollar are the ones requiring the
heaviest capital investment—meat, poultry/ eggs, and
dairy products. These items accounted for $194 billion in
1987, more than half of the $377 billion spent on all
food.

In the other two food areas shown in Table 8–1 farmers
did worse. In 1987 farmers retained a meager 20 cents of
every dollar consumers spent on fruits and vegetables and
a pitiful 7 cents of each dollar spent on grains. No wonder
farmers are eager to connect directly with the consumer
through farmers' markets and the like.

Point-of-Sale and Other Costs.

One of the major costs in distribution includes the final
step, retailing or food service. This increased from $32 bil-
lion in 1970 to $140 billion in 1987, a more than four-
fold increase, substantially larger than the growth in total
food sales, which went from $111 to $377 billion.

Other unusually high increases in costs were labor, up
from $32 billion in 1970 to $131 billion in 1987; advertising and other costs, up from $24 billion to $82 billion;
wholesaling (direct costs), up from $9 billion to $32 billion; and fuels, up from $2 billion to $14 billion.[1]

The Problems of Growing Demand

Demand for Healthy Food. More Americans want to eat
healthy food. In 1985, 90 percent of those polled said
they were concerned about nutrition; over 40 percent said
they worried about fat and cholesterol in foods.[2] In 1988,
half of those surveyed said they were trying to cut down
on food (1) that was high in salt, sugar, fat or cholesterol,
and (2) that was highly processed and was high in preservatives, additives and artificial ingredients.[3]

In response, the national market for healthier food has
grown dramatically. Sales of dietetic and low-calorie

sauces and dressings, and salt substitutes have soared.[4] Consumption of yogurt, with a reputation for being healthy because its cultures aid in the digestion of nutrient-rich milk, has probably grown faster than any other food in the last 35 years, from barely one-tenth of a pound per person in 1955 to 4.6 pounds per person in 1988.[5]

Problems. The growth of demand for healthy food has shown up as a rapid increase in demand for organic produce. The problem is, it takes time to develop new sources of organically grown food. This poses a dilemma. To encourage supply, a national market for wholefoods must be maintained. However, this market requires enormous transportation and related environmental costs that for many people are the antithesis of the objectives of sustainable agriculture.

Organic Labeling Fraud. One solution to the problem of excess demand for organic food is labeling fraud, i.e. identifying a food as organically grown when it is not. Brad McDowell, Publisher of *Food Distribution Magazine*, has given me permission to print his estimate of the proportion of food sold as organic today that is mislabeled: 50 percent.

In our survey of manufacturers, distributors and retailers, we asked them about fraud in the labeling of organic produce. Of the 398 respondents who answered the question, one-fourth (92) said they had personally encountered fraud in the labeling and promotion of organic foods. Most respondents (191 vs. 143) say that they think "much" fraud exists in the area. Of those (153) who chose to guess the percentage of food labeled as organic that is actually organically grown and processed, the average guess was 78 percent.

The respondents have more reason for confidence in what they buy than the average consumer. Of the respondents the great majority (358 vs. 45) place importance on the certification of farmers from whom they buy; a somewhat lesser majority (298 vs. 75) is satisfied with the standards maintained by the certification groups active in their area. These relections on the distribution of organic produce suggest that Senator Leahy's national organic labeling law is overdue.

Think Globally, Buy Locally. Trucking farm produce long distances is expensive; it cost Americans $14 billion of their food bill in 1987.[6] Trucking is also hard on the produce, perhaps even legitimizing in some cases the persistent myth that organic foods must have more cosmetic flaws. Honeysuckle Market in Memphis stopped trucking in produce from long distances to help protect the environment, one of the main arguments for organic and sustainable agriculture. Is so much shipping of fluorocarbon-refrigerated produce thousands of miles in noisy, highway-hogging, diesel-guzzling trucks necessary and justified? Because of the direct and indirect costs of transportation, organic produce and wholefoods will be best distributed in the states or regions where these items are grown and produced.

They will also be best distributed in states where there is a strong market for healthier products. Paradoxically, the more we end-run the Leviathan, the less we may have to. In a state that has a good supply of organic food and a good set of laws and certification programs, buying healthy food is easier.

How Your State Rates. We offer a general picture of which states are best provided with organic foods and wholefoods in Table 8–2. It is based on the strength of certification programs, and concentration of distributors and retail outlets that sell wholefoods and organic produce. We would rank the states as follows, "best" denoting states where the most progressive actions to date have been taken; "poor" describing those where the term "organic farming" would most likely draw a blank stare.

Table 8–2
Availability and Certification of Healthy Food
The Best and Worst States

Best
California, Maine, Texas
Very Good
Colorado, Michigan, Minnesota, Oregon, Washington
Good
Arizona, District of Columbia, Florida, Illinois, Maryland, Massachusetts, Vermont, Wisconsin
Fair
Arkansas, Connecticut, Georgia, New Hampshire, New Jersey, New York, North Carolina, Ohio, Pennsylvania, South Carolina, Virginia
Poor
Alabama, Alaska, Hawaii, Idaho, Indiana, Iowa, Kansas, Kentucky, Louisiana, Mississippi, Missouri, Montana, Nebraska, New Mexico, Rhode Island, Tennessee, Utah
Very Poor
Delaware, Oklahoma, Nevada, North Dakota, South Dakota, West Virginia, Wyoming

Source: Author's qualitative assessment of the data in Chapters 5 and 10.

These rankings are, of course, relative. In an ideal world, the availability and identifiability of organic foods and wholefoods in the least progressive state would be better than what prevails in California and Texas.

Distributors and Turfs. The truth about wholefood stores is that most of them buy almost everything they sell from one distributor, or maybe two. In a small town like Woodstock, NY, lucky enough to have more than one wholefood store, the distributor's tractor-trailer truck roars into town every week or so and drops its merchandise at both stores.

Many medium-sized distributors will ship to individual, non-commercial customers, but they commonly require minimum orders, which in turn encourages consumers to organize into buying co-ops, discussed in Chapter 6. The minimum order is often lower than the $500 that Stow Mills (the largest distributor on the East Coast) and other distributors require of their commercial customers, mostly wholefood stores and supermarket chains. However, the prices and terms may well be less favorable.

Distributors are the key to the wholefood business. Many firms are also not interested in publicity. A benevolent interpretation of their silence is that they are just so busy, and so forth. But with labeling fraud such a major concern, distributors who avoid the spotlight may be seeking to avoid accountability for their product, filling a demand for organic produce with whatever happens to be on hand. With the link broken between producer and customer, who's to know?

The U.S. wholefood industry includes about 700 distributors, of which a half-dozen probably account for half the business.

The only truly national distributor is Tree of Life, based in St. Augustine, FL. It is a subsidiary of a shrewd $4–billion-a-year conglomerate, Wassanen (accent on the second "a") Corp., based in Amstelveen, a suburb of Amsterdam. Tree of Life was originally a $35–million-a-year southern company with a near-monopoly in its region. After being acquired by Wassanen it then purchased $90–million-a-year Balance Foods in New Jersey, and continues to acquire other distributors in every part of the country, divided into eight regions based on the marketing areas of the acquired companies. Tree of Life representatives were much more forthcoming about their business at the 1989 Anaheim Natural Foods Expo than were representatives of other large distributors. They did over $50 million a year in their Southeastern home division alone in 1988, and may have doubled this number in 1989. With all of its divisions together, Tree of Life probably grossed about $300 million in 1989.

East Coast: The Big Three. The three main distributors on the East Coast are Tree of Life, Stow Mills, and Cornucopia. The largest distributor on the East Coast, and probably the largest operation out of a single office, is Stow Mills, in Chesterfield, NH. Stow Mills is highly secretive about its operations, but its competitors say that it is focusing on selling wholefoods to the mass market (supermarkets) rather than the smaller wholefood stores, which require more attention and service.

I spoke with the President, Richard Youngman, at the 1989 Anaheim Natural Foods Expo, and I told him I was writing this book. He said: "We don't want to talk to you at all, but don't take it personally. We don't talk to newspapers either. We don't see what we gain by giving out any information about our business."

Stow Mills is said by competitors and industry specialists to have done about $65 million in business in 1989, significantly less than Tree of Life but probably at a higher profit margin since its operations are less scattered and are oriented to the mass market. It is less well positioned than Tree of Life, however, for taking advantage of the growth in interest in organic food because it already has a high market share in a single region and is battling with strong competitors, while Tree of Life has less competition in other regions.

One significant competitor to Stow Mills in the East is Cornucopia, in Coventry, RI, which did about $50 million in 1989. Cornucopia is the polar opposite of Stow Mills in its attitude toward the legitimacy of consumer in-

terest in information. Norman Cloutier and members of his staff were open and generous with information.

Neshaminy Valley in Pennsylvania and the fast-growing Sherman Foods in New York also serve a large number of stores on the East coast. For organic produce, Organic Farms Inc. of Beltsville, MD is the biggest supplier in the region and probably the country.

West Coast and Pacific Northwest. Rainbow Distributors (with warehouses in Denver, CO and Los Angeles, CA- and Nature's Best in Torrance, CA are the two main competitors of Tree of Life in California (although many small distributors seem to thrive in the state). Nutrasource in Seattle is Tree of Life's main competition in Washington and Oregon.

Midwest. The largest distributors in the Midwest, other than the ones already mentioned, are Blooming Prairie, with bases in Iowa City, IA and Minneapolis, MN, and Health Foods Inc., based in Chicago/Des Plaines, IL.

South. Tree of Life is the main distributor in the deep South and almost single-handedly supplies some of the Southern states, although Cornucopia is considering expansion into the southern region. Further West, Texas Health Distributors (affiliated with Whole Foods Markets) is a major player.

Southwest. Texas Health Distributors and Food for Health in Phoenix, AZ are the two biggest companies in the region. Tree of Life, of course, has a presence as well.

At the end of this chapter we provide details on dozens of other major distributors. In Chapter 10 we provide information about distributors only if they accept orders from non-commercial customers, i.e. buying clubs or food co-ops (or in some cases individuals). The restrictive policies of some distributors may change as the number and strength of individual customers grows—after all, the mail-order catalog business is burgeoning in every other field.

The Best Distributors

Based on our questionnaires to companies in the natural foods industry, the distributors listed in Table 8–3 are the most highly regarded, with at least two surveys mentioning them. Remember the list is partly a function of size— Tree of Life is a good company, but it is probably no coincidence that the largest distributor got the most recommendations. You can use this list to encourage your local food store to consider alternatives, and you may wish to base your decision on where to shop and eat in part on who the distributor is.

Distributors with a heart (♥) at the end of their listing are personal favorites among the top ten, based on our communication with them during the preparation of this book. In the listings later in the chapter we also append a diamond (♦) or two, which indicates third-party testimony to the organization's dedication to the consumer.

Some names in the list are primarily growers or manufacturers and are reviewed elsewhere in this book under the more appropriate heading.

Table 8–3
America's Outstanding Wholefood Distributors

110 Tree of Life, St. Augustine, FL; Cleburne TX; Bloomington IN; Sun Valley CA; Seattle WA; Bergen NJ♥
 59 Stow Mills, Chesterfield, NH
 54 Cornucopia Natural Foods, Coventry, RI♥
 24 Rainbow Distributors, Denver, CO/Los Angeles, CA
 22 Nature's Best, Torrance, CA♥
 19 Organic Farms, Beltsville, MD♥
 18 Blooming Prairie, Iowa City, IA/Minneapolis, MN♥
 18 Neshaminy Valley, Ivyland, PA♥
 17 Health Foods Inc., Chicago/Des Plaines, IL
 15 Food for Health, Phoenix, AZ
 15 Natural Food Wholesalers, Miami, FL
 13 North East Cooperatives, Brattleboro, VT
 13 Sierra Natural Foods, San Francisco, CA
 12 Frontier Co-op Herbs, Norway, IA
 11 Fowler Bros., San Rafael, CA
 10 Nutra Source, Seattle, WA
  9 Garden Spot, New Holland, PA
  9 Whole Food Express, Eureka, CA
  8 Beautiful Foods, Philadelphia, PA
  8 North Farm Co-op, Madison, WI
  7 Mountain People's Warehouse, Grass Valley, CA
  6 Mountain Warehouse, Durham, NC
  6 Roots & Fruits, Minneapolis, MN
  5 Falcon Distributors, Santa Cruz, CA
  5 Feather River, Petaluma, CA
  5 Federation of Ohio River Co-ops, Columbus, OH
  5 Genessee Natural Foods, Genessee, PA
  5 Midwest, Ann Arbor, MI/Bloomington, IN
  4 All Natural, Foxboro, MA
  4 Associated Buyers, Sommersworth, NH
  4 Clear Eye, Savannah, NY
  4 Country Life, Chicago IL/Pullman MI
  4 Frankferd Farms, Valencia, PA
  4 Hatch Natural Foods, Warrentown, VA
  4 Marshall Distrib., Salt Lake City, UT
  4 Natural Foods Inc., Toledo, OH
  4 Natural Food Plus, Minneapolis, MN
  4 Soy Power, Santa Monica, CA
  4 Texas Health, Austin, TX
  3 Albert's Organics, Los Angeles, CA
  3 Arrowhead Mills, Hereford, TX
  3 Fairhill Foods, Suisun, CA
  3 Jaffe Bros, Valley Center, CA
  3 Natural Food Distributors, Newton, CT
  3 Purity Foods, Okemos, MI
  3 Regional Access, Ithaca, NY
  3 Rock Island Foods, Santa Cruz, CA
  3 Something Better, Battle Creek, MI
  3 Star West Botanicals, Sacramento, CA
  3 Tucson Co-operative Warehouse, Tucson, AZ
  2 Alta Dena Certified Dairy, City of Industry, CA
  2 Atlanta Health Drink/Natural Food, Atlanta, GA
  2 Better Foods Foundation, Greencastle, PA
  2 Brandt, Chicago, IL
  2 Deep Root Organic Truck Farmers, Bellows Falls, VT
  2 Dowel Quality Producers, New York, NY
  2 Eden Foods, Clinton, MI
  2 Foodworks, Chicago, IL
  2 Gold Mine Natural Food Co., San Diego, CA
  2 Harvest Day Wholesales, Madison, WI
  2 Hi Profit, Sun Valley, CA
  2 Hudson Valley Federation, Clintondale, NY
  2 Keene, Dallas, TX/Tulsa, OK
  2 Lifesource, Toronto, ON
  2 Little Bear Organic Foods, San Diego, CA
  2 Living Farms, Tracy, MN
  2 Maximum, Toronto, ON
  2 Natural Commodities, Hallandale, FL
  2 Nature's Foods NW, Gresham, OR
  2 Nomadic Organics, Minneapolis, MN
  2 Ontario Federation of Co-ops, Toronto, ON
  2 Orange Blossom Co-op, Gainesville, FL
  2 Red Safron, Minneapolis, MN
  2 Sahara Natural Foods, Berkeley, CA
  2 Super Nutrition, New York, NY
  2 Superior Natural, Detroit, MI

Source: Author's survey, summer and fall, 1989.

Updating Market Information The following sources do regular broad-gauge surveys of the distribution of healthy food, and can be contacted for up-to-date information on the state of the market:

Cooperative Grocer, Box 597, Athens, OH 45701. (614) 448-7333. Dave Gutnecht, Editor. Follows the co-op retail business, circulates to 2,000 co-op stores. Subscription is $18/year, six issues♥♦

Food Distribution Magazine, 1002 South Fort Harrison Ave., Clearwater, FL 34616. (813) 443-2723. Brad McDowell, Publisher. 30,000 controlled circulation, mostly to retail stores with some distributors, importers and brokers. Has actively campaigned against supermarket slotting fees, described in Chapter 9.♥♦♦

Health Foods Business, 567 Morris Avenue, Elizabeth, NJ 07208. (201) 353-7373. Sent to 13,000 subscribing retailers and manufacturers selling natural foods and supplements. Individuals may subscribe for $30/year (U.S. address).♦

New Hope Communications, 1301 Spruce Street, Boulder, CO 80302. Publishers of *Natural Foods Merchandiser* (15,000 circ.), *Organic Times* (15,000 circ.) and *Delicious* Magazine (300,000 circ.). Sponsors of annual Natural

Foods Expos (East and West). Steven Hoffman, Editor: (303) 939-8440. Gil Johnson, Director of Research, 1029 NW 23rd Ave., #300, Portland, OR 97210, (503) 226-0588.♥♦

Whole Foods Magazine, 3000 Hadley Road, South Plainfield, NJ 07080. Dan McSweeney, (201) 769-1160; FAX (201) 494-4851. 12,000 controlled circulation to buyers of wholefoods and supplements. Editorial coverage is focused exclusively on independent wholefood stores and distributors.♦

Quality Distributors, by State

The following state-by-state directory, through the end of this chapter, describes some of the best distributors we came across in our research—especially wholesale distributors of organic produce. If you want whole foods in your supermarkets and corner grocery stores, one way to get them might be to ask the owners of your neighborhood stores to pick up some of the following distributors. In New York City it is becoming increasingly common to find Health Valley and Little Bear products next to Betty Crocker and Nabisco. This trend will, we hope, continue.

Arizona

Chino Valley, **Prairie Sun Farm,** 1145 Granite Creek Lane, Chino Valley, AZ 86323. (602) 636-2922. **Type of Business:** Food producer and distributor. In business since 1975. **Sells to:** Retailers. **Sells:** Fresh fruit (Concord grapes). The #1 Eastern Concord grape sold for table use. **Other:** Certified organic.

Phoenix, **Food For Health Co.,** Sarah L. Adams, Executive Assistant, PO Box 23152, Phoenix, AZ 85063. (602) 269-2371. **Type of Business:** Distributor. **Sells to:** Retailers. **Sells:** Cereals, flour, rice, pasta, breads, oils, nuts and nut butters, fruit juices, preserves, dried fruit, vegetables, salsa, legumes, bagels, cookies, cakes, corn chips, tacos, cheese, ice cream, yogurt, miso, tempeh, tofu, soybean milk and other soy products. **Other:** Asserted 30% organic. Special prices for bulk orders. Delivery by truck west of the Mississippi. Minimum order is $300 freight free or $150 plus freight.♦♦♦

Arkansas

Huntsville, **Ozark Organic Growers Association,** Rt. 4, Box 140-H, Huntsville, AR 72740. **Type of Business:** Distributor. **Sells to:** Retailers. **Sells:** Fresh fruit (blueberries, raspberries, strawberries, apples, pears), fresh and dried culinary herbs, meat ("ethical" veal, beef), Ozark Mountain wildflower honey, fresh and dried shiitake mushrooms. **Other:** Certified organic. Minimum Order is generally 750–1,000 trucking lbs.

California

Bolinas, **Star Route Farms,** Warren Weber, Bolinas, CA 94924. (415) 868-0929. **Type of Business:** Grower. **Sells to:** Retailers, distributors, restaurants, and public. **Sells:** lettuce, arugula, broccoli, cauliflower, spinach, radiccio, leeks, chicory, edible flowers and herbs. **Other:** California

Certified Organic Farmers-certified 100% organic. Shipping by truck in the Bay area 6 days a week; airfreight & Federal Express on request. **Comments:** One of the first organic growers in the Bay Area, Weber sells most of his produce directly to top San Francisco restaurants, whose chefs say they value the *taste* of his vegetables and herbs as much as their chemical-free status.♥♦

Chico, **Knudsen & Sons, Inc.,** Speedway Ave., PO Box 369, Chico, CA 95927. (916) 891-1517. **Type of Business:** Distributor. **Sells to:** Distributors only. **Sells:** Juices (apple, gravenstein, pear, concord grape), wine, non-alcoholic beer, preserves, jams, jellies, soft drinks, spritzers. **Other:** Asserted 8% organic.

Chico, **Ohsawa America,** Lane Seiger, Larry Lenk, 1608-A West Fifth St., Chico, CA 95928. Mail to: PO Box 3608, Chico, CA 95927. (916) 342-6050. **Type of Business:** Distributor. **Sells to:** Retailers. **Sells:** Baked goods (rice crackers), condiments (rice vinegar, pickles), whole grains (brown rice), processed grain products (mochi, noodles, rice crackers), soy products (soy sauce, miso, dried tofu), sweeteners (brown rice syrup powder), teas (kukichtwig tea), also kudzu, dried lotus root, dried daikon. **Other:** Asserted organic; require certification from producers.

Chico, **Solar Fresh,** PO Box 7707, Chico, CA 95927. (916) 891-5723. **Type of Business:** Wholesale distributor. **Sells to:** Retailers. **Sells:** Organic and specialty produce including a wide variety of fresh fruits and vegetables. They also sell some dried fruit. **Other:** Asserted 80% organic, CCOF certified. All prices negotiable. Shipping is by truck to Oregon, California, and Washington. Minimum Order is $500.

City of Industry, **Hansen Foods Inc.,** 14380-G Nelson Ave, City of Industry, CA 91744. (818) 336-7099. **Type of Business:** Processor. **Sells to:** 11 Western states. **Sells:** Natural juices and sodas, No organically grown goods. **Other:** No certification, minimum order is $7,500 for delivery, $2,150 for P/U.

City of Industry, **US Specialties,** Wayne Specht (President), 14320 Bonelli, City Of Industry, CA 91746. (818) 968-0334. **Type of Business:** Distributor. **Sells to:** Retailers. **Sells:** Cereals, grains, flour, pasta, rice, miso, soybean milk, pinto beans, dried fruit, candy bars, chips, fruit juices, coffees and teas. **Other:** Minimum order is $350; catalogue available.

City of Industry, **Gabriele,** 17651 E Railroad St, Industry, CA 91748. (818) 964-2324 FAX: (818) 912-1058. **Type of Business:** Manufacturer. **Sells to:** Retailers. **Sells:** Wholewheat and flavored pasta (macaroni, noodles, spaghetti). **Other:** Minimum order $2500 for truck delivery; $500 for pick-up of shipping.

Coachella, **Great Date in the Morning,** PO Box 31, 85-710 Grapefruit Blvd., Coachella, CA 92236. (619) 298-6171. **Type of Business:** Grower, processor, mail-order distributor, and wholesale distributor. **Sells to:** Wholesalers, retailers, and mail order to the public. **Sells:** Dates, melons, strawberries, fresh vegetables and spices. **Other:**

Certification by CCOF and OCIA. Minimum order is 50 cases for wholesale.

Davenport, **Molino Creek Farming Collective,** Mark Lipson, PO Box 69, Davenport, CA 95017. (408) 458–7886. **Type of Business:** Grower. **Sells to:** Retailers. **Sells:** Dried fruit (tomatoes) fresh fruit, flour (blue and red stoneground corn meal), fresh vegetables (artichokes, dry-farmed summer and winter squashes, peppers, leeks, and other vegetables). **Other:** Certified organic (100%-CCOF).

Davenport, **Odwalla,** Drawer O, Davenport, CA 95017. (408) 425–4557. **Type of Business:** Manufacturer and distributor, **Sells to:** Retailers. **Sells:** Fresh, unpasteurized fruit juices and vegetables juices. **Other:** Asserted 30% organic. They are affiliated with CCOF. They deliver by truck to the Bay Area. Minimum order is $50.

Emeryville, **Tumbleweed Dist,** 6315 Doyle St, Emeryville, CA 94608. (415) 428–9242, FAX: (415) 428–1532. **Type of Business:** Distributor. **Sells to:** Retailers. **Sells:** A variety of wholefoods and organic produce. Cereals (corn, granola, oatmeal, wheat), flour (buckwheat, rye, whole wheat), cookies, cakes, crackers, rice, pasta, oils, chicken, beans, dried fruit, miso, soybean milk, fruit juices and other beverages. **Other:** Asserted 15% organic (CCOF). Minimum order is $100 on established routes.

Encinitas, **Sunwest Naturals Inc.,** John Deters (President), Box 1101, Encinitas, CA 92024. (619) 931–8719. **Type of Business:** Distributor and wholesaler. **Sells to:** Retailers. **Sells:** Baked goods (bagels, cakes, cookies, muffins, tacos and corn chips), breads, cheese, kefir, yogurt, fruit juices, tempeh, tofu, and salsa. **Other:** 15% organic (OCIA certified). Only serves Southern California. Minimum order is $100.

Eureka, **Whole Food Express,** 3134 Jacobs Ave., Eureka, CA 95501. (707) 445–3185. **Type of Business:** Distributor. **Sells to:** Retailers. **Sells:** Dried beans, dried fruit, fresh fruit, whole grains, flour and meals, processed grain products, herbs and spices, condiments,coffee, teas, juices, meats, nuts and nut butters, soy products. **Other:** Asserted 25% organic. They are affiliated with CCOF. M-F 8-5; will-call on Wednesdays. Delivery Sun-Fri; 2% C.O.D. on non-UPS deliveries. Minimum order is $50 to call, $100 within 50–mile radius of warehouse, $300 for rest.♦♦

Fairfax, **Wildwood Natural Foods,** 135 Bolinas Rd., Fairfax, CA 94930. (415) 459–TOFU. **Type of Business:** Manufacturer and Distributor. **Sells to:** Retailers. **Sells:** Macrobiotic products, soy products, Wildwood organic tofu (bulk and vacuum packed), Wildwood organic soymilk, Soyfood Unlimited organic tempeh, Santa Cruz organic tempeh, Grainaissance organic mochi, frozen snacks. **Other:** Asserted organic; products must meet standards in section 26569.11.

Fairfield, **MLO Products,** Inc., Mel Williamson, President, 2351 N. Watney Way, Fairfield, CA 94533. (707) 422–9597. **Sells to:** Retailers. **Sells:** MLO and Pure and Simple brands. **Other:** Asserted 10% organic.

Goleta, **Fairview Gardens,** Michael Ableman, 598 N. Fairview Ave., Goleta, CA 93117. (805) 967–7369. **Type of Business:** Grower and distributor. **Sells to:** Wholesalers, retailers. **Sells:** Condiments (peach butter), fresh fruit (avocados, peaches, lemons, oranges, mandarins, feijoas, cherimoyas, figs, etc.), fresh vegetables (globe artichokes). **Other:** Certified organic.

Grass Valley, **Mountain Peoples Warehouse,** 110 Springhill Bvld., Grass Valley, CA 95945. (916) 273–9531. **Type of Business:** Distributor, since 1976. **Sells to:** Retailers, buying clubs, and other wholesalers. **Sells:** Baked goods, coffee, condiments, dairy products, dried beans, dried fruit, fresh fruit, whole grains, flour and meals, processed grain products, herbs and spices, juices, meat and eggs, nuts and nut butters, oils, seeds, soy products, sweeteners, fresh vegetables. **Other:** Certification varies, organic "preferred". Member of CCOF. Minimum order is $200 for warehouse pick-up, $300 for delivery on regular scheduled routes.♦♦

Los Altos, **Your Land Our Land Inc.,** Kevin C. Martin, PO Box 7037, Los Altos, CA 94022. (415) 821–6732. **Type of Business:** Distributor. **Sells to:** Restaurants. **Sells:** Fresh fruits, fresh herbs and spices, fresh specialty vegetables (lettuces and salad greens). **Other:** Asserted 100% organic; member of CCOF.

Los Angeles, **West Valley Produce Co.,** Murray Cherness (President), 726 South Mateo St., Los Angeles, CA 90021. (213) 627–4131. **Type of Business:** Distributor and broker to health food stores. **Sells to:** Mainly retailers. **Sells:** Organic produce in numerous varieties. Lots of fresh fruits and vegetables, green beans, lima beans, raisins, nuts (almonds, walnuts), herbs and spices. Most of their growers are CCOF certified. Discount for orders by pallet. No minimum order.

Los Angeles, **Albert's Organics Inc.,** 4605 S. Alameda Ave., Los Angeles, CA 90058. (213) 234–4595. **Type of Business:** Distributor, since 1981. **Sells to:** Retailers. **Sells:** A wide variety of organically grown fruits and vegetables. **Other:** Asserted 90% organic. They ship to the entire U.S., Canada, and Europe. **Comments:** Albert's Organics received a large number of recommendations from businesses dispersed throughout the U.S. and Canada. They also put out a quarterly newsletter, *The Organic Advocate.*♦♦

Los Angeles, **Mountain Wholesale Produce Co.,** 726 Mateo Street, Los Angeles, CA 90021. (213) 683-1384, Fax: (213) 683-1274. **Type of Business:** Wholesale distributor. **Sells to:** Retailers—all of U.S. and Canada. **Sells:** Fresh fruits and vegetables. **Other:** Certified organic by CCOF.

Manteca, **Jemolo Enterprises** (Natural Food Products Division), PO Box 378, Manteca, CA 95336. (209) 823-5896. **Type of Business:** Manufacturer, exporter, private label packager, and mail order distributor. **Sells to:** Distributors and retailers. **Sells:** Dairy products (Meadow Maid powdered milk and powdered ice cream mix (predigested & lactose-free), various mixes (cakes, muffins, pancakes, cookies, wholewheat and oat bread), Vita-mac pasta (vegetable protein with amino acid balance), food replacements and protein and isotonic drinks. **Other:** Asserted 50% organic. Special prices for container or truck load lots or private label customers. Minimum order for most products 2000 lbs.

Newport Beach, **Pure Sales Inc.,** PO Box 8708-702, Newport Beach, CA 92658. (714) 540-5455. **Type of Business:** Broker to manufacturers and distributors, import/export company. **Sells:** Gourmet and grocery sauces; grocery pasta, snacks and confections. **Other:** Bulk order discounts. All sales are F.O.B. WHSE; five-day lead time for pick-up. Minimum order is $1,000. Catalogue Available. 25% of goods are organically produced; site visits are made to the premises of producers.

North Hollywood, **R & R Distribution Systems,** 7525 Ethel Avenue, Units B & C., North Hollywood, CA 91605. (818) 982-1020. **Type of Business:** Manufacturer and distributor. **Sells:** Dried fruit, fresh fruit, grains, meats, nuts, seafood, spices, vegetables, bread, cereals, pasta, rice. **Other:** Asserted 50% organic overall. Minimum order is $50.

Oakland, **Alfalfa Omega Express Inc.,** Jaye Preston, Officer, 5427 U. Telegraph Ave., Oakland, CA 94609. (415) 655-2918.

Oakland, **All Organic Produce and Supply,** Joe Blackburn, Michael Mahlanga, Chris Neiman, 368 2nd Street, Oakland, CA 94607. (415) 465-6169. **Type of Business:** Distributor. **Sells to:** Retailers. **Sells:** Dried beans, dried fruits, fresh fruits, grains, herbs, nuts and nut butters, oils, seeds, vegetables and tools of the trade. **Organic?** Asserted 100% organic, member of CCOF.

Ojai, **Highwinds Ranch,** James Rush, PO Box 1294, Ojai, CA 93023. (805) 525-3064. **Type of Business:** Grower and packer. **Sells to:** Retailers only. **Sells:** Fresh fruit (apricots, grapefruit, lemons, oranges), dried apricots, and avocados. **Other:** CCOF certified 100% organic. Buyer normally pays contract trucker $1 per box of fruit delivered to Los Angeles. Minimum order is 1 box.

Orland, **Family Farms,** Wyo Avenue/Road 9, Orland, CA 95963. (916) 865-3865. **Type of Business:** Producer and distributor, since 1982. **Sells to:** Retailers. **Sells:** Organic whole grains (popcorn, wheat, corn), flours and meals (wheat flour, corn meal). **Other:** Certified organic, grown and processed under Section 26569.11 of the California Health and Safety Code, member of CCOF.

Orosi, **Ecology Sound Farms,** 42126 Road 168, Orosi, CA 93467. (209) 528-3816. **Type of Business:** Producer and distributor, since 1968. **Sells to:** Mainly to retailers. **Sells:** Organic fresh produce (navel oranges, kiwifruit, plums, persimmons, asian pears), garlic, nuts, seeds, dried fruit, beans. **Other:** Certified Organic, member of CCOF. They ship at all hours 6 days a week. Minimum order is 1 box. Mail-order catalogue available.

Pacoima, **Natural Oil Imports,** 12350-G Montague St., Pacoima, CA 91331. (818) 897-0536. **Type of Business:** Manufacturer and distributor. **Sells:** Exotic oils. **Other:** Minimum order is one gallon. Catalogue available upon request.

Pescadero, **Jacobs Farm,** Box 508, Pescadero, CA 94060. (415) 879-0508, Fax: (415) 879-0930. **Type of Business:** Grower. **Sells to:** Retailers, distributors, restaurants and the public through farmers markets and mail order. **Sells:** fresh herbs (basil, chives, dill, oregano, parsley, sage, rosemary and thyme), fresh vegetables (English pod peas, sugar snap peas, artichokes, kale, collards, mache, tomatoes), fresh edible flowers. **Other:** Certified and documented 100% organic by CCOF and Merchandising Natural Foods. Hours are 8 a.m.-4 p.m. Answering machine takes order at other times. Minimum order is $50 for mail order.

Petaluma, **Spectrum Marketing, Inc.,** John Goodman, Jethren Phillips, 133 Copeland St., Petaluma, CA 94952. (707) 778-8900, Fax: (707) 765-1026. **Type of Business:** Distributor. **Sells to:** Retailers. **Sells:** Low-fat, low-sodium raw milk, and oils (bean, corn, olive, safflower, sesame, sunflower, and organic oils). **Other:** Asserted organic, to be labelled the product must have a bona fide certification by FVO, CCOF, or OCIA.

Richgrove, **Stephen Pavich & Sons,** Famosa Port Highway and Ave. 4, Richgrove, CA 93261. Mail to: Route 2, Box 291, Delano, CA 93215. (805) 725-1046. **Type of Business:** Grower and distributor, since 1953. **Sells to:** Retailers. **Sells:** Fresh fruits (table grapes and melons), fresh vegetables (squash). **Other:** Certified 100% Organic, member of CCOF. Sales are in pallet quantities.

Riverside, **Natural Choice,** 5015 Canyon Crest Dr. # 107-A, Riverside, CA 92507. (714) 683-4427. **Type of Business:** Distributor. **Sells:** Fresh organically grown fruits and vegetables. They specialize in citrus, avocados, exotic fruits. **Other:** Minimum order, 42 cartons.

San Francisco, **Pacific Soybean & Grain,** 495 De Haro St., San Francisco, CA 94107. (415) 863-0867. **Type of Business:** Distributor. **Sells to:** Retailers. **Sells:** Soybeans, alfalfa. **Other:** Asserted 25% organic. Minimum order is $2,000.

San Francisco, **Sierra Natural Foods,** Ryan Sarnataro, 1330 Fitzgerald Ave., San Francisco, CA 94124. (415) 822-1800. **Type of Business:** Distributor. **Sells to:** Retailers, mail order. **Sells:** Condiments, dairy products (North

Farm cheese), dried beans, dried fruit, whole grains, flours and meals, processed grain products, juices, almond butter, olive oil (Spectrum), sunflower seeds, soy products, sweeteners (honey, maple syrup, brown rice malt syrup). **Other:** They screen the products they label as organic quite rigorously and insist on affidavits as well as certification by CCOF, FVO or Eden Foods.◆◆

San Rafael, **Fowler Brothers,** PO Box 2324, San Rafael, CA 94912. (415) 459-3406. **Type of Business:** Distributor. **Sells to:** Retailers. **Sells:** Baked goods, coffee, condiments, dried beans, dried fruit, fresh fruit, whole grains, flours and meals, processed grain products, juices, nuts and nut butters, oils, seeds, soy products, sweeteners, fresh vegetables, fruit conserves, apple sauce, pickles, granola, chips, rice cakes. **Organic?** Products are certified organic; the business is a member of CCOF and buys products certified by CCOF, FVO, OCIA, and Tilth.◆◆

Santa Barbara, **Exotic Progression Co.,** PO Box 4584, Santa Barbara, CA 93140. (805) 969-1903. **Type of Business:** Wholesale distributor. **Sells:** Baked goods, bread, fruit juice, pasta. **Other:** Minimum order $30. Catalogue available upon request.

Santa Cruz, **Falcon Trading Co., Inc.,** 1955 17th Ave., Santa Cruz, CA 95062. (408) 462-1280. **Type of Business:** Manufacturer and Distributor. **Sells to:** Retailers. **Sells:** A full line of organic whole-wheat pastas, organically grown beans, nut, grain and dried fruit. **Other:** Minimum order on established truck routes—other carriers please inquire.◆◆

Santa Monica, **Soy Power,** 1602 Stanford St., Santa Monica, CA 90404. (213) 829-2331, Fax: (213) 829-1266. **Type of Business:** Wholesale distributor. **Sells:** Soy and other whole-food products. **Other:** They assert that 75% of the products they sell are organic. Minimum order is $125. Catalogue available on request.

Torrance, **Nature's Best,** 19801 S Vermont, Torrance, CA 90502. (213) 327-4244. (800) 765-3141. **Type of Business:** Distributor. **Sells to:** Commercial retailers. **Sells:** A wide variety of wholefoods items by major and minor manufacturers (plus cosmetics and other household items). **Other:** Minimum order is $350. They distribute will-call and through UPS.◆◆◆

Watsonville, **Coke Farm 89,** Madelene, Dale, 17245 Tarpey Rd., Watsonville, CA 95076. (408) 726-3100, Fax: (408) 726-3136. **Type of Business:** Grower. **Sells to:** Retailers. **Sells:** Organic fresh vegetables: Beets, broccoli, cabbage, carrots, cauliflower, celery, corn, cucumbers, garlic, many varieties of lettuce, arugula, bokchoi, chard, cress, dandelion, endive, fennel, kohl rabi, leeks, radichio, onions, tomatoes, squash, zucchini, and more. **Other:** Certified organic (100%-CCOF). Minimum order is $300. They have been growing organically on the central coast since 1981.

Watsonville, **Organic Matters Produce Co.,** Peter Young, 303 Salinas Road, Watsonville, CA 95076. (408) 728-0644. **Type of Business:** Distributor **Sells to:** Retailers

Sells: Dairy products and eggs, dried fruit, fresh fruit, nuts and nut butters, soy products, maple syrup, fresh vegetables. **Other:** Asserted organic (90%).

Woodland, **Yocal Produce Cooperative Inc.,** Chris Hardor or Patricia Echevarria, PO Box 411, Woodland, CA 95695. (916) 668-0701, Fax: (916) 668-0704. **Type of Business:** Distributor. **Sells to:** Retailers and wholesalers. **Sells:** Dried fruit, fresh fruit, fresh vegetables, breads, juices, nuts and nut butters, soy products and spices. **Other:** Asserted 95-100% organic, CCOF certified. Preorders are necessary; they rarely sell direct from stock. No minimum order.

Valley Center, **Valley Center Packing Co. Inc.,** Rocky Calamia or Rudy Monica. **Type of Business:** Grower. **Sells to:** Retailers, mail order to all of the U.S., Canada, Europe, and Japan. **Sells:** Fresh fruit (valencias, navels, grapefuit, lemons, avocadoes). **Other:** Asserted 90% organic. Minimum order is 1 pallet 42 boxes.

Colorado

Denver, **Rainbow Natural Foods Distributing,** 4613 Monaco Parkway, Denver, CO 80216. Offices (303) 320-5459, sales (303) 320-5441, (800) 333-RNFD. They also have a dock in Los Angeles. **Type of Business:** Distributor. **Sells to:** Retailers. **Sells:** Baked goods, coffee, condiments, dairy products, dried beans, dried fruit, fresh fruit (large seasonal selection), whole grains, flours and meals, processed grain products, baking ingredients, mixes, cereals, pastas, herbs and spices, juices, nuts and nut butters, oils, seeds, soy products, sweeteners, teas, fresh vegetables, frozen meat and poultry, jams, sauces, salad dressings, soups, and macrobiotic products. **Other:** They assert that 20% of the goods they sell are organic. Most produce is COPA certified. Volume discounts available. Restricted delivery by truck. Minimum order is $200-$400 depending on location.◆◆◆

Johnstown, **Rieder Brothers,** 23455 WCR 17, Johnstown, CO 80534. (303) 587-4863. **Type of Business:** Grower and distributor. **Sells to:** Primarily to retailers, with some sales to the public. **Sells:** Fresh organic vegetables (including potatoes, onions, beets, peppers, broccoli, carrots, turnips, peas, corn, spinach, squash, lettuce, green beans and leeks). **Other:** Certified 100% organic; member of COPA. If far enough away, they will ship by air-freight. Minimum order is enough to fill one freight unit.

Florida

Edgewater, **Tropical Blossom Honey Co., Inc.,** 106 N Ridgewood Ave., PO Box 8, Edgewater, FL 32132. (904) 428-9027. **Type of Business:** Wholesale distributor. **Sells:** Honey. **Other:** No minimum order; catalogue available upon request.

Fort Lauderdale, **Vitality Distributors, Inc.,** 1010 NW 51 Pl., Fort Lauderdale, FL 33309. (305) 771-0445. **Type of Business:** Distributor. **Sells:** Beans, dairy products, dried fruit, grains, nuts, soy products, baked goods, bread, cereals, flour, oils, rice, pasta. **Other:** Minimum order $250 for free delivery in Southeast U.S. Catalogue available.

Miami, **Natural Food Wholesalers**, 2031 NW 89th Pl., Miami, FL 33172. (305) 594–1041. **Type of Business:** Distributor. **Sells:** Natural foods and cosmetics. **Other:** Minimum order $150.00. Catalogue available upon request.♦♦♦

St. Augustine, **Tree of Life Corp.**, 27 Styertown Rd, St. Augustine, FL 32085. Mail to: PO Box 410, St. Augustine, FL 32085. (904) 824–8181. **Type of Business:** The largest distributor of natural foods in the United States. They also manufacture some of their own products. **Sells to:** Retailers. **Sells:** Baked goods, condiments, dried beans, dried fruit, fresh fruit, processed grain products, herbs and spices, juices, nuts and nut butters, oils, seeds, soy products, sweeteners. **Other:** Member of FVO. Tomatoes, carrots, and garlic ingredients are organically grown in accordance with California Health and Safety Code, section 26569.11. Minimum order is $150. **Comments:** Tree of Life got the most recommendations of any company in our survey. It is a subsidiary of Wassanen, a conglomerate based in Amsterdam, The Netherlands.♥♦♦♦♦

Hawaii

Wailuku, **Maui Style Wholesale Natural Foods**, 250-S Waiehu Beach Rd., Wailuku, HI 96793. (808) 242–4797. **Type of Business:** Distributor. **Sells:** A wide variety of natural foods and fresh produce. **Other:** Asserted 10% organic. Minimum order $100 at wholesale location. Catalogue must be picked up.

Illinois

Algonquin, **Strathmore Farm**, 2400 Spring Creek Road, Algonquin, IL 60102. (312) 550–5077, (312) 658–8200. **Type of Business:** Producer and distributor, since 1966. **Sells to:** Retailers. **Sells:** Dried beans (clear hilium soybeans, black soybeans, adzuki beans), whole grains (soft red and soft white winter wheat, hard red spring wheat, popcorn, field corn, oats), meat (USDA-inspected Black Angus beef). **Other:** Certified by the Organic Growers and Buyers Association (OGBA). Pesticide-free farm since 1976. No drugs or antibiotics used. They prefer to ship in bulk and will clean and bag if necessary.

Chicago, **Food Animals Concern Trust (FACT)**, Robert A. Brown, PO Box 14599, Chicago, IL 60614. (312) 525–4952. **Type of Business:** Distributor, since 1982. **Sells to:** Retailers. **Sells:** Meat and eggs: nest eggs from uncaged layers, Rambling Rose Brand free-range veal. Products raised with humane husbandry.

Chicago, **Health Foods Inc**, Jim Zedella, President, 155 Old Higgins Rd, Chicago, IL 60018. (312) 298–8220.♦♦♦

Indiana

Ft. Wayne, **Zahki Foods**, 272–4 Lofty Drive, Ft. Wayne, IN 46808. (219) 432–7122. **Type of Business:** Distributor, since 1981. **Sells to:** Retailers. **Sells:** Condiments, fresh fruit, processed grain products, juices, soy products, fresh vegetables. **Other:** Asserted 25% organic overall.

Iowa

Iowa City, **Blooming Prairie Warehouse**, 2340 Heinz Road, Iowa City, IA 52240. (319) 337–6448. Sue Futrell is Marketing Manager, shares time with Minneapolis office of Blooming Prairie. **Type of Business:** Organic wholesaler. **Sells to:** Cooperatives and small distributors. **Sells:** Organic produce.♥♦♦♦

Norway, **Frontier Cooperative Herbs**, PO Box 69, Norway, IA 52318. (319) 227–7991. **Type of Business:** Distributor. **Sells to:** Retailers. **Sells:** Herbs, spices, teas, and coffees. **Other:** Certification varies. Minimum order is $20.♦♦

Maryland

Beltsville, **Organic Farms, Inc.**, 10714 Hanna, Beltsville, MD 20705. (301) 595–5151.**Type of Business:** Distributor and manufacturer. **Sells to:** Retailers. **Sells:** Baked goods, coffee, condiments, dairy products and eggs, dried beans, dried fruit, fresh fruit, whole grains, flour and meals, processed grain products, fresh herbs and spices, juices, nuts and nut butters, oils, seeds, soy products, sweeteners, fresh vegetables, frozen fruit and vegetables, wine and beer. **Other:** Asserted 100% organic. OFI is discussing providing organic food to supermarket chains, including A&P, ShopRite, Grand Union and Pathmark.♦♦♦

Massachusetts

Foxboro, **All Natural Sales**, 11 Perry Rd., Foxboro, MA 02035. (508) 543–1160. **Type of Business:** Wholesaler and distributor. **Sells:** A range of grocery items including baked goods, legumes, vegetable juices, soy products, and oils **Other:** They assert that about 50% of their products are organic. Minimum order is $100 Northeast, $150 outside Northeast.♦

Great Barrington, **Berkshire Morganicus, Inc.**, PO Box 896, Great Barrington, MA 01230. (413) 528–9057. **Type of Business:** Organic foods distributor and wholesale outlet. **Sells:** A wide range of organic and/or biodynamic foods many made by local producers, including bread, beans, dairy products, dried fruit, pasta, rice, soy products, nuts, and fresh vegetables. **Other:** They assert that 100% of their products are organic (most certified by NOFA). They serve Connecticut and Southeastern New York (including NYC and Long Island) by truck. Minimum order is $100.

Michigan

Ann Arbor, **Daily Grind Flour Mill** (affiliated with the Michigan Federation of Food Co-ops), Tom Burkman, 220 Felch St., Ann Arbor, MI 48103. (313) 665–3845. **Type of Business:** Distributor, since 1972. **Sells to:** Retailers, other distributors. **Sells:** Whole grains (soft winter wheat/white, hard red winter wheat, and hard red spring wheat, whole corn, oats, pearled barley, hulled barley, whole buckwheat (hulled and unhulled), durum wheat, rye, millet). Grains as flours. **Other:** Asserted 98% organic. Certification has to follow the standards of the Organic Growers of Michigan. Minimum order is 500 units of any one product, 1,000 units of any combination of flour or grain, and 2,000 units from a supplier.

Ann Arbor, **Midwest Natural Foods,** 170 April Dr., Ann Arbor, MI 48103. Mail to: Box 1186 Ann Arbor, MI 48106. (313) 769–8444. **Type of Business:** Distributor, since 1971. **Sells to:** Retailers. **Sells:** Baked goods, condiments, dried beans, dried fruit, processed grain products, herbs and spices, juices, nuts and nut butters, oils, seeds, soy products, sweeteners. **Other:** Asserted organic.♦♦

Clinton, **Eden Foods,** 701 Tecumseh Rd., Clinton, MI 49236. (800) 248–0301. **Type of Business:** Distributor. **Sells to:** Retailers. **Sells:** Condiments (organic shoyu soy sauce), dried beans (dried and packaged in glass), whole grains, flours and meals, processed grain products (salt-free whole grain pasta). **Other:** Eden's in-house certification program recently merged with OCIA.

Okemos, **Purity Foods Inc.,** 4211 Okemos Rd. Suite 21, Okemos, MI 48864. (517) 349–7941, (517) 349–7942, (517) 349–7943, (517) 349–2262. **Type of Business:** Manufacturer. **Sells to:** Retailers and other distributors. **Sells:** Bulk beans, dried fruits (imported organic apricots, figs, raisins (sultanas), nuts (imported hazelnuts from Turkey), seeds; baby food; linseed oil; macrobiotic products. **Other:** Goods are certified organic through the independent ERNTEDANK organic program.

Pullman, **Country Life Natural Foods (Oakhaven Inc.-,** 109 52nd Ave, Pullman, MI 49450. (616) 236–5011. **Type of Business:** Manufacturer and wholesale distributor. **Sells:** Cereals, flours, dried fruits, pasta, oils, soy products, nuts, and beans. **Other:** They assert that 20% of their products are organic. They serve only Michigan, Illinois, and Wisconsin. Minimum order is $50 at warehouse, $250 for delivery. They also operate a restaurant in Kalamazoo.

St. Lawrence, **Sunshower,** 48548 60th St., St. Lawrence, MI 49064. (616) 674–3103. **Type of Business:** Producer and distributor, since 1971. **Sells to:** Retailers. **Sells:** Bulk cereals, grains, juices, preserves, jams, jellies, dairy products, fresh fruit, seitan, herbs and spices, juices, fresh vegetables, and lamb. **Other:** Asserted organic; member of Organic Growers of Michigan Corp.

Sault Ste. Marie, **Haypoint Farm,** Sue Raker, Box 292, Sugar Island, Sault Ste. Marie, MI 49783. (906) 632–1280. **Type of Business:** Producer and distributor, since 1985. **Sells to:** Retailers, mail order (garlic only) and to the public through the farm and a Saturday market at Sault Ste. Marie, July-Sept. **Sells:** Fresh apples, teas, cider, spices, herbs, edible flowers, lamb, garlic, lettuce, honey, apple butter and maple syrup. **Other:** They assert that their produce is 100% organic; they use Tilth, FVO and NOFA organic standards. They are licensed by the Michigan Dept. of Agriculture and will take orders 24 hours a day. They prefer to sell by the case to restaurants, buying clubs, etc. but tailor to needs of customers.

Taylor, **Safe Foods Inc.,** Joseph T. Rogers, 20189 Northline, Taylor, MI 48180. (313) 287–2131. **Type of Business:** Wholesale food distributor. **Sells to:** Retailers. **Sells:**

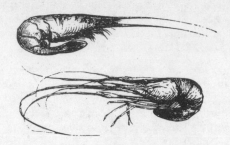

Grains, beans, seafood (shrimp, trout), brown rice, popcorn, fresh fruit (apples, blueberries, grapefruit, melons, nectarines, oranges, strawberries), pecans, vegetables (beets, broccoli, cabbage, carrots, cauliflower, corn, cucumbers, lettuce, garlic, onions, peas, peppers, potatoes, radishes, spinach, squash, tomatoes, zucchini). **Other:** Asserted 100% organic. Special prices for brokers. Deliveries to Michigan, Ohio, Indiana. Minimum order is $100 or more depending on location.

Minnesota

Caledonia, **Sno-Pac Foods,** 379 S Pine St., Caledonia, MN 55921. (507) 724–5281. **Type of Business:** Manufacturer, retail store, co-op and mail order distributor. **Sells to:** Mainly retailers and distributors. **Sells:** Peas, sweet corn, broccoli, cauliflower, green beans. **Other:** Asserted 90% organic. They will ship by Airfreight anywhere in the U.S. but they prefer that customers buy from distributors.

East Bethel, **Nomadic Organics,** 22921 NE Johnson St., East Bethel, MN 55005. (612) 434–8557, Fax: (612) 434–3307. **Type of Business:** Organic wholesaler, distributor, and broker. **Sells:** Organic fruits, vegetables, dried fruit, nuts, and assorted grocery items. **Other:** They assert that 99% of their produce is organic, 1% transitional. Mail order available everywhere UPS goes. Minimum order $100. Orders are shipped the next day if in stock, otherwise in no more than 7 days.

Minneapolis, **Blooming Prairie Natural Foods,** 510 Kasota Ave., SE, Minneapolis, MN 55414. (612) 378–9774. See entry for Iowa City, IA above. Set up under the auspices of Blooming Prairie in Iowa City, and shares senior staff. Sells rice, beans, flour.♥♦♦♦

Minneapolis, **Roots and Fruits Cooperative Produce,** Jo Elliott, 510 Kasota Ave., Minneapolis, MN 55414. (612) 379–3030, Fax: (612) 379–0280. **Type of Business:** Distributor. **Sells to:** Retailers. **Sells:** Coffee, fresh fruit, fresh herbs, soy products, fresh vegetables, cheese. **Other:** Asserted 10% organic, produce certified by OBGA (Organic Buyers and Growers Association) and CCOF. Minimum order is $100.♦♦

Osage, **IKWE Marketing Company,** Margaret Smith, Box 183, Osage, MN 56570. **Type of Business:** Producer and distributor. **Sells to:** Retailers. **Sells:** Whole grains (wild rice, native harvest lake rice—organic certified). **Other:** Asserted 50% organic, member of Minnesota Organic Growers and Buyers Association.

Winona, **Little Bear Trading Co., Inc.**, 226 E. Second St., Winona, MN 55987. (507) 452-6332. Type of Business: Manufacturer and Distributor, since 1975. Sells to: Retailers. Sells: Baked goods (bagels and croissants), fresh and processed beans, cereals, flour (rye and whole wheat), whole wheat noodles, rice, grains and veggie-burger mix. Other: Documented organic, OFPANA standards. Warehouse hours are 8–4. Shipping usually takes 15 days. Minimum order is $2,000 or 5,000 units.

Montana

Big Sandy, **Montana Flour & Grains**, Bob Quinn, Dave Arsenault, Ferry Route, Box 808, Big Sandy, MT 59520. (406) 378 3105. Type of Business: Grower. Sells to: Retailers. Sells: Whole grains (hard red winter and spring wheat, hard and soft white wheat, durum, hull-less barley, hull-less oats, rye, triticale) a 7 grain mix; and kamut, an ancient wheat.) They also sell 100 stone ground whole grain flour from above grains. Other: Asserted 80% organic (OCIA). Most orders are C.O.D. or net 15 days with approved credit.

Corwin Springs, **Royal Teton Ranch**, Box A, Corwin Springs, MT 59021. Type of Business: Grower. Sells: Grains and legumes (dried peas), eggs, meat, fresh vegetables (carrots, potatoes, cabbage, winter squash, beets). Other: Asserted organic (100%). Minimum Order is $200.

Nebraska

Oshkosh, **M & M Distributing**, Mark and Marcy Jones, R.R. 2, PO Box 61-A, Oshkosh, NE 69154. (308) 772-3664. Type of Business: Distributor. Sells to: Retailers, mail order. Sells: Whole grains (amaranth on a large scale, blue corn). Other: Asserted organic (100%).

New Hampshire

Chesterfield, **Stow Mills**. Type of Business: Distributor.♦♦♦ Stow Mills declined to answer any of our queries.

New Jersey

Carlstadt, **Liberty Imports Inc.**, Michell Paetzold-Health Foods Product Manager, 400 Commerce Boulevard, Carlstadt, NJ 07072. (201) 935-6850. Type of Business: Importer. Sells to: Distributors. Sells: Gourmet-health beverages, condiments, coffee substitutes, vegetarian pâtés, and pattie mixes, soups, crackers, cookies and candy. Other: No organic claims. Minimum order is $600 FOB.

Williamstown, **Health Is Wealth Inc.**, Sykes Lane, Williamstown, NJ 08094. (609) 728-1998. Sells: soybean-fed hormone-free chicken and turkey, chicken franks.

New York

Jacksonville, **Finger Lakes Organics (FLO)**, PO Box 549, Jacksonville, NY 14854. (607) 387-3333. Type of Business: Distributor since 1986. Sells to: Retailers. Sells: Fresh fruit, whole grains, fresh herbs, fresh vegetables. Other: Asserted 100% organic. All FLO members NY-NOFA certified. Minimum order depends on delivery distance/route.

Rochester, **Cinagro Produce**, Bob Berch, 166 Public Market, Rochester, NY 14609. (716) 232-6824. Type of Business: Distributor. Sells to: Retailers. Sells: Coffee, dairy products, dried beans, dried fruit, fresh fruit, whole grains, flours and meals, processed grain products, juices, nut and nut butters, seeds, soy products, fresh vegetables. Other: Asserted organic 20%.

North Carolina

Asheville, **Fairglen Farms**, Jim Smith, W.N.C. Farmers Mkt., 570 Brevard Rd., Asheville, NC 28806. (704) 252-4414. Type of Business: Growers—a collection of small mountain farms in western North Carolina. Sells to: Retailers. Sells: Herbs and spices (fresh culinary, fresh ginger), fresh vegetables. Other: Certified organic (Carolina Farm Stewardship).

Asheville, **Great Eastern Sun**, 92 McIntosh Rd., Asheville, NC 28806. (704) 252-3090, (800) 334-5809, (704) 667-8051. Type of Business: Distributor. Sells to: Retailers. Sells: Coffees, teas, grain beverages, snacks, confections, soy products, and macrobiotic products.

Asheville, **The Macrobiotic Wholesale Company**, Bill Fass, 799 Old Leicester Hwy., Asheville, NC 28806. (704) 252-1221. Type of Business: Distributor. Sells to: Retailers. Sells: Coffee, condiments, dried beans, dried fruit, whole grains, flours and meals, processed grain products, herbs and spices, oils, soy products, sweeteners, teas. Other: Asserted 83% organic. First order is C.O.D.

Charlotte, **Tropical Nut & Fruit**, Betty York, PO Box 7507, Charlotte, NC 28214. (704) 588-0400, (800) 438-4470, (800) 532-0414. Type of Business: Distributor. Sells to: Retailers. Sells: Dried beans, dried fruits, whole grains, flours, processed grain products (cereals, pastas), nuts, snack mixes, spices, seeds. Other: Asserted 5% organic.

Durham, **Mountain Warehouse**, Peggie Gunn, Chris Kirkman, 305 S. Dillard St., Durham, NC 27701. (919) 682-9234. Type of Business: Distributor. Sells to: Retailers. Sells: Coffee, dried beans, dried fruit, whole grains, flour and meals, processed grain products, herbs and spices, juices, nut butters, oils, seeds, soy products, sweeteners. Other: Asserted 15% organic. Minimum order is $350.♦♦

Henderson, **Carolina Agro-Tech Corporation**, Marlene Smith, Jack Lebby, Toby Farris, Route 5 Box 84E, Henderson, NC 27536. Type of Business: Manufacturer and distributor. Sells to: Retailers. Sells: Herbs and spices, shiitake and oyster mushrooms, dried and fresh. Other: Certified 100% organic by Carolina Farm Stewardship. Minimum Order is $45.

Rutherfordton, **The American Miso Co. Rt.3**, PO Box 541, Rutherfordton, NC 28139. (704) 287-2840. Type of Business: Distributor. Sells to: Retailers. Sells: Gourmet soups, macrobiotic products, soups, soy products, and refrigerated and frozen soy products.

North Dakota

Butte, **F.U.T.U.R.E. Organic Inc.,** PO Box 228, Butte, ND 58723. (701) 626-7360. **Type of Business:** Grain distributor and processor. **Sells to:** Retailers. **Sells:** Whole grains, processed grain products. Presently developing organic chicken feed. **Other:** Certified organic (90%-OCIA, OGBA). Minimum order is one 50 lb. bag.

Ohio

Toledo, **Toledo Natural Foods Inc.,** 3040-G Hill Ave., Toledo, OH 43607-2931. (419) 537-1713. **Type of Business:** Wholesaler. **Sells to:** Retailers. **Sells:** A wide variety of products from dried fruits, nuts-raw and roasted, candies, popcorn, beans, rice, sesame products, oat bran, soup mixes, and macaroni products. **Other:** Only two products of Natural Foods are organic: Organic Raisin and Organic Oat Bran. Shipping is done through UPS and their own Truck Line. They do not deliver to Alaska or Hawaii.

Oregon

Broadbent, **R. Ransdell,** PO Box 155, Broadbent, OR 97414. (503) 572-5564. **Type of Business:** Distributor. **Sells to:** Retailers. **Sells:** Livestock, grains, produce. **Other:** Certified organic.

Eugene, **Cowboy Produce,** 444 Lincoln Street, Eugene, OR 97401. (503) 343-6581. **Type of Business:** Broker and commission merchant. **Sells to:** Wholesalers, retailers, and other distributors. **Sells:** Organically grown fresh fruits and vegetables. Also juices and processed fruits and vegetables. **Other:** Asserted 100% organic, produce is certified by CCOF. Minimum order is one pallet.

Eugene, **Organically Grown Co-op,** 2545 Prairie Road, Suite I, Eugene, OR 97402. (503) 689-5320. **Type of Business:** Producer, wholesaler, and distributor. **Sells:** 150 or so varieties of fresh organic fruits and vegetables. **Other:** Their products are sold under the "Ladybug" brand name. Produce is certified by Tilth, CCOF, or Washington State. They service only Oregon. Minimum order is $150.

Pennsylvania

Ivyland, **Neshaminy Valley Natural Foods Distributor Ltd.,** 5 Louise Drive, Ivyland, PA 18974. (215) 443-5545. FAX: (215) 443-7087. **Type of Business:** Distributor. **Sells to:** Retailers and buying clubs. **Sells:** Beans (all certified organic), cereals, flour, grains, breads, baked goods, dried fruit, fruit juices, oils, pasta, rice, fresh fruit and vegetables, dairy products, soy products, nuts and nut butters, beverages, candy and sweeteners. **Other:** Asserted 33% organic (CCOF). Orders must be placed by 4 p.m. two days before the truck is due in your area; changes in the order can be made up to 12 noon the day before the due date. Minimum order is $250-$400 depending on shipping area.♦♦♦

Mansfield, **Krystal Wharf Farms,** RD 2, Box 191 A, Mansfield, PA 16933. (717) 549-8194. **Type of Business:** Distributor and mail order distributor. **Sells to:** Mainly retailers. **Sells:** Organically grown fruit and vegetables. Also

wildcrafted herbs. **Other:** They have truck routes in Eastern Pennsylvania, parts of New Jersey, and western upstate New York. Their mail order business has been growing rapidly.

New Holland, **Garden Spot Distributors,** 438 White Oak Road, Box 729 A, New Holland, PA 17557. (717) 354-4936. **Type of Business:** Distributor. **Sells to:** Retailers, distributors, mail order. **Sells:** Baked goods, condiments, dairy products, dried beans, dried fruit, whole grains, flours and meals, processed grain products, herbs, juices, meat, nuts and nut butters, oils, seeds, soy products, sweeteners, teas. **Certification:** Asserted 70% organic, produce certified by OCIA.♦♦

Rhode Island

Coventry, **Cornucopia Natural Food,** Norman Cloutier, President, 8 Industrial Drive, Coventry, RI 02816. (401) 822-2300. **Type of Business:** One of the three largest distributors of wholefoods on the East Coast. **Sells to:** Retailers. **Sells:** Baked goods, condiments, dairy products, dried beans, dried fruit, whole grains, flours and meals, processed grain products, juices, nuts and nut butters, oils, seeds, soy products, fresh vegetables. **Other:** They assert that 15% of their products are organic.♦♦♦

Texas

Austin, **Texas Health Distributors,** Tom Calzone (President), 501 Waller, Austin, TX 78702. (512) 473-2173. **Type of Business:** Distributor. **Sells to:** Retailers. **Sells:** Dried beans, grains, cereals, flour, pasta, rice, pita bread, dried fruit, juices, nuts and nut butters, oils, seeds, fresh fruit and vegetables, dairy products, soy products, baked goods, beverages and spices. **Other:** Asserted 50-60% organic. Certified by Texas Department of Agriculture. 10% discount available for bulk orders. Only services states of Texas and Louisiana. $250 for pick-ups and $1,000 for deliveries.♦

Vermont

Brattleboro, **Northeast Cooperatives,** PO Box 1120, Quinn Road, Brattleboro, VT 05301. (802) 257-5856 in VT (Main warehouse), (617) 389-9032 in MA (produce). **Type of Business:** Distributor. **Sells to:** Retailers, buying clubs. **Sells:** Coffee, dairy products and eggs, dried beans, dried fruit, fresh fruit, whole grains, flour, meals, processed grain products, herbs and spices, juices, nuts and nut butters, oils, seeds, soy products, sweeteners, teas, fresh vegetables. **Other:** Asserted 35% organic, suppliers must provide papers. Minimum order is $400.♦♦

East Hardwick, **Vermont Northern Growers Co-op,** Box 125, East Hardwick, VT 05836. (802) 472-6285. **Type of Business:** Marketing co-op. **Sells:** Organically grown storage vegetables including beets, cabbage, carrots, celery, onions, potatoes, rutabagas, and turnips. **Other:** Asserted 100% organic, all growers certified by Vermont Organic Farmers Association (VOFA). They will arrange trucking anywhere in New England and have shipped as far away as Chicago. They do UPS shipments on Mondays. Minimum order is one 25 lb. bag. Special prices for ton pallets of root crops.

Virginia

Warrenton, **Hatch Natural Foods Corporation,** Robert Wagg, PO Box 888, Warrenton, VA 22186. (703) 987-8551. **Type of Business:** Distributor. **Sells to:** Retailers, buying clubs, co-ops, restaurants, and individuals. **Sells:** A complete assortment of grocery items (including dairy products) and organic produce. **Other:** They are a 20-year--old company, and assert that about 50% of the goods they sell are organically grown and processed. They truck to areas in the Mid-Atlantic region from Pennsylvania to North Carolina. Minimum order $300 for delivery, $50 for pick-up. Requires 2-day lead time for trucking orders, 10-day for UPS. They also have a monthly sales flyer.

Washington

Bremerton, **GMT Inc.,** 245 4th Street, #410, Bremerton, WA 98310. (206) 479-6576. **Type of Business:** Importer and broker. **Sells to:** Retailers, restaurants, and manufacturers. **Sells:** Beans (lentils, pinto, soy, split green, lima, navy and chick peas), grains (barley, popcorn, couscous, oats, rice), rye and wholewheat flour and soybean milk. **Other:** Overall about 50% of products are organic, certified by SGS, CICC and CIO. All prices are direct from manufacturer; special prices available for orders of full container loads. Minimum order is one full container load.

Olympia, **Farmers Wholesale Cooperative,** PO Box 7446, Olympia, WA 98507. (206) 754-8989. **Type of Business:** Farmer-owned cooperative. **Sells to:** Distributors. **Sells:** A wide selection of fresh organic vegetables and some organic fruit. **Other:** Asserted 100% organic. Most of their growers are certified by Washington State. They send weekly trucks to Los Angeles, San Francisco, Chicago, Minneapolis, and Beltsville. They will try to arrange shipping for customers outside current shipping areas. They also do some air shipping. Orders shipped 2 days after received. They sell under the "Farmer's Own" brand name. Minimum order is 1 pallet or LD3 of product.

Seattle, **Northbest Natural Products,** PO Box, 31029, Seattle, WA 98103. (206) 633-2283. **Type of Business:** Wholesaler and distributor. **Sells:** A range of vegetarian products with no processed sugars, low salt, and no artificial additives or preservatives. **Other:** They assert that about 15% of their products are organic. They offer 24 hour delivery "everywhere." The company has been in business 20 years.

Seattle, **NutraSource,** Chan Beauvais, Senior Buyer, 4005 6th Ave. So., Seattle, WA 98018. (206) 467-7190. Largely owned by Puget Consumers Co-op and employees. **Type of Business:** Wholesaler of organics and wholefoods. **Sells to:** Large distributors.♦♦

CANADA

British Columbia

Penticton, **Marathon Natural Foods Ltd.,** 1375 Commercial Way, Penticton, BC V2A3H4. (604) 493-7887. **Type of Business:** Distributor and wholesaler. **Sells to:** Retailers in Western Canada **Sells:** Breads, beverages, candy, cereals, dairy products, oils, fruit, soy products, and fruit drinks. **Other:** 4% discounts for $350 orders of single product groups. Minimum order is $150.

Vancouver, **Horizon Distributors/CRS,** Gordon Truscott, 3450 Vanness, Vancouver, BC V5R5A9. (604) 439-7977. **Type of Business:** Wholesaler and distributor. **Sells to:** Retailers. **Sells:** Baked goods, beans, beverages, candy, fruit, oils, soy products, flour. **Other:** Asserted 20% organic. They do not sell in the U.S. or Canadian Atlantic Provinces. Minimum order is $150.

Ontario

Markham, **Alpha Basics Corp,** Anne Currie, 271 Amber Street, Markham, ON L3R3J7. **Type of Business:** Distributor **Sells to:** Retailers & Restaurants **Sells:** refrigerated and frozen products, shelf (grocery) goods, bulk, organics, macrobiotics, and "all natural" specialty & gourmet items. **Other:** Asserted 10% organic (CHFA, CSFA). Minimum order is $150.

Markham, **Timbuktu Natural Foods,** 173 Denison Street, Markham, ON L3R1B5. (416) 477-7755. **Type of Business:** Wholesaler and distributor. **Sells to:** Retailers. **Sells:** Beans, cereals, processed and dried fruit, beverages, candy, baked goods, flour, nuts and nut butters, pasta, rice, soy products, and grains. **Other:** Asserted 60% organics. Delivery in 2 Days. Minimum order is $100.

Toronto, **Noor,** 9 Hanna Avenue, Toronto, ON M6K1W8. (416) 537-5695. **Type of Business:** Wholesaler and distributor. **Sells to:** Retail stores. **Sells:** Health foods, oils, and New Age music. **Other:** Asserted 5% organic. Shipping is by UPS, post, or (in the Toronto area) truck.

Quebec

Montreal, **Koyo Foods,** Mark L'Ecuyer, 1213 Montee De Liesse, Montreal, PQ H4S1J7. (514) 745-2500. **Type of Business:** Manufacturer/Distributor. **Sells to:** Canadian retailers. **Sells:** Processed fruits, soy products, and fresh beans. Free of additives and pesticides. **Other:** Minimum order is $200.

Montreal, **Mansa M.B. Inc.,** Jean-Pierre Manzoni, 1258 Sherbrooke East, Montreal, PQ H2L1M1. (514) 691-0926. **Type of Business:** Import, export, and distribution. **Sells to:** Retailers in Canada and the southwestern US including Alaska, and Hawaii. **Sells:** Chips, juices, jam, and 13 varieties of Mansa M.B. oil. **Other:** Asserted 40% organic, certified by Nature Et Progres.

Alfalfa's Market in Littleton, Colorado is one of the premier natural foods markets in the United States. Their two stores (the other is in Boulder) received the third highest total of recommendations in our surveys.

CHAPTER
9

RIDING THE LEVIATHAN

*If the 1980–88 rate continues, by 1993 Americans will spend more money on
eating out than on buying food to cook at home.*

Healthy food will become more accessible as the number of wholefoods stores and healthy-food restaurants grows. That will happen as demand for their products continues to increase (see Table 9–1). Meanwhile, the Leviathan is turning, and wholefoods and organic produce are more widely available in local grocery stores, supermarkets and conventional restaurants.

This chapter is organized in two halves: (1) buying food for eating in, and (2) eating out. The first half is on retail stores (wholefoods and supermarkets), the second half on restaurants (ethnic and fast-food). We begin with a brief review of the trend toward more eating out.

Eating in vs. Eating Out

One reason for paying special attention to restaurants is that more people are eating out. While total spending on food increased from $300 billion in 1980 to $475 billion in 1988, the increase was much higher (76 percent) for food eaten away from home than food eaten at home (42 percent).[1]

If the 1980–88 rate continues, *by 1993 Americans will spend more money on eating (or taking) out than on buying food to cook at home.* But growth was faster in the first half of the 1980s than at the end of the decade, so it may take longer. In 1983–84, fast-food chains grew 7 percent, other restaurants a tad under 5 percent. By the end of the decade, growth slowed to one-third the rate for both.[2]

The trend may be seen in the figures for weekly spending on food. Between 1980 and 1986, average consumer spending on food went from $48.39 a week to $59.60 a week. But during this period the amount spent at home went up only 12.8 percent, while the amount spent away from home went up 46.4 percent.[3]

Young adults under 25 will probably be the first age group to spend more money eating out than eating in.

New data may reveal that this has already happened. The people spending the most on eating out are the 34–44 age group; the ones spending the most eating in are the 45–54 age group.[4]

Wholefood Stores and Small Grocery Stores

Industry Profile. The market for wholefoods grew from about $500 million a year in the early 1970s to total wholefood-store sales of nearly $3.5 billion in 1989[5]—over $2 billion if we exclude supplement sales.[6] Table 9–1 shows some recent figures for wholefood stores, along with some traditional small grocery stores that carry some wholefood products.

Table 9–1
Wholefood Retail Sales, $ billions

Year	Grocery Stores	Wholefood Stores
1984	0.5	2.2
1986	0.6	2.4
1988	0.7	2.9

Source: New Hope Communications, *Natural Foods Merchandiser*, 1989.[7]

Reports of a doubling of demand for organic produce sales in 1989 compared to 1988 are common, and a rapid increase in demand is expected to continue in the 1990s.

Retail stores are the backbone of the wholefood distribution system. In 1965 America had only 500 wholefood stores (then called "health-food" stores and now also commonly called natural-food stores). In 1989, the country had about 7,500 wholefood stores, of which 1,500 were organized into five chains, accounting for more than half (i.e. over $2 billion) of the national wholefood-store business. Only about 150 of the wholefood stores can be considered models of their kind; they do about one-third (i.e., over $1.2 billion) of the business. The seven supermarket-style Bread & Circus stores in Boston and Providence are probably the best model for the future; Mrs. Gooch's in the Los Angeles area is also outstanding and has many devotees.

Wholefoods and Supplements. Most wholefood-store managers are very aware of the need to offer relatively unprocessed food, but many of their customers go for the quick fix—the supplements, which crowd out the additive-free fresh food.

Supplements have a relatively long shelf life and high value-to-weight and value-to-shelf-space ratios. No wonder store managers are tempted to cut back on space devoted to perishables when it is so much easier for them to make a living just selling supplements. Wholefood stores have found out what the supermarkets did years ago, that processed foods are easier to ship, store, and sell; many are choosing the path of least resistance.

Wholefood shoppers are similarly tempted. It's easier to take home some supplements than to pay more attention to what we eat. But the cost of supplements over time can be very high, and most people who eat properly don't need supplements. Supplements may be helpful in certain cases (some doctors will often prescribe them) but super-large doses of some vitamin and iron supplements have on occasion been found to be dangerous. The rash of nearly 1,000 cases of L-tryptophan (an amino acid used as a sleeping pill) poisoning at the end of 1989 is a reminder that, as the *Harvard Medical School Health Letter* warns sternly: "There is nothing natural about consuming half a dozen grams a day of a pure amino acid. And the same industrial processes used to produce drugs are required to produce pure tryptophan in large quantities—processes that are subject to failure or contamination."[8]

The Wholefood Cost Factor. For many people, the current state of the food market sometimes poses a dilemma. The less expensive food (treated to minimize loss and maximize transportability) is often the least healthy; the most healthy might be the most expensive.

Healthier food is not *necessarily* more expensive. Many foods processed with unhealthy doses of sugar and salt added, wrapped in ecologically wasteful aluminum or styrofoam trays, are much more expensive per pound than fresh grains or produce.

Grains and legumes, staples of the healthy diet outlined in this book, are cheaper than the meat or poultry that they can replace. Beans are one of the cheapest foods anyone can buy. Learning to shop for fruits and vegetables in season is an important way to save money.

Where wholesome food is in fact more expensive, the extra cost must be weighed against the health benefits. Given the cost of medical care and the income opportunities given up by someone who is sick or fatigued, healthy food is for most people worth some extra cost. A marketing expert says that consumers are willing to spend twice as much in a wholefood store for an organic item than it would cost (not organic) in a supermarket. A high-volume supermarket, which doesn't have a preselected clientèle receptive to organic produce, can only charge 25 to 30 percent more for organic produce because consumers have ample alternatives available to compare prices to.[9]

The more people who make the healthy food choice, the more food suppliers will compete to provide healthy food, and the same economies of scale that bring down the price of processed foods today will bring down the price of wholefoods tomorrow.

Eliminating intermediaries can save a lot of money. Remember from Chapter 8, the farmer only gets 7 cents of the dollar consumers spend on grain products. In choosing a place to shop or eat at a low cost, we suggest you look for co-ops, which tend to be cheaper than regular stores. Also, look for vegetarian restaurants, which tend to be cheaper than regular restaurants unless they are designed to cater to the upwardly mobile, which will be obvious from the size of their menu and pepper grinders, and the glitziness of their decor.

The Best Wholefood Stores. Based on our survey of specialists in the wholefoods industry, the stores considered outstanding by our respondents are shown in Table 9–2. (The figure in the left-hand column indicates the number of "votes"; two or more votes qualified.) Notice that none of the largest supermarket chains were nominated. But many of the wholefoods stores are run like supermarkets—I would argue that the best of them are in this category. Outstanding models of the wholefood supermarket are Bread & Circus, in the Boston area; Mrs. Gooch's, in southern California, Alfalfa's Market, in Colorado; and Whole Foods, in Texas and Louisiana, and northern California.

Table 9–2
America's Outstanding Wholefoods Stores

Votes	Store
57	Mrs. Gooch, Beverly Hills/Glendale/Hermosa Beach/Los Angeles/Northridge/Sherman Oaks/Thousand Oaks, CA
35	Bread & Circus, Brookline/Cambridge/Hadley/Newton/Newton Highlands/Wellesley, MA, Providence, RI♥
28	Alfalfa's, Boulder/Englewood, CO♥
21	Whole Foods, Austin/Dallas/Houston/Richardson, TX, New Orleans, LA, Berkeley/Palo Alto, CA♥
12	Unicorn Village, North Miami Beach, FL♥
11	Real Foods, Emeryville/San Rafael/San Francisco/Sausalito, CA
10	Mother's Market, Costa Mesa/Huntington Beach/Long Beach, CA
9	Living Foods, Marin/San Anselmo, CA
6	Integral Yoga, New York, NY♥
6	Oak Feed Store, Miami, FL
6	Rainbow Grocery, San Francisco, CA
5	Commodities, New York, NY
5	North Co. Co-op, Minneapolis, MN
5	Rainbow Market, Denver, CO
4	The Big Carrot, Toronto, ON
4	Erewhon, Los Angeles, CA
4	Jimbo's, San Diego, CA
4	Molly Stone's, Palo Alto, CA
4	Natural Food, New York, NY
4	Organic Groceries, Santa Rosa, CA
4	Weaver St. Market, Carrboro, NC
4	Wellspring Grocery, Raleigh/Durham, NC
3	Country Life, Litchfield, CT
3	Down to Earth, New York, NY
3	Edge of the Woods, New Haven, CT
3	Natural Food Market, Miami, FL
3	Nature's Fresh, Portland, OR
3	New City Market, Chicago, IL
3	SNFC, Sacramento, CA
3	Takoma Park Co-op, Takoma Park, MD
3	Yes! Natural Gourmet, Washington, DC
2	Arcata Co-op, Arcata, CA
2	Blue Sky Market, Palatine, IL
2	Cassidy's, Encinitas, CA
2	Co-opportunity, Santa Monica, CA
2	Community Foods, Santa Cruz, CA
2	Country Sun, Palo Alto, CA
2	Cup o'Soup, Storrs, CT
2	Dinner for the Earth, Asheville, NC
2	Down to Earth, Honolulu/Wailua, HI
2	East End Food Co-op, Pittsburgh, PA
2	Erie Whole Foods, Erie, PA
2	Fresh Food Market, Asheville/Hendersonville, NC
2	Good Earth The, Atlanta, GA
2	Greentree Grocers, San Diego, CA
2	Hunger Mountain Co-op, Montpelier, VT
2	Nature's Way Food Outlet, Greensburg, PA
2	New Morning, Woodbury, CT
2	NHN, Pittsburgh, PA
2	Oasis, Eugene, OR
2	Puget Consumer Co-op, Seattle, WA
2	Rainbow Foods, Minneapolis, MN
2	Rainbow Grocery, Atlanta, GA
2	Sevananda, Atlanta, GA
2	Sherwyn's, Chicago, IL
2	Somadhara, Ithaca, NY
2	State St. Market, Montpelier, VT
2	Sun Harvest Farms, San Antonio, TX
2	Sundance Natural Foods, Eugene, OR
2	TAU, Montreal, PQ
2	Whole Foods, New York, NY
2	Willimantic Co-op, Willimantic, CT
2	World of Nutrition, Newington, CT

Source: Author's survey, summer and fall, 1989. The "votes" are a tally of the nominations by the businesses we surveyed; 207 stores received one "vote" each. No ballots were used; all nominations were written in.

Most wholefood stores dutifully sell what the distributors supply and the customers ask for, and give a lot of shelf space to supplements because as we have mentioned they are much easier to stock than the produce. Few wholefood stores do their own testing or independent buying. The local yellow pages or newspapers provide information on the run-of-the-mill wholefood stores.

Small Grocery Stores. When most Americans think of shopping for food, they think of cavernous, impersonal supermarkets with bored teen-age cashiers and piped-in music. The stock clerks often know little about the products, the manager is a low-profile hard-to-locate presence, and the whole store can be shut down on the basis of a show of hands in a boardroom 500 miles away.

Because supermarkets are often cogs in huge corporations, attention to the needs of the communities that use them is often a forgotten idea. A supermarket changes the products it sells based on food industry sales projections, rather than on local consumer requests.

But if you check out some of the markets in your area, you might find that they offer some of the wholefoods brands we talk about. You will probably also find that the proprietors have a greater understanding of the products they shelve and a greater appreciation of your business. Patronizing smaller stores and bakeries might cost a little more. If it does, the possibility of getting better food and, perhaps, developing a stronger sense of community can make it worth it.

Supermarkets

As Americans spend relatively more money on eating out, some supermarkets are closing their doors—200 of them in 1986–88. But we still have 30,400 supermarkets left and they continue to be our principal source of food purchases.[10]

One problem that manufacturers of healthy food must confront to get their products on the shelves is the supermarket slotting fee. Since about 1985, supermarket chains have charged fees of as much as $20,000 per product *per store* for the risks of stocking unproven goods, i.e. new products or even products that are faltering in sales. These retailers are not isolated sharks; it is industry practice.

After World War II, food manufacturers were in the driver's seat because goods were scarce. As distributors began to appreciate their central position, they gradually became the dominant force. Supermarkets are now flexing their economic muscle and are essentially telling everyone else "We are the key link in the food chain, and anyone who isn't already making us rich must pay tribute."

What makes this supermarket power possible is something called DPP—Direct Product Profit, an intensely detailed profit-per-product information system. If a new product is to be introduced, or an old product isn't producing the requisite profit for the supermarket, a manufacturer has a choice: (1) Don't ship the product, or (2) Pay $20,000 per store to stock it.

All very well, but consumers end up paying for this. Manufacturers have to pay for the slotting fees by raising their wholesale prices.

The Supermarket Blind Spot: Consumers. As supermarkets look back on their food fiefdom, most have forgotten any responsibility to the consumer. Major exceptions include Giant Foods and Safeway.

An example is the pesticide issue. Fruits and vegetables produced by large orchards or farms are cheaper for the supermarkets to handle and supermarket buyers go for price, so supermarkets have been slow to show interest in organic fruits and vegetables. We will note exceptions, such as Safeway's (and later others) banning of Alar-treated apples from its shelves in 1986, and we will identify some exemplary supermarkets in this chapter. But the number is still small. Consumers need to become better informed and use market forces to raise the number of responsible supermarkets.

Smaller grocery stores often offer better quality fruit and vegetables, along with a somewhat higher price. Their early-morning buyers may hunt for quality in the big-city wholesale markets or find it locally, but they, too, are mostly concerned with the appearance of produce, not with the pesticides that might have been used on it.

Choosing Supermarkets That Care. Some supermarkets are better than others at responding to consumer demand. Particularly with regard to produce, many have begun to pay attention to consumer concerns. In some states, most notably California, Texas, and Massachusetts, supermarkets specializing in organic foods and wholefoods are thriving. Elsewhere, conventional chains are starting to take the problem of pesticide residues seriously. Some question whether this is the best way to monitor produce—certification agencies are probably better equipped—but it is undeniably a step in the right direction.

We sent questionnaires to 300 supermarkets to get a picture of trends in stocking supermarket shelves. Part I asked questions about organic produce: did the stores think sustainable agricultural practices were viable, did they sell organic produce, had they sold it in the past? Part II asked about stocking processed goods: what role should a store take in encouraging good nutrition, are products today healthier than those of 10 years ago, are labeling laws tough enough, did the store have a wholefoods section? Part III asked stores what products they stocked have less than 1.5 milligrams of sodium per calorie, are low in fat (less than 30% of calories), and have none of the 25 additives the Center for Science in the Public Interest says to avoid in *The Complete Eater's Digest and Nutrition Scoreboard*. We wanted to get a picture of what healthy food you could find in supermarkets across the country.

The chains that returned our questionnaire said that the demand for organic produce was growing. They said they either stocked no organic produce or a token amount (5% of overall produce was common), but most said they were thinking about or were definitely planning whole-food sections. The remarkable fact is that *supermarket chains that are so precise when it comes to DPP, the direct product profit, did not have comparable nutritional information on these products.*

One that did have the data was Giant Foods, a large chain in the Baltimore-Washington-Richmond corridor, which included with their questionnaire response a copy of their excellent *Eat for Health* food guide. Part of a program the chain set up in association with the National Cancer Institute, the book shows for every food product data on its calories, milligrams sodium/serving, grams fat/serving, milligrams cholesterol/serving, grams saturated fat/serving, and grams fiber/serving. The labels on Giant Food store shelves are color-coded to support the book, featuring a space where any desirable attributes of the product described (i.e. "high-fiber" or "low-fat") are summarized. The numbers in the book are supplied by manufacturers; the figures checked out reasonably well against other sources. Every supermarket should have a guide or shelf labeling like Giant Foods and should be able to give consumers a succinct comparison of the products it sells.

Many supermarkets take the position that it isn't their job to check on the existence of chemicals in food. In 1986, Safeway took a different position and said it would not sell apples that had been treated with Alar, even though the EPA hadn't yet banned it.

Similarly, in August 1989 five large U.S. supermarket chains and Ben & Jerry's Homemade, the ice cream manufacturer, said they would refuse any milk or dairy item produced with the genetically engineered drug bovine somatotropin, also called bovine growth hormone (BGH). The drug increases milk production in cows by up to 25 percent. Opposition to the drug stems from three sources: (1) concerns that the drug is unsafe, based on research indicating that the drug could get into milk and produce "hormonal and allergic effects" in people (and especially infants) who drink it,[11] (2) concerns that use of the drug will hurt small dairy farmers by giving a disproportionate advantage to big producers, and (3) assertions that consumers do not want adulterated milk products.

The five stores that barred use of the drug on dairy cows are: 1. *Safeway* (110 stores in the West and Washington, DC.), 2. *Kroger* (1200 stores in 30 states), 3. *Stop & Shop* (116 stores in New England), 4. *Supermarkets General* (based in New Jersey), and 5. *Vons* (based in El Monte, Calif.).

Ben & Jerry's Homemade changed its ice cream labels to indicate its opposition to BGH, and offers a phone number for more information (802–BGH-FARM).

Produce Departments. In the early part of 1989 several markets started experimental programs of selling organic produce. Many cut them back or closed them for the winter, when organic food choices were more limited, but one market that has stuck with it is D'Agostino, a chain of 24 stores in the New York City area. The company has been somewhat disappointed in sales, but feels that the future of the experiment is promising. Said Frank Griscavage, manager of the University Place store: "I don't think customers are informed on how good the product is." The store cut back its organics section to about 25 per cent of stock for the winter, but is ready to increase levels in the spring of 1990 and will buy as much organic produce as it can sell.

In September 1989, four supermarket chains and one distributor signed an agreement that strives to phase out by 1995 the use of 64 pesticides considered potential carcinogens by the EPA. The agreement also stated that the companies would (1) refuse to stock foods that had been treated with the fungicide ethylene bisdithio-carbamate (EBDC), the field-crop herbicide alachlor, and the fungicide captan, and (2) ask food suppliers to disclose all pesticides used to grow food and vegetables.[12]

These five organizations have 1,200 outlets and sales of $8 billion (for comparison, total U.S. annual supermarket sales are nearly $300 billion). The participating companies are:

1. *Raley's*, a chain of 57 markets based in Sacramento, California that was also the first major chain to test for pesticide residues and advertise the results (about 10 other markets have followed suit).[13]

2. *ABCO Markets Inc.*, A chain of 75 stores based in Phoenix, Arizona, that has annual sales of $800 million.

3. *Provigo Inc.*, which runs over 1,000 supermarkets in the Province of Quebec, Canada, and 30 stores under the Petrini marquee in the U.S. Midwest.

4. *Bread & Circus*, a chain of five stores in the Boston area that is one of the premier wholefood supermarkets in the country. (Bread & Circus sells organic produce in season, but relies on conventional distributors for much of their winter produce. See Chapter 10, Newton, Massachusetts for more).

5. *American Brothers Produce*, a distributor based in San Jose, California.

Several food industry trade associations and the National Agricultural Chemicals Association criticized the program, saying it was irresponsible. The President of the Produce Marketing Association in Newark, Del., expressed distress that the chains would join in "casting public doubt on

fresh foods and vegetables—some of the most healthful foods people can eat."

Linda Fisher, EPA assistant administrator for pesticides and toxic substances, criticized the move saying, "The coalition puts the onus of pesticide regulation on grocery retailers, who are not and should not be responsible for such decisions." In response to criticism that she was absolutely right—that, indeed, the responsibility should not be with supermarkets but is because the EPA is too slow—she replied that ". . . EPA must balance both the value to society and the risk which may be presented by these pesticides," implying that, because of its complexity, the task cannot be rushed. She added that the EPA is committed to working faster.[14]

Wholefoods Departments. An increasing number of stores are beginning to stock wholefoods and some are creating special sections for relatively unprocessed products. Several of the Boney's Markets in the San Diego area, perhaps taking a cue from the success of Mrs. Gooch's, have started stocking more wholefoods products and, in season, feature significant quantities of organic produce. Rainbow Markets, a chain of 22 stores in Minnesota, has also developed wholefoods sections.

Some supermarkets have opted to use wholefoods exclusively. Mrs. Gooch's in the Los Angeles area was created by a consumer who got tired of searching for additive-free foods. Sandra Gooch (after whom the store is named) had an allergic reaction to a common, FDA-approved food additive which required hospitalization. When she got out, she did more research on additives and allergies and realized just how hard it is to get additive-free foods. Mrs. Gooch's now has seven stores and is the most widely acclaimed retailer in the wholefoods industry.

Some other wholefoods supermarkets that set a standard for the industry are Bread & Circus in the Boston area; Alfalfa's Market, with branches in Boulder and Aurora, Colorado; and Whole Foods, which has branches in Texas, Louisiana, and the Bay Area of California. For more on these markets, see Chapter 10. The complete list of highly regarded wholefoods supermarkets and stores can be found in Chapter 8.

Supermarket Trends. To a certain degree, stores like the ones above, through their enthusiasm and education programs, have influenced consumer demand. However for most stores, the managers are, far from leading it, barely responding to consumer demand. Organic produce has not caught on quickly for two reasons: (1) Properly handled, organic produce requires more effort to ensure rapid turnover, to avoid the faster product deterioration without postharvest treatment, (2) Organic produce is still a novelty in most parts ofthe country and the public is not yet fully informed about the value of the products.[15]

Even so, improvements can be seen in other sections of conventional supermarkets:[16]

1. *Fish.* As supermarket managers see more people buying fresh fish, they have personnel to cut up fish on the spot and offer customers advice on how to prepare it.

2. *Dairy.* In early 1988, few brands of nonfat yogurt were

available in supermarkets; now many are. But it is still hard in some regions to find skim milk in gallon containers.

3. *Rice.* It is now possible to find brown rice—even more than one variety—in most supermarkets. As a mediocre chef, I am pleased to find idiot-proof Success rice comes in the brown variety.

4. *Pasta.* Pastas now come in dozens of varieties, many featuring legume-grain combinations that offer complete protein as well as lots of complex carbohydrates.

5. *Breads.* The selection of whole-wheat breads and other whole-grain breads at supermarkets has increased dramatically over the last decade. Most of it may not be as tasty as fresh bread from a local bakery, but it has more fiber than the fluffy white stuff that used to be the only bread available in supermarkets.

6. *Juices.* Where once many juice-drinks were packed with corn syrup and artificial flavors, now dozens of varieties of pure juice are available in bottles, cartons, and concentrate.

Making Healthy Choices

How to Use Food and Supermarket Labels. We encourage you to use wholefood stores and restaurants, but you can buy healthy food in regular supermarkets and restaurants; it just requires more care.

The key is to learn the basic principles behind a healthy diet, and then to read labels and ask questions. In general, this means, (1) looking for foods low in fat (especially saturated fat), (2) avoiding salty and sugary processed foods low in key nutrients, and (3) eating a variety of foods.

Because fat is probably the most significant problem in the diet of the average American, understanding what the fat/protein/carbohydrate breakdown means is important. The key is to remember that a gram of fat has 9 calories, a gram of protein has 4 calories, and a gram of carbohydrates has 4 calories. So if something has just 10 grams of fat and 10 grams of carbohydrates, it gets more than two-thirds of its calories from fat: 90/130. The total of fat + carbohydrates + protein should approximate to the total calories per serving listed on the package. An example is shown in Table 9–3.

Table 9–3
Sample Calculation, Percent Calories from Fat

Food component, Calories/gram	Grams	Total Calories	Percent
Fat, 9	2*	18	20%
Carbohydrates, 4	17*	68	76%
Protein, 4	1*	4	4%
Total	20	90*	100%

*Information on label; other columns are calculated using the calories/gram multiplier for each food component.

Source: Can of Campbell's Tomato Soup (concentrated).

If the label shows the breakdown between saturated fat and polyunsaturated fat or between simple and complex carbohydrates, all the better; this allows you to be more selective.

Wise Substitutions. Table 9–4 distills the basic principles into practical recommendations for shoppers. (In Chapter 7 we offered advice regarding specific products.)

Table 9–4
Easy Substitutions for a Healthier Diet

Instead of	Substitute	Calories saved	Fat saved (grams)
Beef, 3.5 ounces tenderloin, choice, untrimmed, broiled	Beef 3.5 ounces tenderloin, select, trimmed, broiled	75	10
Chocolate, 1 ounce unsweetened	Cocoa powder, 3 tablespoons	73	13
Cookies, 3 chocolate sandwich	Cookies, 3 fig bar	0	4
Corn chips, 1 ounce	Popcorn, 1 ounce plain air-popped	125	9
Cream cheese, 1 ounce	Cottage cheese, 1 ounce, 1% fat	74	9
Croissant, 1	Bagel, 1 plain	35	10
Doughnut, 1 glazed	Angel-food cake, 1 slice	110	13
Duck, roast 3.5 ounce, no skin	Chicken, 3.5 ounces skinless roast	46	7
Frankfurter, 1 beef	Frankfurter, 1 chicken	67	8
French fries, 1 fast-food serving	Potato, 1 medium-size baked	125	11
Ice cream, 1 cup premium	Sorbet, 1 cup	320	34
Lamb chop 3.5 ounces, broiled	Lamb, leg, 3.5 ounces lean, trimmed	219	28
Peanuts, 1 ounce, oil-roasted	Chestnuts, 1 ounce roasted	96	13
Potato chips, 1 ounce	Pretzels, 1 ounce thin	40	9
Salami, 1 ounce, hard	Ham, 1 ounce extra-lean roast	75	8
Sour-cream dip, 1 tablespoon	Salsa, 1 tablespoon bottled	20	3
Tuna 3 ounces, light, in oil	Tuna, 3 ounces, light, in water	60	6

Source: Excerpted from the *University of California, Berkeley Wellness Letter*, September 1989. Reprinted by permission. © Health Letter Associates, 1989.

Shopping for a Better World. Besides substituting plain popcorn for corn chips, some people will take a larger view of their health to encompass the health of their environment, and will want to substitute products from more responsible food processing companies for products from less responsible ones.

If so, they will want to:

Avoid products made by American Home Products (Chef Boyardee, for example) and Castle & Cooke (Dole Pineapple, for example), which both did very poorly in the ratings of *Shopping for a Better World* (New York: Ballantine, for Council on Economic Priorities, 1990), and

Choose products made by Ben & Jerry's Homemade (Lite brand or sorbet only, we urge), Celestial Seasonings, Dolefam (makes Old Monk olive oil), General Mills, Kellogg's, Newman's Own, Procter & Gamble, Quaker Oats, and Sara Lee (pass up the cheesecake), which all did well on the ratings.

Healthy Restaurant Options

Survey Results. Our survey of restaurants suggests that the following are best bets:

Most Recommended Restaurants

Angelica's Kitchen, New York, NY♥
Common Ground, Brattleboro, VT♥
Good Earth, Berkeley/Glendale/Goleta/Santa Rosa, CA
Green's, San Francisco, CA♥
Milly's, San Rafael, CA♥
New Riverside Cafe, Minneapolis, MN
Paul & Elizabeth, Northampton, MA
Souen, New York, NY
Unicorn Village, Miami/North Miami Beach, FL♥
ABC Cafe, Ithaca, NY
Blind Faith Cafe, Evanston, IL
Bloodroot Cafe & Bookstore, Bridgeport, CT
Cafe Brenda, Minneapolis, MN
Eat Your Vegetable, Atlanta, GA
Emil's Deli, Greensburg, PA
Five Seasons, Jamaica Plains, MA
Fragrant Vegetable, Los Angeles/Monterey Park, CA
Gemini, Denver/Wheatridge, CO
Horn of the Moon, Montpelier, VT
Killer Dogz, Morgantown, WV
Kristos & Drivakis, Cincinnati, OH
Living Springs, New York, NY
Mary's Natural, Philadelphia, PA
Mud Pie, Minneapolis, MN
Pure 'N Simple, Troy/Pontiac, MI
Revelation, Santa Rosa, CA
Spring Street Natural, New York, NY♥
Sunlight Cafe, Seattle, WA
Vegie Foods, San Francisco, CA
Walnut St. Cafe, Erie, PA
Wildflower Cafe, Arcata, CA

Some areas have more interest in "heart-healthy" meals than others. In California's Sonoma Valley such in-terest is strong. A well-reputed restaurant in Santa Rosa, John Ash & Company, says that during the week about 40 percent of diners choose the heart-healthy options; on weekends the percentage drops to 20.[17]

Vegetarian Restaurants. In our listings of restaurants in Chapter 10, we are heavy on vegetarian or pesce-vegetarian restaurants for two reasons: (1) They tend to serve healthier food, and (2) Vegetarian restaurants serving tasty food are for many people harder to find. Hamburgers are easy to make, and the high fat content ensures tastiness. Really tasty vegetable dishes require much more effort. Because the average American consumes too much saturated fat (and, many argue, too much protein as well), we emphasize restaurants that serve nutrient-rich, low-fat foods. The merits of and problems with vegetarian and macrobiotic diets are discussed at length in Chapters 2 and 3.

Spa Cuisine. A few restaurants offer healthy "spa" cuisine. Spa entrées might be an imaginative salad, or a salmon steak surrounded by *nouvelle cuisine* vegetables with no sauce. The stress in spa cuisine is keeping the calories down with *cuisine minceur* (thin cooking) while maintaining the standards of first-class cooking.

Some restaurants offer standard beefeater fare but provide spa *options*. This is not ideal (what a shame to pass up the fatty, delicious Béarnaise sauce, *canard à l'orange*, croissants, or pâté). But better to have the bouillabaisse, fruit, low-fat entrée, and salad options than not.

Restaurants in New York City frequented by the rich and famous that have spa options include the Ambassador Grill, Aurora, the Four Seasons, and "21".[18] As Americans react to government pronouncements by becoming more food-conscious, the number of gourmet restaurants offering spa options is likely to grow. Use of organically grown vegetables will surely spread as the excellence of their taste is appreciated as well as their vitamins.

Chinese Food. [19] A favorite of mine, Chinese food has a well-deserved reputation for being healthy because of its reliance on rice and vegetables. The main foods excluded from the Chinese diet are milk and most milk products. The diet tends to be low in fat and high in fiber.

Avoid crispy noodles set on the table with a dish of duck sauce; in fact don't eat anything that says "crispy"—which means deep-fried—or "fried"; frying adds both calories and saturated fat. The heavy oil sauces used in some

Chinese restaurants are bad enough, but they can be drained off; fried food is irredeemable. Sweet-and-sour pork (or indeed any pork, the most commonly served Chinese meat, or spareribs) and egg rolls are examples of deep-

fried food to be avoided. A crispy beef meal has nearly twice as many calories as a meal of snow peas with water chestnuts and bamboo shoots. Avoid dishes heavily laden with nuts. Avoid high-sodium MSG, monosodium glutamate, by eschewing soy sauce and asking ahead or before you order about MSG in the food; spices are better than salt or MSG for seasoning. Some Chinese restaurants regrettably try to adapt their food to the American palate by adding a lot of sugar—ask, taste, and be guided accordingly.

Choose rice, preferably brown rice, and vegetables like bamboo shoots, bok choi (cabbage), broccoli, mushrooms, and snow peas. Go for the Buddha's Delight, an assortment of vegetables, no meat, in a light sauce. Steamed (not fried) dumplings, grilled (not deep-fried) fish or chicken, moo goo gai pan, and udon noodles are also healthy.

Indian. Many patrons of Indian restaurants are for religious reasons vegetarians, so low-fat vegetarian options are plentiful. But as in Chinese cuisine, a restaurant may saturate the food with fat by frying the food in oils or ghee (clarified butter).

Avoid puri (fried bread), coconut milk curry sauces (or coconut anything), pakoris and samosas (fried appetizers), muglai (creamy curry sauce), yogurt as a main dish unless low-fat, and any creamy or cheese sauces, such as in creamy beef curry (over 500 calories with rice!).

Choose dal (lentils) as in mulligatawny soup or dal palak, chicken or vegetables with yogurt (preferably low-fat; ask), tandoori chicken, fish or vegetable curries, nan (baked bread) or pulka (unleavened bread), basmati rice with vegetables, sweet-and-sour cabbage, onions, tomatoes. Chutney is high in sugar.

Italian. The Italian diet can be very healthy, but in American restaurants the menus are heavy on high-calorie, high-fat cheese and oil.

Avoid crema or fritto food, antipasto, cannelloni (over 800 calories!), fettuccine Alfredo, garlic bread, lasagna, parmesan, pepperoni, and sausage dishes. Instead, choose the plain bread, fresh green salads with dressing reduced or on the side, and seafoods.

Choose pomodora-style food, calamari with vegetables (barely 200 calories), ciappino (seafood soup), minestrone soup, mussels steamed in red sauce, shrimp, chicken cacciatore (tomato sauce), eggplants, pasta primavera, green salad with low-oil dressing, and if you must have a dessert, the fruit ice or just fruit.

Japanese. The diet excludes milk and milk products and is low in fat; it obtains needed nutrients from a variety of fish, vegetables and seaweeds. A danger is the high-salt content of the food.

Avoid the high-salt soy sauce, pickled or smoked fish or vegetables; any "tempura" (deep-fried), "age" or "katsu" (fried) food; surimi, a high-salt pseudo-crab; and fried dumplings. Half of calories in a tonkatsu, fried pork, come from fat.

Choose clear soups such as miso; then, chicken yakitori (shish kebab, 275 calories), or chicken or salmon teriyaki. Shabu-shabu is a healthy plate of meat or seafood tidbits and vegetables for cooking in a broth at your table. Sushi and sashimi, raw fish choices (the sushi comes on top of fingers of rice), are very healthy unless the fish is infected with parasites, which won't be the case if the sushi chef is good (don't try to serve raw fish at home unless you know exactly where the fish came from and how to handle it). If you don't know the sushi chef, order the cooked-crab or shrimp, or vegetable, sushi. Good Japanese restaurants make it easy to develop a taste for tempeh and tofu, which are low in fat unless fried and are a very nutritive substitute for meat.

Mexican. While Mexican food has many healthy features, such as the omnipresence of beans, lettuce, peppers, and tomatoes, it has fat and sugar traps for those who are not careful in their selections.

Avoid flour tortillas; crisp burritos or tacos, fried tortillas or fried anything else; beef enchiladas (especially the enchiladas rancheros, with cheese and sour cream, over 900 calories in a serving of two!; tortilla chips with high-fat guacamole, nachos, flautas, sour cream; desserts such as flan and sopapillas (fried).

Choose gazpacho or black bean soup; soft burrito, taco, or tostada; corn tortillas (one-fourth the fat of flour tortillas); rice; beans in soft tortilla, or beans any other way; chicken with vegetables; marinated fish; lettuce; tomatoes and salsa (a delicious tomato-onion-chile sauce). Soft chicken tacos have only about 225 calories.

Fast-Food Survival Kit

In 1989 the fastest-growing fast-food chain was Subway, a sandwich shop concentrated on the East Coast. McDonald's continued in 1988 to add U.S. units at the rate of 4 percent a year, while growing at over twice that rate internationally. In early 1990 Hardee's absorbed Roy Rogers.

Almost everything served at a fast-food store is highly processed—from the "enriched" white-bread buns to the deadly mixture of beef fat and coconut oil that is melted at high temperature to cook French fries. Many items are laden with sodium. One simple fast-food meal has more salt than the Center for Science in the Public Interest recommends we consume in a day. Sauces are high in sugar.

If you don't think you have to worry about your health just yet, and you love the taste of the fat, sodium, and sugar (and preservatives), fast-food restaurants may be for you. Young people crave fast food. The frenzied lunchtime rush of students to local fast-food chains at one high school (in Gilroy, Calif.) was such a source of traffic hazards and tardiness that school officials threatened to close the campus. This, however, raised students' outcries about the food available for purchase on-campus; they demanded fast food. School district officials contacted McDonald's and Burger King executives to ask if one of their franchises might be built on the high school campus. Fortunately, they declined, or such a restaurant might grace the center of the campus today. James Logan High in Union City, Calif., however, has opened a thriving 7–Eleven.

Fast-food franchises have become so pervasive that they have engendered many reactions. For example, on November 10, 1989 simultaneous news conferences were held in ten cities to issue the Slow-food Manifesto. The manifesto (which was the idea of Italian restaurateur Carlo Petrini) among other things decries the erosion of local cuisines and cultures by the invasion of fast-food franchises.[20]

Efficiency experts at places like McDonald's are seeking ways to reduce the 30–40 seconds of unprofitable "think time" that people use up at the counter, and the 8–10 seconds "talk time" they take to place their order.[21] The information below may help reduce your "think time" while also helping you avoid making an unhealthy decision under pressure from people in line behind you.

Least Healthy Fast Foods. As Americans become more dependent on fast-food outlets for their food, figuring out the healthy choices is becoming increasingly essential. Table 9–5 shows the fattiest of the choices offered by fast food outlets. All of them derive more than half of their calories from fat.

Table 9–5
Survey of Some of the Fattiest Fast Foods

Company Product (Calories)	Fat, grams (% of Calories)
*Arby's**	
Beef 'n Cheddar (455)	27 (53)
*Burger King**	
Whopper with Cheese (711)	43 (54)
Whopper (628)	36 (52)
Specialty Chicken Sandwich (688)	40 (52)
Breakfast Croissant w/Sausage (538)	41 (69)
*Carl's Jr.**	
Super Star Hamburger (770)	50 (58)
Famous Star Hamburger (590)	36 (55)
Sausage, 1 patty (190)	17 (81)
*Dairy Queen**	
Triple Hamburger with Cheese (820)	50 (55)
Triple Hamburger (710)	45 (57)
Chicken Breast Fillet (608)	34 (50)
Hot Dog with Chili (320)	20 (56)
Domino's Pizza	
Double Cheese/Pepperoni, 2 slices (545)	25 (42)
*Jack in the Box**	
Sausage Crescent (584)	43 (66)
Swiss and Bacon Burger (678)	47 (62)
Hot Apple Turnover (410)	24 (53)
Taco Salad (503)	31 (55)
Kentucky Fried Chicken	
Extra Crispy Chicken Thigh (317)	26 (75)
*McDonald's***	
McD.L.T. (580)	37 (57)
Hashbrown Potatoes (130)	7 (51)
*Roy Rogers** (acquired by Hardee's)	
Breakfast Crescent Sandwich,	
Sausage (564)	42 (67)
Egg & Biscuit Platter, Sausage (713)	49 (62)
Subway	
Seafood and Crab Salad (198)	11 (51)
Taco Bell	
Taco Bellgrande (355)	23 (59)

* Cooks everything in highly saturated beef fat (worse).** Uses beef fat for French fries only (better).

Source: Center for Science in the Public Interest, *Fast-Food Guide* and unpublished data.[22]

The dubious winners in total number of grams of fat are Jack in the Box's Ultimate Cheeseburger, with over 70 grams of fat, a day's generous allowance, and Burger King's Double Beef Whopper with Cheese, with 64 grams of fat, a close second.

In terms of percentage of calories, the worst offerings are Roy Rogers's Breakfast Crescent Sandwich with Ham and its Egg and Biscuit Platter with Sausage. Both have over 40 grams of fat and derive two-thirds of their calories from fat.

New Fatty Fast-Food Options. Has the recent upsurge in attention to nutrition had a positive impact on menu additions being made by the fast-food companies? The following examples suggest not:[23]

Arby's. The Roast Chicken Club sandwich gives sandwiches a bad name. It has 610 calories, too much salt, and even more fat (from bacon, cheese, and mayonnaise) than the Big Mac, which has 35 grams of fat (55 percent of calories).

Hardee's. The Big Country (Big Coronary) Breakfast with Sausage has more than 1,000 calories—two-thirds of it from the nearly 75 grams (17 teaspoons) of fat, which would be too much fat for twice the calories! It also has 2 grams of sodium and a day's allowance, 280 milligrams, of cholesterol.

Jack in the Box. The new Ultimate Cheeseburger has even more fat than Burger King's Double Beef Whopper.

McDonald's. The new McChicken sandwich has so much fat in the mayonnaise and deep-fried coating that it has more calories and fat than the Quarter Pounder, which has 427 calories and 24 grams of fat (50 percent of calories).

Taco Bell. The new Taco Light is misleadingly named. It contains more than twice the fat (11 grams, from sour cream and more beef) and calories (183 per taco) as the regular taco.

Healthiest Fast Food. More and more fast-food outlets are offering salad options. If you buy a salad you may get some decently nutritious, low-fat food—provided you don't use a high-fat, high-calorie salad dressing. A nutritional standout is Wendy's inexpensive all-you-can-eat salad bar; other fast-food chains also offer good options.

The healthiest fast-food options are shown in Table 9–6.

Table 9–6
Healthiest (Low-Fat) Fast Foods

Company Product (Calories)	Fat, grams (% of Calories)
Many Chains	
Milk, 2% butterfat, 8 ounces- (121)	5 (35)
Burger King	
Breakfast Bagel Sandwich with Ham (418)	15 (32)
Chicken Salad (140)	4 (26)
Carl's Jr.	
Charbroiler BBQ Chicken Sandwich (320)	5 (14)
Domino's	
Pizza, Cheese, 12″, 2 slices (340)	6 (16)
Hardee's	
Side Salad (21)♥	0 (0)
Jack in the Box	
Chicken Fajita Pita (292)	8 (25)
Kentucky Fried Chicken	
Corn on the Cob (176)	3 (16)
Mashed Potatoes with Gravy (59)	1 (9)
Long John Silver	
Ocean Chef Salad (229)	8 (31)
McDonald's	
Vanilla or Strawberry Shake (352)	8 (21)
Hamburger (260)	10 (33)
Chicken Oriental Salad (140)	3 (22)
Roy Rogers	
Pancake Platter with syrup, butter (386)	13 (30)
Subway	
Subway Club, 6 inches (423)	11 (26)
Turkey Sandwich, 6 inches (357)	10 (26)
Taco Bell	
Bean Burrito with Sauce (354)	10 (26)
Wendy's	
Baked Potato plain (250)	2 (7)
Salad bar, all you can eat ♥ ♥	

* Low-fat milk, baked potatoes, and salads are widely available. Salad has no fat, but the dressing does, unless it is low-calorie.

Source: Center for Science in the Public Interest, *The Fast-Food Guide* and unpublished data[24]

New Healthy Fast-Food Options. Hardee's, Jack-in-the-Box and Carl's Jr. have introduced a grilled chicken sandwich, which has much less fat than fried chicken.

Burger King added a Chicken Salad.

Carl's Jr. Charbroiler BBQ Chicken Sandwich contains only about 4 grams of fat.

Hardee's. Grilled Chicken Sandwich, 13 grams of fat (of which 9 are in the mayonnaise; hold the mayo and it's down to 4 grams of fat), less than half the fat in McDonald's McChicken Sandwich; however, it has 1.2 grams of sodium.

Jack in the Box. Fajita Pita, a healthy choice.

McDonald's. Chicken Salad Oriental, a low-fat option (but the McDonald's Chef Salad is a poor choice, with about 13 grams of fat even before the dressing is added).

Taco Bell. Bean Burrito, with about 9 grams of fat, has less fat than the taco salad.

Wendy's discontinued its unhealthy Triple Cheeseburger.

Summing Up. To sum up what we have been saying, Table 9–7 shows the bad news. The major items in fast-food restaurants are all excessively high in fat. The cheeseburgers are work-makers for heart surgeons. The best of the bad lot is the plain McDonald's hamburger, 33 percent fat. But milk shakes are pretty healthy, as are the new salad offerings, provided a low-fat (clear, not creamy) dressing is used, and sparingly.

Fast-food restaurants, like supermarkets, are starting to respond to the health concerns of customers, but slowly. They still listen more to the marketing people than to the dietitians. As Michael Jacobson and Sarah Fritschner put it in the *Fast-Food Guide*, people in the industry talk out of both sides of their mouth: "From one side, they say the public doesn't want nutritious food; from the other side, they are touting the nutritious qualities of the foods they serve."[25] Of course, as most have little to tout, the claims are put in confusing or irrelevant terms.

Fast-food restaurants say they are responsive to the nutritional concerns of their patrons. But on the most basic levels that is hard to establish. One franchise has three outlets in the vicinity of our office and commuting paths. Over the course of five weeks we paid at least two visits to each of these outlets, seeking to get a nutritional brochure on their products. We were met first with blank stares and, after a few minutes' wait, informed by managers that they had just run out—but they would be getting more shortly. Either the little pamphlet is amazingly popular and we were the victims of consistent bad timing, or the chain simply isn't that committed to informing customers—or maybe, as industry cynics claim, people don't really care.

Table 9–7
Average Values for Fast-Food Items

Item	Average Percent Calories from Fat	Range
Unhealthy, Fatty Items		
Chicken sandwich (fried)	48	32–56
Fish sandwich (fried)	46	38–53
French fries	46	43–49
Hamburger (plain)	38	33–48
Healthy Item		
Milkshake	23	16–34

Source: Derived from Center for Science in the Public Interest, unpublished data. The range includes Arby's, Burger King, Carl's Junior, Dairy Queen, Hardee's, Jack in the Box, McDonald's, and Roy Rogers. Three do not offer every item compared: Arby's, Carl's Junior, and Roy Rogers.

Angelica Kitchen, is in a class by itself, it's committed to an integrated philosophy of the whole. Starting with organically grown wholefoods, filtered water, and stainless steel cookware, innovative and creative dishes are designed daily. They use bio-degradable detergents as part of a determined recycling program, open 7 days a week for breakfast, lunch, and dinner. **Angelica Kitchen** is one of the best vegetarian restaurants on the East Coast.

CHAPTER
10

VENDORS OF HEALTHY FOOD

Criteria: availability of wholefoods, i.e. relatively unprocessed and additive-free foods,
and availability of organic produce; plus for restaurants,
availability of vegetarian options.

Having looked at the components of healthy and un-healthy diets, and products and produce that supply those components, we now list many retail stores and restaurants where you can buy healthy food.

We sent thousands of questionnaires and conducted hundreds of interviews in the U.S. and Canada. We screened responses on two general criteria: (1) availability of wholefoods, i.e. relatively unprocessed and additive-free foods, and (2) availability of and commitment to organic produce. Plus for restaurants, we looked for availability of vegetarian options.

Directory Coverage

The following directory includes top wholefoods retailers, supermarkets with wholefoods departments, outstanding restaurants, and some growers of organic produce. We also listed a few other businesses that do not generally sell directly to the public, but are exemplary in some way.

Wholefoods vendors sell products that contain few synthetic chemical additives, preservatives, flavorings, colorings, and pesticide residues. Many also try to avoid stocking products with processed sugars, MSG, hydrogenated oils, and caffeine. Most establishments listed here do not sell food that has been irradiated. Most avoid selling products that entail cruelty to animals.

If you feel we missed a quality vendor, please use the INFO-FORM at the back of this book to alert us for future editions. You will help your favorite business, us, other consumers, and the industry.

We have taken extraordinary pains to report accurately on the business practices of the vendors we list. However, the wise reader will not allow our information to replace such routine precautions as verifying charges before placing an order.

The following directory focuses on retailers, restaurants, and growers. While we do list some distributors and man-ufacturers here, these businesses are more thoroughly discussed and examined in Chapter 8.

We provide key information in this geographical directory, including the vendor's full address and phone number, the hours it is open, what it sells, how it ships, farming methods used (if appropriate), bulk buying terms, and any credit cards accepted. A brief explanation of our format follows.

Hearts ♥ denote the establishments that are our favorites. Diamonds ♦ indicate how often a company was recommended by firms we surveyed, magazines that write on wholefoods, or by our consultants.

All 50 states as well as the District of Columbia, Puerto Rico, and the Virgin Islands are listed in alphabetical order. Four Canadian Provinces (Alberta, British Columbia, Ontario, and Quebec) are also included at the end of the U.S. directory.

Retailer and Grower Listings

Type of Business: Describes the business. Typical responses will be grower, manufacturer, mail-order distributor, distributor, and retailer.

Sells to: For retailers, this space will usually be answered by "The public." We often use this space to give you some sense of what the vendor's main business is. For instance, a bakery that primarily ships to retailers but also has a small store on the premises might be described as selling: "Primarily to retailers, but also to the public direct."

Sells: Here we try to give a brief description of what a store carries. We put together a list of about 200 fresh and processed items and asked respondents to check what they sold. Rather than list all of these items, we provide an evaluation and summary. We also looked at their response to "please list some of the brands you sell" and, based on these, try to tell you how good their selection of wholefoods is. We then looked at the stores' responses to questions about the certification of their produce to try to give you an idea of how broad their organic selection is.

Organic? Here we give you the vendor's estimate, if provided, of how much inventory (both fresh and grocery) is organically grown and processed. We also provide information about the certification of the organic produce grown or resold by the vendor. "Asserted organic" means the producer says the produce is organic, but has not provided any information to back up this statement. "Documented organic" means the producer has answered a questionnaire from a documentation clearinghouse, describing how the produce is grown. "Certified organic" means the produce is certified as organic by an independent certification organization (see the end of Chapter 5 for a state-by-state list of certification agencies).

Credit: If the vendor accepts credit, we list the cards it accepts. V = Visa, M = Mastercard, AE = American Express, D = Discover, CB = Carte Blanche, DC = Diners Club, and ATM = Automated Teller Machine cards, use of which automatically deducts the cost of purchase from your bank account. We also list any minimum purchase for credit if disclosed to us.

Prices: Here we list any discounts available for bulk orders or senior citizens, or special charges. For example, many co-ops add a small charge to orders from non-members.

Hours: We list hours the business is open, in local time. When placing an order by phone, remember time zone differences.

Shipping: If the retailer also fulfils mail orders on a significant scale, we tell you where they will ship, what carrier they use, and what added charges customers may incur.

Minimum Order: Many vendors will not fulfill mail orders for purchases totalling under $10 or $15. We say so here.

Catalogue Available? We say if the vendor provides a catalogue or price list on request, and list the cost if it was disclosed to us. Often you are asked to send a self-addressed, stamped envelope for the catalogue.

Comments: Here we list any interesting features of the vendor, such as details on how to join a co-op or a Thursday cooking class, or on the in-store homeopathic healer.

Food co-ops appear to be the cheapest source of wholefoods and organic produce. Space constraints kept us from including the smallest co-ops; medium-sized co-ops that we might have included did not always return our questionnaire. You can often identify a local food co-op by contacting one of the cooperative warehouses listed in Chapter 6.

The most direct way to purchase fresh organic produce is through farmers' markets or pick-your-own farms. Ask growers who claim to be organic about their certification (see Chapter 5 for the most important certification agencies). Ideally they will have certification seals on their crates. Sometimes growers will tell you that they don't like the certification agencies for one reason or another (e.g. too expensive, too lax, too strict). We nonetheless recommend that you persist in looking for certification or documentation both for your own sake and because it supports the needed certification agencies, which help maintain standards.

To find out more about farmers' markets or pick-your-own farms in your area, write your state Department of Agriculture. We wrote to all 50 and about two-thirds of them supplied us with comprehensive lists, sometimes with maps. For example, Massachusetts, Rhode Island, and Wisconsin have excellent directories. Not all of these markets will have organic growers, but if you find one on your first visit, he or she will probably be back at the same time and place the following week.

Restaurant Listings

The three questions we asked when deciding whether to include a restaurant are: (1) Do they offer vegetarian options? (2) Do they offer organically grown produce? (3) Do they offer whole-grain options (brown rice, whole wheat pasta)?

Type of Business:

Restaurant.

Sells: We describe the cuisine and say if they offer vegan or macrobiotic options. Sometimes the restaurant will offer macrobiotic or vegan options only.

Organic? We report the restaurant's estimate of how much of the produce it uses is organic. This produce is not necessarily always certified organic; it would be helpful to the industry if you ask when you order.

Specialties: We list the dishes the establishment is most proud of and scan the menu for any unusual items.

Prices: Cost of a middle-priced entrée.

Hours: The hours the business is open, in local time.

Reservations: We say whether reservations are required or even possible. Sometimes reservations are not taken for groups smaller than six. We also use this heading to say how much of the restaurant is reserved for non-smokers, in case that plays a role in making reservations.

Credit: Same as described for retailers.

Commendations: We tell you any awards the restaurant has received, with the year awarded, and summarize news stories about the establishment.

AL

Alabama

Birmingham, **Golden Temple Natural Grocery and Cafe**, H.S. Khalsa, 1901 11th Ave. S, Birmingham, AL 35263. (205) 933-6333. Type of Business: Restaurant and retail store. Sells: Vegetarian, vegan and macrobiotic options. Organic? Asserted 30% organic. Specialties: Made-from-scratch vegetable specials, soups, breads, salads, and sandwiches. Prices: A la carte with salad—$4.25, sandwiches $3-$3.50. Hours: Store M-F 8:30-7, Sat. 10-5:30, Sun. 12-5:30, Restaurant M-Sat. 11:30-2. Reservations: Accepted. 100% Non-Smoking. Credit: M AE. Comments: Take-out orders. They grow many of their vegetables on their own farm.

Huntsville, **Pearly Gates Natural Foods**, Myrna Copeland, 2308 Memorial Parkway SW, Huntsville, AL 35801. (205) 534-6233. Type of Business: Grocery Store, delicatessen, bakery and caterers. Sells: Natural and organic foods, including over 600 bulk herbs. Vegan and macrobiotic foods are available. Organic? Asserted 80% organic. Specialties: International cuisine using organic vegetables grown in the Pearly Gates organic gardens. Hours: M-Sat. 10-6:30. Reservations: Possible. 90% non-smoking. Credit: V M. Shipping: They ship mail orders within 24 hours and prefer Mastercard or Visa to C.O.D.

AK

Alaska

Fairbanks, **Whole Earth Grocery**, Kay and Michael Nolan, Box 80228, Fairbanks, AK 99708. (907) 479-2052. Type of Business: Retail store, deli (lunch service), and bakery. Sells to: The public Sells: An impressive variety of fresh produce as well as baked goods, candy, cereals, dairy products, flour, processed fruit, oils, pasta, rice, soy products, frozen and canned vegetables. Credit: None. Prices: 10% bulk discount, 25% business discount. Hours: M-Sat. 10-7. Catalogue Available? Yes.

Juneau, **Fiddlehead Restaurant & Bakery**, Deborah R. Mayhall, 429 W Willoughby, Juneau, AK 99801. (907) 586-9431. Type of Business: Restaurant. Sells: Vegetarian, organically grown, and vegan options. Organic? 50% organic. Specialties: Alaskan seafood, fresh salmon, homemade breads and pastries, and locally grown produce. Prices: Moderate. Hours: M-F 6-10, S-S 7-10. Reservations: Possible. 100% non-smoking. Credit: V M. Commendations: Fodor's (1988), *Alaska Airlines magazine*, August, 1989).

Juneau, **Rainbow Foods**, David Ottoson, 200 North Franklin St., Juneau, AK 99801. (907) 586-6476. Type of Business: Natural-foods grocery store. Sells to: The public. Sells: A full range of fresh organic produce (seasonal) and wholefood grocery items. They also sell organically raised chicken and nitrate-free bacon. Organic? They assert that 80-90% of their produce is organically grown and about 35-40% of their processed goods. Credit: V M AE. Hours: M-F 10-7, Sat. 10-6, Sun. 12-6.

Petersburg, **Helse Restaurant**, Deb Hurley, PO Box 1551, #17 Singly Alley, Petersburg, AK 99833. (907) 772-3444. Type of Business: Restaurant and retail. Sells: A variety of white meat, fish and vegetarian dishes, including some vegan options. Organic? Asserted 15-20% organic. Specialties: Seafood, soups, fresh bread, salads, sandwiches and daily specials. Hours: M-Sat. 9-5:30. Reservations: Possible. 100% Non-Smoking. Credit: None. Shipping: Being on an island, they have to depend on barge schedules or airlines to deliver. They do some small orders to other villages with the mail plane. Comments: This business recently changed hands and the new owner plans to add more vegetarian dishes and seafoods to the menu, and to use more organic foods.

AZ

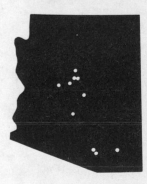

Arizona

Cottonwood, **Mount Hope**, 104 Main St., Cottonwood, AZ 86326. (602) 634-8251. Type of Business: Retail store. Sells to: The public, restaurants, and hotels. Sells: Most goods you would expect to see in a supermarket with a particularly good selection of herbs and spices. Organic?

They assert that about 25% of the goods they sell are organically grown and processed. **Credit:** None. **Prices:** Special prices for bulk orders. **Hours:** M-Sat. 9–6, Sun. 10–5. **Catalogue Available?** Yes, to those interested in buying wholesale. **Comments:** They also sell macrobiotic specialties and books.

Flagstaff, **New Frontiers Market,** 802 South Milton, Flagstaff, AZ 86001. **Type of Business:** Restaurant and retail store. **Sells:** Deli salads, sandwiches, smoothies, cakes, pies, casseroles. **Organic?** Asserted 40%. **Specialties:** Good home cooking; bulk groceries. **Prices:** Entrees—$3.25–$4.50. **Hours:** 9–9. **Credit:** V M. **Commendations:** *Natural Foods Merchandiser* 1985.

Payson, **Arjoy Acres,** HCR Box 1410, Payson, AZ 85541. (602) 474-1224. **Type of Business:** Retail store. **Sells to:** The public. **Sells:** Its own organically grown fresh produce. **Organic?** Asserted 100%. **Credit:** None. **Hours:** 8–5 seven days. **Minimum Order:** 1 lb. **Catalogue Available?** Yes.

Prescott, **Basic Health Foods,** Barbara & Merrill Hardel, 442 W Goodwin, Prescott, AZ 86303. (602) 445-7920. **Type of Business:** Retail store. **Sells to:** The public. **Sells:** Baked goods, fresh beans, beverages and fruit juices, breads, candy, cereals, fresh dairy products, flour, fresh dried fruit, meats, fresh nuts and nut butters, oils, pasta, rice, soy products, frozen vegetables, fresh grains and spices. **Organic?** No organic claims. **Credit:** V M. **Hours:** M-Sat., 9–5:30. **Catalogue Available?** None.

Scottsdale, **Arizona Natural Products,** Michael Hanna, 8281 E Evans Rd. #104, Scottsdale, AZ 85260. (602) 991-4414. **Type of Business:** Manufacturer and mail-order distributor. **Sells to:** The public. **Sells:** Onions and garlic. **Organic?** They say they do not need to use pesticides or synthetic fertilizers so they don't. **Credit:** V M. **Prices:** Open to negotiation for bulk orders. **Hours:** 8–5. **Shipping:** They ship within 48 hrs. Up to 25% discount on select goods ordered large quantities. **Minimum Order:** None. **Catalogue Available?** Yes. **Comments:** They own the first U.S. patent issued for "odorless garlic." They offer a money-back guarantee and free literature with their orders.

Sedona, **Oak Creek Orchards Country Market,** Jim & Jeanine Eddy, Box 132–236 Copper Cliffs Dr., Sedona, AZ 86336. (602) 282-2726. **Type of Business:** Organic farm and retail store. **Sells to:** The public. **Sells:** A wide variety of both fresh produce and grocery items. **Organic?** Asserted 50% organic. **Credit:** V M. **Prices:** Bulk discounts are 10–20% over cost. **Hours:** 9–6 daily, year round. **Minimum Order:** Yes.

Sedona, **Sedona Health Foods,** Ray Briggs, 2081 W Hwy. 89A, Sedona, AZ 86336. (602) 282-5871. **Type of Business:** Retail store. **Sells to:** The public. **Sells:** A selection of wholefood grocery items. **Organic?** Asserted 40% organic. **Credit:** V M AE. **Hours:** M-F 9–6, Sat. 9–5, Sunday closed. **Comments:** Strong in supplements and homeopathic remedies for a small-town store.

Tucson, **Kachina Kuisine,** Frank C. Olmsted, 411-N Ave., Tucson, AZ 85705. (602) 622-1200. **Type of Business:** Manufacturer/Processor. **Sells to:** Health stores, supermarkets. **Sells:** Nuts and vegetarian sandwiches. **Organic?** No organic claims. **Credit:** Cash or 10 days. **Minimum Order:** $15. **Catalogue Available?** No.

Tucson, **Tucson Co-op Warehouse,** Christopher Goodwin, Assistant Manager, 1716 E Factory Ave., Tucson, AZ 85709. (602) 884-9951, FAX (602) 792-3258. **Type of Business:** Co-op distributor. **Sells to:** Retailers and public. **Sells:** Whole grains, cereals, flours, rice, pasta, breads and other baked goods, fresh fruit, vegetables and legumes, meats, dairy products, nuts and nut butters, dried fruit, soy products, fruit juices, and beverages. **Organic?** Asserted 20% organic. **Credit:** None. **Prices:** Volume discount based on dollar amount of purchases. **Hours:** Open seven days. **Shipping:** Serves only the Southwest. **Minimum Order:** $100. **Catalogue Available?** Yes.

Wilcox, **English Family Farm/Orchards,** Dwight and Karla English, Star Rt. 1, Box 150X, Wilcox, AZ 85643. (602) 384-4857. **Type of Business:** Grower. In business since 1983. **Sells to:** Retailers. **Sells:** Fresh fruit (apples—quality tray packed and branded red and gold delicious, Granny Smith and Rome Apples). **Organic?** Documented organic. **Credit:** None. **Shipping:** By truck to Arizona and Nevada only. **Minimum Order:** Wholesale quantities. **Catalogue Available?** No.

AR

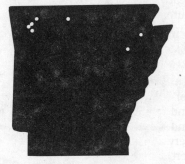

Arkansas

Fayetteville, **Mountain Ark Trading Co.,** Robb Boyd, Frank Head, 120 South East Avenue, Fayetteville, AR 72701. (501) 442-7191, (800) 643-8909. **Type of Business:** Distributor. **Sells to:** Stores and the public—mail order retail all over the world. **Sells:** Organic coffee, condiments (including Umeboshi products, and organic lime vinegar), dried beans (including turtle, pinto, and anazi), dried fruit, whole grains (including teff, and quinoa), flour and meal grains, processed grains (including Japanese pastas and seitan), sourdough bread, herbs, nuts, nut butters (peanut, tahini, sesame, almonds), oils (sesame, corn, olive), soy products (tempeh, natto, soymilk and starters), sweeteners (rice syrup, barley malt, amesake), soups, teas (bancha, barley, lotus root, dandelion, burdock), beer (beer home processing kits), sea vegetables and fish (in season). **Volume:** Approaching $1 million a year. **Or-**

ganic? Asserted 70% organic. Some products are labeled as certified organic, depending on which farm produces them. They look for official state certification or grower documentation. **Hours:** M-F 8–5, Sat. 9–noon (C.S.T.). **Credit:** V M AE. **Prices:** Generally lower than retail. A bulk price list comes with the catalog. **Shipping:** Ships UPS or (especially for those who only have a Post Office box or otherwise can't accept UPS) parcel post. **Minimum Order:** None for retail, $100 for bulk orders. **Catalogue Available?** Yes.♥♦

Fayetteville, **Ozark Cooperative Warehouse,** General Manager, PO Box 1528, Fayetteville, AR 72702. (501) 521–COOP, (501) 521–4920, FAX: (501) 521–9100. **Type of Business:** Distributor. **Sells to:** Stores, buying clubs, church groups, neighborhood groups and others. **Sells:** "Thousands of products"—a wide variety of grains, beans/ legumes, fresh and dried fruits, fruit juices, baked goods, vegetables, vegetable juices, spices, meats, nuts, nut butters, soy products, dairy products, cheeses, flours, pastas, cereals, and beverages (including alcohol-free wines and organically grown coffees). **Organic?** They assert that 20– 30% of their products are organically grown and processed. **Credit:** No credit cards. **Prices:** Discount prices for larger orders and for retail stores. Delivery is included in their prices. **Hours:** M-F 9–6, Sat. 12–4. **Shipping:** They serve the south (AL, AR, GA, LA, KS, MS, MO, OK, TN, and TX) with scheduled refrigerated and frozen delivery; other areas by UPS or common carrier. **Minimum Order:** Depends on your distance from their truck routes. **Catalogue Available?** Yes. **Comments:** In their fifteenth year, they "absolutely guarantee your satisfaction on all purchases." They also put out a free newsletter and sponsor a meeting/health conference each fall.♥

Fayetteville, **Summercorn Foods,** David Druding, 401 Watson, Fayetteville, AR 72701. (501) 521–9338. **Type of Business:** Manufacturer and mail order and truck distributor (AR, OK, KS, LA, MO, TN, TX). **Sells to:** The public and retailers. **Sells:** Baked goods; granola, whole wheat and rye; cookies, crackers, snacks, and confections; grocery and refrigerated/frozen soy products. **Organic?** Asserted 66% organic. **Credit:** None. **Prices:** Discounts up to 10% on orders of $2500+. **Hours:** M-F, 9–4:30 or by prearrangement. **Minimum Order:** None. **Catalogue Available?** Stock pricelist available.

Huntsville, **Eagle Agricultural Products, Inc.,** Gary and Kathy Turner, 407 Church Ave., Huntsville, AR 72740. (501) 738–2203. **Type of Business:** Manufacturer, distributor and retailer. **Sells to:** Retailers and the public both directly and by mail order. **Sells:** Dried beans (kidney, lima, navy, pinto and soy), fresh fruit (apples and melons), whole grains (barley, buckwheat, corn, popcorn, millet, oats, rice, wheat), fresh vegetables (carrots, potatoes, tomatoes), flour and meals (hot and cold wheat, whole wheat, buckwheat, rye), rice (brown and wild), pastas, poultry, cookies, packaged baking mixes, condiments, sodas, and fruit drinks. **Organic?** Asserted organic, 95%. **Credit:** V M. **Prices:** Special prices for bulk orders (500 lbs. or more). **Hours:** M-F 9–6. **Shipping:** Will ship to anywhere in North America. Volume discounts available

on mail order services. **Minimum Order:** None. **Catalogue Available?** Yes.

Weiner, **Southern Brown Rice,** PO Box 185, Weiner, AR 72479. (501) 684–2354. **Type of Business:** Grower and processor. **Sells to:** The public through mail order. **Sells:** Beans (especially soy), rice (long, medium, and short grain; brown and wild varieties; Basmati rice and Southern wild blend), brown rice cream, brown rice flour, and rice bran. **Organic?** Certified 95% organic by Organic Crop Improvement Association. **Credit:** None. **Prices:** Special prices for bulk orders (1,000 lbs. or more). **Hours:** Will sell directly to the public, 8–5 **Shipping:** No restrictions. **Minimum Order:** None. **Catalogue Available?** Yes. **Comments:** Family-owned and managed business since 1907.

CA

California

Arcata, **Arcata Coop,** 811 1st, Arcata, CA 95521. (They, along with the Eureka Coop and the Fortuna Coop are part of North Coast Cooperative, Inc.) **Type of Business:** Retail store, manufacturer, co-op. **Sells to:** The public, retailers, restaurants, buying clubs. **Sells:** A wide range of natural groceries and fresh organic produce. **Organic?** Fresh produce 80% organic (certified by Organic Crop Improvement Association, California Certified Organic Farmers), other goods, 20%. **Credit:** None. **Prices:** Bulk discount 10%. **Hours:** Varies by store. **Catalogue Available?** For wholesale only. **Comments and Commendations:** Consumer Coop Mgmt. Association's Coop Achievement Award, 1989; Arcata County Recycling Center's Recycling Award, 1988.

Arcata, **Casa de Pasa,** Marc Chaton, 854 9th St., Arcata, CA 95521. **Type of Business:** Restaurant. **Sells:** Mexican food. **Organic?** 10%. **Specialities:** Vegelada, Rice & Bean Platter, "Heart Health" items. **Prices:** $3–$6. **Hours:** M-Sat. 11–9:30 (F -10), Sun. 4–9:30.

Arcata, **Mad River Farm Country Kitchen,** Susan Anderson, PO Box 155, Arcata, CA 95521. (707) 822–7150. **Type of Business:** Manufacturer and mail-order distributor. **Sells to:** The public and retailers. **Sells:** Jams (blackberry, red raspberry, strawberry, boysenberry, blueberry, monmorency cherry, red raspberry rhubarb), marmalades (sunshine and lemon), and cranberry conserves. **Organic?** The strawberry jam and marmalades are made from organically grown fruit. **Credit:** None. **Shipping:** Orders are generally shipped within one week to anywhere in the United States. **Minimum Order:** None. **Catalogue Available?** Yes. **Comments:** They use white sugar due to concerns that molasses and "non-sugar" sweeteners (like grape) have high levels of pesticide contamination. They claim the pectin in their jams is good for cholesterol reduction. The business is family-run and has a good record of environmental conscientiousness and charitable donations.

Arcata, **Tofu Shop,** The, 768 18th St., Arcata, CA 95521. (707) 822-7409. **Type of Business:** Take-out restaurant, manufacturer, and retail store. **Sells:** Tofu burgers, cold cuts, sandwiches, salads, breads, soups, and desserts. **Organic?** Asserted 50%, no additives, colorings or preservatives. **Specialties:** Fresh tofu made on premises using traditional methods. **Prices:** $2.75 -$4.10. **Hours:** M-Sat. 8-8, Sun. 11-6. **Reservations:** Not accepted. 100% No smoking. **Credit:** None. **Shipping:** Call them for details. **Comments and Commendations:** Named best natural take-out service in country by Wholelife Times magazine (1985). They say they are one of the few traditional style tofu-shops in the western hemisphere.

Bard, **Western Date Ranches,** Peggy Hartsock, Marketing Manager, PO Box 879, Bard, CA 92222. (619) 572-0192. **Type of Business:** Grower, manufacturer, packer and shipper. **Sells to:** The public and retailers. **Sells:** Medjool dates. **Organic?** Asserted 100% organic. **Prices:** Bulk orders sold at wholesale prices to the public. **Hours:** M-F 8-5. **Shipping:** All orders FOB Bard, CA. **Minimum Order:** 10 cases. **Catalogue Available?** Yes.

Berkeley, **Blue Nile,** The, 2525 Telegraph Ave., Berkeley, CA 94704. (415) 540-6777. **Type of Business:** Restaurant. **Sells:** Authentic Ethiopian cuisine, eaten in the true Ethiopian style, using Injera (Ethiopian bread) to maneuver the food from the plate to the mouth. The Blue Nile offers a wide variety of Ethiopian vegetarian alternatives. **Organic?** Asserted 50% organic. **Specialties:** Vegetarian combinations, with lentils, split peas, cracked wheat, rice, fresh vegetables and salad. **Prices:** Entrees range from $4 to $7. **Hours:** M-Sat. 11:30-10, Sun. 5-10. **Reservations:** Possible. 100% non-smoking. **Credit:** V M. **Commendations:** The Euro-Visitors Guide (Paris); *Evening Magazine; Express Weekly,* Readers Choice; *San Francisco Focus* magazine, Gold Winner, Readers Choice.

Berkeley, **Whole Foods Market,** 3000 Telegraph Ave., Berkeley, CA. (415) 649-9395. (Also in Palo Alto, Austin, Dallas, Houston, and Richardson, TX, and New Orleans, LA.) **Type of Business:** Part of a chain of 8 wholefoods supermarkets in Texas, Louisiana, and California. **Sells to:** The public. **Sells:** A huge variety of wholefood grocery items and organic produce. They claim to have "the most significantly integrated mix of conventional 'clean' food and 'natural' foods" in the country.

Organic? Produce is 30-40% organic in winter and 60-80% in summer. Certified by California Certified Organic Farmers. **Credit:** V M AE. **Prices:** 5% discount for unopened retail cases. **Hours:** 9-11, 7 days a week. **Commendations and Comments:** Whole Foods Markets are known for their informative and relaxing atmospheres and the Whole Foods employees tend to be quite knowledgeable. Lectures and tours are offered to encourage better shopping. They claim (as does Real Foods in San Francisco) to be the largest retailer of organically grown produce in the U.S. Whole Foods was the fourth most recommended retail chain.♥♦♦♦

Beverly Hills, **Mrs. Gooch's Natural Foods Markets, Inc.,** 239 N Crescent Drive, Beverly Hills, CA 90210. (213) 274-3360, Fax (213) 274-8149. (Also in Glendale, Hermosa Beach, Los Angeles, Northridge, Sherman Oaks, and Thousand Oaks.) **Type of Business:** Wholefood supermarket and wholesaler. **Sells to:** The public. **Sells:** A huge variety of wholefoods and organic produce. Their goal is "to offer you products that contain: no chemical additives, no harmful preservative agents, no artificial flavorings, no artificial colorings, no refined sugar, no flour, no caffeine, no chocolate, no hydrogenated oil, and no irradiated foods." **Organic?** They sell 425 organically grown and processed products and are affiliated with Organic Crop Improvement Association and California Certified Organic Farmers. **Credit:** V M and ATM Cards. **Prices:** 10% discount on full-case purchases. **Hours:** 9-9 seven days a week. **Comments and Commendations:** Mrs. Gooch's got the most recommendations of any retailer in the Catalogue and received glowing reviews from almost everyone who mentioned them. They are in the vanguard of healthy food establishments in this country. If you live in Southern California and are seeking a huge variety of healthy foods, Mrs. Gooch's is your best bet.♦♦♦

Bolinas, **Star Route Farms,** Warren Weber, Bolinas, CA 94924. (415) 868-0929. **Type of Business:** Grower. **Sells to:** Retailers, distributors, restaurants, and public. **Sells:** Lettuce, arugula, broccoli, cauliflower, spinach, radiccio, leeks, chicory, edible flowers and herbs. **Organic?** 100% organic (California Certified Organic Farmers). **Shipping:** By truck in Bay area 6 days a week; airfreight and Federal Express on request. **Catalogue Available?** Yes. **Comments:** One of the first organic growers in the Bay Area, he sells 70% of his produce directly to restaurants who say they value the taste of his vegetables and herbs as much as their chemical-free status.♥♦

Calabasas, **Good Earth Restaurant and Bakery,** Mr. E. R. Wilson, 23945 Calabasas Rd. Suite 107, Calabasas, CA 91302. (818) 347-5722. **Type of Business:** Restaurant. **Sells:** Fresh fish, Good Earth burgers, eggplant and salads. Vegetarian and vegan options available. **Organic?** Asserted 4% organic. **Specialties:** Teriyaki chicken, Malaysian stir fried chicken or beef and Country French lasagna. **Prices:** $6.25-$9.75. **Hours:** Daily 7-10 (open until 11p.m. Fri. and Sat.). **Reservations:** Not required. 5% No smoking. **Credit:** V M.

Campbell, **Bread of Life Alternative Food Store,** 1690 S Bascom Ave., Campbell, CA 95008. (408) 371-5000. **Type of Business:** Natural foods supermarket. **Sells to:** The public. **Sells:** An extensive selection of wholefoods, specialty foods, and fresh organic produce. **Organic?** Produce is about 50% organic (California Certified Organic Farmers), 40% of processed goods are organic. **Credit:** V M certain ATM cards. **Prices:** 8% discount on case purchases, 15% on bulk herb purchases. **Hours:** M-F 9-9, S-S 9-8. **Comments and Commendation:** Best Natural Food Store, Best Gourmet Supermarket in Santa Clara Valley— *Metro.* Besides carrying a great selection of foods, they also offer household cleaning supplies, paper products, and much more. "Truly one-stop shopping."

Canoga Park, **Follow Your Heart,** Brooke Ide, 21825 Sherman Way, Canoga Park, CA 91303. (213) 348-0291. **Type of Business:** Restaurant and retail store. **Sells:** Soup. **Organic?** Filtered water. **Specialties:** Vegetarian and vegan dishes available. **Prices:** $5.50-$7.95. **Hours:** Market M-Sat. 7:30 a.m.-9 p.m. Sun. 10-9, Restaurant M-Sat. 7:30 a.m.-8:30 a.m. Sun. 10-8:30. **Reservations:** Not accepted. 100% No smoking. **Credit:** V M.

Carpinteria, **Moore Ranch,** Steve or Ben Moore, 5844 Casitas Pass Rd., Carpinteria, CA 93013. (805) 684-8046. **Type of Business:** Grower, packer and shipper. **Sells to:** Primarily retailers and restaurants. **Sells:** Fresh fruit (lemons, limes, avocados, persimmons), fresh vegetables (green beans, sugar snapper peas, squash, zucchini). **Organic?** Certified 100% organic, California Certified Organic Farmers and Demeter (Bio-dynamic) certified. **Minimum Order:** Negotiable.

Chico, **Weiss's Kiwifruit,** G.E. Weiss, 594 Paseo Companeros, Chico, CA 95928. (916) 343-2354. **Type of Business:** Broker to distributors, mail-order distributor, and retail store. **Sells to:** Retailers and the public. **Sells:** Fresh kiwifruit. **Organic?** California Certified Organic Farmers certified. **Credit:** Check only. **Prices:** Special prices for bulk orders. **Hours:** M-Sat. 8-6. **Shipping:** Lower UPS charges for larger orders. **Minimum Order:** 2.5 lbs., or $8.75. **Catalogue Available?** Yes. **Comments:** They sell fresh kiwifruit from October through December, but they warn that the kiwifruit might freeze in transit, particularly in December.

Clovis, **Healthfood Express,** Lin Martin, 181 Sylmar, Clovis, CA 93612. (209) 252-8321. Mail to PO Box 8357, Fresno, CA 93747. **Type of Business:** Mail-order distributor. **Sells to:** The public. **Sells:** A variety of meat-substitutes, granola products, and dried fruits. **Organic?** No organic claims. **Credit:** V M. **Prices:** Discounts awarded on a points basis for future orders. **Shipping:** Cost depends on order size. A $50 order would cost between $5-$15 depending on region. **Minimum Order:** $30 suggested. **Catalogue Available?** Yes.

Coachella, **Great Date in the Morning,** Jim Dunn, PO Box 31, 85-710 Grapefruit Blvd., Coachella, CA 92236. (619) 298-6171. **Type of Business:** Grower, processor, mail-order distributor, and wholesale distributor. **Sells to:** Wholesalers, retailers, mail order. **Sells:** Dates, melons, strawberries, fresh vegetables and spices. **Organic?** California Certified Organic Farmers and Organic Crop Improvement Association certified. **Credit:** None. **Shipping:** Quantity discounts available. **Minimum Order:** 50 cases for wholesale purchases; none for retail. **Catalogue Available?** Yes.♦

Coachella, **Lee Anderson's Covalda Date Company,** PO Box 908, 51-392 Highway 86, Coachella, CA 92236. (619) 398-3551. **Type of Business:** Manufacturer, wholesaler, mail-order distributor and retail store. **Sells to:** Distributors, retail stores, and the public. **Sells:** Dates (fresh, processed, and dried), citrus fruits, and pecans. **Organic?** "Self-certified" since the 40's. **Credit:** V M. **Prices:** Discounts available at every level. **Hours:** M-F 8-4:30. **Shipping:** UPS to everywhere possible. **Minimum Order:** 750 lbs. for distributors only. **Catalogue Available?** Yes. **Comments:** Lee Anderson, "King of Dates," was a pioneer in sustainable agriculture and built a business that continues to thrive today. Lee celebrated his 101st birthday in July, 1989.♥

Costa Mesa, **Mother's Market & Kitchen,** 225 E 17th St., Costa Mesa, CA 92627. (714) 631-4741. **Type of Business:** Retail store, mail-order distributor, wholesaler, restaurant. **Sells to:** The public. **Sells:** An impressive array of natural groceries and fresh produce. **Organic?** Fresh produce 35% organic (certified by Organic Crop Improvement Association, Farm Verified Organic, NOFA, California Certified Organic Farmers, Demeter/Bio-dynamic); other grocery items 10-20% organic. **Credit:** V M ATM Interlink. **Prices:** 10% off full cases when ordered in advance. **Hours:** 9-9, seven days. Restaurant 9-8:30. **Comments:** The full-service vegetarian restaurant offers "international low-fat, low-salt, high-flavor cuisine."♦♦

Del Mar, **Souplantation,** 3790 Via de la Valle, Del Mar, CA 92014. (619) 222-7404. **Type of Business:** Restaurant. **Sells:** Salads with no additives or preservatives from a 60-item salad bar, homemade soups made daily with no MSG, homemade muffins and fresh fruit salad. **Organic?** Asserted 10% organic. **Prices:** All you can eat dishes for between $5.25 and $6.95. **Hours:** 11-10. **Reservations:** Possible. 90% non-smoking. **Credit:** None.

Desert Hot Springs, **Mallat Family,** Frank and Regina Mallat, Owners, 29930 Desert Charm Rd., Desert Hot Springs, CA 92240. (619) 342-0065. **Type of Business:** Wholesale distributor and grower. **Sells to:** Sale to the public limited to mail orders placed by phone for fresh herbs and Mesclon lettuce. Their primary business is selling to stores and co-ops in Southern California. **Sells:** Fresh fruit, spices, and vegetables; specialty—organic citrus and Mesclon lettuce. **Organic?** Asserted 100% organic, certified by the. Have applied for California Certified Organic Farmers certification. **Credit:** None. **Shipping:** Order by phone. They ship by UPS.

Duncan Mills, **The Blue Heron,** Moscow Rd. & Rte. 116, Duncan Mills, CA 95430. (707) 865-2225. **Type of Business:** Restaurant. **Sells:** Vegetarian dishes. **Organic?**

Asserted 40% organic. **Specialties:** Various vegetarian dishes and fresh fish, especially salmon. **Prices:** $9–$13. **Hours:** M-F 5:30–9, S-S 10–3. **Reservations:** Accepted. 100% No smoking. **Credit:** V M.

El Cajon, **Boney's,** 152 N Second St., El Cajon, CA 92021. (619) 579–8251. (Affiliated stores in Escondido, Hillcrest, Pacific Beach, San Diego, and Vista.) **Type of Business:** Supermarket that carries some wholefood items. **Sells to:** The public. **Sells:** A selection ofwholefood grocery items, conventional grocery items, and a small amount of organic produce. **Organic?** About 5% of produce is organic (California Certified Organic Farmers). **Credit:** None. **Prices:** Discounts on bulk orders. **Hours:** 9–8 daily.

Elk Creek, **Gravelly Ridge Farms,** Star Route 16, Elk Creek, CA 95939. (916) 963–3216. **Type of Business:** Mail-order distributor. **Sells to:** Retail stores and the public. **Sells:** A wide variety of organic fresh fruit, dried fruit, vegetables, and grains. **Organic?** California Certified Organic Farmers certified. **Hours:** M-F and Sun. 9–6. **Shipping:** They ship perishables on the same day they are harvested. Availability depends on season. **Minimum Order:** None. **Catalogue Available?** Yes.♦

Emeryville, **Real Foods,** 5800 Shellmount, 94608, Emeryville, CA 94608. (415) 420–8085. **Type of Business:** Chain of wholefoods markets. **Sells to:** The public. **Sells:** A good selection of fresh organic produce, organic bulk items, and wholefood grocery items. **Organic?** About 95% of produce is organic in summer, less in winter. **Credit:** V M. **Prices:** Discounts on certain bulk orders. **Hours:** 9–8. **Comments:** Real Foods got the fifth most recommendations in our survey.

Encinitas, **The Shepherd Natural Food Restaurant,** John Kanterakis, 1126 1st St., Encinitas, CA 92024. (619) 753–1124. **Type of Business:** Restaurant. **Sells:** Natural foods. From their whole wheat pancakes and eggwhite omelet, to their "mushroom burger", salad bar and nightly dinner specials, the Shepherd aims to provide a tasty menu, low in fat and cholesterol and high in fiber. All the cuisine here is vegetarian, with many vegan options. **Organic?** Asserted 50% organic. **Specialties:** Mushroom burgers, tofu sandwiches, Stroganoff (using mushrooms), Asian Lentil Loaf, Stuffed Cabbage and Cashew Melody (a dairyless lasagna with cashew seed cheese). **Prices:** Entrees range from $4.95 to $7.95 at lunch and from $7.95 to $9.95 at dinner. **Hours:** Sat.-Th 8 a.m.–9:30 p.m., F 8 a.m.–11:30 p.m. **Reservations:** Possible for parties of 6 or more. 100% non-smoking. **Credit:** V M AE. **Commendations:** "Best Health Food Restaurant in North County," *The Entertainer*, 1988. **Comments:** Musicians perform live daily.

Escondido, **Boney's,** 510 W 13th Ave., Escondido, CA 92025. (619) 745–2141. (Affiliated businesses in El Cajon, Hillcrest, Pacific Beach, San Diego, and Vista.) **Type of Business:** Wholefoods grocery market. **Sells to:** The public. **Sells:** A large variety of wholefood grocery items and fresh produce. A soup and salad bar restaurant is attached to the store. They also have an attached bakery that makes breads from their own sprouted grains. **Organic?** About 10% of produce is organic (California Certified Organic Farmers); about 20–25% of grocery items. **Credit:** None. **Prices:** 10% discounts on full cases (except for dairy or sales items). **Hours:** 9–8 daily. **Comments:** Each store in the group is run by a different member of the extended family.

Esparto, **Capay Canyon Ranch,** Leslie Barth, PO Box 508, Esparto, CA 95627. (916) 662–2372, FAX: (916) 662–2306. **Type of Business:** Grower, manufacturer and distributor. **Sells to:** Retailers, mail order to general public. **Sells:** Fresh apricots, cherries and grapes, dried fruit (raisins, apricots, pears, tomatoes), nuts and nut butters (almonds, walnuts). **Organic?** Asserted organic, 50%, member of Farm Verified Organic. All products grown on ranch are organic in accordance with section 26569.11 of the California Health and Safety Code. **Credit:** No credit cards. **Prices:** Discount for bulk orders over 500 lbs. **Hours:** 8 a.m. to 5 p.m. **Minimum Order:** None. **Catalogue Available?** Yes.

Etna, **Black Ranch,** Dave and Dawn Black, 5800 Eastside Rd., Etna, CA 96027. (916) 467–3387. **Type of Business:** Grower, manufacturer and mail-order distributor. **Sells to:** Retailers, and the public. **Sells:** Whole grains (oats, red and white wheat, amaranth and rye), rose hips, red clover sprouts, wholegrain flour (wheat, rye, and amaranth), 6–grain cereal. **Organic?** California Certified Organic Farmers certified. **Credit:** None. **Prices:** Special prices for 40 or 50 lb. bags. **Hours:** Call ahead. **Shipping:** $2 shipping and handling charge. **Minimum Order:** 6 lbs. **Catalogue Available?** Yes.

Eureka, **Eureka Cooperative,** 3134 Jacobs Ave., Eureka, CA 95501. (707) 445–3185. (They, along with the Arcata Co-op and the Fortuna Co-op are part of North Coast Cooperative, Inc.) **Type of Business:** Retail store, manufacturer, co-op. **Sells to:** The public, retailers, restaurants, buying clubs. **Sells:** An all-inclusive range of natural groceries and fresh organic produce. **Organic?** Fresh produce 80% organic (certified by Organic Crop Improvement Association, California Certified Organic Farmers); other goods, 20%. **Credit:** No. **Prices:** Bulk discount 10%. **Hours:** Varies by store. **Catalogue Available?** For wholesale only. **Comments and Commendations:** Consumer Coop Mgmt. Association's Coop Achievement Award, 1989; Arcata County Recycling Center's Recycling Award, 1988.

Fontana, **Smith's Health Foods,** 16920 "A" Orange Way, Fontana, CA 92335. (714) 350–3550. **Type of Business:** Retail store. **Sells to:** The public. **Sells:** A range of wholefood groceries plus fresh beans, grains, nuts, and soy products **Organic?** Fresh produce asserted 100% organic, other grocery, 5%. **Credit:** V M D. **Hours:** M-F 9–6, Sat. 9–5. **Comments:** The store will special-order items not in stock at the customer's request.

Forestville, **Kozlowski Farms—Sonoma County Classics,** Cindy Kozlowski Hayworthy, 5566 Gravenstein

Hwy., Forestville, CA 95436. (707) 887–1587, FAX: (707) 887–9650. **Type of Business:** Grower and manufacturer. **Sells to:** The public, distributors. **Sells:** Jams, jellies, no-sugar-added fruit butters, no-sugar-added chutneys, no-sugar-added conserves, fudge sauces, marmalades, barbecue sauce, vinegars, mustards, syrups, fresh and frozen berries, fresh and unsulfured dried apples, fresh squeezed apple ciders. **Organic?** Certified organic, 75%. Member of California Certified Organic Farmers and Sonoma County Agriculture Marketing Program. **Credit:** V M. **Hours:** Retail—Daily 9–5, except major holidays. **Shipping:** UPS or best carrier for weight and location. Normal delivery two weeks after receipt of order. **Minimum Order:** Varies. **Catalogue Available?** Yes.

Fremont, **Lloyds Natural Foods Market,** 39145 Fremont Hub, Fremont, CA 94538. (415) 792–3000. **Type of Business:** Retail store. **Sells to:** The public. **Sells:** A range of natural grocery items with some fresh produce.

Fullerton, **California Health Foods,** 115 E Commonwealth, Fullerton, CA 92632. **Type of Business:** Retail store. **Sells to:** The public direct and by mail. **Sells:** Fresh fruit, dried fruits (all types unsulfured), vegetables (all varieties including frozen broccoli, corn, carrots, and spinach), nuts and nut butters (all types), grains (all types), cereals (corn, granola, oatmeal, wheat), breads (oat, pita, pumpernickel, rye, whole wheat, sprouted, yeast-free, wheat-free, bagels, bread crumbs, cakes, muffins, crackers, tacos, crackers), flour (buckwheat, rye, whole wheat, pancakes) rice, pasta, oils, beans (all), soy products (miso, milk, tempeh, tofu), cheeses, yogurt, milk, kefir, ice cream, spices (all), beverages (fruit juices, soda, teas, sodas), popcorn, candy bars (no sugar), salsa, and sauces. **Organic?** Asserted organic, 25% overall (all produce is certified 100%). They are affiliated with California Certified Organic Farmers. **Credit:** V M. **Prices:** 10% discount for bulk orders. **Hours:** M-Th 9–6, F 9–7, Sat. 9–5:30. **Shipping:** Ship Parcel Post or UPS, usual time 3 days. **Minimum Order:** No. **Catalogue Available?** No.

Garberville, **Wood Rose Cafe,** Pam Hanson and Leah Linzer, 911 Redwood Dr., Garberville, CA 95440. (707) 923–3191. **Type of Business:** Restaurant. **Sells:** Vegetarian and vegan dishes available. Burgers (wholewheat buns, tofu or sesame burgers), burritos, tostadas, omelets, sandwiches, pancakes, beverages and juices made to order. **Organic?** Asserted 25% organic. **Specialties:** Their menu includes "Tofu Rancheros"—as opposed to huevos (eggs) rancheros—and a variety of omelets. **Prices:** $2.25–$6.25. **Hours:** M-F 8–2:30 p.m., S-S 8–1p.m. **Reservations:** Not accepted. 100% No smoking. **Credit:** None.

Gilroy, **Van Dyke Ranch,** Betty or Peter, 7665 Crews Rd., Gilroy, CA 95020. (408) 842–5423. **Type of Business:** Grower. **Sells to:** Distributors, retailers, and the public by mail order. **Sells:** Dried fruit (bing cherries, apricots), fresh fruit (apricots, cherries). **Organic?** Certified organic (100%—California Certified Organic Farmers). **Minimum Order:** 5 lbs. **Catalogue Available?** Yes. **Comments:** A friendly place; much of their operation has been organic for 70 years. They are also building a fruit stand.♥♦

Glendale, **Mrs. Gooch's Natural Foods Markets, Inc.,** 826 N Glendale Avenue, Glendale, CA 91206, (818) 240–9350, Fax (818) 240–2681. (Also in Beverly Hills, Hermosa Beach, Los Angeles, Northridge, Sherman Oaks, and Thousand Oaks.) **Type of Business:** Wholefoods supermarket and wholesaler. **Sells to:** The public. **Sells:** A huge variety of wholefoods and organic produce. Their goal is "to offer you products that contain: no chemical additives, no harmful preservative agents, no artificial flavorings, no artificial colorings, no refined sugar, no flour, no caffeine, no chocolate, no hydrogenated oil, and no irradiated foods." **Organic?** They sell 425 organically grown and processed products and are affiliated with Organic Crop Improvement Association and California Certified Organic Farmers. **Credit:** V M and ATM Cards. **Prices:** 10% discount on full-case purchases. **Hours:** 9–9 seven days a week. **Comments and Commendations:** Mrs. Gooch's got the most recommendations of any business in the Catalogue and received glowing reviews from almost everyone who mentioned them. They are in the vanguard of healthy food establishments in this country. If you live in Southern California and are seeking a huge variety of healthy foods, Mrs. Gooch's is your best bet.♦♦♦

Goleta, **The Growing Concern,** Paul Garett, Ed Slupski, Rte. 1, Box 286, Goleta, CA 93117. (805) 968–4461. **Type of Business:** Grower. **Sells to:** Wholesalers. **Sells:** Fresh vegetables (lettuces, celery, broccoli, cauliflower, cabbage, tomatoes, strawberries). **Organic?** Certified organic California Certified Organic Farmers.

Grass Valley, **Briarpatch Co-op,** 416 Washington St., Grass Valley, CA 95945. (916) 272–5333. **Type of Business:** Retail store, co-op. **Sells to:** The public. **Sells:** A complete line of wholefood grocery items and fresh organic produce. **Organic?** Produce 80–90% organic. Certified by Organic Crop Improvement Association, Farm Verified Organic, California Certified Organic Farmers. **Credit:** No. **Prices:** 10% discount for members only. **Hours:** M-Sat. 9–7, Sun. 12–5.

Grass Valley, **Mountain Peoples Warehouse,** 110 Springhill Bvld., Grass Valley, CA 95945. **Write to:** PO Box 1027, Nevada City, CA 95959. (916) 273–9531 **Type of Business:** Wholesale natural foods distributor, since 1976. **Sells to:** Retailers, buying clubs, and other wholesalers. **Sells:** Baked goods, coffee, condiments, dairy products, dried beans, dried fruit, fresh fruit, whole grains, flour and meals, processed grain products, herbs and spices, juices, meat and eggs, nuts and nut butters, oils, seeds, soy products, sweeteners, fresh vegetables. **Organic?** Certification varies, organic "preferred": all of their organic growers are certified by California Certified Organic Farmers; almost all of their produce is organic. **Prices:** They pass along specials that their suppliers offer. **Hours:** M-F 7–5. **Shipping:** They serve 10 Western states with their own fleet of trucks and ship by container to Alaska and Hawaii. **Minimum Order:** Depends on area: $300 for nearby or metro locations, $500 for more distant or out of the way locations, and $200 for pick-up. **Catalogue Available?** Yes, for $1.00.

Healdsburg, **Timber Crest Farms,** Ruth Waltenspiel, 4791 Dry Creek Rd., Healdsburg, CA 95448. (707) 433–8251. **Type of Business:** Grower and manufacturer. **Sells to:** Distributors, retailers, and mail order to the public. **Sells:** Dried fruit (apples, apricots, peaches, pears, prunes), dried tomatoes, fruit butters, fancy dried fruit trays. **Organic?** Asserted 70% organic. **Credit:** V M AE. **Prices:** 3 different lists (Distributor price list, Full Case price list, and individual mail order price list). **Hours:** M-F 8–5, Sat. 10–4. **Shipping:** All orders shipped same day received. **Minimum Order:** 5,000 lbs. for distributor accounts, full case for retailers, one package for consumers. **Catalogue Available?** Yes.

Hermosa Beach, **Mrs. Gooch's Natural Foods Markets, Inc.,** 526 Pier Avenue, Hermosa Beach, CA 90254. (213) 376–6931, FAX (213) 376–7651. (Also in Beverly Hills, Glendale, Los Angeles, Northridge, Sherman Oaks, and Thousand Oaks.) **Type of Business:** Wholefood supermarket and wholesaler. **Sells to:** The public. **Sells:** A huge variety of wholefoods and organic produce. Their goal is "to offer you products that contain: no chemical additives, no harmful preservative agents, no artificial flavorings, no artificial colorings, no refined sugar, no flour, no caffeine, no chocolate, no hydrogenated oil, and no irradiated foods." **Organic?** They sell 425 organically grown and processed products and are affiliated with Organic Crop Improvement Association and California Certified Organic Farmers. **Credit:** V M and ATM Cards. **Prices:** 10% discount on full-case purchases. **Hours:** 9–9 seven days a week. **Comments and Commendations:** Mrs. Gooch's got the most recommendations of any business in the Catalogue and received glowing reviews from almost everyone who mentioned them. They are in the vanguard of healthy food establishments in this country. If you live in Southern California and are seeking a huge variety of healthy foods, Mrs. Gooch's is your best bet.◆◆◆

Hermosa Beach, **The Spot,** 110 2nd St., Hermosa Beach, CA 90254. (213) 376–2355. **Type of Business:** Restaurant. **Sells:** Vegetarian Mexican food, salads, and sandwiches. Vegan, dairy-free, and macrobiotic dishes available. **Organic?** Asserted 50% organic. **Specialties:** The menu includes many intriguing dishes from Teri Tofuyaki [sic] to Mexican Spud. **Prices:** $5.50–$6.95 **Hours:** 11–9:30 p.m. **Reservations:** Not accepted. 100% No smoking. **Credit:** V M. **Commendations:** They use Mrs. Gooch's produce. *Easy Reader* Best Vegetarian Restaurant in the South Bay award—1986, 1987, 1988 and 1989.◆

Hillcrest, **Boney's,** 734 University, Hillcrest, CA. (619) 295–4569. (Affiliated businesses in El Cajon, Escondido, Pacific Beach, San Diego, and Vista.) **Type of Business:** Whole foods supermarket. **Sells to:** The public. **Sells:** A full line of wholefood grocery items and some organic fresh produce. **Organic?** 10% produce. **Credit:** None. **Prices:** 10% discounts on cases. **Hours:** 9–9 M-Sat., 9–7 Sun.

Hollywood, **Orean Health Express,** 1320 N Vine, Hollywood, CA 90028. (213) 462–9945. **Type of Business:** Restaurant. **Sells:** Vegetarian, vegan and macrobiotic dishes only. **Organic?** Asserted 30% organic. **Specialties:** Vegiburgers, pancakes, burritos, baked potatoes, tacos, soup, salads and beverages. **Prices:** $2.50–$4.00 **Hours:** 7 a.m.–9 p.m. **Reservations:** Not accepted. 100% no smoking. **Credit:** None. **Commendations:** Their menu is approved by the American Heart Association.

Huntington Beach, **Licata's California Nutrition Centers,** Paul Licata, 5242 Bolsa Ave., Suite 3, Huntington Beach, CA 92647. (714) 893–0017. Retail store located in Anaheim. **Type of Business:** Retail store and mail-order distributor. **Sells to:** The public. **Sells:** A variety of wholefood grocery items: cereals, flours, mixes, breads, oils, beans, dried fruit, dairy products, soy products, salsa, beverages. **Organic?** No organic claims. **Credit:** V M. **Prices:** 10% discount on full cases. **Hours:** M-Sat. 9:30 a.m.–6 p.m. **Shipping:** Mail Order: Volume discounts from 10–25%. All orders add $2.00 shipping. **Minimum Order:** None. **Catalogue Available?** Yes.

Huntington Beach, **Mother's Market & Kitchen,** 19770 Beach Blvd., Huntington Beach, CA 92648. (714) 963–6667. **Type of Business:** Retail store, mail-order distributor, and wholesaler. **Sells to:** The public. **Sells:** See listing for Costa Mesa.◆◆

Laguna Beach, **Boat Canyon Health Foods,** 632 No. Coast Highway, Laguna Beach, CA 92651. (714) 494–6775. **Type of Business:** Retail store. **Sells to:** The public. **Sells:** A full line of natural groceries and fresh produce. **Organic?** Fresh produce 75% organic (certified by Organic Crop Improvement Association), other goods, 90%. **Credit:** V M. **Prices:** 10% discount on case items. **Hours:** M-Sat. 9–6, Sun. 10–5.

Laguna Beach, **The Stand Natural Foods Restaurant,** Edward Brancard, 238 Thalia, Laguna Beach, CA 92651. (714) 494–8101. Also at: 347 Mermaid, 494–9499. **Type of Business:** Restaurant. **Sells:** Vegetarian and vegan dishes only, macrobiotic dishes available. **Organic?** Asserted 80% organic. **Specialties:** Fresh juice, salads, sandwiches, hot foods, and their home-made baked goods and desserts. **Prices:** $1.75–$4.95 **Hours:** 7–7 daily. **Reservations:** Not accepted. 100% No smoking. **Credit:** None.

Laguna Niguel, **The Natural Grocer,** 28062 Klamata Ct., Laguna Niguel, CA 92656. (714) 249–1933. **Type of Business:** Retail store. **Sells to:** The public. **Sells:** A full selection of wholefood groceries and fresh produce. **Organic?** Fresh produce asserted 50–100% organic. Other items 50% estimated organic. **Credit:** V M. **Prices:** Bulk discount usually 10%. **Hours:** 9–9.

Lakeport, **Nature's Food Center,** 601 N Forbes, Lakeport, CA 95453. (707) 263–5359. **Type of Business:** Retail store and mail-order distributor. **Sells to:** The public. **Sells:** A wide variety of natural grocery items and fresh organic produce. **Organic?** Fresh produce 90% organic (certified by California Certified Organic Farmers). Other items, 50% organic. **Credit:** None. **Prices:** For bulk discount information, please inquire. **Hours:** 9–5:30. **Shipping:** Generally within 48 hours. **Catalogue Available?** Yes.

Lathrop, **California Natural Products,** Joseph R. Hall, PO Box 1219, Lathrop, CA 95330. (209) 858–2525. **Type of Business:** Manufacturer. **Sells to:** To retailers and the public. **Sells:** Bulk: honey and syrup; grocery: coffee, tea, grain beverages and macrobiotic products. **Specialties:** Dacopa Instant Beverage—no caffeine, consists wholly of roasted juices from Dahlia tubers. **Organic?** 5% organically grown. **Credit:** None. **Hours:** 8–5. **Shipping:** UPS plus one day. **Minimum Order:** Case of 6 or 12 depending on the product.

Live Oak, **Sowden Bros.,** Buzz or Bud, 8888 Township Rd., Live Oak, CA 95953. (916) 695–3750, Fax: (916) 695–1395. **Type of Business:** Grower and distributor. **Sells to:** Retailers, and the public by mail order. **Sells:** Dried fruit (organic prunes, whole and pitted), juice (organic Mornin' Glory prune juice), fresh fruit (fuyu persimmons). **Organic?** Certified organic, all prune products meet California Certified Organic Farmers and Farm Verified Organic standards.

Los Angeles, **Albert's Organics Inc.,** Albert Lusk, Ric Toth, Bill Zietlow, Steve Boyle, 4605 S Alameda Ave., Los Angeles, CA 90058. (213) 234–4595. **Type of Business:** Distributor, since 1981. **Sells to:** Retailers. **Sells:** A wide variety of organically grown fruits and vegetables. **Organic?** 90%. **Shipping:** They ship to the entire U.S., Canada, and Europe. **Minimum Order:** None, though shippers sometimes have minimums. **Catalogue Available?** Yes. **Comments:** Albert's Organics received a large number of recommendations from businesses dispersed throughout the U.S. and Canada. Albert's appears to be one of the foremost distributor of organic produce west of the Mississippi. They also ship to East Coast distributors like Neshaminy Valley.♥♦♦

Los Angeles, **The Artful Balance,** 525½ N Fairfax Ave., Los Angeles, CA 90046. (213) 852–9091. **Type of Business:** Restaurant. **Sells:** Wholefood. Vegetarian, vegan and macrobiotic dishes are available. **Organic?** When possible. **Specialties:** They specialize in the personal and individual dietary requirements of their customers (including allergy avoidance). **Prices:** $10–$15. **Hours:** 5:30–11. **Reservations:** Accepted. 90% No smoking. **Credit:** V M. **Commendations:** Nathan Pritikin Foundation, 1989.

Los Angeles, **Country Life Buffet Restaurant,** Michael Dernchak, 888 S Figueroa, Los Angeles, CA 90017. (213) 222–0360. **Type of Business:** Restaurant and health food store. **Sells:** Pasta dishes, steamed vegetables, salad and fruit bar, **Organic?** No organic claims. **Specialties:** Eggplant parmesan, fruit salads, and pasta dishes. Vegan dishes are available. **Prices:** $4.00–$5.50. **Hours:** Store 10–8, Buffet 11–3. **Reservations:** Accepted. 100% No smoking. **Credit:** None. **Commendations:** *Los Angeles Downtown News.*

Los Angeles, **Erewhon Natural Food Market,** 8001 Beverly Blvd., Los Angeles, CA 90048–4595. (213) 655–5441. **Type of Business:** Retail store and delicatessen. **Sells:** Organic produce, take-out food from the "healthycatessen", and a variety of wholefood items. They have a large pro-

duce department and a good macrobiotic section. **Organic?** 60% organic, affiliated with California Certified Organic Farmers. **Prices:** $4.50–$7.00 **Hours:** M-F 9–9, Sat. 9–8, Sun. 10–6 **Reservations:** Take-out only. **Credit:** V M. **Comments:** Their take-out food got as many recommendations as their produce and grocery section, which themselves were widely recommended.♦♦

Los Angeles, **Fragrant Vegetable,** 11859 Wilshire Blvd., Los Angeles, CA 90025. (213) 312–1442. (also in Monterey Park). **Type of Business:** Restaurant. **Sells:** Chinese vegetarian dishes. All dishes are made from vegetables, gluten, tofu fungus, mushrooms, and nuts. **Organic?** No organic claims. **Specialties:** Spicy salt and pepper shrimp (mushrooms), Peking ribs (pecan nuts), Buddhist cushion (vegetable, mushroom and tofu). **Prices:** $4.50–$16.50. **Hours:** M-F 11:30–10, S-S 11:30–11. **Reservations:** Not required but are accepted. **Credit:** V M AE; minimum for credit card is $5 for lunch and $10 for dinner. **Commendations:** Widely recommended and described by the *Los Angeles Times* (Rose Dosti) as "One-of-a-kind in Los Angeles, perhaps the United States."♦

Los Angeles, **Golden Temple,** Ranbir S. Bhai, 7910 W 3rd St., Los Angeles, CA 90048. (213) 655–1891. **Type of Business:** Restaurant. **Sells:** Vegan foods with macrobitic options. **Organic?** Asserted organic, 25%. They have filtered water. **Specialties:** Pasta, Tofu Mushroom Sautée, New Mexican Enchilada, Oriental Salad, Mung Bear Rice Casserole. "We present health oriented delicious desserts which could be compared with fine French desserts." **Prices:** $6–$10. **Hours:** M-F 11:30–10, Sat. 5:30–10. **Reservations:** Possible. No smoking allowed. **Credit:** V M. **Comments:** They claim to be oldest vegetarian restaurant in Southern California. **Commendations:** "Best vegetarian restaurant in L.A."—Karan Kaplan. Award of Excellence—Paul Wallace.

Los Angeles, **The Kingsley Garden,** Randy Ellis, 4070 W 3rd St., Los Angeles, CA 90020. (213) 389–5527. **Type of Business:** Restaurant. **Sells:** All natural vegetarian cuisine with vegan options available. **Organic?** Asserted 95% organic. **Specialties:** International cuisine: Mexican, Italian, Indian and Californian. **Prices:** $8–$10. **Hours:** 11:30 to 10 p.m. **Reservations:** Possible. **Credit:** V M.

Los Angeles, **Melissa's Brand** (World Variety Produce Inc.), Manny Duran or Trudy Hernandez, PO Box 21407, Los Angeles, CA 90021. (213) 588–0151. **Type of Business:** Mail-order distributor and wholesaler. **Sells to:** The public, retailers, and distributors. **Sells:** Beans (chick peas, green and lima), fresh fruit (bananas, kiwifruit, mangoes, melons), spices (basil, chives, ginger root, oregano, parsley, rosemary, sage, thyme), vegetables, noodles, wild rice, tofu, and other specialty produce. **Organic?** Asserted 30% organic. They are a member of the United Fresh Fruit & Vegetable Produce Marketing Association. **Credit:** None (M pending approval) **Prices:** May vary for specialities. **Shipping:** Loading and receiving weekdays 1 a.m.–5 p.m., otherwise by special arrangement. **Minimum Order:** Yes, depending on product in question. **Catalogue available?** Yes.

Los Angeles, **Mrs. Gooch's Natural Foods Markets, Inc.,** 3476 Centinela Avenue, Los Angeles, CA 90066. (213) 391-5209. (Also in Beverly Hills, Glendale, Hermosa Beach, Northridge, and Thousand Oaks.) **Type of Business:** Wholefood supermarket and wholesaler. **Sells to:** The public. **Sells:** A huge variety of wholefoods and organic produce. Their goal is "to offer you products that contain: no chemical additives, no harmful preservative agents, no artificial flavorings, no artificial colorings, no refined sugar, no flour, no caffeine, no chocolate, no hydrogenated oil, and no irradiated foods." **Organic?** They sell 425 organically grown and processed products and are affiliated with Organic Crop Improvement Association and California Certified Organic Farmers. **Credit:** V M and ATM Cards. **Prices:** 10% discount on full-case purchases. **Hours:** 9–9 seven days a week. **Comments and Commendations:** Mrs. Gooch's got the most recommendations of any business in the Catalogue and received glowing reviews from everyone who mentioned them. They are in the vanguard of healthy food establishments in this country. If you live in Southern California and are seeking a huge variety of healthy foods, Mrs. Gooch's is your best bet.♦♦♦

Los Angeles, **Nowhere Cafe,** 8009 Beverly Blvd., Los Angeles, CA 90048. (213) 655-8895. **Type of Business:** Restaurant. **Sells:** Vegetarian, vegan and macrobiotic dishes available. **Organic?** 30% organic; whenever available. **Specialties:** Fresh fish, natural chicken, pasta, pizza, burritos, tostadas, stir-fried vegetables, salads and sugar-free desserts. **Prices:** $8.50–$14. **Hours:** Lunch M-Sat. 12–2, Dinner S-S 6–10. **Reservations:** Accepted. 100% No smoking. **Credit:** V M and AE. Minimum for credit is $10. **Commendations:** Certified by California Certified Oragnic Farmers.

Los Angeles, **Rainbow Natural Foods Distributing,** Carol Kachmer, 3055 E 12 St., Los Angeles, CA 90023. (213) 260-7177, Fax: (213) 266-4204. **Type of Business:** Distributor. **Sells to:** Retailers, restaurants and the general public. **Sells:** A wide selection of fresh organic produce (vegetables, fruits, spices and herbs). **Organic?** They buy 95% of their produce from California Certified Organic Farmers-and Tilth-certified suppliers and are members of California Certified Organic Farmers. **Credit:** None. **Prices:** Discount on pallet loads of produce. **Hours:** The public can collect pre-ordered goods Tues.-Thurs., 9–12. **Shipping:** Orders must be placed at least 3 hours before pick-up. **Minimum Order:** $125 for pick-up, $195 for delivery. **Catalogue Available?** Yes.

Los Angeles, **Zen Bakery,** 10988 Pico Blvd, Los Angeles, CA 90064. (213) 475-6727. **Type of Business:** Manufacturer and retail store. **Sells to:** Public and retailers. **Sells:** Baked goods, bread, coffee, cheese, fruits, vegetables, spices, and grains. No artificial additives or preservatives, sweetened using white grape juice. Organic fruit is used but not organic flour. **Organic?** None of their products contains additives or preservatives and they are "97% sure there are no pesticides." **Credit:** None. **Hours:** 7:30-5. **Shipping:** They will deliver anywhere within 100 miles of

any of their three locations. **Minimum Order:** Varies. **Catalogue Available?** Yes.♦

Mendocino, **Old Mill Farm School of Country Living,** mail to: PO Box 463, Mendocino, CA 95460. Farm store at 45124 Ukiah St., Mendocino. (707) 937-0244. **Type of Business:** Grower. **Sells to:** Distributors and the public through a stand and by mail-order. **Sells:** Lamb, chicken, duck, goat cheese, produce. **Organic?** Certified organic by California Certified Organic Farmers, 100%. **Shipping:** UPS, AE. **Minimum Order:** $50. **Catalogue Available?** Yes. **Comments:** Old Mill is as much a school as a farm. It is a non-profit organization offering alternative education to groups that want to experience the farm and rural lifestyle. They have a 300–acre homestead surrounded by 63,000 acres of state forest. They farm 40 acres using "French-intensive" methods and grow most of their own food. They are willing to take work done on the farm as a form of credit to pay for the retreat.♥

Menlo Park, **Flea Street Cafe,** 3607 Alameda de la Pulyas, Menlo Park, CA 94025. (415) 854-1226. **Type of Business:** Restaurant. **Sells:** Predominantly organic dishes, with many vegetarian options. They cook with locally grown, seasonal organic produce as well as organic grains, meats, eggs and any other organic ingredients whenever available. They grow their own organic herbs and edible flowers. **Organic?** 75–80% organic, member of CFSA and California Certified Organic Farmers (the owner is on the CSFA board of directors). **Specialties:** They do their own baking and the menu changes every 2–3 weeks. **Prices:** Entrees range from $13 to $17. They offer a three course meal for $16 to $22. **Hours:** Lunch: Tues.-F, 11:30–2:30, Dinner: Tues-Sat., 6–10, Sunday Breakfast: 9–2. **Reservations:** Recommended. 100% non-smoking. **Credit:** V M. **Commendations:** *Focus* magazine, "Best South Bay Restaurant", 1987, 1988; *Mercury News,* ***½*, 1985–89; National Heart Association for San Mateo County, First Prize in Cooking Competition.♥♦

Mill Valley, **░░░ ░oods,** Joseph Rogoff, 149 Throckmorton, Mill Valley, CA 94941. (415) 383-7121. **Type of Business:** Retail store. **Sells to:** Public. **Sells:** Fresh fruits, fresh vegetables, dried fruits, beans, nuts, nut butters, grains, breads, flour, cereals, pastas, rice, oils, baked goods, dairy products, spices, soy products (miso, sauce, milk, tempeh, tofu), meats (beef, poultry, turkey), seafood, beverages (fruit juices, sodas, coffees, teas, wines), candies. **Organic?** Certified organic, 90%, member California Certified Organic Farmers. **Credit:** No credit cards. **Prices:** 10% off for bulk orders. **Hours:** M-F 9 a.m.–8 p.m., Sat. 9 a.m.–7 p.m., Sun. 10 a.m.–6 p.m.♦♦

Monrovia, **Ferraro's Fine Juices Inc.,** Patricia Earle, PO Box 1315, Monrovia, CA 91017. (818) 357-3339. **Type of Business:** Grower and manufacturer. **Sells to:** Distributor, retailers, and public at retail outlet at plant. **Sells:** Juices (fresh fruit and vegetable) **Organic?** California Certified Organic Farmers certified. **Credit:** None. **Prices:** Special prices for very large orders only. **Shipping:** Next day delivery. **Minimum Order:** $40 for retail stores. **Catalogue Available?** Yes.

Monterey, **Sweet Earth & Company,** PO Box 1211, Monterey, CA 93942. (408) 375-3673. **Type of Business:** Manufacturer. **Sells to:** Retailers and restaurants. **Sells:** Baked goods. **Organic?** They assert that 20% of their products are organic. **Catalogue Available?** Yes.

Monterey Park, **Fragrant Vegetable,** 108 No. Garfield Ave., Monterey Park, CA 91754. (818) 280-4215. (Also in Los Angeles). **Type of Business:** Restaurant. **Sells:** Chinese vegetarian dishes. All dishes are made from vegetables, gluten, tofu fungus, mushrooms, and nuts. **Organic?** No organic claims. **Specialties:** Spicy salt and pepper shrimp (mushrooms), Peking ribs (pecan nuts), Buddhist cushion (vegetable, mushroom and tofu). **Prices:** $4.50-$16.50. **Hours:** M-F 11:30-10, S-S 11:30-11. **Reservations:** Not required but are accepted. **Credit:** V M and AE. Minimum for credit is $5 for lunch and $10 for dinner. **Commendations:** Widely recommended and described by the *Los Angeles Times* (Rose Dosti) as "One-of-a-kind in Los Angeles, perhaps the United States."♦

National City, **National Health & Nutrition,** Veronica Bal, Plaza Bonita, 3030 Plaza Bonita Rd., Suite 2062, National City, CA 92050. (619) 267-6970. **Type of Business:** Retailer (part of a chain). **Sells:** Some wholefood type products, but no organic produce. See listing in Florida (West Palm Beach) for more details.

Navarro, **Mendocino Sea Vegetable Company,** John and Eleanor Lewallen, PO Box 372, Navarro, CA 95463. (707) 895-3741. **Type of Business:** Harvesters, processors and distributors. **Sells to:** Retailers, restaurants and the public via mail order. **Sells:** Sea vegetables from North America, harvested in unpolluted coastal locations. **Organic?** Uncertified. It would be extremely hard to certify businesses harvesting plants from the ocean. They assert that the sea vegetables are sun-dried only and have no additives. **Credit:** After first order. No credit cards accepted. **Prices:** 10% discount for retail orders of $100 worth or more, as well as discounts for any bulk purchase of unpackaged sea vegetables. **Shipping:** Worldwide by UPS or US mail. **Minimum Order:** Orders under $20 (post paid) are subject to a $4 handling charge. **Catalogue Available?** Yes. **Commendations:** *East West* Magazine, 1987. **Comments:** The "kelp" brown sea vegetables, such as wakame and kombu, contain algin, which is thought by some to remove radioactive particles and heavy metals from the human body. Sea vegetables are varied. Wakame and Kombu are very popular with macrobiotic eaters; the latter makes great soup stock. Try Mendocino Grapestone, a deep red sea vegetable with a delicious oyster-like taste, or flaked nori sprinkled on rice.

Nevada City, **Alpine Aire Foods,** Box 926, Nevada City, CA 95959. (800) 322-6325. **Type of Business:** Manufacturer, distributor, and mail-order distributor. **Sells to:** The public. **Sells:** Grains, bulk cereals, packaged convenience mixes, packaged grains, cereals, pasta, soups. **Organic?** No organic claims. Their products are free of sugar, preservatives, artificial colors, and artificial flavors. **Credit:** V M. **Prices:** A "Quick Meal" runs about $6. **Shipping:** Everywhere. **Minimum Order:** None. **Catalogue Available?** Yes.

Northridge, **Mrs. Gooch's Natural Foods Markets, Inc.,** 9350 Reseda Blvd., Northridge, CA 91324. (818) 701-5122, Fax (818) 701-1871. (Also in Beverly Hills, Glendale, Hermosa Beach, Los Angeles, Sherman Oaks, and Thousand Oaks.) **Type of Business:** Wholefood supermarket and wholesaler. **Sells to:** The public. **Sells:** A huge variety of wholefoods and organic produce. Their goal is "to offer you products that contain: no chemical additives, no harmful preservative agents, no artificial flavorings, no artificial colorings, no refined sugar, no flour, no caffeine, no chocolate, no hydrogenated oil, and no irradiated foods." **Organic?** They sell 425 organically grown and processed products and are affiliated with Organic Crop Improvement Association and California Certified Organic Farmers. **Credit:** V M and ATM Cards. **Prices:** 10% discount on full-case purchases. **Hours:** 9-9 seven days a week. **Comments and Commendations:** Mrs. Gooch's got the most recommendations of any business in the Catalogue and received glowing reviews from almost everyone who mentioned them. They are in the vanguard of healthy food establishments in this country. If you live in Southern California and are seeking a huge variety of healthy foods, Mrs. Gooch's is your best bet.♦♦♦

Oakland, **All Organic Produce and Supply,** Joe Blackburn, Michael Mahlanga, Chris Neiman, 368 2nd St., Oakland, CA 94607. (415) 465-6169. **Type of Business:** Distributor. **Sells to:** Retailers. **Sells:** Dried beans, dried fruits, fresh fruits, grains, herbs, nuts and nuta butters, oils, seeds, vegetables and tools of the trade. **Organic?** Certified organic, member of California Certified Organic Farmers.

Oakland, **Macrobiotic Grocery and Learning Center,** Joel Huckins, 1050 40th St., Oakland, CA 94608. (415) 653-6510. **Type of Business:** Restaurant and retail store. **Sells:** Macrobiotic goods and organic produce. **Organic?** 100% organic, certified by California Certified Organic Farmers. **Specialties:** Vegetarian, vegan and macrobiotic dishes only. **Prices:** $6.50-$8.50 **Hours:** Store 8 a.m.-9 p.m. daily, Restaurant-M-Sat. Lunch 11:30-1, Dinner 5:30-7:30, Sun. Brunch 11-1 **Reservations:** Accepted. **Credit:** None.

Oakland, **Spectra,** Francois Gallo, Partner, 484 Lake Park #163, Oakland, CA 94610. (415) 834-8731. **Type of Business:** Importer/Master Distributor. **Sells to:** Distributors. **Sells:** Organically produced juice, yogurt and herbs. **Organic?** Certified organic by Demeter. **Credit:** 30 days with approval. **Hours:** 10-7. **Shipping:** Common carrier. **Minimum Order:** None. **Catalogue Available?** No.

Orange, **Island Products,** 393 N Cypress, Orange, CA 92666. (714) 997-5615. **Type of Business:** Manufacturer, wholesaler and retailer. **Sells to:** Public and retailers. **Sells:** Dried fruits, nuts, and candy, including a range of no-salt and no-preservative brands. **Organic?** Asserted 80% organic. **Credit:** V M AE. **Prices:** Discount for some bulk orders. **Hours:** 8-6. **Shipping:** Only serve LA county. **Minimum Order:** 200 packages. **Catalogue Available?** Yes.

Orland, **Family Farms,** Wyo Avenue/Road 9, Orland, CA 95963. (916) 865–3865. Type of Business: Producer and distributor, since 1982. Sells to: Retailers. Sells: Organic whole grains (popcorn, wheat, corn), flours and meals (wheat flour, corn meal). Organic? Certified organic, grown and processed under Section 26569.11 of the California Health and Safety Code; member of California Certified Organic Farmers.

Orosi, **Ecology Sound Farms,** 42126 Road 168, Orosi, CA 93467. (209) 528–3816. Type of Business: Producer and distributor, since 1968. Sells to: Mainly to retailers. Sells: Organic fresh produce (navel oranges, kiwifruit, plums, persimmons, Asian pears), garlic, nuts, seeds, dried fruit, beans. Organic? Certified organic; member of California Certified Organic Farmers. Credit: None. Shipping: They ship at all hours 6 days a week. Minimum Order: 1 box. Catalogue Available? Yes, for mail order.

Oxnard, **Purepak, Inc.,** Dean Walsh, Jim Willrodt, Brian Pence, PO Box 588, Oxnard, CA 93032. (805) 485–1127. Type of Business: Growers and shippers. Sells to: Mainly distributors. Sells: Organic strawberries. Organic? Member of California Certified Organic Farmers. Credit: None. Hours: 8–5 p.m. Shipping: FOB Oxnard. Minimum Order: None. Catalogue Available? No.

Pacific Beach, **Boney's,** 1260 Garnet Ave., Pacific Beach, CA 92109. (619) 270–8200. (Affiliated businesses in El Cajon, Escondido, Hillcrest, San Diego, and Vista.) Type of Business: Wholefoods supermarket. Sells to: The public. Sells: A selection of wholefood grocery items and some organic produce. Organic? Varies with season. Credit: None. Prices: Discounts some bulk orders. Hours: 9–8 daily.

Pacifica, **Good Health Natural Food,** 80 W Manor, Pacifica, CA 94044. (415) 355–5965. Type of Business: Retail store. Sells to: The public. Sells: A comprehensive range of fresh organic produce and packaged natural foods. Organic? 90–95% organic fresh produce. Certified by Organic Crop Improvement Association, California Certified Organic Farmers. Credit: V M. Prices: 10% off on full cases. Hours: M-Th 9:30–8, F 9:30–7, Sat. 9:30–6, Sun. 12–6.

Palo Alto, **The Good Earth Restaurant and Bakery,** Kathy Jones, 1058 Elwell Ct., Palo Alto, CA 94303. (415) 969–5051. Type of Business: Restaurant. Sells: Fresh fish, Good Earth burgers, eggplant, and salads. Vegetarian and vegan options available. Organic? Asserted 5% organic. Specialties: Sourdough wholegrain berry pancakes, the "Planet Burger", Guatemalan chicken and black beans. Prices: $3.50–$10.00. Hours: Daily 7–10. Reservations: Accepted. 5% No smoking. Credit: V M AE. Commendations: *San Francisco Chronicle,* 10 Best Desserts in Bay Area, 1978 for carrot cake.

Palo Alto, **Whole Foods Market,** Renee Weller, 774 Emerson, Palo Alto, CA 94301. (415) 326–8676. (Also in Berkeley, several locations in Texas, and New Orleans, LA.) Type of Business: Retail store, part of a chain based in Austin Texas. Sells to: The general public. Sells: A wide variety of wholefood grocery items and fresh organic produce; beans, beverages, dairy products, fruit (dried, processed and fresh), grains, meats, nuts, soy products, spices, fresh vegetables, baked goods, breads, confections, cereals, flour, oils, pasta, rice and salsa. Organic? 30–40% in winter and 60–80% in summer. Certified by California Certified Organic Farmers. Credit: V M. Prices: 5% discount on whole cases. Hours: 9 a.m.–10 p.m. daily. Comments: Whole Foods Markets are known for their informative and relaxing atmosphere and the Whole Foods employees tend to be quite knowledgeable. Lectures and tours are offered to encourage better shopping. Whole Foods got the fourth most recommendations in our survey.♦♦♦

Paso Robles, **Jardine Organic Ranch,** Duane Jardine, Owner, 910 Nacemiento Lake Dr., Paso Robles, CA 93446. (805) 238–2365, (805) 239–4334. Type of Business: Grower. Sells to: Distributors, retailers, and public (through own stand). Sells: Nuts (almonds, pistachios, and walnuts) and almond nut butter. Organic? 100% Farm Verified Organic certified. Minimum Order: $500 to retailers and distributors, half pound to public.

Pescadero, **Jacobs Farm,** Sandy, Larry, Box 508, Pescadero, CA 94060. (415) 879–0508, Fax: (415) 879–0930. Type of Business: Grower. Sells to: Retailers, distributors, restaurants and the public through farmers' markets and mail order. Sells: Fresh herbs (basil, chives, dill, oregano, parsley, sage, rosemary and thyme), fresh vegetables (English pod peas, sugar snap peas, artichokes, kale, collards, mache, tomatoes), fresh edible flowers. Organic? Certified 100% organic by California Certified Organic Farmers and documented by Merchandising Natural Foods. Hours: 8 a.m.–4 p.m.—Answering machine takes order at other times. Minimum Order: $50 to mail order. Catalogue Available? Yes.

Petaluma, **Markey's Cafe,** 316 Western Ave., Petaluma, CA 94952. (707) 763–2429. Type of Business: Restaurant. Sells: Vegetarian, vegan, and macrobiotic options. Organic? Asserted 15% organic. Specialties: Soups, entrees, and pastries. Prices: Entrées $4.50–$6.50. Hours: 8 a.m.–9:30 p.m. Reservations: Not taken. Credit: None. Commendations: Bay Area Back Roads (both book and radio program).

Philo, **Dach Ranch,** Mendocino Growers, John Dach, 9201 Hwy. 128, Mail to: PO Box 44, Philo, CA 95466. (707) 895–3173; evenings (707) 895–3382. Type of Business: Grower and distributor. Sells to: Retailers, and the public by mail order. Sells: Fresh fruit (pears, apples, raspberries, grapes), herbs, juices, meat (lamb), JAM-IT low or no-sugar fruit pectins, can be made with honey, too. California Certified Organic Farmers certified apple cider vinegar. Organic? Certified organic, 100%. Member of California Certified Organic Farmers. Credit: No credit cards accepted. Prices: Prices for large orders happily discussed. Hours: There is an answering machine. Shipping: Delivery varies with product. Minimum Order: None. Catalogue Available? Yes.♥

Pleasant Grove, **Pleasant Grove Farms,** Ed or Wynette Sills, PO Box 636, Pleasant Grove, CA 95668. (916) 655-3391. **Type of Business:** Grower. **Sells to:** Distributors and mail order to public. **Sells:** Corn (yellow, white and multicolored), popcorn and elephant garlic. **Organic?** California Certified Organic Farmers certified 70% organic. **Hours:** 7-6. **Catalogue Available?** Yes. **Comments:** By rotating his crops with purple vetch, Sills increases soil fertility while decreasing the onslaught of bugs. He says his organically grown crops earn twice as much as his other remaining crops, even though yields are lower, because input costs are so much lower.

Redwood City, **Mollie Stone's Farm Market,** David Bennett, PO Box 5583, 520 Woodside Rd., Redwood City, CA 94063. (415) 365-8300. (Also in Sausalito.) **Type of Business:** Retail store. **Sells to:** Public **Sells:** Fresh fruits and vegetables, dried fruits, nuts, nut butters, grains, breads, flours, cereals, baked goods, rice, pastas, soy products, beans, spices, dairy products, oils, beverages (fruit and vegetable juice, soda, tea, coffee), meats, and candies. **Organic?** 20% organic, produce certified by California Certified Organic Farmers. **Credit:** V M. **Prices:** 10% off for full cases or sacks. **Hours:** M-F 9-9, S-S 9-7.

Redwood Valley, **Mrs. Densen's Cookie Co. Inc.,** Mike Bielenberg, 9651 Hwy. 101 N, Redwood Valley, CA 95470. (707) 485-0306. **Type of Business:** Private label manufacturer (90% of their business) and retailer. **Sells to:** Distributors and the public. **Sells:** Cookies made from naturally sweetened, wholegrain ingredients. Some products are organic (as is most of the grain and flour they use)—check labels to be sure. **Organic?** Asserted 25% organic. **Credit:** V M AE D. **Hours:** 8:30-5 daily. **Minimum Order:** None. **Catalogue Available?** Yes.

Richvale, **Lundberg Family Farms,** Susan Lundberg, 5370 Church St., Mail to: PO Box 369, Richvale, CA 95974. (916) 882-4551. **Type of Business:** Grower and manufacturer. **Sells to:** Retailers, mail order and direct to the public. **Sells:** Brown rice products (macrobiotic)—including flour, cereal and rice cakes. **Organic?** 50% certified organic. Member of Organic Foods Production Association of North America and pending certification with California Certified Organic Farmers and Organic Crop Improvement Association. **Credit:** None. **Hours:** 7 a.m.-5:30 p.m. **Minimum Order:** Yes. **Catalogue Available?** Yes. **Comments:** The farm engages in a soil-building program. They do not burn the stubble. They plant cover crops to supply nitrogen and organic matter between rice crops. Even non-organic crops are grown with minimal fertilizers and herbicides.♥♦♦

Sacramento, **Mum's,** Juliana Harris, 2968 Freeport Blvd., Sacramento, CA 95818. (916) 444-3015. **Type of Business:** Restaurant. **Sells:** Vegetarian dishes, predominantly vegan and/or macrobiotic. **Organic?** Asserted 30%-50% organic. **Specialties:** California and International Gourmet vegetarian. **Prices:** $5-$10. **Hours:** Lunch Tu-F 11:30-2:00; Dinner Tu-Sat. 5:30-9:30; Brunch Sat. 10-2, Sun. 5:30-9:30. All tables are non-smoking. **Reservations:** Possible for parties of four or more and on holidays. **Credit:**

V M AE. **Commendations:** *East West Restaurant Guide*—1989.♦

Sacramento, **Sacramento Natural Foods,** 2996 Freeport Blvd., Sacramento, CA 95818. (914) 442-0380. **Type of Business:** Retail store and co-op. **Sells to:** The public. **Sells:** A complete line of natural grocery items and organic fresh produce. **Organic?** Fresh produce 50% organic (certified by Farm Verified Organic, California Certified Organic Farmers, Demeter/Bio-dynamic). Of other items, 5-10% are organic. **Credit:** None. **Prices:** Bulk discounts: 10% for non-members, 20% for members. **Hours:** 9 a.m.-10 p.m. daily. **Comments:** They offer their own in-store deli with seating for 60, a florist and coffee shop (tenants). Sales volume is over $5 million annually, with an overall 13,500 sq. ft. of selling space.

San Diego, **Be Wise Ranch,** Bill Brammer, 9018 Artesian Rd., San Diego, CA 92127. (619) 756-4851. **Type of Business:** Grower and distributor, since 1977. **Sells to:** Retailers, mail order. **Sells:** Fresh fruit: navel and Valencia oranges, lemons, limes, tangelos, tangerines, avocadoes, peaches; fresh vegetables: tomatoes, zucchini, and squash. They sell seconds (citrus) to juice companies. **Certification:** Certified organic California Certified Organic Farmers. **Minimum Order:** 25-40 lbs.

San Diego, **Boney's,** 6091 University, San Diego, CA 92115. (619) 582-4344. (Affiliated businesses in El Cajon, Escondido, Hillcrest, Pacific Beach, and Vista.) **Type of Business:** Wholefoods supermarket. **Sells to:** The public. **Sells:** A full line of wholefood grocery items and a small amount of organic produce. **Organic?** About 10-20% on grocery items. **Credit:** None. **Prices:** 10% off on cases (except for products on sale). **Hours:** 9-8 M-Sat., 9-7 Sun. **Comments:** Each Boney's is run by a different member of the extended family.

San Diego, **Cornucopia Restaurant,** Michelle Esmailian, 112 W Washington St., San Diego, CA 92103. (619) 299-4174. **Type of Business:** Restaurant. **Sells:** A menu of all homemade, health-conscious vegetarian dishes. **Organic?** Organic food is used whenever possible. **Specialties:** Tofu fried rice, super tostada and wheat-less corn bread. **Prices:** Entrees range from $4.25 to $6.95. **Hours:** M-F 7:30-9, Sat. 9-9, Sun. 9-2 p.m. **Reservations:** Not possible. 100% non-smoking. **Credit:** None.

San Diego, **Govinda's Natural Foods,** Kelly Fowler, 3102 University Ave., San Diego, CA 92104. (619) 284-4826. **Type of Business:** Restaurant. **Sells:** Vegetarian, vegan and macrobiotic options. **Organic?** Asserted 10% organic. **Specialties:** All you can eat natural foods, gourmet deserts, catering. **Prices:** $3.49-$5.69. **Hours:** M-Sat. 11:30 a.m.-9 p.m. Sun. 5 p.m.-9 p.m. **Reservations:** Possible. **Credit:** V M (minimum of $10). **Comments:** They offer a "video room" for entertainment. The food is cooked by monks in a spiritual atmosphere. "Our food is pleasing not only to the body but to the soul."

San Diego, **Grain Country,** David Jackson, 3448 30th St., San Diego, CA 92104. (619) 298-1052. **Type of Business:** Restaurant, retail store. **Sells:** Vegetarian food with macrobiotic options. **Organic?** 100% from certified suppliers. **Specialties:** Macromeals and noodles. **Prices:** $6.95–$8.95. **Hours:** Restaurant: daily 11:30–3 p.m. Store: M-Sat. 10 a.m.–6 p.m. **Reservations:** No. All tables are no smoking. **Credit:** V M (if less than $25, add 5%). **Comments:** In addition to the store and restaurant, Grain Country offers macrobiotic education on a regular basis: cooking classes, theory classes, lectures, and counseling.

San Diego, **Kung Food,** Frank Russo, 2949 5th Ave., San Diego, CA 92103. (619) 298-7330. **Type of Business:** Restaurant. **Sells:** Vegetarian and deli items with vegan and macrobotic options. **Organic?** Asserted 20% organic. **Specialties:** Layered Tofu Supreme, Tofu Vegetable Enchiladas. **Prices:** $4.95–$8.50. **Hours:** M-F 11:30 a.m.–10 p.m., Sat. and Sun. 8:30 a.m.–10 p.m. **Reservations:** Possible. 100% No Smoking. **Credit:** V M AE. **Commendations:** "Best Healthy Restaurant in San Diego"—1987 *San Diego Home & Gardens.*

San Diego, **Ocean Beach People's Food Co-op,** Joe Sheridan, 4765 Voltaire St., San Diego, CA 92107. (619) 224-1387. **Type of Business:** Retail store and co-op. **Sells to:** The public. **Sells:** A full range of vegetarian natural foods (mostly non-dairy) and organic produce (when available). They sell only "cruelty-free" products. **Organic?** Asserted 80% organic. **Credit:** None. **Prices:** There is a 10% surcharge for non-members (first-time patrons are exempt). **Hours:** 10–8 M-Sat., 10–7 Sun.

San Diego, **Zen Bakery,** 909 Grand Ave., San Diego, CA 92109. (619) 483-4608. Also in Los Angeles and Miami, FL. **Type of Business:** Manufacturer and retailer. **Sells to:** The public. **Sells:** Cookies, muffins, coffee, whole wheat bread, apple juice, fruit drinks, fruit, vegetables, spices, oats and wheat. No additives or preservatives, sweetened with white grape juice. Organic fruit used but not organic flour. **Organic?** None of their products contain additives or preservatives and they are "97% sure there are no pesticides." **Credit:** None. **Prices:** Wholesale prices for orders of 50 dozen or up. **Hours:** 7:30–5. **Shipping:** They will deliver within 100 miles of any of their three locations. **Minimum Order:** Varies. **Catalogue Available?** Yes.

San Francisco, **The Ganges,** 775 Frederick St., San Francisco, CA 94117. (415) 661-7290. **Type of Business:** Restaurant. **Sells:** Indian vegetarian cuisine. **Organic?** No organic claims made. Filtered water. **Specialties:** "Lite" food and non-fried appetizers. **Prices:** $6.50–$10.50. **Hours:** M-Sat. 5–9:30. **Reservations:** Required. 100% non-smoking. **Credit:** None. **Comments and Commendations:** The main chef and proprietor has lived most of her life in India and Kenya. Her book *The Surti Touch* is widely acclaimed. The Ganges is commended by *San Francisco Focus,* May 1988; *Santa Rosa Buyers Guide,* September 28, 1988, and *Image,* February, 1987.

San Francisco, **Greens at Fort Mason,** Ft. Mason, Building A, San Francisco, CA 94123. (415) 771-6222. **Type of Business:** Restaurant. **Sells:** Vegetarian cuisine. Some dishes are macrobiotic, but options may not always be available. **Organic?** Asserted 80% organic. They get produce from Star Route Farms in Bolinas. **Specialties:** The menu changes daily. Special 5-course meals are served Fridays and Saturdays. **Prices:** Lunches range from $7.50–$9.50, dinners from $8.50–$11.50 Tues-Thurs. Friday and Saturday dinners are $30 per person. Sunday brunches run from $4–$8. **Hours:** Tu-Sat 11:30–2:15 and 6–9:30; Sun 10–2. **Reservations:** Accepted. 100% no-smoking. **Credit:** V M and local personal checks. **Commendations and Comments:** *San Francisco Examiner,* 1990; *New York Times,* 1988; *Gourmet,* 1988 and many others. Greens is one of the best vegetarian restaurants on the West Coast and got the second most recommendations from our survey. The restaurant also has a panoramic view of the Bay.♥♦♦♦

San Francisco, **Rainbow Grocery,** Linda Trunzo, Phil Bewley, Tom Darcey, Fred D'Aguilar, 1899 Mission St., San Francisco, CA 94103. (415) 863-0620. **Type of Business:** Retailer and a collective. Their store has three parts: a clothing store, a supplement store, and a food store. **Sells to:** The public. **Sells:** A variety of natural or wholefoods and conventional foods; baked goods, coffee, condiments, dairy products and eggs, dried beans, dried fruit, fresh fruit, whole grains, flours and meals, processed grain products, herbs and spices, juices, nuts and nut butters, oils, seeds, soy products, sweeteners, teas, fresh vegetables. **Organic?** Asserted 25% organic, Most of their producers are small farmers who are generally members of California Certified Organic Farmers, Organic Crop Improvement Association or Farm Verified Organic. **Credit:** None (food stamps accepted). **Prices:** 10% discounts for members. **Hours:** M-Sat. 9:30–7:30. **Comments:** Their store is a center for information on healthy diet, offering books for sale, free magazines, and a bulletin board.♦

San Francisco, **Real Food Company** (4 stores) 1) 1023 Stanyan, (415) 564-2800; 2) 1234 Sutter (415) 474-8488; 3) 3939-24th, (415) 282-9500; 4) 2140 Polk, (415) 673-7420. Also in Emeryville, San Rafael, Sausalito. **Type of Business:** Wholefoods market chain. **Sells to:** The public. **Sells:** A comprehensive selection of organic fresh produce, organic bulk items, and wholefood grocery items. **Organic?** Produce is about 95% organic in the summer, 65%–70% organic in the winter. Around 75% of bulk items are organic. Anything organic that they can get, they carry. **Credit:** None. **Prices:** 10% discount for bulk orders. **Hours:** 9–8 daily (9–9 at Polk street location). **Comments:** The Stanyan, Sutter, and Polk St. stores have an attached deli. Real Foods got the fifth most recommendations in our survey.♦♦♦

San Francisco, **Taste of Honey Bakery,** Rochelle Gottlieb, 751 Diamond St., San Francisco, CA 94114. (415) 285-7979 and 1515 Church St., San Francisco. **Type of Business:** Juice bar/cafe. **Sells:** Vegetarian food only, with vegan and macrobiotic options. **Organic?** Asserted 25–35% organic. Filtered water. **Specialties:** Juices, frozen yogurt and desserts made without sugar or white flour, and many that are wheat-free, dairy-less, oil-less and egg-less. **Prices:** Lunch for around $3. **Hours:** M-F 7:30–9, Weekends 9–9. **Reservations:** Not possible. 100% non-smoking. **Credit:** None.

San Gabriel, **Diwana,** 1381 E Las Tunas Dr., San Gabriel, CA 91776. (818) 287–8743. **Type of Business:** Restaurant. **Sells:** Vegetarian, Indian cuisine. **Organic?** Asserted 90% organic. **Specialties:** Regional specialities from across India. **Prices:** Entrees range from $4 to $9. **Hours:** 11–9. **Reservations:** Possible. **Credit:** V M. **Commendations:** *Star News, Los Angeles Times, Pasadena Weekly.*

San Luis Obispo, **Foods for the Family,** 570–3 Higuera St., San Luis Obispo, CA 93401. (805) 543–5485. **Type of Business:** Retail store. **Sells to:** The public. **Organic?** Fresh produce 90% organic (certified by California Certified Organic Farmers), other grocery, 10%. **Credit:** V M. **Hours:** M-F 9–8, Sat. 9–6, Sunday closed. **Comments and Commendations:** Public choice award—Best Health Food Store—*Newtimes* (local newspaper).

San Rafael, **Milly's,** 1643 Fourth St., San Rafael, CA 94901. (415) 459–1601. **Type of Business:** Restaurant. **Sells:** Vegetarian dishes, mostly vegan, with quite a few macrobiotic options. **Organic?** 75% of the produce they serve in the summer is organically grown. The percentage is somewhat less in the winter. **Specialties:** Tempeh Oscar, Warm Cabbage Salad, Seitan Scaloppine, and nightly special salads and entrees. **Prices:** $6.75–10.50. **Hours:** 5:30–9:30 nightly (dinner only). **Reservations:** Not possible. **Credit:** V M AE. **Commendations:** Milly's got the most recommendations of any restaurant in our survey with accolades coming from as far away as Wisconsin and Georgia. They were also one of the few restaurants given a top rating in the *Vegetarian Times Guide to Natural Foods Restaurants.* ♥♦♦♦

San Rafael, **Real Food Company,** 770 Francisco Blvd. West, San Rafael, CA 94901. (415) 459–8966. (Also in Emeryville, San Francisco, and Sausalito.) **Type of Business:** Part of a chain of seven wholefoods markets. **Sells to:** The public. **Sells:** A comprehensive selection of fresh organic produce and wholefood grocery items. **Organic?** Produce averages around 95% organic in the summer, and 75% in the winter. About 75% of processed goods are organic. **Credit:** V M, $15 and up. **Prices:** Discounts on some bulk orders. **Hours:** M-F 9–8, Sat. 10–8, Sun. 11–7. **Comments:** Real Foods got the fifth most recommendations in our survey.♦♦♦

Santa Barbara, **The Main Squeeze,** 138 E Canon Perdido, Santa Barbara, CA 93101. (805) 966–5365. **Type of Business:** Restaurant. **Sells:** Vegetarian options. **Organic?** Asserted 25% organic. **Specialties:** Seafood, pasta, Mexican vegetarian options, Tempeh Tacos, and Espresso Shakes. **Prices:** $2.25–$8.50. **Hours:** M-F 11–10, S-S 5–10. **Reservations:** Not taken. **Credit:** None.

Santa Cruz, **Dharmas,** Portola Ave., Santa Cruz, CA 95060. **Type of Business:** Restaurant. **Sells:** Natural fast foods; vegetarian with vegan and macrobiotic options. **Organic?** Asserted organic, 50%. Filtered water. **Specialties:** Brahma Burger, American Saute, Bo Thai, Nuclear Bluff.

Prices: $1.85–$6.50. **Hours:** 8 a.m. to 9 p.m. **Reservations:** No. **Credit:** No credit cards.

Santa Cruz, **New Leaf Community Market,** 2335-D Mission St., Santa Cruz, CA 95060. (408) 426–1299. **Type of Business:** Retail store. **Sells to:** The public. **Sells:** A very all-inclusive range of wholefood groceries and fresh organic produce. **Organic?** Fresh produce 80% organic (certified by Farm Verified Organic, California Certified Organic Farmers), other items, 20%. **Credit:** None. **Prices:** 10% discount on case orders. **Hours:** 9–9, seven days. **Comments and Commendations:** Santa Cruz Community Credit Union, "Community Development Recognition," 1988. They donate 10% of profits to local community and non-profit organizations.

Santa Cruz, **Seychelles,** 313 Cedar St., Santa Cruz, CA. (408) 425–0450. **Type of Business:** Restaurant. **Sells:** Mediterranean cuisine; vegan and vegetarian options. **Organic?** Asserted 10–50%. **Specialties:** Vegetarian dishes, fish and chicken entrees, homemade pasta and fresh wheat bread baked daily. **Prices:** $9.50–13.50. **Hours:** Lunch M-F 11:30–2:30, Dinner 5:30–10. Sunday brunch 10–2:30. **Reservations:** Possible. **Credit:** V M. **Comments and commendations:** They offer some musical entertainment. *San Jose Mercury News*—Four-Star Chef, May 1989. Best Vegetarian Restaurant—*Good Times* (local paper) 1985. They also had one of their recipes published in *Bon Appétit* Magazine in August, 1987.

Santa Monica, **Co-opportunity,** 1530 Broadway, Santa Monica, CA 90404. (213) 451–8902. **Type of Business:** Member-owned natural food store. **Sells to:** The public. **Sells:** Almost all lines of food, excepting seafood. The majority of goods are free from artificial additives and low in sugar. **Organic?** They get whatever organic food they can (asserted 25%). They rely on the certification claims of their suppliers. **Credit:** None. **Prices:** Discounts to members. **Hours:** M-Sat., 9–8, Sun., 10–7. **Shipping:** No delivery.♦

Santa Monica, **Col. Sanchez Traditional Foods, Inc.,** Kathryn Bennett, PO Box 5015, Santa Monica, CA 90405. (213) 396–2228, Fax (213) 396–3522. (See also New Mexico, Santa Fe.) **Type of Business:** Manufacturer. **Sells to:** Distributors, retailers, and the public by mail order. **Sells:** Corn Mother Blue Corn Chips, and Col. Sanchez brand tamales (made with no meat, dairy products, or wheat), burritos, Blue Corn Tortillas, Blue Corn Biscuits, Red Chile Tortillas, truffles (sweetened with apple juice), blue and yellow corn masa (for making tortillas). They also distribute some Island Spring products (see listing under Washington, Vashon) including tofu-burgers, maskal teff, kimchi, and salad dressing. **Organic?** Asserted 100% organic. They say they regularly investigate certification and documentation claims to ensure that only organic produce is used. Corn products are also tested for aflatoxin. **Credit:** none. **Shipping:** UPS. **Minimum Order:** $500 for distributors. **Catalogue Available?** Yes. **Comments:** Their goal is to offer an alternative to "chemically corrupted junk food."

Santa Monica, **Oasis,** 1439 Santa Monica Mall #6, Santa Monica, CA 90401. (213) 393–0940. **Type of Business:** Restaurant. **Sells:** Vegan and vegetarian dishes with macrobiotic options. **Organic?** Asserted 10%. **Specialties:** Deli case with 14 salads daily, fresh soups, homemade desserts, hot entrees and fresh juices. **Prices:** $4–$6. **Hours:** 11–11 M-Sun. **Reservations:** Not possible. **Credit:** None.

Santa Monica, **Red Sea Ethiopian Restaurant,** 1551 Ocean Ave. (courtyard), Santa Monica, CA 90401. (213) 394–5198. **Type of Business:** Restaurant. **Sells:** Ethiopian food with vegetarian options. **Organic?** Asserted 20% organic. **Specialties:** Spinach, collard greens, lentils, and a variety of mixed vegetables spiced with garlic, ginger, and onions. **Prices:** $8.95–12.95. **Hours:** Sun.-Th 11:30–11, F-Sat. 11:30–12. **Reservations:** Possible. **Credit:** V M AE DC CB. **Commendations:** *Vegetarian Times,* California Restaurant Writers Association, *Organic Grocer.*

Santa Rosa, **Restaurant Matisse,** 620 5th St., Santa Rosa, CA 95404. (707) 527–9797. **Type of Business:** Restaurant. **Sells:** Fine cuisine. **Organic?** Asserted 30% based on certification and documentation claims of producers. **Specialties:** Duck dishes, desserts. **Prices:** $17.50 (2 course dinner). **Hours:** Lunch: M-F 11:30 a.m.–2 p.m., Dinner: M-Sun. 6 p.m.–9 p.m. **Reservations:** Required. No smoking at tables. **Credit:** V M AE D. **Commendations:** Gourmet Magazine, 1989, Food & Wine, 1988, Wine Spectator, 1988, 1987.

Santa Rosa, **Ristorante Siena,** 1229 N Dutton Ave., Santa Rosa, CA 95401. (707) 578–4511. **Type of Business:** Restaurant. **Sells:** Italian cuisine with vegetarian options. **Organic?** 20% asserted organic. **Specialties:** Homemade pasta, pizzas, salads using fresh local ingredients. **Prices:** $5–$13.95. **Hours:** Breakfast: M-F 7 a.m.–10:30 a.m., Lunch: M-F 11:30 a.m.–2:30 p.m., Dinner W-Sun. 6 p.m.–9:30 p.m. Brunch. **Reservations:** Possible. 5% tables are smoking tables. **Credit:** V M D CB. **Comments:** Family-owned business.

Santa Rosa, **Santa Rosa Health Foods,** 711 4th St., Santa Rosa, CA 95404. (707) 542–0646. **Type of Business:** Retail store. **Sells to:** The public. **Sells:** A wide variety of beans, baked goods, beverages, cereals, dairy products, dried fruit, fresh fruit, grains, nuts, oils, pastas, soy products, and spices. They also sell frozen vegetables: broccoli, carrots, corn, and spinach. **Organic?** 25% of their produce is organic, though not certified. **Credit:** V M AE. **Hours:** M-W, F 9:30–6; Th 9:30–9; Sat. 9:30–5. **Comments:** A family business; they've been around 37 years.♦

Sausalito, **Mollie Stone's Farm Market,** 100 Harbor Drive, Sausalito, CA 94966. (Also in Redwood City) **Type of Business:** Retail store. **Sells to:** The public. **Sells:** Fresh fruits and vegetables, dried fruits, nuts, nut butters, grains, breads, flours, cereals, baked goods, rice, pastas, soy products, beans, spices, dairy products, oils, beverages (fruit and vegetable juice, soda, tea, coffee), meats, and candies. **Organic?** 20% organic, produce certified by California Certified Organic Farmers. **Credit:** V M. **Prices:**

10% off for full cases or sacks. **Hours:** M-F 9–9, S-S 9–7.

Sausalito, **Real Food Company,** 200 Caledonia, Sausalito, CA 94965. (415) 332–9640. Also in Emeryville, San Rafael, and San Francisco. **Type of Business:** Chain of seven wholefood grocery stores. **Sells to:** The public. **Sells:** A comprehensive selection of organic fresh produce, organic bulk items, and wholefood grocery items. **Organic?** Produce is about 95% organic in the summer, 65%-70% organic in the winter. Around 75% of bulk items are organic. Anything organic that they can get, they carry. **Credit:** V M. **Prices:** 10% discounts on special ordered cases. **Hours:** 9–9. **Comments:** Real Foods got the fifth most recommendations in our survey.♦♦♦

Sebastopol, **Appleseed Ranch,** Paul Kolling, 1834 High School Road, Sebastopol, CA 95472. (707) 823–4408. **Type of Business:** Grower and distributor. **Sells to:** Retailers, mail order. **Sells:** Baked goods (organic pies), dried fruit (apples, pears), fresh fruit (apples, raspberries), herbs and spices (edible and medicinal), juices (apple cider-fresh processed-raw-frozen), seeds (old varieties, vegetable and nursery stock), sweeteners (honey, apple syrup), teas (raspberry), fresh vegetables (corn, tomatoes, popcorn, squash, pumpkin), apple-raspberry sauce, apple sauce (pure Gravenstein). **Organic?** Certified organic, member of California Certified Organic Farmers. **Minimum Order:** 3 containers or $45.

Sebastopol, **Wild Rose Ranch,** PO Box 1619, Sebastopol, CA 95473. (707) 823–1480. **Type of Business:** Grower, processor and shipper. **Sells to:** Distributors. **Sells:** Organic apples and apple juice. **Organic?** California Certified Organic Farmers certified, 80%. **Minimum Order:** Wholesale quantities. **Catalogue Available?** Yes.

Sherman Oaks, **Foods For Health,** Jan Ito, 14543 Ventura Blvd., Sherman Oaks, CA 91403. (818) 784–4033. **Type of Business:** Restaurant and retail store. **Sells:** Sandwiches, salads, soups, and desserts including vegan and macrobiotic options. **Organic?** Asserted 65% organic. **Specialties:** Homemade soups and daily roasted turkey. **Prices:** Entrees $2.75–$5.50. **Hours:** M-Sat. 9–7. **Reservations:** Not possible. 100% non-smoking. **Credit:** V M, $10 minimum for credit. **Commendations:** *Daily News,* 1985.

Sherman Oaks, **Mrs. Gooch's Natural Foods Markets,** Inc., 15315 Magnolia Blvd., Suite 320, Sherman Oaks, CA 91403 (818) 501–8484. (Also in West Los Angeles, Hermosa Beach, Northridge, Glendale, Beverly Hills, and Thousand Oaks.) **Type of Business:** Wholefood supermarket and wholesaler. **Sells to:** The public. **Sells:** A huge variety of wholefoods and organic produce. Their goal is "to offer you products that contain: no chemical additives, no harmful preservative agents, no artificial flavorings, no artificial colorings, no refined sugar, no flour, no caffeine, no chocolate, no hydrogenated oil, and no irradiated foods." **Organic?** They sell 425 organically grown and processed products and are affiliated with Organic Crop Improvement Association and California Certified Organic Farmers. **Credit:** V M and ATM Cards. **Prices:** 10% discount on full-case purchases. **Hours:** 9–9 seven days a week. **Comments and Commendations:** Mrs. Gooch's got the most recommendations of any business in the Catalogue and received glowing reviews from everyone who mentioned them. They are in the vanguard of healthy food establishments in this country. If you live in Southern California and are seeking a huge variety of healthy foods, Mrs. Gooch's is your best bet.♦♦♦

Sierra Madre, **Lozano**, 44 N Baldwin, Michelle Lucero, Sierra Madre, CA 91024. (818) 355-5945. **Type of Business:** Restaurant. **Sells:** Mexican, Southwest, Central American and Italian food. **Organic?** No organic claims. **Specialties:** Low-fat and low-calorie foods. **Prices:** Entrees $8–$15. **Hours:** Sun.-Th 11–10, F-Sat. 11–11. **Reservations:** Possible. 60% non-smoking. **Credit:** V M AE DC. **Comments and Commendations:** Their menu is approved by the American Heart Association and has been recommended by the Pritikin Foundation and Weight Watchers.

Solvang, **Santa Barbara Olive Co. Inc. & The Olive House,** 1661 Mission Dr., Solvang, CA 93463. (805) 688-9917 (800) 624-4896—outside CA, (800) 521-0475—inside CA. **Type of Business:** Manufacturer, retail store, and mail-order distributor. **Sells to:** The public through their store and by mail order. **Sells:** Olives, olive oil, grapeseed oil, sesame oil, vinegars, condiments. Their montserrat extra-virgin olive oil is certified organic. **Organic?** Asserted organic, 20%. **Credit:** V M AE D. **Prices:** There are special discounts available on large orders exceeding 50 cases. **Hours:** 10–6. **Shipping:** For less than a truck load (LTL), they ship in trucking consolidators or UPS. For orders exceeding 50 cases, they request one week lead time. Mail order everywhere. **Minimum Order:** None. **Catalogue Available?** Yes. **Comments:** They recently introduced a canned black olive with no chemical preservatives, no MSG, no ferrous glutonate and one-third less salt. "It will be the only one of its kind."

Sonora, **Country Store,** 1979 C Mono Way, Sonora, CA 95370. (209) 532-6146. **Type of Business:** Retail store. **Sells to:** The public. **Sells:** A very impressive range of natural groceries and organic fresh produce. **Organic?** 100% organic fresh produce (California Certified Organic Farmers); 40% for processed items. **Credit:** None. **Prices:** 10% discount for 1 case or 25lbs., 15% for 10 cases or 50lbs. **Hours:** M-Sat. 9:30-6, F 9:30-7, Sun. 11-5. **Comments:** They feature over 300 different herbs and spices.

South Lake Tahoe, **Grass Roots,** Jon McElroy, 2040 Dunlap Dr. (PO Box 10259) South Lake Tahoe, CA 95731. (916) 541-7788. **Type of Business:** Restaurant and retail store. **Sells:** Light meals and snacks, mainly vegetarian, with vegan and macrobiotic options. **Organic?** 50% of the fruit they sell in the restaurant and 90% of their produce is asserted organic. **Specialties:** The menu is mostly vegeburgers, Mexican cuisine, sandwiches, and chili. **Prices:** Entrees range from $3.25 to $4.50. **Hours:** M-F 9:30-7. **Reservations:** Not possible. 100% non-smoking. **Credit:** V M, with a minimum of $10. **Comments and Commendations:** Grass Roots is small, but growing and also has a bakery.

South Pasadena, **Grass Roots,** Meir Pumi, 1119 Fair

Oaks, S Pasadena, CA 91030. (818) 799-0156. **Type of Business:** Restaurant and retail store. **Sells:** Light meals and snacks, mainly vegetarian, with vegan and macrobiotic options. **Organic?** Asserted 50% organic. **Specialties:** Homemade apple walnut muffins, frozen yogurt shakes, assorted brown rice salads, hot soups, gazpacho and sandwiches. **Prices:** Entrees range from $3.25 to $4.95. **Hours:** M-F 8-6, Sat. 9-6. **Reservations:** Not possible. 100% non-smoking. **Credit:** V M, with a minimum of $10.

Thousand Oaks, **Mrs. Gooch's Natural Foods Markets,** Inc., 451 Avenida de los Arboles, Thousand Oaks, CA 91360. (805) 492-5340, Fax (805) 493-0553. (Also in Beverly Hills, Glendale, Hermosa Beach, Los Angeles, Northridge, and Sherman Oaks.) **Type of Business:** Wholefood supermarket and wholesaler. **Sells to:** The public. **Sells:** A huge variety of wholefoods and organic produce. Their goal is "to offer you products that contain: no chemical additives, no harmful preservative agents, no artificial flavorings, no artificial colorings, no refined sugar, no flour, no caffeine, no chocolate, no hydrogenated oil, and no irradiated foods." **Organic?** They sell 425 organically grown and processed products and are affiliated with Organic Crop Improvement Association and California Certified Organic Farmers. **Credit:** V M and ATM Cards. **Prices:** 10% discount on full-case purchases. **Hours:** 9-9 seven days a week. **Comments and Commendations:** Mrs. Gooch's got the most recommendations of any business in the Catalogue and received glowing reviews from almost everyone who mentioned them. They are in the vanguard of healthy food establishments in this country. If you live in Southern California and are seeking a huge variety of healthy foods, Mrs. Gooch's is your best bet.♦♦♦

Tollhouse, **Sun Mountain Research Center,** 35751 Oak Springs Drive, Tollhouse, CA 93667. (209) 855-3710. **Type of Business:** Grower. **Sells to:** Distributors and the public. **Sells:** Herbs. **Organic?** Asserted organic. **Minimum Order:** $10. **Catalogue Available?** No.

Ukiah, **Ukiah Coop,** 308 'B' E Perkins, Ukiah, CA 95482. (707) 462-4778. **Type of Business:** Retail store, co-op. **Sells to:** The public and a few restaurants. **Sells:** A wide range of wholefoods and fresh produce. **Organic?** Fresh produce 75% organic, other items estimated at 40-60%. **Credit:** None. **Prices:** Bulk discount is 20% markup. **Hours:** M-F 9-7, Sat. 9-6. **Minimum Order:** (Bulk) 1lb. on herbs and spices, 25lbs. on grains, case lots for others. **Comments:** "Biggest herb and spice selection in Northern California."

Venice, **I Love Juicy,** 826 Hampton Dr., Hollywood, CA 90291. (213) 399-1318. **Type of Business:** Restaurant and retail store. **Sells:** "All original super-natural 100% vegetarian international cuisine—Tasty and healthy designer food for the human design." Fresh juice, smoothies, soups, salads, quiche, pizza, appetizers, sandwiches, 35 entrees, sushi, desserts, dairyless ice cream, teas, picnic lunches and catering. Everything here is vegan and there is a lot of choice for macrobiotic eaters. **Organic?** Asserted 60% organic. **Prices:** Entrees range from $5 to $10 **Hours:** Open 24 hours. **Reservations:** Possible. There are no non-smoking tables. **Credit:** None. **Commendations:** Many, including Whole Life Times, 1984; *Vanity Fair*, 1985; "Entertainment Tonight," 1986; *Whole Life* magazine, 1987; *Los Angeles Times*, calendar section, 1989. They also sent us a restaurant review in Chinese that we assume to be favorable.♦

Venice, **L.A. Eats**, 1009 Washington Blvd, Venice, CA 90291. (213) 296-5914. **Type of Business:** Restaurant. **Sells:** Vegetarian and vegan options. **Organic?** No organic claims. **Specialties:** Southwest lasagna, homemade bread for sandwiches. **Prices:** $6–$10. **Hours:** M-Sat. 11–10. **Reservations:** Possible. 90% No Smoking. **Credit:** V M. **Commendations:** *Los Angeles Times* 1985, 87, 88; *L.A. Magazine:* 1988, 89; Channel 7 News (ABC): 1985. They are "small, fun, and homey."

Ventura, **Classic Carrot**, 1847 E Main, Ventura, CA 93001. (805) 643-0406. **Type of Business:** Restaurant. **Sells:** Natural foods with vegetarian vegan and macrobiotic options. **Organic?** When available. **Specialties:** Soups, sandwiches, tacos, hot entrees, carrot cake. **Prices:** $3.25–$5.95. **Hours:** M-F 11 a.m.–6:30 p.m. Sat. 11 a.m.–4 p.m. **Reservations:** Possible. 85% of tables are non-smoking. **Credit:** None. **Commendations:** Won many categories in local paper's "Best Of" Contest—decided by reader's voting. **Comments:** Catering available.

Ventura, **Lassen Health Food**, 4013 E Main St., Ventura, CA 93003. (805) 644-6990. **Type of Business:** Retail store. **Sells to:** The public. **Sells:** Baked goods, bread, cereals, flour, fruit juice, nuts, oils, pasta, rice, soy products and frozen vegetables. **Organic?** Fresh produce 80% organic (certified by California Certified Organic Farmers), other goods, 20%. **Credit:** V M. **Prices:** Bulk discount is 10%. **Hours:** M-Sat. 9:30–6:30.

Vista, **Boney's**, 705 E Vista Way, Vista, CA 92083. (619) 758-7175. (Affiliated businesses in El Cajon, Escondido, Hillcrest, Pacific Beach, and San Diego.) **Type of Business:** Wholefoods supermarket. **Sells to:** The public. **Sells:** A full line of wholefood grocery items and some organic produce. **Organic?** 10–20% on produce, about 25% on grocery items. **Credit:** Only for supplements. **Hours:** 9–7 Daily.

Walnut Creek, **Good Nature Grocery**, 1359 N Main St., Walnut Creek, CA 94596. (415) 939-5444. **Type of Business:** Retail store. **Sells to:** The public. **Sells:** Every kind of wholefood product plus a complete line of fresh organic produce. **Organic?** Fresh produce 98% organic (certified by Organic Crop Improvement Association, Farm Verified Organic, California Certified Organic Farmers, Demeter/Bio-dynamic), other items 20–30%. **Credit:** V M. **Prices:** 10% discount for case orders, 5% for bulk (25–50lbs.). **Hours:** M-F 9–8, S-S 10–7. **Comments:** The largest natural foods store in Contra Costa County. They specialize in organic prouduce and bulk.

Watsonville, **Coke Farm 89**, Madelene, Dale, 17245 Tarpey Rd., Watsonville, CA 95076. (408) 726-3100, Fax: (408) 726-3136. **Type of Business:** Grower. **Sells to:** Retailers. **Sells:** Organic fresh vegetables: Beets, broccoli, cabbage, carrots, cauliflower, celery, corn, cucumbers, garlic, many varieties of lettuce, arugula, bokchoi, chard, cress, dandelion, endive, fennel, kohl rabi, leeks, radiccio, onions, tomatoes, squash, zucchini, and more. **Organic?** Certified organic (100%—California Certified Organic Farmers). **Minimum Order:** $300. **Comments:** They have been growing organically on the central coast since 1981.

Watsonville, **Organic Matters Produce Co.**, Peter Young, 303 Salinas Road, Watsonville, CA 95076. (408) 728-0644. **Type of Business:** Distributor **Sells to:** Retailers **Sells:** Dairy products and eggs, dried fruit, fresh fruit, nuts and nut butters, soy products, maple syrup, fresh vegetables. **Organic?** Asserted organic (90%).

Westley, **Just Tomatoes Company**, Karen Cox, PO Box 807, Westley, CA 95387. (209) 894-5371. **Type of Business:** Processor, wholesaler and mail-order distributor. **Sells to:** Retailers, restaurants and the general public. **Sells:** Dried tomatoes, apples and persimmons. **Organic?** Asserted 100% organically processed but not grown. **Credit:** None. **Prices:** 10% discount on orders over 100lbs. **Hours:** Telephone orders taken during the day. **Shipping:** Deliveries by UPS. **Minimum Order:** One case. **Catalogue Available?** Yes.

Winters, **Moon Shine Trading Co.**, Ishai Zeldner, PO Box 896, Winters, CA 95694. (916) 753-0601. **Type of Business:** Manufacturer, retailer, and mail-order distributor. **Sells to:** Distributors, retailers, and public. **Sells:** Honey, preserves, nut butters (almonds and cashews). **Organic?** Asserted 10% organic. **Credit:** V M. **Prices:** Discounts available for large orders. **Hours:** M-F 8–4. **Shipping:** 1–3 weeks for delivery. **Minimum Order:** $15. **Catalogue Available?** Yes.

Yuba City, **Sunflower Natural Foods**, 726 Sutter St., Yuba City, CA 95991. (916) 671-9511. **Type of Business:** Wholefoods market and mail-order distributor. **Sells to:** The public. **Sells:** A wide variety of wholefood grocery items (including non-dairy cakes and unsulfured dried fruit) and some organic produce. **Organic?** Produce is about 20% organic (California Certified Organic Farmers), processed goods are 40–50% organic. **Credit:** V M. **Prices:** 10% discount on bulk orders. **Hours:** M-Sat. 10–6. **Comments:** They strive to offer alternatives to processed "sugared" foods and try to carry products with no refined sugars, chemical additives, or hydrolyzed fats.

CO

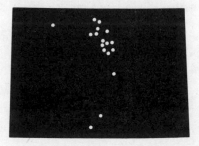

Colorado

Aurora, **Rainbow Grocery**, 2660 E Colfax, Aurora, CO 80206. Type of Business: Retail grocery. Sells to: The public. Sells: A wide array of wholefood grocery items and fresh organic produce. Organic? Organic produce varies between 25% and 70% organic depending on season (mostly California Certified Organic Farmers).Grocery items are about 15–25% organic. Credit: None. Hours: 9–7:30 daily. Comments: They are the sister store of the one in Denver. They try to focus on customer service and have put out a newsletter.♥

Boulder, **Alfalfa's Market,** 1651 Broadway, Boulder, CO 80302. (303) 442-0909. Also in Littleton. Type of Business: Wholefoods supermarket. Sells to: The public. Sells: They have a delicious deli, incredible organic produce, over 350 herbs and spices, meat raised without hormones or antibiotics, supplements, grocery items (plus biodegradable personal and home care products). Organic? Asserted 20% organic. They are affiliated with the Colorado Organic Produce Association and Organic Foods Production Association of North America. Credit: V M. Prices: 10% off bulk bin prices. Hours: 8–9 daily. Comments and Commendations: They offer local delivery within the city limits. Alfalfa's is one of the foremost natural foods supermarkets in the country and got the third most recommendations in our survey.♥♦♦♦

Boulder, **Crystal Market,** Mike Gilliand, 1825 Pearl St., Boulder, CO 80302. (303) 440-9599. Type of Business: Retail store. Sells to: The public. Sells: A full line of wholefood grocery items. Organic? Produce certified by Colorado Organic Producers Association. Credit: V M. Hours: 7–11. Comments: Crystal Market is affiliated with Wild Oats Market and Columbine Market in Ft. Collins under the name Agora Markets.

Boulder, **Wild Oats Market,** 2584 Baseline Rd., Boulder, CO 80303. Type of Business: Retail store. Sells to: The public. Sells: A full line of natural groceries. Organic? Asserted 25–30%. Credit: V M. Prices: 10% discounts on bulk orders. Hours: 7–11. Comments: Crystal Market is affiliated with Wild Oats Market and Columbine Market in Ft. Collins under the name Agora Markets.

Colorado Springs, **Poor Richard's,** 324 1/2 N Tejon St., Colorado Springs, CO 80903. (719) 632-7721. Type of Business: Restaurant. Sells: Wholefoods cuisine with vegetarian options (tofu enchiladas, Vegeritos, and at least two other vegetarian specials per day, plus vegetarian sandwiches) and some dairy-free items. Organic? Asserted about 25% organic. 60% of tables are no-smoking. Specialties: Home-made natural baked goods (baked daily in the restaurant) made from whole-wheat flours, alfalfa, honey, and oat bran. Prices: $4–7. Hours: 10:30–10 daily. Reservations: Possible. Credit: V M. Comments: They occasionally feature plays and comedy. They also own the espresso/dessert bar next door.

Denver, **Jerusalem Restaurant,** Said S. Wahdan, 1890 E Evans, Denver, CO 80201. (303) 777-8828. Type of Business: Restaurant. Sells: Macrobiotic Middle Eastern cuisine with vegetarian and vegan options. Organic? As-serted 50% Organic. Prices: $1.75–$7.45. Hours: 9 a.m.–3 a.m. Reservations: Possible. One-half of tables are no smoking. Credit: V M AE. Commendations: Westwood Paper, 1985–89.

Denver, **The Macrobiotic Center,** 1512 Monaco Pkwy., Denver, CO 80220. (303) 399-9511. Type of Business: Educational center. Sells: Dinners on Friday nights (7:00) and take-out lunches on Mondays, Wednesdays, and Fridays. Specialties: Macrobiotic teaching and food. Hours: See above. Comments: Their primary focus is on education.

Denver, **Rainbow Grocery,** 2660 E Colfax, Denver, CO 80206. (303) 320-1664. (Sister stores in Aurora and Seattle.) Type of Business: Retail grocery. Sells to: The public. Sells: A wide array of wholefood grocery items and fresh organic produce. It is a small store, but it is jam-packed. Organic? Organic produce varies between 25% and 70% organic depending on season (mostly California Certified Organic Farmers). Grocery items are about 15–25% organic. Credit: None. Hours: M-F 8–9, Sat. 9–9, Sun. 9–8. Comments: They are the original health-food store/grocery in Denver and are affiliated with Rainbow Natural Food Distributing that serves much of the south-central part of the country. They try to focus on customer service and have started a newsletter.♥

Denver, **Rosewood Cafe,** Porter Hospital, 2525 S Downing, Denver, CO 80210. (303) 778-5881. Type of Business: Restaurant. Sells: Vegetarian food with vegan options. Organic? No organic claims. Specialties: Haystacks, Mexican Food, nut loaves, casseroles, and desserts. Prices: $1.25-1.65. Hours: 6:15 a.m.–7 p.m. Reservations: Not possible. Credit: None. Comments and Commendations: *Food Management,* 1988. The menu looks inviting, but watch out for fatty, deep-fried items.

Englewood, **Samurai Restaurant & Lounge,** 9625 E Arapahoe, Englewood, CO 80111. (303) 799-9991. Type of Business: Restaurant. Sells: Japanese cuisine; vegetarian, vegan, and macrobiotic options available. Organic? No organic claims. 35% of the tables are no-smoking. Specialties: Sushi, Sashimi, Sukiyaki, and other traditional Japanese dinners. Prices: $8.50–35. Hours: M-F 11–2, M-Th 4–10, F 4–10:30. Reservations: Possible. Credit: V M AE DC.

Fort Collins, **Columbine Market,** 1611 S College Ave., Ft. Collins, CO 80525. Type of Business: Retail store. Sells to: The public. Sells: A full line of natural groceries. Organic? Asserted 25–30%. Credit: V M. Prices: 10% discounts on bulk orders. Hours: 7–11. Comments: Crystal Market is affiliated with Wild Oats Market and Columbine Market in Ft. Collins under the name of Agora Markets.

Fort Collins, **Fort Collins Food Coop (Cooperative Markets Inc.),** Paula Curtis, Manager, 250 East Mountain, Fort Collins, CO 80524. (303) 484-7448. Type of Business: Co-op/Retail store. Sells to: Co-op members and the general public. Sells: A wide variety of processed foods and fresh produce including a very large range of cooking and medicinal herbs. **Organic?** They try to support local farmers; most of their produce is certified by Colorado Organic Producers Association (COPA). **Credit:** None. **Prices:** Bulk discounts as follows: Co-op members 20% above cost, non-members 30% above cost, Co-op discount workers, 10% above cost. **Hours:** M-F 8:30–8, Sat. 9–6:30, Sun. 11–6. **Comments:** Careful consideration given to ecological impact of products carried—e.g. packaging. "Cruelty-free" health and beauty line. In-store deli, featuring homemade sandwiches, cookies, muffins, and granola.

Gardner, **Malachite School and Small Farm,** Alan Mace, ASR Box 21 Pass Creek Road, Gardner, CO 81040. (719) 746–2412. **Type of Business:** Producer and Mail-order distributor. **Sells to:** Retailers, mail order to the general public. **Sells:** Honey, frozen beef, dried herbs and sourdough starter. **Organic?** Asserted 100% organic, the farm is a member of Colorado Organic Producers Association. **Credit:** None. **Prices:** No discount for bulk. **Hours:** Daily, 9–5. **Minimum Order:** None. **Catalogue Available?** Yes. **Comments:** They host bed and breakfast style farmstays and encourage people to join in farm activities and enjoy farm-fresh meals.

Johnstown, **Rieder Brothers,** 23455 WCR 17, Johnstown, CO 80534. (303) 587–4863. **Type of Business:** Grower and distributor. **Sells to:** Primarily retailers, with some sales to the public. **Sells:** Fresh organic vegetables (including potatoes, onions, beets, peppers, broccoli, carrots, turnips, peas, corn, spinach, squash, lettuce, green beans and leeks). **Organic?** 100% certified organic, member of Colorado Organic Producers Association. **Credit:** None. **Hours:** 7–5. **Shipping:** If far enough away, by airfreight. **Minimum Order:** Enough to fill one freight unit. **Catalogue Available?** Yes.

La Jara, **Hamilton Farms,** Tom Hamilton, 23242 Hwy. 371, La Jara, CO 81140. (719) 274–5230. **Type of Business:** Grower and distributor. **Sells to:** Retailers. **Sells:** Fresh vegetables: potatoes (reds, russets, yellow finn) and onions. **Organic?** Certified organic by Colorado Organic Producers Association. **Credit:** None. **Hours:** 7–6. **Minimum Order:** None. **Catalogue Available?** Yes.

Littleton, **Alfalfa's Market,** 5910 South University, Littleton, CO 80121. Also in Boulder. **Type of Business:** Wholefoods supermarket. **Sells to:** The public. **Sells:** They have a delicious deli, incredible organic produce, over 350 herbs and spices, meat raised without hormones or antibiotics, supplements, grocery items, and biodegradable personal and home care products. **Organic?** 20% organic. They are affiliated with the Colorado Organic Producers Association and Organic Foods Production Association of North America. **Credit:** V M **Prices:** 10% off bulk bin prices. **Hours:** Daily, 8 a.m.–9 p.m. **Comments and Commendations:** Alfalfa's is one of the foremost natural foods supermarkets in the country and got the third most recommendations in our survey.♥♦♦♦

Steamboat Springs, **Suzanne's Specialties,** Bart Smith, 116 9th St., Steamboat Springs, CO 80487. (303) 879–

5731. **Type of Business:** Retail store and mail-order distributor. **Sells to:** The public and restaurants. **Sells:** They offer a complete coffee and juice bar w/ a different coffee of the day, specialty teas, carrot juice, seasonal fruit juices, and special protein shakes. The store also offers a variety of fresh organic vegetables and processed foods. **Organic?** Asserted 75% organic. **Credit:** V M. **Hours:** M-F 9:30–5:30, Sat. 10–4. **Shipping:** 10% off on orders up to 25 lbs.; 20% on orders above 25 lbs. **Minimum Order:** None. **Catalogue Available?** Yes.

CT

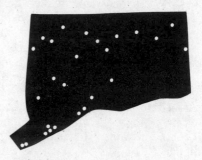

Connecticut

Bolton, **Aux Fines Herbes,** PO Box 9500, Dimock Lane, Bolton, CT 06043. (203)224–3724. **Type of Business:** Restaurant. **Sells to:** Buying clubs, restaurants, and retailers in central Connecticut. **Sells:** Sage, rosemary, thyme, and about 10 other herbs plus eggplant, lettuce (25 varieties), peppers, radishes, squash, tomatoes, and zucchini. **Organic?** 100%, certified by Natural Organic Farmers Association. **Credit:** None. **Shipping:** Deliveries Wednesdays and Saturdays.

Bridgeport, **Bloodroot,** 85 Ferris St., Bridgeport, CT 06605. (203) 576–9168. **Type of Business:** Restaurant. **Sells:** Vegetarian entrees with vegan and macrobiotic options. They have a seasonal menu that changes every three weeks to take advantage of what is freshest. **Organic?** About 60%. **Specialties:** Homemade breads, dairy-free desserts, **Prices:** $7–9.50. **Hours:** Lunch: Tu, Th-Sun. 11:30–2:30. Dinner: Tu, Th 6–9; Wed 7–9 (reservations required); F, Sat. 6–10. **Reservations:** Possible for 5 of more (dinner only). **Credit:** None. Personal checks accepted. **Commendations:** Hailed by the *Vegetarian Times* as one of the eight best vegetarian restaurants in America. They also put out two cookbooks.♦

Burlington, **Blue Twine Farm,** Cipah Shapiro, 21 Polly Dan Road, Burlington, CT 06013. (203) 589–2619. **Type of Business:** Grower. **Sells to:** Retailers (95%), co-ops, and the public. **Sells:** Tofu dips and spreads, and some herbs at the end of the season. **Organic?** Natural Organic Farmers Association certified 100% organic. **Credit:** None. **Hours:** 9–6 out of her home. **Comments:** Her business is a cottage industry serving the local area.

Danbury, **Chamomille Natural Foods Store,** Route 6 Plaza, Danbury, CT 06810. (203) 792–8952. **Type of**

Business: Retailer. Sells to: The general public. Sells: A wide assortment of wholefood grocery items and organic produce. Organic? Asserted 80–85% organic. They rely on the certification claims of their suppliers. Credit: V M. Prices: 10% discount per case or $40 worth of an item. Hours: M-Sat. 9:30–6.

Danielson, **Community Health Foods,** 56 Main St., Danielson, CT 06293. (203) 779-0033. Type of Business: Retail store. Sells to: The public. Sells: A full assortment of wholefood grocery items and organic produce. Organic? 25% overall. Credit: None. Prices: 10% discounts on bulk orders. Hours: M-Th 8:30–5:30, F 8:30–7., Sat. 9–5. Comments: They try to keep their prices down because they believe that good foods should be affordable to everyone. They also have a snack bar at which customers can purchase their lunches.

Durham, **Ronald Capozzi,** Meetinghouse Hill Rd., Durham, CT 06422. (203) 349-1417. Type of Business: Farm. Sells to: Mainly retailers, but also the public through a stand. Sells: Yellow raspberries. Organic? Natural Organic Farmers Association certified 100% organic. Credit: None. Shipping: He personally delivers.

Farmington, **Natural Gourmet,** 5 Melrose Drive, Farmington, CT 06032. (203) 676-9083. Type of Business: Retail store. Sells to: Public. Sells: Beans, fresh fruits, dried fruits, frozen vegetables (broccoli, potatoes), cheeses (150 varieties), yogurt, ice cream, coffees, teas, nuts and nut butters, grains, baked goods, flours, cereals, oils, pastas, rice, soy products, juices, jams, canned tomatoes, salsa. Organic? 25% certified and asserted. Member of National Nutritional Foods Association. Credit: None. Prices: Special prices for case lots. Hours: M-F 9–8, Sat. 9–6, Sun. 10–5.

Goshen, **Four Winds Farm,** Rt. 63 South, Goshen, CT 06756. (203) 491-2650. (203) 491-3178. Type of Business: Grower. Sells to: The public through a stand, farmers markets in Torrington and Plymouth, and pick-your-own. Sells: Strawberries, blueberries, green beans, melons, peaches, oregano, parsley, sage, rosemary, thyme, beets, broccoli, cabbage, carrots, corn, cucumbers, lettuce (several varieties), onions, peas, peppers, potatoes, radishes, spinach, squash, tomatoes, zucchini and pumpkins. Organic? 80% organic, Natural Organic Farmers Association certified. Credit: None. Hours: 9–6 Tues-Sun. from June 15–December 24.

Greenwich, **Greenwich Healthmart,** Chuck Ringel, 30 Greenwich Avenue, Greenwich, CT 06830. (203) 869-9658. Type of Business: Retailer. Sells to: The general public. Sells: A large range of baked goods, beans, beverages, breads, confections, cereals, dairy products, flour, fruit, nuts and nut butters, oils, pasta, rice, soy products, vegetables, grains, beef, turkey, peppers and ginseng. Organic? They rely on the certification claims of their suppliers. Credit: V M AE. Prices: 10% off case lots and bulk grains in full bags. Hours: M-F, 8:30–5:30; Sat., 8:30–5. Minimum Order: Minimum of $20 for mail order. Catalogue Available? No.

Greenwich, **Hay Day Country Farm Market,** Randi Brawley, Vice President, 1050 East Putnam Ave., Greenwich, CT 06878. (203) 637-7600. Type of Business: Retailer. Sells to: The general public. Sells: Baked goods, beans, beverages (roasted on the premises), breads (baked on the premises), confections, cereals, dairy products (including their own ice cream and yogurt), flour, fruit (both processed, fresh and dried), certified Black Angus beef, Hay Day fresh peanut butter, oils, pasta (their own), rice, tofu, fresh vegetables, grains, nuts, herbs and spices. Organic? Asserted 60% organic. Credit: None. Prices: No discount for bulk. Hours: M-Sat. 8–7, Sun. 8–6.

Hamden, **Hay Day Country Farm Market,** 2460 Dixwell Avenue, Hamden, CT 06514. (203) 288-3148. Type of Business: Retailer. Sells to: The general public. Sells: Baked goods, beans, beverages (roasted on the premises), breads (baked on the premises), confections, cereals, dairy products (including their own ice cream and yogurt), flour, fruit (both processed, fresh and dried), certified Black Angus beef, Hay Day fresh peanut butter, oils, pasta (their own), rice, tofu, fresh vegetables, grains, nuts, herbs and spices. Organic? Asserted 60% organic. Credit: None. Prices: No discount for bulk. Hours: M-Sat. 8–7, Sun. 8–6.

Hartford, **Cheese and Stuff,** 550 Farmington Ave., Hartford, CT 06105. (203) 233-8281. Type of Business: Retailer. Sells to: The general public. Sells: Most foods, especially cakes, cheeses and seafood. Asserted 10% organic. Organic? They rely on the certification claims of their suppliers. Credit: V M AE. Prices: 10% discount for bulk. Hours: M-F 9–9, Sat. 9–6, Sun. 10–6. Shipping: We use UPS for their gift baskets, 24-hour advance notice required for preparation.

Kensington, **Nature's Harvest Health Shoppe,** Carolyn Smith, 47 Chamberlain Hwy., Kensington, CT 06037. (203) 828-0404. Type of Business: Retailer. Sells to: The public. Sells: Baked goods, beans, beverages, candy, dairy products, flour, processed and dried fruit, nuts, nut butters, oils, pasta, rice, soy products, frozen vegetables, some fresh fruit (apples, bananas, grapefruit, oranges, strawberries and tangerines), grains, meats, spices and alfalfa seeds. Organic? Certified 85% organic by NOFA. Credit: V M. Prices: 10% discount on 25lb. or 50lb. bags. Hours: M-Sat., 9–6; Late opening, until 8 p.m. on Thursday.

Kent, **Kenko Natural Grocery,** Leonard Urbanowicz, 350 Kent Cornwall Rd. (Rt. 7), Kent, CT 06757. (203) 927-4079. Type of Business: Grower, retailer. Sells to: The public. Sells: Baked goods, beans, cereals, beverages, dairy products, flour, fruit, meats, nuts, oils, pasta, rice, soy products, vegetables, herbs and spices. Organic? Natural Organic Farmers Association Certified. Credit: None. Hours: 8–8, 7 days a week. Shipping: None. Minimum Order: None. Catalogue Available? Yes.

Litchfield, **Marshmallow Saanens,** Cindy Clark, Norfolk Rd., Litchfield, CT 06759. (203) 567-5090. Type of Business: Producer. Sells to: Public. Sells: Veal and chevon. Organic? Asserted 100% organic, listed with Natural Organic Farmers Association but not certified by them. **Credit:** None. **Hours:** 9–6 by telephone, visits by appointment only. **Minimum Order:** Yes, one animal. **Catalogue Available?** No.

Milford, **El Torero Restaurant,** Alber Fournier, Owner, 1698 Boston Post Rd., Milford, CT 06460, (203) 878–7734. **Type of Business:** Restaurant. **Sells:** Texan-Mexican food. **Organic?** Asserted 5% organic. **Specialties:** Seafoods. **Prices:** $6–$14. **Hours:** M 5–10, T-F 11:30–10, Sat. 12–11, Sun. 3–10. **Reservations:** Possible. **Credit:** V M AE DC CB.

Milford, **Natural Foods of Milford,** Yasmine V. Cronin, 232 Boston Post Road, Milford, CT 06460. (203) 877–7275. **Type of Business:** Retailer. **Sells to:** The public. **Sells:** A range of beans, beverages, dairy products, fruit (dried, fresh and processed), grains, meat, nuts, soy products, spices, vegetables, baked goods, cereals, oils, pasta, rice and breads. **Organic?** Asserted 100% organic. **Credit:** V M. **Prices:** No discount for bulk. **Hours:** M-W 10–6, Th-F 10–7, Sat. 10–5, Sun.—seasonal opening times vary. **Minimum Order:** No. **Catalogue Available?** No. **Comments:** Soon to be a retail cooperative and buying club.

North Cornwall, **Ridgeway's Organic Produce,** Town St., North Cornwall, CT 06796. (203) 672–6767, (203) 672–0279. **Type of Business:** Grower. **Sells to:** The public through a farm stand. **Sells:** Organic vegetables, apples, strawberries, and maple syrup. **Organic?** Natural Organic Farmers Association certified.

Oneco, **Wayne's Organic Garden,** Wayne Hansen, 1080 Plainfield Pike, PO Box 154, Oneco, CT 06373. (203)564–7987. **Type of Business:** Grower. **Sells to:** Retailers and the general public. **Sells:** Green beans, strawberries, basil, parsley, beets, broccoli, cabbage, carrots, cauliflower, corn, cucumbers, eggplant, lettuce, peas, peppers, radishes, spinach, squash, tomatoes, turnips, zucchini and arugula. **Organic?** Certified 100% organic by Natural Organic Farmers Association. **Credit:** None. **Hours:** Phone orders, M-F 5 p.m.–8 p.m., all day Sat. and Sun. May to mid-October. **Minimum Order:** None.

Oxford, **Butterbrooke Farm,** 78 Barry Road, Oxford, CT 06483. (203) 888–2000. **Type of Business:** Grower. **Sells:** 75 varieties of chemical-free, open-pollinated, short-maturity seeds; not certified organic. **Catalogue Available?** Yes.

Southbury, **Spruce Brook Farm,** Enid Grant, Owner, 708 Spruce Rd., Southbury, CT 06488. (203) 264–8346. **Type of Business:** Grower and retailer (mainly through farmers markets: Sat., Weston, CT, June-Oct; Sat., Bethel, CT, Aug-Oct; Thurs, Stamford, CT, July-Oct). **Sells to:** The public. **Sells:** Basil, chives, ginseng, parsley, blueberries, cucumbers, eggplant, garlic, lettuce, peppers, radishes, tomatoes, zucchini and leeks. **Organic?** Certified 100% organic by Natural Organic Farmers Association. **Credit:** None. **Comments:** A very small operation, with only 2 acres producing and an orchard which will produce fruit in 1991.

Storrs, **Betterways Marketplace,** Jim Pittman, Holiday Mall Rte. 195, Storrs, CT 06268. (203) 429–4517. **Type of Business:** Retailer. **Sells to:** The public. **Sells:** Vegetarian products, specializing in cruelty free and environmentally sound products. They carry almost all non-meat foods. **Organic?** Asserted about 20% organic. They rely on the certification claims of their suppliers. **Credit:** None. **Prices:** 10% discount for bulk. **Hours:** M-Sat. 9:30–6.

Thomaston, **Cricket Hill Farm,** Kasha and David Furman, 670 Walnut Hill Rd., Thomaston, CT 06787. (203) 283–4707. **Type of Business:** Grower. **Sells to:** Retailers, distributors, restaurants and the public. **Sells:** Garlic and onions. **Organic?** Natural Organic Farmers Association certified 100% organic. **Credit:** None. **Hours:** Phone orders, 8–6 daily. **Shipping:** By mail. **Minimum Order:** 1 lb. **Catalogue Available?** Yes.

Westport, **A Change of Seasons,** 256 Post Rd. E, Westport, CT 06881. (203) 454–0737. **Type of Business:** Restaurant and take-out deli. **Sells:** A menu of health gourmet meals prepared using only cold-pressed oils. Macrobiotic dishes are available. **Organic?** Asserted 30–50% organic. **Specialties:** Fresh pasta, free-range chicken dishes, fresh fish and macrobiotic dishes. **Prices:** Entrees—Lunch $6.25–$7.95, Dinner $10.95–$15.95. **Hours:** 11:30–10. **Reservations:** For Friday and Saturday nights. **Credit:** V M (lowest limit: Lunch $15, Dinner $30).♦

Westport, **Food for Thought,** Ltd., Alex Reznikoff, 221 Post Road West, Westport, CT 06880. (203) 226–5233. **Type of Business:** Retail store, carrying organic produce for the last 21 years. **Sells to:** The general public. **Sells:** All the products sold by a good supermarket, but the difference being that 90% of the goods are organic. **Organic?** Membership of Natural Organic Foods Association, National Nutritional Foods Association, and the Committee for Sustainable Agriculture. **Credit:** V M. **Prices:** All bulk orders are discounted by 10–25%. **Hours:** M-Sat. 7:30–7, Sun. 8–5. **Minimum Order:** No. **Catalogue Available?** Yes.♦

Westport, **Hay Day Country Farm Market,** 1026 Post Road East, Westport, CT 06880. (203) 227–9008. **Type of Business:** Retailer. **Sells to:** The general public. **Sells:** Baked goods, beans, beverages (roasted on the premises), breads (baked on the premises), confections, cereals, dairy products (including their own ice cream and yogurt), flour, fruit (both processed, fresh and dried), certified Black Angus beef, Hay Day fresh peanut butter, oils, pasta (their own), rice, tofu, fresh vegetables, grains, nuts, herbs and spices. **Organic?** Asserted 60% organic. **Credit:** None. **Prices:** No discount for bulk. **Hours:** M-Sat. 8–7, Sun. 8–6.

DE

Delaware

Milford, **The Nature Trail,** Inc. , 809 N Walnut St., Milford, DE 19963. (302) 422–0430. Type of Business: Retail store Sells to: The public. Sells: They specialize in natural foods for the allergy sensitive. They have a fair selection of grocery items (including homemade cakes) and some organic produce. Organic? Produce 100% organic (Farm Verified Organic, Natural Organic Farmers Association); processed goods 75%. Credit: None. Prices: 15% discounts on case lot purchases. Hours: M-F 5 p.m.–8:30 p.m., Sat. 9–2. Comments: The store will do special orders on request. They also carry all-natural supplements, herbs, and books.

Newark, **Nature's Way Health Food Store,** Newark Shopping Center, Newark, DE 19711. (302) 737–7986. Type of Business: Retail store. Sells to: The public. Sells: A range of natural grocery items, plus fresh beans, grains, nuts, soy products and spices. Organic? Fresh produce 100% organic (certified by Organic Crop Improvement Association, Farm Verified Organic), other grocery, 75%. Credit: V M. Prices: Case discounts. Comments: The store also carries vitamins and supplements. They will special order for customers.

Newark, **The Newark Co-op Inc.,** 280 East Main St., Newark, DE 19711. (302) 368–5894. Type of Business: Wholefood store and co-op. Sells to: Members and the public. Sells: A large variety of organically grown produce and wholefood grocery items. They also carry non-toxic cleaning products. Organic? Produce is about 67% organic, about 50% grocery and bulk items are organic. They try to carry every organic product available through East Coast distributors. Credit: None. Prices: Working members pay shelf price, a mark-up of about 35% over wholesale (most stores mark-up 50–67%) and can get bulk orders at 10% over wholesale. Non-working members pay 10% over the shelf price and non-members pay 25% over shelf price. Hours: M-Sat. 10–8, closed Sun. Comments: One of the members offers cooking classes through the Chrysalis Center. The store also offers information on holistic health. Membership costs $100 lifetime payable over 2+ years and is like buying a share of the store.♦

Wilmington, **The Juice-o-mat,** 912 Orange St., Wilmington, DE 19801. (302) 658–1900. Type of Business: Retail

store. Sells to: The public. Sells: Fruit juices, and some wholefoods: bread, rice cakes, granola, flour, pasta, oils, rice, soy products, cheese and yogurt. Credit: V M. Hours: 9–4:30 daily.

Wilmington, **The Vegetarian,** 9 E 8th St., Wilmington, DE 19801. (302) 655–5523 Type of Business: Restaurant. Sells: Vegetarian cuisine with vegan options. Organic? Asserted 10–50%. Water is filtered. Specialties: "Sizzle Burgers" and other huge sandwiches, lasagna, and stuffed baked potatoes. Prices: $3–5. Hours: M-F 11:30–3; from Labor Day to Memorial Day, regular hours plus 12–2:30 on Saturday and dinner on the first Friday of each month. Reservations: Not possible except for the Friday dinners. All tables are no-smoking. Credit: None. Comments: The special Friday dinners usually coincide with musical performances.

DC

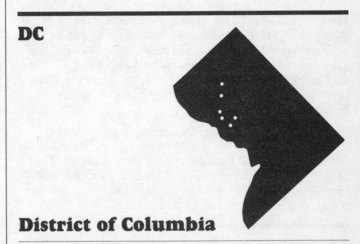

District of Columbia

Washington, **Hugo's Natural Foods Market,** 3813 Livingston St. NW, Washington, DC 20015. (202) 362–0621 (Office), (202) 966–6103 (Store). Type of Business: Retail store. Sells to: The public. Sells: An extensive selection of fresh organic produce and wholefood processed goods. Also, supplements, crystals, health and beauty aids, cookware and more. Organic? About 60% of the produce in the summer and 20% in the winter. Credit: V M. Prices: 10% discount on items purchased in case quantities. Hours: M-Sat. 9–8, Sun. 10–6. Comments: They have a deli section that will make sandwiches, too. They sell everything they can get in organic form.

Washington, **Kalorama Cafe,** Arlene Morris, 1248 Lamont St. NW, Washington, DC 20009. (202) 667–1022. Type of Business: Restaurant. Sells: Vegetarian and macrobiotic options. Organic? 10% organic. Specialties: Italian pastas, seafood, and pizza. Prices: $6.95–$9.95 Hours: Tu-Sat. lunch 11:30–3, dinner 6–10. Fri. and Sat. dinner 6–11. Sun. brunch 11–3. Closed Sun. evening and all day Monday. Reservations: Not required, but possible. 50% non-smoking. Credit: None. Comments: The only place in DC to get food using whole grains exclusively.

Washington, **Naturally Yours,** 2029 P St., Washington, DC 20036. (202) 429–1718. Type of Business: Retail store. Sells to: The public. Sells: A complete line of wholefood groceries and fresh organic produce. **Organic?** Asserted 100% organic on fresh produce, 50% on other items. **Credit:** V M. **Prices:** 10% discount for special case orders. **Hours:** M-Sat. 10–8, Th 10–9, Sun. 11–7.

Washington, **Patrick's Natural Foods,** 1825 Columbia Rd. NW, Washington, DC 20009. (202) 462–5150. **Type of Business:** Retail store. **Sells to:** The public. **Sells:** Baked goods, beans, bread, candy, cereals, dairy products, fruit juice, oils, pasta, rice and soy products. **Organic?** Fresh produce asserted 50% organic. They assert that 90% of their grocery items are organic. **Credit:** V M AE. **Hours:** M-Th 9–8, F-Sat. 9–7:30, Sunday closed.

Washington, **Red Sea,** 2463 18th St. NW, Washington, DC 20009. (202) 483–5000. **Type of Business:** Restaurant. **Sells:** Some vegetarian options. **Organic?** No organic claims. **Specialties:** Vegetarian cuisine. **Prices:** $4.50–8.25. **Hours:** 11:30–11. **Reservations:** Possible. **Credit:** V M and "other". **Commendations:** *Washington* magazine Best 50 Restaurant Award. Red Sea may be the elusive "great Ethiopian restaurant" you always hear about in DC. They do not use organic produce and have predominantly meat-based entrees, but their vegetarian entres are reputed to be fantastic.

Washington, **Yes! Natural Gourmet,** Tom Eoff, 3425 Connecticut Ave. NW, Washington, DC 20008. (202) 363–1559. **Type of Business:** Retail store. **Sells to:** The public. **Sells:** Full service natural food store. **Organic?** 40% organic. **Credit:** V M AE ($15.00 minimum). **Hours:** M-F 9 a.m.–9 p.m., Sat. 9 a.m.–7 p.m., Sun. 12–6.♦

FL

Florida

Boca Raton, **Donigan Nutrition Center,** 3561 N Federal Hwy., Boca Raton, FL 33431. (407) 395–5521. **Type of Business:** Retail store. **Sells to:** The public. **Sells:** A limited range of packaged wholefoods. **Organic?** Asserted 20% organic. **Credit:** V M. **Hours:** M-Sat. 10–5. Closed Sundays. **Minimum Order:** $10 for credit card orders.

Boca Raton, **Whole Earth Market,** 7098 Beracasa Way, Boca Raton, FL 33433. (407) 394–9438. **Type of Business:** Retail store. **Sells to:** The public. **Sells:** A full array of wholefood grocery items and organic produce. **Organic?** Asserted 50% organic. **Credit:** V M. **Prices:** 10% discounts on bulk orders. **Hours:** M-Sat. 9–9, Sun. 10–5.

Clearwater, **Mike's Health Foods,** 2340 Sr. 580, Ste. D., Clearwater, FL 34623. (813) 799–6453. **Type of Business:** Retail store. **Sells to:** The public. **Sells:** An impressive selection of fresh organic fruits and vegetables, wholefood groceries, and organic meats. **Organic?** 100% of their produce is organic (Organic Crop Improvement Association), and about 60% of their processed goods. **Credit:** V M. **Prices:** No discounts on bulk orders. **Hours:** M-Sat. 10–6.

Clearwater, **Nature's Food Patch & Bunny Hop Cafe,** Laurie Powers, 1408 Cleveland St., Clearwater, FL 33515. (813) 443–6703. **Type of Business:** Restaurant and natural-foods supermarket. **Sells:** Natural health foods and vegetarian dishes in the cafe. Filtered water. **Organic?** Asserted 35% organic (produce 100%). They communicate regularly with Organic Crop Improvement Association. Water is filtered. **Specialties:** Excellent range of macrobiotic and gourmet vegetarian dishes. **Prices:** Entrees: $3–$6. **Hours:** M-F 10–9, Sat. 10–7. The cafe is only open for lunches and dinner on Friday on a reserved basis. **Reservations:** Not required except Friday evenings. 100% non-smoking. **Credit:** V M. **Comments:** The menu for the cafe looks intriguing and along with a good assortment of macrobiotic dishes features items like yeast-free non-alcoholic beer, and organic watermelon juice.

Coconut Grove, **The Last Carrot,** Michael Compton, 3420 Main Hwy., Coconut Grove, FL 33133. (305) 445–0805. **Type of Business:** Restaurant. **Sells:** Sandwiches and light meals. **Organic?** Asserted 10% organic, water filtered. **Specialties:** Whole-wheat pita sandwiches and fresh fruit juices. **Prices:** $.95–$3. **Hours:** M-Sun. 11–7. **Reservations:** Not possible. 100% non-smoking. **Credit:** None. **Comments:** They have been at the same location for 17 years.♦

Coconut Grove, **The Macrobiotic Foundation of Florida, Inc.** , 3291 Franklin Ave., Coconut Grove, FL 33133. (305) 448–6625. **Type of Business:** Restaurant (take-out available). **Sells:** Soups, grain and bean dishes, tempeh, seitan, casseroles, desserts, salads, sandwiches and burgers as examples. **Organic?** Asserted almost 100% organic. Filtered water. **Specialties:** International nights, with food from countries around the world. **Prices:** Entrees range from $6 to $12. **Hours:** Lunch, dinner and Sunday brunch. **Reservations:** Usually required. 100% non-smoking. **Credit:** V M AE. **Comments:** Guest speakers lecture on Tuesdays and Thursdays after dinner. They also offer macrobiotic cooking classes.♦

Coconut Grove, **Oak Feed Store,** 3030 Grand Ave., Coconut Grove, Miami, FL 33133. (305) 448–7595. **Type of Business:** Retail store. **Sells to:** The general public. **Sells:** Baked goods, beans, teas, sodas, candy, cereals, dairy products, flour, fruit juices, dried fruit, nuts, oils, pasta, rice, soy products, frozen vegetables, grains, fresh fruit, vegetables and spices. **Organic?** They rely on the certification of suppliers. **Credit:** V M AE. **Prices:** 20% discount for bulk. **Hours:** 9–9, 365 days a year. **Comments:** They have been in business for 19 years and emphasize quality.♦

Edgewater, **Tropical Blossom Honey Co. Inc.,** PO Box 8, 106 N Ridgewood Ave., Edgewater, FL 32132. (904) 428–9027. **Type of Business:** Manufacturer, wholesale distributor and a small retail outlet. **Sells to:** Retailers and the general public. **Sells:** Tropical wild honey, syrup-bulk, preserves, nut butters, preserves, jams, jellies. Asserted 60% organic. **Credit:** None. **Prices:** Special discounts for bulk. **Hours:** 8–5. **Minimum Order:** No. **Catalogue Available?** Yes.

Ft. Lauderdale, **Bread of Life,** Richard Gerber, 2250 Wilton Dr., Ft. Lauderdale, FL. (305) 563–TOFU. **Type of Business:** Natural foods market and restaurant. **Sells:** Vegetarian gourmet cuisine with vegan and macrobiotic options. **Organic?** Asserted 100% organic in retail. **Prices:** Entrees range from $5.50 to $10.95. **Hours:** 7 days a week. **Reservations:** Not required. 100% non-smoking. **Credit:** V M AE DC. **Commendations:** The executive chef, Julie Gerber, was personal chef to Dr. Anthony Sattilaro, author of "Recalled by Life."

Ft. Lauderdale, **Carrot Patch,** Claudia Banks, 1032 E Las Olas Blvd., Ft. Lauderdale, FL 33301. (305) 761–8263. **Type of Business:** Delicatessen (with seating) and retail store. **Sells:** Breakfast bar and sandwich bar, with vegetarian, vegan and macrobiotic options. **Organic?** Asserted 5–50% organic. **Specialties:** Gourmet whole-wheat pizza and stuffed whole-wheat breads. **Prices:** Entrees range from $4 to $7. **Hours:** 8–8. **Reservations:** Possible. 100% non-smoking. **Credit:** V M AE. The minimum for payment by credit card is $20. **Comments:** The store offers cooking classes and is putting together a chapter of Americans for Safe Food.

Gainesville, **Orange Blossom Cooperative Warehouse,** Burt Polansky (buyer), 1601 NW 55th Place, Gainesville, FL 32606, Mail to: PO Box 4159, Gainesville, FL 32613. (904) 372–7061. **Type of Business:** Retail store, Co-op/buying club, and mail-order distributor. **Sells to:** The general public, wholesale to buying clubs. **Sells:** A complete selection of wholefoods and organic produce. Coffee, condiments, dried beans, dried fruit, whole grains, flour and meals, processed grain products, herbs and spices, organic juices, nuts and nut butters, oils, seeds, soy products, sweeteners, and teas. **Organic?** They assert that 100% of their produce is organic. **Credit:** None. **Prices:** Discounts on full pallets. **Hours:** F 9–4, Sat. 10–2. **Shipping:** They only deliver to Florida, Alabama and Georgia. **Minimum Order:** $100 for pick up, $300 for delivery within Alachua County, $500 outside Alachua County. **Catalogue Available?** Yes.

High Springs, **The Great Outdoors Trading Co. and Cafe,** 65 N Main St., High Springs, FL 32643. (904) 454–2900. **Type of Business:** Restaurant and retail store. **Sells:** Soups, quiche, sandwiches, salads, fresh fish, pasta and vegetarian entrees, including vegan options. **Organic?** Asserted 25% organic, a lot of which is home grown. **Specialties:** Seitan and tofu sandwiches and daily special entrees. **Prices:** Entrees range from $6.95 to $14.95. **Hours:** M-Th 10–9, F-Sat. 10–10, Sun. 11:30–9. **Reservations:** Possible. 100% non-smoking. **Credit:** V M AE D.

Comments: Situated just off I-75, this provides a welcome alternative to usual roadside food. The store is an outdoor specialty shop selling tents, canoes, and other camping accessories.

Hollywood, **National Health and Nutrition,** 433 Hollywood Mall, Hollywood Blvd. at I-95, Hollywood, FL 33021. (305) 983–0780. **Type of Business:** Retail store (part of a chain). **Sells:** Some wholefood type items but no organic produce. See the listing under West Palm Beach.

Miami, **Granny Feelgoods at Metrofare,** 111 NW 1st St., Miami, FL 33128. (305) 579–2104. Also: Downtown, at 190 SE 1st St., Miami, FL 33131. (305) 358–6233. **Type of Business:** Restaurant. **Sells:** Fresh natural food vegetarian dishes, including vegan and macrobiotic options. **Organic?** No organic claims made, but they are a member of NNFA. Filtered water. **Specialties:** Seafood, Mexican and Italian. **Prices:** Entrees range from $4.95 to $8.95. **Hours:** 7–6. **Reservations:** Possible. 100% non-smoking. **Credit:** V M AE (a $10 minimum). **Commendations:** *Miami Herald,* "Best Natural Foods Restaurant in Miami" for the last 5 years, and a four-star rating.

Miami, **Sprout Delights Inc.,** Steven Bern, 13090–2702, NW 7th Ave., Miami, FL 33168. (305) 687–5880, (800) 334–2253. **Type of Business:** Manufacturer. **Sells to:** Manufacturer and mail-order distributor. **Sells:** Over 90% organic. Gourmet, grocery, cakes, snacks, confections, grocery crackers, cookies, and other baked goods, including 100% organic breads. **Organic?** Afiliated with the Organic Foods Production Association of North America. **Credit:** None. **Prices:** Discounts on orders over $200. **Hours:** Sun.-Fri., 8–6. **Shipping:** No delivery to Canada. **Minimum Order:** Mail order $20, distributors 1,000 lbs. **Catalogue Available?** Yes.

Miami, **Zen Bakery,** 7384 SW 40th St., Miami, FL 33155. Also in Los Angeles and San Diego. **Type of Business:** Manufacturer and retail store. **Sells to:** Public and retailers. **Sells:** Baked goods, bread, coffee, cheese, fruits, vegetables, spices, and grains. No artificial additives or preservatives, sweetened using white grape juice. Organic fruit is used but not organic flour. **Organic?** None of their products contain additives or preservatives and they are "97% sure there are no pesticides." **Credit:** None. **Hours:** 7:30–5. **Shipping:** They will deliver anywhere within 100 miles of any of their three locations. **Minimum Order:** Varies. **Catalogue Available?** Yes.

Miami Beach, **Our Place,** 830 Washington Ave., Miami Beach, FL 33139. (305) 674–1322. **Type of Business:** Restaurant. **Sells:** Sandwiches, salads and light meals. Vegan and macrobiotic options. **Organic?** Asserted 10% organic, filtered water. **Specialties:** Vegan cuisine. **Prices:** Entrees—$4.50–$6. **Hours:** M-T 11–9, F-Sat. 11–11. **Reservations:** May be made. 100% non-smoking. **Credit:** V M (minimum $10). **Commendations:** American Lung Association, South Florida Vegetarian Association. **Comments:** A coffee house atmosphere, with live entertainment and, they claim, "love at first bite foods."

Miami Springs, **The Garden Restaurant,** Vera Astorini, 17 Westward Dr., Miami Springs, FL 33166. (305) 887–9238. **Type of Business:** Restaurant. **Sells:** Soups, salads, sandwiches, burgers, seafood, chicken and vegetarian entrees, pasta and desserts. **Organic?** Asserted 40% organic. Filtered water. **Specialities:** International vegetarian and seafood cuisine. **Prices:** Entrees range from $5.95 to $8.50. **Hours:** M-Sat. 11:30–3, 5–10. **Reservations:** Possible. 95% non-smoking. **Credit:** V M AE. The minimum for the use of credit cards is $10. **Comments and commendations:** *Miami Herald.* They are family owned and operated and have been in business for 15 years.

Naples, **Martha's Natural Food Market,** 2073 9th St. N, Naples, FL 33940. (813) 261–7838. **Type of Business:** Retail store. **Sells to:** The public. **Sells:** A full range of wholefood grocery items and fresh organic produce. **Organic?** Produce is asserted 95% organic; about 35% of grocery items are organic. **Credit:** V M. **Prices:** 10% discounts on case lots. **Hours:** M-F 9–8, Sat. 9–6, Sun. 1–5.

North Miami Beach, **Artichoke's,** Lorrie Song, 3055 NE 163rd St. (Sunny Isles Blvd.), North Miami Beach, FL 33160. (305) 945–7576. **Type of Business:** Restaurant. **Sells:** Starters, salads, vegetable entrees, seafood entrees and a large selection of chicken entrees. Vegan and macrobiotic options are usually available. **Organic?** Asserted 10% organic. Filtered water. **Specialties:** International fare, as a consequence of the multi-ethnic owners. **Prices:** Entrees range from $6.95 to $12.95. **Hours:** Sun., T-Th, 5:30–10; F-Sat., 5:30–10:30. **Reservations:** Not possible. 100% non-smoking. **Credit:** V M AE. Minimum for payment by credit card is $15. **Commendations:** *Vegetarian Times,* 1988.

North Miami Beach, **Unicorn Village Restaurant and Marketplace,** North Miami Beach, FL. (305) 933–3663. **Type of Business:** Large wholefood grocery store and natural foods restaurant. *Retail store:* **Sells to:** The public. **Sells:** A large range of fresh organic produce, natural and organic meats, and wholefood grocery items. **Organic?** The produce is asserted 33% organic (Organic Crop Improvement Association, Natural Organic Farmers Association, California Certified Organic Farmers, Farm Verified Organic, and others) about 25% of the processed goods are organic. **Credit:** V M AE. **Hours:** 8–Midnight daily. *Restaurant:* **Sells:** "Innovative cuisine," with vegetarian, vegan and macrobiotic options. **Organic?** About 10% of both the produce and processed items are organic. 100% no smoking, water is filtered. **Specialties:** Fresh fish dishes, unusual vegetarian entrees, and delicious natural desserts. **Prices:** $5.95–12.95. **Hours:** 11:30 a.m.–midnight daily. **Reservations:** Possible. **Credit:** V M. **Commendations:** American Heart Association, Restaurant Specialty Awards (5 years), Best Natural Foods Specialty Restaurant, South Florida Magazine (10 years), Recipes printed in the *Miami Herald* regularly. **Comments:** The restaurant offers live jazz and a waterfront view (boat docking possible). The natural foods deli has over 75 items for take out. Unicorn Village also has a boutique that offers books, crystals, self-help tapes, and gifts. They were one of the most widely recommended businesses in our survey for both their restaurant and store, and do a thriving business. One of the top natural foods establishments in the country.♥♦♦♦

Orange City, **Debbies Health Foods,** 816–2 Saxon Blvd., Orange City, FL 32763. (904) 775–7002. **Type of Business:** Retail store. **Sells to:** The public. **Sells:** A full range of packaged natural foods as well as beans, dried fruit, grains, nuts, soy products, and spices. **Credit:** V M. **Hours:** M-Sat. 9–9, Sun., 12–6.

Orange Park, **The Granary Whole Foods,** 1738 Kingsley Ave., Orange Park, FL 32073. (904) 269–7222. **Type of Business:** Retail store/Deli/Bakery. **Sells to:** The public. **Sells:** A full line of wholefood groceries and fresh produce. **Organic?** Produce certified by Organic Crop Improvement Association, Farm Verified Organic. **Credit:** V M. **Prices:** For bulk prices refer to Jan Rawski or Nelson Hellmuth. **Hours:** M-Sat. 9–6.

Orlando, **Florida Hospital,** 601 E Rollins St., Orlando, FL 32803. (407) 896–6611. **Type of Business:** Restaurant and retail store. **Sells:** Vegetarian foods with vegan options. **Organic?** No organic claims. Water is filtered. **Specialties:** Homemade breads, pastries, etc.; Meatless entrees; Buffets, banquets with totally vegetarian menus. **Prices:** $1.00–$2.50. **Hours:** 6:30–7p.m. **Reservations:** Possible. 100% of tables are non-smoking. **Credit:** No credit cards.

Plantation, **National Health & Nutrition,** 610 Broward Mall, Plantation, FL 33324. (305) 473–1790. **Type of Business:** Retail store (part of a chain). **Sells:** Some wholefood type items but no organic produce. See listing under Florida, West Palm Beach.

Sarasota, **The Granary Inc.,** (1st location) 1451 Main St., Sarasota, FL 34236. (813) 366–7906. (2nd location) 1930 Stickney Point Rd., Sarasota, FL 43231. (813) 924–4754. (Cafe) 1400 Main St., Sarasota, FL 34236. **Type of Business:** Retail store/Cafe. **Sells to:** The public. **Sells:** A complete range of wholefood groceries and fresh produce. **Organic?** Fresh produce 25% organic, processed goods 25%. For certification they rely on distributors' assurances, local farmers, and the Florida Organic Farmers Association. **Credit:** V M. **Prices:** 15% discount for case or full bag. **Hours:** 9–9.

Sarasota, **Wildflower,** W Patton, 5218 Ocean Blvd., Sarasota, FL 34242. (813) 349–1758. **Type of Business:** Restaurant. **Sells:** A selection of vegetarian entrees, Mexican food, macrobiotic platters, seafood, sandwiches and salads. Accommodates vegan and macrobiotic diners. **Organic?** Asserted 25–30% organic. **Specialties:** Homemade breads, desserts, soups, casseroles and fresh fish. **Prices:** Entrees range from $5.95 to $12.95. **Hours:** Breakfast (from 8 a.m.), lunch and dinner. **Reservations:** Possible. 100% non-smoking. **Credit:** V M.♦

St. Augustine, **Tree Of Life Corp.,** 27 Styertown Rd., St. Augustine, FL 32085. Mail to: PO Box 410, St. Augustine, FL 32085. (904) 824–8181. **Type of Business:** The largest distributor of natural foods in the United States.

Sells to: Retailers. **Sells:** Baked goods, condiments, dried beans, dried fruit, fresh fruit, processed grain products, herbs and spices, juices, nuts and nut butters, oils, seeds, soy products, sweeteners. **Organic?** Member of Farm Verified Organic. Tomatoes, carrots, and garlic ingredients are organically grown in accordance with California Health and Safety Code, section 26569.11. **Minimum Order:** $150. **Catalogue Available?** Only to natural-food and other retail stores.♥♦♦♦

Tampa, **Monroe Health Foods,** part of Holistic Labs Inc. 5025 E Fowler Ave., Suite 13, Tampa, FL 33617. Office: (813) 988–7788, order desk: (813) 977–1000. **Type of Business:** Manufacturer, distributor, retail store, and holistic health clinic. **Sells to:** Distributors, retailers, and the public through the store. **Sells:** Grains, cereals, breads, flours, baked goods, rice, pasta, dried beans, miso, tempeh, tofu, soy milk, soy sauce, cheeses, ice cream, kefir, yogurt, nuts and nut butters, oils, spices, dried fruits, fruit juices, fruit preserves/jams, salsa, colas, coffee, teas, meats, popcorn, carob snacks, and rice cakes. **Organic?** Assured 85% organic. All herbs are certified organic. **Credit:** V M. **Hours:** Retail store: M-Sat. 9 a.m.–6 p.m. Wholesale accounts. (UPS) M-F 9 a.m.–6 p.m. **Shipping:** UPS and US mail. **Catalogue Available?** Yes. **Comments:** They are much more than a health food store and work to promote certain theories of nutrition intended to increase healthiness and longevity.

Tampa, **The Natural Kitchen,** a.k.a. The N.K. Cafe, 4100 W Kennedy Blvd., Tampa, FL. (813) 287–1385. **Type of Business:** Restaurant. **Sells:** Vegetarian and white meat and fish dishes, including steamed and sauted vegetables, vegetarian casseroles, soups, salads, sandwiches, with grouper and chicken in the evenings. **Organic?** Asserted 10–25% organic. Filtered water. **Specialties:** Vegetable cashew saute, steamed vegetable casserole and clam chowder. **Prices:** Entrees range from $2.25 to $9.50. **Hours:** M 10:30–4, Tu-F 10:30–9. **Reservations:** Possible for large parties. 15% non-smoking. **Credit:** V M AE. **Commendations:** *Bon Appetit,* 1979; *The Tampa Tribune,* 03/18/88.

West Palm Beach, **Natural Health and Nutrition,** Ron Nolan, 224 Datura, Suite 916, West Palm Beach, FL 33401. (407) 833–8992. **Type of Business:** Retailer. Headquarters for a national chain. **Sells to:** The public. **Sells:** Baked goods, beverages, breads, cereals, flour, fruit juices, pasta, rice, oils. Their business seems to lean more toward supplements and body-building aids (some even offer clothes) than other businesses we list. But their locations in some smaller communities may make them the closest reasonable outlet of healthy processed foods for some people. **Organic?** They are affiliated with NNFA. **Credit:** V M AE. **Hours:** M-Sat. 10–9, Sun. 12–6.

Winter Park, **Chamberlin's Natural Foods,** 430 So. Orlando Ave., Winter Park, FL 32789. (407) 647–6661. **Type of Business:** Retail store and restaurant. **Sells:** A full range of wholefood grocery items, baked goods, and organic produce. The restaurant sells vegetarian and macrobiotic options. **Organic?** They assert that 100% of produce is organic and 40% of their offerings overall. **Specialties:** Salads, soups, sandwiches. **Prices:** $4–$8. **Hours:** M -F 11:30–9:00. **Reservations:** Not possible. **Credit:** V M AE ($5 minimum order). **Commendations:** *Natural Foods Merchandiser,* 1986.

Winter Park, **Power House,** Saviz Shafaie, 111 E Lyman Ave., Winter Park, FL 32789. (407) 645–3616. **Type of Business:** Restaurant. **Sells:** Natural foods with vegetarian and vegan options. **Organic?** No organic claims. **Specialties:** Smoothies, shakes, yogurt dishes, vegetarian chili, sandwiches. **Prices:** $1–$5. **Hours:** M-Sat. 10 a.m.–10:30 p.m., Sun. 11 a.m.–7:30 p.m. **Reservations:** No. All tables are non-smoking. **Credit:** No credit cards. **Comments:** Involved in peace movement, environmental groups, and community services.

GA

Georgia

Atlanta, **Ari's Discount Health Market,** 1544 Piedmont Ave., Ansley Mall, Atlanta, GA 30324. (404) 876–4373. **Type of Business:** Retail store. **Sells to:** The public. **Sells:** Baked goods, beans, bread, cereals, dairy products, flour, fruit juice, dried fruits, pasta, and rice. **Organic?** Processed goods asserted 10–20% organic. **Credit:** V M AE. **Prices:** 10% discount for cases. **Hours:** M-F 10–8, Sat. 10–7, Sun. 12–6.

Atlanta, **Cook's Kitchen,** 1395 McLendon Ave., Atlanta, GA 30307. (404) 522–8646. **Type of Business:** Restaurant. **Sells:** Vegetarian, vegan and macrobiotic dishes with a carry-out meal service available. Everything is cooked to order (allowing modifications for special dietary needs) in an open kitchen (customers can watch all aspects of food preparation). **Organic?** Asserted 25% organic. Filtered water. **Specialties:** International vegetarian dishes. **Prices:** Entrees at $4–$8. **Hours:** M-F, 11:30–9. **Reservations:** Not possible. 100% non-smoking. **Credit:** None. **Commendations:** *Atlanta* magazine 1981, 1983, 1984, 1985, 1986; *Gourmet* magazine 1986 and *Atlanta Journal* 1989.

Atlanta, **Good Earth,** 211 Phass Rd. NE, Atlanta, GA 30305. (404) 266–2919. **Type of Business:** Retail store. **Sells to:** The general public. **Sells:** Baked goods, beans, teas, breads, popcorn, chips, rice cakes, cereals (granola, oatmeal, wheat), cheeses, ice cream, yogurt, flour, fruit juices, preserves, dried fruits, nuts, oils, pasta, rice and soy products. **Organic?** Member National Nutritional Foods Association. **Credit:** V M. **Prices:** No discount for bulk purchases. **Hours:** 9–6:30.

Atlanta, **Nuts 'n Berries,** 4568 Peachtree Rd., Atlanta, GA 30909. (404) 237–6829. **Type of Business:** Deli and retail store. **Sells:** Salads, sandwiches, pies and cookies. **Organic?** 10% asserted organic. Filtered water. **Specialties:** Oat bran muffins (rated the best by the *New York Times*) and hot daily specials which are low fat, low salt and made from fresh ingredients daily. **Prices:** Entrees less than $4. **Hours:** M-F 9:30–8, Sat. 9:30–7, Sun., 11–6. **Reservations:** Possible. 100% non-smoking. **Credit:** V M. **Commendations:** They claim their menu is certified by certified nutritionalists. Acknowledged in *The Atlanta Constitution* 1988, *Health* magazine 1988 and *The New York Times* 1989.

Atlanta, **Shipfeifer on Peachtree,** Shelley Shaw, 1814 Peachtree Rd. NW, Atlanta, GA 30309. (404) 875–1106. **Type of Business:** Restaurant. **Sells:** Mediterranean and Middle Eastern cuisine, including vegetarian, vegan and macrobiotic options. **Organic?** No organic claim. **Specialties:** Middle Eastern foods, falafel, hummus, Greek salads, spanikopita, pizzas. **Prices:** Entrees—$3.29–$8.95. **Hours:** M-Th 11–12, F 11 a.m.–1 a.m., Sat. 11:30–12 a.m., Sun. 11:30–12 a.m. **Reservations:** Not possible. 50% non-smoking. **Credit:** V M AE.

Atlanta, **Soul Vegetarian Restaurant,** Yafah Israel, 515 Ashby St., Atlanta, GA 30310. (404) 752–5194. **Type of Business:** Restaurant. **Sells:** Vegetarian dishes that are 100% natural—containing no meat, dairy products, preservatives or chemical additives. **Organic?** No organic claims. Filtered water. **Specialties:** Kalebone, specialty salads and soybean ice cream. **Prices:** Lunch—$3.30–$5. **Hours:** M 11–10, Tu-Sat. 11–11, Sun. 5–11. **Reservations:** Possible. 100% non-smoking. **Credit:** AE. **Commendations:** *Vegetarian Times* 1989.

Atlanta, **Veggie Land,** Eric Sommers, 211 Pharr Road NE, Atlanta, GA 30305. (404) 231–3111. **Type of Business:** Restaurant. **Sells:** Vegetarian and vegan cuisine, with some macrobiotic options. **Organic?** They use a little organic produce. Filtered water. **Specialties:** Rice/vegetarian dishes, lasagna, noodles and soups. **Prices:** Entrees range from $3.95 to $5.95. **Hours:** 11:30–3, 5:30–8:30 daily. **Reservations:** Not possible. 100% non-smoking. **Credit:** None.

Columbus, **Country Life,** 1217 Eberhart Ave., Columbus, GA 31906. (404) 323–9194. **Type of Business:** Restaurant and retail store. **Sells:** Vegan and vegetarian food. **Organic?** No organic claims. Water is filtered. **Specialties:** All vegan entrees prepared fresh daily. **Prices:** $1.49. **Hours:** Restaurant—Sun.-Thurs, 11:30–2:30; Store—Sun.-Thurs, 10–6. **Reservations:** Not possible. 100% non-smoking. **Credit:** V M.

Roswell, **Harry's Farmers Market,** Harry Blazer, 1180 Upper Hembree Road, Roswell, GA 30076. (404) 664–

6300. **Type of Business:** Farmers market and bakery. **Sells to:** The public. **Sells:** Salad bar, hot foods bar and baked goods. The bakery produces over thirty varieties of bread, prepared traditionally. **Organic?** Some breads (5% of the total goods) certified organic by California Certified Organic Farmers, some goods are also certified by Nutriclean. **Credit:** None. **Prices:** Special prices for bulk orders. **Hours:** Tu-F 10–8, Sat. 9–8, Sun. 10–7. **Shipping:** Case and pallet discounts. **Minimum Order:** None. **Catalogue Available?** Yes.

HI

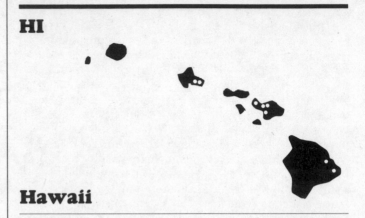

Hawaii

Hilo, **Abundant Life Natural Foods,** Leslie Miki, 90 Kamehameha Avenue, Hilo, HI 96720. (808) 935–7411. **Type of Business:** Retail store. **Sells to:** The public. **Sells:** Baked goods, fresh beans, beverages, fresh breads baked in Hawaii, candy, cereals, dairy products, flour, fresh, processed, and dried fruit, nuts and nut butters, oils, pasta, rice, fresh soy products, fresh spices, fresh vegetables, and a deli department that features fresh sandwiches and salads. **Organic?** Asserted 50% organic. **Prices:** 20% discount on anything in store if ordered by the case or bulk bag. **Hours:** M-F 8:30–6, Sat. 9:30–5, Sun. 10–3. **Comments:** They sell their own deli items and try to carry as much organic as possible.

Honolulu, **Kokua Co-op,** 2357 S Beretania, Honolulu, HI 96826. (808) 941–1922. **Type of Business:** Cooperative and retail store. **Sells to:** Members and the public. **Sells:** A wide range of fresh organic produce and wholefood grocery items. **Organic?** Overall, about 50–60% of the goods they sell are asserted organic. **Credit:** None. **Prices:** Discounts for members. **Hours:** M-Sat. 9–8, Sun. 10–7. **Comments:** They are a not-for-profit corporation and feature a gourmet deli department with self-serve vegetarian take-out dishes only.

Honolulu, **Yen King Chinese Restaurant,** 4211 Waialae Ave., Kahala Mall, Honolulu, HI 96816. (808) 732–5505. **Type of Business:** Restaurant. **Sells:** Szechuan and Peking cuisine with an extensive list of vegetarian options. **Organic?** No organic claims. **Specialties:** Eggplant dishes. **Prices:** Around $10 for a main dish with noodles or rice. **Hours:** 11–9:30 daily. **Reservations:** Possible. 70% non-smoking. **Credit:** V M AE (minimum for credit is $10).

Kihei, **Polli's on the Beach,** 101 N Kihei Rd., Kihei, Maui, HI 96816. (808) 879-5275. **Type of Business:** Restaurant. **Sells:** Mexican dishes, including vegetarian and vegan options. **Organic?** No organic claims made. Filtered water. **Prices:** $3-$12. **Hours:** Sun.-Th, 11:30-10:30; F-Sat., 11:30-12. **Reservations:** Possible. 25% nonsmoking. **Credit:** V M AE D. **Comments:** Their slogan is "We try hotter"!

Makawao, **Maui,** Polli's Mexican Cantina, 1202 Makawao Ave. at Baldwin Ave., Makawao, Maui, HI 96793. (808) 572-7808. **Type of Business:** Restaurant. **Hours:** 11:30-10:30 daily. See listing above for Kihei for more information.

Pahoa, **Hawaiian Exotic Fruit Co., Inc.** , Andy Sarhanis, Box 1729, Pahoa, HI 96778. (808) 965-7154, (808) 965-9021. **Type of Business:** Distributor, retail store and mail-order distributor. **Sells to:** Retailers and the public. **Sells:** Fresh fruit (bananas, lemons, pineapples), fresh vegetables (sweet corn and sweet potatoes), fresh whole ginger and turmeric and dried fruits (white pineapple and exotic bananas). **Organic?** Asserted 100% organic. **Credit:** None. **Prices:** Discounts only when per unit shipping costs make rates for larger packages cheaper. **Hours:** Sun., Wed 8-12 in the morning. **Shipping:** They will ship anywhere. **Minimum Order:** Varies. **Catalogue Available?** Yes.

Paia, **Mana Health Foods Inc.,** Theresa Thielk, Office Manager, PO Box 550, Paia, HI 96779. (808) 579-8137. **Type of Business:** Retail store. **Sells to:** The public and restaurants. **Sells:** A large variety of wholefood items and organic produce. **Organic?** Asserted 50% organic. **Credit:** None. **Hours:** 8-8 daily.

Wailuku, **Maui Style Wholesale Natural Foods,** Tim Anthony, 250-S Waiehu Beach Rd., Wailuku, Maui, HI 96793. (808) 242-4797. Retail store is Westside Natural Foods, 136 Dickenson St., Lahaina, HI 96761. **Type of Business:** Distributor and retail store. **Sells to:** Retailers and the general public. **Sells:** Baked goods, condiments, dairy products, dried beans, dried fruit, fresh fruit, whole grains, flour and meals, processed grain products, herbs and spices, juices, nuts and nut butters, oils, seeds, soy products, sweeteners, fresh vegetables. **Organic?** They assert that about 10% of their goods are organic (California Certified Organic Farmers). **Credit:** None. **Prices:** 10% discount for bulk orders at the retail location. **Hours:** M-Sat. 7:30-9, Sun. 9-7. **Minimum Order:** $100 at the wholesale location. **Catalogue Available?** Yes, but it must be picked up; they do not mail catalogues.

ID

Idaho

Boise, **Mrs. Beesley's,** Lorrain and Richard Kuehn, Owners, 10370 Overland, Boise, ID 83709. (208) 376-8484. **Type of Business:** Retail store. **Sells to:** The public and some buying clubs. **Sells:** A wide variety of fresh organic produce, organic meats, and grocery items, including over 200 varieties of spices and nitrate-free sausages and meats. **Organic?** They assert that 70+% of the goods they sell are organically grown and processed. **Credit:** V M D. **Prices:** Discounts for pre-ordered purchases and pre-paid purchases. **Hours:** M-F 7-9, Sat. 10-9, sun 12-5 **Catalogue Available?** Yes.

Ketchum, **The Kneadery,** 260 Leadville Ave., PO Box 2278, N Ketchum, ID 83340. (208) 726-9462. **Type of Business:** Restaurant. **Sells:** Breakfast and light lunches, all prepared from scratch with minimal use of preservatives, sugars, salt and fats. Vegetarian options are available and also a special low-calorie menu for the weight conscious. **Organic?** No organic claims, filtered water, 100% no-smoking. **Specialties:** Salads, sandwiches, and omelets. **Prices:** Breakfast, $2.95-$5.95; Lunch, $4.50-$5.95. **Hours:** 8 a.m.-2 p.m. **Reservations:** Not possible. **Credit:** V M AE DC. **Comments:** They list their staff on the first page of the menu and even have a hall of fame for retired waitresses.

IL

Illinois

Algonquin, **Strathmore Farm,** 2400 Spring Creek Road, Algonquin, IL 60102. (312) 550–5077, (312) 658–8200. **Type of Business:** Grower, processor, and distributor, since 1966. **Sells to:** Retailers. **Sells:** Dried beans (clear hilium soybeans, black soybeans, adzuki beans), whole grains (soft red and soft white winter wheat, hard red spring wheat, popcorn, field corn, oats), meat (USDA inspected Black Angus beef). **Organic?** Certified by the Organic Growers and Buyers Association. Pesticide-free farm since 1976. No drugs or antibiotics used. **Minimum Order:** Prefer to ship in bulk, will clean and bag if necessary.

Arlington Heights, **Chowpatti Vegetarian Restaurant,** 1035 S Arlington Heights Rd., Arlington Heights, IL 60005. (312) 640–9554. **Type of Business:** Restaurant. **Sells:** A large menu of international vegetarian cuisine, including American, Italian, French, Indian, Mexican and Middle Eastern served in a casual, patio-like atmosphere. Food here is low fat, low calorie, low cholesterol and low sodium. Macrobiotic options and dietary information are available. **Organic?** They say they are trying to make some of their dishes organic. Water is filtered. **Specialties:** Over fifteen combinations of freshly squeezed fruit and vegetable juices, all squeezed after they are ordered. Also, a large selection of non-alcoholic beer and wine is available. **Prices:** Entrees $4–$5. **Hours:** Sun.-Thurs., 12–9; Fri. and Sat., 12–10. **Reservations:** Possible. 100% non-smoking. **Credit:** None. **Commendations:** ". . . an oasis in the northwest suburbs."—Vegetarian Times. Rated *** in the *Guide to Natural Food Restaurants.*

Chicago, **Bread Shop,** 3400 N Halstead St., and 432 W Diversey, Chicago, IL 60657. (312) 528–8108. **Type of Business:** Retail store and delicatessen. **Sells:** Chicago's first vegetarian grocery, delicatessen and whole grain bakery. Vegan and macrobiotic foods are available. **Organic?** Asserted 10% organic. **Specialties:** Whole-wheat burritos, scones and muffins as well as Chicago's first whole grain pizza. **Prices:** $3.99–$4.99/lb. **Hours:** M-F 8–8, Sat. 9–8, Sun. 9–5. **Reservations:** Not possible as seating is limited. **Credit:** None. **Commendations:** Northalstead Merchants Association, 1987; Lakeview East Development Association, 1983 and 1985. **Comments:** The new location at 430 W Diversey is a bakery, deli, and coffee-house with a dozen chairs. They were one of the first natural foods purveyors in the Chicago area and are affiliated with "The Bread Shop Kitchen" vegetarian restaurant.

Chicago, **Food Animals Concern Trust (FACT),** Robert A. Brown, PO Box 14599, Chicago, IL 60614. (312) 525–4952. **Type of Business:** Distributor, since 1982. **Sells to:** Retailers. **Sells:** Meat and eggs—nest eggs from uncaged layers, Rambling Rose Brand free-range veal. Products raised with humane husbandry.

Chicago, **New City Market,** 1810 N Halsted St., Chicago, IL 60614. (312) 280–7600. **Type of Business:** Wholefoods market. **Sells to:** The public direct and by mail. **Sells:** A complete assortment of wholefood grocery items and fresh organic produce. Also bulk organic beans and grains. All products are free of artificial additives and processed sugars. **Organic?** Produce is asserted 99% organic

(even in winter); about 50% of grocery items are organic. **Credit:** V M AE ($20 minimum). **Prices:** 10% discounts on case orders. **Hours:** M 9–9, T-F 9–8:30, S-S 9–7. **Shipping:** UPS. **Catalogue Available?** No. **Comments:** They also have a deli section with a wide variety of macrobiotic foods. New City takes pride in its friendly, knowledgeable staff.♥♦

Chicago, **NEW Cuisine,** Ted Ingram, 360 W Erie, Chicago, IL 60610. (312) 642–8885. **Type of Business:** Restaurant. **Sells:** Natural gourmet food, including a variety of different ethnic cuisines, as well as vegetarian, vegan and macrobiotic options. **Organic?** Asserted 40% organic. The water is filtered. **Specialties:** Fish dishes and different ethnic dishes. **Prices:** Entrees $6.50–$14.75. **Hours:** Tues-Sat., 5 p.m.–10 p.m. **Reservations:** Possible. 100% non-smoking. **Credit:** AE. **Commendations:** *Men's Fitness* magazine, Aug 1989; *Bon Appétit,* Nov 1988; Restaurant Hospitality, July 1989; American Express Goldcard Newsletter, June 1989.♦

Chicago, **Star of Siam,** Eddie Duly, 11 E Illinois, Chicago, IL 60611. (312) 670–0100. (Affiliated to DAO International Inc., 105 E Ontario, Chicago, IL 60611. (312) 664–9600.) **Type of Business:** Restaurant. **Sells:** Thai cuisine. **Organic?** No organic claims. 80% no smoking. **Specialties:** Satay, spring rolls, red Thai mixed vegetables. Vegetarian dishes are available. **Prices:** $3.95–$4.75. **Hours:** S-Thurs. 11–9:30, F-Sat. 11–10:30. **Reservations:** Required. 80% No smoking. **Credit:** V M AE D DC. $10 minimum. **Commendations:** Commended by the Illinois Restaurant Association, 1988.

Chicago, **Vegetaria,** Tom Hoyer, 3182 N Clark St., Chicago, IL 60657. (312) 549–0808. **Type of Business:** Restaurant. **Sells:** Vegetarian cuisine with no egg, fish, or meat products, and pure vegan options. **Organic?** Asserted 60% organic. Filtered water. **Specialties:** Hand-made fresh food, organic bean and grain dishes, no-sugar soft drinks, no-fat, no-cholestrol soft serve desserts, hand made sugar-free desserts, and items for people allergic to wheat, corn, and milk. **Prices:** Entrees $1.75–$4.75. **Hours:** M 12–6, Tu-F 12–12, S-S 10–12. **Reservations:** Possible. 100% no-smoking (also, a Honeywell smoke eater and air cleaner). **Credit:** V M (Minimum $10). **Commendations:** Associated Press 1989.

Cicero, **The Fruitful Yield,** 6126 Cermak, Cicero, IL 60650. (708) 788–9103. **Type of Business:** Retail store (part of a chain of 7 in the Chicago area). **Hours:** M 9–1, Tu W 9–6, Th 9–9, F 9–8, Sat. 9–6, Sun. 11–7. See Downers Grove listing for more.

Downers Grove, **The Fruitful Yield,** Gary Kleinman, 2111 63rd St., Downers Grove, IL 60515. (312) 969–7614. **Type of Business:** Part of a chain of retail stores in the Chicago area. **Sells to:** The public direct and by mail order. **Sells:** A variety of wholefoods items and some frozen organic produce. **Organic?** Asserted 20% organic. **Credit:** V M. **Hours:** M-F 9:30–8:30, Sat. 9:30–5. **Shipping:** The Skokie store handles mail order. There is a $2.00 shipping fee if the purchase is under $20, and a $.25 per pound shipping charge for orders from west of the Rockies. **Minimum Order:** $5. **Catalogue Available?** Yes.

Elmhurst, **The Fruitful Yield,** 214 N York Rd., Elmhurst, IL, 60126. (708) 530–1445. **Type of Business:** Retail store (part of a chain of 7 in the Chicago area). **Hours:** M Th 9–9, Tu W F Sat. 9–6. See Downers Grove listing for more.

Evanston, **The Green Earth,** 2545 Prairie St., Evanston, IL 60201. (800) 322–3662, (312) 864–8949. **Type of Business:** Retail store and mail-order distributor. **Sells to:** The public. **Sells:** They specialize in organic food and have a wide selection of organic produce, organic grains, and meat from organically grown animals. **Organic?** Most of their goods are certified organic, agency varies. **Credit:** V M. **Hours:** 10–7 daily. **Shipping:** They ship Monday through Thursday by UPS or Federal Express (if necessary). They ship their perishable orders in re-usable styrofoam containers within card-board boxes with call tags. **Mininum Order:** None. **Catalogue Available?** Yes. **Comments:** They actively support sustainable agriculture and ecologically sound practices.♦

Glen Ellyn, **Country Life,** 503 Duane, Glen Ellyn, IL 60187. (312) 469–3368. **Type of Business:** Restaurant and retail store. **Sells:** Vegetarian, vegan and macrobiotic foods. **Organic?** Asserted 15% organic. Filtered water. **Specialties:** Falafel, lasagna, sunburgers, chili vegetarian soup, cream soups and tofu cheese cake as well as "all you can eat" specials. **Prices:** Entrees all $6.95. **Hours:** Closed Sundays. **Reservations:** Not required. 100% non-smoking. **Credit:** V M.

Glendale Heights, **The Fruitful Yield,** 2118 Bloomingdale Rd. (Willowood Shopping Center), Glendale Heights, IL 60139. (708) 894–2553. **Type of Business:** Retail store (part of a chain of 7 in the Chicago area). **Hours:** M, Th 9:30–8; Tu, W, F 9:30–6; Sat. 9–5. **Please see Skokie listing for more.**

Lansing, **Sunrise Farm Health Foods,** Lill Chapman, 17650 Torrence Avenue, Lansing, IL 60438. (312) 474–6166. **Type of Business:** Retail store. **Sells to:** The public. **Sells:** An impressive variety of both fresh produce and processed foods. **Organic?** Asserted organic; member of the National Nutritional Foods Association. **Credit:** V M D. **Prices:** 10% discount on bulk. **Hours:** M-Th 9:30–8:30, TWFS 9:30–8:30. **Minimum Order:** None. **Comments:** Established 1967.

Lombard, **The Fruitful Yield,** 727 E Roosevelt Rd., Lombard, IL 60148. (708) 629–9242. **Type of Business:** Retail store (part of a chain of 7 in the Chicago area. **Hours:** M-Th 9–9, Tu W F Sat. 9–6. **Please see Skokie listing for more.**

McHenry, **Natures Cornucopia,** Verne and Ruth Hill, 1259 N Green, McHenry, IL 60050. (815) 385–4500. **Type of Business:** Retail store. **Sells to:** The public. **Sells:** A wide selection of fresh organic produce and processed foods. **Organic?** 40% organic. **Credit:** V M. **Prices:** Discounts on supplement orders over $150. **Hours:** M-Th

8–6, F 8–7, Sat. 8–5. **Shipping:** Normally 1 week. **Minimum Order:** None. UPS charges are added. **Comments:** All the lines they sell are low in fat, and free of additives and pesticides, with possible exception of some athletic supplements. The store is one of the most complete natural and organic food and nutrition centers in the area. Over 100 items in bulk.

Naperville, **Nu-World Amaranth,** Inc. , Larry Walters, PO Box 2202, Naperville, IL 60567. (312) 369–6819, FAX: (312) 416–8316. **Type of Business:** Manufacturer. **Sells to:** Retailers and by mail order to public. **Sells:** Whole grain (amaranth), flours and meals (amaranth flour and toasted amaranth flour), processed grains (puffed amaranth, amaranth bread blends, amaranth muffin mix, amaranth pancake mix), amaranth cereals, amaranth fruit drinks and amaranth cookies. Variety of amaranth seeds for planting (ornamental and edible). **Organic?** Certified by the American Amaranth Institute. Asserted 80% organic. Affiliated with Organic Foods Production Association of North America. Many growers are Organic Crop Improvement Association certified. **Prices:** Special prices available for bulk industrial accounts; wholesale distributor prices and retail case prices for stores or individual customers. **Shipping:** Ship by UPS or truck. Normal delivery time is 2 weeks. Prepayment on first orders until credit reference established. Freight for larger orders are F.O.B. Earlville, IA. **Minimum Order:** None. **Catalogue Available?** Yes.

New Lenox, **Salt of the Earth Natural Foods,** Sue Dite and Barbara Hoyt, Owners, 1340 N Cedar Road, New Lenox, IL 60451. (815) 485–6525. **Type of Business:** Retail store and mail-order distributor. **Sells to:** The public. **Sells:** An impressive selection of organic produce, organic meats, and grocery items—"everything from soup to nuts." **Organic?** They assert that 30% of the goods they sell are organically grown and processed. Much of their produce is certified by California Certified Organic Farmers in California. **Credit:** None. **Prices:** 10% off cases and volume discounts. **Hours:** M-Th 10–6, F 10–8, Sat. 9–5. **Comments:** They work with buying clubs and co-ops who do volume buying. If you live in the area you should drop by—They have an amazing selection of goods.

Oakbrook Terrace, **Country Life,** Kevin, 17 W 717 Roosevelt, Oakbrook Terrace, IL 60181. (312) 629–2454. **Type of Business:** Restaurant and retail store. **Sells:** Vegetarian, vegan and macrobiotic foods. **Organic?** Asserted 15% organic. Filtered water. **Specialties:** Falafel, lasagna, sunburgers, chili vegetarian soup, cream soups and tofu cheese cake as well as "all you can eat" specials. **Prices:** Entrees all $6.95. **Hours:** Closed Sundays. **Reservations:** Not required. 100% non-smoking. **Credit:** V M. **Comments:** Operated by 7th Day Adventists.

Schaumburg, **The Fruitful Yield,** 1113 N Salem Drive, Schaumburg, IL 60194. (708) 679–8975. **Type of Business:** Retail store (part of a chain of 7 in the Chicago area. **Hours:** M Th 9:30–7, Tu W F 9:30–8, Sat. 9–5. See Skokie listing for more.

Skokie, **The Fruitful Yield,** 4950 Oakton, Skokie, IL 60077. (708) 788-9103. **Type of Business:** Part of a chain of retail stores in the Chicago area. **Sells to:** The public direct and by mail order. **Sells:** A variety of wholefoods items and some frozen organic produce. **Organic?** Asserted 20% organic. **Credit:** V M. **Hours:** M 10-7, Tu W F 10-6, Th 10-8, Sat. 10-5. **Shipping:** The Skokie store handles mail orders for the chain. There is a $2.00 shipping fee if the purchase is under $20, and a $.25 per pound shipping charge for orders from west of the Rockies. **Minimum Order:** $5. **Catalogue Available?** Yes.

IN

Indiana

Griffith, **Baum's Specialty Foods,** 210 W Ridge Road, Griffith, IN 46319. (219) 769-3140. (Also in Merrillville.) **Type of Business:** Retail store. **Sells to:** The public. **Sells:** Some wholefoods grocery items; a complete selection of flours, grains, and legumes, and a variety of cereals and juices. **Organic?** Asserted 30%. **Credit:** V M AE. **Prices:** 20% discounts for cases bought in bulk. **Hours:** M-F 10-8, Sat. 10-6, Sun. 12-5. **Comments:** They have three nutritionists, a body-building expert, and an expert in pre-natal care on staff to complement their book selection. The owner also does a lot of public speaking.

Indianapolis, **Georgetown Health Foods,** 3976 Georgetown Rd., Indianapolis, IN 46254. (317) 293-9525. **Type of Business:** Retail store. **Sells to:** The public. **Sells:** A full line of processed foods with a fair selection of fresh produce. **Organic?** Asserted 5% organic. **Credit:** V M AE. **Prices:** 10% discount for bulk cash orders. **Hours:** MTuTh 10-7, WF 10-8, Sat. 10-6. **Comments:** "Probably the largest retail store in Indiana."

Indianapolis, **Good Earth Natural Food Store,** 6350 N Guilford Ave., Indianapolis, IN 46220. (317) 253-3609. **Type of Business:** Retail store. **Sells to:** Public. **Sells:** Grains, cereals, flour, breads, meat, poultry, beans, pasta rice, oils, soy products, dairy products, nuts and nut butters, dried fruit, fresh fruit and vegetables, fruit juices, beverages, bagels, cookies, crackers, candy and other snacks, herbs and spices. **Organic?** Asserted 10% organic. **Credit:** V M AE . **Prices:** Discounts of 10%-25% below retail price available for bulk orders. **Hours:** M-Sat. 9-7, Sun. 12-5. **Shipping:** Mail orders are C.O.D. or charged

on credit card only; any $50 purchase gets a 5% discount if it is not charged, except for juicers, shoes, previously discounted cases, or bulk bags. **Minimum Order:** None. **Catalogue Available?** No.

Merrillville, **Baum's Specialty Foods,** 405 W 81st. Avenue, Merrillville, IN 46410. (219) 769-3140. (Also in Griffith.) **Type of Business:** Retail store. **Sells to:** The public. **Sells:** Some wholefoods grocery items; a complete selection of flours, grains, and legumes, and a variety of cereals and juices. **Organic?** Asserted 30%. **Credit:** V M AE. **Prices:** 20% discounts for cases bought in bulk. **Hours:** M-F 10-8, Sat. 10-6. **Comments:** They have three nutritionists, a body-building expert, and an expert in pre-natal care on staff to complement their book selection. The owner also does a lot of public speaking.

Mishawaka, **Garden Patch Market,** Jay Frederickson, 228 W Edison, Mishawaka, IN 46545. (219) 255-3151. **Type of Business:** Retail store. **Sells to:** The public. **Sells:** A full range of grocery goods and some organic products, including organic meats and Amish chicken. **Organic?** 10% organic. **Prices:** 10% discount off full cases. **Hours:** 10-7, M-F.

West Lafayette, **Goodness! Grocery,** Sheila G. Phillips, General Manager, 307 Sagamore Parkway West, West Lafayette, IN 47906. (317) 463-FOOD. **Type of Business:** Retail store and co-op. **Sells to:** The public. **Sells:** Baked goods, beverages, cereals, 250 herbs, spices, and teas. In season, fresh vegetables and fruit. **Organic?** 20% organic. **Credit:** None. **Hours:** Daily 9-9. **Prices:** 10% off on whole cases or bags. **Minimum Order:** None. **Catalogue Available?** No. **Comments:** They just moved into a newly remodeled store; a beautifully clean 4800 sq. ft. space (including back room and offices) with both a bakery and carry out deli.

IA

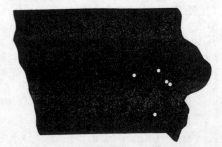

Iowa

Cedar Rapids, **New Pioneer Fresh Food Market,** John Higgins, 5070 Lindale Dr. NE, Cedar Rapids, IA 52240. (319) 338-9441. **Type of Business:** Retail store. **Sells to:** The public. **Sells:** A full line of natural, conventional, and gourmet groceries. **Organic?** Asserted 15% organic. They are affiliated with Iowa Organic Growers and Buyers Association. **Prices:** 5% bulk discount. **Hours:** 9-9 daily.

Comments: They offer lots of written information to shoppers.

Fairfield, **A Taste of India,** 410 W Lowe St., Fairfield, IA 52556. (515) 472–6530. **Type of Business:** Restaurant. **Sells:** Vegetarian Indian cuisine, as well as Mexican dishes, soups, and salads. Vegan options are available. **Organic?** Asserted 40% organic. The water is filtered. **Specialties:** Brunch on Sundays, with pancakes, scrambled tofu, lasagna, and fruit salads as examples of the variety available. **Prices:** $5 for a buffet meal. **Hours:** M-Sat. 11:30–3, 6:30–9; Sun. 10–3, 6:30–9. **Reservations:** Possible. 100% non-smoking. **Credit:** None.

Iowa City, **The Kitchen,** 9 S Dubuque, Iowa City, IA 52240. (319) 337–5444. **Type of Business:** Restaurant. **Sells:** Chicken, fish and seafood dishes, as well as vegetarian, vegan and macrobiotic options, are prepared in an open kitchen where diners can watch their own meal being prepared. **Organic?** Asserted 50% organic. **Specialties:** "Create your own" fresh pasta entrees. **Prices:** Entrees from $2.60 to $14, half orders are available. **Hours:** M-Sat. 11–2:30 and 5–9:30. **Reservations:** Not possible. 100% non-smoking. **Credit:** None. **Commendations:** Given a four spoons rating (the highest) by WMT-TV in 1988.

Iowa City, **New Pioneer Fresh Food Market,** John Higgins, 22 S Van Buren St., Iowa City, IA 52240. (319) 338–9441. **Type of Business:** Retail store. See entry for Cedar Rapids.

Laurel, **Paul's Grains,** Wayne, 2475–B 340 St., Laurel, IA 50141. (515) 476–3373. **Type of Business:** Manufacturer, retail store and mail-order distributor. **Sells to:** Distributors and the public. **Sells:** Whole grains and grain products, apples, various beans and nuts, beef, lamb, chicken and turkey. **Organic?** Asserted 99% organic, "self-certified." **Credit:** None. **Prices:** Discount prices with bulk orders. **Hours:** Daylight hours. **Shipping:** Send check with order plus $1.50 packaging and delivery to the post office, $2.50 packaging and delivery to UPS. **Minimum Order:** None. **Catalogue Available?** Yes. **Comments:** They claim they have been farming organically for 26 years.

KS

Kansas

Bunker Hill, **Cross Seed Co. Inc.,** HC 69, Box 2, Bunker Hill, KS 67626. (913) 483–6163. **Type of Business:** Manufacturer, retail store and mail-order distributor. **Sells to:** Retailers and the public. **Sells:** Grains (barley, buckwheat, popcorn, millet, oats and wheat), flour, and beans (adzuki, chick peas, lentils, pinto and soy). **Organic?** Certified 100% organic by Kansas Organic Producers and awaiting Organic Crop Improvement Association approval. **Credit:** None. **Hours:** M-F 8-5, Sat. 8-2. **Shipping:** Usually UPS. **Minimum Order:** None. **Catalogue Available?** Yes.

Hutchinson, **Helmuth Country Bakery,** 6706 W Mills Road, Hutchinson, KS 67501. (316) 567–2301. **Type of Business:** Grower and manufacturer of flour-based products. **Sells to:** Restaurants, about 45 retail stores, over 30 supermarkets and the public; limited supply. **Sells:** Amaranth and wheat products: flour and bread mixes in 5 and 50lb. bags; pure amaranth flour; puffed amaranth; buns; egg noodles; and snack crackers. **Organic?** All grains asserted organic, all other products asserted natural. **Comments and References:** Cost is somewhat less than double baked goods made with ordinary wheat flour. Samples were provided at the 1989 Anaheim Natural Foods Expo. Helmuth Country Bakery specializes in Amish and Mennonite farm bakery, and may be the only significant U.S. source of baked goods using amaranth flour. See *Baking* Magazine, May 1988, pp. 52–53.

Lawrence, **Pines International,** Ron Seibold, PO Box 1107, Lawrence, KS 66044. (913) 841–6016, (800) 642–7463. **Type of Business:** Processor. **Sells to:** The public. **Sells:** Wheat grass, barley grass, and beet juice powder. **Organic?** Asserted organic, Organic Crop Improvement Association. **Credit:** V M. **Hours:** 9–5. **Minimum Order:** Yes, only for bulk. **Catalogue Available?** Yes. **Comment:** All products are fat-free and pesticide-free.♦

Luray, **Cheyenne Gap Amaranth,** Arris Sigle, H.C. 1, Box 2, Luray, KS 67649–9743. (913) 698–2457 early until 8 a.m. Central Time, (913) 698–2292 all day. **Type of Business:** Farmer, processor, and distributor, since 1978. **Sells to:** Retailers, mail order, pick up orders. **Sells:** Amaranth grain, flour, planting seeds. Also non-organic oats and sheep. **Organic?** Asserted organic. **Credit:** None. **Prices:** Amaranth is generally a bit expensive because of low crop yields. If you buy 5 lbs. or more of grain, it sells for $1.50/lb. Flour is $2.50/lb. for orders over 10 lbs. and $2.00/lb. for orders over 25 lbs. **Hours:** (see above). **Shipping:** World-wide by 4th class mail. Shipments usually made within one week of receiving order. **Minimum Order:** 1lb. for flour, grain, and seeds. **Catalogue Available?** Yes, for $2. **Comments:** He is a one-man operation and generally grinds the flour freshly as orders come in. He has worked in conjunction with the Rodale Research Center on growing Amaranth.

Prairie Village, **Manna Nutrition Store,** Mark Isbell, Owner and Purchasing Manager, 5309 W 94th Terrace, Prairie Village, KS 66207. (913) 381–6604. **Type of Business:** Restaurant and retail store. **Sells:** Groceries, fresh carrot juice, supplements and sandwiches. **Organic?** Asserted 50–80%; member of National Nutritional Foods Association. Filtered water. **Specialties:** Specialty sandwiches and vegetarian options. **Prices:** Sandwiches and salads ranging from $2.70–$3.50. **Hours:** M-F 9:30–6, Sat. 10–5. **Reservations:** Not possible. 100% non-smoking. **Credit:** V M AE D. **Commendations:** *Squire* Magazine's "Best Health Food Store" 1984 and 1985.

KY

Kentucky

Lexington, **Alfalfa,** 557 S Limestone, Lexington, KY 40508. (606) 253–0014. **Type of Business:** Restaurant. **Sells:** A predominantly vegetarian restaurant, serving some fish and poultry dishes and usually at least one vegan option. **Organic?** Asserted 20% organic. Organic flour is used in the baking of bread and whole wheat desserts. **Specialties:** Red beans on rice, bean burritos, lasagna, salads. **Prices:** Entrees—Lunch $3.50–$4.50, Dinner $5.25–$11. **Hours:** Lunch M-F 11–2; Brunch S-S 10–2; Dinner Tues-Thurs 5:30–9, F-Sat. 5:30–10. **Reservations:** Not possible. 40% non-smoking. **Credit:** None. **Commendations:** *Lexington Herald Leader* Oct 28, 1988.♦

Lexington, **Everybody's Natural Foods,** Hetty Carriero, 503 Euclid Ave., Lexington, KY 40502. (606) 255–4162. **Type of Business:** Restaurant and retail store. **Sells:** Vegetarian and non-dairy meals. **Organic?** They assert that 20–70% of their food is organically grown and processed. All tables are non-smoking. **Credit:** V M. **Prices:** Entrees are $4.00 and up. **Hours:** M-F 8–8, Sat. 10–6, Sun. 12–5. **Reservations:** No.

LA

Louisiana

New Orleans, **The Apple Seed Shoppe,** 346 Camp St., New Orleans, LA 70130. (504) 529–3442 **Type of Business:** Restaurant. **Sells:** A natural foods restaurant serving soups, salads, sandwiches, smoothies and natural fruit juices. Delivery is possible with orders over $10. **Organic?** No organic claims. **Specialties:** Crabmeat dishes and apple-yogurt delight. **Prices:** Entrees $3–$7. **Hours:** M-F 10:30–3. **Reservations:** Possible. 100% non-smoking. **Credit:** None.

New Orleans, **Whole Foods Market,** 3135 Esplanade Ave., New Orleans, LA 70119. (504) 943–1626. (Also in Austin, Dallas, Houston, and Richardson, TX, and Berkeley and Palo Alto, CA). **Type of Business:** Wholefood supermarket; Part of a chain of eight wholefood supermarkets in Texas, Louisiana, and California. **Sells to:** The public. **Sells:** A huge variety of wholefood grocery items and organic produce. They claim to have "the most significantly integrated mix of conventional 'clean' food and 'natural' foods" in the country. **Organic?** They are a part of the program run by the Texas Department of Agriculture. **Credit:** V M AE. **Prices:** 5% discount for unopened retail cases. **Hours:** 9–11, 7 days a week. **Commendations and Comments:** Whole Foods Markets are known for their informative and relaxing atmosphere and the Whole Foods employees tend to be quite knowledgeable. Lectures and tours are offered to encourage better shopping. They claim (as does Real Foods in San Francisco) to be the largest retailer of organically grown produce in the U.S. Whole Foods got the fourth most recommendations in our survey.♥♦♦♦

Shreveport, **Ethereal Living Foods,** John, Peter or Katie Koellen, 3309 Line Ave., Shreveport, LA 71104. (318) 865–8947. **Type of Business:** Restaurant. **Sells:** Vegetarian food (except for the chicken and tuna salad) with a macrobiotic special on Wednesdays. **Organic?** The grains, tofu and sprouts used are organic. **Specialties:** Daily vegetarian specials such as eggplant spinach lasagna, vegetarian quiche, roulades, crepes and enchiladas. **Prices:** Entrees range from $2.49 to $5.99. **Hours:** M-F 9:30–4, Sat. 10:30–3. **Reservations:** Not possible. 100% non-smoking. **Credit:** V M. **Commendations:** *Louisiana Life,* 1989.

ME

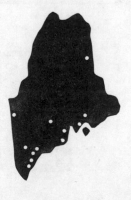

Maine

Albion, **Johnny's Selected Seeds,** Barbara Kennedy, 310 Foss Hill Road, Albion, ME 04910. (207) 437-9294. Type of Business: Mail-order distributor. Sells to: Retailers and the public. Sells: Vegetable, herb, and farm seeds. Organic? Certification varies. Credit: V M AE. Prices: 5% discount on orders over $100. Hours: 7-4:30. Minimum Order: None. Catalogue Available? Yes.

Belfast, **Fiddler's Green Farm,** Nancy Galland and Richard Stander, Owners, RR 1, Box 656, Belfast, ME 04915. (207) 338-3568. Type of Business: Processor (milling, mixing and packing). Sells to: Retailers, distributors, buying clubs and the public (mail orders). Sells: Organic baking mixes and hot cereals: pancake and muffin mix, with toasted buckwheat and buttermilk, Irish Soda Bread mix, Buttermilk Spice Cake mix, Penobscot Porridge (four grain hot cereal) and Toasted Brown Rice Cream with oat bran. Organic? Certified by Maine Organic Farmers and Gardeners Association. All ingredients certified by Organic Crop Improvement Association, Farm Verified Organic, or Natural Organic Farmers Association. Credit: V M. Hours: Phone orders, 7 days a week, 9-5. Shipping: Only to continental U.S. Allow 2 weeks for mail order to the West Coast, less for closer addresses. Minimum Order: None for mail order, 2 cases for wholesale. Catalogue Available? Yes. Commendations: *The New York Times,* January 27, 1988.

Blue Hill, **Hay's Farm Stand,** Dennis King and Jean Hay, PO Box 92, Blue Hill, ME 04614. (207) 374-2822. Type of Business: Grower. Sells to: Public from own store, restaurants, and retailers. Sells: Beets, broccoli, cabbage, carrots, cauliflower, celery, corn, cucumbers, eggplant, lettuce, onions, peas, peppers, potatoes, radishes, spinach, squash, tomatoes, turnips, zucchini, chard, kale, mustard greens, bok choi, yellow/purple/romano beans, melons, raspberries, strawberries, basil, dill, parsley, cheese, coffees, lamb and poultry. Organic? 100% organic, certified by Maine Organic Farmers and Gardeners Association. Credit: V M. Hours: July through October: M-Sat. 10-4, closed Sundays. Shipping: They only sell locally.

Bridgewater, **Wood Prairie Farm,** Jim and Megan Gerritsen, RFD 1, Box 164, Bridgewater, ME 04735. (207) 429-9765. Type of Business: Grower. Sells to: Processors, distributors, retailers, and the public (by mail order and through a stall at Houlton Farmers Market, Fridays, August-October). Sells: Green beans, strawberries, oats, wheat, lamb, beets, cabbage, carrots, garlic, onions, potatoes, squash, tomatoes and turnips. They specialize in season-long subscription vegetable farming for local consumers; plus direct to consumers mail order sales of Yukon Gold potatoes and other winter vegetables. Organic? Asserted 100% organic, certified by Organic Crop Improvement Association and Maine Organic Farmers and Growers Association. Credit: V M. Hours: 7-9 for phone orders. Shipping: Goods are delivered by UPS. Canada, Alaska and Hawaii are not normally served. Minimum Order: None. Catalogue Available? Yes.

Cape Elizabeth, **Ram Island Farm Herbs Inc.,** Ann Deleharty, Ric Marshall (President), Ram Island Farm, Cape Elizabeth, ME 04107. (207) 767-5700. Type of Business: Grower and manufacturer. Sells to: Direct to retailers, and mail order to other consumers. Sells: Bulk teas, herbs, condiments, spices, and salt substitutes. Organic? Asserted 40% organic certified by Maine Organic Farmers and Gardeners Association. Credit: V M. Prices: No special prices for bulk orders. Hours: Appointment only. Shipping: Within 48 hours of receipt of order. Minimum Order: Even cases. Catalogue Available? Yes.

Franklin, **Maine Coast Sea Vegetables,** Shep Erhart or Carl Karush, Shore Rd., Franklin, ME 04634. (207) 565-2907. Type of Business: Grower and manufacturer. Sells: Sea vegetables (alaria, kelp, dulse, nori), sea chips, sea seasonings and condiments; all macrobiotic products. (Sea vegetables supply a balanced source of 57 minerals as trace elements essential to bodily functioning. They also are a great source of protein, natural fiber and vitamins.) Organic? No organic claims. Prices: Special bulk prices for sea vegetables over 50 lbs. Shipping: 2 week delivery time. Minimum Order: $25. Catalogue Available? Yes.

Freeport, **The Corsican,** 9 Mechanic St., Freeport, ME 04032. (207) 865-9421. Type of Business: Restaurant. Sells: Salads served with home-baked bread, a selection of homemade pizzas on unbleached white or wheat crusts, calzones and sandwiches. Vegetarian options are available. Organic? No organic claims. Specialties: Pizza-pesto and tomato pizza, sandwiches on fresh-baked bread, homemade soups, and seafood. Prices: Entrees—$3.50-$12.95. Hours: 11-9. Reservations: Not possible. Credit: None.

Freeport, **USM Wolfe's Neck Farm,** RR 1, Box 71, Burnett Road, Freeport, ME 04032. (207) 865-4469, outside Maine, (800) 346-9540. Type of Business: Producer. Sells to: Predominantly to the public. Sells: Frozen organic beef, since 1959, and frozen organic lamb. Organic? Certified organic by Maine Organic Farmers and Gardeners Association. Credit: None. Hours: Orders should be phoned in advance (8-5) and can be picked up Monday through Saturday noon. Shipping: Truck deliveries are made to southern New Hampshire, Rhode Island, and Connecticut when orders justify; generally once a month. Charges are $5 each for 42lb. cartons (for 5 or more) and $4 each for 20lb. cartons (for 10 or more). Delivery on smaller orders is slightly more expensive. Air shipments are also possible, with the price based on weight. Minimum Order: None. Catalogue Available? Yes.

Otisfield, **Morin's Rosewood Farm Unlimited,** Marianne Izzo-Morin and Donald Morin, 5770 Scribner Hill Road, Otisfield, ME 04270. (207) 539-4273. Type of Business: Grower. Sells to: Retailers and the public (via a farm shop or "pick-your-own"). Sells: Apples, apple leathers, blueberries, cider, apple wine and champagne, spices and fresh vegetables. They produce lamb which is 75% organic and are seeking organic grain distributors in the state to make it 100% organic. Organic? Asserted 100% organic. They go by MOFGA standards but are not certified by them because of the cost. The only fertilizer used is derived from the sheep raised on the farm or from plant material. Credit: None. Hours: 9-5 daily throughout the summer until mid-November. **Minimum Order:** None for public, one bushel for retailers. **Catalogue Available?** Yes.

Portland, **The Whole Grocer,** 118 Congress St., Portland, ME 04101. (207) 774-7711. Type of Business: Retail store. Sells to: Public. Sells: Vegetables, fruits, dried fruits, grains, beans, nuts and nut butters, soy products, spices, rice, pasta, oils, breads, cereals, flours, meats, dairy products, beverages, and candies. **Organic?** 10–20% of products are certified organic (Maine Organic Farmers and Gardeners Association, Organic Crop Improvement Association, Organic Foods Production Association of North America). **Credit:** No credit cards. **Prices:** Special prices for bulk orders in advance, 10% discount. **Hours:** M-F 10–8, Sat. and Sun. 10–7. **Minimum Order:** None.♦

Rockland, **Good Tarn Co-op,** Sheryl Cooper, 216 S Main St., Rockland, ME 04841. (207) 594-9286. Type of Business: Retail store and co-op. Sells to: Members and the public. Sells: Cereals, grains, flour, beans, nuts and nut butters, oils, rice, pasta, dairy products, soy products, dried fruit, salsa, fresh fruit and vegetables when in season, spices, breads, candy, crackers, cookies and beverages. **Organic?** Asserted 80–90% organic, associated with MOFGA. **Credit:** None. **Prices:** Special prices for bulk orders; 25% discount for members, 15% discount for non-members. **Hours:** M-F 9:30–6, Sat. 9:30–5. (9:30–4 in winter).♦♦

Upton, **Heritage Farm,** Box 345, Upton, ME 04261. (207) 533-2820. Type of Business: Grower. Sells to: The public through a stand. Sells: Fresh fruit and vegetables in season; beans (adzuki, kidney, pinto, sulfer, turtle, soldier, Jacobs cattle and Red Mexican beans); melons, plums, raspberries, strawberries, blackberries, loganberries and elderberries; asparagus, beets, broccoli, cabbage, carrots, cauliflower, celery, corn, cucumbers, lettuce, peas, peppers, potatoes, spinach, snow peas, squash, pumpkin, tomatoes, turnips, zucchini, and amaranth. **Organic?** Asserted 100% organic (uses no sprays or synthetic fertilizers).

MD

Maryland

Baltimore, **Golden Temple Natural Foods,** 2322 N Charles St., Baltimore, MD 21218. (301) 235-1014. Type of Business: Retail store and Cafe. Sells to: The public. Sells: A complete range of natural groceries and fresh pro-

duce. **Organic?** 25% of fresh produce is organic (certified by Farm Verified Organic). They estimate that about 5% grocery items are organic. **Credit:** V M. **Prices:** 10–20% discounts on bulk or full cases. **Hours:** M-F 9:30–7, Sat. 9:30–6, Sun. 11–5. **Comments:** The store also features a yoga and massage center.

Baltimore, **Good Things Cafe,** 11 W Preston St., Baltimore, MD 21201. (301) 685-7110. Type of Business: Restaurant. Sells: International wholefoods cuisine with vegetarian, vegan, and macrobiotic options. **Organic?** Asserted 50% organic. **Prices:** Dinner: $8.95–11.95. **Hours:** Lunch and dinner. **Reservations:** Possible. **Credit:** V M AE. **Comments:** The restaurant opened in February, 1990.

Beltsville, **Organic Farms, Inc.,** Brad Eishold, Joseph Dunsmoore, owner, 10714 Hanna, Beltsville, MD 20705. (301) 595-5151. Type of Business: Distributor. Sells to: Retailers. Sells: Baked goods, coffee, condiments, dairy products and eggs, dried beans, dried fruit, fresh fruit, whole grains, flour and meals, processed grain products, fresh herbs and spices, juices, nuts and nut butters, oils, seeds, soy products, sweeteners, fresh vegetables, frozen fruit and vegetables, wine and beer. **Organic?** Certified organic. They test their food at every step. OFI is discussing providing organic food to supermarket chains, including A&P, ShopRite, Grand Union, and Pathmark.♦♦♦

Beltsville, **Organic Foods Express,** Scott Nash, 11003 Emack Road, Beltsville, MD 20705. (301) 937-8608. Type of Business: Mail-order distributor, retail store, and delivery service. Sells to: The public. Sells: Cereals, grains, flour, beans, nuts and nut butters, pasta, rice, oils, fruit juices, preserves, canned vegetables, fresh fruit and vegetables, dried fruit, dairy products, soy products, cookies, muffins, breads, candy, chips, fresh herbs and beverages. **Organic?** Asserted 80% organic. **Credit:** V M. **Prices:** Special prices available for bulk orders. **Hours:** Orders generally taken on Wednesdays between 9 and 6:30 or Fridays between 11 and 4, though special arrangements can be made. **Shipping:** UPS delivery during the week anywhere UPS goes or home delivery on weekends within the Washington D.C. vicinity. **Minimum Order:** None. **Catalogue Available?** Yes.

Cabin John, **Bethesda Community Food Store/Bethesda Co-op,** Kim Coletta, 7945 Mac Arthur Blvd. No. 102, Cabin John, MD 20818. (301) 320-2530. Type of Business: Retailer and cooperative. Sells to: Members and the general public. Sells: A wide selection of baked goods, beans, beverages, confections, cereals, dairy products, flour, fruit, meats, nuts, nut butters, oils, pasta, rice, soy products, vegetables, salsa, spices and grains. **Organic?** Asserted 50% organic. They rely on the certification claims of their suppliers. **Credit:** None. **Prices:** Discounts for volunteer members. **Hours:** M-Sat. 9–8, Sun. 11–6.

Catonsville, **Bamboo Inn,** 1111 N Rolling Rd., Catonsville, MD 21228. (301) 788-4777. Type of Business: Restaurant. Sells: Cantonese and Szechuan foods. **Organic?** No organic claims. **Specialties:** Vegetarian dishes are available. Prices: $5–$10. Hours: 11–11. Reservations: Not required but are accepted. 30% No smoking. Credit: V M.

Eldersburg, **A Touch of Nature,** 6482 Ridge Rd., Eldersburg, MD 21784. (301) 795–8986. Type of Business: Retail store. Sells to: The public. Sells: A range of packaged wholefoods. Organic? Processed goods, 70% organic (Organic Crop Improvement Association). Credit: V M. Prices: 10% discount on all case orders or 10 lbs. of bulk items. Hours: M-Sat. 10–9, Sun. 12–5.

Forestville, **LD Greengrocer,** 3430 Donnell Dr., Forestville, MD 20747. (301) 735–2310. Type of Business: Retail store. Sells to: The public. Sells: A full line of wholefoods and non-organic fresh produce. Organic? Asserted 15% organic for processed foods. Credit: V M. Prices: 10% discount for cases. Hours: M-Sat. 6–9, Sun. 6–8. Comments: 4,000 sq. ft.—largest store in area.

Frederick, **Common Market Coop,** 11 Commerce St., Box 3415, Frederick, MD 21701. (301) 663–3416. Type of Business: Retail store, co-op. Sells to: The public, co-op members. Sells: A complete range of wholefood grocery items and fresh organic produce. Organic? Fresh produce 100% organic (certified by Organic Crop Improvement Association, Farm Verified Organic, Natural Organic Farmers Association), 40% of other goods asserted organic. Credit: None. Prices: Members entitled to a reduced mark-up of 20–25%. Hours: M-W 10–6, Th 10–8, F-Sat. 10–6, Sun. 12–3. Comments: The co-op strives to offer wholefoods at the lowest prices. (They also stock "cruelty-free" body care products and cosmetics).

Frederick, **It's only Natural,** 43 E Patrick St., Frederick, MD 21701. (301) 662–7277. Type of Business: Retail store and mail-order distributor. Sells to: The public. Sells: A range of wholefood grocery items and selected fresh produce. Credit: V M. Prices: 10% off on case lots. Hours: M-F 10–6, Sat. 10–5. Shipping: UPS. No COD's. Shipping charge.

Hunt Valley, **Parsley Patch (subsidiary of McCormick & Co.,** Inc.), Bill Pappas, 211 Schilling Circle, PO Box 208, Hunt Valley, MD 21031. (301) 527–6007. Type of Business: Processor and distributor. Sells to: Retail stores and the public. Sells: Salt-free spice and herb blends and seasonings: garlic, lemon pepper, Oriental, Italian, Mexican, popcorn, dill, cinnamon and seafood. Organic? No organic claims. Credit: Personal checks or money orders only. Prices: No special prices for bulk orders. Shipping: Delivers to 48 states only. Minimum Order: 1 bottle for a consumer, 1 case for a business. Freight will be added if order is less than $200. Catalogue Available? Yes.

Silver Springs, **Takoma Park-Silver Spring Co-op,** Sue DeLettera, 623 Sligo Ave., Silver Spring, MD 20910. Type of Business: Retail store, co-op. Sells to: The public. Sells: Various processed foods and fresh produce. Organic? Affiliated with Organic Foods Production Association of North America, 20–30% of products organically grown. Credit: None. Hours: T-Sat. 10–8, Sun. 10–6, Closed Monday. Comment: Community food store.

Smallest mark-up possible. Caters to the community as much as possible.♦

Timonium, **Mathias Foods,** Inc. , 2139 York Rd., Timonium, MD 21093. (301) 252–2060. Type of Business: Retail store. Sells to: The public. Sells: A wide range of wholefood grocery items and fresh organic produce. Organic? Fresh produce 100% organic (certified by Organic Crop Improvement Association, Farm Verified Organic, Demeter/Bio-dynamic), other goods, 30–40%. Credit: V M. Prices: 15% discount oncase or bulk purchases. Hours: M-F 10–7, Sat. 10–6, Sun. 12–5.

Westminster, **Harvestin' Natural Foods,** 12 Locust Lane, Westminster, MD 21157. (301) 876–3585. Type of Business: Restaurant. Sells: Natural foods. Organic? Asserted 50% organic. Specialties: Vegan and macrobiotic dishes are available. Prices: Sandwiches are around $2.50. Hours: M-F 10–6, Sat. 10–5. Reservations: Not possible. Credit: None.

MA

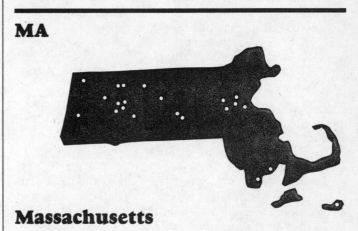

Massachusetts

Amherst, **Maplewood Organic Farm,** David Holm, 132 Belchertown, Amherst, MA 01002. (213) 256–8384 (Store) (413) 256–0926. Type of Business: Grower, delicatessen, and retailer (through the farm shop and a Saturday morning market, Northampton, MA, May-Oct). Sells to: The general public. Sells: Green beans, peanuts, coffees, teas, dairy products, fruit (dried and fresh), poultry, nuts, soy products, basil, dill, ginger, parsley, fresh vegetables (most of which are grown on the farm), baked goods, granola, oatmeal, oils, pasta and organically grown bedding plants. Organic? Certified organic by Natural Organic Farmers Association (NOFA). Credit: V M. Hours: M-F 7–8, Sat. 8–7, Sun. 9–6.

Amherst, **Snyder's Farm,** Dana Snyder, 870 Bay Rd. Amherst, MA 01002. (413) 253–3230. Type of Business: Growers/manufacturers. Sells to: Retailers, others. Sells: Soy, grains, and legume hay. Organic? Certified by Natural Organic Farmers Association. Credit: None. Shipping: Deliver only within 50 mile radius of Amherst.

Barre, **Many Hands Organic Farm,** Julie Rawson and Jack Kittredge, RFD #2, Sheldon Rd., Barre, MA 01005. (508) 355–2853. Type of Business: Grower. Sells to: Retailers, farmers' market and to public on own stand. Sells:

Braided garlic and flowers. On a local scale, sells poultry, turkey, pork, fresh produce (beets, broccoli, cabbage, cauliflower, celery, corn, cucumbers, lettuce, onions, peas, potatoes, radishes, spinach, squash, tomatoes, zucchini, leeks, brussel sprouts, kale and chard), raspberries, strawberries, basil, parsley, bagels, cookies and wholewheat bread. **Organic?** Natural Organic Farmers Association (NOFA) certified 30% organic. **Hours:** 8–8. **Shipping:** They are a small business and make their own deliveries. **Catalogue Available?** Yes. **Comments:** The owners are officers in NOFA and planned the 1989 NOFA Summer Conference in Williamstown, Mass.♥

Belchertown, **White Oak Market Garden,** Alex Stone and Lance Minor, Box 937, Belchertown, MA 01007. (413) 323-7130. **Type of Business:** Grower. **Sells to:** Retailers, restaurants and to the public via local markets in Newton (Tuesdays, July-Oct), Brookline (Thursdays, June-Oct) and Northampton (Saturday, May-Oct). **Sells:** Vegetables, salad greens, garlic, spices and flowers. **Organic?** Certified 100% organic by Natural Organic Farmers Association. **Credit:** No credit cards are accepted but credit is possible. **Prices:** Variable. **Hours:** 24 hour answering machine for telephone orders. **Shipping:** Possible. **Minimum Order:** $40 for retailers and restaurants. **Catalogue Available?** No.

Boston, **Milk Street Cafe,** Marc Epstein (owner), Stephanie Joliet (chef), 50 Milk St., Boston, MA 02109. (617) 542-3663. **Type of Business:** Restaurant and catering company. **Sells:** Salads, pasta, pizza, quiches, crepes, sandwiches, desserts and beverages. **Organic?** Asserted 10% organic. Water is filtered. **Specialties:** Soups, Middle Eastern salads, seafood and Italian entrees. Vegetarian, vegan, and macrobiotic dishes are available. **Prices:** $4.95–$6. **Hours:** M-F 7-3. **Reservations:** Not accepted. 75% No smoking. **Credit:** None. **Commendations:** "Best of Boston" awards, 1982–1987.

Boston, **Souper Salad, Inc.,** Larry Reinstein, 80 Ashford St., Boston, MA 02134. (617) 254-7687. **Type of Business:** Restaurant. **Sells:** Homemade soups and salads. **Organic?** No organic claims. Water is not filtered. **Specialties:** Vegetarian dishes are available. **Prices:** $4.95–$7.95. **Hours:** 11-11 (although stores will vary). **Reservations:** Not accepted. 50% No smoking. **Credit:** V M AE, $10 minimum. **Commendations:** Commended by the *Boston Globe.*

Brookline, **Bread & Circus,** 392 Harvard St., Brookline, MA 02146-2983. (617) 738-8187. Also in Cambridge (115 Prospect St.), Hadley (Mountain Farms Mall), Newton (45 Kenneth St. and 916 Walnut St.), Wellesley (278 Washington St.) and Providence, RI. **Type of Business:** Wholefood supermarket chain and wholesaler. Part of a chain of seven supermarkets. They also sell wholesale to other supermarket chains. **Volume:** About $50 million retail, $30 million wholesale. They saw a 30–50 percent increase in organic products in the February-March 1989 period. **Sells to:** The public through 6 stores in the Boston area. **Sells:** "You'll find just about everything you expect in a major supermarket—all made with wholesome ingredients, without chemical additives." They sell organic fruits and vegetables in season and natural (i.e. hormone free) meat. None of their products have artificial colors, artificial flavors, or artificial preservatives. Their products are also void of processed sugars, nitrates, nitrites, and MSG. **Hours:** M-Sat. 9-9, Sun. 12-8 **Comments and Commendations:** Bread & Circus is one of the foremost purveyors of healthy food in the country. In our surveys they were among the leaders in peer recommendations. The commendations Bread & Circus receives from newspapers, magazines, and patrons we've encountered are universally glowing. If you live near Boston or Providence or are visiting either area you should definitely drop in on one of their stores.♥♦♦♦

Brookline, **Open Sesame,** Rob Chihara, 48 Boylston St., Brookline, MA 02146. (617) 277-9241. **Type of Business:** Restaurant. **Sells:** Specializes in non-dairy and no-meat dishes and in macrobiotic foods. **Organic?** Some organic produce. Water is filtered. **Specialties:** Vegetarian, vegan, and macrobiotic dishes available. **Prices:** $6–$13. **Hours:** M-Sat. Lunch 11:30–4:30, Dinner 4:30–10; Sun. Dinner 4–10. **Reservations:** Not accepted. 50% No smoking. **Commendations:** Commended by the "Best of Boston" awards, 1987.♦

Cambridge, **Bread & Circus,** 115 Prospect St., Cambridge, MA 02139-2597. (617) 492-0071. Also in Brookline (392 Harvard St.), Hadley (Mountain Farms Mall), Newton (45 Kenneth St. and 916 Walnut St.),Wellesley (278 Washington St.), and Providence, RI. **Type of Business:** Wholefood Supermarket. **Commendations and Comments:** An oft-praised and innovative chain that sets an impressive example of what supermarkets can be. (Please see Brookline listing.)♥♦♦♦

Cambridge, **Cambridge Food Co-op,** 580 Massachusetts Ave., Cambridge, MA 02139. (617) 661-1580. **Type of Business:** Retail store. **Sells to:** The public. **Sells:** A full line of wholefood groceries and fresh produce. **Organic?** Produce is asserted 60% organic (Organic Crop Improvement Association, Farm Verified Organic, California Certified Organic Farmers); 30% of processed goods are asserted organic. **Credit:** None. **Prices:** 10% discount on case prices. **Hours:** M-Sat. 9-9, Sun. 12-9.

Cambridge, **Equal Exchange,** PO Box 2652, Cambridge, MA 02238. (617) 482-4995. **Type of Business:** Manufacturer, wholesaler, broker to wholesalers, and mail-order distributor. **Sells to:** Retailers, the public. **Sells:** Cashews, coffees, teas, banana chips, unrefined organic sugar and Cape Verdean tuna fish. (Equal Exchange provides a link between Third World farmers and U.S. consumers. They offer farmers more control over the marketing of their products and the possibility of earning more for them. Products come from democratically run cooperatives where profits are shared equitably and from Third World governments that place importance on the well-being of all people through job-creation, healthcare, literacy programs and land reforms.) **Organic?** Organic Crop Improvement Association certified 40% organic. **Credit:** Personal checks only. **Prices:** 10% discount available for orders over $50. Different price lists for stores and for wholesalers. **Shipping:** Within 24 hours of receipt of order. **Minimum Order:** None. **Catalogue Available?** Yes.

Cambridge, **Northeast Cooperatives,** Cynthia Moore, purchasing manager, Leonard Dankner, produce manager, 5 Cameron Ave., Cambridge, MA 02140. (617) 389-9032. MA (802) 257-5856 (VT). **Type of Business:** Distributor, since 1984. **Sells to:** Retailers, individuals with $400 or more ordered. **Sells:** Coffee, dairy products and eggs, dried beans, dried fruit, fresh fruit, whole grains, flour and meals, processed grain products, herbs and spices, juices, nuts and nut butters, oils, seeds, soy products, sweeteners, teas, fresh vegetables, organic cheese line. **Organic?** They use recognized certification programs and require papers from suppliers. **Minimum Order:** $400.

Cambridge, **Satori,** Patricia Alfaro, 95 Prescott St. #41, Cambridge, MA 02138. (617) 864-4116. **Type of Business:** Restaurant. **Sells:** Crepes, pancakes, soups, salads, sandwiches, seafood, noodles, rice and tempura. **Organic?** Asserted 50% organic. Water is filtered. **Specialties:** Tofu lasagna, fish dinners and wholesome desserts. Vegetarian, vegan, and macrobiotic dishes available. Musical entertainment is also offered occasionally. **Prices:** $6–$10. **Hours:** T-Sat. 12–9, Sun. 11–9. **Reservations:** Not required but accepted. 100% non-smoking. **Credit:** Personal checks only. **Commendations:** Commended by the *Boston Globe.*

Conway, **South River Miso,** Christian Elwell, South River Farm, Conway, MA 01341. (413) 369-4057. **Type of Business:** Processor and mail-order distributor. **Sells to:** Wholesalers, retailers, and the public. **Sells:** Organic, unpasteurized miso and organic, brown rice koji. **Organic?** Asserted 100% organic. **Credit:** Payment by check only. **Shipping:** By UPS and by USPS outside the UPS area. No shipping during June, July and August. **Minimum Order:** None. **Catalogue Available?** Yes.

Greenfield, **Franklin Community Co-op,** Patti Waters, 32 Chapman St., Greenfield, MA 01301. (413) 772-2513. **Type of Business:** Retail store, Co-op. **Sells to:** The public. **Sells:** Variety of fresh produce and processed foods. **Organic?** No organic claims. **Credit:** None. **Hours:** M, Tues, W, F-Sat. 9:30–6, Thurs. 9:30–8.

Greenfield, **Joyce's Jungle,** Joyce R. Young, 36 Birch St., Greenfield, MA 01301. (413) 772-0641. **Type of Business:** Grower. **Sells to:** The public through their own store and, Saturday mornings, at the Greenfield farmers' markets. **Sells:** Fresh vegetables (beets, broccoli, cabbage, carrots, cauliflower, celery, cucumbers, eggplant, lettuce, onions, peppers, radishes, spinach, squash, tomatoes, turnips and zucchini), fresh cut flowers and perennial flowering plants. **Organic?** Natural Organic Farmers Association certified 100% organic.

Hadley, **Bread & Circus,** Mt. Farms Mall, Rt.9, Hadley, MA, 01035. **Type of Business:** Wholefood supermarket **Commendations and Comments:** Part of an oft-praised and innovative chain that sets an impressive example of

what supermarkets can be. (Please see Brookline listing.)♥♦♦♦

Housatonic, **Berkshire Mountain Bakery Inc.,** Richard Bourdon, PO Box 785, Housatonic, MA 01236. (800) 274-3412, (413) 374-3412. **Type of Business:** Manufacturer and mail-order distributor. **Sells:** Natural sourdough bread: wholewheat, rye, sesame, rice, raisin and other types. **Organic?** Asserted 100% organic. **Shipping:** $1.50 handling plus UPS shipping charge. If customer is more than 5 days away via UPS, we must ship 2nd day by air. **Minimum Order:** None, but minimum of 12 loaves to get wholesale price. **Catalogue Available?** Yes.

Marion, **Jonathon's Agricultural Enterprises Inc.,** PO Box 270, Marion, MA 02738. (617) 763-2577. **Type of Business:** Grower and distributor. **Sells to:** Retailers and restaurants. **Sells:** Alfalfa, muna bean, radish, clover, onions, lentil, pea, wheat, adzuki, dill sprouts, and mixes of sprouts. **Organic?** Asserted 100% organic. **Catalogue Available?** Yes.

Nantucket, **Something Natural,** 50 Cliff Rd., Nantucket, MA 02554. (508) 228-0504. **Type of Business:** Bakery and sandwich shop. **Sells:** Wholegrain breads, herb breads, carrot cake, sandwiches and salads. **Organic?** Water is not filtered. **Specialties:** Vegetarian dishes available. **Prices:** $3–$7. **Hours:** Seasonal; 10–6:30. **Reservations:** Not required.

New Bedford, **Down To Earth Natural Food,** 751 Kempton St., New Bedford, MA 02740. (508) 996-1995. **Type of Business:** Retail store. **Sells to:** The public. **Sells:** Baked goods, fresh beans, beverages,breads, candy, cereals, dairy products, flour, processed and fresh dried fruit, meats, fresh nuts and nut butters, pasta, rice, fresh soy products, frozen vegetables, fresh grains and spices. **Organic?** No organic claims. **Hours:** M-F 9–7, Sat. 9–6. **Comments:** There is a natural-foods cafeteria next door, M-Sat. 11–2:30, Fri also 4:00–8:00.♦

Newton, **Bread and Circus,** 916 Walnut St. or 45 Kenneth St., Newton, MA 02161-1135. Also in Brookline (392 Harvard St.), Cambridge (115 Prospect St.), Hadley (Mountain Farms Mall), Wellesley (278 Washington St.) and Providence, RI. **Type of Business:** Wholefoods supermarket. **Commendations and Comments:** Part of an oft-praised and innovative chain that sets an impressive example of what supermarkets can be. (Please see Brookline listing.)

Northampton, **Paul & Elizabeth's Restaurant,** Paul Sustuk, 150 Main St., Northampton, MA 01060. (413) 584-4832. **Type of Business:** Restaurant. **Sells:** Vegetarian food; fresh fish, tempura, salads, homemade breads, and muffins. **Organic?** Asserted 10% organic. Water is filtered. **Prices:** $10–$16. **Hours:** M-Sat. 11:30–9:45. **Reservations:** Not required but accepted. 80% No smoking. **Credit:** V M.♦♦

Phillipston, **Baldwin Hill Corporation,** Phil Leger, Baldwin Hill Road, Phillipston, MA 01331. (508) 249-4691. **Type of Business:** Manufacturer, retail store, and mail-order distributor. Sells to: Retailers and the public. Sells: Traditionally prepared, organic, sourdough bread. The grain is stone-ground and then the bread is baked in wood-fired brick ovens. **Organic?** Asserted 100% organic. Member of Organic Foods Production Association of North America (which does not certify but acts as an umbrella organization). **Credit:** None. **Prices:** Discount prices on 500 loaves or more. **Hours:** 7–9. **Shipping:** UPS. **Minimum Order:** 12 loaves for retailers. **Catalogue Available?** Yes.

Wellesley, **Bread & Circus,** 278 Washington St., Wellesley, MA 02181-4999. (617) 235-7262. Also in Brookline (392 Harvard St.), Cambridge (115 Prospect St.), Hadley (Mountain Farms Mall), Newton (45 Kenneth St. and 916 Walnut St.), and Providence, RI. **Type of Business:** Wholefoods supermarket. **Commendations and Comments:** One of the stores in an oft-praised and innovative chain that sets an impressive example of what supermarkets can be. (Please see Brookline listing.)♥♦♦♦

Williamstown, **Caretaker Farm,** Sam and Elizabeth Smith, Hancock Rd. (Route 43), Williamstown, MA 01267. (413) 458-4309. **Type of Business:** Grower and retailer (through their farm shop). **Sells to:** Distributors, retailers and the public. **Sells:** Green beans, strawberries, basil, dill, parsley, beets, carrots, cucumbers, lettuce, potatoes, spinach, squash, zucchini and breads (rye, whole wheat and sourdough). **Organic?** Certified 100% organic by Natural Organic Farmers Association. **Credit:** None. **Hours:** 7–7. **Minimum Order:** $50 for retailers, $100 for distributors. **Catalogue Available?** No.

Worcester, **Annapurna,** 483 Cambridge St., Worcester, MA 01610. (508) 755-7413. **Type of Business:** Restaurant. **Sells:** Lacto-vegetarian Indian cuisine. **Organic?** 10% asserted. **Specialties:** Udipi cuisine. **Prices:** $3.80–$5. **Hours:** Lunch: M-F 11:30–2p.m., Dinner: Daily 5p.m.–10p.m. **Reservations:** Possible for parties of 4 or more. 30% of tables are non-smoking. **Credit:** V M. **Comments:** The restaurant celebrates Sri Krishna Janmashtami, the birth of Krishna, with a sumptuous feast around the second week in September. Deepawali (Festival of Lights) is celebrated on November 11th and 12th. Celebration dinners are for those with prepaid reservations only.

Worcester, **Living Earth,** Albert Maykel and Frank Phelan, 232–234 Chandler St., Worcester, MA 01609. (508) 753-1896. **Type of Business:** Retail store. **Sells to:** Public. **Sells:** Cereals, grains, flours, beans, pasta, rice, oils, meat, poultry, seafood, soy products, nuts and nut butters, fresh fruit and vegetables, dried fruit, fruit juices, processed vegetables, preserves, dairy products, breads, cookies, crackers, candy, beverages, herbs and spices. **Organic?** Natural Organic Farmers Association certified 60–90% organic for produce, 35% organic for dry goods. **Credit:** V M. **Prices:** 10–20% discounts available for bulk orders. **Hours:** M-F 9:30–6 (–8 Thurs.), Sat. 9–5, Sun. 12–5. **Comments:** They claim to have the largest selection of organic foods in central New England.♦

MI

Michigan

Ann Arbor, **Arbor Farms Market,** Leo Fox, 2215 W Stadium Blvd., Ann Arbor, MI 48103. (313) 996-8111. **Type of Business:** Retail store. **Sells to:** The public. **Sells:** Baked goods, beans, beverages, breads, candy, cereals, dairy products, flour, processed fruit, dried fruit, meats, nuts and nut butters, oils, pasta, rice, soy products, frozen and fresh vegetables, fresh fruit, grains, spices. **Organic?** 20% organically grown goods. **Credit:** None. **Prices:** 10% discount on full cases. **Hours:** M-Sat. 9–8, Sun. 10–6. **Comments:** All additive-free products.

Ann Arbor, **Michigan Federation of Food Cooperatives,** Doug Grigg, Janelle Hope, 727 W Ellsworth St., Ann Arbor, MI 48108. (313) 761-4642. **Type of Business:** Distributor, since 1971. **Sells to:** Retailers. **Sells:** Coffee, condiments, dried beans, dried fruit, whole grains, flour and meals, processed grain products, herbs and spices, juices, nuts and nut butters, pasta, seeds, soy products, sweeteners, teas. **Organic?** Asserted organic (10%), member of Organic Foods Production Association of North America. **Minimum Order:** $250 (see Chapter 6 for more).

Ann Arbor, **Seva Restaurant and Market,** Steven F. Bellock, 314 E Liberty St., Ann Arbor, MI 48104. (313) 662-1111. **Type of Business:** Restaurant and retail store. **Sells:** Vegetarian food; Mexican and Oriental cuisine. **Organic?** No organic claims. Water is filtered. **Specialties:** Vegan and macrobiotic dishes available. Comedy club downstairs for entertainment. **Prices:** $5.25–$7.25. **Hours:** M-F 11–9, Sat. 10–10, Sun. 10–9. **Reservations:** Not required but accepted. 100% No smoking. **Credit:** V M. **Commendations:** Recommended by *Ann Arbor News* as Best Value Restaurant, 1986, 1987 and 1989, and as Most Comfortable Restaurant in 1989.♦

Berrien Springs, **Andrews University Cafeteria,** Bennett Chilson, U.S. 31 North, Berrien Springs, MI 49104. (616) 471-3161. **Type of Business:** Restaurant. **Sells:** Lacto-ovo-vegetarian food only. **Organic?** No organic claims. Water is not filtered. **Prices:** $4.95. **Hours:** daily 6:30–8, 11:30–1, 5–6. **Reservations:** Not accepted. 100% No smoking.

Clinton, **Eden Foods,** 701 Tecumseh Rd., Clinton, MI 49236. (800) 248-0301. **Type of Business:** Distributor. **Sells to:** Retailers. **Sells:** Soy products, condiments (organic shoyu soy sauce), dried beans (dried and packaged in glass), whole grains, flours and meals, processed grain products (salt-free whole grain pasta). **Organic?** Accepts Organic Crop Improvement Association (OCIA) certified products and conducts an in-house certification program; its certification program is being certified by OCIA ("double-certified").

Dearborn, **Specialty Grain Company,** Steve Boese, president, 1903 Monroe St., Dearborn, MI 48124. Mail to: PO Box 2458 Dearborn, MI 48123. (313) 561-0421. **Type of Business:** Distributor, since 1976. **Sells to:** Retailers, mail order. **Sells:** Dried beans (black, soybean, adzuki), dried fruit, whole grains, flours and meals (wheat flakes, rye flakes, oat flakes, rolled oats, oat bran), processed grain products, nuts and nut butters, seeds. Gourmet popcorn, biodynamically produced commodities. **Organic?** Asserted organic. **Minimum Order:** None.

East Lansing, **East Lansing Food Coop,** Inc. , 4960 Northwind, East Lansing, MI 48823. **Type of Business:** Retail store, co-op. **Sells to:** The public. **Sells:** Variety of fresh produce and processed foods. **Credit:** None. **Hours:** 10–8 daily.

Grand Rapids, **Harvest Health Inc.,** Henry Diedering, 1944 Eastern Ave. SE, Grand Rapids, MI 40507. (616) 245-6268. **Type of Business:** Retail store, mail-order distributor and wholesaler (herbs and spices). **Sells:** Baked goods, beans, breads, cereals, flours, soy products, rice, pasta, oils, dairy products, fruit juices, dried fruits, nuts, spices. **Organic?** Affiliated with the National Nutritional Foods Association. **Credit:** V M. **Prices:** Call for quantity price. **Hours:** M-Sat. 9–5:30, Fri. until 9 p.m. **Shipping:** Anywhere covered by UPS and US mail. 25% on wholesale orders. 1-to-2 week delivery. **Minimum Order:** $10 net. **Catalogue Available?** Yes. **Comments:** A family-owned business started in 1952.

Kalamazoo, **Country Life,** Tom Rudnik, 233 Portage St., Kalamazoo, MI 49007. (616) 343-7421. **Type of Business:** Restaurant and retail store. **Sells:** Natural-foods vegetarian restaurant. **Organic?** Asserted 10% organic in the restaurant, cooking is done with well water. Asserted 40% organic in the store. **Specialties:** Salad bar, sandwiches, entrees and blended drinks. **Prices:** Entrees at $3.50+. **Reservations:** Not possible. **Credit:** None. **Comments:** The business is non-profit, "operated solely for the health and happiness of our customers."

Pullman, **Country Life Natural Foods,** Div. Oak Haven Inc., 109 52nd Ave., Pullman, MI 49450. (616) 236-5011. **Type of Business:** Manufacturer and wholesale distributor. **Sells to:** Retailers and the public. **Sells:** Bulk dried fruit, corn chips, crackers, sodas, candy,grains, cereals, nuts, oils, flours, beans, soybean milk, seeds, applesauce and sugar-free preserves, rice and gourmet pasta. **Organic?** Asserted 20% organic, relying on the certification of suppliers. **Credit:** None. **Prices:** Special prices for bulk orders. **Hours:** M-Thurs. 9–1:30 and 3-6, Fri. and Sun., 9-1. **Shipping:** Serves only Michigan, Illinois, and

Wisconsin. **Minimum Order:** $50 at warehouse, $250 for delivery. **Catalogue Available?** Yes.

Royal Oak, **Cuisine Couriers,** Lynn Marie Hinososa, 508 S Washington, Royal Oak, MI 48067. (313) 541-2002. **Type of Business:** Natural Foods Delicatessen. **Sells:** Vegetarian light lunches, soups, salads, and baked goods, with a carry-out service. Vegan and macrobiotic options are available. **Organic?** Asserted 30% organic. **Specialties:** Vegetarian pizza, curry coleslaw, lasagna made with tofu, "chic-un" salad with tempeh instead of chicken and vegetarian stuffed grape leaves. **Prices:** Entrees—$4–$5. **Hours:** M-F 10-6, Sat. 9-5. **Reservations:** Not required. 100% non-smoking. **Credit:** None. **Commendations:** *Detroit Monthly* January 1989 (front page).

Royal Oak, **Inn Season Cafe,** George Chek (owner), 500 E Fourth St., Royal Oak, MI 48062. (313) 547-7916. **Type of Business:** Restaurant. **Sells:** Vegetarian cuisine and seafood. **Organic?** Asserted 60% organic. Water is filtered. **Specialties:** Swiss chard pecan rolls with tomato mint sauce; vegetable paella; linguine with shiro miso and fresh basil sauce; stuffed eggplant; pepper, leek and mushroom stew with corn and cheese dumplings. Vegan and macrobiotic dishes available. **Prices:** Lunch $6.95-$8.95, Dinner $10.95-$13.95. **Hours:** M-Sat. 11-10. **Reservations:** Not accepted. 100% no smoking. **Credit:** None. **Commendations:** Widely recommended; local papers' Best Vegetarian Restaurant for last five years.

Sault Ste. Marie, **Haypoint Farm,** Sue Raker, Box 292, Sugar Island, Sault Ste. Marie, MI 49783. (906) 632-1280. **Type of Business:** Producer and distributor, since 1985. **Sells to:** Retailers, mail order (garlic only), and to the public through the farm and a Saturday market at Sault Ste. Marie, July-Sept. **Sells:** Fresh apples, teas, cider, spices, herbs, edible flowers, lamb, garlic, lettuce, honey, apple butter, and maple syrup. **Organic?** Asserted 100% organic. They say they use Tilth, Farm Verified Organic and Natural Organic Farmers Association organic standards, licensed by the Michigan Dept. of Agriculture. **Credit:** None. **Prices:** Yes. **Hours:** 24 hours. **Minimum Order:** Prefers to sell by the case to restaurants, buying clubs, etc. but tailors to needs of customers. **Catalogue Available?** Yes.

Taylor, **Safe Foods Inc.,** Joseph T. Rogers, 20189 Northline, Taylor, MI 48180. (313) 287-2131. **Type of Business:** Wholesale food distributor. **Sells to:** Retailers. **Sells:** Grains, beans, seafood (shrimp, trout), brown rice, popcorn, fresh fruit (apples, blueberries, grapefruit, melons, nectarines, oranges, strawberries), pecans, vegetables (beets, broccoli, cabbage, carrots, cauliflower, corn, cucumbers, lettuce, garlic, onions, peas, peppers, potatoes, radishes, spinach, squash, tomatoes, zucchini). **Organic?** Asserted 100% organic. **Prices:** No special prices for bulk orders, although special broker prices. **Shipping:** Deliveries to Michigan, Ohio, Indiana. **Minimum Order:** $100 or more depending on location. **Catalogue Available?** Yes.

West Cassopolis, **Roseland Farms,** John and Merill Clark, 27427 M-60 West Cassopolis, MI 49031. (616) 445-8769, (616) 445-8987. **Type of Business:** Producer and distributor, since 1976. **Sells to:** Retailers, mail order to the general public. **Sells:** Meat (bulk and individual cuts, beef and pork), fresh apples and pears, flours and meals, fresh vegetables (tomatoes and corn), soy and navy beans, whole grains (corn, oats, rye), and canola oil. **Organic?** Certified organic by the Organic Growers of Michigan. **Credit:** V M. **Prices:** Minimum order of 100 lbs. for a 10% discount to retailers and distributors. **Hours:** M-Sat. 8–5, Sun. 1–5. **Shipping:** Overnight delivery or 1–2 days UPS on ice. **Minimum Order:** None, but 10% discount with an order of 100 lbs.+ and 20% on 300 lbs.+. **Catalogue Available?** Yes.

MN

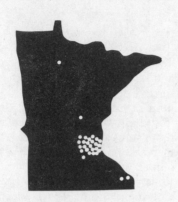

Minnesota

Apple Valley, **Rainbow Foods,** Marj. Anderson, 15125 Cedar Avenue S, Apple Valley, MN 55124. (612) 431–4000. **Type of Business:** Retail store. Please see entry for Minneapolis.

Bemidji, **Harmony Food Co-op,** Greg Klave, 722 Beltrami Ave., Bemidji, MN 56601. (218) 751–2009. **Type of Business:** Cooperative. **Sells to:** Members and the general public. **Sells:** A wide variety of baked goods, beans, beverages, candy, cereals, dairy products, flours, fruit, meats, nuts, oils, pasta, rice, soy products, vegetables, grains and spices. **Organic?** Asserted 30% organic. **Credit:** None. **Prices:** Special prices for bulk orders. **Hours:** M-Sat. 9–6. **Minimum Order:** None. **Catalogue Available?** Yes.

Blaine, **Rainbow Foods,** 12493 Central Avenue NE, Blaine, MN 55434. (612) 755–9160. **Type of Business:** Retail store. Please see entry for Minneapolis.

Burnsville, **Valley Natural Foods,** 1401 S Grand Ave. So., Burnsville, MN 55337. (612) 892–6661. **Type of Business:** Retail store and co-op. **Sells to:** Members and the public. **Sells:** A wide variety of wholefood groceries and fresh produce. **Organic?** Processed goods asserted to be 50% organic. **Credit:** None. **Hours:** M-F 9–8, Sat. 9–5:30, Sunday closed.

Columbia Heights, **Rainbow Foods,** Barb Beise, 4300 Central Avenue NE, Columbia Heights, MN 55421. (612) 781–6916. **Type of Business:** Retail store. Please see entry for Minneapolis.

Eagan, **Rainbow Foods,** Linda Maki, 1276 Town Centre Drive, Eagan, MN 55123. (612) 452–9506. **Type of Business:** Retail store. Please see entry for Minneapolis.

East Bethel, **Nomadic Organics Inc,** Bill Krahn, Edward Brown, 22921 NE Johnson St., East Bethel, MN 55005. **Type of Business:** Distributor. **Sells to:** Wholesaler, broker, distributor and mail-order distributor. **Sells:** Cheeses, organic corn chips, dried dates, apricots and raisins, organic almonds and almond butters, pistachio nuts, coconuts, walnuts, soy products, organic chicken, fresh fruits, fresh vegetables and spices. **Organic?** Certified organic (99%—Organic Growers and Buyers Association). **Credit:** None. **Prices:** Mail orders must be prepaid. **Hours:** 8–5. **Shipping:** No more than 7 days; goods in stock are shipped the next day. **Minimum Order:** $100.00. **Catalogue Available?** Yes.

Eden Prairie, **Rainbow Foods,** Stacy Jacobson, 970 Prairie Center Drive, Eden Prairie, MN 55344. (612) 934–6595. **Type of Business:** Retail store. Please see entry for Minneapolis.

Garrison, **Life-Renewal Inc.,** Div. Garrco, Inc., Ronald M, Holmquist, Hwy. 18, Box 92, Garrison, MN 56450. (612) 692–4498. **Type of Business:** Manufacturer, retail store and mail-order distributor. **Sells to:** Retailers and the public. **Sells:** Processed and fresh beans, teas, breads, popcorn, cereals, flour, dried fruit, oils, pasta, grains, nuts, spices and medicinal herbal products. **Organic?** Asserted 100% organic. **Credit:** None. **Prices:** Discounts for bulk orders. **Hours:** M-F 8–5. **Shipping:** Small orders are shipped the same day they are received. **Minimum Order:** None. **Catalogue Available?** Yes.

Hopkins, **Rainbow Foods,** Debbra Manske, 1515 Excelsior Avenue E, Hopkins, MN 55343. (612) 931–1100. **Type of Business:** Retail store. Please see entry for Minneapolis.

Maplewood, **Rainbow Foods,** Barb Manship, 2501 White Bear Avenue, Maplewood, MN 55109. (612) 777–7849. **Type of Business:** Retail store. Please see entry for Minneapolis.

Minneapolis, **Cafe Brenda,** Brenda Langton, 300 1st Ave. N, Minneapolis, MN 55401. (612) 342–9230. **Type of Business:** Restaurant. **Sells:** Gourmet natural foods. **Organic?** Around 40%. **Specialties:** A variety of daily specials and fresh seafoods. **Prices:** Lunch $5–$8, Dinner $8–$14. **Hours:** M-F, 11:30–2:00; M-Thurs, Dinner 5:30–9:30 **Reservations:** Possible. 85% non-smoking. **Credit:** V M AE. **Commendations:** Claim citation in numerous publications.♦♦

Minneapolis, **Jardin,** Kevin Hudalla, 1614 Harmon Place, Minneapolis, MN 55403. (612) 338–2363. **Type of Business:** Restaurant, opened in July, 1989. **Sells:** Vegetarian cuisine. **Organic?** Asserted 50% organic. Filtered water. **Specialties:** Organic vegetarian dishes. **Prices:** $6.95–$11.95. **Hours:** 11–10. **Reservations:** Possible. 100% non-smoking. **Credit:** V M.

Minneapolis, **Linden Hills Co-op,** Tree Li, 4306 Upton Ave. S, Minneapolis, MN 55410. (612) 922–1159. **Type of Business:** Retail Co-op. **Sells to:** Co-op members and the public. **Sells:** Cookies, corn chips, crackers, muffins, pancakes, tacos, a large variety of beans, beverages, breads, candy, cereals, dairy products, flour, fruit juices, dried fruits, meats, nuts, oils, pasta, rice, soy products, fresh and processed vegetables and spices. **Organic?** Asserted 30% organic. **Organic?** Member of Organic Growers and Buyers Association. **Credit:** None. **Prices:** 5% off for bulk orders to non-members, 10% over cost for members. **Hours:** M-Sat. 9–8, 9–6 Sun. **Shipping:** Deliveries made once or twice weekly. **Minimum Order:** The minimum of the supplier. **Catalogue Available?** No.

Minneapolis, **Mud Pie Vegetarian Restaurant,** Debra-Johnson, 2549 Lyndale Ave. S, Minneapolis, MN 55405. (612) 872–9435. **Type of Business:** Restaurant. **Sells:** Multi-ethnic, 10 page, vegetarian menu, with vegan and macrobiotic options. **Organic?** Asserted 25% organic. Filtered water. **Specialties:** The Mud Pie vegie burger and Mexican, Arabian, Oriental, Italian, French and Hungarian dishes. **Prices:** Entrees range from $4–$8. **Hours:** M-F 11–11, Sat. 8–11, Sun. 8–10. **Reservations:** Possible for parties of 5 or more. 25% non-smoking. **Credit:** AE. **Comments:** Mud Pie vegetable patties are also sold frozen through some wholefoods stores.♦♦

Minneapolis, **New Riverside Cafe,** Erik Riese, 329 S Cedar Ave., Minneapolis, MN 55454. (612) 333–4814. **Type of Business:** Restaurant. **Sells:** Vegetarian dishes, including vegan and macrobiotic options. **Organic?** Asserted 30% organic. A member of Organic Growers and Buyers Association. Water for drinks is filtered. **Specialties:** Wok dishes, seasonal/regional dishes and health-and-allergy conscious desserts. **Prices:** $3–$6.50. **Hours:** M-F 7–11, Sat. 8–12, Sun. 9–1:30. **Reservations:** Not possible. 60% non-smoking. **Credit:** None. **Commendations:** Four stars, *St. Paul Pioneer,* Minneapolis, 1988; 'Best Health Food', *Twin Cities Reader,* Minneapolis, 1988; 'Best Vegetarian Cafe', *City Pages,* Minneapolis, 1988.♦♦

Minneapolis, **Nigels's,** Nigel or Ellen, 15 S 12th St., Minneapolis, MN 55403. (612) 338–2235. **Type of Business:** Restaurant. **Sells:** Vegetarian, vegan and macrobiotic dishes. **Prices:** Entrees—$2.75–$8.95 (Lunch), $7.95–$21.95 (Dinner) **Hours:** 11–11. **Reservations:** Possible. **Credit:** V M AE D DC. **Commendations:** *City Pages* Readers Poll: "Best Restaurant 1989."

Minneapolis, **North Country Coop,** 2129 Riverside Ave., Minneapolis, MN 55454. (612) 338–3110. **Type of Business:** Retail store and co-op. **Sells to:** Public. **Sells:** A wide selection of baked goods, beans, beverages, candy, cereals, dairy products, flour, fruit (processed, dried and fresh), nuts, oils, pasta, rice, soy products, vegetables (fresh and frozen), salsa, grains, meats and spices. 40% of the produce is organic and 10% of the processed goods. **Organic?** Certified by Organic Growers and Buyers Association. **Credit:** None. **Prices:** Discount for whole bags ordered in advance. **Hours:** M-F 9–9, Sat. 9–8, Sun. 10–8.

Comments: North Country got the most recommendations of any co-op in our survey.♦♦

Minneapolis, **Rainbow Foods,** 2919 26th Avenue South, Minneapolis, MN 55406. (612) 724–4605. Also: 8020 Brooklyn Blvd., Minneapolis, MN 55445. (612) 424–6331. Also: 1104 Lagoon, Minneapolis, MN 55408. (612) 823–1563. **Type of Business:** Supermarket with natural-foods dept. **Sells to:** The public. **Sells:** A full line of wholefoods grocery items, beans, grains, nuts, soy products, and spices. **Organic?** They asserted that 15% of their grocery items come from organically grown food. **Hours:** 24 hours. **Comments:** Chain of 22 supermarkets with natural-foods departments. Some stores with organic produce.

Minneapolis, **Roots and Fruits Cooperative Produce,** Jo Elliott, 510 Kasota Ave., Minneapolis, MN 55414. (612) 379–3030; FAX: (612) 379–0280. **Type of Business:** Co-op distributor. **Sells to:** Retailers. **Sells:** Coffee, fresh fruit, fresh herbs, soy products, fresh vegetables, cheese. **Organic?** Asserted organic (10%) by Organic Growers and Buyers Association. **Credit:** None. **Minimum Order:** $100. **Catalogue Available?** Yes.

Minneapolis, **Seward Co-op Grocery,** Gail Graham, 2201 E Franklin Ave., Minneapolis, MN 55404. (612) 338–2465. **Type of Business:** Natural-foods grocery. **Sells to:** The public. **Sells:** A full-line natural-foods grocery. **Organic?** 30–40% organic, certified by Organic Growers and Buyers Association. **Prices:** Bulk orders—5% discount for non-members, 10% discount for members. **Hours:** Daily 9–9. **Comments:** Features a natural food deli, with fresh hot soups daily, sandwiches, soft serve non-fat frozen yogurt. Filtered water is used in deli.♦

Oakdale, **Rainbow Foods,** Dawn Bauer, 7053 10th St. N, Oakdale, MN 55119. (612) 739–9570. **Type of Business:** Retail store. Please see entry for Minneapolis.

Plymouth, **Rainbow Foods,** Diane Kaczmarek, 10200 6th Avenue N, Suite 100, Plymouth, MN 55441. (612) 541–9044. **Type of Business:** Retail store. Please see entry for Minneapolis.

Robbinsdale, **Rainbow Foods,** Ellen Engemansen, 3505 W Broadway, Robbinsdale, MN 55422. (612) 522–4445. **Type of Business:** Retail store. Please see entry for Minneapolis.

St. Charles, **Diamond K Enterprises,** Jack Kranz, R.R. 1, Box 30, St. Charles, MN 55972. (507) 932–4308. **Type of Business:** Manufacturer, retailer, wholesaler, broker, and mail-order distributor. **Sells to:** Retailers and the public. **Sells:** Dried and fresh beans, flours and meals, grains, nuts, processed grain products, seeds, oils, and dried fruits. **Organic?** Asserted organic. **Credit:** V M. **Prices:** Discount for large orders. **Hours:** M-Sat., 8–5. **Shipping:** All U.S. areas served usually allow 1–2 weeks for delivery. **Minimum Order:** None. **Catalogue Available?** Yes.

St. Paul, **Mill City Sourdough Bakery,** Mary Ann Mattox, 1566 Randolph Ave., St. Paul, MN 55105. (612) 698–4705. **Type of Business:** Manufacturer, retail store and mail-order distributor. **Sells to:** Retailers and the public. **Sells:** Baked goods (sourdough breads: whole wheat, French peasant, French, raisin almond, Finnish rye, rye, sesame, rice). **Specialities:** Authentic handmade sourdough bread; no added yeast, fats, oils, sweeteners, or dairy products. **Organic?** Certified organic by the Organic Growers and Buyers Association (member) and Organic Crop Improvement Association. **Credit:** V M AE. **Prices:** Wholesale prices if 12 loaves are ordered. **Hours:** M-Thurs, 3–6; Fri, 9–6. **Shipping:** By UPS, usual delivery time 3 days. **Minimum Order:** 6 loaves (12 loaves for wholesale). **Catalogue Available?** Yes.

St. Paul, **Old City Cafe,** Berkeh Mishulovin, 1571 W Grand Ave., St. Paul, MN 55116. (612) 699-5347. **Type of Business:** Restaurant. **Sells:** Kosher, vegetarian cuisine, with Israeli and Middle Eastern delicacies. **Organic?** No organic claims made. **Specialties:** Hummus, tabbouli, ratatouille, falafel, vegetarian chili, bab ghanouj and baklava, as examples. **Prices:** $3.50–$10. **Hours:** Sun.-Th, 11:30–8:30; Sat., from two hours after sundown to 12:30. Closed Fridays. **Reservations:** Possible. 100% non-smoking. **Credit:** No credit cards accepted. **Commendations:** *Twin Cities Entertainment, Star Tribune, Twin Cities Reader* and *Jewish World.* **Comments:** Minnesota's only kosher restaurant.

St. Paul, **Rainbow Foods,** 1660 Robert St. S, St. Paul, MN 55118. (612) 457-8540, **and** 1566 University Ave., 55104, (612) 644-4321 **and** 892 Arcade St., St. Paul, MN 55106. (612) 776-5808. **Type of Business:** Retail store. Please see entry for Minneapolis.

Stillwater, **Valley Coop,** 215 No. William, Stillwater, MN 55082. (612) 439-0366. **Type of Business:** Retail store and co-op. **Sells to:** The public. **Sells:** A huge range of wholefoods, fresh fruit and vegetables. **Organic?** Processed goods asserted 5% organic. **Credit:** No. **Hours:** M-F 9–8, Sat. 9–6, Sun. 12–5. **Comments:** This is a large, thriving co-op that welcomes new members (who are entitled to discounts) but also has about 50% non-member customers. They will not carry foods containing artificial additives. They also stock high quality kitchen wares, health and beauty aids.

Winona, **Little Bear Trading Co., Inc.,** 226 E Second St., Winona, MN 55987. (507) 452-6332. **Type of Business:** Manufacturer and distributor, since 1975. **Sells to:** Retailers. **Sells:** Baked goods (bagels and croissants), fresh and processed beans, cereals, flour (rye and whole wheat), whole wheat noodles, rice, grains and veggie burger mix. **Organic?** Documented organic, Organic Foods Production Association of North America standards **Credit:** None. **Prices:** Negotiable with the size of the order. **Hours:** Warehouse hours are 8–4. **Shipping:** Usually 15 days. **Minimum Order:** $2,000 or 5,000 units. **Catalogue Available?** Yes.

MS

Mississippi

Jackson, **Rainbow Whole Foods Co-op and High Noon Cafe,** 4147 Northview Dr., Jackson, MS 39206. (601) 366-1602. **Type of Business:** Retail store and cafe. **Sells to:** Members and the public (10% surcharge for non-members). **Sells:** A wide range of wholefood grocery items and fresh organic produce. The cafe sells macrobiotic lunch-plates and sandwiches. **Organic?** Produce is about 90% organic, bought locally when possible. Most comes from Texas and California and is certified by the Texas Agriculture Department or California Certified Organic Farmers. About 20% of the processed goods are organic (and increasing all the time). **Credit:** None. **Prices:** Members can earn discounts by volunteering hours to the store. 4, 8, and 12 hours volunteered earn 10%, 20%, and 30% discounts respectively. **Hours:** M-W, F, Sat. 10–6; Th 10–7; Sun. closed. **Comments:** Membership costs $15 a year for individuals, $20 for families, and $100 for lifetime. They also supply a few local restaurants and put out a newsletter.♥

Ocean Springs, **Russell's,** 1302 Government St., Ocean Springs, MS 39564. (601) 875-8882. **Type of Business:** Natural foods grocery store. **Sells to:** The public. **Sells:** A wide selection of organic, wholefood grocery items (especially beans, nuts, seed, grains, and flours) and some fresh organic produce. **Organic?** Processed goods are about 90% organic. Very little of their produce is organic, that coming from local growers. **Credit:** None. **Prices:** Discounts on special orders and senior citizen discounts. **Hours:** 9–5:30 6 days a week. **Comments:** They carry a complete line of macrobiotic foods and offer classes in wholefoods cooking and nutrition. They also have an extensive book department and try to emphasize education.

Oxford, **Community Good Foods,** 1112 Van Buren Ave., Oxford, MS 38655. (601) 234-8064. **Type of Business:** Retail store and cooperative. **Sells to:** The public and Co-op members. **Sells:** Wholefood grocery items and some organic produce. They sell a lot of bulk rice, beans, flours, grains, spices, and oils and also offer goods from pasta and yogurt to home brewing supplies and local honey. **Organic?** They estimate that 20% of their grocery items are organic. **Credit:** None. They do take checks and sometimes will give charge accounts to co-op members.

Prices: 10% discounts for co-op members. Further discounts for senior citizens. Hours: 10–5:30 M-F, 10–5 Sat. Comments: Membership costs $20 for individuals, $30 for households, and $5 for students (per semester). They also have a vegetarian cafe on the premises.

MO

Missouri

Kansas City, **Clearly Nature's Own,** 4301 Main, Kansas City, MO 64111. (816) 931–1873. Type of Business: Retail store. Sells to: The public. Sells: A complete line of natural groceries and fresh organic produce. Organic? Asserted 75% organic for produce, 10–15% other. Credit: None. Prices: 5% discount for case. Hours: M-F 9–8, Sat. 9–7, Sun. 10–6.

Mountain View, **Morningland Dairy,** Jim or Margie Reiners, Rt.1, Box 188–B, Mountain View, MO 65548. (417) 469–3817. Type of Business: Manufacturer and mailorder distributor. Sells to: Retailers and the public. Sells: Dairy products (raw milk cheddars, colbys, jacks, and herb cheeses), meat. Organic? Asserted 100% organic. Credit: None. Prices: 5% discount on 40 lbs.; 10% discount on 250 lbs. Hours: 8–5. Shipping: By UPS. Minimum Order: None. Catalogue Available? Yes.

St. Louis, **Brandt's Market,** 6525 Delmar, St. Louis, MO 63130. (314) 727–3663. Type of Business: Retailer. Sells to: The general public. Sells: Asserted 60% organic. Muffins, beans, coffee, sodas, teas, wines, breads, 'natural' chocolate and other confections, cereals, dairy products, flour, fruit juices, nuts, oils, pasta, rice, soy products, frozen and fresh vegetables (organic as available), dried and fresh fruit, free-range poultry, Irish oak smoked salmon and spices. They concentrate on natural/gourmet foods, which must be as appealing to the palate and the eye as they are natural. Organic? They rely on the certification of suppliers. Credit: V M AE D. Prices: Discounts for bulk. Hours: M-F 10–8, Sat. 9–6, Sun. 12–5. Shipping: They deliver products and custom made gift baskets via UPS, within 24 hours of order.

St. Louis, **Golden Grocer,** John LaRico, 335 N Euclid, St. Louis, MO 63108. (314) 367–0405. Type of Business: Retail store. Sells to: The public. Sells: Over 300 varieties of processed and fresh groceries,herbs and spices. Organic? They assert that they sell about 33% organic. Credit: V

M D. Prices: 15% bulk discount. Hours: M-Sat. 10–6:30, Sun. 12:30–4:30. Comments: They also have a hot and cold salad bar, pizza by the slice, and whole-grain bakery goods.

St. Louis, **The Natural Way,** 8110 Big Bend Blvd., St. Louis, MO 63119. (314) 961–3541. Type of Business: Retailer. Sells to: Public. Sells: Products free of chemical additives, added sugars and meat. Organic? Asserted 20% organic (100% organic produce). Organic? They sell some goods from certified producers. Credit: V M. Prices: 15% discount on bulk orders. Hours: M-F 9:30–8, Sat. 9:30–6:30, Sun. 12–5.

St. Louis, **Sunshine Inn,** 8 1/2 S Euclid, St. Louis, MO 63108. (314) 367–1413. Type of Business: Restaurant. Sells: White meat and vegetarian dishes, including vegan and macrobiotic options. Organic? Asserted 5% organic. Specialties: Sesame tempeh, Garden of Eden, Gold Lion veggie burger and Broccoli Blossom. Prices: Entrees— $3.50–$8.95. Hours: Tues-Sat. 8–10, Sun. 10–12:30, 5–9. Reservations: Possible. Credit: V M AE. Commendations: *Vegetarian Times,* 1984.

Willow Springs, **Plumbottom Farm,** Rt. 3, Box 129, Willow Springs, MO 65793. Type of Business: Grower and vendor. Sells to: The public (direct and by mail), distributors, retailers, and restaurants. Sells: Over 100 varieties of organic produce. Organic? Certified 100% by Ozark Organic Growers Association. Credit: None. Hours: 7–7 for their stand and for mail orders by phone. Shipping: Details on price list. Minimum Order: $50 for retailers, restaurants, and distributors. Catalogue Available? Yes. Comments: Most of their mail orders are garlic braids decorated with flowers. They sell in the Willow Springs farmers market on Wednesdays and Saturdays.

MT

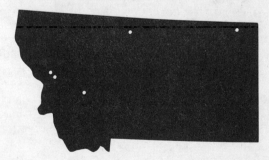

Montana

Big Sandy, **Montana Flour & Grains,** Bob Quinn, Dave Arsenault, Ferry Route, Box 808, Big Sandy, MT 59520. (406) 378–3105. Type of Business: Grower. Sells to: Retailers. Sells: Whole grains (hard red winter and spring wheat, hard and soft white wheat, durum, hull-less barley, hull-less oats, rye, triticale, a 7–grain mix, and kamut). They also sell 100% stone ground whole grain flour from above grains. Organic? Certified 80% organic (Organic

Crop Improvement Association). **Minimum Order:** Most orders are C.O.D. or net 15 days with approved credit.

Helena, **Real Food Store,** Laughing Water, Owner/Manager, 1090 Helena Avenue, Helena, MT 59601. **Type of Business:** Retail store. **Sells to:** The public direct and through the mail (small volume). **Sells:** A wide variety of organic and wholefoods—a variety comparable to that of an average supermarket. The store also has a huge variety of bulk herbs. **Organic?** He sells as much organic produce as is available and is vice-president of the Organic Certification Association of Montana (OCAM), a chapter of Organic Crop Improvement Association. **Credit:** None. **Prices:** 20% off on items purchased by the case and 10% off for orders over $100. **Hours:** 9:30–6 M-Sat. **Shipping:** Usually within 2 days, depending on availability. **Minimum Order:** None. **Catalogue Available?** Not at present. **Comments:** They place a premium on being honest and truthful with customers and go to great lengths to find good research support for the items and brands they sell.

Missoula, **Good Food Store,** Diana Reetz-Stacey/Cheryl Loberg, 920 Kensington Ave., Missoula, MT 59801. (406) 728–5823. **Type of Business:** Retail store. **Sells to:** Public. **Sells:** Natural foods with a minimum of additives, processing and packaging. This is the largest natural foods store in Montana, so it stocks almost everything. **Organic?** The Good Food Store is a member of the Organic Certification Association of Montana. 15% of the goods sold here are certified organic brands. **Credit:** None. **Prices:** 10% discount on full cases or full bags. **Hours:** M-Sat. 9–8. **Minimum Order:** None. **Catalogue Available?** Yes.♦

Missoula, **Mammyth Bakery,** Kimberly L. Kuethe, Owner, 131 W Main, Missoula, MT 59802. (406) 549–5542. **Type of Business:** Bakery, restaurant, and retail store. **Sells:** The restaurant features vegetarian, seafood and poultry entres, plus four special entrees daily; often including vegan or macrobiotic options. There is also a salad bar. The bakery produces a wide variety of baked goods, including some organic breads. Their wholesale business to local restaurants constitutes a large percentage of their business. **Organic?** Asserted 25–35% organic. **Specialties:** Crusty Italian peasant breads, a variety of honey sweetened, sugarless bars and cookies, cheesecakes, hommos sandwiches on fresh pita bread and Mandarin chicken on a freshly baked Kaiser rolls. **Prices:** At lunch, entrees are $3.25–$5. **Hours:** M-Sat. 8–6. **Reservations:** Not possible. 100% non-smoking. **Credit:** V M AE.♦

Scobey, **Great Grains Milling Co.,** Alvin Rustebzkke, PO Box 427, Scobey, MT 59262. (406) 783–5588. **Type of Business:** Manufacturer and retail store and mail order. **Sells to:** Retailers, distributors, and the public. **Sells:** Stone-ground hard red spring wheat products. **Organic?** In the process of getting certified by Farm Verified Organic, Organic Crop Improvement Association. **Credit:** No credit cards. **Shipping:** Mails by UPS. **Catalogue Available?** Yes. **Comments:** "I grow hard red spring wheat organically, grind it into a stone wisk, then seal it in a plastic bag after flushing the bag with nitrogen. The flour will stay fresh with no bugs for a long time—over a year."

NE

Nebraska

Lincoln, **Open Harvest Natural Foods Coop & Bakery,** Cynthia Taylor, 2637 Randolph, Lincoln, NE 68510. (402) 475–9069. **Type of Business:** Retail store. **Sells to:** The public. **Sells:** A comprehensive range of processed foods and fresh produce. **Credit:** None. **Prices:** 10% discount for bulk orders. **Hours:** M-F 9–8, Sat. 9–5:30, Sun. 12–5. **Comments:** Whole-grain bakery in house.

Rosalie, **Do-R-Dye Organic Mill,** Richard Dye, Box 50, Rosalie, NE 68055. (402) 863–2248. **Type of Business:** Processor and mail-order distributor. **Sells to:** Retailers, mail order to the public. **Sells:** Grains (oats, wheat, rye, corn, sweet corn, blue corn), oatmeal, flour (rye and whole wheat). **Organic?** Certified organic (100%—Organic Crop Improvement Association). **Credit:** No credit cards, large orders can get at least 50% credit for up to 10 days after delivery. **Prices:** Wholesale prices on orders over 500 lbs. **Hours:** M-F, 8–5. **Shipping:** Throughout the mainland USA, mainly by commercial truck. The average transit time is 7–10 days. **Minimum Order:** $5 plus postage. **Catalogue Available?** Pricelist available on request.

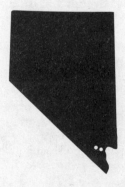

NV

Nevada

Las Vegas, **Ira's Organic Foods Market,** Ira Lovitch, 5643 W Charleston Blvd #3, Las Vegas, NV 89102. (702) 258–4250. **Type of Business:** Retail store, mail-order distributor, and wholesale distributor (selective lines). **Sells to:** The public, retailers, restaurants, and buying clubs/co-ops. **Sells:** A wide variety of organic produce and wholefoods, and some specialty items, such as yeast-free bread. **Organic?** They assert that 100% of their stock is organic and the store is a supporting member of California Certified Organic Farmers. **Credit:** Soon. **Prices:** Lower prices for bulk orders. Write for more details. **Hours:** Tu-W 9-7, Th-F, Sat. and M 9-6. **Shipping:** UPS (customer pays freight costs). **Minimum Order:** None. **Catalogue Available?** Yes. **Comments:** They strive to be 100% organic—one of only two stores we know of that make that claim. They pick up all of their produce with their own trucks and will send a newsletter upon request.

Las Vegas, **J & J Health Foods,** 3870 E Flamingo, Las Vegas, NV 89121. (702) 456-7807. **Type of Business:** Retail store. **Sells to:** The public direct and by mail order. **Sells:** A range of processed wholefoods. **Organic?** No organic claims. **Credit:** None. **Prices:** 10% discounts on case orders. **Hours:** M-F 9-7, Sun. 12-5.

NH

New Hampshire

Hanover, **Hanover Consumer Cooperative,** Robert P. Briggs, 45 So. Park St., Hanover, NH 03755. (603) 643-2667. **Type of Business:** Cooperative food store. **Sells to:** The general public. **Sells:** Almost all food products. 5% of the goods are organic, including fresh produce, yogurt, cream, cheeses, juices, applesauce, peanut butter, raisins, rice cakes, and corn chips, and the range and percentage of organic goods is increasing. **Organic?** Their suppliers are certified by Vermont Organic Farmers or the State of New Hampshire. **Credit:** None. **Prices:** Discounts available for bulk orders. **Hours:** M-F 8-8, Sat. 8-6. **Comments:** People can join the co-op with a one time membership fee of $35, which is redeemable.

Keene, **Butternuts,** Jay Smelts, 15 Court St., Keene, NH 03431. (603) 352-8818. **Type of Business:** Restaurant. **Sells:** They serve fresh, seasonal foods with an interesting selection of appetizers, soups, pasta, vegetable stir fries, salads, shellfish, and meat and poultry entres. Their menu features a lot of variety. **Organic?** Some of the food used is organic, depending on seasonal availability. **Specialties:** Fresh seafood, pasta, stuffed dumplings and vegetarian specialties such as Butternuts Vegetarian Grill. On Sunday nights, Butternuts serves an exclusively Japanese menu,

featuring authentic sushi and tempura. **Prices:** Entrees, at dinner, range from $8.95 to $16.95. **Hours:** Lunch, Tues-Fri, 11-2; Brunch, Sat. and Sun., 10-2; Dinner, Tues-Sun., 5-9:30. **Reservations:** Recommended. 100% non-smoking. **Credit:** V M AE DC CB. **Commendations:** Getaways for Gourmets, 1989.♦

Wolfeboro, **East of Suez,** Charles G. Powell, RR1 Route 28, Wolfeboro, NH 03894. (603) 569-1648. **Type of Business:** Restaurant. **Sells:** A large range of vegetarian dishes as well as poultry and seafood. **Organic?** Asserted 25% organic, grown by the owners. **Specialties:** Japanese tempura with or without shrimp, stir-fried vegetables, chicken dishes and Thai steamed seafood. **Prices:** Entrees—$10-$12. **Hours:** Tues-Sun., 6-10. **Reservations:** Not possible. **Credit:** None.

NJ

New Jersey

Avon, **Healthfair,** 216 Main St., Avon, NJ 07717. (201) 774-2016. (Please see listing for Little Silver, NJ for more.) **Type of Business:** Retail store. **Sells to:** The public. **Sells:** A wide variety of wholefood groceries and fresh organic produce. **Hours:** M-Sat. 10-6.

Bridgewater, **Colloides Naturels,** 1170 Rt. 22 Suite 106, Bridgewater, NJ 08807. (201) 707-9400. **Type of Business:** Sales/distributor for manufacturer. **Sells to:** Retailers, processors and the public. **Sells:** Gums: Arabic, agar, guar, tragacath, carrageenen, locust bean and karaya. **Organic?** Asserted 100% organic. **Credit:** None. **Prices:** Very large orders permit price reduction. **Hours:** M-F 9-5. **Shipping:** All the U.S. states. **Minimum Order:** Depending on the gum type, 55 or 110 lbs. **Catalogue Available?** Yes.

Cherry Hill, **Mrs. Emm's All Natural Health Food Stores,** Marketplace Shopping Center, Route 70, Cherry Hill, NJ 08003. (609) 424-1177. **Type of Business:** Retail store. **Sells to:** The public. **Sells:** A full array of wholefood grocery items, including canned and frozen vegetables. **Organic?** Produce is asserted 100% organic (Organic Crop Improvement Association, Farm Verified Organic, Natural Organic Farmers Association, California Certified Organic Farmers); they assert that about 80% of processed items are organic. **Credit:** V M. **Prices:** 10% discounts on case purchases. **Hours:** M-F 10-9, Sat. 10-6, Sun. 11-4. **Com-**

ments: They are part of a chain of 12 stores that stretches through much of New Jersey and Pennsylvania.

Closter, **Total Health Nutrition Center, Inc.,** 90 Closter Plaza, Closter, NJ 07624. (201) 767-7541. **Type of Business:** Retail store. **Sells to:** The public. **Sells:** Baked goods, beans, bread, candy, cereals, dairy products, fruit juice, dried fruit, meat, nuts, oils, pasta, rice, soy products and some vegetables. **Organic?** Produce 100% organic, certified by Organic Crop Improvement Association, Farm Verified Organic, Demeter/Bio-dynamic. Processed food asserted 60% organic. **Credit:** V M AE D. **Prices:** 10% discount for case orders. **Hours:** M-Sat. 10-6. **Minimum Order:** $20 for credit card users.

East Rutherford, **Park and Orchard,** Buddy Coebhardt, 240 Hackensack St., East Rutherford, NJ 07073. (201) 939-9292. **Type of Business:** Restaurant. **Sells:** Seafood, poultry and vegetarian dishes. Vegan and macrobiotic options are also available. **Organic?** Non-organic. **Specialties:** Seafood, Chinese, Italian, grilled food and vegetarian casseroles. **Prices:** $10.95-$18.95. **Hours:** Tues-F 12-2, M and Sat. 5-10, Sun. 2-9. **Reservations:** Not possible. **Credit:** V M AE D. **Commendations:** Two stars—*New York Times;* Three stars—*New Jersey Monthly;* Two stars—*Bergen Record;* Award of excellence—*Wine Spectator.*♦♦

Emerson, **Old Hook Farm, Inc.,** 650 Old Hook Rd., Emerson, NJ 07630. (201) 265-4835. **Type of Business:** Retail store and organic farm. **Sells to:** The public. **Sells:** A comprehensive range of organically grown fresh produce and natural grocery items. **Organic?** Produce 75% organic (Organic Crop Improvement Association, Farm Verified Organic, Natural Organic Farmers Association, California Certified Organic Farmers, Demeter/Bio-dynamic), processed goods about 90% organic. **Credit:** None. **Prices:** 10-15% discount on case orders. **Hours:** Tu-Sun. 9-6, closed Mondays.

Hightstown, **Nutrition Center,** Becky Russell, Rte. 130, Warren Plaza West, Hightstown, NJ 08520. (609) 448-4885. **Type of Business:** Retailer. **Sells to:** Public. **Sells:** A variety of baked goods, beans, breads, cereals, dairy products, flour, fresh, dried and processed fruit, meats, nuts, oils, pasta, rice, soy products, fresh and processed vegetables, beverages, supplements, herbs, natural remedies, biodegradable household goods, grains and spices, about 50% organic. **Organic?** Reliant on the certification of suppliers. **Credit:** V M. **Prices:** No discount for bulk. **Hours:** M-Tues. 10-6, W-F 10-9, Sat. 10-5, Sun. 12-4. **Shipping:** UPS mail orders only.

Hightstown, **Nutrition Center,** Rte. 130, Warren Plaza West, Hightstown, NJ 08520. (609) 448-4885. **Type of Business:** Retail store. **Sells to:** The public. **Sells:** A complete range of wholefood grocery items and fresh organic produce. **Organic?** Fresh produce 100% organic (certified by Organic Crop Improvement Association, Farm Verified Organic, Demeter/Bio-dynamic), other goods, 50%. **Credit:** V M. **Prices:** 10% discount for case purchases. **Hours:** M-Tues. 10-6, W and F 10-9, Sat. 10-5, Sun.

12-4. **Comments:** They carry pet supplies, organic baby foods, cosmetics, books.

Hoboken, **Hoboken Farmboy,** Roy North, 229 Washington St., Hoboken, NJ 07030. (201) 656-0581. **Type of Business:** Retailer. **Sells to:** Public. **Sells:** A large variety of baked goods, breads, beans, beverages, confections, dairy products, flour, fresh, dried and processed fruit, meats, nuts, oils, pasta, rice, soy products, fresh and processed vegetables, grains and spices. **Organic?** Rely on the certification claims of suppliers. **Credit:** V M D. **Prices:** 10% off case orders or equivalents. **Hours:** M-F 10-10, Sat. 10-9, Sun. 11-8.

Little Silver, **Healthfair,** 625 Branch Ave., Little Silver, NJ 07735. (201) 747-3140. **Type of Business:** Retail store. **Sells to:** The public. **Sells:** A wide variety of wholefood groceries and fresh organic produce. **Organic?** Fresh produce 99% organic (Organic Crop Improvement Association, Farm Verified Organic, California Certified Organic Farmers) processed goods 20%. **Credit:** V M D. **Prices:** 10% discount for case orders. **Hours:** M-Sat. 9-6, Fri 9-8. **Minimum Order:** $20 for UPS. **Comments:** Will not knowingly sell irradiated foods. Caters to special dietary needs with wheat-free, gluten-free, and sugar-free products.

Matawan, **Healthfair,** Rte. 34 & Broad St., Matawan, NJ 07747. (201) 583-3800. (Please see listing for Little Silver, NJ for more). **Type of Business:** Retail store. **Sells to:** The public. **Sells:** A wide variety of wholefood groceries and fresh organic produce. **Hours:** M-Sat. 10-6, Th 10-8.

Mays Landing, **Mrs. Emm's All Natural Health Food Stores,** Festival at Hamilton, Rt. 322 and Rt. 40, Mays Landing, NJ 08043. (609) 625-3377. **Type of Business:** Retail store, part of a chain of 12 in NJ and PA. **Sells:** A full array of wholefood grocery items, including canned and frozen vegetables. **Organic?** Produce is asserted 100% organic (Organic Crop Improvement Association, Farm Verified Organic, Natural Organic Farmers Association, California Certified Organic Farmers); they assert that about 80% of processed items are organic. **Credit:** V M. **Prices:** 10% discounts on case purchases. **Hours:** Varies depending on store.

Medford, **Mrs. Emm's All Natural Health Food Stores,** Taunton Forge Shopping Center, Taunton and Tuckerton Roads, Medford, NJ 08055. (609) 596-7171. See entry for Mays Landing above.

Mercerville, **Black Forest Acres,** 724 Rt. 33, Mercerville, NJ 08619. (609) 586-6187. **Type of Business:** Retail store. **Sells to:** The public. **Sells:** A complete array of wholefood groceries and fresh produce. **Organic?** 100% organic for produce, 90% for processed foods. Certified by Farm Verified Organic, Demeter/Bio-dynamic. **Credit:** V M. **Prices:** Case lots get a 10% discount. **Hours:** M-F 9:30-7:30, Sat. 9:30-6. **Catalogue Available?** Upon request. **Comments:** Full-service deli, serving vegetarian meals, organic, turkey, chicken, meat. They also cater to special dietary concerns.

Middletown, **Healthfair,** Rte. 35 and Harmony Rd., Middletown, NJ 07748. (201) 671–3334. (Please see listing for Little Silver, NJ for more). **Type of Business:** Retail store. **Sells to:** The public. **Sells:** A wide variety of wholefood groceries and fresh organic produce. **Hours:** M-Sat. 10–6, F 10–8.

Montvale, **Chestnut Ridge Health Food,** 26F Chestnut Ridge Rd., Montvale, NJ 07645. (201) 391–6173. **Type of Business:** Retail store. **Sells to:** The public. **Sells:** A full range of wholefood grocery items and fresh beans, cheese, yogurt, grains, nuts, soy products, spices, and selected vegetables. **Organic?** 100% organic (produce) certified by Organic Crop Improvement Association, Farm Verified Organic, or Demeter/Bio-dynamic; 40% of processed goods. **Credit:** V M AE. **Prices:** 15% discount for case or bulk orders. **Hours:** 10–6 daily.

Oakhurst, **Healthstar,** Rt. 35 and West Park Ave., Oakhurst, NJ 07755. (201) 531–3141. **Type of Business:** Retail store. **Sells to:** The public. **Sells:** A wide range of wholefood groceries and fresh beans, dairy products, grains, nuts, soy products, spices, frozen vegetables. **Organic?** Fresh produce 100% organic (certified by Organic Crop Improvement Association, Farm Verified Organic), other goods, 70%. **Credit:** V M. **Prices:** Discounts on case lots. **Hours:** M-Sat. 10–6.

Ocean City, **Adele's Natural Foods,** 511 8th St., Ocean City, NJ 08226. (609) 398–6391. **Type of Business:** Retail store. **Sells to:** The public. **Sells:** Bakery items, beans, bread, candy, dairy products, flour, fruit juice, dried fruit, oils, pasta, rice, soy products and some frozen vegetables. **Organic?** Produce 100% organic (certified by Organic Crop Improvement Association), other goods 5%. **Credit:** V M AE D. **Prices:** 10% off on case lots. **Hours:** M-Sat. 10–6. **Comments:** The store went up for sale at the end of 1989 and may have changed.

Pennsville, **Simply Delicious,** 243–A N Hook Rd., Box 124, Pennsville, NJ 08070. (609) 678–4488. **Type of Business:** Retail store and mail-order distributor. **Sells to:** The public direct and by mail. **Sells:** An impressive range of wholefood grocery items, with some fresh produce. **Organic?** 95% organic for produce (Organic Crop Improvement Association, California Certified Organic Farmers, Natural Organic Farmers Association, Demeter/Bio-dynamic); processed goods are about 50% organic. **Credit:** V M D. **Prices:** 10% discount for case orders. **Hours:** 9–7, seven days. **Shipping:** Same day whenever possible. **Minimum Order:** For credit cards, $15. **Catalogue Available?** Yes.

Rahway, **Heartymix Company 1231 Madison Hill Rd.,** Rahway, NJ 07065. (201) 382–3010. **Type of Business:** Manufacturer and mail-order distributor. **Sells to:** Public only by mail order. **Sells:** "We manufacture and sell naturally fortified baking and food mixes which are made from, as far as we can manage, natural ingredients of high food value–unbleached or whole wheat flour, wheat germ, brewers' yeast, buttermilk powder, corn oil, natural nuts and dried fruits (dried fruits may have sulfur dioxide added). Natural carotene is added for vitamin A and as a colorant, with perhaps vitamin C as a perservative." Mixes include: bread mixes, wheatless bread mixes, dry soup mixes, cake/cookie/muffin mixes, pancake mixes and fruit snack mixes. **Organic?** No organic claims. **Prices:** Special prices for wholesale orders. **Shipping:** Ususally ship within one week. **Minimum Order:** None.

Red Bank, **Victory Market,** 31 W Front St., Red Bank, NJ 07701. (201) 747–0508. **Type of Business:** Retail store. **Sells to:** The public. **Sells:** A full range of wholefoods and natural produce. **Organic?** Asserted 15% for processed goods. **Credit:** V M AE. **Prices:** 20% bulk discount. **Hours:** M-Sat. 8–6, Sunday closed. **Shipping:** $1 per mile charge for deliveries. **Catalogue Available?** Yes. **Comments:** A gourmet/specialty store which evolved from a meat market. They also provide nutritional advice.

Ringwood, **Food for Thought,** Ringwood Plaza, Skyline Drive, Ringwood, NJ 07456. (201) 962–6355. **Type of Business:** Retail store. **Sells to:** The public. **Sells:** Full range of fresh produce and wholefood groceries. **Organic?** 3% organic for fresh (Farm Verified Organic), 20% for processed food. **Credit:** V M D. **Prices:** 15% above cost for bulk; 10% off 1 case items. **Hours:** M, Tu, Th, F 10–7; W 10–6; Sat. 9:30–5; Sun. 11–3. **Minimum Order:** $100 to get bargain rate of 15% above cost. **Comments:** The store specializes in bodybuilding assistance and preventive health.

Toms River, **Natural Products, Inc.,** 675 Bachelor St., Toms River, NJ 08753. (201) 240–0024. **Type of Business:** Retail store and distributor. **Sells to:** The public, co-ops. **Sells:** A full line of natural groceries and fresh organic produce. **Organic?** Fresh produce 100% organic (Organic Crop Improvement Association, Natural Organic Farmers Association), processed goods 60%. **Credit:** V M. **Prices:** 15% discount for case orders, monthly specials and circulars. **Hours:** M-F 10–6, Sat. 10–5. **Comments:** Fresh sandwiches, soup, fresh organic juices, fresh bakery bread.

Vineland, **Your Heart's Content,** Inc. , Shop-Rite Shopping Center, 3630 E Landis and Lincoln Aves., Vineland, NJ 08360. (609) 794–3366. **Type of Business:** Retail store. **Sells to:** The public. **Sells:** A variety of packaged wholefoods, fresh beans, dairy products, grains, meats, nuts and soy products. **Organic?** 10% of processed goods asserted as organic. **Credit:** V M. **Hours:** M-Sat. 9–9, Sun. 9–6. **Comments:** This is a recently established "diet" Gourmet Food Shoppe. The staff also prepares fresh foods—hot and cold—for take-out.

Voorhees, **Mrs. Emm's All Natural Health Food Stores,** Eagle Plaza Shopping Center, 205 Haddonfield - Berlin Rd., Store No. 28, Voorhees, NJ 08043. (609) 627–5151. **Type of Business:** Retail store, part of a chain of 12 in NJ and PA. **Sells:** A full array of wholefood grocery items, including canned and frozen vegetables. **Organic?** Produce is asserted 100% organic (Organic Crop Improvement Association, Farm Verified Organic, Natural Organic Farmers Association, California Certified Organic

Farmers); they assert that about 80% of processed items are organic. **Credit:** V M. **Prices:** 10% discounts on case purchases. **Hours:** Varies depending on store.

West End, **Healthfair,** 139 Brighton Ave., West End, NJ 07740. (210) 229–6636. (Please see listing for Little Silver, NJ for more) **Type of Business:** Retail store. **Sells to:** The public. **Sells:** A wide variety of wholefood groceries and fresh organic produce. **Hours:** M-Sat. 9:30–6, Th 9:30–8, Sun. 10–4.

NM

New Mexico

Albuquerque, **LaMontanita Co-op Supermarket,** Lee Barbour, General Manager, 3500 Central SE, Albuquerque, NM 87106. (505) 265–4631. **Type of Business:** Retail store. **Sells to:** The public, retailers, and restaurants. **Sells:** It is a full-scale supermarket featuring organic meats and vegetables. **Organic?** 50% organic. **Prices:** Special orders for members vary on quantities over a certain amount. **Hours:** M-F 8:30–7:30, S-S 8:30–6:30. **Minimum Order:** For special orders only. **Comments:** One price for all.♦

Las Vegas, **Semilla Natural Foods,** Jane Lumsden, 510 University Avenue, Las Vegas, NM 87701. (505) 425–8139. **Type of Business:** Retail store and cafe. **Sells to:** The public. **Sells:** Fresh Produce—beans, beverages, dairy products, dried fruit, grains, turkey, chicken, nuts, soy products, spices, carrots. Processed Foods—Some baked goods, beans, beverages, cereal, dairy products, flour, processed fruit, dried fruit, salmon, oils, pasta, rice, soy products. **Organic?** 30–50% organic. **Prices:** Low mark-up on full and partial cases, full sacks. **Hours:** M-F 9:30–5:30, Sat. 10–3. **Shipping:** By mail; small orders are called in and then check is mailed. **Minimum Order:** None. **Comments:** They've been in business for 19 years.

Santa Fe, **Natural Cafe,** 1494 Cerrillos Rd., Santa Fe, NM 87501. (805) 983–1411. **Type of Business:** Restaurant. **Sells:** International cuisine, vegetarian dishes, fresh seafood and organic chicken. **Organic?** Varies seasonally. **Specialties:** New Mexican black bean enchiladas, grilled polenta with red chile, fresh pasta with lemon cream sauce, chicken teriyaki and fresh grilled salmon au poivre. **Prices:** Entrees—$4.95–$13.95. **Hours:** Lunch Tues-F, 11:30–2:30; Dinner Tues-Sun., 5–9:30. **Reservations:** Not

possible. **Credit:** None. **Commendations:** *New York Times,* 1989.♦

NY

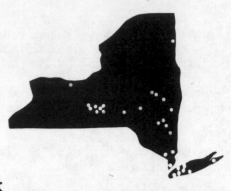

New York

Albany, **Dean's Incredible Edibles,** Westgate Shopping Center, 911 Central Ave., Albany, NY 11206. (518) 489–5723. **Type of Business:** Retail store. **Sells to:** The public. **Sells:** A range of wholefood groceries plus fresh beans, grains, nuts, soy products, apples, and dates. **Organic?** Fresh produce 100% organic (certified by Organic Crop Improvement Association, Farm Verified Organic, Demeter/Bio-dynamic). **Credit:** V M. **Prices:** 10% discount on orders of a case or more. **Hours:** M-W 10–6, Th-F 10–8:30, Sat. 10–5:30.

Boiceville, **Bread Alone,** Rte. 28, Boiceville, NY 12412. (914) 657–3328. **Type of Business:** Manufacturer and retail store. **Sells to:** Public through store, farmers' markets, and mail order. **Sells:** Delicious whole-wheat breads made from organic ingredients. **Organic?** 90% organic. Member of Organic Foods Production Association of North America. **Credit:** V M. **Prices:** Wholesale prices to stores and distributors. **Hours:** M-F 9–9, Sat. 9–5. **Shipping:** They deliver in Hudson Valley area and NYC. UPS elsewhere. **Catalogue Available?** Yes.♥♦♦

Brooklyn, **Myrna's Natural Shoppe,** 713 Fulton St., Brooklyn, NY 11217. (718) 858–6145. **Type of Business:** Retail store. **Sells to:** The public. **Sells:** A selection of natural grocery items plus fresh beans, grains and nuts. **Credit:** V M AE. **Hours:** M-Th 10–7:30, F-Sat. 10–8, Sun. 12–5. **Comments:** New kid on the block and still growing.

Brooklyn, **Park Slope Food Co-op,** 782 Union St., Brooklyn, NY 11215. (718) 622–0560. **Type of Business:** Co-op. **Sells to:** Members. **Sells:** A very impressive array of wholefoods and fresh produce. **Organic?** Produce 20% organic (Organic Crop Improvement Association, Farm Verified Organic, Natural Organic Farmers Association); 15% for grocery items. **Comments:** They have 2,500 members. They don't offer reciprocal shopping privileges to members of other co-ops. New members are welcomed (but be prepared to volunteer some time to work at the store).

Cedarhurst, **Nutrition Learning Ctrs.,** 445 Central Ave., Cedarhurst, NY 11516. (516) 374–3438. **Type of Business:** Retail store. **Sells to:** The public. **Sells:** A limited range of wholefood groceries. **Organic?** Fresh produce 100% organic (certified by Organic Crop Improvement Association, California Certified Organic Farmers), other items, 25%. **Credit:** V M. **Hours:** M and F 9–3, Tu 8–8:30, W 11–9, Th 9–7. **Comments:** They also sell books, cookbooks, videos and kitchenware.

Ghent, **Hawthorne Valley Farm,** R.D. No.2, Box 225A, Ghent, NY 12075. (518) 672–7500. **Type of Business:** Grower. **Sells to:** The public (60% of sales). **Sells:** Fresh fruit and vegetables (most varieties), dried fruit, fruit juices, beans, grains, baked goods, breads, cereals, oils, rices, pasta, dairy products, nuts and nut butters, spices, soy products, meats, beverages. **Organic?** 80% of products are Certified Organic/Biodynamic (Demeter Assoc.). 100% of farm acreage is certified. **Credit:** No credit cards. **Hours:** M-Sat 9–5. **Shipping:** Delivers only locally, within 100 miles. **Catalogue Available?** No. **Comments:** Sells at NYC's Union Square Farmers' Market every Saturday.

Great Neck, **Beyond Food, Inc.** , 215 Middleneck Rd., Great Neck, NY 11021. (516) 466–7991. **Type of Business:** Retail store. **Sells to:** The public. **Sells:** A wide range of fresh produce and wholefood grocery items. **Organic?** Fresh produce: 100% organic, certified by Organic Crop Improvement Association, Farm Verified Organic, or Demeter/Bio-dynamic. Processed goods 40% organic. **Credit:** AE. **Prices:** Discounts for case orders. **Hours:** M-F 10–7, Sat. 10–6. **Comments:** Fresh juice bar, protein shakes, expanding soup and sandwich bar. Deliveries in Great Neck, King's Point Area.

Guilford, **Deer Valley Farm RD #1,** Guilford, NY 13780. (607) 764–8556. **Type of Business:** Grower, manufacturer, and distributor since 1947. **Sells to:** Retailers and mail order to the public. **Sells:** Dried beans, dried fruit, whole grains, flours and meals, sweeteners, fresh vegetables, baked goods, processed grain products, and meat. **Organic?** Asserted organic (50%). Member of Natural Organic Farmers Association. (See Chapter 6 for more.)

Hicksville, **Good Life Natural Foods,** 339 S Broadway, Hicksville, NY 11801. (516) 935–5073. **Type of Business:** Retail store, mail order. **Sells to:** The public. **Sells:** An impressive variety of natural grocery items and fresh organic produce. **Organic?** Fresh produce 100% organic (certified by Farm Verified Organic, California Certified Organic Farmers, Demeter/Bio-dynamic); other items, 75%. **Credit:** V M. **Prices:** 10–20% off case orders. **Hours:** M-F 9:30–6, Sat. 10–5. **Catalogue Available?** Yes. **Comments:** They offer custom-tailored diets to fit individual needs and food allergies.

Himrod-on-Seneca, **Four Chimneys Farm Winery,** Walter Pedersen, Scott Smith, R.D. #1, Hall Rd., Himrod-on-Seneca, NY 14852. (607) 243–7502. **Type of Business:** Grower of grapes, manufacturer of wines. **Sells to:** Retailers, mail order. **Sells:** Grapes, grapejuice (red and white), wine, wine vinegar. **Organic?** Certified organic (100%—Natural Organic Farmers Association, IFOAM, NFA). **Credit:** None. **Prices:** 5% discount on 3 or more cases. **Hours:** At the winery, M-Sat., 10–6; Sun., 1–6. Alternatively at Greenmarkets, Union Square, NY (17th and Broadway) W, F, Sat., 9–5. Also, Saturdays at Ithaca Farmers Market, Ithaca, NY, May-Dec. **Shipping:** They do not deliver to Canada as deliveries are by UPS. Orders are shipped out the day after paid order is received. **Minimum Order:** To retailers and restaurants, 1 case, by mail order to the public, 1 bottle. **Catalogue Available?** Yes.

Hyde Park, **Mother Earth Storehouse,** Rt. 9 Colonial Plaza, Hyde Park, NY 12538. (914) 329–5541. (Please see listing for Kingston for more). **Type of Business:** Retail store. **Sells to:** The public. **Sells:** A range of wholefood grocery items and organic produce.

Ithaca, **ABC Cafe,** Patricia Lockwood, 308 Stewart Ave., Ithaca, NY 14850. **Type of Business:** Restaurant. **Sells:** Vegetarian dishes, vegetarian stir fries, homemade tofu burgers, homemade hummus and salads. The dishes made from scratch have no preservatives or additives in them. **Organic?** Asserted 20% organic. **Specialties:** Fresh baked pastries daily, ethnic dinner specials, Tues, Japanese; Wed., Greek; Thurs., Mexican; Fri., Lasagna; Sat., Varies seasonally; Sun., Pesto. **Prices:** Entrees range from $1.95 to $7.95 **Hours:** Tu-Th 11–12, Fri 11–1 a.m., Sat. 9:30–1 a.m., Sun. 9:30–10. **Reservations:** Possible. There are no non-smoking tables. **Credit:** None. **Commendations:** "Best Coffee in Town", *Ithaca Times* Readers Poll, 1984, 1985, 1986, 1987 (then category removed).

Ithaca, **Cabbagetown Cafe,** Sharon Kuehn, 404 Eddy St., Ithaca, NY 14850. (607) 273–2847. **Type of Business:** Restaurant. **Sells:** Vegetarian cuisine. **Organic?** Asserted up to 50% seasonal organic produce. **Specialties:** Homemade soups, fresh bread (baked on the premises), speciality salads, nightly dinner specials, excellent Sunday brunch. **Prices:** Entrees $4.25–$7.95. **Hours:** Lunch: M-F 11:30–2:30; Dinner: M-Thurs 5–9, F-Sat., 5–10; Sun. 10–2, 2–9. **Reservations:** Possible for large parties (5 or more). 100% non-smoking. **Credit:** None. **Commendations:** *Ithaca Times*—"Best Salads in Ithaca" 1988.

Ithaca, **Moosewood Restaurant,** 215 N Cayuga, Dewitt Mall, Ithaca, NY 14850. (607) 273–9610. **Type of Business:** Restaurant. **Organic?** Whenever possible in season (asserted around 40%). **Specialties:** Fresh pasta on Wednesday nights, ethnic specialities on Sunday nights, homemade desserts. Vegetarian, vegan and macrobiotic options are available. **Prices:** Entrees range from $4.50 to $9.50. **Hours:** Lunch: M-Sat. 11:30–2; Dinner: Sun.-Th 5:30–8:30; F-Sat., 6–9. **Reservations:** Possible. **Credit:** None. **Commendations:** They say their commendations are "too numerous to list." **Comments:** Cooperatively managed and owned. Outdoor terrace dining in the summer. They also offer a 302–page cookbook available for $12.95.♥♥

Jackson Heights, **Jackson Heights Health Foods,** 83–06 37th Ave., Jackson Heights, NY 11372. (718) 429–7511. **Type of Business:** Retail store. **Sells to:** The public. **Sells:**

A selection of wholefood grocery items. **Organic?** Asserted 65% organic for processed foods. Some stock certified by Organic Crop Improvement Association, Farm Verified Organic. **Credit:** V M AE. **Prices:** 10% discount for bulk. **Hours:** 10–6:30, six days (closed Sundays).

Jamaica, **Annam Brahma**, 84–43 164th St., Jamaica, NY 11432. (718) 523-2600. **Type of Business:** Restaurant. **Sells:** Ethnic vegetarian cuisine, with vegan options available. **Organic?** No organic claims. Filtered water. **Specialties:** East Indian dishes, Italian cuisine (Sun. and Thurs.), and Chinese (Tues.). **Prices:** Entrees range from $3.50 to $8. **Hours:** M, Tues., Th-Sat., 11–10; W 11–2; Sun. 12–10. **Reservations:** Possible only for large parties. 100% non-smoking. **Credit:** None. **Commendations:** *Queens Tribune*—"Best Vegetarian Restaurant". **Comments:** The owners and employees are all studying Sri Chinmoy and offer free meditation classes daily.

Kingston, **Mother Earth Storehouse**, Rt. 9W North Kings Mall, Kingston, NY 12401. (914) 336-5541. **Type of Business:** Retail store. **Sells to:** The public. **Sells:** A range of wholefood grocery items and organic produce. **Organic?** Produce 90% organically grown (Organic Crop Improvement Association, Farm Verified Organic, Natural Organic Farmers Association, California Certified Organic Farmers, Demeter/Bio-dynamic), processed food 40%. **Credit:** V M D. **Prices:** 10% discount on case buying.

New York, **Angelica Kitchen**, 300 E 12th St., New York, NY 10003. (212) 228-2909. **Type of Business:** Strict vegan restaurant. **Sells:** Dishes made with a majority of macrobiotic and organic foods. **Organic?** Asserted 98% organic. The water is filtered. **Specialties:** Daily specials created by the chefs, homemade amazaki, walnut lentil pate, hiziki caviar, Dragon Bowl, nori maki, soba sensation, dashi and soba. **Prices:** Entrees are $7–$8.75. **Hours:** 11:30–10:30, 7 days a week. **Reservations:** For parties of 6 or more. 100% non-smoking. **Credit:** Cash only. **Commendations and Comments:** They use only biodegradable dishwashing detergents and diligently recycle all they can. No alcoholic beverage license, but liquor stores in the area are open late, and you can bring in your own bottles. Very inexpensive for the top quality of the food; it's hard to miss ordering something delicious, although you may not be enthusiastic about the dairy-free cakes and sauces. One of the very best vegetarian restaurants on the East Coast. The lentil soup with wakame is a glorious meal in itself. Recommended by The *New York Daily News*, *Vegetarian Times*, The *Village Voice*, *Macromuse*, *Whole Life Times* and others.♥♦♦

New York, **Au Natural**, Linda Lorusso, 1043 2nd Ave. at 55th St., New York, NY 10022. (212) 832-2922. **Type of Business:** Restaurant. **Sells:** Free range poultry and vegetarian dishes. **Organic?** Asserted 80% organic. **Prices:** Entrees $8–$20. **Hours:** 8 a.m.-Midnight, 7 days a week. **Reservations:** Not possible. 25% non-smoking. **Credit:** AE DC, $20 minimum.

New York, **Blazing Salads**, David Feldman, 228 W 4th St., New York, NY 10014. (212) 929-3432. **Type of Busi-** ness: Restaurant. **Sells:** Salads, sandwiches, omelets and hot dishes, including a lot of vegetarian food and some vegan and macrobiotic options. Fresh food, well prepared and presented. **Organic?** Asserted 35% organic. **Specialties:** Salads, stuffed fresh flounder, and vegetarian specialties like sesame vegetable saute. **Prices:** Entrees from $7 to $14. **Hours:** 12 p.m.-12 a.m. **Reservations:** Not possible. 50% non-smoking. **Credit:** V M AE, the minimum for credit card payment is $10. **Commendations:** *Gourmet*, 1983; *Working Woman*, 1988. **Comments:** A second branch is at 1135 First Avenue (between 62nd and 63rd) New York City.

New York, **Boostan**, Mike Ofier, 85 MacDougal St., New York, NY 10012. (212) 533-9561. **Type of Business:** Restaurant. **Sells:** A selection of vegetarian Mediterranean cuisine. All entrees and salads are made to order. **Organic?** Asserted 80% organic. Filtered water. **Specialties:** Boostan specializes in providing a very extensive choice of authentic Mediterranean dishes, particularly appetizers and soups. **Prices:** Entrees range from $5.95 to $9.95. **Hours:** Noon to early morning. **Reservations:** Possible. 50% non-smoking. **Credit:** None. **Commendations:** *Cue* magazine, 1982; *New York* magazine, 1982.

New York, **Cheese on Second**, Richard Kahn, 1731 Second Ave., New York, NY 10128. (212) 996-4516. **Type of Business:** Retailer. **Sells to:** Public. **Sells:** A huge selection of cheeses, whole wheat bread, candy, cereals, whole wheat flour, fruit juices, pasta, rice, tofu, teas, and fresh fruit, vegetables and spices. **Organic?** Asserted 40% organic, they rely on the certification of suppliers. **Credit:** None. **Prices:** Special discounts on bulk orders and a 20% discount for caterers. **Hours:** M-F 11-7:30, Sat. 11-6, Sun. 11-6:30.

New York, **Commodities**, Bruce MacDonald, 117 Hudson St., New York, NY 10013. (212) 334-8330. **Type of Business:** Retail store, wholesaler of natural foods. **Sells to:** The public. **Sells:** One of the best selections of fresh produce and wholefood grocery items in Manhattan. **Organic?** Asserted 40% organic, Eden Food Certification (also Organic Crop Improvement Association). **Credit:** V M. **Prices:** Special prices for wholesale orders of $150 or more in full cases. **Hours:** 10-8 daily. **Comments:** They specialize in organically grown foods and macrobiotic foodstuffs.♦♦

New York, **Greenmarket. Administrative office: 130 E 16th St.,** New York, NY 10003. (212) 477-3220. **Type of Business:** Farmers Markets at Cadman Plaza (Court and Montague), City Hall (Park Row), Federal Plaza (Broadway and Worth), Union Square (Broadway and 17th), West 57th St. (9th ave), West 77th (Columbus Ave.), and World Trade Center (Church St.). **Sells to:** Farmers sell to the public, out of stands or, often, trucks. **Sells:** A wide variety of baked goods, produce, cheeses, and some crafts. **Organic?** Not all are organic, but there are often a few organic growers at a market (their signs usually state this fact). **Credit:** Generally none. **Prices:** Usually inexpensive. **Hours:** Generally early morning to sundown. **Comments:** The goods sold are usually quite fresh and the baked goods I have purchased at the Union Square Farmers' Market have been without exception quite good (especially the bread from Bread Alone).

New York, **House of Vegetarian,** Chung Fong Chu, 68 Mott St., New York, NY 10013. (212) 226-6572. **Type of Business:** Restaurant. **Sells:** Vegetarian cuisine. **Organic?** Asserted 100% organic. Filtered water. **Specialties:** Vegan food only, macrobiotic options. **Prices:** Entrees $5–$8. **Hours:** 11–10:30. **Reservations:** Possible. 100% non-smoking. **Credit:** None. **Commendations:** *Whole Life,* 1987.

New York, **Integral Yoga Natural Foods,** 229 West 13thSt. (near 8th Avenue), New York, NY 10011. (212) 243-2642. (Locations also in Charlottesville and Richmond, Virginia.) **Type of Business:** This is reputed to be one of the best health food stores in New York City. (They will soon open a mail order business as well.) **Sells to:** The public. **Sells:** An impressive variety of fresh organic produce, wholefood grocery items, and macrobiotic foods. They are a vegetarian store and carry no meat fish, chicken, or eggs (they do carry some dairy products). They also have a salad bar, a gourmet bar, and a "Fountain of Youth" juice bar. **Organic?** Asserted 60–80% of produce and 25–30% of processed goods. **Credit:** V M AE. **Prices:** 10% discount on bulk purchases (as long as the product is not one of the monthly specials). **Hours:** M-F 10–9:30, Sat. 10–8:30, Sun. 12–6:30. **Shipping:** UPS. **Minimum Order:** None. **Catalogue Available?** They offer a partial list now and will soon offer a more complete catalog. **Comments:** They also run the Integral Yoga Institute, and the Integral Yoga Natural Apothecary (located across the street), which sells supplements, homeopathic remedies and books. I took the evening series on yoga food categories. The atmosphere at the store is very pleasant and friendly, which could help account for its popularity—the register line sometimes runs all the way to the back of the store.♥♦♦

New York, **Living Springs,** Daniel Thomas, General Manager, 116 E 60th St., New York, NY 10022. (212) 319-7850. **Type of Business:** Restaurant and retail store. **Sells:** Vegetarian cuisine and goods. **Organic?** This restaurant grows some of its own fresh produce. Currently this is just lentil and sunflower sprouts, and in summer, greens and squash, but more of the fresh produce will be organic in the future, as the farm expands. **Specialties:** A wide variety of fruits, nuts, seeds, grains and vegetables, prepared simply and tastefully at a reasonable price. **Prices:** All-you-care-to-eat prices for a buffet meal, breakfast, $6; lunch, $8.50; dinner, $10. Food may also be purchased by the pound. **Hours:** Open for lunch and dinner. **Reservations:** Not possible. 100% non-smoking. **Credit:** AE, the minimum for payment by credit card is $20. **Comments:** In conjunction with the restaurant they also offer a variety of health education classes, either at no cost, or (in the case of cooking classes) at a price set to cover their expenses. Subjects include how to stop smoking, stress control, weight control, vegetarian cooking and nutrition, and home remedies. Nature slides and videos are shown during the meal.

New York, **Luma's 200 Ninth Avenue (22nd street),** New York, NY 10011. **Type of Business:** Restaurant. **Sells:** Macrobiotic food. **Organic?** "Whenever possible." **Specialties:** Tempeh scallopine, homemade vegetarian ravioli, charcoal-broiled seitan. **Prices:** Moderate to expensive. **Hours:** Tu-Th 5:30–10:30, F-Sat. 5:30–11, Sun. 5–10. Closed Mondays. **Reservations:** Recommended. **Commendations and Comments:** Nicely decorated; alcoholic-beverage license. The food itself isn't as tasty as, and is more expensive than, other restaurants like Angelica Kitchen. You need to select with care from the menu; avoid the cream substitutes, go for the fish and pasta.

New York, **Mitali Restaurant Inc.,** 334 East 6th St., New York, NY 10003. (212) 533-2508. **Type of Business:** Restaurant. **Sells:** Northern Indian Cuisine with vegetarian options. **Organic?** No organic claims. **Specialties :** Exotic Gourmet food prepared from own family recipe. **Prices:** $6.95 to $11.95. **Hours:** 12 p.m.-12 a.m. **Reservations:** Possible. 55% of tables are non-smoking. **Credit:** V M AE.

New York, **Nowhere Cafe,** 11 Waverly Place, New York, NY 10003. (212) 475-0255. **Type of Business:** Restaurant and Bar. **Sells:** Vegetarian cuisine. **Organic?** Asserted 90–95% organic. **Specialties:** Veggie burgers, whole wheat pizza, puffed pastries and saute vegetables. **Prices:** Entrees range from $6.95 to $12.95. **Hours:** Restaurant hours: T-Sun. 6 p.m.–11 p.m.; Bar –4 a.m. daily. **Reservations:** Possible. 20% non-smoking. **Credit:** V M AE, minimum for payment by credit card is $15. **Commendations:** *Elle* magazine, 1988; *City* magazine, 1988; *Rolling Stone,* 1989; *New York Post,* 1989. **Comments:** Set up by a rock star, another restaurant of the same name exists in Los Angeles. Live music is performed here.

New York, **Pumpkin Eater,** 2452 Broadway, New York, NY 10024. (212) 877-0132. **Type of Business:** Restaurant and catering. **Sells:** Pasta, vegetarian and seafood dishes, and a large selection of sandwiches at lunch. **Organic?** When available. **Specialties:** Vegetarian lasagna and fish (salmon, scrod, sole and bluefin). **Prices:** Entrees range from $6.95 to $14.95. **Hours:** M-F 9–11, Sat. 11–12, Sun. 11–11. **Reservations:** Possible. 100% non-smoking. **Credit:** V M AE (the minimum for the use of credit cards is $15). **Commendations:** *Whole Life Times,* 1989; *Free Spirit Magazine,* 1989; *Village Voice,* 1987.

New York, **Souen,** 28 East 13th St., New York, NY 10003. (212) 627-7150. Also at 210 Sixth Ave., New York, NY 10014. (212) 807-7421. **Type of Business:** Restaurant. **Sells:** Natural foods and macrobiotic cuisine with a Japanese flair. Many vegetarian options. **Organic?** Asserted 90% organic. **Specialties:** Weekend brunches and daily specials which include seitan cutlets, brown rice sushi, tempeh croquettes, salmon teriyaki, and steamed fish. They also serve beer and organic wine. **Prices:** $6.50–$18. **Hours:** M-Sat. 12–11, 12–10 Sun. **Reservations:** Possible. **Credit:** V M AE DC. **Commendations and Comments:** The Macrobiotic Center of New York, *Whole Life Times,* 1986, *New York Times,* 1982. "We do our best to serve the best quality delicious tasting natural food in harmony with the environment and to create a pleasant harmonious environment in which to eat it." They have been in business since 1969.♦

New York, **Spring St. Natural Restaurant,** Robert Schoenholt, 62 Spring St., New York, NY 10012. (212) 966–0290. **Type of Business:** Restaurant. **Sells:** White meat, fish and vegetarian foods, with vegan and macrobiotic options. No freezing or artificial additives used in the preparation of the food. **Organic?** Asserted 30% organic. **Specialties:** Vegetarian dishes. **Prices:** Entrees range from $5 to $12. **Hours:** 11:30 a.m.-2 a.m. **Reservations:** Not possible. 60% non-smoking. **Credit:** V M AE D, minimum for payment by credit card is $10.

New York, **Vegetarian's Paradise,** Sikay Tang, 48 Bowery, New York, NY 10013. (212) 571–1535. **Type of Business:** Restaurant. **Sells:** Chinese vegetarian cuisine prepared according to the Buddha's tradition, with no dairy products or fish. **Organic?** Asserted 20% organic. **Specialties:** Vegetarian "meat" dishes that are made with yams, soy products, bean curd and baby corn, soups made with a bean-sprout base and fresh vegetable dishes. **Prices:** Entrees range from $5.50 to $10. **Hours:** Sun.-Th 11:30–10:30, F-Sat., 11:30–11:30; Closed Wed. **Reservations:** Not possible. No non-smoking tables. **Credit:** None. **Commendations:** *Whole Life Times,* 1981; *Village Voice,* 1981 and 1982.

New York, **Whole Foods Soho,** 117 Prince, New York, NY 10012. (212) 673–5388. (Not affiliated with the Texas chain). **Type of Business:** Retail store. **Sells to:** The public direct and by mail. **Sells:** A range of wholefood grocery items and fresh organic produce. **Organic?** Asserted 12% of produce and about 15% of grocery items. **Credit:** V M AE. **Prices:** 10% discounts on bulk orders. **Hours:** 9–9:30 daily. **Shipping:** UPS. **Minimum Order:** None. **Catalogue Available?** Yes. **Comments:** They also have a deli section. They had trouble keeping up with the demand for organic produce last year, so they started bringing it in from California and Colorado.

Newfield, **Dawes Hill Honey/Bee Supreme Nutritional Products,** Steven Zimmerman, 1143 Elmira Rd., Newfield, NY 14867. (607) 273–7173. **Type of Business:** Manufacturer and retailer. **Sells to:** Anyone. **Sells:** Varietal Honeys, honeyfruit spreads, nutritional products from the hive and beeswax candles. **Organic?** Asserted 95% organic. **Credit:** V M AE. **Hours:** A small, self-service honey stand is open all day, every day. **Shipping:** Deliveries made across the U.S. **Minimum Order:** None. **Catalogue Available?** Yes, for distributors and stores.

Oneonta, **Autumn Cafe,** Nancy or Tim Johnson, 244 Main St., Oneonta, NY 13820. (607) 432–6845. **Type of Business:** Restaurant. **Sells:** "An American Bistro" serving wholefood cooking, vegetarian, chicken, and fish. Vegan options are available. **Organic?** Asserted 50% organic, but this varies seasonally. **Specialties:** Daily, seasonal specials and soups (always vegetarian). **Prices:** Entrees—Lunch, $3.45-$6.95; Dinner, $3.45-$12.95. **Hours:** M 11-3:30 p.m., Tues.-Sat. 11–12, limited menu

after 9 p.m. **Reservations:** Possible. 75% non-smoking. **Credit:** V M AE, minimum for credit is $5.

Oyster Bay, **The Right Stuff,** 15 West Main St., Oyster Bay, NY 11771. (516) 922–2604. **Type of Business:** Retail store. **Sells to:** The public. **Sells:** A full line of wholefood grocery items and fresh produce. **Organic?** Fresh produce 100% organic, processed goods 85%. **Credit:** AE. **Hours:** M-F 10–7, Th 10–7:30, Sat. 10–6, Sun. 10:30–430.

Penn Yan, **Spring Wheat,** Terrie Sautter, 108 Elm St., Penn Yan, NY 14527. (315) 536–7981. **Type of Business:** Retail store. **Sells to:** The public. **Sells:** Grains, dried fruits, cereals, breads, oils, flours, fruit juices, dairy products: yogurts and cheese (over 40 types), beans, pastas, nuts and nut butters (peanut, almond, cashew), rice, soy products, spices, herbs, and teas. **Organic?** 8% organic. **Credit:** V M (in the process). **Prices:** Discount: 15% over cost for one whole unit: bag, box, case. 25% over cost for split package. **Hours:** M-F 9:30–5:30, Sat. 9:30–3, Closed Sundays. **Comments:** A small natural food store in a small, rural community. Participates every Saturday in local Farm Market. They will do catering for groups from 2 people to 200.

Rochester, **Lori's Natural Foods Center, Inc.,** 900 Jerfferson Rd., Rochester, NY 14623. (716) 424–2323. **Type of Business:** Retail store. **Sells to:** The public. **Sells:** A wide range of wholefood groceries. **Organic?** 30–35% organic for processed foods (Farm Verified Organic, Natural Organic Farmers Association). **Hours:** Tu-W 7:30–3:30, Th 7:30–6, F 7:30–6:30, Sat. 7:30–1:30, Closed Sunday and Monday. **Comments:** Specializes in assisting customers with food allergies. They carry many hard-to-find items.

Rockville Centre, **Natural Choice,** 287 Merrick Rd., Rockville Centre, NY 11570. (516) 766–1703. **Type of Business:** Retail store. **Sells to:** The public. **Sells:** A complete range of natural grocery items and fresh organic produce. **Organic?** Fresh produce 100% organic (certified by Organic Crop Improvement Association, Farm Verified Organic), other goods, 50%. **Prices:** 10% off bulk and case orders. **Hours:** M-Th 10–6, F-Sat. 10–9. **Comments:** This is a young store (in business for two years) with a very enthusiastic attitude toward the community it serves. They buy organic products whenever possible.

Sag Harbor, **Provisions,** Main St., Sag Harbor, NY 11963. (516) 725–2666. **Type of Business:** Retail store and Cafe. **Sells:** A wide range of wholefood items and the largest selection of organic produce on the east end of Long Island. **Cafe Specialties:** Soups, sandwiches, whole wheat pancakes with maple syrup, fresh carrot juice, and cheeses. **Organic?** 100% of produce (certified by Organic Crop Improvement Association, Farm Verified Organic, Natural Organic Farmers Association, California Certified Organic Farmers, or Demeter) and 40% of processed goods. **Credit:** AE. **Prices:** 10% discount on bulk orders. **Hours:** (Winter) M-Sat. 8–7, Sun. 9–5; open later in the evenings in summer.♥

Schenectady, **Earthly Delights Natural Foods, Inc.,** 162 Jay St., Schenectady, NY 12305. (518) 372-7580. **Type of Business:** Retail store. **Sells to:** The public. **Sells:** A wide range of wholefood grocery items with a selection of fresh fruit and vegetables. **Organic?** Produce 100% organic, certified by Farm Verified Organic, Demeter/Bio-dynamic, processed goods asserted to be 50% organic. **Prices:** 10% discount on a case. **Hours:** M-Sat. 9–5:30, Th till 9 p.m. **Comments:** Offers homemade soups, salads, and sandwiches, 20 different types of coffee plus complete macrobiotic section.

Scotia, **Mothers Cupboard, Inc.,** 309 Mohawk Ave., Scotia, NY 12302. (518) 372-2863. **Type of Business:** Retail store. **Sells to:** The public. **Sells:** A full line of wholefood grocery items, plus a selection of fresh produce. **Organic?** Produce certified by Farm Verified Organic. **Credit:** Planned. **Hours:** M-F 10–5:30, Th 10–7, Sat. 10–5. **Comments:** A gourmet health food store, selling gourmet pastas and custom-made gift baskets. They cater to the needs of the individual and will special-order items.

Suffern, **Natura Whole Food Market,** 41 Lafayette Ave., Suffern, NY 10901. (914) 357-9200. **Type of Business:** Retail store and Cafe. **Sells to:** The public. **Sells:** A good range of wholefoods and fresh produce. **Organic?** Estimated 35–40% organically grown produce, 25% for processed food. **Credit:** None. **Prices:** 10% discount on case orders. **Hours:** M-Th 9:30–6, F 9:30–7.

Trumansburg, **MacDonald Farm,** Thomas MacDonald, RD1, Trumansburg, NY 14886. (607) 387-6632. **Type of Business:** Grower. **Sells to:** Mainly retailers and distributors. **Sells:** Whole grains (rye), fresh vegetables (winter vegetables, beets, carrots), pickles from their own cucumbers, sauerkraut from their own cabbage, celtic salt. **Organic?** Asserted organic (100%).

Westport, **Champlain Valley Milling,** Samuel M. Sherman, President, PO Box 454, 110 Pleasant St., Westport, NY 12993. (518) 962-4711 Fax: (518) 962-8799. **Type of Business:** Manufacturer, broker to Purity Foods Inc., and retail store. **Sells to:** The general public. **Sells:** Whole grain flours (rye, whole wheat, durum, organic white bread, organic, white pastry, red and white bulgur, corn, couscous, wheat, soy flour. **Organic?** Asserted 75% organic, uncertified. **Credit:** None. **Prices:** Special discounts to wholesalers and on whole trailerloads. **Hours:** M-F 9–3:30. **Shipping:** Truck service to New England and New York State and UPS to NYC and the rest of the USA. Deliveries are every other week into New England. **Minimum Order:** 2,000 lbs. for delivery, no minimum if picked up by the buyer. **Catalogue Available?** Yes.

Woodbury, **Earth's Bounty,** 8031-33 Jericho Tpke., Woodbury, NY 11797. (516) 364-1171. **Type of Business:** Retail store. **Sells to:** The public. **Sells:** A very impressive array of natural groceries and fresh organic produce. **Organic?** Fresh produce 100% organic (certified by Organic Crop Improvement Association, Farm Verified Organic, Natural Organic Farmers Association, Demeter/Biodynamic), other goods, 50%. **Credit:** No. **Prices:** 10% discount on cases. **Hours:** M-Sat. 10–6, Th 10–6:30. **Comments:** Their first choice is always organic. 95% of their fruit juices are organic, all grains and flours. They sell nothing with refined white sugar, white flour or fructose.

Woodstock, **Sunflower Natural Foods,** Bradley Meadows Plaza, Woodstock, NY 12498. (914) 679-5361. **Type of Business:** Retail store. **Sells to:** The public. **Sells:** A full line of wholefoods and organic fresh produce. **Organic?** Fresh produce, 60% organic (Farm Verified Organic). Processed goods, 20–30%. **Credit:** None. **Hours:** M-Sat., 9–9, Sun., 10–7.

Yorktown, **Earthlight Food,** 100 Triangle Center, Yorktown, NY 10598. (914) 962-4462. **Type of Business:** Retail store. **Sells to:** The public. **Sells:** An impressive array of natural grocery items and fresh produce. **Organic?** 100% organic for produce (Organic Crop Improvement Association, Farm Verified Organic), 20% for processed goods. **Credit:** None. **Prices:** 10% discount for all case orders. **Hours:** M-W 10–6, Th-F 10–8, Sat. 9–5, Sunday closed. **Comments:** "The largest natural-food store in Westchester County."

NC

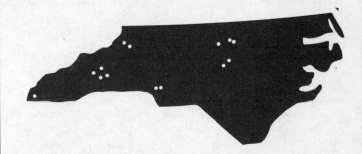

North Carolina

Asheville, **Fairglen Farms,** Jim Smith, W.N.C. Farmers Mkt., 570 Brevard Rd., Asheville, NC 28806. (704) 252-4414. **Type of Business:** Growers—a collection of small mountain farms in western North Carolina. **Sells to:** Retailers. **Sells:** Herbs and spices (fresh culinary, fresh ginger), fresh vegetables. **Organic?** Certified organic (Carolina Farm Stewardship).

Blowing Rock, **Ambrosia Health Products,** Box 887, Blowing Rock, NC 28605. (704) 295-3013. **Type of Business:** Retail store. **Sells to:** The public. **Sells:** A range of wholefood groceries and selected fresh produce. **Organic?** Fresh produce 90% organic (certified by Farm Verified Organic), other goods, 70%. **Credit:** V M. **Prices:** 20% discount on orders of $100 or more. **Hours:** 10–6. **Shipping:** Credit card and phone orders O.K. **Catalogue Available?** In the works.

Boone, **Bare Essentials,** Mary Underwood, 200 W King St., Boone, NC 28607. (704) 264-5220. **Type of Business:** Retailer. **Sells to:** Public. **Sells:** Asserted 10–20% organic. Beans, beverages, breads, candy, cereals, dairy products, flour, fresh and dried fruit, nutd and nut butters, pasta, rice, soy products, salsa, grains, poultry, spices and fresh vegetables. **Organic?** Rely on the certification of suppliers. **Credit:** V M. **Prices:** 10% discount on full case purchases. **Hours:** M-Sat., 10–6.

Charlotte, **Berrybrook Farm Natural Foods,** Gayle Dover, 1257 East Blvd., Charlotte, NC 28203. (704) 334–6528. **Type of Business:** Retailer. **Sells to:** The public. **Sells:** 15–20% of the goods are organic. They sell most products that would be stocked by a good supermarket as well as a large range of beans and peas, cheeses, oils (including specialties like almond, apricot, advocado and walnut) and organic fruit juices. **Organic?** Member of the Carolina Farm Stewardship Association. **Credit:** V M. **Prices:** 10% discount on full bags or cases. **Hours:** M-Sat. 9:30–6.

Charlotte, **People's Natural Foods,** Dick Harrell, 617 S Sharon Amity Rd., Charlotte, NC 28211. (704) 364–1919. **Type of Business:** Restaurant and retail store. **Sells:** The restaurant serves soups, salads, whole wheat sandwiches, filled croissants, Mexican favorites, melts, quiche and whole wheat pizzas. **Organic?** 20–25% of the food served is asserted organic (including 100% of the produce). **Specialties:** Quiches, filled jumbo Idaho bakers and macrobiotic rice specialities. **Prices:** $2–$5. **Hours:** Restaurant: M-Sat. 11–5; Retail: M-Sat., 9:30–6. **Reservations:** Not possible. 100% smoking. **Credit:** V M.

Durham, **New American Food Co,** David Johnson, PO Box 3206, Durham, NC 27705. (919) 682–9210. **Type of Business:** Mail-order distributor. **Sells to:** Public. **Sells:** Baked goods, beans, beverages, candy, cereals, whole wheat flour, apple juice, applesauce, nuts (peanuts, cashews and almonds), oils, pasta, rice, soy products and salsa. **Organic?** Asserted 60% organic, rely on the certification of suppliers. **Credit:** V M AE. **Prices:** No discount for bulk. **Hours:** 24 hours. **Minimum Order:** None. **Catalogue Available?** Yes.

Durham, **Wellspring Grocery,** Lex Alexander, 737 9th St., Durham, NC 27705. (919) 286–2290. **Type of Business:** Retail store. **Sells to:** The general public. **Sells:** All the food products you would expect a good grocery store to stock. 20% organic. **Organic?** They assert their produce is grown by the standards of the Organic Foods Production Association of North America. **Credit:** V M. **Prices:** No discount for bulk. **Hours:** M-Sat. 9–8, Sun. 10–7. **Catalogue Available?** No.

Fletcher, **Homestead Farms,** Box 5410 Naples Rd., Fletcher, NC 28732. (704) 684–1155. **Type of Business:** Retail store. **Sells to:** The public. **Sells:** A wide range of wholefood groceries with some fresh produce. **Organic?** Fresh produce asserted 95% organic, other goods, 25%. **Credit:** V M AE. **Prices:** Discounts available. **Hours:** 9–6.

Hillsborough, **Regulator Cafe,** John Troy, 108 S Churton St., Hillsborough, NC 27278. (919) 732–5600. **Type of Business:** Restaurant. **Sells:** New American cuisine, mainly vegetarian, with vegan and macrobiotic options.

Organic? Asserted 30% organic. Water filtered. **Specialties:** Vegetarian, fresh seafood and soyfoods. **Prices:** Entrees range from $7 to $13. **Hours:** Lunch, 11:30–2:30; Dinner, 6–9:30. **Reservations:** Possible. 30% nonsmoking. **Credit:** V M AE.

Lynn, **Nature's Storehouse,** Doug or Shelly Woodward, Highway 108, POBox 69, Lynn, NC 28750. (704) 859–6356. **Type of Business:** Retailer and mail-order distributor (breads only). **Sells to:** Public. **Sells:** Freshly baked breads, beans, beverages, cereals, dairy products, fresh blueberries, apples and apple juice, dried fruit, nuts, freshly ground peanut butter, oils, rice, soy products, grains, spices, alfalfa and sprouts. **Organic?** Asserted 80% organic overall. Rely on certification of suppliers. **Credit:** None. **Prices:** Discounts for bulk. **Hours:** M-F 8–5, Sat. 8–12. **Shipping:** Continental USA by overnight express as breads have no preservatives. **Minimum Order:** 10 loaves. **Catalogue Available?** Yes.

Murphy, **The Whole Store,** 211 Tennessee St., Murphy, NC 28906. (704) 837–3552. **Type of Business:** Retail grocery and book store. **Sells to:** The public. **Sells:** A good range of natural grocery items, with some seasonal fresh produce. **Organic?** 100% organic fresh produce (Organic Crop Improvement Association). Processed goods are approximately 80% organic. **Credit:** V M. **Prices:** 20% discount for bulk orders. 10% discount for senior customers. **Hours:** M-F 10–5:30, Sat. 10–3:30. **Catalogue Available?** Soon. **Comments:** Pronounced "story," the store has grown rapidly since its September 1988 opening. They claim to have the largest selection of natural foods in a 100–mile radius (their natural soft-drink selection is particularly good). They also offer free herbal tea to shoppers.

Raleigh, **Irregardless Cafe,** 901 W Morgan St., Raleigh, NC 27603. (919) 833–9920. **Type of Business:** Restaurant. **Sells:** Vegetarian, seafood and poultry dishes, with daily menu changes. Vegan and macrobiotic options are available. **Organic?** No organic claims. Water is filtered **Prices:** Entrees range from $9 to $12. **Hours:** M-F, lunch, 11:30–2:15; M-Sat., dinner, 5:30–9:30; Sun. brunch, 10–2. **Reservations:** Not possible. 100% non-smoking. **Credit:** V M. **Commendations:** Voted the best restaurant in the Triangle by *Spectator* magazine, for the last 5 years.

Raleigh, **Noah's Co-op Grocery,** Bart Hamburg, PO Box 12523, Raleigh, NC 27603. (919) 834–5056. **Type of Business:** Retailer and co-op/buying club. **Sells to:** Members and the public. **Sells:** Baked goods, processed beans, beverages, breads, candy, cereals, dairy products, flour, processed fruit, dried fruit, nuts and nut butters, oils, pasta, rice, soy products, salsa, fresh fruit and vegetables, spices and grains. **Organic?** Asserted 75% organic. **Organic?** Rely on the certification of suppliers. **Credit:** None. **Prices:** 15% above wholesale discount for bulk orders. **Hours:** M-F 10–8, Sat. 10–6, Sun. 1–6.

Waynesville, **Zoolie's Natural Food Market, Inc.,** 208 Haywood Square, PO Box 869, Waynesville, NC 28786. (704) 452–3663. **Type of Business:** Retail store. **Sells to:** The public. **Sells:** Baked goods, fresh beans, beverages, candy, cereals, dairy products, flour, processed and fresh dried fruit, meats, fresh nuts and nut butters, oils, pasta, rice, soy products, grains, spices. **Organic?** No organic claims. **Credit:** V M AE. **Prices:** Discount for case lots. **Hours:** M-F 9:30-6, Sat. 9:30-5. **Shipping:** Immediate, mail or UPS.

ND

North Dakota

Fargo, **Tochi Products,** 1111 2nd Ave. N, Fargo, ND 58102. (701) 232-7700. **Type of Business:** Retail store. **Sells to:** The public. **Sells:** A full line of natural groceries with fresh vegetables in season. **Organic?** Fresh produce 100% organic (Organic Crop Improvement Association, Farm Verified Organic). Other items, 25%. **Credit:** None. **Prices:** Discounts for 25-50 lb. orders. **Hours:** M-W, F-Sat. 10-6, Th 10-8, Sunday closed. **Comments:** In business 18 years. Also sells books and herbs.

OH

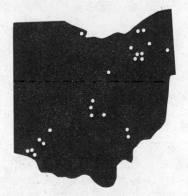

Ohio

Akron, **Cooperative Market,** Steve Torma, 590 West Market St., Akron, OH 44303. (216) 762-2667. **Type of Business:** Retailer and Cooperative buying club. **Sells to:** The general public. **Sells:** Natural foods, herbs, produce, baked goods and supplements. 10% of the goods are asserted to be organic (mainly meat, cheese, beans, flour and rice). **Organic?** They trust, and rely on, the certification claims of their suppliers, with whom they have had a long business relationship (15 years). **Credit:** None. **Prices:** Discount to members. **Hours:** M-Sat., 10-6 (late opening on Thursday, until 8). **Catalogue Available?** No.

Akron, **Millstream Natural Health Supplies,** Jonathan D. Miller, 1310-A E Tallmadge Ave., Akron, OH 44310. (216) 630-2700. **Type of Business:** Broker and distributor to health food stores and co-ops. Also a mail-order distributor and retailer. **Sells to:** Retailers and the general public. **Sells:** Baked goods, condiments, dairy products, including eggs and a wide variety of cheeses, dried beans, dried fruit, fresh fruit, whole grains, flours and meals, processed grain products, herbs and spices, juices, nut and nut butters, oils, seeds, soy products, sweeteners, teas, fresh vegetables. **Organic?** Asserted 90% organic. They rely on the certification claims of their suppliers. **Credit:** None. **Prices:** An 8% discount is available on full bags and cases and 6% on half bags or cases. **Hours:** M-W, 10-5; Th-F, 10-7; Sat., 10-4. **Shipping:** They do not send the most perishable items (e.g. lettuce, spinach, broccoli) more than two shipping days away from May through to mid-October. **Minimum Order:** None. **Catalogue Available?** Yes.

Akron, **Mustard Seed Market,** Phillip Nabors, 3885 W Market St. (Rt.18), Akron, OH 44313. (216) 867-3833. **Type of Business:** Restaurant and retail store. **Sells:** A wide variety of gourmet natural foods sold in the store. The restaurant offers vegetarian, vegan and macrobiotic options. **Organic?** Asserted 30% organic. **Prices:** Entrees— $3.95-$11.95. **Hours:** M-Sat. 9-9, Sun. 10-6. **Reservations:** Possible. 100% non-smoking. **Credit:** V M.♦

Amesville, **New Morning Farm,** Joan Kraynanski, Rt. 1 Box 25, Amesville, OH 4571. (614) 448-4021. **Type of Business:** Grower. **Sells to:** Retailers, distributors, restaurants and the public (mail order and through a Saturday market in Athens, Ohio from June to November). **Sells:** Fresh strawberries, dried tofu pasta, fresh garlic, green beans and squash, and spicy pastas made with organic flour. **Organic?** Certified by Organic Ecological Food and Farm Association. **Credit:** None. **Hours:** 7-7. **Shipping:** Do not deliver to Canada. 14 days maximum delivery time on order. **Catalogue Available?** Yes.

Cincinnati, **Clifton Natural Foods,** Aline Kuhl, 207 W McMillan St., Cincinnati, OH 45219. (513) 651-5288. **Type of Business:** Retail store. **Sells to:** The public. **Sells:** A very large selection of processed and fresh produce, which is organic whenever possible. Their specialty is vegetarian chili. **Organic?** 75% organic. **Credit:** V M **Prices:** 15% discount for bulk dry goods, 10% discount for bulk refrigerated and frozen goods. **Hours:** M-Sat. 10-7, Sun. 11-4. **Comments:** Features a full service deli/juice bar serving fresh hot/cold soups (vegetarian) sandwiches, salads, fresh carrot juice, made to order smoothies, protein shakes, hot organic coffee and "fresh daily" eggless muffins.

Cincinnati, **New World Foodshop and Restaurant,** Sherry Tizzano, 347 Ludlow Ave., Cincinnati, OH 45220. (513) 861-1101. **Type of Business:** Restaurant and retail store. **Sells:** Continental breakfast, soups, salads, omelets, sandwiches, rice, noodles and vegetables. Vegetarian, vegan and macrobiotic options available. **Organic?** Asserted 60% organic. Member, National Nutritional Foods

Association. Water is filtered. **Specialties:** Macrobiotic soups, brown rice and vegetables, vegeburger and muffins. **Prices:** Entrees—$3-$6. **Hours:** M-F 10-8:30, Sat. 10-7, Sun. 11-5. **Reservations:** Possible. 100% non-smoking. **Credit:** None. **Commendations:** *East West* magazine, *Vegetarian Times*.

Cincinnati, **Wooden Shoe Gardens,** David Rosenberg, 5115 Wooden Shoe Lane, Cincinnati, OH 45232. (513) 681-4574. **Type of Business:** Broker, retail store and wholesale distributor. **Sells to:** Retailers and the general public. **Sells:** Organically grown produce and horticultural supplies. **Organic?** Organic (100%), affiliated with Ohio Ecological Food and Farm Association. **Credit:** None. **Prices:** Special prices for bulk orders. **Hours:** W 1-7, Th 9-1, Sun. 10-3.

Clarksville, **Todd's Fork Creek Company,** 885 N George Rd., Clarksville, OH 45113. (513) 289-2040. **Type of Business:** Grower, miller, retailer, and mail-order distributor. **Sells to:** Retailers, and the public. **Sells:** Organic flours (soy, wheat), soft white wheat, yellow, red, blue, and white corn **Organic?** 100% organic, Ohio Ecological Food and Farm Association certified. **Hours:** Call for apointment. **Minimum Order:** None. **Catalogue Available?** Yes.

Cleveland, **Cleveland Food Co-op,** 11702 Euclid Ave., Cleveland, OH 44106. **Type of Business:** Retail store and cooperative. **Sells to:** Co-op members and the public (30% surcharge that goes toward membership if you decide to join). **Sells:** A full range of wholefood grocery items and fresh organic produce. They also have an in-house kitchen that makes "carry-out" goods that include macrobiotic sweets and entrees. **Organic?** Produce 20% organic in summer, about 10% in winter (Ohio Ecological Food and Farm Association); Processed goods about 20%. **Credit:** None. **Prices:** 10% off case orders. **Hours:** M-F 9-8, Sat. 9-5, Sun. 10-5. **Comments:** There is a $5 non-refundable membership fee and $20 ($10 for senior citizens) refundable deposit required to join. They are very ecologically conscious and promote recycling. They are also socially conscious and regularly donate food to the poor.♥♦

Cleveland Heights, **The Noble Bean,** Lynne McAlister, 2159 Lee Rd., Cleveland Heights, OH 44118. (216) 397-0202. **Type of Business:** Restaurant, delicatessen and producer of tempeh. **Sells:** Purely vegan food (except cheese—non-dairy is available), with a lot of familiar "meat" dishes made with soy products, particularly tempeh, which is made by the company and supplied to health food stores throughout the area. There are dishes suited to macrobiotic eaters, and sugarless desserts for diabetics to enjoy. **Organic?** Asserted 75% organic, including organic coffee. **Specialties:** Tempeh fingers served over brown rice (tastes like chicken fingers), soysage and soysage balls (like Swedish meatballs). **Prices:** Entrees range from $5.95 to $8.95. **Hours:** Lunch: M-Sat. 11:30-3, Dinner: M-Th 5-9, Fri-Sat. 5-10. **Reservations:** Recommended. 100% non-smoking. **Credit:** None. **Commendations:** Most recently, *The Plain Dealer*, June 23, 1989; *Spotlight* magazine, May, 1989; *Cablevision Magazine*.♦

Columbus, **Federation of Ohio River Cooperatives,** Mark Novak, Linda Grove, 320 Outerbelt St., Columbus, OH 43213. (614) 861-2446. **Type of Business:** Distributor. **Sells to:** Retailers, Markets. **Sells:** Coffee, condiments, dairy products, dried beans, dried fruit, fresh fruit, whole grains, flours and meals, processed grain products (pasta), herbs, juices, meats and eggs, oils, seeds, soy products, sweeteners, fresh vegetables. **Organic?** Asserted organic (25%). **Minimum Order:** $600. Free delivery outside of Franklin Co., OH; $200 free delivery inside Franklin Co.

Columbus, **Bexley Natural Food Coop,** Vivian Stockman, 508 N Cassady Ave., Columbus, OH 43209. (614) 252-3951. **Type of Business:** Retail co-op. **Sells to:** The public. **Sells:** A variety of baked goods, beans, beverages (including no-sugar sodas and no-alcohol wines), breads, candy, cereals, dairy products (including low-fat, low-salt cheeses), flour, fruit, meats (Amish chicken, Albacore tuna), nuts, oils, pasta, rice, soy products, vegetables and spices. **Organic?** Asserted about 60% organic, Member of NNFA. **Credit:** None. **Prices:** No discount for bulk. Members work for shelf prices, non-members and non-working members pay a surcharge. **Hours:** M 9-8, T 9-5, W 9-8:30, Th 9-8:30, F 9-6, Sat. 10-5.

Crestline, **Beam Road Berry Farm and Supply,** Saundra "Lyn" Chapis, 5493 Beam Rd., Crestline, OH 44827. (419) 683-2136. **Type of Business:** Grower. **Sells to:** Public only. **Sells:** Fruits: blueberries, grapes, raspberries. Vegetables: asparagus, corn, tomatoes. **Organic?** 100% certified by Ohio Ecological Food and Farm Association. **Credit:** V M. **Hours:** March 15 through Oct 15 10 a.m.-6 p.m. **Comments:** They cultivate 3 acres (certified each year) and customers pick their own produce.

Cuyahoga Falls, **Zardow's Health Foods,** 2425 State Rd., Cuyahoga Falls, OH 44223. (216) 929-2415. **Type of Business:** Retailer. **Sells to:** The public. **Sells:** A wide variety of goods from anazi beans to organic meat to yogurt. **Organic?** Asserted 30-40% organic, but "growing with the industry." **Credit:** V M D. **Prices:** Reduced prices for bulk orders. **Hours:** 10-6 M-Sat. **Comments:** They have been in business over 30 years and also carry juices, books, and a complete line of skin care items.

Hiram, **Silver Creek Farm,** Molly and Ted Bartlett, 7097 Allyn Rd., Hiram, OH 44234. (216) 569-3487, (216) 569-4381. **Type of Business:** Grower. **Sells to:** Retailers, restaurants and the public (mail order and through a market at W 9th and St. Clair Ave., Warehouse District, Cleveland from June to October). **Sells:** Fresh blueberries, popcorn, lamb, poultry, basil, dill, mushrooms, peppers, squash, heirloom tomatoes, shallots, shiitake mushrooms and honey. **Organic?** 60% organic. Certified by Ohio Ecological Food and Farm Association. **Credit:** None. **Hours:** 8-6. **Minimum Order:** None. **Catalogue Available?** Yes. **Comments:** This is a specialty crop farm and will grow whatever individuals or the market desires.

Litchfield, **Infinite Garden Farm,** Larry Luschek, 8102 Crow Road, Litchfield, OH 44253. (216) 725-6762. **Type of Business:** Grower. **Sells to:** Retailers, Restaurants and the general public. **Sells:** Broccoli, cabbage, cauliflower, eggplant, garlic, green beans, lettuce, peppers, potatoes and tomatoes. **Organic?** Certified 90% organic by Ohio Ecological Food and Farm Association. **Credit:** None. **Hours:** Goods sold through a farm shop and a market at West 9th and St. Clair, Cleveland, Ohio, July-Oct. **Shipping:** Goods only sold locally, no shipping. **Minimum Order:** None. **Catalogue Available?** No.

Morrow, **Magella Homestead,** Karen Magella, 8455 US 22 and 3, Morrow, OH 45152. (513) 289-2436. **Type of Business:** Grower and pick-your-own organic farm. **Sells to:** The public. **Sells:** Beans (lima and split green), goose egg/oatmeal cookies, lamb, poultry (goose, duck, turkey), spices, fresh vegetables, eggs (duck, goose, turkey, chicken) and pick your fruit (blackberries, raspberries, strawberries, melons, grapes and, in 1991, cherries, apples, peaches and pears). **Organic?** Asserted only, uncertified because of the cost, they use Ohio Ecological Food and Farm Association standards. **Credit:** None. **Hours:** 9-9. **Shipping:** Goods delivered directly only in the local area. **Minimum Order:** None. **Catalogue Available?** Yes.

Port Clinton, **Karen Messner,** 230 Alice St., Port Clinton, OH 43452. (419) 734-4296. **Type of Business:** Grower. **Sells to:** Retailers and the public. **Sells:** Beans (green, lima, navy, split green), applesauce, green tomato mincemeat, dried apples, fresh apples, grapes, melons, strawberries and raspberries, hay, wheat, spices and fresh vegetables. **Organic?** Asserted 100% organic, soon to be certified by Ohio Ecological Food and Farm Association. **Credit:** None. **Hours:** 8-8. **Shipping:** Local deliveries within a 10-mile area. **Minimum Order:** Varies. **Catalogue Available?** No.

Rockbridge, **Rockbridge Farms,** Mark McClelland, 11464 Cantwell Cliff, Rockbridge, OH 43149. (614) 385-4308. **Type of Business:** Grower and retailer. **Sells to:** Restaurants and the general public. **Sells:** Beets, broccoli, cabbage, carrots, cauliflower, celery, corn, cucumbers, eggplant, garlic, lima beans, lettuce, onions, okra, peas, peppers, potatoes, radishes, spinach, tomatoes, turnips and zucchini. **Organic?** Certified 100% organic by Ohio Ecological Food and Farm Association. **Credit:** None. **Hours:** As well as through the farm shop, goods are sold at a Saturday market in Worthington, Ohio, from mid-May to the end of October. **Minimum Order:** None.

Roseville, **Rober L. Forgrave,** 8185 A Butcher Knife Road, Roseville, OH 43777. (614) 849-2249. **Type of Business:** Organic farm. **Sells to:** Mainly retailers and the public through farmers' markets (Saturdays in Lancaster and Lanesville, May-October). **Sells:** Green beans, lima beans, chestnuts, broccoli, cabbage, cauliflower, corn, garlic, lettuce, onions, peppers, squash, tomatoes, and zucchini. **Organic?** Asserted 100% organic. **Credit:** None.

Tippecanoe, **Riverbend Farm,** Gene Sacha, 82900 Tippecanoe Rd., Tippecanoe, OH 44699. (614) 922-4691. **Type of Business:** Grower. **Sells to:** The public pick-your-own and a membership club. **Sells:** Blueberries, blackberries, raspberries, strawberries, corn, peppers, pumpkins, squash,

tomatoes, hay and beef. **Organic?** Asserted 100% organic. They are not certified, but are members of OEFFA (Ohio Ecological Food and Farm Association). **Credit:** None. **Comments:** The organic beef and hay is sold under the name of Windy Knoll Farm.

Yellow Springs, **Wind's Cafe,** Mary Kay Smith, 230 Xenia Ave., Yellow Springs, OH 45387. (513) 767-1144. **Type of Business:** Restaurant. **Sells:** A menu that changes monthly and always has at least one vegetarian entree, often vegan. **Organic?** Asserted 20% organic. Water filterd. **Specialties:** Scrambled tofu at lunch. **Prices:** Entrees range from $9 to $16. **Hours:** M-Sat. 11:30-2, 6-10; Sun. 10-2. **Reservations:** Possible for parties of 7 or more. 30% non-smoking. **Credit:** V M. **Commendations:** Listed as one of the ten best restaurants in the Dayton area, 1988 and 1989.

Youngstown, **Good Food Co-op,** Kate Cullum, Manager, 62 Pyat St., Youngstown, OH 44502. (216) 747-9368. **Type of Business:** Retail store and co-op. **Sells to:** The public directly. **Sells:** An extensive variety of organic produce and grocery items including low sodium and nitrate-free items. **Organic?** They assert that 50% of the goods they sell are organically grown and processed. **Credit:** None. **Prices:** 2% discounts on bulk orders. **Hours:** M, Tu, W, F 10:30-6, Th 10:30-8, Sat. 9-6. **Comments:** While they do have a small supplement section, they emphasize that they specialize in whole, natural, and organic *foods.*♥

OK

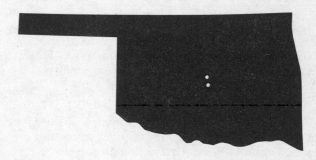

Oklahoma

Norman, **The Earth Natural Foods,** Tempie Nichols, 309 S Flood, Norman, OK 73069. (405) 364-3551. **Type of Business:** Restaurant and retail store. **Sells:** Sandwiches, baked potatoes, tacos, rice, soups, salads, bread, smoothies and other beverages. **Organic?** As much as possible. Water is filtered. **Specialties:** Special vegetarian dish in addition to main menu each day. Vegetarian, vegan and macrobiotic dishes are available. **Prices:** $1.50-$4.50 **Hours:** M-F 10-7, Sat. 10-6, Sun. 1-5. **Reservations:** Not accepted. 100% No smoking. **Credit:** V M.

Oklahoma City, **The Earth Natural Foods,** Tempie Nichols, 1101 NW 49th (and Western), Oklahoma City, OK 73118. (405) 840-0502. **Type of Business:** Retail store and deli. **Sells:** Sandwiches, baked potatoes, tacos, rice, soups, salads, bread, smoothies and other beverages. **Organic?** Asserted 100% organic in the produce case; 1% in deli. Water is filtered. **Specialties:** Special vegetarian dish in addition to main menu each day. Vegetarian, vegan and macrobiotic dishes are available. **Prices:** $1.50–$4.75 **Hours:** M-F 10–6:30, Sat. 10–5, Sun. 1–5. **Reservations:** Possible for groups of 6 or more. 100% no smoking. **Credit:** V M.

OR

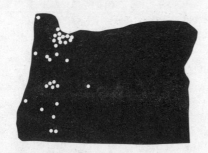

Oregon

Ashland, **Ashland Community Food Store,** 37 Third St., Ashland, OR 97520. (503) 482-2237. **Type of Business:** Retail store. **Sells to:** Retailers and the general public. **Sells:** More than 50% organic. Baked goods, beans, beverages, breads, confections, cereals, dairy products, flour, fruit (dried, fresh, processed and juices), nuts, oils, pasta, rice, soy, salsa, canned tomatoes, grains, frozen poultry and seafood, spices and fresh vegetables. **Organic?** Products certified by Oregon Tilth and California Certified Organic Farmers. **Credit:** None. **Prices:** Discount for bulk orders is generally 15% above cost price. **Hours:** 9–8. **Minimum Order:** By the case or bag generally.♦

Ashland, **North Light Vegetarian Restaurant,** 36 South 2nd St., Ashland, OR 97520. (503) 482-9463. **Type of Business:** Restaurant. **Sells:** Vegetarian, with vegan and macrobiotic options. **Organic?** 85% organic. They prefer to use organic whenever possible, unless it is not cost effective. **Specialties:** Vegan menu with cheese option on some dishes. International Gourmet Cuisine: Thai, Mexican, Indian (Eastern and American), etc. **Prices:** $5.50–$7.25 for entrees. **Hours:** Daily, 8 a.m.–9 p.m. **Reservations:** Not possible. **Credit:** V M. **Comments:** Offers musical entertainment.

Astoria, **The Community Store,** Beth Kandell, 1389 Duane St., Astoria, ON 97103. (503) 325-0027. **Type of Business:** Retail store and co-op. **Sells to:** Members and the public. **Sells:** A wide variety of fresh produce and processed foods, specializing in fresh fruit, fresh dried fruit, and fresh flours. **Organic?** Member of Oregon Tilth. 50% organic. **Prices:** Members "mark-up" is half "shelf" mark up. Volunteer members get an even better break. **Hours:** M-Sat. 10–6. **Catalogue Available?** Yes, but without price

list. **Comments:** Specialize in as much organically grown bulk food as they can get.

Bend, **Good Food Store,** 1124 NW Newport Ave., Bend, OR 97701. (503) 389-6588. **Type of Business:** Retail store. **Sells to:** The public. **Sells:** A full range of natural groceries and fresh produce. **Organic?** asserted 40% organic. **Credit:** None. **Hours:** M-Sat. 9:30–6:30.

Corvallis, **First Alternative, Inc.,** 1007 SE Third St., Covallis, OR 97333. (503) 753-3115. **Type of Business:** Retail store. **Sells to:** The public. **Sells:** A comprehensive array of natural groceries and fresh produce. **Organic?** Asserted 20% organic. **Credit:** None. **Prices:** 4% discount for case or bag buy. **Hours:** M-Sat. 9–9, Sun. 11–8.

Corvallis, **Nearly Normals,** 109 NW 15th St., Corvallis, OR 97330. (503) 753-0791. **Type of Business:** Restaurant. **Sells:** "Gonzo" vegetarian cuisine. Soups, salads, sandwiches, Mexican and other ethnic entrees, burgers, omelets and breakfast served all day. There is a children's menu, and vegan and macrobiotic options are available. **Organic?** Asserted 50–75% organic. Filtered water. **Specialties:** Falafel, sunburgers, burritos, creative nightly specials, organic honey lemonade and frozen fruit smoothies. **Prices:** Entrees range from $3–$6.25. **Hours:** M-F, 8–9; Sat., 9–9. **Reservations:** Possible. 100% non-smoking. **Credit:** None.♦

Eugene, **Cowboy Produce,** Pat J. Leonard, 444 Lincoln St., Eugene, OR 97401. (503) 343-6581, California address: 2999 Hose Rd., Imperial, CA 92251. (619) 355-1810. **Type of Business:** Distributor. **Sells to:** Retailers. **Sells:** Fresh vegetables (row-crop vegetables, carrots, winter hard squash, cantaloupes, sharlyn, juan canary, casaba, honeydew, orange flesh honeydew, watermelon, broccoli, cauliflower). **Organic?** Certified organic (100%—California Certified Organic Farmers). **Minimum Order:** Pallet sales only.

Eugene, **Food Connection,** 1060 Green Acres Rd., Eugene, OR 97401. (503) 344-1901. **Type of Business:** Supermarket. **Sells:** Some organic produce (10–20% of total). **Organic?** Produce locally grown and distributed by Organically Grown Co-op.

Eugene, **Friendly Foods & Deli,** Gerry Segal, 2757 Friendly St., Eugene, OR 97405. (503) 683-2079. **Type of Business:** Retail store. **Sells to:** The public. **Sells:** Baked goods, fresh beans, fresh beverages, breads, candy, cereals, fresh dairy products, flour, processed, dried, and fresh fruit, fresh meats, oils, nuts and nut butters, pasta, rice, fresh soy products, fresh, frozen and canned vegetables, fresh grains, and fresh spices. **Organic?** Member of Oregon Tilth. 30% organic. **Prices:** 10% off for pre-order full case bag lots. **Hours:** 7 days—8 a.m.–10 p.m. **Comments:** Hot and cold natural foods in deli with indoor and outdoor seating.

Eugene, **Oasis Fine Foods,** 2489 Williamette, Eugene, OR 97405. (503) 345-1014. **Type of Business:** Retail store. **Sells to:** The public. **Sells:** Very wide range of processed foods as well as fresh beans, fruit, spices, and vegetables. **Organic?** Produce is certified by Tilth. **Credit:** None. **Prices:** Bulk discounts as follows: For large orders, cost plus 10%, for small special orders, cost plus 20%. **Hours:** 8 a.m.–10 p.m. **Minimum Order:** One case. **Comments:** They sell specialty items, gift baskets. Features own bakery and chemical-free meat shop.

Eugene, **Surata Soyfoods Inc.,** Peter Chabarck, Sales Manager, 302 Blair Blvd., Eugene, OR 97402. (503) 485–6990, (503) 343–8434. **Type of Business:** Manufacturer and retailer. **Sells to:** Distributors, retailers and the general public. **Sells:** Soy products, including tempeh, soysage, tofu, Szechuan-baked tofu and hickory-smoked tofu. **Organic?** Certified organic by Organic Crop Improvement Association. **Credit:** None. **Prices:** Bulk soy tempeh $1.25/lb. (minimum order 100 lbs.). 10% discount for orders of 100 cases or more. **Hours:** M-Th 9–5, F 9–1. **Minimum Order:** None. **Catalogue Available?** Yes. **Comments:** Surata is worker owned and operated. This cooperative business was involved in the lobbying effort for stricter organic standards and regulation in Oregon.

Glide, **McCord Apiaries,** Stephen Mc Cord, Sales Rep., 1805 Glide Loop Dr., Glide, OR 97443. (503) 496–3277. **Type of Business:** Processor, retailer and mail-order distributor. **Sells to:** The general public. **Sells:** Honey and pollen, 100% organic. **Organic?** Certified organic by the State of Oregon, Department of Agriculture. **Credit:** None. **Prices:** $4.25 lb. for 25 lbs. or less, $4 above 25 lbs. **Hours:** Not limited, retail is out of the family home. **Shipping:** By UPS. **Minimum Order:** None. **Catalogue Available?** Yes.

Lake Oswego, **Nature's Deli,** 333 South State St., Lake Oswego, OR 97034. (503) 635–3374. See Nature's Fresh Northwest, Portland.

Lincoln City, **Trillium Natural Grocery,** 1026 SE Jetty Avenue, Lincoln City, OR 97367. (503) 994–5665. **Type of Business:** Retail store. **Sells to:** The public. **Sells:** Wide selection of processed foods and fresh produce. **Organic?** Member of Oregon Tilth. 50% organic. **Prices:** Bulk orders are cost plus 10% **Hours:** Daily, 10:30–6:30. **Shipping:** Weekly. **Minimum Order:** $2.00 on bulk orders.

North Bend, **Coos Head Food Store,** 1960 Sherman Avenue, North Bend, OR 97459. (503) 756–7264. **Type of Business:** Retail store co-op. **Sells to:** The public. **Sells:** A wide selection of processed foods and fresh produce. **Organic?** Oregon Tilth. 95% of produce organic, 40% of coffee, 30% of bulk foods. **Prices:** 5% discount for case or bulk bag, 10% for $200 or more bulk, cost plus 10% for other businesses that resell the product or make a product from the purchased product. **Hours:** M-F 9–7, Sat. 10–6, Sun. 12–5. **Catalogue Available?** No, but price list available.

Portland, **Cafe Tierra,** 2181 NW Nicolai, Portland, OR 97210. (503) 227–4490, (800) 547–0474 **Type of Business:** Restaurant, manufacturer, and retailer. **Sells:** Coffee (35 selections available). **Organic?** Certified Organic (Organic Crop Improvement Association) **Minimum Order:** 20 lbs. bulk or $75.00 of 8 ounce or 2 ounce containers.

Portland, **Food Front,** Dennis McLearn, General Manager, 2375 NW Thurman, Portland, OR 97210. (503) 222–5658. **Type of Business:** Retail store, co-op Grocery. **Sells to:** The public. **Sells:** A very wide variety of fresh produce and processed foods. **Organic?** Member of Oregon Tilth. 30% organic. **Credit:** V. **Hours:** Daily 9–9. **Comments:** They are a 5,500 sq ft retail natural foods grocery with annual sales exceeding $3 million. They offer a 5% discount to their members and members of other co-ops.◆

Portland, **G's Herb International,** Ltd., Gary Halfant, Jeff Anders, 2344 NW 21st Pl.,Portland, OR 97210. (503) 241–1131, outside Oregon (800) 547–4233, Fax: (503) 227–5446. **Type of Business:** Distributor. **Sells to:** Mainly retailers and restaurants. **Sells:** Herbs and spices. **Organic?** Asserted organic (5–8%). **Minimum Order:** Minimum quantity 1 lb., minimum order $50.

Portland, **Happy Harvest Grocers,** 2348 SE Ankeny, Portland, OR 97214. **Type of Business:** Retail store and vegetarian cafe. **Sells to:** The public. **Sells:** An impressive range of processed foods and fresh produce (except meat). **Organic?** 50% organic. They are affiliated with the Oregon Tilth. **Credit:** No. **Prices:** 10% discount on pre-orders bag/box lot. **Hours:** Mon-Sat. 10–8. **Minimum Order:** No. **Comments:** The restaurant focuses on organically grown ingredients and makes use of alternative sweeteners (e.g. fruit juice). The Happy Harvest is a small, owner-operated, friendly place to dine.

Portland, **Nature's Beaverton,** 4000 SW 117th, Portland, OR 97224. (503) 646–3824. **Hours:** Daily 9–9. See Nature's Fresh Northwest, Portland.◆

Portland, **Nature's Corbett,** 5909 SW Corbett, Portland, OR 97201. (503) 244–3934. **Hours:** Daily 9–8. See Nature's Fresh Northwest, Portland.◆

Portland, **Nature's Fremont,** 3449 NE 24th, Portland, OR 97211. (503) 288–3414. **Hours:** Daily 9–9. See Nature's Fresh Northwest, Portland.◆

Portland, **Nature's Fresh Northwest,** Theresa Marquez, 3449 NE 24th Ave., Portland, OR 97212. (503) 281–7489 (office), (503) 288–3414 (store). **Type of Business:** Chain retail store. **Sells to:** The public. **Sells:** A great selection of organically grown produce. During season, they carry 75% organic produce. **Organic?** Asserted 10 -15% organic overall (depends on time of year). Produce certified by Oregon Tilth and California Certified Organic Farmers. **Prices:** 10% off for full cases of grocery products. For wine, full cases are sold at cost plus 10%. **Hours:** 7 days. 9–9.◆

Portland, **Nature's Snack Bar,** Metro YMCA, 2831 SW Barbur Blvd., Portland, OR 97201. (503) 227–0928. See Nature's Fresh Northwest, Portland.◆

Portland, **Oregon Spice Co. Inc.,** 3525 SE 17th Ave., Portland, OR 97202. (503) 238–0664, FAX (503) 238–3872. **Type of Business:** Manufacturer, wholesaler, retail store and mail-order distributor. **Sells to:** Retailers, restaurants, and the general public. **Sells:** Coffee, teas, all culinary herbs and spices, and salt-less seasoning. **Organic?** Asserted 10% organic. **Credit:** None. **Prices:** Discount for bulk. **Hours:** M-F 8–5. **Shipping:** By UPS or private carriers. **Minimum Order:** $50. **Catalogue Available?** Yes.

Portland, **Portland Adventist Medical Center,** Dietary Dept., 10123 SE Market St., Portland, OR 97216. (503) 257-2500. **Type of Business:** Restaurant. **Sells:** Nutritionally balanced vegetarian cuisine. The Portland Adventist Medical Center has been delivering its from-scratch vegetarian menu for the past 96 years. It is now looked to by hospital-food-service directors throughout the western U.S. for advice on vegetarian catering. **Organic?** No organic claims made. **Specialties:** Vegetarian entrees, legume and homemade soups, full service short order grill, salad and deli bar. **Prices:** Entrees $1–$1.75 (not a full meal). **Hours:** 6:30–6:30. **Reservations:** Not possible. 100% nonsmoking. **Credit:** None. **Commendations:** *Food Management,* July 1989.

Roseburg, **Elderflower Farm,** 501 Callahan Road, Roseburg, OR 97470. (503) 672-9803. **Type of Business:** Grower and mail-order distributor. **Sells to:** Consumers and retailers, mail order. **Sells:** Dried culinary herbs, culinary herb blends, herb vinegars and related books. **Organic?** Asserted organic, 100%; they claim to follow the State of Oregon's organic requirements. **Credit:** V M. **Prices:** No special prices for bulk. **Hours:** M-F 9–5. **Shipping:** Normal UPS—7–10 days. **Minimum Order:** None.

Salem, **Heliotrope Natural Foods,** 2060 Market St. NE Salem, OR 97301. (503) 362-5487. **Type of Business:** Retail store, just starting wholesale. **Sells to:** The public and a few restaurants. **Sells:** A very wide range of organic produce and wholefood grocery items, including fresh bakery products. **Organic?** Overall, about 15% of the products they sell are organically grown (produce is Tilth-certified). **Credit:** None. **Prices:** 15% discount on case orders, 10% off bulk cheese. They sell certain staple items at cost. **Hours:** M-Sat. 9–9, Sun. 11–6. **Comments:** They recycle plastic and encourage customers to bring in bags and bottles. They also have a self-service deli renowned for its Indian foods and salsa. Their newspaper is mailed out to customers once a month and they are very community-oriented, sponsoring monthly speakers at the public library and promoting dietary education.

Tillamook, **Tillamook County Creamery Association,** Gary Sauriol, PO Box 313, Tillamook, OR 97141. (503) 842-4481, (503) 842-3102. **Type of Business:** Manufacturer and mail-order distributor. **Sells to:** Wholesalers, retailers and the general public. **Sells:** Dairy products, all are made without artificial additives and preservatives and many are low in sodium. **Organic?** Non-organic. **Credit:** V M. **Prices:** Discount for bulk, 500 lb.–2,500 lb. minimum. **Hours:** 8–5. **Minimum Order:** None for mail-order, 1,500 lb.–2,500 lb. for truck delivery. **Catalogue Available?** Yes.

Williams, **Herb Pharm,** PO Box 116, Williams, OR 97544. **Type of Business:** Grower. **Sells to:** Distributors, retailers, and the public by mail. **Sells:** Herbs and spices.

Organic? Asserted organic. **Credit:** None. **Minimum Order:** None.

PA

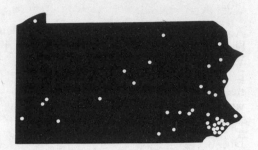

Pennsylvania

Allentown, **Garden Gate Natural Foods,** 17 S 9th St., Allentown, PA 18102. (215) 433-8891. **Type of Business:** Retail store. **Sells to:** The public. **Sells:** An impressive range of wholefood groceries and fresh organic produce. **Organic?** Produce 100% organic, certified by Organic Crop Improvement Association, California Certified Organic Farmers, Demeter/Bio-dynamic. **Credit:** M. **Prices:** 10% discount for cases. 10% discount for senior citizens ($5 minimum). **Hours:** M-Th 9–8, TWF 9–6:30, Sat. 9–5:30.

Altoona, **Millenial Health & Books,** 1718 12th Ave., Altoona, PA 16601. (814) 949-9108. **Type of Business:** Retail store and mail order business. **Sells to:** The public. **Sells:** Some wholefood grocery items; kosher yogurt, bulk herbs, snack-foods, coffee, teas, and juices, supplements, books, bibles, and novelties. **Organic?** Asserted 5–15%. **Credit:** None. **Prices:** Special prices for pastors and missionaries. **Hours:** M-F 11:30–6. **Shipping:** U.S. Postal Service or UPS. **Minimum Order:** $5 for mail order. **Catalogue Available?** Yes. **Comments:** The owner is an Associate Pastor of a Baptist Church, who said on his questionnaire that he hopes to see us in heaven. The store's slogans are "Millenial—come on in and get your root and toot and spiritual gluten!" and, "We have everything you need to make you happy, healthy, or holy."

Ardmore, **Mrs. Emm's All Natural Health Food Stores,** 11 W Lancaster Avenue, Ardmore, PA 19003. (215) 896-7717. **Type of Business:** Retail store, part of a chain of 12 in Pennsylvania and New Jersey. **Sells:** A full array of wholefood grocery items, including canned and frozen vegetables. **Organic?** Produce is asserted 100% organic (Organic Crop Improvement Association, Farm Verified Organic, Natural Organic Farmers Association, California Certified Organic Farmers); they assert that about 80% of processed items are organic. **Credit:** V M. **Prices:** 10% discounts on case purchases. **Hours:** Varies depending on store.

Chalfont, **Mrs. Emm's All Natural Health Food Stores,** 11 W Lancaster Avenue, Ardmore, PA 19003. (215) 896-7717. See entry for Ardmore above.

Collegeville, **Cook's Natural Foods,** Collegeville Shopping Center, Collegeville PA 19426. (215) 277-8841. **Type of Business:** Retail store. **Sells to:** The public. **Sells:** A wide variety of processed wholefoods as well as fresh beans. **Organic?** Asserted 75% on packaged goods. **Credit:** V M AE D. **Prices:** 10% off case lots. **Hours:** M-Th 10-6, F 10-7, Sat. 10-4. **Comments:** They cater to special diet needs (e.g. low-fat, low cholesterol, milk-free, yeast-free, wheat-free). They will also special-order any product.

Dresher, **Mrs. Emm's All Natural Health Food Stores,** Dresher Plaza, 1650 Limekiln Pike, Dresher, PA 19025. (215) 628-4440. **Type of Business:** Retail store, part of a chain of 12 in Pennsylvania and New Jersey. See entry for Ardmore, PA.

Easton, **Nature's Way,** 145 Northampton St., Easton PA 18042. (215) 253-0940. **Type of Business:** Retail store. **Sells to:** The public. **Sells:** A complete line of fresh produce and wholefood grocery items. **Organic?** Produce, 95% organic. Processed goods, 5-10%. Certified by Organic Crop Improvement Association, Farm Verified Organic, Natural Organic Farmers Association, California Certified Organic Farmers. **Credit:** V M. **Prices:** For bulk foods in original packing, at least 10% discount. **Hours:** M, W, Th 9:30-5:30, Tu, F 9:30-8, Sat. 9:30-5. **Comments:** Established 15 years ago, 2800 sq. ft., parking in rear of store.

Elkins Park, **Mrs. Emm's All Natural Health Food Stores,** Elkins Park Square, Old York and Church Roads, Elkins Park, PA 19117. (215) 635-1107. **Type of Business:** Retail store, part of a chain of 12 in Pennsylvania and New Jersey. See entry for Ardmore, PA.

Erie, **Whole Foods Co-op Association.,** 560 East 14th Street, Erie, PA 16503. (814) 456-0282. **Type of Business:** Co-op. **Sells to:** Co-op members. **Sells:** A full range of wholefood grocery items, plus a selection of fresh produce. **Organic?** 99% organic fresh produce (California Certified Organic Farmers); estimated 50% for other items. **Prices:** 5% off 20 lbs. or more if picked up within 2 days. **Hours:** M-W 12-5, Th-F 10-7:30, Sat. 10-3:30.

Gettysburg, **Nature's Food & Restaurant,** 48 Baltimore St., Gettysburg, PA 17325. (717) 334-7723. **Type of Business:** Restaurant and retail store. **Sells:** Vegetarian food; soups, sandwiches, salads, shakes and other beverages. Retail store sells bulk foods and packages items, dietary supplements, herbs and homeopathic remedies and other environmentally-kind products. **Organic?** Fresh produce asserted 100% organic (Organic Crop Improvement Association, Demeter); Asserted 70% organic overall. Water not filtered but bottled water available. **Specialties:** Vegan and macrobiotic dishes also available. All dishes listed with calorie estimates. **Prices:** $1 -$2.50. **Hours:** M-T 8:30-5, F 8:30-7, Sat. 9-2. **Reservations:** Not accepted. 100% No smoking. **Credit:** V M AE, $25 mini-

mum. **Commendations:** Listed in *Vegetarian Times Guide to Natural Food Restaurants,* 1988.

Greensburg, **Nature's Way Food Outlet,** 796 Highland Ave., Greensburg, PA 15601. (412) 836-3524. **Type of Business:** Retail store. **Sells to:** The public. **Sells:** A range of wholefood groceries and produce plus fresh apples and carrots. **Organic?** Asserted 100% organic on fresh produce, 90% on other items. **Credit:** No. **Prices:** 10% discount for case orders. **Hours:** M-F 10-6, Th 10-8, Sat. 10-5.

Harrisburg, **Genesee Natural Foods,** 5405 Locust Lane, Harrisburg, PA 17109. (717) 545-3712. **Type of Business:** Retail store. **Sells to:** The public. **Sells:** A comprehensive line of both fresh produce and wholefood grocery items. **Organic?** Produce 100% organic. Certified by Organic Crop Improvement Association, Farm Verified Organic, Natural Organic Farmers Association, or California Certified Organic Farmers. **Credit:** None. **Prices:** Case discounts, wholesale orders. **Hours:** M-Tu 10-6, W-F 10-7, Sat. 10-5.

Hellertown, **Frey's Better Foods,** 648 Main St., Hellertown, PA 18055. (215) 838-6889. **Type of Business:** Retail store. **Sells to:** The public. **Sells:** A comprehensive range of wholefood groceries and organically grown fresh produce. **Organic?** 100% organic for fresh food, certified by Organic Crop Improvement Association, Farm Verified Organic. 40% for processed items. **Credit:** None. **Prices:** 15% bulk discount. **Hours:** M-Th, 9:30-5:30, Fri 9:30-8, Sat., 9:30-4. **Comments:** Will special order items not usually in stock.

Honesdale, **Nature's Grace,** 110 7th St., Honesdale, PA 18431. (717) 253-3469. **Type of Business:** Retail store/ Deli. **Sells to:** The public. **Sells:** A wide variety of natural groceries with selected fresh fruit and vegetables. **Organic?** Fresh produce 5% organic (Organic Crop Improvement Association, Farm Verified Organic, Demeter/Biodynamic); processed goods about 10% organic. **Credit:** None. **Prices:** 10% discount for case or over 10 lbs. **Hours:** M-Sat. 10-5, F 10-8:30.

Ivyland, **Neshaminy Valley Natural Foods Distributor Ltd.,** Phil Margolis, President, 5 Louise Drive, Ivyland, PA 18974. (215) 443-5545, FAX: (215) 443-7087. **Type of Business:** Distributor. **Sells to:** Retailers and buying clubs. **Sells:** Beans (all certified organic), cereals, flour, grains, breads, baked goods, dried fruit, fruit juices, oils, pasta, rice, fresh fruit and vegetables, dairy products, soy products, nuts and nut butters, beverages, candy and sweeteners. **Organic?** California Certified Organic Farmers certified 33% organic. **Credit:** Does not accept any credit cards. Send a check, or leave one to be picked up when the truck driver delivers the goods. **Prices:** Special prices for bulk orders. **Shipping:** Order must be placed by 4 p.m. two days before the truck is due in your area; changes in the order can be made up to 12 noon the day before the due date. **Minimum Order:** Yes. $250-$400 depending on shipping area. **Catalogue Available?** Yes.♦♦♦

Kimberton, **Kimberton Hills Farmstore,** Box 155, Kimberton, PA 19442. (215) 935-0214. **Type of Business:** Retail store, Producer. **Sells to:** The public, retailers, restaurants, and buying clubs. **Sells:** An impressive variety of seasonal fresh fruit and vegetables, with additional packaged wholefoods. **Organic?** 100% organic for fresh produce (certified by Organic Crop Improvement Association, Farm Verified Organic, or Demeter/Bio-dynamic); 90% for processed foods. **Credit:** None. **Hours:** W and F 10-6, Sat. 10-3. **Shipping:** Delivers to Philadelphia on Thursdays. **Minimum Order:** $40. **Catalogue Available?** Yes. **Comments:** They have a tea room on the premises, and use their own products whenever possible.

Lansdowne, **La Bar's Natural Foods,** 12 N. Lansdowne Ave., Lansdowne, PA 19050. (215) 626-3667. **Type of Business:** Retail store. **Sells to:** The public. **Sells:** A range of wholefood grocery items, and fresh beans, grains, nuts and soy products. **Organic?** Asserted 10% organic. **Credit:** D. **Prices:** 5% off a full case; 10% off any order over $40. **Hours:** M-S, 10:30-5:30.

Lebanon, **L M Zellers Health Prod.,** 977 York St., Lebanon, PA 17042. (717) 272-6969. **Type of Business:** Retail store. **Sells to:** The public. **Sells:** A limited selection of natural foods. **Organic?** Fresh produce 100% organic (Organic Crop Improvement Association), processed goods 80%. **Hours:** M-F 9-5, Sat. 9-12.

Manheim, **Weavers Natural Food, Inc.,** 15 Market Square, Manheim, PA 17545. (717) 665-6871. **Type of Business:** Retail store and mail-order distributor. **Sells to:** The public. **Sells:** A full line of wholefood items, except fresh fruit and vegetables. **Organic?** 10% organic for processed food, certified by Farm Verified Organic. **Credit:** V M. **Prices:** 10-20% discount for bulk purchases. **Hours:** M-Th 9-5, F 9-8, Sat. 9-3. **Shipping:** Same day when possible.

Mansfield, **Krystal Wharf Farms,** RD 2, Box 191 A, Mansfield, PA 16933. (717) 549-8194. **Type of Business:** Distributor and mail-order distributor. **Sells to:** Mainly retailers. **Sells:** Organically grown fruit and vegetables. Also "wildcrafted" herbs. **Organic?** Asserted organic. **Credit:** None. **Shipping:** They have truck routes in Eastern Pennsylvania, parts of New Jersey, and western upstate New York. **Comments:** They say that their mail order business has been growing rapidly.

Marshall's Creek, **Naturally Rite,** Rt. 209 Box 1187, Marshall's Creek, PA 18335. (717) 223-1133. **Type of Business:** Retail store and restaurant. **Sells to:** The public. **Sells:** A complete range of wholefood groceries and fresh organic produce. **Organic?** Produce 100% organically grown (Organic Crop Improvement Association), about 40% of processed goods are organic. **Credit:** V M AE D (planned). **Prices:** Case discount 10-15%. **Hours:** M-F 10-9, Sat. 9-9, Sun. 10-9. **Comments:** A natural foods restaurant is attached to the store.

Milesburg, **Rising Sun Organic Produce,** Hope P. Woodring, Box 627 I-80 and Pa-150, Milesburg, PA 16853. (814) 355-9850. **Type of Business:** Retail store

and mail-order distributor. **Sells to:** The public. **Sells:** Fresh fruit, vegetables, dried fruit, grains, flour, cereals, pasta, nuts, beans, meat (seafood by special order only), soy products, cheese, yogurt, fruit juices, jellies, oils, bread, candy, muffins, tacos, herbs, spices and beverages. **Organic?** Asserted 98% organic. **Credit:** None. **Prices:** 10% discount available for bulk orders. **Hours:** F 10-8, S 10-5. **Shipping:** Only within UPS areas; orders shipped Mondays in insulated boxes and ice packs which must be returned. **Minimum Order:** None. **Catalogue Available?** Yes.

New Holland, **The Community Store,** 1065 W Main St., New Holland, PA. (717) 656-4256. **Type of Business:** Retail store and restaurant. **Sells to:** The public. **Sells:** A wide variety of natural groceries and fresh produce. **Organic?** Fresh produce asserted 100% organic, other items, 50%. **Credit:** No. **Prices:** 10% discount on full cases. **Hours:** M-W 9-5, Th 9-7, F 9-5, Sat. 9-4, 2nd and 4th Friday each month 9-9. **Comments:** Offers wholefood lunches M-Sat. 11:30-3 and macrobiotic dinners 2nd and 4th Friday evening each month. Reservations required for dinners, which are served family style.

Newfoundland, **White Cloud Restaurant and Inn,** George or Judy Wilkinson, RD1, Box 215, Newfoundland, PA 18445. (717) 676-3162. **Type of Business:** Restaurant. **Sells:** Vegetarian dishes only; soups, salads, sandwiches and beverages. **Organic?** Asserted 70% organic. Water not filtered. **Specialties:** Nutburgers, pancakes, tahini, cheesebake, tofu parmesan, steamed or sauteed vegetables on brown rice; vegan and macrobiotic dishes also available. **Hours:** Summer, S-S 8-10, 12-2, 6-8. **Reservations:** Possible. 100% No smoking. **Credit:** V M. **Commendations:** Originally founded as a retreat for members of Self-Realization Fellowship. Offers guests "peace, quiet and good food".

Newtown, **Mrs. Emm's All Natural Health Food Stores,** Village at Newtown, Rt. 413 at Rt. 532, Newtown, PA 18940. (215) 579-9601. **Type of Business:** Retail store, part of a chain of 12 in Pennsylvania and New Jersey. **Sells:** A full array of wholefood grocery items, including canned and frozen vegetables. **Organic?** Produce is asserted 100% organic (Organic Crop Improvement Association, Farm Verified Organic, Natural Organic Farmers Association, California Certified Organic Farmers); they assert that about 80% of processed items are organic. **Credit:** V M. **Prices:** 10% discounts on case purchases. **Hours:** Varies depending on store.

Penns Creek, **Walnut Acres,** Walnut Acres Road, Penns Creek, PA 17862. (717) 837-0601. **Type of Business:** Grower, manufacturer, mail-order distributor and retailer. **Sells to:** Distributors, retailers and mail order to public. **Sells:** Baked goods (cookies, breads, muffins, pancakes), dried beans, whole grains, flours, pasta, rice, cheese, oils, nuts and nut butters, dried fruit, soy products, spices, fruit juices, canned soups and canned vegetables. Fresh fruit, meat, vegetables, tempeh, tofu and yogurt available at store only. **Organic?** 100% organic for fresh produce (Organic Crop Improvement Association), and 80% for processed goods. **Credit:** V M. **Prices:** 25% off retail for wholesale orders. **Hours:** M-Sat. 8–5. **Shipping:** Orders shipped worldwide within 3 working days of receipt. **Minimum Order:** $300 for wholesale; none for retail. **Catalogue Available?** Yes. **Comments:** Walnut Acres, one of the oldest organic farms in the country (dating back to 1946), is one of the most frequently recommended mail-order distributors we have come across and they make or sell a lot of terrific products.♦♦♦

Philadelphia, **Center Foods,** Cynthia & Dennis Tice, 337 S Broad Street, Philadelphia, PA 19107. (215) 735-5673. **Type of Business:** Retail store and co-op. **Sells to:** The public. **Sells:** A wide selection of processed foods and fresh produce. **Organic?** Asserted 70% organic. **Prices:** 10% discount on case amounts. **Hours:** M-Sat. 10-7, Sun. 11:30-5. **Minimum Order:** 1 case. **Comments:** Features a deli on premises, where they feature all organic take out meals, fresh organic juices, organic soups, organic baked goods, organic coffee and teas, organic salads. All of their goods are prepared with spring water.

Philadelphia, **European Dairy Restaurant,** Michael Matcis, 2000 Sansom St., Philadelphia, PA 19103. (215) 568-1298. **Type of Business:** Restaurant. **Sells:** Kosher cuisine. **Organic?** No organic claims. Water is not filtered. **Specialties:** Homemade soups, potato pirogen, matca brie and strudel; vegetarian dishes are available; musical entertainment is also offered. **Prices:** $4-$10. **Hours:** S-T 11-9, F 11-3, closed Sat. **Reservations:** Possible. 20% No smoking. **Credit:** AE and DC. **Commendations:** *Baltimore Jewish Times,* October 28, 1988.

Philadelphia, **Health Foods International,** 3585 Aramingo Ave., Philadelphia, PA 19134. (215) 289-5750. **Type of Business:** Retail store, wholesaler, mail-order distributor. **Sells to:** The public, retailers, restaurants. **Sells:** A range of wholefood grocery products. **Organic?** Produce asserted 10% organic; processed 50%. **Credit:** V M 30-day credit when qualified. **Prices:** Discounts for large orders. **Hours:** M-F 8-6, Sat. 10-6. **Minimum Order:** 200 cases for wholesale, none for retail. **Catalogue Available?** Yes.

Philadelphia, **Keyflower Dining Room,** Divine Tracy Hotel, 20 S 36th St., Philadelphia, PA 19104. (215) 386-2207. **Type of Business:** Restaurant. **Sells:** Menu changes daily; tofu, tempeh, beans, baked chicken, fish and fresh vegetables. **Organic?** Asserted 40% organic. Water is filtered. **Specialties:** Brown rice with every meal; vegetarian and macrobiotic dishes are available. **Prices:** $4-$7 for complete meal including designated health drink. **Hours:** M-F 11:30-2, 5-8. **Reservations:** Possible. 100% no smoking. **Credit:** Travelers check or cash only.

Philadelphia, **Mrs. Emm's All Natural Health Food Stores (3 locations),** 1) 704 South Street, Philadelphia, PA 19147. (215) 922-4118; 2) 7940 Bustleton Avenue (near Rhawn Street) 19152. (215) 725-3881; 3) Krewstown Shopping Center, Krewstown Rd. and Grant Ave., 19115. (215) 934-7711. **Type of Business:** Retail store, part of a chain of 12 in Pennsylvania and New Jersey.

Sells: A full array of wholefood grocery items, including canned and frozen vegetables. **Organic?** Produce is asserted 100% organic (Organic Crop Improvement Association, Farm Verified Organic, Natural Organic Farmers Association, California Certified Organic Farmers); they assert that about 80% of processed items are organic. **Credit:** V M. **Prices:** 10% discounts on case purchases. **Hours:** Varies depending on store.

Philadelphia, **Tang Yean Restaurant,** Charles Chen, 220 N 10th St., Philadelphia, PA 19107. (215) 925-3993, (215) 922-8636. **Type of Business:** Restaurant. **Sells:** Chinese cuisine. **Organic?** No organic claims. Water is filtered. **Specialties:** Seafood, imitation meat entrees, white meat chicken only served (no beef, pork, or MSG is used); vegetarian dishes are available. **Prices:** $4.75-$10.95 **Hours:** M-T 3-10, F-S 3-12, Sun. 3-10:30. **Reservations:** Accepted. 100% No smoking. **Credit:** V M AE, $15 minimum. **Commendations:** Widely recommended; Best of Philly, 1986.

Pittsburgh, **East End Food Co-op,** Sandra E. Greene, 7516 Mead St., Pittsburgh, PA 15208. (412) 242-3598 **Type of Business:** Co-op, retailer, and processor. **Sells to:** Members and the public. **Sells:** A full line of natural groceries and organic produce—dairy, soy, meat plus poultry, books, and crafts. **Organic?** Produce is about 35-50% organic (Organic Crop Improvement Association, Farm Verified Organic, California Certified Organic Farmers), about 50% of processed goods are organic. **Credit:** None. **Prices:** Members get a 10% discount off the shelf price and can save up to 30% by ordering bulk in advance. **Hours:** M-F 10-8, Sat. 11-8, Sun. 12-5.♦

Pocono Summit, **Near East Lebanese Restaurant,** Rte. 940, Box 201, Pocono Summit, PA 18346. (717) 839-8993. **Type of Business:** Restaurant. **Sells:** Salads, hummus, boma and kebabs. **Organic?** Asserted 45% organic. Water not filtered. **Specialties:** Near Eastern dishes; vegetarian dishes available; belly-dancing on Saturday nights. **Prices:** $7.95-$11.25 **Hours:** Lunch 11:30-3, Dinner 5-9 (Sat. 5-10). **Reservations:** Required. 50% No smoking. **Credit:** None. **Commendations:** Recommended by the *Vegetarian Times.*

Reading, **Nature's Garden,** Susanne Fiori, Reading Mall, Reading, PA 19606. (215) 779-3000, (215) 987-6905. **Type of Business:** Restaurant and retail store. **Sells:** Vegetarian only with vegan and macrobiotic options. **Organic?** 50-60% certified organic. Water is filtered. **Specialties:** Grain and bean burgers, soups, pasta salads, and "yogi hogi." **Prices:** $2.59-$4. **Hours:** Retail: M-W 10-7, Th-Sat. 10-9. Snack bar: M-W 11-6, Th-Sat. 11-7. **Reservations:** No. 100% of tables are non-smoking. **Credit:** V M. **Comments:** "We are 13 years old . . . People who are not familiar with natural foods can taste dishes expertly prepared, buy the raw ingredients, and be told how to prepare them at home."

Sinking Spring, **Health Basket,** Rt. 422 West, Sinking Spring, PA 19608. (215) 670-9550. **Type of Business:** Retail store. **Sells to:** The public. **Sells:** A selection of wholefoods and fresh produce. **Organic?** Asserted 100% organic for all stock. **Credit:** V M. **Prices:** 20% off list price for 3 or more items. **Hours:** 10–5. **Comments:** Specializes in vitamins, minerals, herbs.

State College, **Granary Natural & Ethnic Foods,** 2766 W College Ave., State College, PA 16801. (814) 238–4844. **Type of Business:** Retail store. **Sells to:** The public. **Sells:** A full line of wholefood groceries, as well as fresh organic carrots and low-spray apples. **Credit:** V M. **Prices:** 10% discount on cases or full bags. **Hours:** MHHP Sat. 10–6. **Comments:** Offers home brewing supplies, dietary supplements. Many local products.

Tamaqua, **Dutch Country Gardens,** Joseph Yasenchek, Box 1122 Rd. #1, Tamaqua, PA 18252. (717) 668–0441. **Type of Business:** Grower and mail-order distributor. **Sells to:** Distributors and public. **Sells:** Produce: blueberries, melons, beets, carrots, corn, cucumbers, potatoes, squash, tomatoes, turnips, zucchini and sweet potatoes. **Organic?** Asserted 100% organic. **Credit:** None. **Prices:** No special discounts. **Hours:** 9–5. **Minimum Order:** $25.00 Catalogue Available? No.

Valencia, **Frankferd Farms,** T. Lyle or Betty Ferderber, 318 Love Rd., Rd.#1, Valencia, PA 16059. (412) 898–2242. **Type of Business:** Manufacturer, distributor and mail order. **Sells to:** Public only through ordering. **Sells:** Baked goods, beans, breads, cereals, dairy products, flour, fruit juices, dried fruit, oils, pastas, rice, soy products, salsa, beverages and candies. **Organic?** About 35% certified organic (Organic Crop Improvement Association, Western PA Organic Growers Assn.) **Credit:** No credit cards. **Hours:** Friday 9–5:30, Sat. 9–12. on a preorder or appointment only basis. **Shipping:** Trucks serve PA, eastern Ohio, WV, MD, and D.C. Mailing by UPS and US postal. **Minimum Order:** On the trucks—depending on how far. No minimum on pick-up or UPS. **Catalogue Available?** Yes. **Comments:** "We're a three-generation family-owned food distributor, one of a handful who actually grow and process some of their own products. We rely on customer service and good products to keep us going. Our farm/warehouse is humble, but real."

Washington, **Health World,** 310 Oak Spring Rd., Washington, PA 15301. (412) 225–7520. **Type of Business:** Retail store. **Sells to:** The public. **Sells:** A selection of wholefood grocery items. **Organic?** Asserted 50% organic. **Credit:** V M. **Hours:** M-Sat. 10–9, Sun. 11–5.

Williamsport, **Freshlife,** 2300 East 3rd St., Williamsport, PA 17701. (717) 322–8280. **Type of Business:** Retail store. **Sells to:** The public. **Sells:** A very impressive range of both natural groceries and organically grown fresh produce. **Organic?** Fresh produce asserted 95% organic; processed goods 20%. **Credit:** V M. **Prices:** 20% plus off retail for bulk orders. **Hours:** M-W, Sat 9:30–6, Th-F 9:30–8. Sunday closed. **Minimum Order:** $150 for wholesale. **Catalogue Available?** Planned. **Comments:** Largest natural-food store in a "200–mile radius."

Wyomissing, **Naturally Gourmet,** 1101 Woodland Rd., Wyomissing, PA 19610. (215) 376–3188. **Type of Business:** Retail store and cafe. **Sells to:** The public. **Sells:** A limited selection of natural grocery items. **Credit:** None. **Hours:** M-F 10–8, Sat. 10–5.

PR

Puerto Rico

Humacao, **Nutrilife,** Calle Miguel Casillas, Num. 9, Humacao, PR. **Type of Business:** Retail store and restaurant. **Sells to:** The public. **Sells:** A full range of fresh organic produce and wholefood grocery items. Also vegetarian meals and take-out. **Organic?** "Most products; almost all the flours rice and cereals" are asserted organic. **Credit:** None. **Prices:** Occasional bargain sales. **Hours:** 8–6 daily.

RI

Rhode Island

Coventry, **Cornucopia Natural Food,** Norman Cloutier, President, 8 Industrial Drive, Coventry, RI 02816. (401) 822–2300. **Type of Business:** One of the three largest distributors of health foods on the East Coast. **Sells to:** Retailers. **Sells:** Baked goods, condiments, dairy products, dried beans, dried fruit, whole grains, flours and meals, processed grain products, juices, nuts and nut butters, oils, seeds, soy products, fresh vegetables. **Organic?** Asserted Organic (15%). **Catalogue Available?** Free to approved customers (stores only).♥♦♦♦

East Greenwich, **Hartman's Back to Basics,** 250 Main St., East Greenwich, RI 02818. (401) 885–2679. **Type of Business:** Retail store. **Sells to:** The public. **Sells:** A variety of natural grocery items and fresh produce (excepting fruit and vegetables). **Organic?** Fresh produce 100% organic (certified by Organic Crop Improvement Association, Farm Verified Organic), processed goods 65%. **Credit:** No. **Hours:** M-W 10–5:30, Th-F 10–7, Sat. 9–5:30. Closed Sunday.

Middletown, **Au Natural—Natural Food Market,** 700 Aquidneck Ave., Middletown, RI 02840. (401) 846–4146.

Type of Business: Retail store. Sells to: The public. Sells: A complete range of wholefood groceries and fresh organic produce. Organic? Fresh produce 80% organic (certified by Organic Crop Improvement Association, Farm Verified Organic), other grocery, 40–50%. Credit: V M. Hours: M-Sat. 8–7.

Newport, **Harvest Natural Foods,** 1 Casino Terrace, Newport, RI 02840. (401) 846–8137. Type of Business: Retail store, deli, and caterer. Sells to: The public direct and by mail. Sells: A full range of wholefood grocery items and fresh organic produce. Their take out deli features a variety of soups, salads, sandwiches, and entrees. Organic? Produce 90% organic (Organic Crop Improvement Association, Farm Verified Organic, Natural Organic Farmers Association, California Certified Organic Farmers, Demeter/Bio-dynamic); processed goods 40%. Credit: V M AE. Prices: 10% discounts on cases (5% if already featured on sale). Hours: M-Sat. 9:30–6, Sun. 12–5. Shipping: They will ship anywhere in the U.S., Canada, or the Caribbean by U.S. mail or UPS. Minimum Order: None. Catalogue Available? No. Comments: They have 9 years of catering experience and handle all types of events. They promise "stocking-stuffers galore" at Christmas time and ready-made or made-to-order gift baskets.

Newport, **Nature's Goodness,** 199 Connell Highway., Newport Mall, Newport, RI 02840. (401) 847–7480. Type of Business: Retail store. Sells to: The public. Sells: A range of wholefood groceries. Organic? Estimated 50% organic for fresh produce and 50% for other. Certified by Farm Verified Organic. Credit: V M. Hours: M-F 10–9, Sat. 10–8, Sun. 12–5.

Providence, **Bread & Circus,** 261 Waterman St. Providence, RI 02904. (401) 272–1690. Also in Brookline, Cambridge, Hadley, Newton (2), and Wellesley, MA. Type of Business: Wholefood supermarket chain and wholesaler. Part of a chain of seven supermarkets. They also sell wholesale to other supermarket chains. Volume: About $50 million retail, $30 million wholesale. They saw a 30–50 percent increase in organic products in the February-March 1989 period. Sells to: The public through six stores in the Boston area and one in Providence. Sells: "You'll find just about everything you expect in a major supermarket—all made with wholesome ingredients, without chemical additives." They sell organic fruits and vegetables in season and natural (i.e. hormone-free) meat. None of their products has artificial colors, artificial flavors, or artificial preservatives. Their products are also void of processed sugars, nitrates, nitrites, and MSG. Hours: M-Sat. 9–9, Sun. 12–8 Comments and Commendations: Bread & Circus is one of the foremost purveyors of healthy food in the country. In our surveys they were among the leaders in peer recommendations. The commendations Bread & Circus receives from newspapers, magazines, and patrons we've encountered are universally glowing. If you live near Boston or Providence or are visiting either area you should definitely drop in on one of their stores.♥♦♦♦

Westerly, **Sandy's Fruit,** 15 Post Rd., Westerly, RI 02891. (401) 596–2004. Type of Business: Retail store. Sells to: The public. Sells: An expanding variety of wholefood grocery items and some organic fruit. Organic? They assert that less than 1% of their produce is organic and that about 15% of their other items are guaranteed pesticide free. Credit: V M AE. Prices: Discounts for bulk orders. Hours: M-Th and Sat. 8–6, F 8–7:30, Sun. 8–5. Comments: They also have a deli and prepare a variety of entrees and salads.

SC

South Carolina

Charleston, **Raspberry's Natural Food Store,** 1331 Ashley River Rd., Charleston, SC 29407. (803) 556–0076. Type of Business: Retail store. Sells to: The public. Sells: An impressive range of wholefoods and natural produce. Organic? Asserted 20% organic produce. Credit: No. Prices: 10% discount on prepaid full case orders. Hours: M-F 9:30–6:30, Sat. 9:30–5:30, Sun. 1–5.

Columbia, **The Basil Pot,** Richard Schwartz, 928 Main St., Columbia, SC 29201. (803) 799–0928. Type of Business: Restaurant. Sells: Basic plate of rice, beans, vegetables and pizza. Organic? Asserted 20–50% organic. Water is not filtered. Specialties: Vegetarian, vegan and macrobiotic dishes available. Prices: $3.75–$8.95 Hours: Breakfast M-F 7–10, S-S 9–2:30. Lunch S-S 11–2:30. Dinner M-Sat. 5:30–9:30. Reservations: Not accepted. 100% No smoking. Credit: V M. Commendations: Columbia's Good Food Spot, July 1989.

Columbia, **Nice-N-Natural,** 1217 College St., Columbia, SC 29201. (803) 799–3471. Type of Business: Restaurant. Sells: Fresh fruit salads, spinach salads, chicken and tuna salad sandwiches, vegetarian sandwiches, soups, mint iced tea and fresh limeade. Organic? Asserted 15% organic. Water is filtered. Specialties: Vegetarian dishes available. Prices: $1.75–$4.35. Hours: M-T 11–3:30, F 11–3. Reservations: Not accepted. 100% No smoking. Credit: None. Commendations: Listed as one of Columbia's "Ten Best Restaurants".

North Myrtle Beach, **The Natural Food Store,** 3320 S King's Hwy., N Myrtle Beach, SC 29582. (803) 272–4436. Type of Business: Retail store. Sells to: The public. Sells:

A good range of natural grocery items plus fresh dates, figs, carrots and tomatoes. **Organic?** Produce 50% organic (certified by Organic Crop Improvement Association, Farm Verified Organic, California Certified Organic Farmers) other goods, 30%. **Credit:** V M AE D. **Prices:** 10% discount on full case or bulk orders. **Hours:** M-Sat. 9–7.

SD

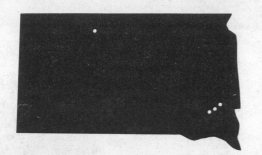

South Dakota

Hartford, **Skunk Creek Honey,** Robert or Shirley Smith, RR 2 Box 231, Hartford, SD 57033. (605) 528–6651. **Type of Business:** Manufacturer. **Sells to:** Wholesalers; retailers; and public on the farm. **Sells:** Honey products; fudge or spun honey with peanut butter or cinnamon or apricots, also a "Very Berry Strawberry Spun Honey Spread" and hand-rolled beeswax candles. **Organic?** South Dakota Beekeepers Association. **Credit:** None. **Prices:** Wholesale and retail price list. Wholesale involves sales to those customers who have a sales tax number and will use the product for resale. The retail price listing is for those wishing to buy individual items for their own use or for gifts.) **Hours:** 7:30 a.m.–8 p.m. **Catalogue Available?** Yes.

Olivet, **Willow Hill Italian Veal,** Kent Wintersteen, PO Box 16, Olivet, SD 57052. (605) 387–2307. **Type of business:** Producer/farmer. **Sells to:** Retailers and the public. **Sells:** Natural free-range veal (produced without the use of any hormones, meat dyes or any other artificial additives). **Organic?** Asserted 100% "naturally" grown. **Prices:** Special prices for sides of veal ordered in quantity. **Shipping:** UPS delivery areas only covered; July -December. **Minimum Order:** 50 lbs. **Catalogue Available?** No.

Parker, **Honey World, Inc.,** PO Box 458, Parker, SD 57053. (605) 297–4181. **Type of Business:** Manufacturer and retail store. **Sells:** Honey. **Organic?** 100% organic. **Credit:** No credit cards. **Prices:** Special 55–gallon prices. **Hours:** 8 a.m.–4 p.m. every Tuesday. **Minimum Order:** No. **Catalogue Available?** Yes.

Wakonda, **Bullseye Honey Farms,** Roger Starks, PO Box 272, Wakonda, SD 57073. (605) 361–0493. **Type of Business:** Apiary and distributor. **Sells to:** Retailers and the public by mail order. **Sells:** Honey. **Organic?** Asserted 100% organic. **Credit:** None. **Prices:** Honey is sold by the serving container or by 55–gallon container. Price per

pound is better on the the 55–gallon drums. **Minimum Order:** None. **Catalogue Available?** Yes.

TN

Tennessee

Chattanooga, **The Vitality Center,** 1150 Hixson Pike, Chattanooga, TN 37405. (615) 266–5016. **Type of Business:** Retail store. **Sells to:** The public direct and by mail order. **Sells:** A full range of wholefood groceries including: 7–grain, millet, ezekiel, sunflower, and herbal breads; a good selection of dried fruits; and infant-care products from organic baby-food to biodegradable diapers. **Organic?** They estimate that about 20% of their processed goods are organic. **Credit:** V M D. **Prices:** 10% discounts for bulk orders. **Hours:** M-Sat. 10–6. **Comments:** They also offer cooking classes and herbal information classes. They pride themselves on having a knowledgeable staff.

Cookeville, **Greenside Grocery Juice Bar,** 201 S Willow, Cookeville, TN 38501. (615) 526–4860 **Type of Business:** Restaurant and retail store. **Organic?** 10% asserted organic. Water is filtered. **Specialties:** Sandwiches on homemade bread. **Hours:** M-Th, Sat. 10–5:30, Fri 9–6. 100% of tables are non-smoking. **Reservations:** Not possible.

Johnson City, **Natural Foods Market/Eatwell Cafe,** Patsy Meridith, 216 E Main St., Johnson City, TN 37604. (615) 929–8570. **Type of Business:** Restaurant and retail store. **Sells:** Vegetarian food; soups, salads and sandwiches. **Organic?** Asserted 30% organic. Water is filtered. **Specialties:** Vegan and macrobiotic dishes are available. **Prices:** $1.55–$3.25 **Hours:** M-F 10–6 Sat. 10–5 (Lunch M-Sat. 11–3) **Reservations:** Possible. 100% No smoking. **Credit:** V M. $10 minimum. **Commendations:** The owners are members of the Center for Science in Public Interest (Americans for Safe Food).

Knoxville, **Knoxville Food Co-op,** 937 N Broadway, Knoxville, TN 37917. (615) 525–2069. **Type of Business:** Retailer. **Sells to:** Members and the public. **Sells:** A full range of wholefood grocery items, including organic cereals, canned goods, and flour, and fresh organic produce. They also have an arrangement with a local bakery to supply them with bread made from organic ingredients. **Organic?** Produce is asserted 70% organic in spring, summer, and fall; less in winter. **Credit:** None. **Prices:** Members pay shelf price. Working members receive coupons that give them 20% discounts on purchases up to $50 (the coupons can be used many times, if necessary, until $50 is reached). Non-members pay shelf-price plus 10%. **Hours:** M-Sat. 9:30–7:30, Sun. 1–6. **Comments:** Membership requires the purchase of one share ($15) a year; lifetime membership costs $100. The co-op is run on a democratic basis, has open membership, and sometimes offers cooking classes.

Knoxville, **Nature's Pantry,** Ann Yates, 4928 Homberg Dr., Knoxville, TN 37919. **Type of Business:** Retail store. **Sells to:** The public direct and by mail. **Sells:** A good selection of wholefood type items and some organic frozen vegetables. **Organic?** Asserted 20% organic. **Credit:** V M AE. **Hours:** M-Sat. 10–8. **Shipping:** UPS. **Minimum Order:** None. **Catalogue Available?** Soon. **Comments:** They also offer massage, neuro-muscular, polarity, and acupuncture therapy and nutritional guidance.

Madison, **Tennessee Christian Medical Center,** 500 Hospital Dr., Madison, TN 37115. (615) 865-2373. **Type of Business:** Restaurant. **Sells:** Vegetarian dishes only. **Organic?** No organic claims, water is filtered. **Specialties:** They offer two vegetarian entrees daily and "healthy desserts." **Prices:** $0.95–$1.65 **Hours:** 6–6:30 **Reservations:** Possible. 100% No smoking. **Credit:** None.

Memphis, **Honeysuckle Health Foods,** 4741 Poplar, Memphis, TN 38117. (901) 682-6255. **Type of Business:** Wholefoods supermarket with a small restaurant section. **Sells to:** The public direct and by mail. **Sells:** A full range of wholefood grocery items and organic produce in season (much of it grown on their own farm). They also have an open-kitchen vegetarian restaurant known for its spicy (and good) food. **Organic?** All their produce is organic, but they will not sell winter produce for the immediate future (it is often too battered when trucked from California and the trucking subtracts from the environmental benefits accrued by the sustainable agriculture.) **Credit:** V M AE. **Prices:** Bulk prices are low, case or bag quantities get an additional 10% discount. **Shipping:** UPS or U.S. mail (they prefer payment by credit card because it is easier for them and cheaper for the customer than COD. They will ship COD on request.) **Minimum Order:** None. **Catalogue Available?** No. **Comments:** Women from The Bible School of Health (renowned for its bread) come to the store once a month—the third Tuesday as of presstime—to offer samples of their wares and to take blood and cholesterol readings. The group then does cooking classes in the evening ($10 gets you a delicious meal and a class). Co-owner Jitendra Agrawal offers his own Indian cooking classes to overflow crowds once a month. The store has just started selling its own free-range eggs, poultry, and pork. They try to emphasize teaching and environmental concerns. A great store.♥

Nashville, **Slice of Life Bakery and Restaurant,** Hae Yung Popkin (Owner) or Scott Merrick (Manager), 1811 Division St., Nashville, TN 37203. (615) 329-2525. **Type of Business:** Restaurant. **Sells:** Vegetarian casseroles, soups, muffins, desserts, breads, poultry and seafood. Organic? Asserted 50% organic. Water is filtered. **Specialties:** Vegetarian and macrobiotic dishes available. Musical entertainment also offered. **Prices:** $2.50–$11.95 **Hours:** M-Sat. 7–9:30, Sun. 8–3. **Reservations:** Not accepted: 100% No smoking. **Credit:** V M AE DC Carte Blanche.

Nashville, **Sunshine Grocery,** Lin Cameron, 3201 Belmont Blvd., Nashville, TN 37212. (615) 297-5100. **Type of Business:** Retail store. **Sells to:** The public. **Sells:** Fresh organic produce and wholefoods. **Organic?** They say that they carry as many organic items as possible and that the percentage is constantly growing. **Credit:** None. **Prices:** Grocery purchases totaling over $35 before tax receive 5% discounts. Orders on case lots get 16–25% off. **Hours:** M-Sat. 9–7, Closed Sun.

TX

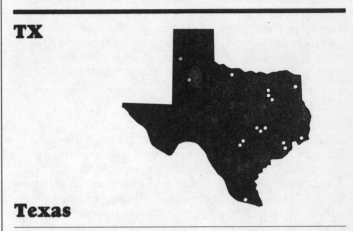

Texas

Atlanta, **J. Francis Co.,** Rt. 3, Box 54, Atlanta, TX 75551. (214) 796-3364. **Type of Business:** Growers. **Sells:** Pecans. **Organic?** Asserted organic. **Minimum Order:** 5–10 lbs.

Austin, **Mother's Cafe and Garden,** 4215 Duval, Austin, TX 78751. (512) 451-3944. **Type of Business:** Restaurant. **Sells:** Vegetarian food only; pancakes, omelets, tacos, stir-fry vegetables, enchiladas, pasta, salads, soups, beer, wine, smoothies and other beverages. **Organic?** Asserted 5% organic. **Specialties:** Vegan and macrobiotic dishes are available. Musical entertainment also offered. **Prices:** $2.50–$6.95 **Hours:** M-F 11:30–10, S-S 10–10. **Reservations:** Possible for groups of 6 or more. 100% No smoking. **Credit:** V M DC Carte Blanche. $10 minimum. **Commendations:** *Austin Chronicle*—Best Vegetarian Restaurant in Austin (from readers' poll), 1989; *Texas Monthly* magazine, May 1987.

Austin, **Treaty Oak Cafe,** Charles Mayes, 1101 W 5th St., Austin, TX 78703. (512) 482-8226. **Type of Business:** Restaurant. **Sells:** Fresh seafood and vegetables, pastas, enchiladas, natural meats and poultry. **Organic?** Asserted 5% organic. Water is not filtered. **Specialties:** Vegetarian, vegan and macrobiotic dishes are available. **Prices:** $5.95–$16.95 **Hours:** Lunch M-F 11:30–3, Dinner M-T 5:30–9:30 (F-Sat–10), Sun. Brunch 10–2. **Reservations:** Possible. 100% No smoking. **Credit:** V M AE. **Commendations:** Reviewed by Diane Payton Gomez in *The American-Statesman*, 1989.

Austin, **Whole Foods Market,** 4006 South Lamar, Austin, TX 78704. (512) 448–3884, **and** 914 North Lamar, 78703, (512) 476–1236 and 9070 Research Blvd. 78703, (512) 451–0275. (Also in Dallas, Houston, Richardson; New Orleans, LA; and Berkeley and Palo Alto CA.) **Type of Business:** Part of a chain of eight wholefood supermarkets in Texas, Louisiana, and California. **Sells to:** The public. **Sells:** A huge variety of wholefood grocery items and organic produce. They claim to have "the most significantly integrated mix of conventional 'clean' food and 'natural' foods" in the country. **Organic?** They are a part of the program run by the Texas Department of Agriculture. **Credit:** V M AE. **Prices:** 5% discount for unopened retail cases. **Hours:** 9–11, 7 days a week. **Commendations and Comments:** Whole Foods Markets are known for their informative and relaxing atmosphere and the Whole Foods employees tend to be quite knowledgeable. Lectures and tours are offered to encourage better shopping. They claim (as does Real Foods in San Francisco) to be the largest retailer of organically grown produce in the U.S. Whole Foods was the fourth most recommended chain in our survey.♥♦♦♦

Dallas, **Kalachandji's,** 5430 Gurley Ave., Dallas, TX 75223. (214) 821–1048. **Type of Business:** Restaurant. **Sells:** Gourmet vegetarian and Indian cuisine, homemade bread, pies, desserts and salads. **Organic?** Water is filtered. **Specialties:** Vegetarian dishes available. Musical entertainment is also offered. **Prices:** $4.95–$8.95. **Hours:** Tu-Sun. 5:30–9:30. **Reservations:** Possible. 100% no smoking. **Credit:** V M AE D. **Commendations:** Listed as one of the top ten restaurants in U.S by *The Vegetarian Times,* April 1987.

Dallas, **Whole Foods Market,** 2218 Lower Greenville, Ave., Dallas, TX 75206. (214) 824–1744. (Also in Austin, Houston, Richardson, New Orleans (LA), and Palo Alto and Berkeley (CA). **Type of Business:** Wholefood supermarket, part of a chain of eight in Texas, Louisiana, and California. **Comments and Commendations:** Whole Foods was one of the most highly and broadly recommended businesses in our survey. Their stores are known for their relaxed atmospheres and their employees tend to be very knowledgeable. (Please see Austin listing.)♥♦♦♦

Hereford, **Arrowhead Mills Inc.,** Boyd Foster, PO Box 2059, 110 South Lawton, Hereford, TX 79045. (806) 364–0730. (806) 364–8242. **Type of Business:** Manufacturer and retail store. **Sells to:** Retail stores and public. **Sells:** Beans (chickpeas, kidney beans, pinto beans, anazi, adzuki, lentils, soy, split green), grains, cereals, flour, seeds, brown rice and oils. **Organic?** Asserted 75% organic. Certified by Texas Department of Agriculture. **Credit:** V M. **Prices:** Special prices for bulk orders. **Hours:** Retail store: M-F 8–5 **Shipping:** Bulk orders are shipped only within Texas and adjacent states. Orders usually shipped within 5 days. Delivery can take up to 10 days. **Minimum Order:** $5 for mail order (provided only for those who cannot buy their products locally), 300 lbs. for bulk orders. **Catalogue Available?** Yes.♥♦♦♦

Houston, **The Macrobiotic Center of Texas,** Janis Jamail or Catherine Willhite, 3815 Garrott St., Houston, TX 77006. (713) 523–0171. **Type of Business:** Restaurant, retail store and nutrition center. **Sells:** Lunch—One-plate meal includes soup, grain, legumes, variety of vegetables, salad, greens and tea. Dessert optional. Dinner—Pasta, seitan stroganoff and burgers, tofu lasagna and quiche, steamed vegetables, sauces and beverages. **Organic?** Asserted 75% organic. Water is filtered. **Specialties:** Macrobiotic dishes only; Mexican tamales, blackbean tacos, vegetarian tofu quiche, pasta and spring rolls. Nutrition and cooking classes offered. **Prices:** $5.25–$7.25 **Hours:** Office and store M-F 10–4; Lunch 12–2, Dinner (T-Sat.) 5:30–8. **Reservations:** Possible. 100% No smoking. **Credit:** None. **Commendations:** Articles in the *Chronicle, Post, Time* magazine, and other Houston city magazines.

Houston, **Whole Foods Market,** 2900 South Shepherd, Houston, TX 77098. (713) 520–1937. (Also in Austin, Dallas, Richardson, New Orleans (LA), and Palo Alto and Berkeley (CA).) **Type of Business:** Wholefood supermarket, part of a chain of 8 in Texas, Louisianna, and California. **Comments and Commendations:** Whole Foods was one of the most highly and broadly recommended businesses in our survey. Their stores are known for their relaxed atmospheres and their employees tend to be very knowledgeable. See Austin listing.♥♦♦♦

Lubbock, **Well Body Natural Foods,** Susan Alderson, 3651 34th, Lubbock, TX 79410. (806) 793–1015. **Type of Business:** Retail store. **Sells to:** The public. **Sells:** A wide variety of fresh produce and processed foods. **Organic?** 50% organic. **Credit:** V M. **Prices:** 20% discount on bulk orders. **Hours:** M-Sat. 10–6. **Minimum Order:** 1 case or 1 lb. **Comments:** Features a deli and restaurant. Has been in the *Texas Monthly* a number of times (January 1989). Renovations are being undertaken in 1990.

Mauriceville, **The Crawdad Farm,** PO Box 395, Mauriceville, TX 77626. (409) 745–2388. **Type of Business:** Grower. **Sells to:** Retailers. **Sells:** Rice (long grain), live crawfish. **Organic?** Asserted organic (100%). **Minimum Order:** Wholesale quantities only.

Mission, **Stanley and Marina Jacobson,** 1505 Doherty, Mission, TX 78572. (512) 585–1712. **Type of Business:** Grower. **Sells to:** Mostly public by mail order. Some wholesale. **Sells:** Oranges and Texas Ruby Red Grapefruit. **Organic?** 100% certified organic by the Texas Department of Agriculture. **Credit:** No credit cards. **Prices:** "Price is very close to supermarkets and less than a healthfood store—and picked fresh!" **Shipping:** "We pick tree-ripe and ship within 24 hours, usually less." Citrus is packed in shredded paper that protects against freeze and other climate changes. **Minimum Order:** 1/4 bushel (about 15 pounds). **Catalogue Available?** Yes.

Richardson, **Whole Foods Market,** 60 Dal-Rich Village, Richardson, TX 75080. (214) 699–8075. Also in Austin, Dallas, Houston, New Orleans (LA), and Palo Alto and Berkeley (CA). **Type of Business:** Wholefood supermarket, part of a chain of 8 in Texas, Louisianna, and California. **Comments and Commendations:** Whole Foods was one of the most highly and broadly recommended businesses in our survey. Their stores are known for their relaxed atmospheres and their employees tend to be very knowledgeable. See Austin listing.♥♦♦♦

San Antonio, **Artesia Waters Inc.,** Richard M. Scoville (President), 4671 Walzem Rd., San Antonio, TX 78218. (512) 654–0293 FAX: (512) 654–3027 **Type of Business:** Manufacturer. **Sells to:** Distributors, wholesalers, retailers and by mail order to public. **Sells:** Bottled mineral water (sparkling, still, naturally flavored and distilled). **Organic?** Asserted 100% organic. Sodium, sugar and calorie-free. **Credit:** None. **Prices:** Special prices available for bulk orders. **Hours:** 8–5. **Shipping:** Delivery time by truck is 10 working days and for mail orders 6 weeks. **Minimum Order:** None. **Catalogue Available?** Yes.

San Antonio, **Gini's Home Cooking and Bakery,** Gini or Tol Crowley, 7214 Blanco, San Antonio, TX 78216. (512) 342–2768. **Type of Business:** Restaurant. **Sells:** Pritikin style prepared soups, vegetables, breads, lasagna, spaghetti, curry, fresh fish, salads and desserts. **Organic?** Asserted 10% organic. Water is not filtered. **Specialties:** Vegetarian, vegan and macrobiotic dishes available. **Prices:** $5.95–$9.95 **Hours:** M-F 7–10, Sat. 8–10, Sun. 9–9 **Reservations:** Possible. 100% No smoking. **Credit:** V M AE DC. $5 minimum. **Commendations:** *San Antonio* magazine's Silver Spoon Award, 1988. (readers vote for "Best Alternate Dining.")

Wichita Falls, **Sunshine Natural Foods,** Parker Square, Wichita Falls, TX 76308. (817) 767–2093. **Type of Business:** Retail store. **Sells to:** The public. **Sells:** A full line of fresh produce and grocery items. **Organic?** Asserted 30% organic. **Credit:** V M. **Prices:** 10% discount on bulk. **Hours:** M-F 9–6, Sat. 10–5. **Salad Bar:** M-Sat. 11–2. **Comments:** They grind their own flour daily and bake whole wheat breads, cookies, muffins, and pies. Salad Bar offers Santa Fe-style Mexican Buffet first Friday of each month.

UT

Utah

Ogden, **Bright Day Health Foods,** Elizabeth W. Shafer, 952 28th Street, Ogden, UT 84403. (801) 399–0260. **Type of Business:** Retail store. **Sells to:** The public. **Sells:** A wide variety of processed food as well as fresh grains, nuts, soy products, and spices. **Credit:** V M AE. **Prices:** 10% discount if ordered in case lots. **Hours:** M-Sat. 9:30–6:30 (store), M-Sat. 11–4 (Lunch Bar). **Comments:** Deli/Lunch Bar provides sandwiches, soups, hot entrees, cookies, muffins, carrot juice, green drink (celery, spinach, parsley) made fresh daily. One of very few health food restaurants in Salt Lake/Ogden area.♦

Provo, **Govinda's Buffet,** Peter Corbett, 260 N University Ave., Provo, UT 84601. (801) 375–0404. **Type of Business:** Restaurant. **Sells:** Sandwiches, salads, soups, rice dishes and desserts—all vegetarian. **Organic?** No organic claims. **Specialties:** Everything fresh daily. **Prices:** All you can eat buffet, Lunch $3.75, Dinner $5.25. **Hours:** 11–2:30, 5–9 daily. **Credit:** V M AE CB.

Salt Lake City, **New Frontier Natural Foods,** Steve Anderson, 1029 Second Ave., Salt Lake City, UT 84103. (801) 355–7401. **Type of Business:** Restaurant and retail store. **Sells:** Deli salads, sandwiches, smoothies, cakes, pies, casseroles, **Organic?** Asserted 40%. **Specialties:** "Good home cooking," and bulk groceries. **Prices:** Entrees—$3.25–$4.50 **Hours:** 9–9. **Credit:** V M. **Commendations:** *Natural Foods Merchandiser* 1985.♦

Salt Lake City, **New Frontiers Market,** 1026 Second Avenue, Salt Lake City, UT 84103. See New Frontiers Market, 2454 South 700 East, Salt Lake City, UT.♦

Salt Lake City, **New Frontiers Market,** Jake Collier, 2454 South 700 East, Salt Lake City, UT 84106. (801) 359–7913. **Type of Business:** Retail store. **Sells to:** The public. **Sells:** A very wide selection of fresh produce and processed foods. **Organic?** 10–40% organic, depending on the time of year. **Credit:** V M AE. **Prices:** 5–15% discounts on bulk orders depending on quantity and item. **Hours:** M-Sat. 9–9, Sun. 10–5.

VT

Vermont

Barre, **Cherry Hill Cooperative Cannery,** Ken Davis, General Manager, MR 1, Barre, VT 05641. (802) 479–2555. **Type of Business:** Manufacturer and distributor. **Sells to:** Distributors, retailers, wholesalers and public. **Sells:** Apple sauces, apple butters, maple syrup, marinara sauce, mustards, pickles, salsa and dressings. **Organic?** Asserted 25% organic. **Credit:** V M for retail sales only. **Prices:** No special prices for bulk orders. **Hours:** M-F 8–5. **Shippping:** By common carrier and UPS. Lead time 2–3 days. **Minimum Order:** None for retail or wholesale orders; 150 cases for distributor orders. **Catalogue Available?** Yes.

Bethel, **Rathdowney Ltd.,** Brendan Downey-Butler, 3 River St., Bethel, VT 05032. (802) 234-9928. **Type of Business:** Manufacturer, mail-order distributor and retail store. **Sells:** Thai peanut sauce, apple sauce, preserves, fruit juices, coffee, tea, salsa, popcorn, chips, muffins, pancakes, crackers, cake mixes, herbs and spices. **Organic?** Certified 100% organic. **Credit:** V M AE and personal checks. **Prices:** Prices negotiable for bulk orders on a per order basis; discounts between 7.5%–12%. **Hours:** M-Sat. 9–5, Sun. 11–4 **Shipping:** Delivery between 5–8 days. **Minimum Order:** $75. **Catalogue Available?** Yes.

Brattleboro, **The Common Ground,** 25 Eliot St. Brattleboro, VT 05351. (802) 257-0855. **Type of Business:** Restaurant. **Sells:** Natural foods cuisine with vegetarian and macrobiotic options. **Organic?** Estimated 50% organic in the winter, 80–100% in the summer. **Specialties:** Miso, vegetarian chili, cashew burgers, wholegrain desserts. Other specials vary meal to meal, depending on who is cooking. **Prices:** A self-serve people's meal costs $3.60 and up. Scallops and the catch-of-the-day can cost up to $11. An average meal runs $5–$7. **Hours:** M, W-Sat lunch, 11:30–2:30; closed-grill, 2:30–5:30; dinner, 5:30–9 (5:30–8 in winter). Sun brunch, 10:30–1:30; dinner 5:30–9 (5:30–8 in winter). Closed Tuesdays. **Reservations:** Possible. 100% no-smoking. **Credit:** None; cash or check. **Comments:** The restaurant has good food and a lively, friendly atmosphere. They feature live dinner music on weekends (often really good folk musicians) and after-dinner dancing about twice a month. Common Ground has been a worker-owned collective for 18 years.♥♦♦

Brattleboro, **Northeast Cooperatives,** Cynthia Moore (purchasing agent), Leonard Danker (produce manager), PO Box 1120, Quinn Road, Brattleboro, VT 05301. (802) 257-5856 in VT (main warehouse), (617) 389-9032 in MA (produce). **Type of Business:** Distributor. **Sells to:** Retailers, buying clubs. **Sells:** Coffee, dairy products and eggs, dried beans, dried fruit, fresh fruit, whole grains, flour and meals, processed grain products, herbs and spices, juices, nuts and nut butters, oils, seeds, soy products, sweeteners, teas, fresh vegetables, organic cheese. **Organic?** 30–40% of grocery and dairy items asserted organic. 50% of produce asserted organic; suppliers must provide papers. **Minimum Order:** $400.

Burlington, **Origanum Natural Foods,** Catherine Camp, 227 Main St., Burlington, VT 05401. (802) 863-6103. **Type of Business:** Retailer. **Sells to:** The public. **Sells:** A full range of wholefood grocery items, bulk items, and organic produce. **Organic?** Produce is 50–60% organic (75–80% in summer), about 40% of bulk items and grocery items are organic. **Credit:** V M. **Prices:** Discounts for cases, 25 or 50 pound bags. **Hours:** M-F 9:30–7:30, Sat.

9:30–7 Sun., 11–5. **Shipping:** They will do mail orders, but have no formal mail-order operation as of January 1990.

Chester, **Gourmet Produce Co.,** Richard D. Rommer, RR 3, Box 348, Chester, VT 05143. (802) 875-3820. **Type of Business:** Grower and mail-order distributor. **Sells to:** Retail stores and individuals. **Sells:** Fresh wheatgrass, frozen wheatgrass juice, sunflower sprouts, radish sprouts, wheatgrass juicers and growing supplies. **Organic?** Vermont Organic Farmers Association certified 100% organic. **Credit:** V M AE. **Prices:** Wholesale prices available for bulk orders. **Shipping:** Most orders shipped same day via UPS throughout Continental U.S. **Minimum Order:** None.

East Hardwick, **Vermont Northern Growers Co-op,** Lou Pulver, Box 125, East Hardwick, VT 05836. (802) 472-6285. **Type of Business:** Marketing Co-op for members. **Sells:** Fresh fruit and vegetables (beets, cabbage, carrots, celery, onions, potatoes, turnips and rutabagas, cauliflower, broccoli, parsnips, squash and apples). **Organic?** Vermont Organic Farmers Association certified 100% organic. **Credit:** None. **Prices:** Special prices for ton pallets of root crops. **Hours:** Wed 10–1. **Shipping:** Delivers by truck and UPS. UPS shipped on Mondays. **Minimum Order:** One $25 bag. **Catalogue Available?** Yes.

East Thetford, **Longwind Farm,** David Chapman, Box 203, East Thetford, VT 05043. (802) 785-2793. **Type of Business:** Retail store, farmstand and tomato wholesaler. **Sells to:** The public. **Sells:** Fresh vegetables (tomatoes, beets, broccoli, carrots, cauliflower, corn, cucumbers, eggplant, garlic, lettuce, onions, peas, peppers, potatoes, radishes, spinach, squash and zucchini), strawberries and basil; also sells bedding plants and perennials. **Organic?** Vermont Organic Farmers Association certified 98% organic. **Hours:** S-S 10–6. **Shipping:** Deliver only in Northeast.

Jacksonville, **Coombs Maple Products Inc.,** Dana Coombs, Maple La., HCR 13, Box 50, Jacksonville, VT 05342. (802) 368-7301. **Type of Business:** Manufacturer and retail store. **Sells:** Pancakes, apple juice, jelly, maple syrup, popcorn, chocolate, snacks, candy bars and other confection. **Organic?** Asserted 75% organic. **Credit:** V M. **Prices:** Special prices for bulk orders available depending on volume. **Hours:** 7:30–5 daily. **Shipping:** Orders shipped within 24 hours. **Minimum Order:** None. **Catalogue Available?** Yes.

Middlebury, **Earth's Best,** Susan Smiley, Pond Lane, Mail to: PO Box 887, Middlebury, VT 05753. (802) 388-7974. **Type of Business:** Distributor. **Sells to:** Retailers. **Sells:** Fruit (apples in bulk bins; plums, peaches, pears and apricots in 40 unit frozen IQF; bananas in 30 unit frozen boxes); whole grains (barley, rice, millet, and oatmeal in 50 unit bags); vegetables (sweet potatoes and carrots in bulk bins or 25 unit bags; green peas and green beans in 30 unit frozen IQF; spinach 30 unit frozen; onions 30 unit frozen or dehydrated); baby food (fruit and vegetable purées, fruit and grain combinations in 4.5 ounce glass jars; rice and mixed grain cereals in 8–ounce canisters). Organic? Certified organic by the Organic Crop Improvement Association, California Certified Organic Farmers, Organic Growers and Buyers Association, and Natural Organic Farmers Association. Produce must be grown on soil free from pesticides for three years. **Minimum Order:** Baby food minimum is 286 cases.

Middletown Springs, **The Herb Patch,** Diane Copley, Pawlet Road, PO Box 1111, Middletown Springs, VT 05757. (802) 282-HERB. **Type of Business:** Manufacturer. **Sells to:** Retailers and some limited retail sales. **Sells:** Herbs, spices, herbal vinegars, mulling spices, honey, salt-free dip mixes, salt-free classic culinary blends, and herbal teas. **Organic?** Asserted 30% organic. **Credit:** V M. **Prices:** Special prices for blends ordered in bulk. **Shipping:** 2-3 days delivery. **Minimum Order:** 1 case. **Catalogue Available?** Yes.

Montpelier, **Horn of the Moon Cafe,** 8 Langdon St., Montpelier, VT 05602. (802) 223-2895. **Type of Business:** Restaurant. **Sells:** Vegetarian dishes; soups, salads and baked goods. **Organic?** Asserted 50% organic. Water is not filtered. **Specialties:** Vegan and macrobiotic dishes available. Musical entertainment also offered. **Prices:** $4-$8. **Hours:** M 7-3, Tu-Sat. 7-9. **Reservations:** Not accepted. 100% no smoking. **Credit:** None. **Commendations:** New England Monthly magazine.

Montpelier, **Hunger Mountain Co-op,** Inc. , 403 Barre St., Montpelier, VT 05602. (802) 223-6910. **Type of Business:** Retail store. **Sells to:** The public. **Sells:** A complete line of natural groceries and fresh produce. **Organic?** Fresh produce 40% organic (certified by Organic Crop Improvement Association, Farm Verified Organic), other grocery 20%. **Credit:** None. **Prices:** Bulk discount approximately 10% below retail. **Hours:** M-Sat. 9-6, F 9-7, Sun. 10-4.

Plainfield, **Littlewood Farm,** Joe Klein, RFD 1, Box 1400, Plainfield, VT 05667. 454-8466. **Type of Business:** Grower. **Sells to:** Mostly to distributors. To public through farmers market (Plainfield Village—Every Sat. from July to October). **Sells:** Vegetables: beets, broccoli, cabbage, carrots, cauliflower, celery, corn, cucumbers, eggplant, garlic, lettuce, onions, peppers, potatoes, radishes, spinach, squash (winter and summer), tomatoes, turnips, zucchini, daikon, chinese cabbage, and bok choi. Fruits: strawberries. **Organic?** Certified 100% Organic by the Vermont Organic Farmers Association (NOFA-VT). **Credit:** None. **Comments:** Littlewood has recently planted a small orchard of apples, plums, and pears that they expect to market locally.

Randolph Center, **David Carpenter,** RR 1, Box 130, Randolph Center, VT 05001. (802) 728-3782. **Type of Business:** Grower. **Sells to:** 95% of sales are to co-ops under the name: Deep Root Organic Truck Farmers Assoc. **Sells:** Vegetables (beets, broccoli, cabbage, carrots, cucumbers, lettuce, onions, peas, potatoes, spinach, squash, turnips, and zucchini) **Organic?** Certified Organic 100% by the Vermont Organic Farmers Association. **Credit:** No credit cards accepted. **Hours:** 8-6:30.

South Royalton, **Jasmine & Bread,** Sherrie Maurer, RR#2, Box 256, South Royalton, VT 05068. (802) 763-7115. **Type of Business:** Grower, sells direct to the public. **Sells:** Condiments. Tomato apple ketchup, chili sauce, mustard, plum sweet and sour, and other preserves, condiments almost all "no-sugar, no-salt". **Organic?** Asserted organic: fruits and vegetables are grown entirely without pesticides." **Prices:** Her mustard goes for $3.75/jar through the mail, or for $4.25-$4.98 at a city health-food store. She mails two jars for $1.75. **Comments:** The name of the company comes from a medieval poem.

St. Johnsbury, **Dancing Bears Farm,** Stewart Hoyt and Grace Gershuny, Box 84, RFD 3, St. Johnsbury, VT 05819. (802) 633-4152. **Type of Business:** Market gardeners. (Grace Gershuny is also involved in consulting to the organic food industry, is a board member of the Organic Foods Production Association of North America and co-author of its "Guidelines for the Organic foods Industry".) **Sells to:** Public at St. Johnsbury Farmers Market only. **Sells:** Poultry, fresh vegetables (beets, broccoli, cabbage, carrots, cauliflower, cucumbers, garlic, lettuce, onions, peas, peppers, potatoes, radishes, squash, tomatoes, zucchini and oriental greens), fresh herbs and spices (basil, chives, dill, oregano, parsley, sage, thyme.) **Organic?** Vermont Organic Farmers Association certified 100% organic. **Credit:** None. **Prices:** Wholesale discounts available for orders in case quantities. **Shipping:** Local delivery only. **Minimum Order:** $10 for delivery. **Catalogue Available?** No.

USVI

United States Virgin Islands

Christiansted St. Croix, **Good Health,** Antoine or Pat Murray, United Shopping Plaza, Christiansted St. Croix, Virgin Islands, USVI 00820. (809) 778-5565. **Type of Business:** Retail store, mail-order distributor, and wholesaler. **Sells:** Beans, dried fruits, grains, cheeses, nuts, soy product, spices, flour, oils, rices, pastas. **Organic?** 25% asserted organic. **Credit:** V M. **Prices:** Special prices for high volume (over $1,000 gets 15% discount). **Hours:** M-Sat. 9-7. **Shipping:** Not serving Canada. **Minimum Order:** Only for wholesale: $100. **Catalogue Available?** Yes.

VA

Virginia

Blacksburg, **Eats Natural Foods,** 1200 N Main St., Blacksburg, VA. (703) 463-2279. **Type of Business:** Retail store, co-op, mail order, and distributor. **Sells to:** The public, restaurants, and buying clubs. **Sells:** An impressive range of natural grocery items and fresh organic produce. **Organic?** Fresh produce asserted as 95% organic, other items, 75%. **Credit:** V M. **Prices:** 10% discount on pre-orders. **Hours:** M-Sat. 9–8, Sun. 12–6.

Charlottesville, **Integral Yoga Natural Foods** (formerly Blue Mountain) 923 Preston Ave., Charlottesville, VA 22901. (Locations also in Richmond and New York City.) **Type of Business:** A vegetarian/wholefood grocery store. **Sells to:** The public. **Sells:** An impressive variety of fresh organic produce, wholefood grocery items, and macrobiotic foods. They are a vegetarian store and carry no meat fish, chicken, or eggs (though they do carry some dairy products and some foods contain egg-whites). **Organic?** Asserted 60–80% of produce and 25–30% of processed goods. **Credit:** None. **Prices:** 10% discount on bulk purchases (as long as the product is not one of the monthly specials). **Hours:** M-F 9:30–6:30, Sat. 9:30–5:30, Closed Sun. **Shipping:** UPS. **Minimum Order:** None. **Catalogue Available?** They offer a partial list now and will soon offer a more complete catalogue. **Comments:** They emphasize customer service and special orders.♦

Edinburg, **Magic Garden Produce,** Robert Peer, Rt. 3, Box 304, Edinburg, VA 22824. (703) 459-3376. **Type of Business:** Producer, shipper and mail-order distributor. **Sells to:** Retailers, restaurants, and the public. **Sells:** Rainbow trout, range-fed chickens, watercress, sprouts and tomatoes. **Organic?** Asserted 100% organic. **Prices:** Discount prices available based on volume. **Shipping:** Delivery overnight by air freight, 1 to 3 days by UPS, and next day by truck. Trout are always shipped on Mondays. **Minimum Order:** 5 lbs. for rainbow trout and poultry; depends on distance for fresh produce. **Catalogue Available?** Yes.

Hamilton, **Natural Mercantile Store,** 154 E Colonial Hwy., Hamilton, VA 22068. (703) 338-7080. **Type of Business:** Retail store. **Sells to:** The public. **Sells:** A comprehensive range of wholefood groceries and fresh organic produce. **Organic?** Fresh produce 100% organic (certified

by Natural Organic Farmers Association, California Certified Organic Farmers), other grocery 85%. **Credit:** V M. **Prices:** Bulk discounts require 10% advance payment. **Hours:** M-F 10–7, Sat. 10–6, Sun. 11–4. **Comments:** Established in 1972. This store is situated in a rural area, but has stayed full-service (offering bulk, organic foods and herbs) even, sometimes, at the cost of turning a profit.

Lexington, **Healthy Foods Market,** 110 W Washington, Lexington, VA 24450. (703) 463-6954. **Type of Business:** Retail store and co-op. **Sells to:** The public. **Sells:** A full line of natural groceries and fresh produce. **Organic?** Asserted 100% organic for fresh produce, 60–70% for processed goods. **Credit:** None. **Prices:** Bulk discount for members—cost plus 10%. **Hours:** M-F 10–6, Sat. 11–4.

McLean, **Sprouts,** 6216 Old Dominion Dr., McLean, VA 22101. (703) 241-7177. **Type of Business:** Retailer and deli. **Sells to:** The public and retail stores. **Sells:** A wide array of wholefood groceries and produce (fresh fruit by special order only). **Organic?** Fresh produce 50% organic (certified by Organic Crop Improvement Association), other grocery 50%. **Credit:** V M. **Prices:** Bulk discounts: 10% for cases ordered in advance and purchases over $100, 20% for purchases over $200. Senior citizens' discount—10%. **Hours:** M-Sat. 10 a.m.–1 a.m., Sun. 12–5. **Minimum Order:** 15 items for sandwiches available wholesale. **Catalogue Available?** Yes (price list). **Comments:** This is a two-in-one business. A retail health food store, but also a wholesale sandwich supplier to 25 other stores.

Newport News, **Health Trail,** 10846 Warwick Blvd., Newport News, VA 23601. (804) 596-8018. **Type of Business:** Retail store. **Sells to:** The public. **Sells:** A good range of natural foods and fresh produce. **Organic?** Produce asserted 95% organic; processed foods 75%. **Credit:** V M AE. **Prices:** 10% discount on case lots. **Hours:** M-Sat. 10–6, F 10–9.

Norfolk, **Health Food Center,** (1st location) 400 E Indian River Rd., Norfolk, VA 23523. (804) 545-7357. (2nd location) 210 E Plume St., Monticello Arcade, Norfolk, VA 23510. (804) 625-6656. (3rd location) 7639 Granby St., Norfolk, VA 23505. (804) 489-4242. (4th location) 700 N Military Hwy., Norfolk, VA 23502. (804) 461-2883. **Type of Business:** Retail store. **Sells to:** The public. **Sells:** Beans, dairy products, dried fruit, grains, nuts, soy products, spices, organic apples and carrots. **Organic?** Asserted 85–90%. **Credit:** V M. **Hours:** 10–9.

Richmond, **City Markets Inc.,** 5602 Patterson Ave., Richmond, VA 23226. (804) 266-7410. **Type of Business:** Retail store and deli. **Sells to:** The public. **Sells:** A complete selection of organic produce and wholefood grocery items. **Organic?** Produce is about 65% organic (Organic Crop Improvement Association, Farm Verified Organic, California Certified Organic Farmers, Demeter). About 60% of processed goods are organic. **Credit:** V M. **Prices:** Discounts on case orders and bulk foods. **Hours:** M-Sat. 9–8, Open Sundays starting in early 1990. **Commendations and Comments:** They also carry only cruelty-free cosmetics and body-care products. The deli has a wide selection of soups and salads. They also boast a knowledgeable staff.

Richmond, **Grace Place Restaurant,** 826 W Grace St., Richmond, VA 23220. (804) 353-3680. **Type of Business:** Restaurant. **Sells:** Vegetarian only with vegan and macrobiotic options. **Organic?** Asserted 50-75% organic. Water is filtered. **Specialties:** Soups, desserts, bread, and nightly specials. **Prices:** $5.50-$7.50 **Hours:** T-Sat. 11:30-3, 5:30-9 **Reservations:** Not accepted. 100% no smoking. **Credit:** None.

Richmond, **Integral Yoga Natural Foods,** 3016 W Cary St., Richmond, VA 23221. (Locations also in Charlottesville and New York City.) **Type of Business:** A vegetarian/wholefood grocery store. **Sells to:** The public. **Sells:** An impressive variety of fresh organic produce, wholefood grocery items, and macrobiotic foods. They are a vegetarian store and carry no meat, fish, chicken, or eggs (though they do carry some dairy products and some foods contain egg-whites). **Organic?** Asserted 60-80% of produce and 25-30% of processed goods. **Credit:** None. **Prices:** 10% discount on bulk purchases (as long as the product is not one of the monthly specials). **Hours:** M-F 9:30-6:30, Sat. 9:30-5:30. **Comments:** They emphasize customer service and special orders. (Because this store is relatively new, information was derived from the questionnaires received from its sister stores in Charlottesville and NYC.)

Virginia Beach, **The Fresh Market & Deli,** 550 First Colonial Rd., #309 Hilltop Sq. Shopping Center, Virginia Beach, VA 23451. (804) 425-5383. **Type of Business:** Retail store and Deli. **Sells:** Baked goods, beans, breads, cereals, dairy products, flour, fruit juices, nuts, oils, pasta, rice, soy products, and fresh vegetables when in season. Deli sells pita sandwiches, salads, chilis, yogurt, crackers and beverages. **Organic?** Asserted 75% organic. Water is filtered. **Specialties:** Vegetarian, vegan and macrobiotic dishes available. **Prices:** $2.95-$6.95 in the deli. Discounts on special retail orders. **Hours:** 9-8. 100% No smoking. **Credit:** V M AE. $10 minimum. **Commendations:** Mentioned in the Coastal Pathways brochure, summer 1989.

Virginia Beach, **Health Food Center,** (1st location) 4584-10 Pembroke Mall, Virginia Beach Blvd., 23462. (804) 499-0002. (2nd location) 738 Hilltop North Shopping Center, Laskin Rd., Virginia Beach, VA 23451. (804) 425-8680. **Type of Business:** Retail store. **Sells to:** The public. **Sells:** See listings for Norfolk.

Virginia Beach, **Heritage Store,** Box 444, Virginia Beach, VA 23458. (804) 428-0100. **Type of Business:** Retail store, manufacturer, mail-order distributor, and holistic center. **Sells to:** The public, retailers, and distributors. **Sells:** A range of wholefood groceries plus selected produce items. **Organic?** Fresh produce asserted 80% organic, other grocery, 25%. **Credit:** V M AE. **Prices:** Discounts for commercial accounts. **Hours:** M-Sat. 10-7, Sun. 12-6. **Minimum Order:** $50 minimum for wholesale customers. **Catalogue Available?** Yes. **Comments:** The company also

offers a variety of other items. The items are mostly derived from an interpretation of the teachings of the late evangelist, Edgar Cayce.

Warrenton, **Hatch Natural Foods Corporation,** Robert Wagg, PO Box 888, Warrenton, VA 22186. (703) 987-8551. (Physical location is Sperryville, VA 22740.) **Type of Business:** Distributor. **Sells to:** Retailers, buying clubs or co-ops, restaurants and public (by appointment only). **Sells:** Baked goods, dairy products, dried beans, dried fruit, fresh fruit and vegetables, whole grains, cereals, flour and meals, breads, pasta, rice, herbs and spices, meat, nuts and nut butters, oils, seeds, soy products, fruit juices and other beverages. **Organic?** Asserted 50% organic. **Credit:** None. **Shipping:** Truck deliveries to Mid-Atlantic only (PA-NC). 2 day lead time for delivered orders, 10 days for UPS, 2 days for pick-up customers. **Minimum Order:** $300 for truck deliveries, $50 for pick-up customers. **Catalogue Available?** Yes.

WV

West Virginia

Birch River, **Brier Run Farm,** Rt. 1, Box 73, Birch River, WV 26610. **Type of Business:** Growers. **Sells to:** **Sells:** Goat cheeses. **Organic?** Asserted organic.

Parkersburg, **Mother Earth Foods,** 1638 19th St., Parkersburg, WV 26101. (304) 428-1024. **Type of Business:** Retail store. **Sells to:** The public direct and by mail. **Sells:** A good selection of wholefood groceryitems and some fresh organic produce. **Organic?** Produce 95% organic (Organic Crop Improvement Association, Farm Verified Organic); processed goods about 50-60%. **Credit:** V M. **Prices:** 20% discounts on bulk orders. **Hours:** M-Th 9-6, F 9-7, Sat. 9-5. **Shipping:** UPS anywhere. **Minimum Order:** $25. **Catalogue Available?** No.

WA

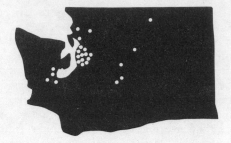

Washington

Bainbridge, **Natural Gourmet**, Willow Helton, 345 Winslow Ave. East, Bainbridge, WA 98110. (206) 842-2759. Type of Business: Retail store/Restaurant/Deli. Sells to: The public. Sells: Fresh beans, beverages, grains, nuts, soy products and spices as well as a selection of processed foods. Credit: V M. Prices: Bulk discount—10%. Hours: M-Sat. 10-7:30, Sun. 11-6.

Bainbridge Island, **Town and Country Market, Inc.,** Margaret Clark, Organics Consultant, 343 East Winslow Way, Bainbridge Island, WA 98110. (206) 842-3848. Type of Business: Retail store. Sells to: The public. Sells: An impressive variety of fresh organic produce and processed foods. Organic? California Certified Organic Farmers, staff member on Advisory Board to Washington Dept. of Agriculture Organic Certification Program. Prices: 10% discounts on case orders. Hours: Daily, 7a.m.–11p.m. Comments: This is a "conventional" supermarket which integrates natural and organic foods.

Chehalis, **Mt. Capra Cheese**, 279 SW 9th St., Chehalis, WA 98532. (206) 748-4224. Type of Business: Manufacturer and mail-order distributor. Sells to: Public at local markets. Sells: Dairy products; cheese (Greek style, cheddar style, jack style). Organic? Asserted 100% organic. Credit: None. Prices: No special prices for bulk orders. Hours: M-F 9-5. Shipping: Ship UPS and Parcel Post worldwide. Minimum Order: None. Catalogue Available? Yes.

Chelan, **Bear Foods Wholesale / Golden Florins General Store**, Charlie Bear, PO Box 2118, 125 E Woodin Ave., Chelan, WA 98816. (509) 682-5535. Type of Business: manufacturer, mail-order distributor, wholesaler, and, retail store. Sells to: The public, retailers, restaurants, and co-ops. Sells: A large selection of fresh produce and processed foods. Organic? 50% organic. Prices: Discounts for bulk orders by the case. Hours: M-Sat. 9-7, Sun. 12-5. Minimum Order: None. Catalogue Available? Yes.

Concrete, **Cascadian Farm**, 311 Dillard, Mail to: PO Box 568, Concrete, WA 98237. (206) 853-8175. Type of Business: Grower and distributor. Sells to: Retailers, mail order. Sells: Fresh fruit, frozen fruit, fresh vegetables, condiments (jams, pickles), whole grains, sweeteners, potato chips and frozen vegetables. Organic? Certified organic, member of Tilth.

Corville, **North Country People's Cooperative**, Gregory Mohr, 282 Weat Astor, Colville, WA 99114. (509) 684-6132. Type of Business: Retail store / Bakery. Sells to: Retailers / The public. Sells: Fresh produce—beans, beverages, dairy products, dried and fresh fruit, grains, nuts, soy products, spices. Processed goods—baked goods, beans, beverages, wide variety of breads, candy, cereals, dairy products (including 20 types of cheese), flour, processed fruit juices and drinks, dried fruits, nuts and nut butters, oils, pasta, rice, soy products. Organic? 30% organic. Prices: If prepaid, an additional 10% discount is given. Hours: M-F 9-6, Sat. 9-5. Minimum Order: None—unless a product they do not regularly carry is available only in case lots. Catalogue Available? Yes.

Ellensburg, **Better Life Natural Foods**, 111 West 6th St., Ellensburg, WA 98926. (509) 925-2505. Type of Business: Retail store/Mail-order distributor. Sells to: The public. Sells: A wide variety of processed foods and fresh produce (excluding vegetables). Credit: V M. Prices: Case packs discounted. Hours: M-W 9:30-6, Thurs 9:30-8, Fri 9:30-4, Sun. 12-4, Sat. closed. Shipping: Same day shipping. Minimum Order: $65 prepared freight. Catalogue Available? Yes.

Ellensburg, **Better Life Natural Foods**, 111 West 6th St., Ellensburg, WA 98926. (509) 925-2505. See Wenatchee Natural Foods, Wenatchee WA.

Everett, **Heritage Flour Mills**, J. Kreps, 2925 Chestnut, Everett, WA 98020. (206) 258-1582. Type of Business: Manufacturer and retailer. Sells to: Wholesalers, retailers and the public. Sells: Mixes (cake, muffins, pancakes and waffles), beans, teas, cereals (corn, granola, oatmeal and wheat), flour (buckwheat, rye and whole wheat), fruit drinks, oils, pasta and rice. Organic? Asserted 15-20% organic. Credit: None. Prices: Discounts for bulk. Hours: M-F, 9-5:30; Sat., 10-5. Shipping: Experienced bulk supplier to bakeries. Minimum Order: For wholesale, minimum order is one case. Catalogue Available? Yes. Comments: Free tours of the mills are available.

Everett, **The Sisters**, Victoria or Martha, 2804 Grand Ave., Everett, WA 98201. (206) 252-0480. Type of Business: Restaurant. Sells: Soups, salads, quiches, sandwiches, desserts, bagels, fresh squeezed juices and espresso. Organic? Water is not filtered. Specialties: Vegetarian dishes available. Prices: from $3-$5 Hours: M-F 7-4. Reservations: Not accepted: 66% no smoking. Credit: V M. Commendations: Listed in *Northwest Best Places*, 1988.

Mount Vernon, **Skagit Valley Food Co-op**, 202 1st St., Mount Vernon, WA 98273. (206) 336-9777. Type of Business: Retail store and 35-seat Deli. Sells to: The public. Sells: Wide selection of processed foods and fresh produce. Organic? 20% organic. Prices: 15% off retail price for full case orders. Hours: M-F 9-7, Sat. 9-6, Sun. 10-4. Comments: Community owned.

Olympia, **Olympia Food Co-op,** 921 North Rogers, Olympia, WA 98502. (206) 754-7666. Type of Business: Co-op. Sells to: The public. Sells: A full line of wholefood grocery items and organic produce. Organic? 40-70% of their produce is certified organic by Tilth. Credit: None. Prices: There is a 10% mark-up for non-members. Hours: 9-8 seven days a week. Comments: The business is member owned. Members must invest at least $29. There are volunteer opportunities available.

Seattle, **Charlie's Produce,** Diane Dempster, Carrie West, 4123 2nd St., Seattle, WA 98134. Mail to: PO Box 24606, Seattle, WA 98124. (206) 625-1412. Type of Business: Distributor. Sells to: Retailers. Sells: Fresh fruit, fresh vegetables. Organic? Certified organic. Priority is to buy certified organic by California Certified Organic Farmers, Oregon Tilth, Washington Dept. of Agriculture, and Texas Dept. of Agriculture.

Seattle, **Ener-G Foods Inc.,** PO Box 84487, Seattle, WA 98124. (206) 767-6660, (800) 331-5222, in WA (800) 325-9788), FAX: (206) 767-4088. Type of Business: Manufacturer and mail-order distributor. Sells: Dietetic foods (gluten-, wheat-, egg- and milk-free): Baked goods (bread crumbs, buns, cakes, cookie mixes, pancackes, waffles), breads, cereal (granola), flour (buckwheat), grains (bulgur, millet and oats), nuts and nut butters, oils, pasta, brown rice, tapioca and soybean milk. Organic? No organic claims. Credit: V M AE. Prices: No special prices for bulk orders. Hours: 8-5 Shipping: 2-5 weeks delivery time. Minimum Order: None. Catalogue Available? Yes.

Seattle, **Gravity Bar,** Laurrien Gilmore, 86 Pine, Seattle, WA 98101. (206) 443-9694. Type of Business: Restaurant. Sells: Gravity bar spans a large range of healthy foods, offering vegetarian, vegan and macrobiotic dishes. Organic? Asserted 25% organic. Filtered water. Specialties: Fresh juices made to order, salads and brown rice and steamed vegetables with sauces. Prices: Entrees range from $3.50 to $6.25. Hours: M-Sat. 7-6, Sun. 8-noon. Reservations: Not possible. 100% non-smoking. Credit: None. Commendations: Recently, Bite of Seattle, 2nd place entrée, 1989; Group Health Organization, 1st place juice bar, 1989; *The Weekly,* Most unusual wait-people award.

Seattle, **Honey Bear,** 2106 N 55th, Seattle, WA 98103. (206) 545-7296. Type of Business: Restaurant and retail store. Sells: A whole-grain natural-foods bakery. Everything is made on the premises. A lunch special M-F and a dinner special 7 nites a week. Serves deli-type salads plus black bean chili, and a soup every day. Organic? 50% (certified). Hours: 6 a.m.-11 p.m. daily. 100% of tables are no smoking. Reservations: No. Credit: No credit cards. Commendations: Best bakery in Seattle, 1988—*The Weekly* readers' poll. Comments: Music 4 nights a week.

Seattle, **Larry's Markets,** Bob Meyers, VP, 14900 Inerurban Ave. S, Seattle, WA 98168. (206) 243-2951. Type of Business: Retail store. Sells to: The public. Sells: A wide variety of processed foods and fresh produce. Credit: V M. Hours: 24-hour operation. Comments: Offers healthy

cooking classes in a cooking school. Also weekly food demos and nutritional walks.

Seattle, **New Orleans Creole Restaurant,** Gaye E. Anderson, 114 1st Ave. So., Pioneer Square, Seattle, WA 98104. (206) 622-2563. Type of Business: Restaurant. Sells: Soups, salads, sandwiches, gumbos, frogs' legs and various seafood and chicken entrees. Organic? Water is not filtered. Specialties: Creole and cajun cuisine. Musical entertainment is also offered; piano at lunchtime and live jazz every night. Vegetarian dishes are available. Prices: $4.25-$12.50 Hours: S-T 11-11, Fri/Sat. 11-2a.m. Reservations: Possible. 50% No smoking. Credit: V M AE DC.

Seattle, **Northbest Natural Products,** Saul Fortunoff, PO Box 31029, Seattle, WA 98103. (206) 633-2283. Type of Business: Distributor and wholesaler. Sells: Teas, fruit juice concentrates, nuts and nut butters, oils (safflower, sesame, sunflower, walnut, peanut), pasta, quinoa products, spirulina products, chlorella products, sesame seeds, herbs and herb products, bee pollens, candy bars, vegetarian vitamins and supplements. Organic? Asserted 15% organic by the standards of the Organic Foods Production Association of North America. Credit: None. Prices: Special prices for bulk orders available according to volume. Shipping: 24-hour delivery. Rarely out of stock and will ship everywhere. Minimum Order: None. Catalogue Available? Yes.

Seattle, **Pilgrim's Garden Grocer,** 4217 University Way NE, Seattle, WA 98105. (206) 634-3430. Type of Business: Retail store. Sells to: The public. Sells: A wide variety of wholefood grocery items and organic produce. They also carry bodycare products that are not animal-tested and a selection of supplements, herbs, and tinctures. Organic? Asserted 30-35% organic. Credit: V M. Hours: M-F, 10-7; Sat. 10-6; Sun. 12-6.

Seattle, **Puget Consumer's Co-op (Ravenna),** 6504 20th NE, Seattle, WA 98115. (206) 525-1450. Type of Business: Co-op. Sells to: The public. Sells: Every variety of fresh produce and processed food. Credit: No. Prices: "Case" discounts—variable. Hours: 9-9, 7 days a week. Comments: Publishes weekly newspaper, offers extensive range of food preparation classes. Seattle's largest wholefood retailer, they also own part of NutraSource.♥♦

Seattle, **Rainbow Grocery,** Allen Yoder, 409 15th Avenue, Seattle, WA 98112. (206) 329-8440. (Also in Aurora and Denver, Colorado, and Kansas City Missouri.) Type of Business: Retail store. Sells to: The public. Sells: A wide variety of fresh produce and processed foods. Organic? 25% organic. Credit: None at the moment. Prices: 10% discounts for products bought by the case. Hours: Daily, 9-8.

Seattle, **Silence-Heart-Nest,** Nandita Polissar, 5247 University Way NE, Seattle, WA 98105. (206) 524-4008. Type of Business: Restaurant. Sells: Vegetarian and vegan dishes. Organic? No organic claims. Specialties: East Indian. Prices: $3.75-$13. Hours: M-T-Th, 11-8 p.m.; W, 11-3 p.m.; F-Sat., 11-9 p.m. Reservations: Possible for parties over 4. Credit: None. Commendations: Silence-

Heart-Nest is locally owned and operated by students of Sri Chinmoy, who has led meditations for peace at the United Nations and in the U.S. Congress. Sri Chinmoy teaches inner and outer peace and dynamism through meditation, service, and physical fitness.

Seattle, **The Sunlight Cafe,** Jan Noone, 6403 Roosevelt Way NE, Seattle, WA 98115. (206) 522–9060. **Type of Business:** Restaurant. **Sells:** Vegetarian cuisine: eggless waffles, nutburger, sauteed vegetables, Mexican entrees, salads and bread. **Organic?** Asserted 20% organic. Water is filtered. **Specialties:** Vegan and macrobiotic dishes available. **Prices:** $4–$7.95 **Hours:** 7–10 **Reservations:** Not accepted: 100% No smoking. **Commendations:** Listed in reader polls of 1989 in *Seattle Weekly, Pacific Northwest* magazine and *View* magazine.♦

Tonasket, **Okanogan River Natural Food Co-op,** 21 West Fourth, Box 591, Tonasket, WA 98855. (509) 486–4188. **Type of Business:** Retail store / Co-op. **Sells to:** The public. **Sells:** Huge selection of fresh produce (no meats), and a wide selection of processed foods. **Organic?** Washington State Tilth. 25% organic. **Prices:** Bulk discount 10% above wholesale for members, 20% above wholesale for non-members. **Hours:** Summer 9 a.m.–7 p.m., Winter 9 a.m.–6 p.m. **Minimum Order:** $25 for bulk orders. **Catalogue Available?** None.

Trout Lake, **Trout Lake Farm,** 149 Little Mountain Rd., Trout Lake, WA 98650. (509) 395–2025. **Type of Business:** Manufacturer, Producer. **Sells to:** The public. **Sells:** Rice, teas, organically grown spices, onions, and potatoes. **Organic?** Asserted organic, certified by Oregon Tilth, Washington Department of Agriculture. **Credit:** None. **Prices:** Varied. **Hours:** 8–5 p.m. **Minimum Order:** 10. **Catalogue Available?** Yes.

Wenatchee, **Wenatchee Natural Foods,** 107 Palouse St., Wenatchee, WA 98801. (509) 662–6413. **Type of Business:** Retail store. **Sells to:** The public. **Sells:** A large selection of fresh and processed foods. **Organic?** Washington Tilth. 10% organic. **Prices:** 10–15% discount plus, depending on size of order. **Hours:** M-Thur 9:00–6:00, Fri 9:00–4:00, Sun. 12:00–4:00. **Shipping:** Will ship anywhere. **Minimum Order:** None. **Comments:** They claim to have the largest selection in Central Washington and the most knowledgeable service.

WI

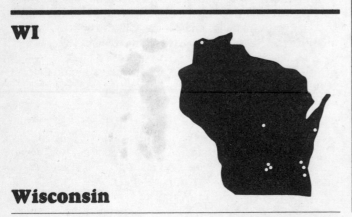

Wisconsin

Brookfield, **Omega-Life Inc.,** PO Box 208, 15355 Woodbridge Rd., Brookfield, WI 53005. (414) 786–2070. **Type of Business:** Distributor and mail-order distributor. **Sells to:** Distributors, health food stores, physicians and nutritionists. **Sells:** Muffin, pancake, and waffle mixes, candy bars and flax seed products. **Organic?** Asserted 90% organic. **Credit:** Terms available. **Prices:** No special prices for bulk orders. **Shipping:** Most orders sent via UPS, generally within 48 hours of receipt. **Minimum Order:** None. **Catalogue Available?** Yes.

Madison, **Ovens of Brittany,** Tim J. Virnig, 305 State St., Madison, WI 53703. (608) 233–7700. **Type of Business:** Restaurant. **Organic?** Asserted 20%. Water is filtered. **Specialties:** Homemade natural bakery (bran muffins), vegetarian stirfrys, salads. **Prices:** $4.95–$16.95. **Hours:** M-Th 7 a.m.–11 p.m., Fri. and Sat. 7 a.m.–12 p.m., Sun. 8 a.m.–11 p.m. **Reservations:** Possible on request. **Credit:** V M AE DC. **Commendations:** "Best Awards" from independent readership poll taken 1981–88 by *Madison* magazine, Madison Newspapers, Inc. and *The Isthmus* magazine. **Comments:** Four other locations in Madison: 1831 Monroe St., 3244 University (Shorewood), 1718 Fordem Ave. (Camelot Square), 1 S Pinckney St. (First Wisconsin Plaza).

Madison, **Sunprint Cafe and Gallery,** Rena Gelman or Linda Derrickson, 638 State St. and 2701 University Ave., Madison, WI 53705. (608) 231–1111. **Type of Business:** Restaurant. **Sells:** Vegetarian food; char-grilled fish and chicken, and gourmet desserts. **Organic?** No organic claims. Water is not filtered. **Prices:** $6 -$12. **Hours:** 7–10. **Reservations:** Not accepted: 100% No smoking. **Credit:** V M. **Commendations:** *Isthmus* magazine, 1989 and *Madison* magazine, 1989.

Madison, **Williamson Street Co-op,** Anya Havsner, 1202 Williamson St., Madison, WI 53703. (608) 251–0884. **Type of Business:** Retail store. **Sells to:** The public and some restaurants. **Sells:** A large variety of fresh produce and processed foods. **Organic?** 50% organic. **Prices:** Discount 10% off shelf price for bulk orders. **Hours:** Daily, 8 a.m.–9 p.m.

Manitowoc, **National Ovens of Manitowoc Inc.,** Paul, Barbara and Todd Stitt, 4300 Hwy. C.R., PO Box 2137, Manitowoc, WI 54221. (414) 758–2500. **Type of Business:** Manufacturer and retail store. **Sells:** Baked goods; buns, cookies, muffins, bread (oat, rye and whole wheat), granola cereal and whole wheat flour. **Organic?** Asserted 50% organic by the standards of the Organic Foods Production Association of North America. **Credit:** V M. **Prices:** No special prices for bulk orders. **Hours:** M-F 8–5 Sat. 9–12. **Shipping:** Deliver to 48 contiguous states only. **Minimum Order:** $30 for free shipping. **Catalogue Available?** Yes.

Milwaukee, **Outpost Natural Foods,** Pam Mehnert, 100 E Capitol Drive, Milwaukee, WI 53212. (414) 961–2597. **Type of Business:** Retail store and co-op. **Sells to:** The public. **Sells:** A wide variety of processed foods and in-season fresh produce. **Organic?** 30% organic. **Credit:** V M

AE. **Prices:** Bulk orders receive 10% off co-op member price. **Hours:** M-Sat. 7a.m.–10p.m., Sun. 10a.m.–7p.m.

Pleasant Prairie, **Br. Ron Corporation,** PO Box 77, Pleasant Prairie, WI 53158. **Type of Business:** Manufacturer. **Sells:** Baked goods; sprouted brownies and cookies. **Organic?** Asserted 25–45% organic. **Credit:** V M and AE. **Prices:** No special prices for bulk orders. **Shipping:** 4 days delivery time. **Minimum Order:** None. **Catalogue Available?** Yes.

Pleasant Prairie, **Kanoa: A Free Spirit,** Stuart Harian Doblin, PO Box 77, Pleasant Prairie, WI 53158. **Type of Business:** Manufacturer. **Sells:** Soy products; soy yogurt. **Organic?** Asserted 70% organic. **Prices:** No special prices for bulk orders. **Hours:** 10–4. **Shipping:** 1 week delivery. **Minimum Order:** None. **Catalogue Available?** Yes.

Stevens Point, **Copps Food Corporation,** 2828 Wayne St., Stevens Point, WI 54481. (414) 344–5900, (414) 734–1918. **Type of Business:** Retail store. **Sells to:** The public. **Sells:** Baked goods, beans, beverages, breads, candy, cereals, dairy products, flour, fresh dried fruit, meats, oils, pasta, rice, soy products, fresh dairy products, fresh grains, fresh nuts, and fresh spices. **Organic?** 15% organic. **Hours:** 24 hours, with staffing in natural foods from 8 a.m.–8 p.m. **Comments:** A full-service, staffed program—the only one of its kind in the Wisconsin grocery mass market. Full line natural wholefoods department with cooler, freezer, HBA, supplement, athletic, bulk, grocery and educational products.

Superior, **Common Health Warehouse Cooperative-Association,** 1505 N 8th St., Superior, WI 54880. (715) 392–9862. FAX: (715) 392–4517. **Type of Business:** Distributor. **Sells to:** Public by appointment only. **Sells:** Cereals, flour, breads, oils, pasta, rice, beans, soy products, dried fruit, fresh fruit and vegetables, nuts and nut butters, meats, poultry, seafood, dairy products, baked goods, candy bars, herbs and spices, fruit juices and other beverages. **Organic?** Asserted 35% organic by the standards of the Organic Foods Production Association of North America; Organic Growers and Buyers Association certified. **Credit:** None. **Prices:** Volume discounts available according to order size. **Hours:** M-F 8:30–4. **Shipping:** Deliver to northern Minnesota, northern Wisconsin, upper peninsula of Michigan, North Dakota, Montana, parts of South Dakota and Wyoming. **Minimum Order:** $100 for pick-up orders and orders on their regular truck routes. For new customers, minimums are negotiable; trucking depends on how well orders fit with existing routes. **Catalogue Available?** Yes.

WY

Wyoming

Caspar, **Wyoming Natural Foods,** 242 S Wolcott, Caspar, WY 82601. (307) 234–4196. **Type of Business:** Natural foods store and juice bar. **Sells to:** The public direct and some by mail. **Sells:** A full range of wholefood grocery items, herbs, and supplements. **Organic?** Asserted 100% organic. **Credit:** V M. **Prices:** Discounts available on bulk orders. **Hours:** M-F 9–5, Sat. 9–4. **Comments:** The proprietor has been in business for over 26 years.

Cheyenne, **Mosher Products,** Leonard Mosher, Owner, PO Box 5367, Cheyenne, WY 82003. (307) 632–1492. **Type of Business:** Grower. **Sells to:** Wholesalers and mail order to public. **Sells:** Wholewheat grain; also sells grinders to make flour. **Organic?** Asserted 100% organic. **Credit:** None. **Prices:** Special prices for bulk orders of 500 bags or more. **Hours:** 8–8. **Shipping:** Shipment on customer terms within UPS delivery area. **Minimum Order:** None. **Catalogue Available?** Yes.

CANADA

Alberta

Medicine Hat, **Nutters Fruit & Nut Co.,** Donald A. Cranston, 107–1601 Dunmore Road SE Medicine Hat, Alberta T1A 1Z8. (403) 529–1664. **Type of Business:** Retail store, and wholesaler. **Sells to:** The public. **Sells:** Beans, tea, coffee, candy, cereals, cheeses, flour, fruit, meats, nuts, oils, pasta, rice as well as fresh grains and a hundred different spices. **Certification:** Canadian Health Food Assoc., Canadian Specialty Food Assoc., Organic Foods Production Association of North America. **Credit:** V. **Prices:** Bulk discount is 10% below retail price. **Hours:** M-Th, Sat. 9–6, Fri 9–9, Christmas M-Sat. 9–9. **Com-**

ments: Specializes in organically and chemically grown bulk items.

British Columbia

North Vancouver, **Jentash Marketing,** Nickey Ahmed, 1563 Columbia St., North Vancouver, BC V7J1A3. (604) 980-3663. Type of Business: Retail store, broker, co-op. Sells to: Western Canada retailers. Sells: Herbal teas, non-alcoholic wines, dried bananas, pasta, oils, rice, fresh Nile spices, fresh dairy products. Certification: 40% organic. Credit: V. Minimum Order: $300. Catalogue Available? Yes.

Vancouver, **Naam Restaurant,** P.B. Keith, 2724 W 4th Avenue, Vancouver, BC. (604) 738-7151. Type of Business: Restaurant. Sells: Vegetarian options. Organic? Varies. Specialties: Chef's Special. Prices: $3.00-$7.95 Hours: 24 hours, 7 days a week. Reservations: Possible. Credit: V M.

Ontario

Elora, **Desert Rose Cafe,** Resa Lent, 42 Mill St. W, Elora, ON N0B1S0. (519) 846-0433. Type of Business: Restaurant and bed-and-breakfast. Sells: Vegetarian, vegan, and macrobiotic options (24-hour notice needed for macrobiotic). Organic? No organic claims. Specialties: Mexican, soups, homemade desserts. Prices: $3.50-$8. Hours: 7 days, 11:30-8:30. Reservations: Possible. Credit: V M.

Kingston, **Sunflower Natural Foods Restaurant,** Katie Scaife, 20 Montreal St., 2nd Floor, Kingston, ON K7L3G6. (613) 542-4566. Type of Business: Restaurant. Sells: Mostly vegetarian, with vegan and macrobiotic options. Organic? 50-75%. Prices: $4.95-$9.95. Hours: Tues.-Sat. 11:30 a.m.–Midnight. Reservations: Possible. Credit: V M. Commendations and Comments: "Where to Eat in Canada", 1981–present. They also have periodic dinner-theater and art shows.

Kitchener, **Full Circle Foods,** Eileen Grogan, 46 King St. W, Kitchener, Ontario N2G 1B7. Type of Business: Retail store. Sells to: The public. Sells: Many fresh produce and processed foods. Certification: Organic Crop Improvement Association. Credit: None. Hours: M-W 9-6, Th-F 9-9, Sat. 9-6.

Markham, **Timbuktu Natural Foods,** David Dennis, 173 Denison St., Markham, ON L3R1B5. (416) 477-7755. Type of Business: Wholesaler and distributor. Sells to: Retailers. Sells: Beans, cereals, processed and dried fruit, beverages, candy, baked goods, flour, nuts and nut butters, pasta, rice, soy products, and grains. Certification: 60% organic. Credit: None. Shipping: Delivery in 2 Days. Minimum Order: $100. Catalogue Available? Yes.

Oakville, **Alternatives Market,** 453 Reynolds St., Oakville, ON L6J3M4. (416) 844-2375. Type of Business: Retail store. Sells to: The public. Sells: A large retailer and full-line store featuring fresh and frozen dinners and entres, salads, and soups that are made on the premises. Over 100 types of bread, and over 75 types of cheese. Certification: Organic Crop Improvement Association member. 10+% organic and growing rapidly. Credit: V M. Hours: M-F 9-9, Sat. 9-6.

Orangeville, **Harmony Wholefoods,** 10 1st St., Orangeville, ON L9W2C4. (519) 941-8961. Type of Business: Retail store. Sells to: The public. Sells: A complete range of wholefood groceries and fresh organic produce. Certification: Estimated 15% organic. Credit: V M. Prices: 10-30% discount on case lot orders and bulk. Hours: M-Sat. 9:30-6, Fri 9:30-9. Comments: Also publishes a monthly newsletter.

Sault Ste. Marie, **Life Supports Natural Food Service,** Glen Shepherd, 21 King St., Sault Ste Marie, ON P6A6K3. (705) 942-4030. Type of Business: Retail store and restaurant. Sells: Vegetarian and vegan options. Organic? Asserted 50%. Water filtered, 100% no smoking. Prices: $4.95 all you can eat. Hours: 9-5:30 daily. Reservations: Possible. Comments: They are a non-profit organization dedicated to teaching good health and nutrition.

Toronto, **United Bakers Dairy Restaurant,** Thornhill location: 390 Steeles Ave. W, Thornhill, ON L4J 6X2. Also in Toronto. Type of Business: Restaurant. Sells: Vegetarian foods with some dairy. Organic? No organic claims. Specialties: Cheeze blintzes, gefilte fish, cabbage borscht soup, vegetarian chopped liver. Prices: $6.95 and up. Hours: M-Th 7 a.m.-10 p.m., F 7 a.m.-8 p.m., Sat. 7 a.m.-9 p.m., Sun. 8 a.m.-9 p.m. Reservations: Not possible. Credit: V M. Commendations: Recommended in *Bon Appétit*'s article on Ethnic Restaurants in Toronto (August, 1988).

Toronto, **Annapurna Vegetarian,** Devavira, 1085 Bathurst St., Toronto, ON M5R3G8. (416) 537-8513. Type of Business: Restaurant. Sells: Strictly vegetarian cuisine, with vegan and macrobiotic options. Organic? Asserted 10-20% organic. Specialties: Masala Dosai, Indian Assortment. Prices: Entree range, $2.50-$5.50. Hours: daily 12-9, except Wed: 12-6:30, closed Sun. Reservations: Possible. 100% non-smoking. Credit: None. Commendations and comments: listed in Where to Eat in Canada. Their menu says that the restaurant is dedicated to the spiritual philosophy of Sri Chinmoy.

Toronto, **Baldwin Natural Foods,** Young Ha, 20 1/2 Baldwin St., Toronto, ON M5T1L2. (416) 979-1777. Type of Business: Retail store. Sells to: The public. Sells: Fresh produce—beans, teas and organic coffees, dairy products, fresh and dried fruit, grains, meats and seafood, nuts, soy products, spices, and a huge selection of fresh vegetables. Processed foods—baked goods, beans, a large selection of breads, candy, hot corn cereal, dairy products, flour, processed and dried fruits, chemical free poultry, nuts and nut butters, oils, pasta, rice, soy products, and frozen vegetables. **Certification:** 95% of produce, 70% of grains, 50% of dry fruits and legumes are organic. **Credit:** V M. **Prices:** 10% off for bulk orders. **Hours:** M-W 10 a.m.–7 p.m., Th-F 10 a.m.–8 p.m., Sat. 9 a.m.–6 p.m.

Toronto, **Bangkok Garden Restaurant,** Sherry Brydson, 18 Elm St., Toronto, ON M5G1G7. (416) 977-6748. **Type of Business:** Restaurant. **Sells:** Vegetarian options. **Organic?** No organic claims. **Specialties:** Thai cuisine freshly prepared from fresh local ingredients and curry pastes made for Bangkok Garden in Thailand. They use no MSG and try to use "more natural sugars" like fructose and honey. **Prices:** $12.95–$16.95 **Hours:** M-Sat., 11:30–11:00 **Reservations:** Suggested. **Credit:** V M AE Diner's Enroute. **Commendations:** *Travel/Holiday* magazine award of excellence 1985–1989. Enroute magazine Readers' Top 100: 1987, 1988.

Toronto, **Big Carrot,** Kent Wakely, 348 Danforth Avenue, Toronto, ON M4K1N8. (416) 466-2129. **Type of Business:** Natural foods supermarket and deli. They are a worker-owner cooperative. **Sells to:** The public and members. **Sells:** An extensive selections of fresh organic produce, wholefood groceries, and organic meat. **Certification:** Asserted 30% for grocery and bulk, 75% for produce (Organic Crop Improvement Association). **Credit:** V M. **Hours:** M-W 9:30-7, Th-F 9:30-9, Sat. 9:30-6, Sun. 11-5. **Comments:** The deli carries over 70 kinds of vegetarian take-out items and desserts (there are a few tables in the store for those who want to eat there). They also publish their own cookbook. Big Carrot is reputed to be one of the top wholefoods stores in Canada.♦♦

Toronto, **East West,** Ron Rosenthal, 807 Bloor St. West, Toronto, ON M6G1L8. (416) 530-1571. **Type of Business:** Restaurant and retail store. **Sells:** Vegetarian and macrobiotic options. **Organic?** Asserted 80% organic. **Specialties:** Macrobiotic self serve buffet including tofu quiche, meatless and dairyless lasagna. **Prices:** Charges by weight. **Hours:** Restaurant Tu-Sun. 12-2:30, 5-9; Store M 12-5, Tu-Sun. 12-9. **Reservations:** Not possible. **Credit:** V M. **Commendations and Comments:** *Toronto Star* 1989. They also offer macrobiotic cooking classes, sell a variety of macrobiotic books and foods, and host seminars.

Toronto, **United Bakers Dairy Restaurant,** Uptown location: 506 Lawrence Avenue W, Toronto, ON M6A1A1. (416) 789-0519. Also in Thornhill. **Type of Business:** Restaurant. **Sells:** Vegetarian foods with some dairy. **Organic?** No organic claims. **Specialties:** Cheese blintzes, gefilte fish, cabbage borscht soup, vegetarian chopped liver. **Prices:** $6.95 and up. **Hours:** M-Th 7 a.m.–10:00 p.m., F 7 a.m.–8 p.m., Sat. 7 a.m.–9 p.m., Sun. 8 a.m.-9 p.m. **Reservations:** Not possible. **Credit:** V M. **Commendations:** *Bon Appétit*—recommended in their article on ethnic restaurants in Toronto (August 1988).

Toronto, **The Vegetarian Restaurant,** 4 Dundonald St., Toronto, ON M4Y1K2. (416) 961-9522. They also have a location at 2849 Dundas St. W, Toronto, M6P146. **Type of Business:** Restaurant. **Sells:** Strictly vegetarian foods.

Organic? They assert that some of the soy products are presently organic and that they are moving toward using more and more organic produce as it becomes more available. All eggs used are free range, all cheeses (with the exception of the parmesan) are free of animal rennet. They avoid foods with chemicals, preservatives, or additives. **Specialties:** Protein loaf, entrees with organic tofu and grain, fresh salads, homemade soups and desserts. **Prices:** $3.00–$5.50. **Hours:** Dundonold St.: M-Th 11:30–9:30, F-Sat. 11:30–10:30, Sun. 4:30–9. Dundas St.: M-Th 11:30–9, F-Sat., 11:30–10, Sun. 4:30–9. **Reservations:** Possible for parties of 6 or more. 100% non-smoking. **Credit:** V M DC. **Commendations:** Two awards from the *Dining Out* magazine; listed in top 400 restaurants of *Toronto Life Epicure;* listed in top 400 restaurants of the *Stoddard Restaurant Guide.*

Toronto, **Yofi's Restaurant & Patio,** Yasmine or Charles Chung, 19 Baldwin St., Toronto, ON. (416) 977-1145. **Type of Business:** Restaurant. **Sells:** Vegetarian and vegan options **Organic?** Asserted 50% organic. **Specialties:** Hummus, tabouleh, babaganoush, falafel pita, falafel plate, vegetarian chili, lasagna, burritos, veggie burger, mushroom burger (all homemade). **Prices:** $5.50–$6.95. **Hours:** M-F 11 a.m.–9 p.m., Sat. 12–7:30, Sun. 12–6:30. **Reservations:** Possible. **Credit:** V M. **Commendations and Comments:** *Toronto Life* magazine 1988 and 1989 recommendations. *Now* magazine (July 27, 1989). They are also renowned for their fresh-fruit frozen yogurt.

Quebec

Montreal, **Restaurant "Au Jardin",** Andie Hardy, 330 Marie-Anne, Montreal, PQ H2W1B1. (514) 849-8867. **Type of Business:** Restaurant. **Sells:** Strictly vegetarian with some vegan and macrobiotic dishes. **Organic?** Asserted 35% organic. **Specialties:** "Homemade" meals. **Prices:** $4.00–$6.50. **Hours:** Lunch: M-F 11:30–2:30; Dinner: daily 4:30–10. **Reservations:** Required. **Credit:** None.

Montreal, **Tau,** 4238 St. Denis St., Montreal, PQ H2J2K8. (514) 843-4420. **Type of Business:** Retail stores. **Sells to:** The public direct and by mail. **Sells:** A fantastic selection of fresh organic produce and wholefood grocery items. **Organic?** 75% of produce (Organic Crop Improvement Association), and 50–55% overall. **Credit:** None. **Prices:** 10% discount on case orders. **Hours:** M-F 9-9, S-S 9-7. **Catalogue Available?** Yes. **Comments:** They are partners in their own organic farms and are very active in promoting ecological awareness.♥

NOTES

CHAPTER ONE:
DIET AND DISEASE

1.   With great gratification I note, as this book goes to press, that the *University of California, Berkeley Wellness Letter* passed the one-million subscriber mark, having had a mere 28,000 subscribers to its first issue in October 1984. People do care about wellness. See *University of California, Berkeley Wellness Letter*, 6:5 (February 1990), p.1.

2.   Lubert Stryer, *Biochemistry* (New York: W.H. Freeman and Co., 1988).

3.   Eva May Nunnelley Hamilton, Eleanor Noss Whitney and Frances Sienkiewicz Sizer, *Nutrition: Concepts and Controversies* (St. Paul: West Publishing Company, 4th edition, 1988), p. 221.

4.   This is a residual item for all diseases that don't fit into other categories; this item does not include "all other external causes," which is a separate item. It may show how disease classifications can become outdated as newer diseases like AIDS become more prominent.

5.   National Center for Health Statistics, Public Health Service, *Vital Statistics of the United States, 1986*, Vol. II, *Mortality*, Part B (Washington, D.C.: U.S. Government Printing Office, DHHS Pub. No. PHS 88-1114, 1988). Derived from Section 8, Geographic Detail, Table 8-9 "Deaths from 34 Selected Causes," pp. 528-529. Heart diseases include ischemic heart disease, 2.7%; cancer includes lung, 6.2%; digestive, 5.5%; genitals/breast, 4.4%. The 11th leading cause of death was chronic liver disease and cirrhosis, 1.2%.

6.   Figures are deaths from the "chronic but largely preventable" disease areas per 100,000 population. States add up to 51 because the District of Columbia is included. CDC is located in Atlanta, Ga. The data are cited in Michael deCourcy Hinds, "Delaware Tries to Erase Image of Its Poor Health," *The New York Times*, January 21, 1990, p. 22. The full citation of the source information is Robert Hahn, Ph.D., "Chronic Disease Reports: Deaths from Nine Chronic Diseases—United States, 1986, *Morbidity and Mortality Weekly Report*, 39:2 (January 19, 1990), pp. 17-20. The MMWR is available from the U.S. Government Printing Office in Washington, D.C. for $70 per year; phone (202) 783-3238. Identical information is available from MMS Publications (at *The New England Journal of Medicine*) for $48 per year; phone (617) 893-3800, 8 a.m. to 4 p.m. EST.

7.   Cause of death data for 1900-04, 1958, and sample intermediate years, are from *Information Please Almanac, 1960* (New York: McGraw-Hill, 1959), p. 346. Data for 1970 and 1983 are from *Reader's Digest Almanac, 1987* (Pleasantville, NY: Reader's Digest Association, Inc., 1986), p. 454. Data for 1988 (preliminary, and based on a 10 percent sample) from Mark S. Hoffman, editor, *The World Almanac and Book of Facts, 1990* (New York: World Almanac, imprint of Pharos Books, Scripps Howard, 1989), p. 836. The 1900 figure is actually an average of 1900-1904 data. The peak in deaths from heart diseases was not necessarily 1970.

8.   *Loc. cit.*

9.   *World Almanac 1990*, Table 188, p. 117. The five-year survival rate is based on the period 1979-84. The average five-year survival rate was the same in 1979-84 as it was in 1974-76.

10.   Anna Bradley, *Healthy Eating: Fact and Fiction* (London: Hodder & Stoughton for Consumers' Association, 1989), p. 16.

11.   M. G. Marmot, F.F.C.M., and George Davey Smith, M.B., "Why Are the Japanese Living Longer?" *British Medical Journal*, 299, December 23-30, 1989, p. 1551.

12.   Japanese men aged 45 to 79 had 2,406 strokes per 100,000 population in 1980 and only 1,329 in 1986. The figures for women were 1,647 and 566. Derived from *ibid.*, p. 1548.

13.   Japanese data from *ibid.*, p. 1547. U.S. data (1988 figures are preliminary) from National Center for Health Statistics, U.S. Department of Health and Human Services, as cited in *World Almanac 1990*, p. 852.

14.   Marmot and Smith, *op. cit.*, pp. 1549 and 1551. The comparisons are to the British diet, but other sources indicate that British dietary fat consumption is not greatly different from that of the United States.

15.   Some say as many as half of Americans are dieting. Others say that they aren't dieting, they are only trying to control their weight. See Chapter 3, footnote 18, for references.

16.   Trish Hall, "And Now, the Last Word on Dieting: Don't Bother," *The New York Times*, January 3, 1990, p. C1. Yo-yo dieting has been said to produce metabolism changes that make each successive effort to lose weight harder.

17.   In order of frequency, non-flu respiratory illnesses are colds, 68.6 million people; other infections, 21.9 million; acute bronchitis, 8.1 million; pneumonia, 3.0 million; other, 4.3 million.

18.   High blood pressure.

19.   National Center for Health Statistics, "Current Estimates from the National Health Interview Survey," *Vital and Health Statistics Survey, 1988,* No. 10, October 1989. Data for 1986 provided in *Statistical Abstract of the U.S., 1989,* 109th ed., Tables No. 182 and 183, p. 114.

20.   The 1979 figure is the average annual rate for the four previous years. The information on use is collected and reported by the FDA. See Myra Alperson, "More Bark, More Bite," CEP Research Report N88–6 (July/August 1988), p. 1.

21.   *Ibid.,* p. 4.

22.   *Ibid.,* pp. 1, 4.

23.   See Sir Robert McCarrison, *Studies of Deficiency Diseases,* London, 1922, and McCarrison and H.M. Sinclair, *Nutrition and Health,* London, 1953.

24.   Michael F. Jacobson, Ph.D. and Sarah Fritschner, *The Fast-Food Guide* (New York: Workman Publishing, 1986), pp. 114, 117, 219.

25.   Steven Findlay and Joanne Siberner, "The Truth About Cholesterol," *U.S. News & World Report,* Nov. 27, 1989, p. 90.

26.   David M. Conning, et al., *Food Fit to Eat: How to Survive Processed Food* (London: Penguin Group/Sphere Books Limited for the British Nutrition Foundation, 1988), pp. 10, 211.

27.   U.S. Department of Commerce, Bureau of the Census, *Statistical Abstract of the United States: 1980,* 101st ed. (Washington, D.C.: GPO, 1980), Table No. 211, p. 131. *The World Almanac: 1990,* p. 121.

28.   Desmond Julian, cited in Ann Kent, "Health: Fit for the Nineties?" *Times (London),* December 28, 1989.

29.   Anna Bradley, *op. cit.,* pp. 118–123. Kent, *loc. cit.*

30.   Americans for Safe Food (Center for Science in the Public Interest), "Some Chemicals Found in Food," *Eating Clean: Overcoming Food Hazards* (Washington, D.C.: Center for Study of Responsive Law, 1987), p. 16.

31.   "Pesticides" refers broadly to herbicides, insecticides and fungicides. Most pesticides in use on U.S. farms are petroleum derivatives. Herbicides are compounds used to kill weeds before planting or during the growth season. Insecticides are used to kill insects. Fungicides are used to kill fungi on fruits, nuts and vegetables during growth or after harvest. We take up the subject of pesticides in Chapter 4.

32.   In 1980, only 30 of 125 U.S. medical schools required a single course in nutrition. Philip Kapleau, *To Cherish All Life* (New York: Harper & Row, 1981), p. 59.

33.   These figures and their sources are cited in more detail in Chapter 3.

34.   J. W. T. Dickerson, G. J. Davies, and M. Crowder, "Disease Patterns of Individuals with Different Eating Patterns," *Journal of the Royal Society of Health,* December 1985, pp. 191–194. Cited in Hamilton, Whitney, and Sizer, *op. cit.,* p. 53.

35.   Muesli has long been used in Switzerland. It was originally composed of soaked raw oatmeal, grated apples, lemon juice, sweetened milk and topped with grated nuts, berries and other fruits. The formula was developed by Swiss natural-food pioneer Dr. Max D. Bircher-Benner (1867–1939), whose work is discussed further in Chapter 3.

CHAPTER TWO:
HOW TO IDENTIFY HEALTHY FOOD

1.   "The unexamined life is not worth living for man." Socrates as quoted by Plato, *Apology,* in *Five Dialogues,* translated by G. M. A. Grube (Indianapolis, In.: Hackett Publishing Co., 1981), p. 41.

2.   Annemarie Colbin, *Food and Healing* (New York: Ballantine Books, 1986), pp. 64, 125.

3.   Herman Aihara, *Learning from Salmon and Other Essays* (Oroville, Calif.: George Ohsawa Macrobiotic Foundation, 1980), p. 1.

4.   *Ibid.,* pp. 83–84.

5.   *Ibid.,* p. 26.

6.   Colbin, *op. cit.,* pp. 125–126.

7.   Rudolph Ballentine, *Diet & Nutrition: A Holistic Approach* (Honesdale, Pa.: The Himalayan International Institute, 1978), p. 563. Colbin, *op. cit.,* p. 65.

8.   Macrobiotics also avoids *non-local* fruits, vegetables, or grains. Besides eliminating meat and dairy products, Kushi puts on the prohibited list sugar, honey, corn syrup, salt, refined (white) flour, canned foods, artificial additives and chemicals (such as saccharin) of any kind including food that has been sprayed during growth with chemicals, tomatoes and potatoes, eggplant, peppers, coffee and tropical fruits. Colbin, *op. cit.,* pp. 65, 126–127.

9.   "Myth: A Macrobiotic Diet Can Cure Cancer," *University of California, Berkeley Wellness Letter,* 6:5 (February 1990), p. 8.

10.   Henry E. Sigerist, *A History of Medicine,* Vol. II: Early Greek, Hindu, and Persian Medicine, pp. 149–160. This brief summary does not do justice to the wealth of information in Sigerist's book.

11.   Buddhists believe that people can be reborn as animals and vice versa. So for them all life, even of the smallest creatures, is sacred. When the Dalai Lama, leader of Tibetan Buddhism, visited Los Angeles in 1989 and saw a plate of shrimp, he shook his head sadly: "So many souls."

12.   Quoted in John Robbins, *Diet for a New America* (Walpole, N.H.: Stillpoint Publishing, 1987), p. 170.

13.   Ballentine, *op. cit.,* pp. 546–551.

14.   Sigerist, *op. cit.,* p. 293.

15.   *Ibid.,* p. 282.

16.   *Ibid.,* pp. 241–242.

17.   Kretschmer, *Körperbau und Charakter* (Berlin, 1921), cited *ibid.,* pp. 324–325.

18.   Albert Einstein, "Science and Religion," *Out of My Later Years* (1950). In fairness, he added: "Religion without science is blind."

19.   Edward Espe Brown, *Tassajara Cooking* (Berkeley, Calif.: Shambhala, a Zen Center Book, 1973), p. 16.

20.   Harold McGee, *On Food and Cooking* (New York: Colliers Books/Macmillan Publishing Company, 1984), p. 582.

21.   Colbin, *op. cit.,* pp. 74–75.

22.   William T. Keeton and Carol Hardy McFadden, *Elements of Biological Science* (New York: W. W. Norton & Company, 3rd edition, 1983), pp. 11–16.

23.   *Ibid.,* pp. 112–119.

24.   *Ibid.,* p. 111.

25. Norman Taylor, ed., *Taylor's Encyclopedia of Gardening* (Boston: Houghton Mifflin Company, 4th ed., 1961), p. 16.

26. Besides specific citations to follow, sources of the food groups are Appendices IV and V in Jonathan Brostoff and Linda Gamlin, *The Complete Guide to Food Allergy and Intolerance* (London: Bloomsbury Publishing Company Limited, 1989), pp. 293–298, and Norman Taylor, ed., *Taylor's Encyclopedia of Gardening* (Boston: Houghton Mifflin Company, 4th ed., 1961).

27. Consulted for vegetable families: Brown, *op. cit.*, p. 17.

28. McGee, *op. cit.*, p. 42.

29. *Ibid.*, pp. 31, 34.

30. *Ibid.*, pp. 54, 61.

31. *Ibid.*, pp. 372–377. McGee says five spoonfuls of sugar have the sweetness of four of honey (p. 380). Annemarie Colbin tells me she advises students in her Natural Gourmet Cooking School to give honey a sweetness indicator of 110 to sugar's 100.

32. The table comes from Marian Burros, "Brand Name Beef: Is It Really Better?" *New York Times*, January 31, 1989, p. C8.

34. The earlier regular semi-decennial updating of the RDAs was disbanded in 1985 because of a philosophical conflict among members of the committee. National Research Council, "Research Council Publishes New RDAs: Major Tool for Nutrition Programs and Policy," press release, October 24, 1989. For an external view of what happened, see Eliot Marshall, "The Academy Kills a Nutrition Report," *Science*, 230:4724, October 25, 1985, pp. 420–421. Reprinted in Paul Saltman, Ph.D. and Yvonne Baskin, editors, *The New Nutrition* (La-Jolla, Calif.: University of California, San Diego, 1987), pp. 111–113.

34. The full table of RDAs covers the following population groups: infants up to six months, and six months to one year; children 1–3, 4–6, 7–10; males 11–14, 15–18, 19–24, 25–50, 51+; females 11–14, 15–18, 19–24, 25–50, 51+; pregnant women; lactating women first six months and second six months. One of the major differences among population groups is that a 50 percent increment in calcium and phosphorus is recommended for all adolescents and young adults 11–24, pregnant women, and lactating mothers. The recommended amount of vitamin C for smokers was almost doubled, from 60 milligrams for nonsmokers, to 100 milligrams.

35. RE means Retinol Equivalent. 1 RE = 1 microgram of retinol or 6 micrograms of beta-carotene.

36. 1 niacin equivalent equals 1 milligram of niacin or 60 milligrams of dietary tryptophan.

37. As cholecalciferol. 10 micrograms of cholecalciferol = 400 international units of vitamin D.

38. Alpha-tocopherol equivalents. 1 milligram d-alpha-tocopherol = 1 alpha-tocopherol.

39. Since the toxic levels of trace elements may be only a few times larger than the normal range of intake of these elements, the upper levels should not be frequently exceeded. National Research Council, *Recommended Dietary Allowances*, 10th ed. (Washington, D.C.: National Academy Press, 1989), p. 284.

40. *Ibid.*, p. 253.

41. *Ibid.*, p. 3.

42. National Cancer Institute, *Diet, Nutrition and Cancer Prevention: A Guide to Food Choices* (Washington, D.C.: U.S. Department of Health and Human Services, Public Health Service, National Institutes of Health, NIH Publication 87–2878, revised ed., 1987), p. 7.

43. Mary Enig, "Is Margarine a Menace?" *Goldbecks' True Foods*, 2:3 (Fall 1989), pp. 1, 2, 5.

44. *Ibid.*, p. 17.

45. Daniel Steinberg, M.D., Letter to the Editor (in response to Thomas Moore's article in the September 1989 issue), *Atlantic Monthly*, January 1990, p. 12.

46. Lubert Stryer, *Biochemistry* (New York: W.H. Freeman and Co., 1988).

47. Lappé, *Diet for a Small Planet* (New York: Ballantine, 1982), p. 172.

48. Patricia Hausman and Judith Benn Hurley, *The Healing Foods* (Emmaus, Pa.: Rodale, 1989), p. 425.

49. National Cancer Institute, *op. cit.*, p. 6. Hausman and Hurley, *op. cit.*, pp. 422–444. "What's Up, Doc? Beta Carotene," *University of California, Berkeley Wellness Letter*, 6:5 (February 1990), p. 7.

50. Information on Vitamin B$_{12}$: B.S. Schweigert, "Significance of Vitamin B$_{12}$ and Related Factors," *Journal of American Dietetic Association*, Oct. 1950; R. Bircher, "Das Fleisch-vitamin (B$_{12}$)", *Der Wendepunkt* (Journal of the Bircher-Benner Clinic), March, 1951; National Research Council, *op. cit.*, pp. 158–163, esp. pp. 161 and 163. Of 431 Australian vegetarians tested, only 21 had unacceptable blood levels of B$_{12}$ (*ibid.*, p. 161).

51. National Research Council, *op. cit.*, p. 150.

52. *Ibid.*, pp. 150–153.

53. McGee, *op. cit.*, p. 543. National Research Council, *op. cit.*, p. 167.

54. *Ibid.*, p. 171.

55. *Ibid.*, pp. 118–119.

56. Jorge C. Rios, *Heart Miracles Today: From the "Front Lines" of Heart Research* (Potomac, Md.: Phillips Publishing for Cardiac Alert, 1989), p. 28.

57. See, for example, Brostoff and Gamlin, *op. cit.*, p. 80.

58. National Research Council, *op. cit.*, pp. 255–256.

59. *Ibid.*, p. 253.

60. Ann E. Przybyla, "Nutrition Education: Whose Responsibility?" *Food Engineering*, February 1989, p. 58.

61. Charles Schaeffer, *Changing Times*, July 1989, p. 35.

62. Nikki and David Goldbeck, "How to Read a Food Label," *Goldbecks' True Foods*, Newsletter, Special Edition, December 1989, p. 4.

63. *Ibid.*, p. 3.

64. Janis F. Swain et al., Brigham Women's Hospital, Boston, cited by Jane E. Brody, "Small Study Challenges Role of Oat Bran in Reducing Cholesterol," *The New York Times*, January 18, 1990, p. A24.

65. Marian Burros, "Decoding a Nutrition Label," *The New York Times*, July 12, 1989, p. C4.

66. Goldbecks, *op. cit.*, p. 4.

67. Przybyla, *op. cit.*, p. 59. Stephen B. Schmidt, "Reform Food Labels Now!" *Nutrition Action Healthletter*, Center for Science in the Public Interest, 16:2 (March 1989), pp. 8–9.

68. Marian Burros, "The Heart Association's Seal of Approval Faces Opposition," *The New York Times*, October 25, 1989, p. C4. Also, Joanne Lipman, "AHA's Seal of Approval Dealt a Blow," *The Wall Street Journal*, January 25, 1990, pp. B1 and B4, and Lipman, "Health Claims for Some Foods May Be Shelved as Doubts Grow," *The Wall Street Journal*, January 29, 1990, pp. B1 and B10.

69. "Foodbusters," Editorial, *The New York Times*, February 2, 1990, p. A30.

70. Schaeffer, *op. cit.*, p. 35. Schaeffer says the actual amount of calcium was equivalent to under 2 ounces of milk; the Center for Science in the Public Interest says it wasn't quite as bad as that, about 3 ounces.

71. Surgeon General, *Report on Nutrition and Health* (Washington, D.C.: U.S. Department of Health and Human Services, Public Health Service, 1988, Publication No. 88–50210, GPO Stock No. 017–001–00465–1), p. 18.

72. *Loc. cit.*

73. Robbins, *op. cit.*, p. 149 paraphrased Mark Braunstein and I paraphrased Robbins.

CHAPTER THREE:
THE HEALTHY DIET

1. Becky Gillette and Kate Dumont, "The Maximum Life Span Plan," *East West*, December 1989, p. 58.

2. Janet Helm, "EN Looks at the 80's: A Decade Devoted to Counting Cholesterol, Beating Obesity and Preventing Cancer," *Environmental Nutrition*, 12:12 (December 1989), p. 5.

3. National Cancer Institute, *Diet, Nutrition & Cancer Prevention: A Guide to Food Choices* (Washington, D.C.: U.S. Department of Health and Human Services, Public Health Service, National Institutes of Health, NIH Publication 87–2878, revised ed., 1987), pp. 1 and 14. Previous edition published as "Diet, Nutrition & Cancer: The Good News" (1986).

4. The McGovern Committee report, the second edition of *Dietary Goals for the United States*, also recommended reducing dietary cholesterol to 250–350 milligrams per day. This was endorsed by the American Heart Association but for the next six years either no specific number was given or the importance of dietary cholesterol was minimized, or both. Except for statements with specific citations, the summaries of the ten guidelines are based on a table in Patricia M. Behlen and Frances J. Cronin, "Dietary Recommendations for Healthy Americans—Summarized," *Family Economics Review*, 3 (July 1985), USD Agricultural Service, Family Economics Research Group. Article reprinted in Paul Saltman, Ph.D. and Yvonne Baskin, eds., *The New Nutrition* (La Jolla, Calif.: University of California, San Diego, 1987), p. 98.

5. The American Heart Association's report was entitled *Diet and Coronary Heart Disease: General Dietary Recommendations*. Two reports in 1979 were unexceptional. The Surgeon General, in *Healthy People—Report on Health Promotion and Disease Prevention* added the need for varied diet, and stressed exercise in addition to diet for weight control. In the same year, the American Medical Association, Council on Scientific Affairs, *Concepts of Nutrition and Health* made recommendations similar to Surgeon General's report. Both were very general. See Behlen and Cronin, *loc. cit.*, in Saltman and Baskin, *loc. cit.*

6. Eliot Marshall, "The Academy Kills a Nutrition Report," *Science*, 230:4724, October 25, 1985, pp. 420–421. Reprinted in Saltman and Baskin, *op. cit.*, p. 112. An egg has 5–6 grams of fat to begin with; when cooked in butter it can be a real diet-buster. McDonald's Egg McMuffin, which most people would view as one of the chain's healthier offerings, has 16 grams of fat, accounting for 42 percent of calories. The cholesterol adds up to 259 milligrams, a day's allowance. See Chapter 9 for more examples.

7. Briefly: Saturated fat is linked to cancer of the breast, colon and prostate. Fiber helps prevent cancer of the colon by speeding the passage of food. Orange and dark-green fruits and vegetables contain beta carotene, which appears to protect against lung, skin and digestive tract cancers. National Academy of Sciences, *Diet, Nutrition and Cancer*, 1982.

8. The same year, the American Cancer Society chimed in with *Nutrition and Cancer: Cause and Prevention—A Special Report*, which recommended avoiding obesity and reducing fat intake. The Academy-Institute guidelines were updated in 1988.

9. Helm, *op. cit.*, p. 4. The publication of the CPPT study was marked by a classic *Time* cover with two fried eggs for eyes and a piece of bacon for a mouth, turned down to suggest a frown (March 26, 1984), with the prophetic conclusion: "Our diet may never be the same."

10. The Surgeon General, *Report on Nutrition and Health* (Washington, D.C.: GPO, 1988), U.S. Department of Health and Human Services, Public Health Service, Publication No. 88–50210, GPO Stock No. 017–001–00465–1, p. v. The language on "dietary excess and imbalance" recurs throughout the report, e.g. on p. 2.

11. *Ibid.*, p. 18.

12. *Nutrition and Your Health: Dietary Guidelines for Americans* (Washington, D.C.: U.S. Department of Agriculture and U.S. Department of Health and Human Services, Home and Garden Bulletin 232, 2nd ed., 1985). The 1985 version updates the 1980 edition.

13. *Ibid.*, p. 2.

14. *Ibid.*, p. 3.

15. The influence of the protein-rich food industries on an unquestionable past U.S. over-emphasis on animal protein is very well presented in John Robbins, *Diet for a New America* (Walpole, N.H.: Stillpoint Publishing, 1987), pp. 170–202.

16. Eva May Nunnelley Hamilton, Eleanor Noss Whitney, and Frances Sienkiewitz Sizer, *Nutrition: Concepts and Controversies* (St. Paul: West Publishing Company, 1988, 4th edition), p. 42.

17. National Cancer Institute, *op. cit.*, p. 2.

18. Three different views of the dieting situation: (1) "*Half of adult Americans are 'dieting'* at any one time," say J. Christian and J. Greger, *Nutrition for Living* (Benjamin-Cummings, 1988) and R. D. Friedman, "Fad Diets," *Postgraduate Medicine*, 1986; cited in The Hume Company, "The New Pritikin Program, Briefing Book 4: Introduction to Weight Control" (Atlanta, Ga.: Hume, 1989), p. 3. (2) "*One-fourth are 'dieting'*," says a 1988 survey for the Calorie Control Council by John P. Foreyt of Houston's Baylor College of Medicine. (3) "*Weight reduction is the plan*, not dieting," is indicated by the consistent growth of low-calorie food consumption, a longer-term commitment. Jennifer Stoffel, "What's New in Weight Control: A Market Mushrooms as Motivations Change," *The New York Times*, November 26, 1989, p. 17.

19. Hamilton, Whitney, and Sizer, *op. cit.*, pp. 512–513.

20. National Cancer Institute, *op. cit.*, p. 2.

21. National Center for Health Statistics, NHANES II (1976–1980), cited in National Research Council, *Recommended Dietary Allowances* (Washington, D.C.: National Academy Press, 10th Edition, 1989), p. 15. Subjects were 18–74 years old. Height and weight was determined without shoes, whereas the Metropolitan Tables allow for an addition of one inch to height for shoes and also allow for five pounds of clothes for men and three pounds of clothes for women. The NHANES subjects were shoeless and were allowed only .2 pound to .6 pound of clothing. Adding shoes adds height but also weight, so the two tables are roughly comparable.

22. *Loc. cit.*

23. The following information is from Erik Eckholm, "Health Benefits of Lifelong Leanness are Challenged," *The New York Times*, August 6, 1985. Reprinted in Saltzman and Baskin, *op. cit.*, pp. 162–166.

24. "Health Risks of Overweight," *Consumer Reports Health Letter*, February 1990, p. 11.

25. Richard E. Ostlund, Jr., *New England Journal of Medicine*, cited in Associated Press, "Weighing Health: Big Derrière vs. Fat Belly, *The New York Times*, January 27, 1990, p. 28.

26. Gillette and Dumont, *loc. cit.*

27. National Institutes of Health, Consensus Development Conference, Statement, "Health Implications of Obesity," *Annals of Internal Medicine*, 1985. Cited in The Hume Company, "Briefing Book 4," p. 3.

28. A. P. Simopolous, "Obesity and Carcinogenesis: Historical Perspective," *American Journal of Clinical Nutrition*, 1987. Cited in The Hume Company, "Briefing Book 4," p. 3.

29. William Bennett and Joel Gurin, "A Matter of Fat," *New York Times*, March 16, 1985, reprinted in Saltman and Baskin, *op. cit.*, p. 171.

30. "EN Speaks with Obesity Expert" [Interview with Wayne Calloway, M.D., Associate Clinical Professor of Medicine at the George Washington University School of Medicine, previously Director of Clinical Nutrition in the Department of Medicine], *Environmental Nutrition*, 13:1 (January 1990), p. 3.

31. *Journal of the American Medical Association*, November 3, 1989, pp. 2395–2401, as summarized in "Fit, Fitter, Fittest," *Harvard Medical School Health Letter*, 15:4 (February 1990), p. 2.

32. "Beyond the Longevity Taboo: An Interview with Roy Walford, M.D.," *East West*, December 1989, p. 58.

33. Walford, *Maximum Life Span* (New York: W. W. Norton, 1983)

34. William Bennett, [M.D.,] "Gurus of Longevity: Living Past 100 is Harder than it Looks," *American Health*, May 1984, pp. 85–86, 88. Reprinted in Saltman and Baskin, *op. cit.*, pp. 417–418.

35. *Ibid.*, p. 419.

36. Donald F. Tapley, M.D., et al., *The Columbia University College of Physicians and Surgeons Complete Home Medical Guide* (New York: Crown Publishers, Inc., 1985), p. 371.

37. Hamilton, Whitney, and Sizer, *op. cit.*, p. 108, based on S. M. Grundy, "Cholesterol and Coronary Heart Disease," *Journal of the American Medical Association*, 256 (1986), pp. 2849–2858.

38. *Loc. cit.*

39. Johnson, "Is Cholesterol . . . ," p. 3.

40. "HDL: How 'Good' Is It?" *Consumer Reports Health Letter*, February 1990, p. 14.

41. *Loc. cit.*

42. Walford: "Beyond the Longevity Taboo . . . ," *op. cit.*, p. 96. Pritikin, *op. cit.*, p. 9. The Hume Company, "The New Pritikin Program, Briefing Book 6: Moving on to Lunch" (Atlanta, Ga.: The Hume Company, 1989), p. 5, citing as a support for the 10 percent level Helen A. Guthrie, *Introductory Nutrition*, 1986. The Pritikin program has many supporters among orthodox physicians. For a critical view of the diet, which was apparently based on the short-term diet for untreated diabetics at the Lexington, Kentucky, Veterans Administration Medical Center, see Victor Herbert, "Megavitamins, Food Fads, and Quack Nutrition in Health Promotion: Myths and Risks," in R. Chernoff and D. A. Lipschitz, editors, *Health Promotion and Disease Prevention in the Elderly* (New York: Raven Press, Ltd., 1988), pp. 48–51. Herbert cites a 1982 (October) issue of *Consumer Reports* questioning Pritikin program claims.

43. Catherine F. Adams, *Nutritive Value of American Foods: In Common Units*, Agriculture Handbook No. 456, prepared by the Agricultural Research Service, USDA (Washington, D.C.: GPO, 1988, originally published 1975), pp. 75, 97. Low-fat, 1% milk information, not provided by the source, is from Tuscan Farms milk carton.

44. The addition of vitamin A palmitate adds fat. Tuscan's fortified skim milk, sold in New York City, has a gram of fat per cup, 9 calories—i.e., over 11 percent of the cup's calories.

45. Derived from the Hume Company, "The New Pritikin Program, Briefing Book 1: Introduction to Nutrition" (Atlanta, Ga.: Hume Company, 1988), table on p. 6.

46. Adams, *op. cit.*, p. 225.

47. *Ibid.*, p. 224.

48. National Cancer Institute, *op. cit.*, p. 5.

49. Helm, *op. cit.*, p. 4.

50. The original article was Thomas J. Moore, "The Cholesterol Myth," *Atlantic Monthly*, September 1989. For one of many fair-minded critiques of Moore's article, see Rodney Johnson, "Is Cholesterol a Real Danger, or Just a Myth?" in *Cardiac Alert*, 11:12 (November 1989), pp. 3, 6. The preponderance of high-powered correspondence to the *Atlantic*, sampled in its January 1990 issue, was critical of Moore's thesis and use of research.

51. For example, a 50–year-old man with a blood cholesterol level of 180 and no risk factors has a 10 percent chance of having a heart attack in his 50's—whereas if the same man had a high-risk blood cholesterol level of 260, his risk would rise to 17 percent.

52. Gina Kolata, "Major Study Aims to Learn Who Should Lower Cholesterol," *The New York Times*, September 26, 1989, Section C (Science Times), p. C1.

53. Notably Moore, *op. cit.*

54. *Ibid.*, p. C11, for deBakey. The new study is by Drs. Richard Benfante and Dwayne Reed of the Kuakini Medical Center in Honolulu; see Jane E. Brody, "High Cholesterol Poses Heart Risk in Older Men, Study Says," *The New York Times*, January 19, 1990, p. A19.

55. Also, while diet and drugs can lower cholesterol levels, the side effects of reduced cholesterol and anti-cholesterol drugs (which can be unpleasant to take, as well) are not fully investigated.

56. The report adds magnesium, but Norman Kaplan says that "in well-controlled studies, magnesium doesn't seem to have an effect." He also wonders about calcium. Bonnie Liebman, "Tackling High Blood Pressure," Cover Story (Interview with Norman Kaplan), *Nutrition Action Healthletter*, 16(4), May 1989, p. 7.

57. James W. Long. M.D., *The Essential Guide to Prescription Drugs* (New York: Harper & Row, Perennial Library, 1989), p. 46.

58. Liebman, *op. cit.*, pp. 5, 6.

59. Unprocessed foods have more potassium in them and have little salt. The potassium is leached out and the salt is routinely added in processing, says Norman Kaplan. Liebman, *op. cit.*, p. 7.

60. About half of people who reduce their sodium intake by 50 percent will be rewarded by a significant drop in blood pressure, says Norman Kaplan. See Liebman, *op. cit.*, p. 6.

61. National Cancer Institute, *op. cit.*, p. 2.

62. American Institute for Cancer Research (AICR), *Dietary Fiber to Lower Cancer Risk*, (Washington, D.C.: AICR, Information Series, 1988), pp. 2, 5.

63. National Cancer Institute, *op. cit.*, p. 4 (recommends against fiber pills). Hamilton, Whitney, and Sizer, *op. cit.*, pp. 75, 77. AICR, *op. cit.*, p. 4. Most at risk of consuming *too much* fiber are the poorly nourished, elderly, or children on a strict vegetarian diet.

64. AICR, *op. cit.*, pp. 2, 4, 6–7. National Cancer Institute, *op. cit.*, p. 8, based on Elaine Lanza and Ritva R. Butrum, "A Critical Review of Food Fiber Analysis and Data," *American Journal of Dietetics*, June 1986.

65.   Hamilton, Whitney, and Sizer, *op. cit.*, p. 38.

66.   By comparison, the Bircher-Benner Clinic has for decades kept its patients below 20 grams of refined sugar per day—that's one level tablespoonful per day. One soda would use up nearly a fortnight's sugar allowance.

67.   Economic Research Service, cited in *Statistical Abstract of the U.S.: 1989*, 109th ed., Table 196, p. 121.

68.   National Cancer Institute, *op. cit.*, p. 3.

69.   Herbert, *op. cit.*, p. 47. Herbert cites an earlier paper of his, which has one reference to sodium, citing in turn H. P. Dustan, "Nutrition and Hypertension," *Annals of Internal Medicine*, 98 (1983), p. 660.

70.   USDA, Economic Research service, cited in *Statistical Abstract of the U.S.: 1989*, 109th ed., Table 196, p. 121.

71.   American Heart Association, *The American Heart Association Diet, An Eating Plan for Healthy Americans* (Dallas, Tex.: AHA, 1985).

72.   Beryl Lieff Benderly, "Saving the Children," *Health*, December, 1989, pp. 74–75.

73.   Ken Ausubel, "The Silent Treatments," *New Age Journal*, September/October 1989, p. 4.

74.   Morris Fishbein, M.D. and William Engle, "Medical Huckster: Blood Money," *American Weekly* [a contemporary *Parade* Magazine], *Herald-American* and other Hearst chain papers including the San Antonio *Light*, 1948. Hoxsey sued the *Light* as well as Fishbein.

75.   Ken Ausubel, "The Troubling Case of Harry Hoxsey," *New Age Journal*, July/August 1988, pp. 46, 49.

76.   Ausubel, "Silent Treatments," p. 5.

77.   Ginia Bellafante, "EPA's Pesticide Panel," *Garbage*, 1:2 (November/December 1989), p. 15. The senators claimed that seven of the eight panelists worked as consultants to the chemical industry during their tenure on the panel.

78.   National Academy of Sciences, *Nutrition Education in U.S. Medical Schools* (Washington, D.C.: National Academy Press, 1985), pp. 59, 74, 75, 78. As of 1985 the situation did not appear greatly improved over five years earlier when of the 125 schools of medicine in the United States, only 30 required a single course in nutrition. Philip Kapleau, *To Cherish All Life* (New York: Harper & Row, 1981), p. 59. Cited by John Robbins, *op. cit.*, p. 150.

79.   William J. Kassler, President, American Medical Student Association, "Testimony: Nutrition Education in the Undergraduate Medical Curriculum," January 1, 1985, in National Academy of Sciences, *op. cit.*, p. 121. Emphasis added.

80.   Paper in the *Journal of the American Medical Association*, January 1990, reported by Lawrence K. Altman, "Wide Abuse of Medical Students Found," *The New York Times*, January 26, 1990, p. B7.

81.   Conversation with Lori Silver, R.D., M.P.H., February 7, 1990.

82.   Butterworth, "The Skeleton in the Hospital Closet," *Nutrition Today*, March/April 1974, pp. 4–8. Cited in Hamilton, Whitney, and Sizer, *op. cit.*, p. 59.

83.   "Prescription Drug Prescribing Bribing," *The Public Citizen Health Research Group Health Letter*, 6:1 (January 1990), p. 12.

84.   *Loc. cit.*

85.   R. L. Weinsier et al., "Nutrition Knowledge of Senior Medical Students: A Collaborative Study of Southeastern Medical Schools," *American Journal of Clinical Nutrition*, 43 (1986), p. 66. Cited in Hamilton, Whitney, and Sizer, *op. cit.*, p. 60.

86.   Haydn Bush, "Cure: Despite Claims to the Contrary, Treatment Today Offers Little More Hope Than It Did a Generation Ago," *Science*, September 1984, p. 34. Two later studies came to the same conclusion: J. Cairns, "The Treatment of Diseases and the War Against Cancer," *Scientific American*, 253:5 (1985), pp. 51–59; and John C. Bailar III and Elaine M. Smith, "Progress Against Cancer?" *New England Journal of Medicine*, 314 (May 8, 1986), pp. 1226–1232. Cairns uses a clinical and biological analysis. "Ours is largely epidemiologic and statistical, yet we come to similar conclusions about the poor rate of success to date . . . ," *ibid.*, p. 1231.

87.   This summary is based on an interview with Mark Hornbrooke, Center for Health Research of Kaiser Permanente in Portland, Ore.

88.   Robbins, *op. cit.*, p. 151.

89.   H. Bailey, *A Matter of Life or Death* (New York: McFadden, 1964), p. 169. Cited in Robert G. Houston, *Repression and Reform in the Evaluation of Alternative Cancer Therapies* (Washington, D.C.: Project CURE, 1989), p. 7.

90.   F. K. Storm and D. L. Morton, *Ca* (Journal of the American Cancer Society), 33, pp. 44–56. Cited in Houston, *op. cit.*, pp. 10, 11.

91.   Louis Harris and Associates, *op. cit.*, Executive Summary, p. 3.

92.   *The Doctor's Dilemma . . .* (London: Constable and Company Ltd., 1911; 6th printing, 1921), p. lxxxviii.

93.   David Aldridge, "Europe Looks at Complementary Medicine," *British Medical Journal*, 299: November 4, 1989, pp. 1121–1122. However, many of Britain's 8,000 healers rely on free-will contributions, even though a few serve officially part-time in National Health Service clinics.

94.   The community was Avon. Of the 200 physicians surveyed, 145 responded. Of these, 41 percent had become interested in complementary medicine by observing benefits in their patients, 38 percent had experienced benefits for themselves or their families, and 38 percent had received some training in complementary techniques. See Richard Wharton, M.R.C.G.P., and George Lewith, M.R.C.P., M.R.C.G.P., "Complementary Medicine and the General Practitioner," *British Medical Journal*, June 7, 1986, pp. 197–1500.

95.   *Ibid.*, p. 1122.

96.   *Loc. cit.*

97.   For a sample of what he says about fat, see Null, *Gary Null's Complete Guide . . .* , pp. 42–43. "If you have a diet high in fat, you are likely to be obese, with greasy skin and oily hair . . . . Nearly half the average American diet consists of fat, but only 5 to 10 percent is required for good, balanced nutrition" (*ibid.*, p. 299). For a sample of what he says about supplements, see *ibid.*, pp. 49–51. For a balanced review of Null's work, see Tom Monte, "The Gary Null Show: Turning the Mike Back at the Author and Popular Radio Spokesman for Alternative Health," *East West: The Journal of Natural Living*, September 1989, cover story, pp. 53–57, 109.

98.   Null, *op. cit.*, p. 5.

99.   His "Resource Guide," in Null, *op. cit.*, pp. 307–313, just lists the names and addresses of alternative physicians he has interviewed, and the date interviewed!

100.   Herbert, "Megavitamins. . . ," p. 48. Herbert cites another source to the effect that about 50 percent of the elderly may be using nutrient supplements, with the strong implication that few of them are taking adequate account of the interaction between the supplements and other foods or any prescription drugs they may be ingesting. See S. C. Hartz and J. Blumberg, "Use of Vitamin and Mineral Supplements by the Elderly," *Clinical Nutrition*, 5, pp. 130–136.

101.   Herbert, "Towards Healthful Diets: The Role of Health Foods," in *Proceedings of the European Nutrition Conference*, edited by

E. M. E. van den Berg, W. Bosman, and B. C. Breedveld (The Hague, Holland: Voorlichtingsbureau voor de Voeding, 1985), p. 85.

102.   Dr. Herbert's pets had, for a fee, been made "professional members" of the American Association of Nutritional Consultants. The gimmick was used in a Herbert lecture in November 1989; it was also reported on by the American Council on Science and Health back in 1983, in "Meet Sassafras Herbert, Professional Nutritionist," *ACSH News and Views*, September/October 1983, p. 3. See Hamilton, Whitney, and Sizer, *op. cit.*, p. 63.

103.   Of 138 unorthodox cancer treatment practitioners studied recently, 60 percent were conventionally trained M.D.s. Cassileth et al., *op. cit.*, p. 105. In its introduction to *Unproven Methods of Cancer Management* (New York: ACS, 1971 and 1982), the American Cancer Society says that the practitioners of alternative therapies have "multiple unusual degrees" received from "correspondence schools," and that only "a few" have M.D. or Ph.D. degrees. In fact, 78 percent of such practitioners had M.D. or Ph.D. degrees; of the 65 percent M.D.'s, 10 percent also hold Ph.D.s. See R. W. Moss, *The Cancer Syndrome* (New York: Grove Press, 1980), cited in Houston, *op. cit.*, p. 7.

104.   Dr. Herbert appeared on television to speak his mind about Dr. Berger on February 8, 1990.

105.   World Health Medical Group, "Dr. Levin Charged with Professional Misconduct," *Newsletter*, September 1989, p. 6.

106.   Lawrence K. Altman, "The Doctor as Guinea Pig," *The New York Times*, Sunday Magazine, April 6, 1986.

107.   Government intervention against complementary therapies limits the accountability of conventional medicine by controlling entry and competition, leading one commentator to suggest that for some would-be protectors of the public from fraud, "the greater fraudulence may lie with the attacker." Houston, *op. cit.*, p. 56.

108.   Barrie R. Cassileth, Edward J. Lusk, Thomas B. Strouse and Brenda J. Bodenheimer, "Contemporary Unorthodox Treatments in Cancer Medicine: A Study of Patients, Treatments, and Practitioners," *Annals of Internal Medicine*, 101:1 (July 1984), pp. 105, 107, 109.

109.   See the entry for the National Health Federation at the end of this chapter, under Health Freedom Lobbyists.

110.   Project CURE, *Report* (1988), p. 11.

111.   Alexander Pope, *An Essay on Criticism* (1711). Without getting into the issue of whose knowledge is "little," it may be worth hitting this dogma with a stigma. In his preface to *The Doctor's Dilemma* (1906), Bernard Shaw considers the attitude of professionals who use this quote to put down the layperson ridiculous. English biologist T. H. Huxley, in *On Elemental Instruction in Physiology* (1877), gave the perfect riposte: "If a little knowledge is dangerous, where is the man [we would say "person" today] who has so much as to be out of danger?"

112.   The Bircher-Benner Clinic since 1936 has offered a lacto-vegetarian diet, with a high raw food content. The main components are organically grown fruits and vegetables and selected dairy products; since 1936 it has offered no meat, poultry or fish. Leafy green vegetables are served daily. Bircher-Benner believed milk was acceptable as an addition to the diet, not a main food. He considered yogurt nutritionally superior to plain milk. Ruth Bircher, *op. cit.*, p. 29.

113.   Ruth Bircher, translated from the German and edited by Claire Loewenfeld, *Eating Your Way to Health: The Bircher-Benner Approach to Nutrition* (London: Faber & Faber, 1966, paperback edition, 5th printing 1977); originally written in 1954; p. 15.

114.   This semi-health is also called mesotrophy. A British bestseller, *Raw Energy*, relies heavily on Dr. Bircher-Benner's work, and that of the long-time head of the Bircher-Benner Clinic, Dr. Dagmar Liechti von Brasch. See Leslie and Susannah Kenton, *Raw Energy* (London: Arrow Books, 1984).

115.   A Senate investigation revealed that the average American doctor received less than three hours instruction on nutrition in four years of medical school. John McDougall, *The McDougall Plan* (New Century Publishers, 1983), p. 7.

116.   Meat is said to have approximately 14 times more pesticide concentrations than do plant foods; dairy products contain 5½ times more. L. Regenstein, *How to Survive in America the Poisoned* (Acropolis Books, 1982), p. 273. Cited in Robbins, *op. cit.*, p. 343.

117.   Goleman, *op. cit.*, pp. C1, C11.

118.   Colbin, *op. cit.*, p. 124, based on Benjamin T. Burton, *Human Nutrition*, and Sharon Ann Rhoads, *Cooking with Sea Vegetables*.

119.   Colbin, *op. cit.*, p. 157.

120.   The sale of raw, i.e. unpasteurized, milk has for good reason (it may be contaminated with tuberculosis bacilli or brucellae bacteria) been banned in most U.S. states, and since 1987 the FDA has been under a court order to ban interstate shipment of packaged and unpasteurized milk.

121.   Dr. Bircher-Benner prescribed raw food for sick patients, and 50 percent raw food for maintenance. Ruth Bircher, *op. cit.*, p. 25.

122.   Colbin, *op. cit.*, pp. 65, 129.

123.   "Ask the Experts. Myth: A Macrobiotic Diet Can Cure Cancer," *University of California, Berkeley Wellness Letter*, 6:5 (February 1990), p. 8.

124.   Communication from Paul Bergner, President, Bergner Communications, Portland, Ore., January 12, 1990. Bergner is a consultant to the American Association of Naturopathic Physicians, but was writing in his personal capacity.

125.   National Research Council, *op. cit.*, pp. 176, 202, 161.

126.   P.C. Dagnelie, *European Journal of Clinical Nutrition*, 42 (1988), p. 1007, as cited in Bonnie Liebman, "Macrobiotic Kids," *Nutrition Action Healthletter*, May 1989, p. 4. Hippocrates observed that being taller was impressive in youth, but could be a burden in old age. Dr. Bircher-Benner believed that rapid growth from high-protein diets was unnatural.

127.   Stan Sesser, "Who Needs a Personal Nutritionist?" *American Health*, December 1984, pp. 64–66, 68, 70. Reprinted in Saltman and Baskin, *op. cit.*, pp. 259–262.

128.   As Bernard Shaw put it, homeopathy operates on the principle that "the drug that gives you a headache will also cure a headache if you take little enough of it." *The Doctor's Dilemma . . .* (London: Constable and Company Ltd., 1911; sixth printing, 1921), p. xci. Homeopathic physicians take more careful case histories than conventional doctors, and their doses are much lower than pharmaceuticals, but the doctor-patient relationships are similar.

129.   American Council on Science and Health, "The Unhealthy Alliance," p. 15.

130.   American College of Physicians, "Clinical Ecology: A Position Paper," *Annals of Internal Medicine*, 111:2 (July 15, 1989), pp. 168–177.

131.   Louis Harris and Associates, for the FDA, *Health, Information and the Use of Questionable Treatments: A Study of the American Public* (Washington, DC: U.S. Department of Health and Human Services, Study No. 833015, September 1987).

132.   National Academy of Sciences, *op. cit.*, p. 65.

133.   *Ibid.*, p. 136.

134.   Hamilton, Whitney, and Sizer, *op. cit.*, pp. 61–62.

135.   Information on state laws from "Issues in Nutrition: Dietician Licensure Update," *East West*, December 1989, p. 16. See also "NNFA

Represented at First-of-a-Kind South Carolina Hearing," *NNFA Monitor*, 3:10 (October 1989), p. 3.

136.   Louis Harris and Associates, for the FDA, *op. cit.* Executive Summary, "Survey on the Use of Questionable Treatments" (FDA, paper, 1986), p. 7. Doctors and retail stores rank No. 2 and No. 3. Questionable treatments are defined as those that lack "a body of scientific evidence to support their effectiveness," in the opinion of the advisory group. Victims of non-traditional or "questionable" treatment are most likely to complain to a friend or relative (57 percent); unfortunately the accumulation of information from reports to friends and relatives is not institutionalized.

137.   American Association of Naturopathic Physicians, "Naturopathic Medicine, What It Is, What It Can Do for You." See also "Holistic Therapies: Naturopathy," *East West*, December 1989, p. 11.

138.   Hamilton, Whitney, and Sizer, *op. cit.*, p. 65.

139.   *Ibid.*, p. 62.

140.   *Ibid.*, p. 65. See also Richard A. Kunin, "Principles That Identify Orthomolecular Medicine: A Unique Medical Specialty," *Journal of Orthomolecular Medicine*, 2:4 (1987), pp. 203–206, esp. p. 204. Advocates of vitamin C go beyond the orthomolecular community; University of California at Berkeley researchers recommend quadrupling the current 60mg Recommended Dietary Allowance for vitamin C. "Vitamin C Attacks the Body's Worst Enemy," *Health*, December 1989, p. 14. The researchers found that vitamin C is the best weapon against free radicals, which are thought to contribute to cancer, heart disease and aging.

141.   Alain Entoven, "Managed Competition of Alternative Delivery Systems," *Journal of Health Politics, Policy, and Law*, 13:2 (Summer 1988), pp. 305–321.

142.   Lucy Moll, "Medical Care: Where's the Choice," *Vegetarian Times*, reprint, p. 5.

143.   Dr. Herbert is in his non-advocacy life a distinguished research scientist specializing in hematology, employed by the Bronx Veterans Administration Hospital.

144.   Victor Herbert, "Good Health, Good Lives, and $25,000,000,000+," *Privileged Information*, 5:3 (February 1, 1989), p. 2.

145.   For more background on the history of the FDA's handling of health claims on food, see *Disease-Specific Health Claims on Food Labels: An Unhealthy Idea*, House Report 100-561, Government Operations Committee, April 4, 1988. The report was prepared by the Subcommittee on Human Resources.

146.   Victor Herbert, "Health Claims in Food Labeling and Advertising: Literal Truths but False Messages; Deception by Omission of Adverse Facts," *Nutrition Today*, 22:3 (May/June 1987), pp. 25–30.

147.   Philip J. Hilts, "F.D.A. is Preparing New Rules to Curb Food Label Claims: Health is Central Issue," *The New York Times*, October 31, 1989, pp. A1, C18; and Hilts, "F.D.A. Acts to Limit Food Health Claims," *The New York Times*, December 15, 1989, p. D17.

148.   "Federal Council Bill Introduced . . . Sen. Harkin Places Bill in Congressional Hopper," *NNFA Monitor*, 3:10 (October 1989), p. 1.

149.   Cassileth et al., *op. cit.*, pp. 107, 109, 111–112.

150.   Professor Farnsworth directs NAPRALERT, an international database of botanical medicine. See Ausubel, "The Silent Treatments," p. 5.

151.   Anthony Robbins, *Scientific American*, December 1989. Cited in the Public Citizen Health Research Group, *Health Letter*, 6:1 (January 1990), p. 7.

152.   Correspondence from Paul Bergner, President, Bergner Communications, Portland, Ore., January 12, 1990.

153.   For an extensive listing of alternative health clinics, see John M. Fink, *Third Opinion* (Garden City Park, NY: Avery Publishing Group, Inc., 1988), the only book of its kind at the time we went to press; the book is available from Project CURE.

154.   AMA, Council on Long Range Planning and Development, *Policy Compendium, 1989*, pp. 98–102. Unfortunately, the resolutions are very weak and general, such as "The AMA recommends that instruction on nutrition be included in the curriculum of medical schools in the United States." (Resolution 34.019.) Or: "The AMA encourages effective education in nutrition at the undergraduate, graduate, and postgraduate levels." (Resolution 34.023.) The AMA's ties to the food industry are bared by such resolutions as 34.016, which supports legislation that would classify irradiation as a food process, rather than an additive (and would thereby remove it from Federal oversight), and 34.027, which links a call for better disclosure of the fat content of food with an appeal for removal of restrictions on marketing replacements for high-fat products.

155.   Bailar and Smith, *op. cit.*, pp. 1226–1232.

156.   "The Unhealthy Alliance: Crusaders for 'Health Freedom,' " Special Report (New York: ACSH, 1988), Appendix II, p. 16.

157.   William T. Jarvis, "Food Faddism, Cultism, and Quackery," *Annual Review of Nutrition*, 3 (1983), pp. 35, 37–41, 43–48. Excerpted in Saltman and Baskin, *op. cit.*, pp. 247–253. In his non-Quackbuster life Jarvis is a Professor in the Department of Preventive Medicine of Loma Linda University.

158.   *Ibid.*, pp. 4–6.

159.   "New NHF Board Members," *Health Freedom News*, p. 4.

160.   Daniel Goleman, "Life-Style Shift Can Unclog Ailing Arteries, Study Finds," *The New York Times*, November 14, 1989, pp. C1, C11.

161.   See Ken Ausubel, "The Silent Treatments," *New Age*, September-October 1989, p. 2.

162.   American Council on Science and Health, *op. cit.*, Appendix II, p. 16.

163.   Bonnie Liebman, "Palm Oil: Can PR Pay Off?" *Nutrition Action Healthletter*, May 1989, p. 8.

164.   "Too Much Fuss About Pesticides?" *Consumer Reports*, October 1989, p. 656.

165.   As recently as 1985 the American Council on Science and Health found "insufficient evidence to warrant establishment of a public policy of guidelines for diet modification for all Americans for the purpose of reducing the risk of cancer." ACSH, *Diet and Cancer* (Summit, NJ: ACSH, 1985), p. 28. The publication denied that cancer incidence would decline from reduced U.S. consumption of fat, meat (including cured or smoked meat), caffeine, alcohol, or food additives and contaminants; or from increased consumption of vegetables and fruits, fiber, vitamins or minerals. Since 1985 the weight of orthodox medicine, as exemplified by the 1988 Surgeon General's Report as well as individual studies and national organization reports, has definitively linked groups of the above factors to cancer as well as heart disease.

166.   Colbin, *op. cit.*, pp. 80–88, and "The Natural Gourmet," *East West*, February 1989, pp. 32–35. The five-phase approach also uses seasons, adding a "late summer" to the four basic seasons.

167.   American Council on Science and Health, *op. cit.*, pp. 13–14.

168.   Philip J. Hilts, "F.D.A. Commissioner Reassigned In Aftermath of Agency Scandals," *The New York Times*, November 14, 1989, p. A21.

169.   Fink, *op. cit.*, pp. 141–143.

CHAPTER FOUR:
FOOD HAZARDS AND HOW TO AVOID THEM

1. Hippocrates, *Hippocratic Writings* (Chicago: Encyclopaedia Britannica, Inc., 1952), p. 2.

2. Thomas Hobbes, *Leviathan: Or the Matter, Forme and Power of a Commonwealth Ecclesiasticall and Civil*, edited by Michael Oakeshott (New York: Collier Books, Division of Macmillan Publishing Co., Inc., 1962), p. 100.

3. Ames was the lead author of "Ranking Possible Carcinogenic Hazards," *Science*, April 1987. The summary of his article appears in John Tierney, "Not to Worry," *Hippocrates*, January/February 1988, p. 29.

4. *Ibid.*, p. 34.

5. "Too Much Fuss About Pesticides?" *Consumer Reports*, October 1989, pp. 655, 657.

6. *Ibid.*, p. 657.

7. *Ibid.*, p. 658.

8. Tierney, *op. cit.*, p. 37.

9. David M. Conning et al., *Food Fit to Eat: How to Survive Processed Food* (London: Penguin Group/Sphere Books Ltd. for the British Nutrition Foundation, 1988), pp. 100–101.

10. Ken Ausubel, "Planting Seeds of Change," unpublished paper, October 2, 1989. Ausubel is a founder of Seeds of Change, an organic seed bank based in Santa Fe, New Mexico (see Chapter 10).

11. Susan Gilbert, "America Tackles the Pesticide Crisis," *The Good Health Magazine*, Supplement to *The New York Times Magazine*, Part 2, October 8, 1989, p. 54.

12. *Loc. cit.*

13. *Ibid.*, pp. 54–55.

14. *Ibid.*, p. 55. Carole Sugarman, "Getting the Bugs Out: In California, Farmers are Experimenting with Alternatives to Chemicals," *Washington Post*, May 24, 1989, p. E16.

15. Robert McCoy, ed., *State of the Environment: A View Toward the Nineties* (Washington, D.C.: Conservation Foundation, 1987), pp. 143–149.

16. Sugarman, *op. cit.*, p. E16.

17. Daphne White, "A Crop of New Ideas," *Foundation News*, September/October 1989, p. 36.

18. For a full list of pesticides and detailed information on their use and hazards, see Lawrie Mott and Karen Snyder, *Pesticide Alert: A Guide to Pesticides in Fruits and Vegetables* (San Francisco: Sierra Club Books for the Natural Resources Defense Council, 1987), pp. 12–15, 18–20. We updated the information in this book by calling the Pesticide Hotline and U.S. EPA, both listed alphabetically in the directory at the end of the chapter.

19. Mott and Snyder, *op. cit.*, p. 58.

20. Rose Gutfeld, "Grocers Plan Their Own Ban on Pesticides," *Wall Street Journal*, September 11, 1989, pp. B1 and B9; and Keith Schneider, "5 Supermarket Chains Open Effort Against Pesticide Use," *The New York Times*, September 12, 1989, p. B9.

21. In each case the pesticide is one of the five pesticides with the heaviest residue traces for that crop, based on data from the State of California and the FDA. For some commodities, especially root crops like carrots, onions, potatoes and sweet potatoes, DDT is still on the list of the five worst offenders, even though it has been banned from use since the beginning of 1973. See Mott and Snyder, *op. cit.*, pp. 11–15.

22. Interview with pesticide specialist at EPA, February 7, 1990.

23. Mott and Snyder, *op. cit.*, p. 7.

24. *Ibid.*, pp. 137–138.

25. Irvin Molotsky, "Antibiotics in Animal Feed Linked to Human Ills," *New York Times*, February 22, 1987. Cited in John Robbins, *Diet for a New America* (Walpole, N.H.: Stillpoint Publishing, 1987), p. 303.

26. Samuel S. Epstein, cited in "Ban on Drug-Produced Milk," *East West*, November 1989, p. 13.

27. *Loc. cit.*

28. Sources include Conning et al., *op. cit.*, pp. 230–236, which was in turn based on a U.K. Government document, *Food Additives: The Balanced Approach*. We appreciate the cooperation of the Center for Science in the Public Interest in helping pick the best examples of additives.

29. *Ibid.*, pp. 129–130.

30. "An Inside Look at Food Labels: Health Valley Natural Spice Uncured Cooked Sausage Made with Beef Bologna Flavoring Added," *East West*, December 1989, p. 12.

31. "Group Launches Drive to Ban Food Irradiation," *The Consumer Affairs Letter*, 10:2 (June 1989), p. 2.

32. See Tony Webb and Dr. Tim Lang, *Food Irradiation: The Facts* (Wellingborough, Northamptonshire, England: Thorsons Publishing Group, 1987), pp. 44, 48, 55, 83–85.

33. "Two States Move to Ban Irradiated Foods," *East West*, November 1989, p. 12.

34. Michael Durham, "Market Traders to Fight Food Irradiation," *Sunday Times* (London), December 31, 1989, p. A5.

35. *Loc. cit.*

36. Conning et al., *op. cit.*, pp. 120–121.

37. *The Times* (London), July 28, 1989.

38. Richard Mackarness, *Not All in the Mind* (London: Pan Books Ltd., 1976), p. 79.

39. Jonathan Brostoff and Linda Gamlin, *The Complete Guide to Food Allergy and Intolerance* (London: Bloomsbury Publishing Company, Limited, 1989), pp. 8–9.

40. Although little hard evidence is available, "the general impression among doctors who treat food intolerance is that it *has* become increasingly widespread." See *ibid.*, p. 236.

41. Guy Garrett and Kit Norman, *The Food for Thought Cookbook* (Wellingborough, Northants., England: Thorsons Publishing Group, 1987), p. 27. Conning et al., *op. cit.*, p. 143.

42. Brostoff and Gamlin, *op. cit.*, pp. 26–27, 77–80.

43. *Ibid.*, p. 188.

44. The toxicity of this poison is so high that one ounce could kill one million people, according to R. Nordland and J. Friedman, "Poison at Our Doorstep," *Philadelphia Inquirer*, September 23–28, 1979. They and Courtney are cited in Robbins, *op. cit.*, pp. 321–322, 416.

45. "EPA Advisors on the Industry Payroll," *Pesticides and You*, Newsletter of NCAMP, 9:3 (August 1989), p. 1. Senator Harry Reid (D-NV), Chairman of the EPA's Senate oversight subcommittee, wrote to the EPA saying that the two individuals appeared to be "in violation of the conflict of interest laws set forth in 18 U.S.C. 207(a)."

46. Conning et al., *op. cit.*, pp. 101–102.

47. David Goldbeck, *The Smart Kitchen* (Woodstock: Ceres Press, 1989), p. 70.

48.   Harry Goldstein and Jay Walljasper, "A Selective Guide to Environmental Groups," *Utne Reader*, November/December 1989, p. 96.

49.   Goldstein and Walljasper, *op. cit.*, p. 96.

50.   "Food Group Launches Drive to Ban Food Irradiation," *The Consumer Affairs Letter*, 10:2 (June 1989), p. 1.

51.   Goldstein and Walljasper, *op. cit.*, p. 97.

52.   Marian Burros, "Eating Well: A Nutritionist Assesses Two Decades of Change in the U.S.," *The New York Times*, November 29, 1989, p. C4.

CHAPTER FIVE:
ORGANIC FARMING AND ITS IMPORTANCE

1.   For an interesting review of the history of the word "organic," see Robert Rodale, "Internal Resources and External Inputs—The Two Sources of All Production Needs" (Emmaus, Pa.: Rodale, unpublished paper, 1989), p. 1. Rodale credits his father, J. I. Rodale, with popularizing the word in the United States.

2.   Nikki and David Goldbeck, *The Goldbecks' Guide to Good Food* (New York: New American Library, 1987), p. 50.

3.   David Goldbeck, "The State of the Plate: Of Oats and Eggs," *Goldbecks' True Food: Wholefoods for Modern Times*, 2:3 (Fall 1989), pp. 1, 7.

4.   Neill Schaller, "Alternative Approaches to Management Systems," paper presented at Conference on Alternative Uses of Highly Erodible Agricultural Land, Memphis, Tenn., November 17–19, 1987. See also Garth Youngberg, "Reassessing Our Goals," *Family Farm Northeast*, January 1988, p. 5.

5.   Dan Howell, *Organic Agriculture: What the States are Doing* (Washington, DC: Center for Science in the Public Interest, 1989), p. 2.

6.   Marian Burros, *The New York Times*, March 29, 1989, Living Section, p. C1.

7.   The poll was conducted for *Organic Gardening* magazine. See Daphne White, "A Crop of New Ideas," *Foundation News*, September/October 1989, p. 41.

8.   Keith Schneider, "Science Academy Recommends Resumption of Natural Farming: Subsidies Found to Encourage Chemical Overuse," *The New York Times*, September 8, 1989, pp. A1, B5.

9.   White, *op. cit.*, p. 36.

10.   Ken Ausubel, "Planting Seeds of Change" (Santa Fe, N.M.: Seeds of Change, 1989, paper), p. 4.

11.   White, *op. cit.*, p. 36.

12.   Allan R. Gold, "Company Ends Use of Apple Chemical," *New York Times*, October 18, 1989, p. A18.

13.   Goldbecks, *op. cit.*, p. 23.

14.   "Alternative Farming has Economic & Environmental Benefits, National Council Reports," *Alternative Agriculture News*, 7:10 (October 1989), p. 1. The story is based on a report of the National Research Council, Board of Agriculture, *Alternative Agriculture* (Washington, D.C.: National Academy Press, 1989). See also Goldbecks, *loc. cit.*

15.   Gail Feensta, "Who Chooses Your Food?—A Study of the Effects of Cosmetic Standards on the Quality of Produce." Cited in Tomàs Nimmo, "Quality Overshadowed by Cosmetic Concern," *Ontario Farmer*, August 2, 1989.

16.   Howell, *op. cit.*, pp. 2, 3. Howell cites Susan DeMarco, former Assistant Commissioner of Agriculture, arguing in *The Progressive* that state leaders deserve most of the credit for the turnaround in public consciousness of the need for fewer toxic chemicals in farming.

17.   This section relies heavily on Howell, *op. cit.*, Part II, pp. 3–5.

18.   Patrick Madden, "Can Sustainable Agriculture Be Profitable?", *Environment*, 29:4, May 1987, p. 33.

19.   *Ibid.*, p. 33.

20.   Susan Gilbert, "America Tackles the Pesticide Crisis," *The Good Health Magazine*, Supplement to *The New York Times Magazine*, Part 2, October 8, 1989, p. 54.

21.   Estimate by organic farming expert Tomás Nimmo of Organic Farm Services (see listing in directory at the end of this chapter).

22.   See the popular Council on Economic Priorities book, Ben Corson et al., *Shopping for a Better World: 1990* (New York: Ballantine Books, 1989), p. 43. Castle & Cooke refuses to disclose its corporate record in four areas. In the seven areas where the information is a matter of public record, the company gets *the worst possible rating in every category*. No other food company comes close to having such a bad record.

23.   Carole Sugarman, "Getting the Bugs Out: In California, Farmers are Experimenting with Alternatives to Chemicals," *Washington Post*, May 24, 1989, p. E16.

24.   California Action Network, *1989 Organic Wholesalers Directory & Yearbook*, p. 125.

25.   Gilbert, *op. cit.*, p. 56.

26.   Among the many sources used for the state-by-state material, in addition to those specifically acknowledged, the two most frequently consulted were: Howell, *op. cit.*, and California Action Network, *Organic Wholesalers Directory & Yearbook*, 1988 and 1989 editions. The author made dozens of phone calls to verify addresses and phone numbers in late 1989, and found a high overall level of turnover in organizations and officers.

27.   "Low-Input/Sustainable Agriculture (LISA) Research and Education Program," Fact Sheet, USDA/Cooperative State Research Service, August 1989.

28.   Tracy Frisch, "How Does Your State Rate?", *The Natural Farmer*, Fall 1989, p. 14. New York is compared to the five New England states and New Jersey, all of which have much better relations with NOFA.

29.   Sources: NOFA chapter information sheets and telephone followup. For the latest information on the identity and whereabouts of volunteer NOFA officers, ask for their annual conference program. In preparation for this book, Domenick Bertelli attended the summer 1989 conference, for which NOFA prepared *Earth.Body.Spirit: 15th Annual Summer Conference & Celebration of Rural Life*, July 14–16, 1989. The NOFA chapter addresses and phone numbers listed are from this book, updated by phone.

30.   Barbara Carroll, "The Texas Organic Certification Program," *Natural Food & Farming*, January 1989, p. 16.

31.   *Ibid.*, p. 20.

CHAPTER SIX:
END-RUNNING THE LEVIATHAN

1.   "Grow Your Own," *Whole Life* Magazine, March 1984, excerpted in Jeffrey Hollender, *How to Make the World a Better Place* (New York: William Morrow, Quill Edition, 1990), p. 134.

2. Rod Nilsestuen, Chair, National Rural Cooperative Task Force, testifying before the House Agriculture Committee hearings on the problems facing rural America. Quoted in The National Cooperative Business Association's NCBA *Cooperative Business Journal*, August 1989, and reprinted in *Workplace Democracy*, 66 (Fall 1989), p. 15.

3. Estimate by Paul Hazen, National Cooperative Business Institute. Cited in Hollender, *op. cit.*, p. 133.

4. The club is the Seikatsu Club Consumers Cooperative, 2–26–17, Miyasaka, Setagaya-ku, Tokyo, Japan. Phone (03) 706–0031. Cited in Hollander, *op. cit.*, p. 137.

5. Ozark Cooperative Warehouse, *Buying Club Manual* (Fayetteville, Ark.: OCW, 1985), pp. 4–6.

6. *Ibid.*, pp. 11–12.

7. *Ibid.*, pp. 13–14.

8. *Mountain Ark Trader*, October-December 1989, p. 26.

9. Conversation with FTC Office of Public Affairs, January 25, 1990.

10. Barry Meier, "Caveats on Ordering by Phone," *The New York Times*, November 4, 1989, p. 50.

11. Ben Corson et al., *Shopping for a Better World* (New York: Ballantine, for the Council on Economic Priorities, 1989).

CHAPTER SEVEN:
PRODUCT GUIDE

1. Derl I. Derr, President of the International Apple Institute, quoted in *New York Times*, May 15, 1989, p. 1.

2. Lawrie Mott and Karen Snyder, Natural Resources Defense Council, *Pesticide Alert: A Guide to Pesticides in Fruits and Vegetables* (San Francisco, Sierra Club Books), 1987, p. 31. For many of the statistics drawn from this book it should be noted that USDA tests do not even register many pesticides available for use, suggesting that residues are underestimated.

3. Rebecca Wood, *The Whole Foods Encyclopedia* (New York, Prentice-Hall Press) 1988, p. 8.

4. "A High Fat Fruit," *University of California, Berkeley Wellness Letter*, January, 1990, p. 6.

5. From "Eater's Digest," *Nutrition Action Healthletter*, published by The Center for Science in the Public Interest, April, 1989, p. 13.

6. The table comes from Marian Burros, "Brand Name Beef: Is It Really Better?" *The New York Times*, January 31, 1989, p. C8.

7. Marian Burros, *op. cit.*, p. C1.

8. For a free and informative (though aggressively partisan) book on the new beef, write to the National Cattlemen's Association, 5420 S. Quebec Street, Englewood, CO 80155. (303) 694-0305.

9. *Guide to Retail and Mail Order Sources of Beef Produced without Growth Hormones*, Washington D.C., Center for Science in the Public Interest, Washington D.C., 1989.

10. U.S. Bureau of the Census, *Statistical Abstract of the United States: 1989* 109th edition (Washington, DC, 1989) p. 120.

11. Mary Abbott Hess, Ms., R.D. and Anne Elise Hunt, *Pocket Supermarket Guide* (Chicago: American Dietetic Association, 1989).

12. Briggs and Calloway, *Nutrition and Physical Fitness, 11th Edition* (New York: Holt, Rinehart, and Winston, 1984) p. 450.

13. *University of California, Berkeley Wellness Letter*, October, 1989, p. 6.

14. Edmund L. Andrews, "Patents: Using Flax to Get Benefit of Fish Oils," *The New York Times*, August 19, 1989.

15. Mary Enig, Ph.D., "Is Margarine A Menace? No One Knows, and Worse, No One Cares," *Goldbeck's True Food*, Fall 1989, p. 2.

16. Mott and Snyder, *op. cit.*, p. 47.

17. From "In Brief", *Environmental Nutrition*, CSPI, October, 1989, Vol 12, No. 10, p. 3.

18. Mott and Snyder, op. cit., p. 59.

19. *University of California, Berkeley Wellness Letter*, June, 1989, p. 1.

20. *The New York Times*, May 18, 1989, p. B-8.

21. Diane Ackerman, "O Muse! You Do Make Things Difficult," *The New York Times Book Review*, November 12, 1989, p. 56.

22. "Caffeine Fix: Coffee, Tea, or Kids?" *Vegetarian Times*, April 1989, p. 9.

23. "Decaffeinated Coffee, It's Not the Same Brew it Used to Be," *The New York Times*, Wednesday, October 25, 1989, p. C6.

24. *University of California, Berkeley Wellness Letter*, October, 1989, p. 3.

25. Loc. cit.

26. Loc. cit.

27. Wood, *op. cit.*, p. 57.

28. *Nutrition Action Healthletter*, CSPI, December, 1989, p. 3.

29. *USA Today*, May 15, 1989.

30. Jane Brody, "Fish Diet Fights Heart Disease, Study Confirms," *The New York Times*, November 9, 1989, p. B23.

31. Lisa Y. Lefferts, "The Truth About Seafood," *Garbage*, Sept/Oct 1989, p. 25.

32. Nikki and David Goldbeck, *The Goldbecks' Guide to Good Food* (New York, New American Library Books, 1987) p. 266.

33. "Knowing How to Read Labels is the Key to Buying 100% Juice," *Environmental Nutrition*, October, 1989, p. 4-5.

34. Jayne Hurley and Stephen Schmidt, *Nutrition Action Healthletter*, CSPI, December, 1989, p. 9.

35. See *Heinerman's Encyclopedia of Fruits, Vegetables, and Herbs* (West Nyack NY, Parker Publishing Company, 1988), p. 147 for a list of journal articles about the mechanisms by which garlic can serve as a remedy.

36. Wood, op. cit. p. 73.

37. Data drawn from the Giant Food Inc., *Eat for Health Food Guide*, 1989, p. 127.

38. *University of California, Berkeley Wellness Letter*, July, 1989, p. 1.

39. From "Ask the Experts," *University of California, Berkeley Wellness Letter*, 6:5 (February 1990) p. 8.

40. Rochelle Green, "Full of Beans . . . and Better for It," *Health Magazine*, December, 1989, pp. 58–61.

41. Julie Sahni, "The Mango Looks Beautiful Enough to Eat (and It Is)," *The New York Times*, May 17, 1989, p. C4.

42. Wood, *op. cit.*, p. 100.

43. These particular statistics were taken from a synopsis of Robbins's book by Ken Ausubel included in his "Planting the Seeds of Change," (Santa Fe, NM: Seeds of Change, unpublished paper), p. 3. Robbins's book is loaded with poignant statistics and disquieting accounts about the meat and poultry industries.

44. From "The Realities of Animal-Based Agriculture," distributed by People for the Ethical Treatment of Animals (with data from John Robbins).

45. "Let the Seller Beware," *Consumer Reports Health Letter*, 2:2, Consumers Union, February, 1990, p. 14.

46. Bruce Ingersoll, "FDA Detects but Then Fails to Confirm Contaminations in 51% of Milk Samples," *The Wall Street Journal*, February 6, 1990, p. B6.

47. Philip J. Hilts, "FDA Chemist Asserts Agency Is Stalling on Tests for Milk Purity," *The New York Times*, February 7, 1990, p. A22.

48. Philip J. Hilts, *loc. cit.*

49. John Robbins, *Diet for a New America* (Walpole, NH, Stillpoint), 1987, pp. 109–121.

50. Nikki and David Goldbeck, *op. cit.*, p. 177.

51. From "Fascinating Facts," *University of California, Berkeley Wellness Letter*, September, 1989. Published in association with the School of Public Health, p. 2.

52. From "Eater's Digest," *Nutrition Action Healthletter*, CSPI, April, 1989, p. 13.

53. Marian Burros, "'Oat Bran' May Be on the Label, but How Much Is in the Box?'" *The New York Times*, March 22, 1989, p. C4.

54. The study was done by Janis F. Swain et al. at Brigham and Women's Hospital in Boston. Cited by Jane E. Brody in "Small Study Challenges Role of Oat Bran in Reducing Cholesterol," *The New York Times*, January 18, 1990, p. A24.

55. *Loc. cit.*

56. Edmund L. Andrews, "Using Flax to Get Benefits of Fish Oils," *The New York Times*, August 9, 1989.

57. From "Fish Oil Revisited," *Edell Health Letter*, 8:11 (November, 1989). Published by Hippocrates magazine.

58. Quotation and some of the information taken from "Shopper's Guide to Natural Foods," by Dan Seamens and David Wollner. Published by *East West*, Brookline, MA, 1989, p. 31.

59. Wood, *op. cit.*, p. 114.

60. From "Vital Statistics," *Hippocrates*, November/December, 1989, p. 14.

61. *Nutrition Action*, CSPI, November, 1989, p. 16.

62. Wood, *op. cit.*, p. 130.

63. From "Fascinating Facts," *University of California, Berkeley Wellness Letter*, 6:5 (February 1990), p. 1.

64. U.S. Bureau of the Census, *Statistical Abstract of the United States: 1989* 109th edition (Washington, DC, 1989) p. 120.

65. From "Kentucky Roast Chicken?" *Nutrition Action Healthletter*, CSPI, April, 1989, p. 3.

66. Carrie Dolan, "Federal Agents Lay Down the Law to Some Chicken-Livered Rangers" *The Wall Street Journal*, January 29, 1990, p. B1.

67. *The New York Times*, March 16, 1989, p. A-16.

68. Sonia L. Nazario, "Are Organic Foods Spiritual Enough? Not for Everyone," *The Wall Street Journal*, July 21, 1989, pp. A1, A11.

69. Rebecca Wood, *op. cit.*, p. 138.

70. *Nutrition Action Healthletter*, CSPI, September, 1989, p. 6.

71. John David Mann, Anna Bond, and David Yarrow, "Seeds of Hope," *Solstice*, Sept/Oct, 1989, p. 11.

72. Wood, *op. cit.*, p. 97.

73. "The Soymilk Face-off," *East West*, June, 1989, p. 53.

74. Jayne Hurley and Stephen Schmidt, "Sorting Out the Soups", *Nutrition Action Healthletter*, December, 1989, p. 10–11.

75. *Environmental Nutrition*, 12:11 (November, 1989) pp. 5–6.

76. Dean Edell, M.D. "Q & A," *The Edell Health Letter*, October, 89, p. 8.

77. Lawrie Mott and Karen Snyder, *Pesticide Alert: A Guide to Pesticides in Fruits and Vegetables* (San Francisco, Sierra Club Books, 1987), p. 119.

78. *Loc. cit.*

79. U.S. Bureau of the Census, *Statistical Abstract of the United States: 1989*, 109th edition (Washington, DC, 1989), p. 120.

80. Barbara Rodriguez, *Organic Gardening*, September, 89, p. 20.

81. Daniel P. Puzo, "A Directory for Organic Products," *Los Angeles Times*, April 12, 1989.

82. Michael deCourcy Hinds, "Concern Over Water Safety Is Growing," *The New York Times*, March 25, 1989, p. 44.

83. "E.P.A. Finds Pesticides in Water of 38 States," *The New York Times*, December 14, 1989, p. A28.

CHAPTER EIGHT:
THE DISTRIBUTION OF HEALTHY FOOD

1. *Statistical Abstract of the U.S.: 1989*, 109th ed., Table 1104, p. 639.

2. Louis Harris poll reviewed in "America's Changing Diet," *FDA Consumer*, October 1985, pp. 4–25, and cited in Jo Anne Cassell, "Commentary: American Food Habits in the 1980s," *Topics in Clinical Nutrition* (4:2), April 1989, p. 52.

3. National Restaurant Association survey, reviewed in National Research Council (Board of Agriculture, Committee on Technological Options to Improve the Nutritional Attributes of Animal Products), *Designing Foods: Animal Product Options in the Marketplace* (Washington, D.C.: National Academy Press, 1988), p. 65, cited in Cassell, *op. cit.*, p. 52.

4. In the mid-1980s they were growing about 10 percent a year. National Research Council, *op. cit.*, p. 65.

5. Figure for 1955 from "America's Changing Diet," *loc. cit.* Figure for 1988 from Economic Research Service, USDA, "Consumption of Major Food Commodities per Person," *The World Almanac and Book of Facts 1990* (New York: Scripps Howard, Pharos Books, 1989), p. 121.

6. *Statistical Abstract of the U.S.: 1989*, 109th ed., Table 1104, p. 639.

CHAPTER NINE:
RIDING THE LEVIATHAN

1.   Lynette D. Hazelton, "Fast Food and Mini-Marts Bite Into Grocers," *The New York Times*, June 1989, Business Section, p. 11.

2.   Michael S. McCarthy, "Restaurants Search for Winning Recipes," *The Wall Street Journal*, January 29, 1990, p. B1.

3.   *Statistical Abstract of the U.S.: 1989*, Tables 709–710, pp. 438–439.

4.   *Ibid.*, Table 709, p. 438.

5.   Estimates from Gil Johnson, Director of Research, *Natural Foods Merchandiser*, interviews, November 7, 1989 and January 9, 1990.

6.   Figures from Johnson; they are consistent with those offered by Marian Burros, "Eating Well," *The New York Times*, August 17, 1988 and cited in Cassell, *op. cit.*, p. 53.

7.   Cited in *The New York Times*, Business Section, July 16, 1989, p. 13.

8.   "Tryptophan: Natural Disaster," *Harvard Medical School Health Letter*, 15:4 (February 1990), p. 2.

9.   John Mejia, in *Supermarket News*, October 30, 1989. Cited in "High Prices Slow Organics," National Nutritional Foods Association, *Newsletter*, 3:12 (December 1989) p. 5.

10.   Hazelton, *op. cit.*, p. 11.

11.   The research was conducted by Professor Samuel S. Epstein of the University of Illinois Medical Center in Chicago.

12.   Rose Gutfeld, "Grocers Plan Their Own Ban on Pesticides," *Wall Street Journal*, September 11, 1989, pp. B1 and B9; and Keith Schneider, "5 Supermarket Chains Open Effort Against Pesticide Use," *New York Times*, September 12, 1989, p. B9.

13.   Schneider, *op. cit.*, p. B9.

14.   *Loc. cit.*

15.   An information gap is the reason a D'Agostino's supermarket manager in New York City gave for the initially slow response it has had to its organic food department. Not enough consumers were sufficiently appreciative of the quality of the produce to be willing to pay a premium for them in 1989. As certification labeling becomes better known, consumer attitudes should shift perceptibly in 1990.

16.   Parts of this list were taken from Marian Burros, "Eating Well: For Careful Buyers, Today's Supermarket Aisle Can be a Road to Good Eating," *The New York Times*, June 28, 1989, p. C8.

17.   Marian Burros, "Eating Well: Menus in California that Go Easy on the Heart," *The New York Times*, January 17, 1990, p. C8.

18.   This list was assembled by comparing the "Health/Spa Menus" listing and the "Power Scenes" listing in the *1989 Zagat New York City Restaurant Survey* (New York: Zagat Survey, 1988), pp. 171, 178.

19.   The following reviews of ethnic cuisine are based heavily on an excellent article by Densie Webb, "Eating Well: In Ethnic Fare, Beware of the Hidden Fats and Calories," *The New York Times*, May 31, 1989, p. C4. Also Hamilton, Nunnelly, and Sizer, *op. cit.*, pp. 49–51.

20.   Florence Fabricant, "A Faintly Amused Answer to Fast Food," *New York Times*, November 15, 1989.

21.   Dena Kleiman, "Fast Food? It Just Isn't Fast Enough Anymore," *The New York Times*, December 6, 1989, pp. A1, C-12.

22.   Derived from computer-generated data graciously provided to us by the Center for Science in the Public Interest. the data represent an update of information in Michael F. Jacobson, Ph.D. and Sarah Fritschner, Center for Science in the Public Interest, *The Fast Food Guide* (New York: Workman Publishing, 1986). See p. 49 for list of products as of 1986; see detailed company-product tables later in the book for data on these products relating to calories, fat, and percent of calories from fat.

23.   Sarah Fritschner, "Finding Healthy Fast Food is Slow Process," *Gannett Westchester Newspapers*, October 11, 1989, p. C-1. Fat content, Jacobson and Fritschner, *op. cit.*, p. 115.

24.   Derived from computer-generated data graciously provided by the Center for Science in the Public Interest, updating Jacobson and Fritschner, *op. cit.*, p. 53 for list of products; detailed company-product tables later in the book for data on calories, fat, and percent of calories from fat. Three low-fat but high-sodium chili (over 1 gram sodium), cottage cheese (over 400 milligrams sodium, 41 of calories from fat), and soup (over 500 milligrams sodium) options were omitted.

25.   Jacobson and Fritschner, *op. cit.*, p. 33.

SOJA BEAN, OR "GERMAN COFFEE BERRY."

INDEX

C

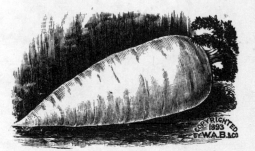

F

O

FOR OUR READER: THIS SPACE IS FOR YOU. Expand this book by noting distributors, stores, restaurants and products that have given you good value. When you fill a page, you may want to photocopy it and sent it to us, (see page 288) for inclusion in future editions of this book.

INFO-FORM

TO: JTM REPORTS, Inc.
30 Irving Place, 9th Floor
New York, NY 10003

Here are my suggestions for the next edition of your book, **The Catalogue of Healthy Food:**

☐ Suggested Deletions: _____

_____

_____

☐ Suggested Additions: _____

_____

_____

☐ Suggested Changes: _____

_____

_____

☐ Comments: _____

_____

_____

Use Additional Sheets as needed

NAME: _____

ADDRESS: _____

CITY: _____ STATE: _____ ZIP: _____

PHONE: _(day)_ _____ _(evening)_ _____

To avoid damaging your book, and to leave the form in place for the next reader, please copy this form before filling it in and returning it.